Clinical Negligence

Second Edition

Clinical Negligence

Second Edition

General Editor

Paul Balen

Published by
Jordan Publishing Limited
21 St Thomas Street
Bristol BS1 6JS

British Library Cataloguing-in-Publication Data

A catalogue record for this book is available from the British Library.

ISBN 978 1 84661 822 2

Typeset by Letterpart Limited, Caterham on the Hill, Surrey CR3 5XL

Printed in Great Britain by Hobbs the Printers Limited, Totton, Hampshire SO40 3WX

PREFACE TO THE SECOND EDITION

The last few years have seen a veritable tsunami of reforms, which have changed the face of the clinical negligence claims process. Jackson, the abolition of legal aid and the inquest reforms amongst others have produced new challenges and opportunities for those willing to secure access to justice for patients.

This book is designed to bring a practical view of the current regime and to encourage practitioners to understand the very special requirements of that sadly increasing number of patients who believe, often with justification, that they have been let down by the very specialists they had relied upon to treat them.

Once again I thank my team of expert commentators for their cooperation and my wife, Helen, for her support.

Paul Balen

PREFACE TO THE FIRST EDITION

I still vividly remember my first big clinical negligence case. I was the second solicitor instructed, the first firm having advised that there was no case leading to the discharge of the client's legal aid certificate. When I read the previous solicitors' file it was evident that no medical records had been obtained; expert evidence had, it is true, been obtained but it took the form of a report from the consultant in charge of the A & E department of the hospital in which the act of negligence was alleged to have taken place (presumably explaining why it was not thought necessary for the solicitor to obtain the medical records). A short advice had been supplied by a non-specialist barrister who opined that on the papers provided there was no evidence of negligence. That was correct because none had been obtained. When I obtained the medical records and an independent medical expert's report everything fell into place.

Clinical negligence work and expertise has come a long way since those days. I hope that this contribution helps those practising in this field in the future.

This book is an unashamedly practical guide through the clinical negligence maze. Each chapter has been compiled by an experienced practitioner or practitioners and culminates in some 'top tips'. These are not intended to be a summary of the chapter but gems of advice derived from the author's years of experience in the field. Statutes and cases are referred to but not quoted in full as all are available for reference purposes in other publications especially the World Wide Web.

Particularly with the advent of the Human Rights Act and the recoverability of the costs of attendance in a resultant successful clinical negligence claim in recent years, the inquest has become of much greater importance. Funding for both clinical negligence and inquest representation remains problematic. Frequently access to justice is only gained by the claimant's lawyer taking risk or effectively acting pro bono. Both inquest work and funding are explored in detail, as is the interface between clinical negligence work and medical product liability claims brought under the Consumer Protection Act.

Work in the clinical negligence field provided for many firms the first step into the multidisciplinary field through the employment of doctors or nurses within the legal team. Whilst all cases are naturally against doctors or hospitals, without a doctor to give expert evidence no claim can get off the ground – a point frequently overlooked by so-called experts commenting critically of lawyers working in this field. Medical input in the compilation of this book is provided by Dr Tom Boyd who provides a GP expert's view and some pointers on common abbreviations found in medical records and on anatomy, whilst my own in-house nurse Jennifer Foster SRN explains how to get the best out of trauma victims and charts the way round the mass of copies apparently masquerading as the client's medical records which are disclosed by health care providers.

Case work in these complex cases is often best served by team work between solicitors and counsel experienced in the field. In similar vein, I particularly welcome the involvement of Phillip Havers QC and Margaret Bowron QC from 1 Crown Office Row; Robin Oppenheim QC and Christopher Gibson QC from Doughty Street; Jalil Asif from 4 New Square and an array of talent under the stewardship of Adrian Hopkins QC from 3 Serjeants' Inn.

Clinical negligence claims are some of the most difficult and complex to resolve. An experienced practitioner will recognise the various tensions which characterise this work. Unlike the generality of personal injury claimants, victims of clinical negligence are usually driven by a number of very different motives. As research[1] and indeed the National Audit Office report[2] demonstrates, although litigation itself is designed to deliver compensation the shopping list of a clinical negligence claimant is far more varied.

Apologies; an explanation; an assurance that lessons have been learnt so that their loved one's life has not been in vain; action taken to improve the quality of healthcare; and disciplinary action against the medical staff involved, all feature heavily. All these can be secured for a client but not simply by blindly following the White Book and the Civil Procedure Rules.

A clinical negligence claimant's expectations may be fuelled by media stories and his respect for the professions or institutions of state destroyed by the breach of trust he may have so recently experienced. An experienced practitioner should be able to start recreating that trust; find ways of providing an explanation and, if that is the client's wish, establish what lessons may have been learnt and action taken, and if not satisfied find ways of publicising the healthcare shortfalls observed in the particular case.

There is nothing so devastating for client and practitioner alike to see exactly the same error in healthcare lead to yet another life ruined.

The law is also very different from general personal injury law. Not only is the *Bolam* test far removed from the simple negligence required to found liability in, say, a road traffic accident but the real battle ground is often causation and not negligence at all.

---

[1] Mulcahy L, Selwood M, Summerfield L, Netten A, *Mediating medical negligence claims: an option for the future?* (Stationery Office, 2000) at p 11.

[2] *Handling Clinical Negligence Claims in England*, HC 403 (National Audit Office, 3 May 2001).

The *Bolam* test is the equivalent of having asked an athlete to run the 110 metres hurdles in the Olympic Games and making the first hurdle the height of a pole vault. Apart from family planning and cosmetic surgery cases, by the very nature of clinical negligence claims, the victim was ill or injured before receiving any treatment and is ill or injured, if not dead, thereafter. Only, of course, the extra illness or injury suffered by the victim as a result of the act of negligence will found a claim for compensation and much argument is likely amongst medical experts seeking to define that 'extra' element. To the claimant it may seem obvious that but for the act of negligence he would be perfectly healthy but in reality that is seldom the situation and careful explanation and handling of expectations may be required.

It was the then Health Secretary Frank Dobson[3] who commented that 'as far as I am concerned the best place for a lawyer in the NHS is on the operating table not sliding around causing trouble for other people'. Most lawyers practising in the clinical negligence field will make no apologies for causing trouble on behalf of their clients. Public exploration of the breaches of duty identified serve to maintain standards and fairly compensate those let down by those failings.

Blaming the lawyer for the fact that cases are brought rather than examining the underlying causes is a tactic as old as Shakespeare: 'first thing we do is kill all the lawyers'[4]. Organisations such as AvMA and APIL have tirelessly worked to destroy that reaction. I hope that this book will contribute to that work.

My thanks go to all the contributors whose hard work and enthusiasm has made my work so easy; to Denise Kitchener APIL's tireless Chief Executive for promoting the idea for the book and Tony Hawitt at Jordans for putting it all together and keeping me in check. The success of this book is down to the authors but the errors and omissions are mine.

Paul Balen

---

[3]   26 February 1998.
[4]   Henry VI Pt II.

ASSOCIATION OF PERSONAL INJURY LAWYERS (APIL)

APIL is the UK's leading association of claimant personal injury lawyers, dedicated to protecting the rights of injured people.

Formed in 1990, APIL now represents around 4,000 solicitors, barristers, academics and students in the UK, Republic of Ireland and overseas.

APIL's objectives are:

- to promote full and just compensation for all types of personal injury;
- to promote and develop expertise in the practice of personal injury law;
- to promote wider redress for personal injury in the legal system;
- to campaign for improvements in personal injury law;
- to promote safety and alert the public to hazards;
- to provide a communication network for members.

APIL is a growing and influential forum pushing for law reform, and improvements, which will benefit injured people.

APIL has been running CPD training events, accredited by the Solicitors Regulation Authority and Bar Standards Board, for nearly 20 years and has a wealth of experience in developing the most practical up-to-date courses, delivered by eminent leading speakers, either publicly or in-house.

APIL training now runs almost 200 personal injury training events nationally each year, plus up to a further 100 meetings of our regional and special interest groups. Topics cover a wide range of subjects and are geared towards giving personal injury lawyers a thorough grounding in the core areas of personal injury law, whilst keeping lawyers thoroughly up to date in all subjects.

APIL is also an authoritative information source for personal injury lawyers, providing up-to-the-minute PI bulletins, regular newsletters and publications, information databases and online services.

For further information contact:

APIL
3 Alder Court
Rennie Hogg Road
Nottingham NG2 1RX
DX 716208 Nottingham 42
Tel 0115 9580585
Email mail@apil.org.uk

CONTRIBUTORS

Jalil Asif QC
Kobre & Kim

Paul Balen
Solicitor and Consultant, Freeths

David Body
Solicitor and Partner, Irwin Mitchell

Dr Tom Boyd
General Practitioner

Ian Christian
Solicitor and Partner, Irwin Mitchell

Laura Craig
Solicitor, Slater & Gordon

Simon Cridland
Barrister, Serjeants' Inn Chambers

Robert Dickason
Barrister, Outer Temple Chambers

Claire Fazan
Solicitor and Partner, Leigh Day & Co

Christopher Gibson QC
Outer Temple Chambers

Philip Havers QC
1 Crown Office Row

Adrian Hopkins QC
Serjeants' Inn Chambers

Jeremy Hyam
Barrister, 1 Crown Office Row

Mandy Luckman
Solicitor and Partner, Irwin Mitchell

David Marshall
Solicitor and Partner, Anthony Gold

Tom Mather
Solicitor and Partner, Irwin Mitchell

Claire McGregor
Barrister, 1 Crown Office Row

John McQuater
Solicitor and Partner, Atherton Godfrey

Jon Nicholson
Solicitor and Partner, Anthony Gold

Aaron Rathmell
Barrister, Serjeants' Inn Chambers

Rosamund Rhodes-Kemp
Solicitor and Partner, Pattinson Brewer

Suzanne Staunton
Barrister, Guildhall Chambers

First Edition Only

Margaret Bowron QC, 1 Crown Office Row

Jennifer Foster (SRN), formerly of Freeths

Tim Meakin, Barrister, 7 Bedford Row

Michael Mylonas QC, Serjeants' Inn Chambers

Fiona Neale, Barrister, Hailsham Chambers

John Pickering, Solicitor, formerly Managing Partner, Irwin Mitchell

Sarah Simcock, Barrister, Serjeants' Inn Chambers

CONTENTS

Chapter 7
The Duty of Care, Standard of Care and Establishing Breach of Duty   157

Chapter 8
Causation   181

TABLE OF CASES

References are to paragraph numbers.

TABLE OF STATUTES

References are to paragraph numbers.

TABLE OF STATUTORY INSTRUMENTS

References are to paragraph numbers.

CHAPTER 1

COPING WITH TRAUMA

In this chapter Jennifer Foster, a State Registered Nurse and trained counsellor, who for 20 years worked in the medico-legal team at Freeths LLP, explains why lawyers and their staff dealing with trauma victims need to understand the psychological effect of the trauma on victims and on themselves and gives guidance on coping strategies. The importance of this for the clinical negligence practitioner cannot be understated. Unless the practitioner understands the client's real concerns and where they come from it is unlikely that that particular client will feel satisfied with the service provided.

1.1 WHAT IS TRAUMA?

Trauma is a psychological wound that results from an emotionally demanding circumstance or incident. It results from the inability of the particular person concerned to cope adequately with what he or she has experienced and/or witnessed. Because it is very much an individual reaction a circumstance experienced as traumatic for one person may not be experienced as traumatic by another. For instance, a person witnessing the death of an individual in a road traffic accident might be traumatised by what that individual has seen, whereas a paramedic on the scene of several deaths each week may not be traumatised by witnessing a similar event.

A key feature of whether an event or circumstance is likely to be experienced as traumatic is whether it is perceived by the person as a threat to their physical or psychological integrity.

People involved in overwhelming disasters and incidents often report typical reactions. Knowledge about these reactions can be useful because it can help us see that we are not going crazy or that we are not weak and inadequate. Such experiences are normal reactions to an abnormal event. Also, it is important to realise that each person deals with trauma in a slightly different way because each situation is unique.

Some people may experience episodes of repeated re-living of some aspects of the trauma. Sometimes these can be intense memories often called 'flashbacks'. Others can also experience nightmares and frightening thoughts. They may also experience physical reactions to situations that remind them of traumatic events. Repeated re-living of traumatic events can disturb day-to-day activities and functioning and result in a lack of interest in normal activities.

1.2   INDIVIDUAL REACTIONS

It is important to understand that each person is an individual and each person will react to trauma and its consequences in his own individual ways. Some people may experience a sense of numbness, an emotional blunting, perhaps even a feeling that they do not care about anything any more. Some people feel detached from other people and then very frustrated that no-one seems to understand how they feel.

The emotions that people can suffer following trauma vary immensely. They can take the form of fear, anger, sadness, guilt. In an immediate aftermath an individual can feel vulnerable. The world might seem threatening and the future very uncertain. It is important to understand that fear and panic are normal emotional responses.

1.2.1   Anger

Anger is a very common and natural response. A person may feel angry because of what has happened to him; angry because he does not feel in control of his life anymore; angry with others for making him suffer either deliberately or unwittingly.

Some people start blaming themselves for what has happened and feel guilty about the event. Some people may experience survivor guilt (guilt over surviving whilst others did not), although in reality there is nothing they could have done and they bear no responsibility for the event at all. A survivor can be angry that he survived particularly when other loved ones perished.

1.2.2   Physical symptoms

The traumatic experience can trigger physical symptoms such as palpitations, patchy sleep, poor concentration, agitation, and dizziness. Another common reaction is for feelings to be rekindled about a previous trauma or loss which have perhaps been buried or denied for many years.

1.2.3   Vulnerability

Trauma may lead to the victim experiencing a feeling of vulnerability and questioning the meaning of life. This is because the event which has been experienced can overturn so much that was previously held dear, and rendered uncertain things which had been prior to the incident either taken for granted or assumed to have been concrete certainties.

1.3 RECOVERY

The first lesson is that recovery does take time. A psychological wound cannot be forced to heal quickly. It is no different from a physical wound. Flowing with the healing process is better than fighting it. This process can be described as moving from victim to survivor.

There are some common elements in this period of healing. First of all it may be seen that the individual starts to sleep better, perhaps not waking in the early hours or managing to get off to sleep only to find that a few hours later he lies awake unable to get back to sleep. As the healing process commences the normal sleep pattern returns. As the victim begins to feel refreshed from sleep he begins to take an interest in himself once again. He may have put weight on because he may have used food as a comfort for his sadness. He may have been unable to eat and lost weight as a result. As his appearance becomes of interest to him once again he may start to regain his appetite and with it his weight.

Some victims describe how they find colour different using expressions such as 'I never realised the sky was so blue'. As the victim's mind starts to clear colours may appear to become sharper and clearer.

1.4 DEALING WITH THE TRAUMATISED CLIENT

Typically the person who is the first point of contact for the client on the first occasion he makes contact with his solicitor will have little or no knowledge of the victim or his background or of the type of problem or experience that has occurred. It is crucial that the interviewer realises that every person is an individual and because of this will deal with or cope with the traumatic events in different ways.

Some solicitors may prefer to deal with a traumatic client on the telephone; others will prefer to deal with the client in an interview room. Sometimes of course the option is not available. However, whichever the method adopted there is very little difference in the approach required.

Whether a solicitor is dealing with a traumatised person at the end of a telephone line or at a face to face meeting, the fact remains that he has to be able to understand his client, take on board information that the client may be trying desperately to get over and at the same time calm him down and convey to him the message that his solicitor is an experienced trained professional who is there to help him, who is on his side, who cares and who the client can trust. This then paves the way for advice to be given both as to the law and prospects of success but probably of equal importance at this stage for an explanation of the various procedures involved in setting up a legal case and of the timetable involved. The creation of a bond of trust may be very important and difficult to achieve for a client whose faith in the institutions of society may have been dealt a terrible blow by the event in question.

Following a traumatic experience the victim may ask a close relative or friend to contact a solicitor on his behalf. It is often easier to deal with a member of the family or a close friend but at the end of the day it is important to remember that it is the traumatised person who must be advised and helped and not necessarily the intermediary who may not be in possession of the whole picture or indeed may have a conflicting agenda.

1.4.1   Telephone interviewing strategies

So how is it best to cope with a person who is sobbing uncontrollably down the telephone and who may well be embarrassed because he cannot stop crying?

First of all adopt a very calming, slow tone. Speak to the client quietly and much slower than in a normal conversation.

In the office where I work, I often have my door shut because I feel that if I am dealing with somebody who is emotionally upset, particularly on the telephone, it is unfair for them to hear laughter or day-to-day office activities in the background. At that particular moment, the client is likely to be deeply upset and emotionally overloaded. For that reason, I advise that these types of telephone calls are taken in an isolated office where the background is peaceful.

My first step is to identify who I am. I never say that I am Mrs Foster. I always say 'my name is Jennifer'. The mere fact of using my first name sets the scene for the traumatised person to perceive that I am adopting a less formal approach then perhaps he expected and may already have experienced from other authorities with whom he has become involved since the event in question. I then ask the person his or her name. If she says 'Mrs Smith' I ask her for her first name and then I say, 'Do you mind if I call you Susan'. The usual response is 'not at all'.

One of the best ways of dealing with trauma is for the person who is traumatised to talk and talk and talk. It is only by talking to others that he will be able to get it off his chest. The more he talks the more he is likely to gain control in remembering the event. Memory and emotions are joined. He will then find that the memory is re-examined and he will start to be able to file his memory of the events in question away. Eventually although the trauma may obviously still affect him it no longer seems overwhelming.

As this process continues the traumatised person will find that the troublesome post-traumatic symptoms become more tolerable and predictable and gradually with the passage of time fade away. This is the origin of the old saying 'time heals'.

I always find that when I am dealing with someone on the telephone, it is best to encourage them to spill out all that has happened. During that time I say very little. Perhaps the only thing that I will do is to encourage them to keep talking.

Even though I may be under time constraints in order to achieve the best results both for me and my client I really have to forget that a clock is ticking. I remember only too well, many years ago, a doctor who was training me saying that if you have a patient who has come in for the first time for a particular symptom you need to give them all the time they need. If you listen to their symptoms, hear what they have to say and then discuss the treatment, you are more likely on the review appointment to have them come in and say, 'well that is fine, doc, those tablets worked well' and you can move on. However, if you look at your watch and you have 6 minutes to be with a patient and you portray that to that individual patient by not really taking in all that they are saying and not really giving them the time to unload their concerns to you; and you merely write a prescription and say 'see how it goes, if it does not work, come back in a month', that individual will feel 'fobbed off'. If that is the approach taken, very often that person will be back in the surgery, 2 or 3 days later with the problem still unresolved. It is therefore better to spend the initial time with the patient/client and understand what the burden and the problems are, and then deal with them.

I always use my voice tone to get the client to tell me what I need to know. During that conversation I need to obtain from them all the information necessary for us to advise on the next step. If a person is sobbing uncontrollably down the telephone I will speak very quietly with gaps in between my words and phrases. Using this method means that the person who is sobbing cannot hear me and so after a few minutes he will start to stop crying because he really wants to listen to what I have to say. By putting breaks in what I am saying, the gaps then become silences. The traumatised person will fill in the gaps and eventually I will be able to take control of the conversation.

There is another voice tone that I use as well which is firmer. This is necessary sometimes if I have a person on the phone who cannot stop talking but is not otherwise showing overt signs of distress. By speaking louder, but again using breaks, I again take control of the conversation. Perversely taking control is exactly what the traumatised victim may be desperately asking you to do but often their trauma creates difficulties in achieving this.

1.4.2 Interview room strategies

How should we deal with the trauma victim in an interview room on a person-to-person basis?

My own tactic is first to prepare the room itself. I have asked that in each of our interview rooms there is a box of paper tissues. When I meet the client I go right up to him, shake hands and then lead him to the interview room and ask him if he would like to take a seat. I try and place myself near the door. There is a very good reason for this. If the traumatised person should begin to feel unwell or faint, he will not collapse to the floor because he is seated and therefore less of a danger to himself.

If you are positioned near the door you can get help if necessary. Sometimes, fortunately rarely, the victim may become aggressive. If this were to happen, a position near the door facilitates a speedy exit.

I also find that traumatised people often fidget. One of the best ways of dealing with this is to ask them if they would like a cup of tea or coffee or maybe a glass of water. I find that they then place their hands round the cup or glass and then feel more confident because they are actually holding on to something.

Again I use the same voice tone as I would during a telephone conversation.

When I am dealing with a client in an interview room it is important to understand that we all have what is called 'our air space'. This is normally about a three foot globe, so if you can imagine putting a glass dome over an individual which is three foot in dimension that is the individual's 'air space'. Crossing into an individual's air space will make that person feel at risk.

To try and explain this, imagine what it is like when you use a bus to get to work during the normal busy rush hour. You are sitting peacefully in your seat, maybe reading a book or just looking out of the window, but as bus stops go by, the bus gets fuller and fuller and eventually people are standing in the aisle. So far this is not a problem, but what happens if a person gets up and has to squeeze past people standing in the aisle to get off at the bus stop. The people in the aisle have to lean forward to let them pass. Automatically people then look up and may feel hemmed in and in some cases even claustrophobic. This is because the people in the aisle have encroached on the individual's 'air space'. In the interview situation I try never to do that unless I am invited.

It is, therefore, much more comfortable if I am sitting in an interview room with a desk between us, or even in a room without a desk where I like the seats arranged so they are not side by side but there is a distance between them.

I have the tissue box strategically placed, probably on a nearby shelf, so if the client starts to cry I can just reach for the box and pop it on the table. I would pull two or three tissues out and hand them to him. This encourages him to cry to get it out of his system.

It is not possible to get accurate information from a person in a distressed state. I find it is best to let the client cry. I talk calmly and give him space and time. Once he has started to calm down, I can then start to talk to him about events. If the client has brought someone with them – a husband, wife, or close friend it is at this time that my questions can be directed to the other person. The traumatised person might say, 'my daughter knows what has happened' and then it is quite easy to turn to her and say 'can you fill me in on some of the information so that I can try and help'.

Whilst I am talking to the individuals concerned I try to be gentle and to comfort them in non-verbal ways. I have already mentioned a drink because when people feel a little agitated or a little stressed about a particular circumstance they often find that their mouth has gone really dry. A traumatised person also often forgets to eat and because this can make blood sugar levels drop, it is helpful to have a plate of sweet biscuits around and to encourage him to eat one.

In some cases it is necessary for the traumatised person to feel that somebody is with them by touch. This of course does involve an invasion of space and is a difficult situation to explain. I often find that it is instinct that tells me what to do. For example, as the sobs start I may very gently offer to hold the client's hand so that he feels the warmth of someone there and realises that he is not alone. If the client is with a friend or a relative I normally find that they will do that. By continuing to speak to them in a very calm, slow voice the tears will pass. I talk to them and ask them about their experiences, because it is by expressing these and talking about them, I can acquire the information that I need. Once they start the flow of conversation they find it easier to talk and I can then ask specific questions.

How do I explain to a traumatised person how long I can spend with them? If someone is upset I could be with them for hours. I actually start the conversation with 'I want to spend the next hour with you ...' Or mention that I can be with them 'for as long as it takes'. The client then knows that I am prepared to help. I may also say that (as I am not a lawyer myself) at the end of the interview I will need to go away and write up my notes and one of our solicitors will then advise how we can help. The traumatised person should then relax because they know how long they have.

Sometimes a victim finds the idea of speaking to a lawyer intimidating and I effectively act as a bridge between the victim and his lawyer making the introduction hopefully that much easier. There is a shortage of access to bereavement counsellors through the NHS and often I may be the first trained person in this discipline that the victim will have met.

Towards the end of the conversation I ask the client to write down any thoughts or feelings that may come to mind after the meeting or the telephone consultation and I find that really helps. Many people who have attended a meeting or a hospital appointment come out and think, 'oh, I forgot to say ...' or 'I wish I had said ...'. For this reason I do two things. During the initial telephone conversation, I advise the client that I will call him back at a later date to discuss any thoughts or any further information that may well have come to his mind since our first conversation. At the time that the event has happened a lot will be pushed to the back of his mind because of the emotional turmoil. I also find that asking a traumatised client to write down his thoughts and feelings can actually serve as a coping mechanism and a way of the individual expressing his emotions.

I always advise clients to re-establish if possible their normal routines and activities. This will help them to restore order in to their lives and allow them to feel more in control.

1.4.3 Homework

During a conversation with a traumatised person I try to access positive memories to counter-balance the negative ones. Unfortunately trauma can make this difficult but our health depends on balancing negative memories with positive ones. I will encourage a client to list his priorities and to deal with them one at a time. I advise the client what we are going to do next and tell him that we are going to give him 'homework'.

The 'homework' may well be to find an insurance policy to see if the client has legal expenses funding. It might be that he has to find a birth certificate or a death certificate or a national insurance number. If I require medical records the traumatised person may wish to deal with this himself but more usually will ask me to arrange to obtain them. If so, I will need authorities signed by the appropriate person as well as details of the relevant health care providers. I need to find out what the client really wants to achieve. I also advise the client to leave important decisions until later but often ask him to start a diary of events or expenses or to continue one if he has already compiled one.

Giving 'homework' is important. Not only does it supply me with the relevant information I need but also it makes the client feel he is participating and is doing something constructive to help in circumstances when previously he may have been swept along by the aftermath of the traumatic event feeling helpless and out of control. So even if the information I require is not really necessary or at least not urgent at that stage I may set the client 'homework' anyway simply in order to provide a practical link with the client and help cement our relationship.

In the same way if for any reason it is immediately clear that we cannot help rather than simply turn the client away it is best to try and be positive by referring them on to other agencies and systems or coming up with other positive suggestions of a way forward.

1.4.4 Time

As I have explained dealing with trauma can leave the affected individual feeling vulnerable and unable to cope. It is for this reason that I always tell my clients to give themselves at least 6 months before they make really important decisions. During that time, life will swing around like a pendulum. If they have to make a decision during this period they may need help from us or other agencies before doing so. I always advise my clients to give themselves time and if possible not to rush into decisions. If we can deal with agencies on the client's behalf and offer to do so the relief is often palpable. There are also often support groups for like affected people which helps the client to realise that he or she is not alone or unique with this experience.

When dealing with traumatised people we also have to be aware that we cannot take on all their trauma and concerns. It is very easy for a traumatised person to try and put everything on to another person. This is actually unhelpful as that person then becomes emotionally and then physically ill.

It is important therefore to take control of every situation. Never give your own personal telephone number or personal address. Make sure that the client is seen in the right environment, and advise him when it is best to telephone. As I have mentioned earlier, I follow the initial telephone call with a second telephone call. I have previously advised that I am going to do this and give the date and time so that the client or witness/relative is aware that I am going to telephone. It is surprising how much more information that individual person will then have.

Remember that after a period of time the victim will re-evaluate his life. Certain things that he does on a day-to-day basis will not matter to him anymore. If he has experienced a bereavement he will realise that life is short and precious. Doing the washing the following day may not matter to him any more.

When I am counselling people I like to try and put life in perspective. At the end of the day I am trying to help someone and to do that I need to give him time and need to be understanding and practical. It is amazing how clients respond if I am supportive and give them encouragement

1.4.5   What not to do!

- Don't try to get them to stifle their expressions or emotions.
- Don't try to suppress their negative feelings.
- Don't try to cheer them up by making jokes about the event or circumstances.
- Don't try to change the subject when they wish to talk.
- Don't tell them that someone else is worse off.
- Don't tell them to 'get a grip'.
- Don't pretend that nothing has happened.
- Don't keep asking them questions about the event in a way that makes them feel as if they are being interrogated.

1.5   COPING STRATEGIES FOR INTERVIEWERS

Feeling stressed after the initial encounter with a traumatised person is perfectly normal. Give yourself time and be reasonable with yourself. It is quite usual to feel upset. We are all human beings. Even professionals whether paramedics or solicitors experience a reaction to trauma. Take time out to go through the emotions that you have just experienced. Have a cup of coffee, relax for a few minutes, chat with a work colleague or friend and try to deal with something pleasant to get it out of your system.

1.6   REFERRAL AGENCIES

It is important to have available a number of referral agencies to which the trauma victim can be referred for further advice and counselling if necessary. There may also be support groups for specific illnesses and diseases. Some examples are given in the table below.

- Age Concern
  www.ageconcern.org.uk
- Association for Improvements in Maternity Services (AIMS)
  www.aims.org.uk
- Breast Cancer Care
  www.breastcancercare.org.uk
- British Heart Foundation
  www.bhf.org.uk
- Cancerbacup
  www.cancerbacup.org.uk
- Changing Faces
  www.changingfaces.co.uk
- Child Death Helpline
  www.childdeathhelpline.org.uk
- Clinical Disputes Forum
  www.clinical-disputes-forum.org.uk
- Compassionate Friends
  www.tcf.org.uk
- Contact a Family
  www.cafamily.org.uk
- Crossroads
  www.crossroads.org.uk
- CRUSE Bereavement Care
  www.crusebereavementcare.org.uk
- Headway – The Brain Injury Association
  www.headway.org.uk
- Inquest
  www.inquest.org.uk
- Macmillan Cancer Relief
  www.macmillan.org.uk
- MIND
  www.mind.org.uk

- MRSA Action UK
  www.mrsaactionuk.com
- MRSA Support
  www.mrsasupport.co.uk
- National Association of Citizens Advice Bureaux (NACAB)
  www.citizensadvice.org.uk
- Pancreatitis Supporters Network
  www.pancreatitis.org.uk
- Patients Association
  www.patients-association.com
- Prevention of Professional Abuse
  www.popan.org.uk
- Royal Hospital for Neuro-disability
  www.rhn.org.uk
- Samaritans
  www.samaritans.org.uk
- Saneline
  www.sane.org.uk
- SCOPE
  www.scope.org.uk
- Self Help UK
  www.self-help.org.uk
- TACT (Trauma Aftercare Trust)
  www.tacthq.demon.co.uk
- Women's Health
  www.womenshealthlondon.org

Action against Medical Accidents (AvMA) is the independent charity which promotes better patient safety and justice for people who have been affected by a medical accident. It is of course not just an organisation for doctors and lawyers.

AvMA believes that whatever the cause of a medical accident, the people affected deserve explanations, support, and where appropriate, compensation. Furthermore, they deserve to know that the necessary steps will be taken to prevent similar accidents being repeated.

Of particular interest to those affected by clinical negligence may be the AvMA discussion forum for people who have been affected by medical accidents to exchange their experiences, ideas and comments with others who have registered as 'friends of AvMA'.[1]

AvMA provides free and confidential advice and support to people affected by medical accidents, via its helpline and casework service and can refer to

---

[1]   See www.avma.org.uk.

specialist clinical negligence solicitors or other sources of support where appropriate. Helpline: 0845 123 2352 (Monday to Friday, 10am–5pm).

TOP TIPS

- Clients will react to trauma in their own individual ways.
- Fear, panic and distrust are normal reactions.
- It is important to create a bond with the client.
- Adopt a slow calm tone of voice.
- Use first names.
- Prepare the interview room.
- Provide the client with 'homework'.

CHAPTER 2

MEDICAL RECORDS

In this chapter solicitor Paul Balen explores a patient's entitlement to access to his medical records and Jennifer Foster SRN describes the format of medical records and what to do with them when obtained.

2.1 OBTAINING THE RECORDS

The law governing the production of medical records and the entitlement of patients or relatives of deceased patients is different. If the patient is alive the production of his records is governed by the data protection legislation.[1] If the patient is deceased production is governed by the Access to Health Records Act 1990.

2.1.1 Surviving patients

The implementation of data protection legislation in early 2000 changed patients' statutory rights of access to their health records which had previously been governed by the Access to Health Records Act 1990 (for records pre-dating 1991) and common law.[2] This Act was repealed except for records of deceased patients by the Data Protection Act 1998 which covers a patient's right of access to all manual and computerised health records regardless of when they were made.

Health records are specified as accessible records under the Act.[3] They are defined as being:

> 'any record which consists of information relevant to the physical or mental health or condition of an individual' which 'has been made by a health care professional in connection with the care of that individual.'[4]

Competent patients may apply for access to their own records, or may authorise a third party, such as their solicitor, to do so on their behalf. This is termed a 'subject access request'. There is no direct power authorising parents to have access to their child's records or to instruct solicitors on their behalf,

---

[1] Data Protection Act 1998, s 1(1).
[2] *Stobart v NHA* [1992] 3 Med LR 284.
[3] DPA 1998, s 68(1)(a).
[4] DPA 1998, s 68(2).

but applying the data protection principles set out in the Act, parents or representatives on their behalf are able to gain access to a child's records if this is in the child's best interests and not contrary to a competent child's wishes. In the same way a person appointed by a court to manage the affairs of mentally incapacitated adults may have access to information necessary to fulfil this function.

The General Medical Council (GMC) has published guidance that sets out a doctor's role and responsibilities towards children and young people[5] which includes guidelines relating to the principles of confidentiality and access to medical records by children, young people and their parents. The guidance explicitly states that young people with capacity have the legal rights to access their own health records and can allow or prevent access by others, including their parents.

The guidance also states[6] that parents should ordinarily access their child's medical records if the child or young person consents or lacks capacity and it does not go against the child's best interests. If the records contain information given by the child or young person in confidence, such confidential information should not normally be disclosed without the consent of the child or young person. This indicates that the consent of a child under the age of majority who is *Gillick*[7] competent should be obtained for the release of medical records in relation to a clinical negligence claim being investigated for that child. There is a reminder that a balance needs to be struck between respecting a child's confidentiality and that child being given access to information that would cause him harm. Further guidance can be sought from the GMC.

The Data Protection Act gives patients the right of access;[8] the right to correct inaccurate information[9] and the rights to know the source of and purpose of the records.[10]

Records must not be disclosed if they:[11]

• are likely to cause serious physical or mental harm to the patient or another person; or

• relate to a third party who has not given consent for disclosure (where that third party is not a health professional who has cared for the patient).

---

[5]   GMC *Guidance for Doctors in relation to children and young people (0 – 18 years)*, 15 October 2007.

[6]   Ibid, para 54.

[7]   The phrase 'Gillick competent' derives from the House of Lords case of *Gillick v West Norfolk and Wisbech Area Health Authority* [1986] AC 112, in which it was determined that children under the age of 16 years could give consent for medical treatment provided they had the cognitive and emotional maturity to understand the implications of the decision being taken.

[8]   DPA 1998, s 7.

[9]   DPA 1998, s 14.

[10] DPA 1998, s 7.

[11] Data Protection (Subject Access Modification) (Health) Order 2000, SI 2000/413.

2.1.2 Right to privacy

Under Art 8 of European Convention on Human Rights everyone has a right to privacy subject to qualifications. There are some circumstances where the data holder may require the court to rule whether disclosure should be made in circumstances in which the records contain sensitive material about third parties.

In these rare cases the court has to balance the public and private rights involved in maintaining the confidentiality of that material against the public and private rights in allowing disclosure for the purposes of a clinical negligence investigation.[12] One solution in these sensitive cases is for disclosure only to be made to the parties' legal representatives and medical experts although a party's lawyer may well finding himself in an ethical dilemma and require guidance from the court before agreeing to such a course of action.

2.1.3 Fees

Patients are entitled to be provided with copies of their records, for example a photocopy of paper records or a print-out of computerised records. It should not be necessary for the solicitor to prove his client's identity when applying for records on that client's behalf as this will already have been carried out by the solicitor for money laundering purposes before the client's file was opened.

Fees are chargeable under the Act and vary dependent on the type of record and whether the patient wants copies of the records or just to see them.[13]

If copies are required the fees chargeable are as follows:
- Records held totally on computer: £10
- Records held in part on computer and in part manually: a reasonable fee of up to £50 unless the records have been added to in the last 40 days when no charge can be made
- Records held totally manually: a reasonable fee of up to £50 unless the records have been added to in the last 40 days when no charge can be made.

If the patient simply needs access to read the original records the charges are:
- Records held totally on computer: £10
- Records held in part on computer and in part manually: £10
- Records held totally manually: £10 unless the records have been added to in the last 40 days when no charge can be made.

---

[12] See eg *Re R (a child)* per Sumner J (unreported) 3 Sept 2004.
[13] Data Protection (Subject Access) Fees and Miscellaneous Provisions) Regulations 2000, SI 2000/191, reg 6.

The maximum fee chargeable for the production of copies of medical records of a living person is therefore £50.

VAT is not chargeable on this fee.[14]

The £50 is not a standard fee. It is the maximum. If the cost of copying is less than £50, the actual cost should be charged. The time for production of the records only starts to run when the fee is paid although some healthcare record holders invoice afterwards.

The Act provides[15] that the copies must be in permanent form unless either that is not possible or would involve disproportionate effort. The maximum fee and the exception where production would require disproportionate effort must not be confused with disproportionate costs.

Most medical records are required for medical treatment and it must be a rare case where their production would require disproportionate effort. The cost of production incurred by a health care provider may well be more than the maximum fee it is entitled to charge under the Act but that does not create an exception. In fixing the maximum chargeable fee for disclosure the Government was well aware that in some cases it would not cover the costs of production but a maximum fee is required in order to balance the patient's right to disclosure of data held about him. Setting the maximum fee too high would have the effect of preventing disclosure and effectively reduce the patient's rights.

2.1.4   Failure to disclose

Records should be disclosed within 40 days although government guidance for healthcare organisations says they should aim to respond within 21 days. Failure of a health care provider to disclose records in accordance with the Act leaves the patient or his representatives with the option of making a complaint to the Data Protection Commissioner (but see below) or an application to the court under Pt 31.16 CPR for pre-action disclosure or for non-party production under Pt 25.

Sometimes a patient may believe that the records disclosed are incomplete. The courts have suggested[16] that that whilst it would be more usual for deficiencies in disclosure to be resolved by cross-examination at trial the court's powers under Pt 3 are wide enough in appropriate circumstances for a pre-action oral hearing to be ordered giving the patient or his representative the opportunity to cross examine medical staff as to the existence or otherwise of the records it is

---

[14]   Customs and Excise Notice 701/57: Health Professionals January 2007 in para 3 medico-legal work.
[15]   DPA 1988, s 8(2).
[16]   *Barnes v Bassetlaw NHS Trust* 2000 MLC 0203.

alleged have not been produced. In his Costs Review Final Report,[17] Jackson LJ, under recommendation 26, suggested that there should be financial penalties for any health authority that, without good reasons, failed to provide copies of medical records requested in accordance with the Pre-Action Protocol for the Resolution of Clinical Disputes. In its consultation paper[18] the Ministry of Justice in response stated that the current system of enforcement under the Data Protection Act via the Information Commissioner was sufficient. However, the Information Commissioner denies this, indicating that late or inadequate disclosure of medical records is not a matter his office can handle.

2.2 DECEASED PATIENTS

The Data Protection Act 1998 only covers the records of living patients. If a person has a claim arising from the death of an individual, he or she has a right of access to information in the deceased's records necessary to fulfil that claim. These rights are set out in the Access to Health Records Act 1990.[19] The provisions and fees are slightly different from those in the Data Protection Act.

2.2.1 Right to privacy

A patient's right to privacy and confidentiality extends after death.

The Access to Health Records Act provides that only information which is directly relevant to the claim may be released.[20] Thus a personal representative or executor can access information to benefit the deceased's estate, as can an individual who was a dependant of the deceased and who has a claim relating to that dependency which has arisen from the death, but the holder of the records may require information to enable him to judge what records are relevant.

In most clinical negligence claims it is likely that the entirety of the medical records will be required either to trawl through for evidence to substantiate a claim or to enable an assessment of life expectancy to be made. It may be extremely difficult for the relatives' solicitor to identify which documents may or not be relevant to the inquiry and the same therefore would be true of the record holder. Provided the nature of the proposed or actual claim is explained the holder should not resist disclosure. The remedy for obstruction is an application to the court for production.

There are certain exemptions to this right to production. A medical record may be withheld if:[21]

---

[17] Jackson, *Review of civil litigation costs*, Final Report (March 2014), www.judiciary.gov.uk/publications/review-of-civil-litigation-costs/.

[18] CP13/10 para 277.

[19] DPA 1988, s 9.

[20] Access to Health Records Act 1990, s 9(1).

[21] AHRA 1990, s 9(3).

- it identifies a third party without that person's consent unless that person is a health professional who has cared for the patient;

- in the opinion of the relevant health professional, it is likely to cause serious harm to somebody's physical or mental health; or

- the patient gave information whilst alive on the understanding that it would be kept confidential after death. Similarly no results of examinations or investigations which the patient thought would be confidential at the time they were carried out can be disclosed. No information at all can be revealed if the patient requested non-disclosure.

Although doctors are advised to explain to their patients the possibility of disclosure after death and solicit views about eventual disclosure where it is obvious in the circumstances that there may be some sensitivity and record such discussions in the medical records, this is rarely done. If there is a noted objection and the record appears to be relevant it may be necessary for the holder of the records to insist on an application for production being made to the court. In that eventuality the court may decide to read the relevant records before deciding on production to the deceased's representatives.

However, the deceased's litigation representative stands in the shoes of the deceased and places his entire medical history in issue at least in so far as it is relevant to the claim. As a result there should be no bar to disclosure to the solicitors instructed on behalf of the deceased's estate.

2.2.2 GP records

If general practice records are required application should be made to the GP's practice where the patient was last registered. A suitably qualified and experienced health professional should review the records before disclosure. If the request is made by a solicitor acting for the patient for clinical negligence purposes this should be a formality.

2.2.3 Fees

Once the person holding the records is satisfied that the person requesting the information is entitled to it, access must then be given within specified time limits. Where the application concerns access to records any of which were made in the 40 day period immediately preceding the date of application access must be given within 21 days. Where the information concerns information all of which was recorded more than 40 days before the date of application, access must be given within 40 days.

An access fee of up to £10 may be charged for providing access to information where all of the records were made more than 40 days before the date of the application. No access fee may be charged for providing access to information if the records have been amended or added to in the previous 40 days.[22]

In the more usual case where copy records are supplied, a fee not exceeding the cost of making the copy may be charged. The charges for copies should be reasonable and can include the cost of posting[23] but unlike a request for production by a person still alive under the Data Protection Act, an applicant for production of a deceased's records under the Access to Health Records Act faces unlimited charges although they still have to be 'reasonable'.

2.3   THE RECORDS

A patient's records include all sudden unexpected incident and inquiry reports as well as reports made to statutory authorities such as the Care Quality Commission. All these documents are disclosable by the holder of the records unless the main reason they were brought into existence was for the purposes of litigation. It also does not matter that the record itself cannot be interpreted by the patient providing it contains a record of the patient's condition which others can interpret.[24]

2.3.1   X-rays

Medical records include x-rays and these are all governed by the costs restrictions under the Data Protection Act. A challenge was made by one health trust that x-rays were not included in the definition of medical records but this was roundly defeated.[25]

The considerable costs involved in copying x-rays has led to trusts adopting a practice of submitting schedules of x-rays leaving it for the claimant's solicitor to identify those which may be relevant so that when notified only relevant scans and x-rays need be copied. Increasingly these days such items are supplied electronically.

2.3.2   Accuracy

The rule regarding the authenticity of records is that the records are assumed to be accurate unless challenged by the other party. When a document is disclosed in a list of documents it is deemed to be authentic unless challenged.

---

[22]   AHRA 1990, s 9(9).
[23]   AHRA 1990, s 9(10).
[24]   Per Mr Recorder Butler, *Hubble v Peterborough Hospitals NHS Trust* (unreported) 21 March 2001.
[25]   *Hubble v Peterborough Hospital NHS Trust* (unreported) 21 March 2001.

2.4   APPLYING FOR RECORDS

The two main sources of records are the patient's GP and treating hospitals. If treatment has been provided privately then records may be held by the patient himself, the clinic or hospital concerned and each treating doctor.

2.4.1   GP records

Applications should be directed in writing to the GP practice concerned. The Law Society has agreed a standard form of application with the BMA a copy of which can be downloaded from the BMA website.[26]

2.4.2   NHS trust hospital records

The Clinical Disputes Forum[27] produced standard forms of application and acknowledgement which are designed to standardise the disclosure procedure and thereby save costs all round. Although use of the forms is voluntary it is better practice to adopt these forms and there should be no need for trusts to supply their own versions. The guidance accompanying the standard forms which was produced in 1998 is now somewhat out of date but the forms themselves are still appropriate They do require the applicant to set out the reason for disclosure and in particular whether a claim is anticipated against the trust or whether the application is for third party disclosure.

2.4.3   Private treatment

Applications for medical records for patients who received private or dental treatment should be directed to the holder of the records. It is usual practice for private patients to be given their own x-rays after treatment. Apart from these private records are likely to be held by both the surgeon and the clinic or hospital concerned. The former is likely to have the operation records and the latter the nursing and after-care records.

2.5   AMENDING RECORDS

A client may well consider that information recorded in his medical records is incorrect.

If instructed in such a case then the advice is that the patient should firstly make an informal approach to the health professional concerned to discuss the situation in an attempt to have the records amended.

---

[26]   See www.bma.org.uk/ap.nsf/Content/bmalawsocform.
[27]   See www.clinical-disputes-forum.org.uk/files/publications/Appendix1.pdf.

If this approach is unsuccessful then the client should be advised to pursue a complaint under the NHS complaints procedure in an attempt to have the information corrected or erased.

If this fails the patient has the right under the Data Protection Act to request that personal information contained within the medical records is rectified, blocked, erased or destroyed if this has been inaccurately recorded. To achieve this he may apply to the Data Protection Information Commissioner[28] or pursue an application for rectification through the courts.

2.6 COMPLAINTS AND INQUIRY RECORDS

All complaints and inquiry/risk management records relating to the client should be requested and produced. Privilege does not apply unless a document was brought into existence for the purposes of legal proceedings.[29]

2.7 CONTENTS OF MEDICAL RECORDS

A client's medical records should be treated with care and respect. They are confidential and that confidentiality should also be respected except for the purposes of putting forward the potential claim.

It is a good idea to keep records so that the exact location of copy records and x-rays can be known at any one time. The record should reveal where they are in the office and when they have been sent to experts and counsel. When the case has finished originals should be returned to the relevant health care provider and copies kept in store or destroyed as appropriate. The client should be made aware of what is happening to his records. They contain data about him and the same protection which a health care provider has to maintain for the patient should apply to the patient as a client.

2.7.1 GP records

GP records in particular tell an individual's life story.

2.7.1.1 *Checking the records*

One of the first things which needs to be checked on receiving medical records is that they all belong to the patient concerned. This may seem strange, but it quite frequently happens that if a husband and wife see a GP together, entries may well be written on just the husband's or just the wife's medical records. Often in a family a son or daughter will be given the first name of one of their parents and a test result or letter or some other document may be filed in the

---

[28] Wycliffe House, Water Lane, Wilmslow, Cheshire SK9 5AF, telephone number 01625 545 700.
[29] *Waugh v British Railways Board* [1980] AC 521.

wrong records by mistake. Some surnames and first names are very common and human error can easily lead to documents being misfiled.

A good starting point is to check the date of birth of the patient in the records against the client's date of birth. If the wrong records have been disclosed contact should be made with the surgery to ascertain whether they should be destroyed (if copies) or returned safely if originals. If only some of the records are of the incorrect patient they again should be returned or destroyed but it is wise to alert the surgery so if copies have been supplied the surgery staff can remove the incorrect records from the originals held at the surgery.

2.7.1.2   Sorting the records

It is a good idea to start by sorting the records into date order into sections as follows:
- computer records
- Lloyd George cards (the actual GP cards)
- correspondence
- lifestyle questionnaires and past medical history
- any clinic cards – ie diabetic, blood pressure etc
- on call duty doctors
- accident and emergency
- temporary resident
- discharge letters
- repeat prescriptions
- nurse documentation – ie health checks, stitches being removed etc
- ECG forms
- test results
- x-rays/scans/ultrasounds
- complaints records.

Unfortunately records are often not dated so the sorter has to become Sherlock Holmes trying to match handwriting or if it is one of the old Lloyd George cards trying to match an entry at the bottom of one card with an entry on the top of the next. This may reveal that some information is missing.

2.7.1.3   Cross-checking

Having sorted the records there are two key tasks. The first is to check that records are complete. The second is to pick up key pointers if the basis of the client's medical complaint is already known.

Obviously incomplete records should be referred back to the surgery with a request for further production. However, some of the documents already disclosed may give a lead to the whereabouts of other documents. These may also be held by the surgery or PCT such as community nurse or midwifery records or by other trusts or agencies which then need to be approached.

When checking the GP records it is often beneficial to look at lifestyle questionnaires and past medical history documents. There may be clues hidden here revealing conditions which should have been acted upon or discovered by others. These may reveal, for example high blood pressure or drug allergies which may turn out to be significant to the investigation ahead.

2.7.2 Hospital records

Hospital records are normally very different from GP records. They too can show a person's life history if they are suffering from a condition that requires regular hospital intervention, but more often they tend to deal with a particular event or a series of different events which may be totally unconnected. It is amazing how often copy hospital records arrive looking as though they have been thrown together randomly making it not only a seemingly daunting task to reassemble the jigsaw but also raising questions as to how the clinicians were ever able to make sense of them during treatment. Indeed poor record keeping is frequently the cause of the adverse event being investigated.

2.7.2.1 *Checking the records*

When dealing with hospital records some of the same points as mentioned above with the GP records applies. The frequency of records being disclosed relating to different patients may be even greater as these records are not a life history kept by stable staff but records dipped in and out of and filed centrally by records clerks with no knowledge of the individual patient. It is surprising how often female records can appear in a man's file and vice versa causing much scratching of heads until the error is realised.

Once again check the date of birth, name and address and remember that patients (particularly female patients) do change their names!

2.7.2.2 *Sorting the records*

It is a good idea to stack the records into a pile and then sort them into sections as follows:
- identification information
- correspondence
- clinical notes
- multi disciplinary
- intensive care
- nursing notes
- clinics

- consent forms and operations
- day case procedures
- accident and emergency
- ambulance service
- maternity
- prescription charts
- charts
- physiotherapy
- occupational therapy
- discharge letters
- discharge summaries
- rehabilitation
- cardiology
- test results
- x-rays/scans/ultrasounds
- traces
- complaints and risk management records.

Once the records have been placed in the piles take a section at a time in as near to the above order as possible depending on the type of case to be dealt with and then sort each section into date order.

Again contrary to all tenets of good record keeping many records will not be dated and Sherlock Holmes therefore has to come into action once again.

Looking at the writing and reading the narrative can sometimes give clues allowing entries to be matched and placed in the correct location. If this does not work, sometimes records will have timed entries referring to other health care workers involved in the patient's care whose own entries may not be dated but can now be correctly positioned in the time-line.

If a particular page still cannot be identified either as to timing or location put it to one side and then at the end of sorting the records, if there are only a few pages left whose correct place in the scheme of things is still unascertained, the task will seem less daunting and by the time the medical case is understood or the expert has reviewed the records their position may become clear. Indeed it is often at this point that some medical knowledge or input is really helpful.

When dealing with test results a decision needs to be made as to whether to file them using the report date and time or just the date when the test was ordered. This is a matter of personal preference but should be applied consistently when dealing with that client's records.

Each section can then be labelled with a divider and placed in a lever arch file.

2.7.2.3 Cross-checking

It will be necessary to check if the records are complete. As well as internally cross checking the records a useful tool will be the client or relative's witness statement or an attendance note giving information as to when the patient attended the hospital, what it is felt went wrong and so on.

It should then be possible to go through the records and follow the chain of events. If a client states that they attended the accident and emergency department three times in two days, there should be three separate accident and emergency sets of records. Another useful pointer is the timing written in records. Sometimes individuals will use a 24 hour clock and others will use a 12 hour clock. Sometimes people forget to move on a year and if the patient attended hospital say in the January of each of two years it is often worth checking the writing and events very carefully just in case the date is wrongly recorded.

When a patient is first seen on a ward a detailed history is usually taken. This can provide useful background material but often the note-taker is a junior doctor in training and key points may be incorrect. There is a danger then that the same inaccuracies are repeated as true history by subsequent entries.

2.7.3 Pagination

Once all the records are placed in their sections it helps if they are paginated. This really does make life much easier for fee earners, experts and eventually counsel and the courts. This obligation is now contained in the standard clinical negligence case management directions. Experts should be encouraged to adopt the pagination in references in their reports. Sometimes case management directions will specify that the claimant's solicitors should keep a running paginated bundle of medical records.

The question of course arises as to whether pagination should still take place if records are known to be incomplete or will be added to, for example, if treatment is continuing. One solution is to number each section and paginate in sections starting at 1 at the beginning of each section so later records can be added and paginated easily.

The solution for missing records is more difficult but there is no reason, for example, why pages 86 a, b, c, d, etc could not be inserted between pages 86 and 87 when missing records are located and added at a later date.

Care should be taken to ensure that copy records are full copies and not truncated or indistinct. If poor quality copies have been supplied send them back or compare them with the originals to ensure everyone is working from as comprehensive set of records as possible. If writing is incomprehensible there is no reason why a transcript should not be requested.

2.7.4   Chronology

The next useful step is to create a chronology or time-line. This can be done by date and or time dependent on the circumstances. Sometimes it is useful to cross-reference entries to other documents, such as statements or reports. Differences and inconsistencies should be highlighted, explained by the client or pointed out to the expert advising on the case. The expert cannot make findings of fact but can indicate which version is likely in his view to be medically credible and explain the impact of each version on his opinion.

2.8   UNDERSTANDING THE RECORDS

It is absolutely fundamental to the successful conduct of a claim even if the advice eventually given is negative that the conducting solicitor understands the medical issues and hence the records even if the sorting and checking is carried out by a medical member of staff or an external agent. Help of course can be at hand from an expert or medically trained member of staff but a library of medical books or guides is vital.

2.8.1   Supplying records

It is accepted by the courts that, absent exceptional circumstances, the claimant's solicitor should organise and manage the disclosure of medical records to third parties[30] so it should not be necessary for a client to be asked to sign an authority for production in favour of a defendant. The claimant's solicitor is entitled to levy a copying charge.

In *Coveney v P&O Ferries*[31] Master Whittaker did not consider it appropriate to cap copying charges and 35p per sheet was approved. The defendant's argument that any copying charge should be capped at the £50 Data Protection Act maximum was also rejected. In *DH v South Devon Healthcare NHS Foundation Trust*[32] the defendant trust refused to pay 35p per sheet for copies of the claimant's GP records arguing that 25p was more reasonable and absent agreement on payment applied for a direct authority. Master Roberts dismissed the defendant's application with costs.

2.8.2   Hearsay evidence

In the case of *Fifield v Denton Hall*,[33] Buxton LJ considered the issue of the use of the evidence arising out of the medical records. In this case a secretary developed a repetitive strain injury during the course of her employment. One of the main issues of fact was the date on which the symptoms manifested

---

30   *Bennett v Compass Costs* [2002] EWCA Civ 642.
31   (unreported) 15 February 2010.
32   (unreported).
33   *Denton Hall Legal Services v Fifield* [2006] EWCA Civ 169, [2006] All ER (D) 104 (Mar), (2006) *The Times*, 22 March, CA.

themselves. The only witness as to this was the claimant herself. The Court of Appeal had to consider whether it could differ from the judge's acceptance of her account. The defendants argued that the judge should have attached proper weight to the contemporaneous medical notes and the history given by the claimant to the defendant's doctor.

He went on to consider the evidential status of such material and set out the following:

- When a doctor makes notes based on what he has been told by a patient (as opposed to his medical opinion), this is hearsay evidence.
- If the doctor's record contradicts the claimant's evidence as to fact, the record is of a previous inconsistent statement allegedly made by the claimant.
- For this 'statement' to be proved as evidence, the witness can admit to making it when it is put to him/her (or if he does not admit that he made the statement it can be proved under s 4 of Criminal Procedure Act 1865).
- Or the statement can be proved under s 1 of the Civil Evidence Act 1995.

If the court concludes that such a statement has been made that is inconsistent, the statement cannot be treated as evidence of its contents, it only goes to the credibility of the witness.

He was critical of the fact that in this case, these steps were not taken. He held that part of the confusion was that the areas of dispute had not been identified before the trial. The defence had simply stated: 'neither admitted nor denied, as the Defendant has no knowledge of the matters pleaded therein and the Claimant is put to strict proof'.

He found that even if the defendants could not have pleaded any more before disclosure, the defendants could have revisited their defence before the trial by which time they knew that they would be advancing a positive case on the basis of inconsistent statements.

He set out the proper procedure to be followed as follows:

- First, a party who sought to contradict a factually pleaded case on the basis of medical records or reports should indicate this in advance, either by amending the pleadings or by informal notice.
- Then the other party must indicate the extent to which they object to the accuracy of the records.
- When the area of dispute has been identified, then the party needs to decide whether the records need to be proved and by which means.

If these precautions have not been taken, the judge at trial may be reluctant to allow reference to the claimant's statements in the medical records for the purpose of contradicting her evidence. Alternatively if there is an unreasonable failure to admit that such statements were made, to the extent that it is necessary to call busy doctors to court simply to prove them, then such failure to co-operate is likely to be punished in costs.

2.8.3 Abbreviations

The meanings behind common abbreviations found in medical records are revealed by Dr Tom Boyd in Appendix 1.

TOP TIPS

*   If the patient is alive the production of records is governed by the data protection legislation; if the patient is deceased by the Access to Health Records Act 1990.
*   The £50 Data Protection Act fee is not a standard fee. It is the maximum.
*   A patient's right to privacy and confidentiality extends after death.
*   Records are assumed to be accurate unless challenged.
*   Check the date of birth of the patient in the records disclosed against the client's date of birth to ensure the correct records have been disclosed.
*   It is fundamental to the successful conduct of a claim that the conducting solicitor understands the medical issues and hence the records even if the sorting and checking is carried out by a medical member of staff or an external agent.

CHAPTER 3

NHS COMPLAINTS PROCEDURE AND REDRESS

Since first writing on this subject in 1998 solicitor Rosamund Rhodes-Kemp has tracked various reviews and reports all of which have highlighted problems with the complaints process and called for reform. The recent Clwyd-Hart report on NHS complaints makes further key recommendations, which are explained later in this chapter.

3.1 INTRODUCTION

The legislation governing the NHS complaints procedure is the Local Authority, Social Services and National Health Service Complaint (England) Regulations 2009.

These regulations set out the obligations on healthcare providers when dealing with complaints.

The NHS Complaints system is designed to provide:
- explanations of what happened
- if appropriate, apologies
- information about action taken to prevent similar incidents happening again.

The complaints process introduced in April 2009 now has two stages:
(1) local resolution
(2) independent review by the Health Service Ombudsman.

It is worth noting that complaint documentation and the findings of professional bodies can form an important part of the solicitor's risk assessment before deciding whether to take on a case, the CFA risk analysis or when applying for funding. So always bear in mind that there may have been an investigation into an incident and a serious untoward investigation report or response to complaint or suspension or referral to a professional body and, if so, all the relevant information should be requested.

Any errors identified can help support a letter of claim and or allegations of negligence and can be an invaluable tool in seeking an early admission of liability.

3.2 SERVICES COVERED BY THE NHS COMPLAINT PROCEDURE

The services covered by the NHS complaint procedure are:

- all NHS and NHS Foundation Trusts
- clinical care commissioning groups (CCCG) (formerly primary care trusts) covering GPs, dentists, opticians and pharmacists working within the NHS
- private healthcare paid for by the NHS.

Also since April 2009, patients subject to certain aspects of the Mental Health Act 1983 have had statutory access to an independent mental health advocate (IMHA). IMHAs help and support patients to understand and exercise their legal rights. They are available to most detained patients as well as patients under supervised community treatment of guardianship.

It is worth noting that the total number of NHS written complaints reported in 2011–12 equates to more than 3,000 a week representing an increase of 8% on the previous year. The Parliamentary and Health Service Ombudsman reported a similar increase and a significant increase of 50% of complainants who felt that the NHS had inadequately acknowledged mistakes in care.

3.3 STAGE ONE: LOCAL RESOLUTION

Since April 2009, there is a duty on NHS bodies to provide a written response to complaints.

3.3.1 Time limits

The complaint should be made within six months of the date of the incident, or within six months of discovering the problem, provided this is within 12 months of the incident. In other words, the overall time limit is 12 months.

NHS organisations have a discretion to waive this time limit if there are good reasons to do so; for example, delay due to mental or physical illness, but as a general rule the complaint should be made as soon as possible after the incident occurs.

Whereas previously the procedure was subject to strict time limits for the investigation, these seem to have been relaxed and this means that while the complainant may get an acknowledgment fairly quickly, the investigation and formal response may take some time. A lot depends on the complexity of the issues, the period of the complaint and the number of staff involved in the investigation/complaint.

3.3.2 The process

- Ask the NHS provider for a copy of its complaints procedure, which will explain exactly how to proceed.

- A complaint can be made orally, in writing or electronically, but all must be answered in writing and it is advisable to make a complaint in writing and addressed to the chief executive or, in the case of clinical commissioning groups, to the complaints manager for that group.

- The complaint should include who or what the complainant is complaining about, where and when the event happened and who was involved.

- It is advisable to include what the complainant would like to achieve as a result of the complaint.

- The healthcare provider must provide a response to the complaint within three working days after receipt and in that response the complainant should also be told:
  - of an opportunity to discuss the complaint, for example at a meeting;
  - information about the way in which the complaint is going to be investigated;
  - the time period within which the investigation of the complaint is likely to be completed including updates in the event of a delay in concluding the investigation and an explanation as to why that delay has occurred.

- At the end of the investigation the complainant receives a formal written response.

3.3.3 Meetings

Complainants can be asked to attend meetings by the NHS provider and it is important prior to such meetings that the complainant asks the NHS provider:

- The format of the meeting.

- Who will be attending the meeting because they usually involve members of staff and hospital or NHS provider management and these may not be those directly involved with the care that is being complained about. In some instances complainants prefer not to meet the person that they are complaining about face to face, but in other circumstances the complainant and/or family and relatives may wish for a particular individual to be at the meeting and it is important to ask for this at the time of notification of the meeting:
  - Many complainants or family and relatives take a friend or someone to support them at the meeting and to take notes.
  - Increasingly these meetings are recorded, minutes are not necessarily taken, and the recording is put on a CD, which is subsequently given to the complainant. Therefore if the complaint would prefer to have a written record, it is important to explain this, again upon notification of the meeting, and when asking for details of the format and attendance.

Previously there were strict time limits for NHS providers to investigate and respond to complaints, but these are no longer set in stone, which is why it makes sense to obtain a copy of the NHS providers' complaints procedure before starting the complaints process. However, the whole process should be discussed with the complainant and agreed including any extensions and, where there is an unreasonable amount of time being taken, the complaint can appeal to the Health Service Ombudsman.

Although compensation is not normally part of the NHS complaints process, it is the case that NHS bodies do have the discretion to make modest 'ex gratia' payments. If the matter is complex, the injury suffered is serious or the amount involved substantial then arguably the NHS complaints process is not the appropriate route and legal advice should be sought. Likewise if compensation is offered as part of the NHS complaints process, most NHS bodies will recommend, and arguably should recommend, that the complainant seek legal advice before accepting that payment.

Until April 2009, the NHS complaints process and legal action were mutually exclusive, but since April 2009 it is possible for a complainant to be taking legal action and making an NHS complaint at the same time.

3.3.4   Serious Untoward Investigations – SUIs

SUIs are becoming more frequent and, on the positive side, many trusts are carrying out very thorough internal investigations following a serious untoward incident.

This involves interviewing staff and preparing witness statements, assessing all the documentation and the history and then preparing a chronology, a root cause analysis of how the error came to occur and an action plan of changes to be made with a time frame. The main purpose of the SUI is to ascertain how the mistake has occurred, learn from it and prevent it happening again.

A cynic may say that the internal investigation can pre-empt criticism of a trust or, in fatal cases, a report under reg 28 of the Coroners (Investigation) Regulations 2013[1] demanding change and/or an enhanced inquest under s 2 of the Human Rights Act. However, it is clear that many trusts take their responsibility to investigate internally very seriously and make genuine efforts to learn from mistakes and put in place preventative measures to avoid recurrence, some even going so far as to try and change the culture or systems if either of these are found to be one of the root causes of the problem.

From a claimant's solicitors point of view, the SUI and report are an important stage of the investigation into a legal claim.

---

[1]   SI 2013/1629.

All the documentation relating to the SUI including preparatory documents or those associated with the investigation including e-mails and minutes of meetings should all be requested. It is important also to ask for draft documents so, for example, all drafts of the witness statements and the root cause analysis because it is quite surprising how this evidence can change over the course of the SUI and can be far more revealing than the final documentation.

The best advice is, if in doubt as to whether an SUI has been conducted, ask for an SUI report.

There are also now what are described as 'never event' errors in the NHS. There is up-to-date list that can be found at www.dh.gov.uk/publications.

3.4 STAGE TWO: THE PARLIAMENTARY AND HEALTH SERVICE OMBUDSMAN

If the complainant remains unhappy after the NHS complaint has been processed or indeed is unhappy about the way the NHS complaint is being processed then the matter can be referred to the Parliamentary and Health Service Ombudsman who is independent of the NHS and the Government.

The office of the Parliamentary and Health Service Ombudsman was created by the NHS Re-Organisation Act 1973 and then modified by the Parliamentary and Health Service Commissioners Act 1987, the Health Service Commissioners Act 1993 and the Health Service Commissioner (Amendment) Act 1996.

The 1996 Act increased the scope of the investigations by the Health Service Commissioner allowing an investigation into all aspects of NHS care and treatment, including clinical judgment.

The aim of the Act was to effectively put the Ombudsman at the top of a unified NHS complaints procedure.

The Health Service Commissioners Act 1993 (as amended) gives the Ombudsman power to investigate in the following circumstances:

(1) On a complaint duly made to (the Commissioners) by or on behalf of a person that he or she has sustained injustice or hardship in consequence of:
   • a failure in a service provided by a Health Service body,
   • a failure of such a body to provide a service which is was a function of the body to provide, or
   • maladministration connected with any other action taken by or on behalf of.

(2) Any failure or maladministration as above includes:
   • the Health Service body
   • a person employed by that body
   • a person acting on behalf of that body, or

- a person whom that body has delegated in functions.

3.4.1 Making a complaint to the Parliamentary and Health Service Ombudsman

This is the final stage of the NHS complaints process and the Parliamentary and Health Service Ombudsman's office would normally only accept a complaint if a complainant has already been through the local resolution stage.

- The Parliamentary and Health Service Ombudsman's website provides a ste-by-step guide to making a complaint including a form that can be downloaded and either completed manually or online.
- The Ombudsman also asks for all the evidence about the complaint in particular letters to and from the organisation about which the complaint has been made.
- In the alternative a complaint can be made in writing:
    - The Parliamentary and Health Service Ombudsman, Millbank Tower, Millbank, London SW1P 4QP.
    - E-mail: phso.enquiries@ombudsman.org.uk or telephone 0345 0154033. The telephone lines are open between 8.30am and 5.30pm, Monday to Friday excluding public holidays.

By referring the matter to the Parliamentary and Health Service Ombudsman, the complainant is asking for an independent review and this may include obtaining independent medical experts' opinion if the matter relates to perceived errors of clinical judgment.

NB. Advice for complainants on the two stages of the standard NHS complaints process is set out on the NHS Choices website.

3.4.2 Potential outcome of the NHS complaint procedure

- At both stages the complainants will receive a written response either from the NHS provider if stage one or the Parliamentary and Health Service Ombudsman if stage two.
- A meeting, conciliation or mediation may be offered.
- Referral to statutory bodies including, for example, the General Medical Council (GMC) or the Nursing and Midwifery Council (NMC).
- Referral for inspection which would now be the remit of the Care Quality Commission.
- A recommendation that no further action be taken.

3.5 APPEALS

It is possible to challenge the refusal to investigate or the findings of a trust or disciplinary body. The process involves an application for judicial review, but the time and costs involved need to be carefully considered in terms of the benefit to any legal case and with a view to proportionality.

Any application for judicial review would be based on the ground that the decision was unlawful or Wednesbury unreasonable.

Examples include:

- a decision-maker does not have the power to make the decision or is using the power they do have improperly;
- the procedure adopted was unfair or biased;
- the decision is irrational;
- the decision is in breach of the Human Rights Act; or
- the decision breaches European Community law.

Obviously the application for judicial review is concerned with how the decision itself was made and anyone claiming for judicial review must have a direct, personal interest in the action or decision being challenged.

3.6 RECENT OR FORTHCOMING CHANGES TO THE NHS COMPLAINTS PROCEDURE

Even in the process of writing this chapter, there have been a number of changes that are likely to influence the way NHS complaints are handled in the future.

3.6.1 The Care Quality Commission

The Care Quality Commission (CQC) has been set up to provide independent regulation of all health and social care services in England. The CQC regulates and inspects hospitals, care homes, GP surgeries, Dentists, ambulance and mental health services and details of their activities and reports and updates can be found on their website.

The CQC does not have a role in handling individual complaints, but it does have power to ensure registered service providers are handling complaints properly. It will also use feedback from users of NHS services to spot patterns of incidents indicating that there could be a more widespread problem.

3.6.2 Healthwatch

New local Healthwatch organisations and Healthwatch England, a new independent consumer body within the CQC, were introduced by the Health and Social Care Act 2012.

The thrust of this Act was to introduce measures intended from April 2013 to strengthen the voice of patients.

Local Healthwatch groups have been set up as part of the local community in order to work in partnership with other local organisations. Essentially the role of Healthwatch is to ensure that the voices of patients and those using services reach the ears of decision-makers.

They offer useful information to those wishing to make a complaint including a complaints tool and leaflet which can be obtained from a complainants local Healthwatch.

3.6.3   Redress

The Redress Scheme has its origins in the NHS Redress Act 2006, but in fact the proposed reforms can be traced back even further to a paper published by Government in July 2000 entitled: *A Plan for Investment, A Plan for Reform*, which committed the Department of Health to look at ways to improve the system for handling and responding to clinical negligence claims that were perceived as being too slow, cumbersome and costly.

The NHS Redress Act 2006 was due to come into force in 2009 with the Redress Scheme up and running shortly afterwards.

The purpose of the Scheme was to establish a process to enable early resolution by providing a quick and appropriate response for low monetary value clinical negligence cases without the need to commence court proceedings.

As at the time of writing, there is a pilot for a Redress Scheme in Wales currently working its way through the system and, according to those involved, the introduction of the Scheme has greatly increased the number of claims being received by the Health Service in Wales and this has resulted in significant delays in dealing with those claims.

Whether it is cognisance of this reality that has further delayed the introduction of the Redress Scheme in England is not clear, but negotiations do seem to have stalled for two main reasons:

(1)   Whether entry to the Scheme should be defined by reference to value or type of case with the claimant's side arguing that the Scheme should be open to:
   (a)   claims for the claimant's physical and psychiatric health is wholly recovered to the pre-existing injury health within 12 months from the date of occurrence and there is no ongoing financial loss;
   (b)   fatal accident cases without dependency claims;
   (c)   any other claims by agreement.

(2)   Whether the Scheme should be truly voluntary and therefore there be no costs consequences to any participants for choosing the court system instead.

It is also true that there have been significant disagreements as to whether or not the Scheme should have fixed costs.

So at the time of writing the NHS Redress Scheme has not been introduced in England and there is some doubt as to whether it will be in the foreseeable future.

3.6.4 The Francis Report 2013 and more recently the Clwyd-Hart Report on NHS complaints published in November 2013

Tricia Hart and Ann Clwyd were commissioned by the Secretary of State for Health for legal review as part of a response to the Francis Report which highlighted that complaints are a warning sign of problems in a hospital and that their importance should be escalated to board level to ensure that complaints were effectively monitored, problems identified and action taken.

Key recommendations of the Clwyd-Hart Report are as follows:
- Chief executives need to take responsibility for signing off complaints. The trust board should also scrutinise all complaints and evaluate what action has been taken. A board member with responsibility for whistle-blowing should also be accessible to staff on a regular basis.
- Trusts must publish an annual complaints report in plain English, which state the complaints made and changes that have taken place.
- The trusts should ensure that there is a range of basic information and support on the wards of patients, such as a description of who is on the ward and what time visiting and meals take place.
- Patients and communities should be involved in designing and monitoring the complaints system in hospitals.
- Trusts should provide patients with a means of feeding back comments and concerns about their care on a ward, including putting a pen and paper by the bedside and making sure patients know who they can speak to, to raise a concern.
- The Patient Advice and Liaison Service should be rebranded and reviewed so its offer to patients is clearer and it should be adequately resourced in every hospital.
- The Independent Advocacy Services should also be rebranded and reorganised.
- Staff need adequate support and training on listening to and acting on feedback, with appraisals linked to their communication skills.

Whether or not these recommendations will be implemented and, if so, when is unclear. What is apparent is that complaints are in future going to form a more pivotal role in monitoring and informing healthcare provision.

3.7 PROFESSIONAL REGULATIONS

There may be occasions when a complainant feels that the treatment, attitude or behaviour of a health care professional might call into question his or her fitness to practice and, in this case, a complaint can be made to the relevant professional body.

The two main organisations are the General Medical Council and the Nursing and Midwifery Council.

3.7.1 The General Medical Council Complaints Procedure

It may be appropriate in certain circumstances to report a doctor to the General Medical Council (GMC).

If, however, a patient or relative is unhappy with the doctor's treatment or care and wants an apology, explanation or review of the treatment received, then the first point of contact would be the person in charge of the care at local level. A complaint should first of all be made to that individual, whether that be the ward manager or the consultant or head of the department, or for GPs, the practice manager.

The GMC is responsible for ensuring doctors maintain good practice in accordance with the standard set by the GMC itself.

It is possible to contact the GMC direct by telephone if the person wishing to complain is unsure whether the doctor is fit to practise or not. These telephone calls are confidential.

The doctor can also be reported in writing to the GMC Fitness to Practise Directorate. It is possible to download the complaint form from the website then complete it and send it by post or email.

All complaints are reviewed carefully to see if there are any issues to be investigated.

If it is decided not to investigate, the GMC may pass the complaint to the doctor's employers so that it can be looked into more closely at local level.

If the GMC do decide to investigate then it will send a copy of the complaint to the doctor and ask for comments. The complainant is then given a chance to respond. At this stage a fact sheet will be sent to the complainant entitled 'Investigating Concerns'.

Once the GMC Fitness to Practise Directorate has full details of the complaint and the doctor's comments the case will be considered by two case examiners (one medical and one non-medical). They will consider whether the concerns are serious enough to warrant a hearing.

If the matter goes to a hearing then a panel will be convened to hear the case and decide if a doctor is fit to practise or not. These hearings are held in private.

The information required by the GMC is:

- doctor's name and work address;
- an explanation of the complaint with dates;
- copies of any supporting documentation, eg medical records or correspondence;
- name and address of anyone else who can support the facts surrounding the complaint.

3.7.1.1   What will the GMC investigate?

The GMC will not investigate all complaints. The trigger is whether or not there is a question as to the doctor's fitness to practise.

Examples of when the GMC will investigate include:

- prescribing drugs in a dangerous way;
- serious and repeated mistakes in making the right diagnosis;
- failure to examine the patient properly;
- failure to respond reasonably to a patient's needs;
- fraud or defamatory conduct;
- serious breach of a patient's confidentiality;
- serious criminal offence.

3.7.1.2   Possible action by the GMC

This will depend on the severity of the complaint. But the GMC can:

- issue a warning;
- impose conditions on the doctor's registration so that they are only allowed to treat patients under supervision or that they are restricted to certain areas of practice;
- agree undertakings, for example to retrain or work under supervision.

3.7.1.3   What the GMC cannot do

It is important for a potential complainant to realise the limits on what the GMC can do. Examples of what the GMC cannot do include:

- explain in detail what happened;
- order a doctor to provide the treatment a patient might want;
- pay compensation;
- fine a doctor;

- order a doctor to give access to medical records;
- order a doctor to apologise.

3.7.2 Nursing and Midwifery Council complaints procedure

The Nursing and Midwifery Council (NMC) is the regulatory body for nurses and midwives and specialised community public health nurses. The aim of the NMC is to protect the public by setting and maintaining standards for all those regulated by the NMC.

- The vast majority of complaints should be made at local level either orally or in writing with supporting documentation if available.
- However, there may be situations where the complaint is so serious, ie the nurse or midwife is unsafe and poses a danger to patients, that the NMC should be contacted direct by telephone or letter.
- A complaint form is available from the NMC from their website or by telephone.
- Once the form is completed it needs to be posted to the NMC.
- It is vital that the complainant identifies the name of the health professional, details of the complaint with dates and the complainant's name and contact details.
- The NMC will acknowledge the letter and the completed form within five working days of receipt by the Fitness to Practise Department.
- If it falls within the remit of the Fitness to Practise Department it will be investigated but if it falls outside or there is insufficient evidence the case will be closed. In any event the NMC will endeavour to put a complainant in touch with someone who can help and support him with the process.
- If the evidence is upheld and a complaint is investigated further then a nurse or midwife may have to appear at a formal nursing and midwifery hearing. This will be convened by the NMC and consists of a panel of specialists who will hear the evidence in private and then adjudicate.

The purpose of NMC proceedings is to protect the public rather than to punish registrants. Registrants who appear before panels are judged against the NMC's Code of Professional Conduct, Standards of Conduct, Performance and Ethics. The panels look for a level of conduct and competence expected of the average registrant.

3.7.2.1 *What will the NMC investigate?*

The NMC will not investigate every complaint but the ambit is extensive.

Examples of when the NMC will investigate include:
- hitting or assaulting a patient;
- stealing money or property from a patient;
- sexually or racially abusing a patient;

- a serious criminal offence;
- having an improper relationship with the patient;
- downloading child pornography;
- administering drugs in a dangerous manner;
- shouting or swearing at a patient;
- failing to ensure patient hygiene or neglect;
- poor quality of care;
- failing to obtain consent;
- failing to keep proper and accurate records.

3.7.2.2 *Possible sanctions by the NMC*

Sanctions will be considered in the following order:

- Take no further action.
- Caution the registrant and direct that the caution be noted against the registrant entry in the Registry for a period of not less than one and not more than five years (a 'caution order').
- Impose conditions with which the registrants must comply for a specified period of not more than three years (a 'conditions of practice order').
- Suspend the individual's registration for a period up to one year (a 'suspension order').
- Strike the individual off the Register (a 'striking-off order').

3.7.3 Other professional organisations

Professional bodies can and do suspend doctors, nurses and midwives pending an investigation often to protect the public, but the individual under investigation is frequently re-instated once the investigation is complete if they are not to be a risk or are prepared to work under supervision or undergo further training. To patients this can seem very unjust especially if it is possible that the mistake, act or omission of the individual under investigation may have contributed to injury or death.

3.7.4 Complaints about private health treatment

The complaints process for private health care is very similar to that of the NHS.

Private hospitals and clinics carrying out medical treatment are regulated by the Care Standards Act 2000. Under this Act all hospitals and clinics must operate a complaints procedure that should follow the same pattern as the NHS Complaints Procedure. Presumably this means that it will be reviewed at the same time as the NHS Complaints Procedure is reviewed.

The key points are as follows:

- A potential complainant needs first to try to deal with the issue at local level and discuss concerns with the treating consultant or care provider in order to obtain an explanation and advice regarding future treatment or care.

- If that is unsuccessful the complainant should make a formal complaint to the hospital or clinic that provided the treatment or care. To do this the complainant should ask for details of the complaints procedure.

- The complaint should then be addressed to the organisation concerned complete with any documentation in support.

- The same time-limits apply as for the NHS.

- If a complainant remains unhappy about the lack of response or what the response contains it is possible to complain to the Healthcare Commission that is responsible for regulating private health care providers as well as the NHS.

- Unlike the NHS there is no third stage as the Health Service Ombudsman's remit does not cover private health treatment.

NB. If a complaint is about a healthcare professional's fitness to practice then the complainant should make a complaint to the relevant regulatory body, for example the GMC.

3.7.5   Other organisations that can help

(1) Local Healthwatch.

(2) The Patients Association, which is a charity set up to tackle poor care and the causes of poor care and which operates a Patient Helpline and can be contacted on 0845 608 4455 or email helpline@patients-association.com.

(3) Actions Against Medical Accidents (AvMA): AvMA is an independent UK-wide charity. It can help patients to consider the options that may be open to them after suffering a medical accident, including providing contacts for specialist solutions. AvMA have a helpline: 0845 123 2352 (open Monday to Friday, 10am to 5pm).

(4) The Care Quality Commission (CQC) is the independent regulator of health and social care in England. The CQC does not have a role in handling individual complaints, but it does have powers to ensure registered providers are handling complaints properly. It will also use feedback from users of NHS services to spot patterns of incidents indicating that there could be a problem.

(5) Citizens Advice Bureau: CAB can advise on NHS complaints.

TOP TIPS

- A patient has a right to make a complaint.
- The NHS Complaints Process and a legal claim are no longer mutually exclusive.

- Complaints can be a very useful source of information on which to base advice on whether there is a viable claim for compensation.
- Complaints should be addressed and resolved at local level.
- A complainant may now obtain small ex-gratia sums of compensation through the NHS Complaints Procedure.
- Keep a close watch on the time-limits if legal action is also being contemplated.
- The Health Service Ombudsman's role has been extended to include consideration of clinical competence.

CHAPTER 4

THE FUNDING OF CLINICAL NEGLIGENCE CLAIMS

Lawyers are business people and clinical negligence practitioners are no exception. Financing an action is essential yet often problematic. In this chapter solicitor David Marshall reviews the pitfalls and possibilities of funding a clinical negligence claim.

4.1 INITIAL INSTRUCTIONS AND FUNDING

This chapter considers only the funding of new clinical negligence claims after 1 April 2013 when the landscape fundamentally changed. This was because of:

- the severe reduction in eligibility for legal aid; and
- the abolition of recoverability of success fees and after the event insurance premiums as costs from the loser under the Legal Aid, Sentencing and Punishment of Offenders Act 2012.

For the very different landscape affecting cases begun before 1 April 2013, please refer to the corresponding chapter in the first edition of this work. Transitional provisions relating to conditional fee agreements and one-way cost shifting are considered briefly in **4.2.7.1** and **4.3.1**.

4.1.1 The retainer

The solicitor needs to be clear about how a client is liable to pay for the work that is to be done so that:

- the solicitor can charge for that work, whether those charges are to be paid by the opponent or by the client;
- the client knows what they will have to pay the solicitor, if anything, and when;
- to ensure that it is a lawful method of funding legal work.

For clinical negligence claims, this is even more important than usual because the overall costs are likely to be much higher than in many other types of litigation for individuals. So there is more potentially at risk if the retainer is wrong. It is essential that this is resolved at the earliest opportunity.

If the case succeeds, it is usual under the English 'loser pays' rule for the defendant to be liable for most of the claimant's costs on top of the damages. The order for costs in the claimant's favour is by way of an indemnity for the costs the claimant has incurred ('the indemnity principle'). If the claimant has incurred no legal liability for costs to the solicitor, then there is nothing to indemnify and the costs order is worthless. As the solicitor cannot enforce a costs claim against the client in these circumstances and can recover nothing from the defendant, it is the solicitor who will go unremunerated despite the considerable efforts the solicitor has made. And, furthermore, in a clinical negligence case success is uncertain. If the case fails, the solicitor needs to know whether or not he is to be paid and, if so, how much and by whom. If he is not to be paid at all, the solicitor should be compensated for taking this risk by a success fee under a conditional fee agreement or, subject to the comments as to their present efficacy in 4.2.8, a damages-based agreement.

4.1.2   Pre-screening work

Clinical negligence enquiries have a notoriously high overall turn-down rate. Many potential clients who telephone a solicitor with an enquiry have no legal case for clinical negligence. There may have been a poor outcome, but that may have been due to the patient's underlying condition. There may have just been a poor explanation by medical staff. There may have been poor 'service delivery', but no loss. There may have been loss, but no breach of duty. There may have been breach of duty but no causation. There are commonly limitation issues.

The client may have no real knowledge of what happened and have obtained no medical records. Few potential clients would be able or prepared to pay privately for a full medico-legal investigation into their case and, in a number of cases, even if they did, they would be quite obviously wasting their money from the outset. Similarly, legal expense insurers expect skilled practitioners to undertake some pre-screening rather than take every potential clinical negligence claim at face value and undertake a full review.

That said practitioners should be slow to advise there is no case or indeed decline to investigate further on inadequate evidence. It is often a fine balance. If instructions are declined, it always safest from a professional indemnity insurance perspective to advise in general terms on limitation and stress that the firm is simply declining instructions, rather than giving a view on the merits, even an informal one.

4.1.3   Available funding options

The following are the main ways in which a client might choose to fund a clinical negligence claim. They are not mutually exclusive and can sometimes be used in combination:

- Private client (see 4.2.1).
- BTE ('Before the event' insurance) (see 4.2.2).

- Trade Union (see **4.2.3**).
- 'Litigation Funding' or 'Third Party Funding' (see **4.2.4**).
- Litigation loan (see **4.2.5**).
- Legal Aid/Public Funding (see **4.2.6**).
- Conditional Fee Agreement (CFA) (see **4.2.7**).
- Damages-based Agreement (DBA) (see **4.2.8**).

4.1.4   Preliminary investigations

The firm might:

- investigate pro bono (and never seek costs for this work); or
- sign a conditional fee agreement immediately; or
- seek to recover costs prior to the date of the conditional fee agreement retrospectively; or
- enter into a 'pre-litigation costs agreement'; or
- enter into a full or partial (eg disbursements only) private client retainer.

Pro bono investigation is simple, but expensive to the firm. A limit on time to be spent and money expended should be set.

An immediate conditional fee agreement is relatively simple. The downside is that the firm is committing to a retainer before undertaking a risk assessment. Although it is of course possible to terminate in accordance with the terms of the conditional fee agreement (eg because the solicitor no longer believes the case will 'win'), the risk being assumed may turn out to be much greater than anticipated and the success fee too low. Conversely, it may be difficult to properly set a success fee prior to investigation.

On current authority a conditional fee agreement can operate retrospectively.[1] It is important to make it clear on the face of the conditional fee agreement that it is dated when signed and operates retrospectively (and not actually to 'backdate' it by implying that the conditional fee agreement was signed at an earlier time than it in fact was).[2] If using the Law Society's model conditional agreement it is important to amend this to provide for the agreement to operate from an earlier date (the standard provision is for it to cover ongoing work only). The model agreement might also be amended to make it a contentious business agreement, as s 59(1) Solicitors Act 1974 expressly allows for a contentious business agreement to be in respect of work 'done or to be done'.

It might be possible to enter into a 'pre-litigation agreement' (which provides for normal costs if the case is won and nothing if the case is abandoned after investigation, or lost) following the Court of Appeal's decision in *Gaynor v*

---

[1]   *Forde v Birmingham* [2009] EWHC 12 (QB), [2009] All ER (D) 64 (Jan).
[2]   See *Holmes v McAlpine* [2006] EWHC 110 (QB).

Central West London Buses Ltd,[3] but care should be taken as this applied only to 'modest pre-litigation services' and is a somewhat peculiar decision perhaps rather on its own facts rather than for general application. The line of cases leading to *Geraghty & Co v Awwad*[4] remains good law that such an agreement will normally be an unenforceable contingency fee.

It is possible to enter into a private retainer for the investigation which might be a full retainer or one which provides for disbursements and maybe a fixed fee. If so, only costs that the client is liable to pay can be recovered as costs from the defendant at the end of the case. In addition, the client's potential liability both for the immediate costs and some explanation as to what might happen at the end of the investigation must be given at the outset.

4.1.5   The Solicitors Code of Conduct

The SRA Code of Conduct was introduced in 2011 and applies a new form of 'outcomes focused regulation'. Solicitors have to abide by the spirit of the code, and cannot look for loopholes to avoid its specific provisions. The overriding principles, many of which must apply to entering into a funding agreement with a client, are:

'You must:
1. uphold the rule of law and the proper administration of justice;
2. act with integrity;
3. not allow your independence to be compromised;
4. act in the best interests of each *client*;
5. provide a proper standard of service to your *clients*;
6. behave in a way that maintains the trust the public places in you and in the provision of legal services;
7. comply with your legal and regulatory obligations and deal with your regulators and ombudsmen in an open, timely and co-operative manner;
8. run your business or carry out your role in the business effectively and in accordance with proper governance and sound financial and risk management principles;
9. run your business or carry out your role in the business in a way that encourages equality of opportunity and respect for diversity; and
10. protect *client* money and *assets*.'

The main outcomes that relate to funding agreements are:

'O(1.1) – you treat your *clients* fairly;

O(1.3) – when deciding whether to act, or terminate your instructions, you comply with the law and the Code;

---

3   [2006] EWCA Civ 1120.
4   (2000) 3 WLR 1041, [2000] 1 All ER 608.

O(1.6) – you only enter into fee agreements with your *clients* that are legal, and which you consider are suitable for the *client's* needs and take account of the *client's* best interests;

O(1.12) – *clients* are in a position to make informed decisions about the services they need, how their matter will be handled and the options available to them;

O(1.13) – *clients* receive the best possible information, both at the time of engagement and when appropriate as their matter progresses, about the likely overall cost of their matter;

O(1.14) – *clients* are informed of their right to challenge or complain about your bill and the circumstances in which they may be liable to pay interest on an unpaid bill;'.

It is mandatory to achieve these outcomes.

The Code of Conduct also provides a number of 'indicative behaviours' that will be evidence of compliance with the Code. The most relevant are:

'IB(1.2) – explaining your responsibilities and those of the *client*;

IB(1.5) – explaining any limitations or conditions on what you can do for the *client*, for example, because of the way the *client's* matter is funded;

IB(1.6) – in taking instructions and during the course of the retainer, having proper regard to your *client's* mental capacity or other vulnerability, such as incapacity or duress;

IB(1.10) – if you have to cease acting for a *client*, explaining to the *client* their possible options for pursuing their matter;

IB(1.13) – discussing whether the potential outcomes of the *client's* matter are likely to justify the expense or risk involved, including any risk of having to pay someone else's legal fees;

IB(1.14) – clearly explaining your fees and if and when they are likely to change;

IB(1.15) – warning about any other payments for which the *client* may be responsible;

IB(1.16) – discussing how the *client* will pay, including whether public funding may be available, whether the *client* has insurance that might cover the fees, and whether the fees may be paid by someone else such as a trade union;

IB(1.17) – where you are acting for a *client* under a fee arrangement governed by statute, such as a conditional fee agreement, giving the *client* all relevant information relating to that arrangement;

IB(1.19) – providing the information in a clear and accessible form which is appropriate to the needs and circumstances of the *client*;

IB(1.26) – ceasing to act for a *client* without good reason and without providing reasonable notice;

IB(1.27) – entering into unlawful fee arrangements such as an unlawful contingency fee;'.

Likely disbursements should be clearly included in estimates. This is particularly important in clinical negligence cases as disbursements, especially medical reports, are likely to be particularly high.

It is possible that the SRA Code of Conduct will be further amended to add indicative behaviours to deal with the new post-Jackson CFA regime.

In practice, solicitors need to be transparent with their clients about alternative funding methods. If a success fee is to be charged to the client, the solicitor does need to consider whether the client might be better advised to explore other funding where no such charge would be made:

- If the client has sufficient funds, and has a very strong claim, the client might choose to pay privately to avoid having to pay a success fee (see **4.2.1**);

- If the client has the benefit of before the event legal expenses insurance (see **4.2.2**);

- Similar considerations may apply if the client is the member of a trade union (see **4.2.3**);

- In a rare clinical negligence case where legal aid is still available for the client this must also be explored as an alternative funding method with the client, even if the solicitor has to refer the client on to another solicitor for legal aid as his firm does not have a contract (see **4.2.6**).

In making a comparison between a CFA and a Damages-based Agreement ('DBA'), it should be noted that solicitors are not required to offer DBAs to clients. However, to ensure that they comply with the Code of Conduct at the very least they should explain that such funding mechanism exists, but that is not offered by their firm, and briefly setting out the pros and cons. Where the solicitor does offer both a DBA and a CFA to the client, it will be important to explain clearly and transparently the advantages and disadvantages of both funding options so that the client can make a proper and informed choice (see **4.2.8**).

Solicitors usually pay particular attention to costs and funding issues at the outset (backed by their firm's precedents and procedures). But the duties are ongoing and must be particularly borne in mind near settlement (particularly with regard to any likely deductions from the damages).

4.2   ALTERNATIVE METHODS OF FUNDING CASES

4.2.1   Private client

It is not intended to deal in detail with pure private client retainers. The risk and expense of a clinical negligence claim is so great that few clients would be wealthy enough to be well advised to risk this. However, the decision is not quite as straightforward as it would have been prior to 1 April 2013. When the additional liabilities of the success fee and an after the event premium were recoverable as costs from the opponent if the case was won (with usually no liability to pay anything if it were lost or abandoned), there was little point in any client forgoing these advantages for the risk of a private retainer. However, for conditional fee agreements after 1 April 2013 the success fee is not recoverable and the client is liable to pay personally any success fee specified in the conditional fee agreement. It is possible that a client who has (or believes that he has) a very strong claim indeed, and the liquid funds to finance a case while it proceeded, might prefer a private client retainer so that all the damages are retained by him at the conclusion.

Any such choice would still be unusual and should be carefully recorded by the solicitor to avoid any allegation of failure to properly advise at the end of a case which turns out to be unsuccessful. It might be appropriate, for example, where there is an open admission of breach of duty and of some causation following the completion of the NHS complaints process.

A private client retainer might also be appropriate for initial investigations only (see **4.1.3**).

If a private client retainer is used, it is essential to provide:
- advice as to alternative funding options
- client care letter
- terms of business
- estimate.

4.2.2   Cases funded with legal expenses insurance

4.2.2.1   *Fundamental terms*

Before the event ('BTE') insurance polices are legal expense insurance policies which have been taken out prior and unrelated to the event which requires legal assistance. They can be stand-alone, but are more typically an add-on to motor or contents or other insurance policies. BTE policies are contracts as between the insurer and the insured client. Insurance contracts are subject to the principles of insurance law such as, for example, the concepts of utmost good faith and subrogation. In theory, at least, it is a contract of indemnity so that the insurer's obligation is to make good the insured's loss (ie legal expenses) for which the insured has primary liability. However, because the legal expenses insurer is paying the bills, there is a third party in the solicitor–client relationship. Indeed, that third party often seeks to influence that relationship such as by directing the client to its own panel of solicitors and refusing to indemnify full hourly rates (or sometimes at all) in cases where there is no costs recovery from the defendant.

The solicitor should first check that the policy is valid and advise about the risk of avoidance (eg for the failure to disclose known claims on inception or on renewal which may entitle the insurer to avoid the policy).

BTE cover is rarely retrospective and written confirmation of cover is required before cover is granted. This usually requires the solicitor to certify reasonable prospects of success. Where BTE insurers require solicitors to report on the merits, solicitors need to consider and agree with the client the initial basis of charging for advising on the scope of the policy, the investigatory work in connection with the claim itself and the report to the insurers.

4.2.2.2　*Scope of policy*

In clinical negligence cases in particular, it is essential for the solicitor to check the policy document including the schedule and all the terms and conditions relating to legal expense insurance. Typically, the main insurer for motor or home contents will have sub-contracted the legal expenses element to a specialist legal expenses insurer.

It is first essential to check that clinical negligence claims are within the scope of the cover. In respect of most add-ons to motor insurance, cover is limited to personal injury arising out of the use of the vehicle so would not cover a clinical negligence claim. The scope of stand-alone BTE and add–ons to household contents and other policies vary widely. The wording of exclusions can often be quite opaque.

Then it is necessary to consider the amount of the indemnity. With a BTE policy, this is for both sides costs. It can range from £5,000 to £100,000. A policy with £25,000 cover for both sides costs is, for example, unlikely to cover the costs of both sides taking a clinical negligence claim to trial.

The limit of indemnity is very likely to be inadequate. However, the BTE policy may be useful for initial investigation. Consider how it can be topped up (eg use it as insurance against for other side's costs only and sign a conditional fee agreement for own costs; or use it to purchase after the event insurance) at the outset and get the consent of the BTE provider (and any top up ATE insurer). All this must be clearly explained to the client and documented to ensure compliance with the Solicitors Code of Conduct.

4.2.2.3 Panel solicitors

The most controversial requirement of BTE insurance is usually panel solicitor restrictions. The Insurance Companies (Legal Expenses Insurance) Regulations 1990[5] provide that the insured has freedom to choose their lawyer 'to defend, represent or serve the interests of the insured in any enquiry or proceedings' whenever recourse is had to BTE with certain exceptions.[6] This has been interpreted as giving freedom of choice once proceedings are imminent or on foot or there is a conflict of interest between the insurer and the insured. The Financial Services Ombudsman has indicated that he would expect a restriction of choice of solicitor to be made clear to the client on inception of the policy. In practice, the insurer rarely does this. However, the Ombudsman has more recently interpreted this more restrictively so that with simple cases (such as low value road traffic accident claims) the insured may be required to use a panel solicitor, but with more substantial claims freedom of choice from the outset may be allowed (an anonymised decision of the Financial Services Ombudsman described as that of the case of Mrs A and B Company of 10 January 2003). However with regard to more substantial claims: 'I would expect insurers to agree the appointment of the policyholder's preferred solicitors in cases of large personal injury and claims that are necessarily complex such as medical negligence ...'

In *Brown-Quinn (1) Webster Dixon LLP (2) v Equity Syndicate Management Limited (1) Motorplus Limited (2)*[7] ('the *Webster Dixon* case') although the Court of Appeal did not allow the solicitors to insist on being appointed under the policy at their usual hourly rates, the court found in favour of the solicitors in respect of many points of principle. The court was particularly scathing of the insurance industry's attempts to avoid the spirit of freedom of choice. The solicitors failed in their attempt to replace the insurers rate with the guideline hourly rate only because they had not adduced at an earlier stage any evidence of the 'going rate' and the court was not prepared to accept that the guideline hourly rates were the correct figures. It may be said that it would be difficult for an individual insured to obtain such evidence but the problem is only likely to surface after the individual insured has been to see a solicitor and a discussion about how any potential litigation is to be paid for has already occurred. In such circumstances a solicitor will already be involved and, if the requisite evidence is available, it will not be too difficult for that solicitor to find it.

4.2.2.4 Retainer

The solicitor's retainer should provide that the client is primarily liable for their fees even if they have BTE insurance. The insurer may object to paying some part of the solicitors' fees on the basis that the client has been unreasonable. Alternatively, it may transpire that the insurer is entitled to avoid the policy.

---

[5] SI 1990/1159.
[6] See reg 7 of the Insurance Companies (Legal Expenses Insurance) Regulations 1990, SI 1990/1159.
[7] [2012] EWCA Civ 1633.

The retainer proposed by the BTE insurer should be checked particularly for hourly rates and compliance with the indemnity principle. Many BTE insurers propose no costs or fixed costs or lower rate costs if a claim is made to the BTE insurer and 'normal costs' (payable by the losing opponent) if the case is won. A partner must sign the bill at the end of the case to confirm that there has been no breach of the indemnity principle. If there has been a breach, the solicitor will be limited only to the costs payable by the BTE insurer.

The retainer with the client might be in the form of a standard private paying client retainer, but with reference to the indemnity from the BTE insurer, but it might be difficult to explain to the client why they have to pay 'normal' rates but their insurer will pay nothing or much less towards them. Best is a conditional fee agreement without a success fee which specifies the firm's normal fees if the claim is successful and the lower fees payable by the BTE insurer if the claim fails.

It is arguable that a success fee can instead be applied to the difference between the rates (which is the amount of the fees risked). But it is also arguable that this does not comply with the statute and, in any event, success fees in this context do not sit well with prior insurance from a client care perspective.

If the solicitor wishes to render interim bills to the BTE insurer or seek payments on account of disbursements, it is sensible to say so at the outset, although some insurers only provide for payment at the end of the case or after specified periods. In practice, many BTE insurers expressly or impliedly refuse to pay at all if the case is unsuccessful (or at best a very low hourly rate). The BTE insurance is then little more than insurance against third party costs and a referral to a solicitor willing to take a no win, no fee case without a success fee.

4.2.2.5 *Acting for a BTE client under a CFA*

If the BTE insurer refuses to allow the client's own solicitor to act, a client can still use a CFA instead of BTE. After all the checks and inquiries have been made the solicitor must make clear to the client the contrast between their liability for costs with BTE when compared with proceeding on a CFA with or without additional liabilities and give appropriate advice and costs warnings to his client on the advantages and/or disadvantages of using any BTE policy. After the advice has been given (confirmed in writing) if the client chooses not to use the BTE the solicitor should be able to sign up an enforceable CFA.

After 1 April 2013, if the solicitor offers equivalent terms to the BTE insurer the client can be advised not to use the BTE insurance. If equivalent terms are to be offered:

- any success fee should be waived (as the BTE panel solicitor will presumably not normally be allowed to charge this to an insured client);
- QOCS will normally protect the client against adverse costs if the case is lost so BTE insurance is irrelevant here;

- there should be a check as to what the BTE insurer offers in respect of Part 36 risk and adverse costs if the case is won and the CFA should replicate this;
- the solicitor will need to indemnify, or insure at his own cost, the risk of own disbursements if the case is lost.

The advent of QOCS should mean that after 1 April 2013 solicitors should not have to lose many cases to BTE panel solicitors where they wish to keep them by offering equivalent terms, provided that they are prepared to waive any success fee.

It is of course also open to the client to make an informed choice to instruct a particular solicitor on less advantageous financial terms than would be available to them through their BTE policy. This might be so because of the particular expertise of the solicitor compared to that of the selected panel solicitor. Any such choice by the client should be fully informed and carefully recorded by the solicitor.

It may also be possible to agree with the legal expense insurer not to make a claim under the legal expenses policy until after proceedings are issued. If the BTE cover is limited and it is reasonable to reserve this for an opponent's costs and own disbursements, then it may be reasonable to do so.

4.2.2.6 Continuing duties to insurer

The solicitor must ensure the client understands the duty of utmost good faith and the importance of full disclosure of material facts, otherwise cover will be avoided. It is irrelevant whether non-disclosure arises from indifference or a mistake. It is irrelevant that the reason for non-disclosure is the client's failure to understand that a fact was material.

Solicitors must themselves, as the client's agent, disclose those material facts which are in their knowledge. Check the policy for reporting requirements about, for example, costs and the prospects of success. In one case[8] a legal expenses insurer successfully sued a firm of solicitors for misrepresentation. The solicitors had obtained, but not disclosed, an unfavourable counsel's opinion. Also check for warranties about future conduct, for example, to the effect that information is and will remain accurate. Ensure that the client understands that the duty of utmost good faith is continuing. Breach of a warranty will entitle the insurer to avoid the policy and repudiate liability from the date of breach.

4.2.3 Cases funded by trade unions

Most trade unions offer a legal assistance scheme to their members. These schemes usually require the union member to instruct the union's panel solicitor. Unions can enter into collective conditional fee agreements (CCFAs)

---

[8] *DAS Legal Expenses Insurance Co Ltd v Hughes Hooker & Co* (unreported) 1994.

with their solicitors with individual union members pursuing their claims on those terms (other than individual success fees, as appropriate).

The requirements for formality and explanations with regard to individuals are relaxed to reflect the protections likely to be provided to their members by the unions in negotiating the generic terms with their lawyers.

If the solicitor is not a panel solicitor for the client's trade union, it is necessary for the client to establish what the terms are on which the union solicitor will act and, in particular, whether a success fee is payable to the solicitor and whether any administration or other such charge will be made by the trade union.

Similar considerations then apply as for BTE insurance as to whether and how a non-panel solicitor can continue to act for a client notwithstanding the availability of trade union funding (4.2.2).

4.2.4   Cases funded by 'litigation funding' or 'third party funding'

'Litigation funding' or 'third party funding' is where an unconnected party (usually a professional litigation funding company) backs the case of a litigant who could not otherwise afford to bring it in exchange for an agreement to share the proceeds of the litigation with the client. Previously such arrangements would have been maintenance or champerty and would have been held to be illegal and unenforceable agreements. However, in *Arkin v Borchard Line Limited and others*[9] the Court of Appeal reviewed the existing case-law and set down guideline as to when such arrangements will be permitted. In particular, the funder must usually accept liability for adverse costs. There is a code of best practice for 'litigation funders' which is presently voluntary, but to which most reputable funders will subscribe.

However, it is not intended to deal in detail here with 'litigation funding' or 'third party funding'. This is because:

* outside commercial litigation, it is not usually available for one-off single issue cases as opposed to group actions;
* third party funders usually prefer to deal with commercial litigants who are more likely to take commercial rather than emotional views of the merits and any settlement;
* disbursements in clinical negligence, although large, are usually capable of funding by the client or the solicitor;
* if the case is meritorious, it will be usually be possible to find a solicitor and barrister who will operate under a conditional fee agreement and qualified one-way cost shifting (combined where appropriate with after the event insurance) will usually mean that exposure to adverse costs risks will usually be limited.

---

[9]   [2005] 3 All ER 613.

4.2.5 Cases funded by litigation loans

Litigation loans are to be distinguished from 'litigation funding'. Here the client takes out a private loan with a third party lender to pay legal fees. The solicitor will treat the client as a normal private paying client. The loan might be to cover all of the costs of the claim. Or it may be to cover disbursements only. There are a number of specialist lenders in the clinical negligence market, particularly offering the client funding for disbursements alongside the solicitor acting under a conditional fee agreement for his costs. The recoverable element of after the event insurance assists here as the lender has some protection if the case loses by taking an assignment of or charge over the after the event insurance policy.

The interest charged by specialist lenders is likely to be high. Clinical negligence cases tend to last longer than most litigation so that the total cost to the client could be very high indeed. Some clients with a good credit history may be able to borrow more cheaply elsewhere (eg from their bank or general financial company).

If a specialist lender is used, the solicitor should check what duties the solicitor owes to the lender and also check if the lender has recourse to the solicitor if loan is not repaid by the client. Obviously this should be avoided where possible.

4.2.6 Cases funded with public funding

4.2.6.1 Overview

After 1 April 2013 very few clinical negligence cases will be funded by legal aid. Under the Legal Aid, Sentencing and Punishment of Offenders Act 2012 ('LASPO') only those matters specified in Sch 1 to the Act, or which qualify for exceptional funding under s 10 LASPO (ie human rights grounds), are in scope, subject to financial eligibility.

However, government proposals for a 'Supplemental Legal Aid Scheme' (which would have made a fixed charge of 25% of general damages and past loss recovered in such cases) are not being proceeded with for the time being.

4.2.6.2 Neurological birth injuries

LASPO Sch 1 para 23 states that public funding will be available for 'a neurological injury ... as a result of which V is severely disabled provided clinical negligence occurred while the victim was in his or her mother's womb, or [within 8 weeks of birth]':

'23 Clinical negligence and severely disabled infants

(1) Civil legal services provided in relation to a claim for damages in respect of clinical negligence which caused a neurological injury to an individual ('V') as a result of which V is severely disabled, but only where the first and second conditions are met.

(2) The first condition is that the clinical negligence occurred –

   (a)   while V was in his or her mother's womb, or
   (b)   during or after V's birth but before the end of the following period –
        (i)   if V was born before the beginning of the 37th week of pregnancy, the period of 8 weeks beginning with the first day of what would have been that week;
        (ii)   if V was born during or after the 37th week of pregnancy, the period of 8 weeks beginning with the day of V's birth.

(3) The second condition is that –

   (a)   the services are provided to V, or
   (b)   V has died and the services are provided to V's personal representative.

General exclusions

(4) Sub-paragraph (1) is subject to –

   (a)   the exclusions in Part 2 of this Schedule, with the exception of paragraphs 1, 2, 3 and 8 of that Part, and
   (b)   the exclusion in Part 3 of this Schedule.

Definitions

(5) In this paragraph –

   •   "birth" means the moment when an individual first has a life separate from his or her mother and references to an individual being born are to be interpreted accordingly;
   •   "clinical negligence" means breach of a duty of care or trespass to the person committed in the course of the provision of clinical or medical services (including dental or nursing services);
   •   "disabled" means physically or mentally disabled;
   •   "personal representative", in relation to an individual who has died, means –
        (a)   a person responsible for administering the individual's estate under the law of England and Wales, Scotland or Northern Ireland, or
        (b)   a person who, under the law of another country or territory, has functions equivalent to those of administering the individual's estate.'

This limits legal aid in effect to cerebral palsy cases at or around birth. But severe neurological damage resulting from negligence of the NHS is sadly not limited to birth injury cases. So, by way of example, children who suffer severe brain damage from failure to monitor and control hyperbilirinaemia, or from a delay in diagnosis and treatment of meningitis or as the result of negligent resuscitation are no longer entitled to legal aid.

To apply for legal aid, solicitors will need to have a civil contract covering the clinical negligence category of work. The client will have to be financially eligible. But this will rarely be an issue in such cases as this is assessed on the child's own means.

The Legal Aid Agency proposes to revise the supervisor standard for clinical negligence to reflect the revised and now highly restricted nature of the category.

4.2.6.3 Exceptional funding

The only clinical negligence cases that remain formally within scope are the severe neurological birth injury cases detailed in **4.2.6.2**. However, under s 10 of LASPO there is the possibility of 'exceptional funding'. The Director of Casework must have made an exceptional case determination relating to the individual and the services required by the individual. Under s 10(3), this is where:

> '(a) that it is necessary to make the services available to the individual under this Part because failure to do so would be a breach of –
>
> > (i) the individual's Convention rights (within the meaning of the Human Rights Act 1998), or
> >
> > (ii) any rights of the individual to the provision of legal services that are enforceable EU rights, or
>
> (b) that it is appropriate to do so, in the particular circumstances of the case, having regard to any risk that failure to do so would be such a breach.'

It can be seen that the nature of this exceptionality is extremely limited. With the availability of conditional fee agreements, in practice the solicitor would have to show why in the particular circumstances the case could not be funded other than by legal aid so that the client had no effective remedy. It is submitted that in single issue clinical negligence cases such circumstances will be very rare. Under s 10(4), where there is a wider public interest, there is a somewhat greater possibility of obtaining funding for inquest representation.

4.2.6.4 VHCC contracts

Each individual case will be the subject of a VHCC (Very High Cost Case) individual case contract. This will be entered into when the certificate is first amended. 'The VHCC – Legal Aid Agency Clinical Negligence Funding Checklist April 2103 v1' issued by the Special Cases Unit sets out the principles on which such cases can be run under legal aid.

Cost/benefit ratios continue to apply under the Civil Legal Aid (Merits Criteria) Regulations 2013:[10]

- 50-60%: 1:4

---

[10] SI 2013/104.

- 60%- 80%: 1:2
- 80%+ : 1:1

The costs allowed under the contract can be revised downwards at the solicitor's request to maintain compliance with the ratios. However, it is unlikely that the ratios will in practice provide a problem in birth injury cases as the likely damages are likely to be very substantial.

There are six stages under the contract:
- the investigative stage
- issue of proceedings to mutual exchange
- settlement
- trial
- quantum investigations
- quantum trial.

4.2.6.4.1   Stage 1: The investigative stage

This includes attendance on the client, medical records, taking client statements, instructing experts, considering reports, raising supplementary questions, instructing counsel, attending conference, the protocol letter and considering the response. Fees allowable against the fund depend upon the number of experts:

Total costs allowed:
- 1 expert: £4,500
- 2 experts: £6,750
- 4 experts: £9,000 – £13,500
- 4 experts: £13,500 – £18,000
- 5/6 experts: £20,250 – £22,500

4.2.6.4.2   Stage 2: Issue of proceedings

This includes statements of case, issue and service, allocation, consideration of defence (including by experts), case management conference, conference with counsel and experts, revising reports, exchanging statements and reports.

Total costs allowed:
- 1 expert: £6,750
- 2 experts: £9,000
- 4 experts: £10,750 – £13,500
- 4 experts: £14,250 – £16,750
- 5/6 experts: £16,750 – £19,000

4.2.6.4.3   Stage 3: Settlement

This includes quantum reports, Part 36 offers and settlement meetings.

Total costs allowed:
- 1 expert: £6,750
- 2 experts: £6,750 – £9,500
- 4 experts: £12,000 – £14,250
- 4 experts: £19,000
- 5/6 experts: £21,750

4.2.6.4.4   Stage 4: Full trial or liability only trial

This includes pre-trial review, finalising statements and reports, trial preparation and attendance.

Total costs allowed:
- 1 expert: £6,750 – £9,500
- 2 experts: £12,000 – £14,250
- 4 experts: £19,000 – £28,500
- 4 experts: £35,750
- 5/6 experts: £40,000

4.2.6.4.5   Stage 5: Quantum investigations

This includes instructing experts and considering reports (including defendant's experts), schedule of loss, conference and negotiations.

Total costs allowed:
- 8–10 quantum expert case: £34,000

4.2.6.4.6   Stage 6: Quantum trial

This includes the pre-trial review, finalising witness statements, conference, trial preparation and attendance at trial where there is a separate quantum trial

Total costs allowed:
- 8–10 quantum expert case: £41,000

4.2.6.5   Prescribed rates for lawyers

The indemnity principle is abrogated for legal aid cases. If the case is won, the solicitor is entitled to be remunerated at 'normal' rates (usually guideline hourly rates with enhancement, if appropriate) rather than prescribed legal aid hourly rates. If a claim for costs is made against the legal aid fund the following rates apply for the lawyers:

Up to £25,000

- Solicitor: £108 per hour
- QC: £180 per hour
- Senior junior counsel alone: £135 per hour
- Led junior counsel: £112.50

Post £25,000

- Solicitor: £70 per hour
- Senior counsel: £90 per hour
- Junior counsel: 350 per hour

Claims must be made under form claim 1 together with the funding checklist, time recording sheets for each stage, counsel's fee notes and disbursement vouchers.

4.2.6.6   Prescribed rates for experts

Expert fees payable out of the fund are prescribed by the Community Legal Service (Funding) (Amendment No 2) Order 2011[11] as amended by the Civil Legal Aid (Remuneration) (Amendment) Regulations 2013.[12] These regulations reduced the maximum fees paid to experts by 20% except for neurologists, neonatologists and neuro-radiologists in cerebral palsy cases. The maximum fees payable are set out in Sch 2 to the 2013 Regulations.

The rates payable to experts are much lower than those commonly commanded by many reputable experts. Many solicitors wish therefore to agree to 'top up' the expert fees at their own risk to ensure that they can instruct the best expert who will give the best prospects of winning the case at all or of maximising the damages for the client. The lawfulness of this is not entirely free from doubt as, for example, clients are not normally permitted to top up legal aid payments to lawyers. However, as we have seen, the indemnity principle is abrogated for legal aid cases so that the solicitor can recover 'normal' between the parties costs if the case is won rather than be limited to the prescribed costs. Similarly, a limitation on a certificate as to the number of experts or the scope of work does not restrict recovery of their costs 'between the parties'. It therefore seems likely that solicitors can choose to 'top up' prescribed expert rates taking the risk that they cannot recover the excess from the fund, but can recover the full cost, subject to reasonableness and proportionality, on assessment 'between the parties'.

---

[11]   SI 2011/2066.
[12]   SI 2013/2877.

The Legal Aid Authority has a strong preference for split trials in contested cerebral palsy cases. The Legal Aid Authority is likely to authorise a maximum claim against the fund of £178,250 for a fully contested cerebral palsy case with a split trial with five liability and ten quantum experts where all six stages are completed.

4.2.6.7   Notice of public funding

Copies of the certificate and any amendments (which are now, often confusingly, implemented by a complete copy of the amended certificate rather than a notice of the amendment) are sent to both the solicitor and the client.

Notice of issue of a legal aid certificate in prescribed form must be filed at court and served on all the parties. The notice should not detail the certificate's limitations. So far as opponents are concerned, this applies even before proceedings have commenced. The client might be at risk with regard to costs protection if notice is not served.

Requests for change of solicitor will only be authorised exceptionally.

With regard to ending funding, this does not take place until after any review of Funding Code procedures has completed. Notice of discharge/revocation must then be served and filed to terminate the retainer.

4.2.6.8   Costs protection in publicly funded cases

One of the principal benefits of public funding is the costs protection that is given to the client in the event of an adverse costs order if the claim is lost or discontinued. The changes to public funding implemented by the Access to Justice Act 1999 reduced this protection a little, so care is needed to explain the remaining risks to clients, although in most cases it will remain intact.

In practice, Qualified One-way Cost Shifting means that adverse costs orders against clients who lose clinical negligence cases will now be rare in any event.

4.2.6.9   Public funding or CFA?

It is important not to forget that public funding is still available for claims arising out of clinical negligence causing severe neurological damage at or around the time of birth. Now that success fees will be irrecoverable for CFAs made on or after 1 April 2013, if a CFA is to be used for such cases the client will be worse off unless the success fee is waived and equivalent cost protection to legal aid is arranged at no cost to the client (because of Qualified One-way Cost Shifting this is likely to only relate to own disbursements if the case is lost).

4.2.7   Cases funded with conditional fee agreements

4.2.7.1   Statutory requirements

Conditional fee agreements (CFAs) were originally introduced to provide a means of access to justice for 'middle England'. It was argued that only the very rich and the very poor (through legal aid, now known as public funding) had access to the courts. For many years public policy, expressed through the offences of champerty and maintenance and enforced through court decisions and practice rules, had prevented lawyers from having an interest in the outcome of a case. Although the crime was abolished in the 1960s, any such agreement remained unenforceable at law. Fears about an ever-reducing access to justice led to a fundamental change of view. The means by which this policy change was implemented was a very 'English' compromise. Parliament did not want to introduce a US-style system of contingency fees for fear of creating a 'compensation culture'. The 'loser pays' costs rule was to be maintained.

Parliament enacted that the lawyer could charge a percentage increase on his normal fee with a maximum success fee of 100%. The Courts and Legal Services Act 1990, s 58 was not brought into force until 1995.[13] The legality of the CFA regime for all clients, not just the impecunious, was upheld by the House of Lords in *Campbell v MGN*[14] (although not without some regret and not without criticism of some of the effects of Parliament's decision). The government has now put into effect the Jackson reforms to remove recoverability of success fees for CFAs made on or after 1 April 2013. These reforms deal for the future with the criticisms of the regime in *Campbell*.

It is very important to determine which regulatory framework applies to the CFA as this will have different consequences as to form, advice and effect (eg recoverability of success fee):

*   The 1995 Regulations:[15] apply to CFAs entered into between 5 July 1995 and 31 March 2000.

*   The 2000 Regulations:[16] apply to CFAs between 1 April 2000 and 1 November 2005.

*   The 2003 Regulations[17] only apply to a 'CFA Lite' which expressly complies with those Regulations between 1 July 2003 and 1 November 2005.

*   The 2005 Regulations[18] revoke the 2000 Regulations and the 2003 Regulations for CFAs entered into after 1 November 2005 and before 1 April 2013.

---

[13]   Conditional Fee Agreements Regulations 1995, SI 1995/1675.
[14]   [2005] UKHL 61.
[15]   Conditional Fee Agreements Regulations 1995, SI 1995/1675.
[16]   Conditional Fee Agreements Regulations 2000, SI 2000/692.
[17]   Conditional Fee Agreements (Miscellaneous Amendments) Regulations 2003, SI 2003/1240.
[18]   Conditional Fee Agreements (Revocation) Regulations 2005, SI 2005/2305.

- Section 44 of LASPO ends recoverability of success fees and the Conditional Fee Agreements Order 2013[19] imposes a cap on the amount of the success fee that can be taken from damages for CFAs entered into on or after 1 April 2013.

The transitional provisions for CFAs relating to the new LASPO regime are set out in Part 48 of the Civil Procedure Rules. Rule 48.1 provides that the CPR in force 'immediately before 1 April 2013' (with any modifications made by Practice Direction) shall apply to a 'pre-commencement funding arrangement'. This is defined as a CFA providing for a success fee which was entered into before 1 April 2013 (or as an individual matter under a CCFA taken on before 1 April 2013).

4.2.7.2 Conditional Fee Agreements Order 2013

The Conditional Fee Agreements Order 2013[20] made under the Legal Aid, Sentencing and Punishment of Offenders Act 2012 repeals the Conditional Fee Agreements Order 2000. It maintains the maximum permitted success fee of 100% of base costs. However, it also provides for a statutory cap on the amount of the success fee by reference to the damages recovered for the client in personal injury proceedings (including clinical negligence) as recommended by Jackson LJ:

> 'The descriptions of damages specified for the purposes of section 58(4B)(d) of the Act are –
>
> (a) general damages for pain, suffering, and loss of amenity; and
> (b) damages for pecuniary loss, other than future pecuniary loss,
>
> net of any sums recoverable by the Compensation Recovery Unit of the Department for Work and Pensions.' [Article 5(2)]

The cap applies only to first instance proceedings. In relation to an appeal the cap can be 100% of the damages. But this is a matter of contract. The CFA must provide for the appropriate level of the cap, whether 25% or less at first instance or 100% or less on appeal. The statutory cap is only a maximum. Although Parliament and Jackson LJ seem to have expected solicitors to compete on the level of success fee, this is a complicated calculation at the best of times. It seems more likely that clients will better understand the cap. It is entirely possible that solicitors will therefore instead compete on a level of cap; in some cases solicitors might offer 10%, 15% or 20% rather than 25% the statutory maximum for personal injury cases. And some solicitors may offer a zero success fee for some cases.

It is essential that the CFA itself provides that the success fee cannot exceed 25% of general damages and past pecuniary loss. If it does not then the CFA

---

[19] SI 2013/689.
[20] SI 2013/689.

will be unenforceable so that no success fee can be claimed from the client and, even more importantly, no base costs recovered from either client or from the opponent.

One obvious problem with this provision is that most cases are not in fact decided by a judge who would apportion the award of damages between different heads of loss. Most cases are settled on a global basis with a single figure agreed to cover all heads of loss.

Even provided that the CFA itself is compliant with the Order, so is enforceable, there is therefore the issue of how to ensure that success fee is capped appropriately in practice.

The pre-Access to Justice Act 1999 cap was a voluntary one recommended by the Law Society and was 25% of all damages recovered. There is a particular concern about the compensation awarded for future care being used to pay lawyers' fees and thus leaving the claimant out of pocket to fund the care required. But, of course, if the litigation cannot be brought at all the claimant recovers no compensation to pay for future care.

It will be best practice to set out for the client a calculation of the success fee whenever an offer is to be approved and made by the claimant or is received from the defendant. The decision to make an offer or to accept an offer will therefore be shown to have been a fully informed one by the client. Such a calculation of the effect of the cap would of course still be subject to solicitor and client assessment by the court if requested by the client.

It should be noted that although Jackson LJ and the government say they are seeking to protect damages payable for future loss, in practice success fees will often still be paid out of damages for future loss. This is for the obvious reason that by definition compensation for past loss will often have already been spent by the claimant. It is therefore not going to be available to pay the success fee. So, notwithstanding the intentions of the Jackson report and the statutory instrument, claimants will have little option than to pay lawyers success fees out of sums earmarked for the future.

In a serious injury case the claimant often requires new suitable accommodation. The damages will not include the full purchase price of the property (*Roberts v Johnston*[21]). This means that the claimant already usually has to 'borrow' from other heads of loss to pay the purchase price. With the increasing prevalence of periodic payment orders for future care, and past losses awards often having been spent, usually only general damages and future loss of earnings are available. If up to 25% of general damages and past loss are to be used to pay lawyers' success fees, this problem will be exacerbated. There will be significant pressure on a claimant's ability to purchase accommodation and/or to maintain a sufficient lump sum for future contingencies.

---

[21]   [1989] QB 878.

There are no new CFA Regulations made under LASPO. The government was apparently concerned about a risk of a return of the costs wars if regulatory non-compliance could be raised by opponents (looking to avoid paying base costs) rather than simply by clients. So far as consumer protection is concerned, the solicitor must comply with the Solicitors Code of Conduct (see **4.1.4**). The client can also seek a solicitor and client assessment of costs, including the success fee (see **4.4.1**).

4.2.7.3 Risk assessment

Risk assessment is crucial. Solicitors must go back to the basics: will this case win? Before entering into a CFA this question is fundamental; nothing else matters more. Although there will be many unknowns and it might be easier to shy away from facing this challenge, the issues of the case have to identified and a concerted effort must be made to identify at the outset what proof will be available to clear each of the evidential hurdles. This is the purpose of risk assessment procedures – although this has been somewhat muddied by the use of risk assessment forms to justify success fees before the advent of fixed success fees.

No CFA case should be taken on without the approval of another fee earner, usually a partner and often a panel. No decision to take any case should be taken by one fee earner with no one checking the decision. But the process must be proportionate and effective. Decisions (even if it is to refer back for more investigation) should be made quickly.

4.2.7.4 Setting success fees under CFAs made on or after 1 April 2013

Any success fee that is charged must be related to the solicitor's 'usual' base costs. Although the amount of the success fee might be capped by reference to the damages, the fee itself cannot be charged by reference to the damages. An American-style contingency fee (a straight cut of the damages) cannot be a CFA. Any such agreement would have to be for non-contentious work or, subject to the provisions of LASPO, a damages-based agreement (see **4.2.8**).

The Courts and Legal Services Act 1990 allows the lawyer to charge a success fee in 'specified circumstances' (ie as specified in the written CFA). The 'specified circumstances' will usually be success in the litigation, although these are not the only 'specified circumstances' that might be agreed between lawyer and client.

Under the statute itself the lawyer is not required to explain the reasons for the level of the success fee. However, the lawyer may have to justify these to the client at the outset, to the client on payment at the end of the case, to the Legal Ombudsman or the Solicitors Regulation Authority after a client complaint, or to the court on a solicitor and client costs assessment. It therefore is good practice to record the reasons for setting a success fee at a particular level at the time it is set.

The lawyer may be taking an additional risk if a Part 36 offer is made. If this is given as a reason, it is important that the CFA does actually create a risk of non-payment for the lawyer in such circumstances.

If the lawyer is agreeing to fund disbursements during the course of the case this is another good reason to include in setting the level of the success fee. There is a cost to the lawyer in tying up capital or borrowing money which is of great benefit to most clients who will not want or be able do so themselves. The lawyer might additionally agree to waive charging any unrecovered disbursements (if the case is lost or if the cost of the disbursement is not awarded between the parties even when the case is won).

The lawyer might also offer the client an indemnity against adverse costs orders in the litigation (see **4.3.4**). The risk of adverse costs orders might be relatively low in personal injury cases where qualified one-way cost shifting applies (see **4.3.1**), but there may still be a residual risk. Expressly charging for the risk as an element within the success fee might, however, render such an indemnity 'insurance' and take the CFA outside the protection afforded by the decision in *LB Southwark v Morris & Sibthorpe*.

The SRA Code of Conduct operates to prohibit overcharging (see **4.1.4**). Overcharging is potentially a disciplinary offence. The client is also entitled to seek a solicitor and client assessment of the solicitor's costs. Although a costs judge must not use hindsight, he is entitled to assess the reasonableness of the solicitor's charges after the event.

The usual starting point for calculation of the success fee required to compensate for the risk of losing is the 'revenue neutral' approach. In cases where the facts are very different, what the court has done in the past is to estimate the probability of success in the particular case (without using hindsight) and then apply a ready reckoner to calculate the success fee required to compensate for the risk of losing cases with a similar level of risk. The individualised ready reckoner approach is therefore most likely to reflect overall risk and be accepted as reasonable practice by the court.

The lawyer also needs to consider how to charge for any other reasons for the setting of the success fee.

As well as assessing the overall level of risk (and other reasons), the lawyer then should also consider whether to apply a flat success fee or to stage the success fee depending upon when the case is resolved. Such staging is likely to find favour with the court on a solicitor and client assessment, and also with a client on negotiation of the success fee, even if the mathematical basis is not necessarily sound.

The claim should be individually risk assessed and an appropriate success fee agreed. However, an experienced practitioner will be expected to have a good knowledge of the risks of clinical negligence claims and the overall failure rate.

The pre-Jackson case-law is still likely to be relevant on any solicitor and client assessment of the success fee. In *Boyd v MOD*[22] a clinical negligence claim was hotly contested with the experts completely at odds. The claim settled for £725,000 just before trial. Liability was admitted but causation and damage were still in dispute. A 100% success fee was upheld. But in *Bensusan v Freedman*[23] where a dentist dropped an instrument down the patient's throat and both breach of duty and causation were clear from the outset, only 20% was allowed (and perhaps this would be even lower today). The Court of Appeal have made it clear in judgments in respect of personal injury claims that they usually prefer staging of success fees rather than a single success fee that applies throughout (see, for example, *Atack v Lee*[24]). Whilst a single stage success fee, particularly at 100%, is still permissible in an appropriate case, it is likely to be more difficult to defend on assessment. However, in *Oliver v Whipps Cross University Hospital NHS Trust*[25] Jack J (sitting with assessors Master Rogers and Greg Cox) held that solicitors are entitled to assess a single stage success fee for a clinical negligence claim at 100% if, on the basis of information supplied by the claimant at the outset, the claim might reasonably be assessed at having no more than a borderline prospect of success.

Calculation of the success fee a solicitor would like to charge to accept the case, subject to the impact of any cap on the damages, can only ever be the starting point. The intention behind the Jackson reforms is that clients will negotiate the level of success fee and indeed shop around to find the best deal. It is open to question whether this will happen in practice.

4.2.7.5 Base costs

The usual focus in a CFA is the success fee. However, it is also important to consider the question of base costs.

The solicitor needs to consider what hourly rate to charge. This does not have to be the local guideline hourly rate, but should be a proper market rate agreed with the client.

Although it is anticipated that much of the base costs will be recovered from the opponent when the case is won, this is by way of indemnity so in principle any unrecovered base costs will be paid by the client.

Alternatively, it is possible to enter into a 'CFA Lite' whereby the client is promised that there will be no charge (other than the success fee, if any).

---

[22] SCCO Deputy Master James, 16 December 2003.
[23] SCCO Master Hurst, 20 September 2001.
[24] [2004] EWCA Civ 1712.
[25] [2009] EWHC 1104 (QB), [2009] All ER (D) 199 (May).

However, the new emphasis on proportionality and 'between the parties' costs budgets means that this is a much greater risk of non-recovery being accepted by the solicitor than prior to 1 April 2013. Solicitor should be cautious of agreeing to a CFA Lite without fully understanding the risks of non-recovery of costs they are now running.

Another option is to agree a voluntary cap on all deductions from the client's damages (success fee, irrecoverable base costs, irrecoverable disbursements, ATE premium). This is more meaningful to the client than the statutory cap which relates to the success fee only. However, the statutory cap must also be incorporated to ensure the CFA is lawful in accordance with statutory requirements. And care needs to be taken not to inadvertently turn the CFA into a damages-based agreement. The Law Society's model agreement gives suggested wording to give effect to this. The level of any voluntary cap should be considered.

4.2.7.6   Form of the CFA

Although the Law Society's model conditional fee agreement is stated to be 'for use in personal injury cases (excluding clinical negligence)' there is in fact no technical reason why it cannot be so used, with minor modifications.

There is likely to be less danger of home-made variations rendering the conditional fee agreement unenforceable now that there are no requirements imposed by regulations. However, the indemnity principle still applies, so it is important that nothing is altered that might affect the client's ultimate liability to pay as this might affect recoverability from the defendant.

If the client is to pay disbursements, the model agreement needs to be amended to provide for this.

It is, however, very important to decide at the outset how to deal with a Part 36 offer that is rejected following the solicitor's advice, but which is subsequently not beaten. There are two widely used options – 'the shared risk clause' (where the solicitor waives success fees, but not basic costs after the offer) and 'the ring-fenced damages clause' (where the solicitor waives all costs after the date of the offer). The ring-fenced damages clause is obviously more risky for the solicitor. It is important to check the position with after the after the event insurance in such circumstances and whether the insurers require a particular clause in the CFA. Barristers will usually not be prepared to accept the 'ring-fenced damages clause' in their CFAs.

4.2.7.7   Transfer of cases

Extreme care needs to be taken in signing a new CFA dated on or after 1 April 2013 when the client has previously entered into a CFA before 1 April 2013. The transitional provisions seem to provide that the success fee under the new CFA would not be recoverable in these circumstances. The client would therefore be worse off. However, the previous solicitors may be reluctant formally to assign the existing CFA. And it is not entirely clear that such an assignment would necessarily be valid in any event. If an after the event policy is linked to the earlier CFA there may be an additional problem as the client may lose the benefit of this policy on transfer of solicitor, but the transitional provisions appear to deprive the client of qualified one-way cost shifting. However, it cannot be right effectively to force a client to stick with a solicitor in which he has lost confidence. One option might be to threaten the first solicitor with a complaint to the legal services ombudsman. If there are genuine service complaints against the first solicitor, it might be possible to seek an award for inadequate service from the ombudsman to compensate for the irrecoverable success fee. The threat of an application to the ombudsman might be sufficient to persuade the first firm to agree to assign the existing CFA.

4.2.7.8   Cancellation of Contracts made in a Consumer's Home or Place of Work etc Regulations 2008 and the Consumer Contracts (Information, Cancellation and Additional Charges) Regulations 2013

The Cancellation of Contracts made in a Consumer's Home or Place of Work etc Regulations 2008[26] came into force on 1 October 2008. These are widely drafted and therefore appear to be capable of including CFAs where the client was signed up at home after 1 October 2008.

The contract (ie the CFA) is unenforceable against the consumer unless the trader has given the consumer a notice of the right to cancel and the information required in accordance with the Regulations. Failure to give the notice is also a criminal offence punishable by a fine of up to £5,000.

It seems likely that a failure to give notice in the appropriate case may render the CFA unenforceable, meaning that no costs will be recoverable by the solicitor against the paying party.

The Regulations were revoked for new CFAs on 13 June 2014 by the Consumer Contracts (Information, Cancellation and Additional Charges) Regulations 2013.[27] References should be made to the helpful Law Society Practice Note. However, it seems that non-compliance does not render the whole agreement unenforceable.

The point was taken albeit unsuccessfully by a disgruntled client in a commercial matter in *Rees v Gateley Wareing*.[28] There seemed little doubt that the Regulations potentially applied, but on the facts of the particular case the judge found that the contract had not been 'made' at the client's home, but rather over a series of contractual transactions, including the office. Such an escape may not be straightforward in a clinical negligence case. It is therefore

---

[26]   SI 2008/1816.
[27]   SI 2013/3134.
[28]   [2013] EWHC 3708 (Ch).

sensible to include the statutory notice on all CFAs unless perhaps one is certain that it will be signed up at the solicitor's office.

4.2.7.9   Counsel

Most of the matters relating to funding covered elsewhere in this section apply equally to counsel as to solicitors. However, a few points arise specifically with regard to counsel and CFAs.

As counsel is usually brought into a case after the solicitor has accepted the case on a CFA basis, different considerations prevail. Counsel should undertake his own risk assessment and not rely upon that conducted by his instructing solicitor. It is recommended that use is made of the APIL/PIBA model CFA.

Now that success fees are payable by the client, it will be necessary to agree with client and with counsel whether counsel is to be paid in any event (and if so whether the fees are covered by an after the event insurance product or not) or is acting under a CFA. Any success fee has to be agreed (involving the client as the client has to pay it). There needs to be thought given as to how the cap will operate on success – presumably if it bites it should do so pro rata to the relative success fees of solicitor and counsel.

4.2.8   Cases funded by damages-based agreements

DBAs are damages-based agreements (contingency fees) which are lawful under s 45 of the Legal Aid, Sentencing and Punishment of Offenders Act 2012 ('LASPO'). DBAs are *not* a US style contingency fee. The so-called 'Ontario' model is intended and operates on the basis that:

- costs shifting applies;
- base costs recovered from a losing opponent belong to the client; and
- the base costs are set off against the agreed contingency fee.

The Damages-Based Agreements Regulations 2013[29] are poorly drafted and difficult to interpret.

However, for personal injury cases the same method of calculating the amount of damages that can be taken by way of fees under a DBA is proposed for DBAs as for the cap on a success fee in a CFA (ie the contingent fee cannot be more than 25% of general damages and past pecuniary loss for proceedings at first instance):

> 'In a claim for personal injuries –
>
>   (a)   the only sums recovered by the client from which the payment shall be met are –
>
>   (i)   general damages for pain, suffering and loss of amenity; and
>
>   (ii)   damages for pecuniary loss other than future pecuniary loss,

---

[29]   SI 2013/609.

net of any sums recoverable by the Compensation Recovery Unit of the Department for Work and Pensions; and

(b) subject to paragraph (4), a damages-based agreement must not provide for a payment above an amount which, including VAT, is equal to 25% of the combined sums in paragraph (2)(a)(i) and (ii) which are ultimately recovered by the client.'

(Regulation 4(2))

The following chart sets out how the DBA operates and how it does not operate:

25% DBA	Base Costs	Damages	Fee	Client retains
SO =	2,000	10,000	2,500 (2,000 + 500)	9,500
NOT	2,000	10,000	4,500 (2,000 + 2,500)	7,500
NOT	2,000	10,000	3,000 (12,000 x 25%)	9,000

Under CPR 44.18 the indemnity principle applies so that the recovered costs cannot exceed the DBA fee. In these circumstances, the client pays nothing extra and keeps all of the damages. If the 'between the parties' costs would have exceed the contingent fee, the solicitor cannot claim these from the opponent. His costs are capped at the amount of the contingent fee.

25% DBA	Value of time	Damages	Fee	Client retains
SO =	5,000	10,000	2,500	10,000
NOT	5,000	10,000	5,000 (2,500 + 2,500)	7,500
NOT	5,000	10,000	5,000 (inter partes)	10,000

The question of whether solicitor or client will be better or worse off in a particular case with a CFA or a DBA is a complex one, dependent upon the likely amount of compensation and the costs to be incurred in achieving this.

There is no obligation on any individual solicitor or firm to offer a choice of CFA or DBA. However, the possibility of others offering a DBA should be mentioned when advising the client about funding options. At present, it seems likely that a DBA will be very disadvantageous to the solicitor compared to a CFA in most low value claims (unless the small claims limit is raised), and very disadvantageous to the client compared to a CFA in most large claims. It seems at present unlikely that DBAs will become a major part of the personal injury funding landscape, unless and until the small claims limit for personal injury claims is significantly lifted, but until the practical reality of life after 1 April 2013 becomes clear, it is impossible to be certain how the market will develop.

4.3   ADVERSE COSTS

As well as clarifying payment of the solicitor's own costs, it is equally important to consider with the client at the outset what will happen if they case is lost with regard to opponent's costs and own disbursements.

4.3.1   Qualified one-way costs shifting

Jackson LJ proposed that cost shifting should generally be abolished in personal injuries litigation for claimants only, which would remove the need for after the event insurance. The government accepted his recommendation. However, QOCS does not appear in the Legal Aid, Sentencing and Punishment of Offenders Act 2012. Rules about liability for and the quantum of costs are generally matters for the Civil Procedure Rules Committee. The Ministry of Justice set out its policy points in the course of debates on the Act in the House of Lords and also by a number of written ministerial statements. It was then left to the civil procedure rules committee to draft the necessary rules to give effect to Jackson LJ's proposal.

Section 2 of Part 44 deals with qualified one-way cost shifting ('QOCS'). It is limited to claims which include claims for personal injury or death. This includes clinical negligence claims.

The approach taken by the Rules is that costs orders can still be made against claimants, but they will not usually be enforced where the claimant has not recovered any damages and never until the end of the case. So, in a claim for 'personal injuries' CPR 44.14 provides (subject to CPR 44.15 & 16): '… orders for costs made against a claimant may be enforced without the permission of the court but only to the extent of [damages and interest]'.

So, if the client recovers no damages, no costs order can be enforced.

Rule 44.14(3) deals with the problem that an unsuccessful personal injury claimant might therefore have a county court judgment registered, even though he had the benefit of QOCS: 'An order for costs which is enforced only to the extent permitted by paragraph (1) shall not be treated as an unsatisfied or outstanding judgment for the purposes of any court record.'

There are a number of qualifications to the one-way cost shifting.

First, under CPR 44.15, QOCS is lost and costs can be enforced without permission of the court being required where the claim is struck out:

- for no reasonable grounds for the proceedings;
- for abuse of process;
- for conduct 'likely to obstruct the just disposal of the proceedings'.

Second, under CPR 44.16(1) QOCS is lost and costs can be enforced against the claimant, but only with the leave of the court, where 'the claim is found on the balance of probabilities to be fundamentally dishonest'.

Third, under CPR 44.16(2) QOCS is lost and costs can be enforced against the claimant, but only with the leave of the court, and only to the extent the court thinks just, where:

- where the claim includes a claim which is made for the financial benefit of a person other than the claimant or a dependent under the Fatal Accidents Act (CPR 44.16(2)(a)). Costs can be enforced in these circumstances against a person for whose benefit the proceedings were brought. But this does not include claims for 'gratuitous provision of care, earnings paid by an employer or medical expenses';
- where the claim includes claims other than a claim for personal injuries (so-called mixed claims).

Under CPR 44.14(1) orders for costs made against a claimant who has recovered damages may be enforced without the permission of the court. However, the sums payable are (unless the circumstances outlined in CPR 44.15 and 44.16 apply) limited to the amount of damages and interest awarded to the claimant.

So, where a claimant wins damages, but on the way has:

- interim costs orders made against him;
- a costs order made against him at trial (eg a partial costs order or an issued based costs order);
- an order for costs against him for failure to beat a Part 36 Offer;

then those costs can be set against the damages and interest otherwise payable to the claimant. Costs orders in favour of the claimant are not brought into the equation.

Under CPR 44.17, QOCS cannot benefit a claimant who 'has entered into a pre-commencement funding arrangement'.

Under CPR 48.2 this means:

- a CFA made before 1 April 2013 (or an individual matter under a CCFA begun after 1 April 2013); or
- an after the event insurance policy taken out before 1 April 2013 (or notional premium from a membership organisation).

It is ambiguous as to whether having made a CFA before 1 April 2013, but not having taken out an ATE policy by then, disapplies QOCS or not, but it seems most likely that it does.

Does a claimant with the benefit of QOCS need ATE insurance? It seems very unlikely that many ATE policies will provide protection for loss of QOCS for fraud or struck out claims. The partial loss of QOCS for mixed claims or claims for another's financial benefit will be rare, and may not be insurable. That leaves only the risk of paying their own disbursements if the case is lost and the risk of losing some of the damages to adverse costs orders if the case is won. Whether clients will want to insure against these risks will depend upon their attitude to risk and the price of the premium. Jackson LJ clearly expects that they will not need ATE insurance. In clinical negligence cases, own disbursements are likely to be much higher than for ordinary personal injury cases. Part of the premium remains recoverable from the opponent as an additional liability (see **4.3.3**).

4.3.2 Before the event insurance policy

If the client has the benefit of BTE cover, this might be utilised to provide protection against adverse costs (in particular the liability to pay own disbursements (see **4.2.2**).

4.3.3 After the event insurance

For cases where the CFA (or other retainer) was made on or after 1 April 2013, the advent of qualified one-way cost shifting should significantly reduce the need for after the event insurance, except to preserve damages following a Part 36 offer, own disbursements if the case is lost and interim costs orders when the overall claim is successful (see **4.3.1**). It is particularly important to check that any ATE purporting to protect the client from the loss of qualified one-way cost shifting after a Part 36 Offer does in fact do so in practice.

Save as set out below, the premium for an ATE policy taken out after 1 April 2013 is payable by the client and is not recoverable as an additional liability from the opponent.

In clinical negligence cases it is often not possible for the claimant or his solicitor to know that a case is viable until expert evidence has been obtained. Most clinical negligence cases are now removed from the scope of legal aid under LASPO (see **D8**). The government was under pressure to come up with a solution with regard to protecting claimants who had to spend significant sums in obtaining such reports. Jackson LJ did not agree with their proposed solution, which was to retain an element of recoverability for such after the event insurance premiums. Jackson LJ's solution was to extend legal aid instead. Of course, the government rejected this.

Section 46 of LASPO inserts a new s 58C of the Courts and Legal Services Act 1990 which makes provision for statutory instrument from providing recoverability of certain after the event insurance premiums related clinical negligence.

The Recovery of Costs Insurance Premiums in Clinical Negligence Proceedings Regulations 2013[30] provide that a costs order may provide for:

> 'payment of an amount in respect of the relevant part of the premium of a costs insurance policy taken out by that party which insures against the risk of incurring liability to pay for one or more expert reports in connection with the proceedings(or against that risk and other risks).'

The recoverable element of the premium relates only to reports (not attendance at trial or at any conference) and is further limited so that costs are not recoverable where:

'(a) the report was not in the event obtained;
(b) the report did not relate to liability or causation; or
(c) the cost of the report is not allowed under the costs order.'

The Recovery of Costs Insurance Premiums in Clinical Negligence Proceedings (No 2) Regulations 2013[31] restrict this to claims exceeding £1,000 (implemented only following parliamentary queries as to the legality of the unlimited provision in the first Regulations).

If after the event insurance is obtained for other elements of the claim, the premium must split out the recoverable element from the part that is payable by the client out of damages.

4.4 CLIENT'S PERSONAL RISK AND/OR SOLICITOR INDEMNITY

It is not compulsory to take out after the event insurance in a case funded under a conditional fee agreement. The premium may be large and the client may decide not to incur it. Alternatively, after the event insurance may not be available, because insurers decline to accept the risk. In normal circumstances, a client is personally at risk for adverse costs if the case is lost. However, qualified one-way cost shifting substantially mitigates this risk. But can a solicitor be held liable for costs because he acted under a conditional fee agreement? In

---

[30] SI 2013/92.
[31] SI 2013/739.

Hodgson v Imperial Tobacco[32] the solicitors for the claimants in the tobacco litigation were acting under CFAs but had been unable to obtain after the event insurance.

Unfortunately, in *Myatt & Others v National Coal Board (No 2)*[33] the court had previously decided (in *Myatt (No 1)*) that the CFA was unenforceable and so 'outside the statutory protection'. The after the event insurance policy was avoided, because it was dependant upon a valid CFA being in force. The defendants sought a wasted costs order under s 51 of the Senior Court Acts 1981. Dyson LJ held that the solicitors had a significant interest in the appeal where some £200,000 profit costs were at stake. It had been thought following *Tolstoy-Miloslavsky v Aldington*[34] that a solicitor could not be liable to a wasted costs order in such circumstances unless 'he acts outside the role of solicitor, eg in a private capacity or as a true third party funder for someone else'. However, the court held that solicitors could fall within the definition of the third category of funders of litigation in *Dymocks v Todd*,[35] namely a non-party who 'not merely funds the proceedings but substantially also controls or at any rate is to benefit from them'. The defendant had not given prior notification of their intention to seek a wasted costs order and the claimants did themselves have some financial interest in the appeal. The court ordered the solicitors to pay 50% of the defendant's costs. Lloyd LJ did, however, add that such an order 'could be common in relation to cases where the enforceability of a CFA is at stake but would be most unusual in any situation'. Brooke LJ agreed 'with both judgments'.

In *Germany v Flatman/Barchester Healthcare v Weddall*[36] the Court of Appeal held that merely by funding the client's disbursements a solicitor do not render himself liable to pay adverse costs as a funder.

The lawyer might specifically offer the client an indemnity against adverse costs orders in the litigation. This is allowed in principle under *Sibthorpe & Morris v LB Southwark*.[37] The Court of Appeal held that such an agreement was not champerty. They also agreed with MacDuff J at first instance that the promise was not a contract of insurance (which would require compliance with separate strict statutory regulations), but was ancillary to the contract of retainer for legal services. Solicitors giving such an indemnity must be sure that they can meet it if called upon (either by having sufficient resources available to meet any claims, or by reinsuring the risk as a practice). If a solicitor's indemnity is provided, the solicitor needs to have in mind under the SRA Code of Conduct Outcome 7.4 that 'you maintain systems and controls for monitoring the financial stability of your firm ...'.

---

[32] [1998] EWCA Civ 224.
[33] [2007] EWCA Civ 307.
[34] [1996] 1 WLR 736.
[35] [2004] 1 WLR 2807, [2004] UKPC 39.
[36] [2011] EWHC 2945 (QB).
[37] [2011] EWCA Civ 25.

Furthermore, if a separate fee (or element of success fee) was charged to the client in exchange for the indemnity against adverse costs, it is perhaps arguable that this would make it more likely that the indemnity would be severed from the contract to provide legal services making it a contract for insurance. If this was so then unless the solicitor was regulated as an insurer then that promise would be void and the solicitor may be committing a criminal offence.

4.5   CLIENT REMEDIES

A lawful and transparent retainer at the outset is vital. If the client is unhappy, there are the following potential remedies:

- The Code of Conduct: breaches of the Code of Conduct could lead to disciplinary action against the solicitor by the Solicitors Regulation Authority.
- Solicitor and client assessment of costs: the client can challenge both the amount of the base costs and the level of success fee and ask the court to decide on reasonableness of either or both.
- The Legal Ombudsman can order the solicitor to pay compensation up to £50,000, which would cover most fee related disputes (note the Ombudsman report 'Complaints in focus: "No win, no fee" agreements' January 2013).

TOP TIPS

- Consider all funding options available to client and evaluate them properly.
- Remember professional duties (and not simply seek to maximise income earned).
- Public funding is largely restricted to birth injury cerebral palsy cases.
- Beware damages-based agreements unless and until the DBA Regulations are amended.
- If using a CFA, consider an additional voluntary cap on all deductions from damages as this is clearer and more comprehensive than only including the statutory cap on the success fee.
- Think about how and why a success fee is being charged.
- Make sufficient charges to enable the solicitor to be able to stay in business.

CHAPTER 5

THE INQUEST

In this chapter Paul Balen explores how to use the inquest system to help bereaved relatives understand how their loved one died and to garner evidence to advise them on the merits of a clinical negligence claim.

5.1 BACKGROUND

Relatives of deceased patients are unlikely to understand the mechanics and limitations of the inquest system unless you can explain some of the historical background to them. Preparing them for the ordeal of the inquiry (and make no mistake about it an inquest can be an ordeal) is an important part of a clinical negligence lawyer's armoury of skills.

Although historically the courts have ruled that inquests are not the appropriate forum at which to consider questions of clinical negligence,[1] the advent of the Human Rights Act has, as we will see, given greater impetus to the use of the inquest as the state's method of providing an investigation following a sudden death during medical treatment.

A coroner's inquest can be an extremely useful part of the evidence gathering exercise prior to presentation of a claim. It is however a mediaeval system struggling to exist in the 21st century world and as a result all parties agreed that the system was ripe for reform. This culminated in the passing of the Coroners and Justice Act 2009 and its associated Rules and Regulations which apply to all uncompleted and new coroner's investigations from 23 July 2013. However these reforms left many features of the coronial process untouched.

5.1.1 History

The office of coroner dates back to 1194 when officers were appointed by King Richard I to help him administer justice and raise money. These officers were known as *custos placitoreum coronae* or custodians of the pleas of the Crown. Their names became abbreviated to coroners. A coroner was elected by a meeting of freemen of the county and was an independent officer, the status which carries down to the present day.

---

[1] *R v HM Coroner for Birmingham ex p Cotton* (1996) 160 JP 123.

In the Middle Ages the coroner was a revenue collector for the Crown, one of whose most important duties was the investigation of death. Deaths were a profitable source of revenue for the Crown.

As a judicial officer, the coroner administered justice and raised revenues for the Crown by fining criminal offenders. It was also the coroner who supervised the practice of trial by ordeal. If a suspected criminal was unharmed then he was innocent. The coroner would record the event and preserve forfeited property for the Crown.

The coroner's role evolved into an inquiry and evidence taking position originally principally involved in recording criminal events. From the sixteenth century onwards he was almost exclusively concerned with the investigation of sudden death.

In 1836, the coroner became responsible for registering all deaths and for arranging medical witnesses to examine bodies in cases of sudden death.

5.1.2 Statute

Coroners Acts were passed between 1897 and 1980 setting out the rules and regulations governing the coroner's jurisdiction. These were eventually consolidated in the 1988 Coroners Act. The Coroners Rules[2] of 1984 remained unaffected by the Consolidation Act until the Coroners and Justice Act 2009 when they were replaced in 2013 by the Coroners (Investigations) Regulations 2013;[3] the Coroners (Inquests) Rules 2013;[4] and the Coroners Allowances, Fees and Expenses Regulations 2013.[5] These are set out in the Appendix and are essential reading for all those advising a client on the inquest process.

The Coroners Rules set out a framework for inquest case management but frequent reference also needs to be made to the Regulations and occasionally the Act. This new regime for the first time recognised the holding of pre-inquests hearings; advance disclosure and specified target time limits for the completion of the investigation. The bereaved relatives are now placed at the centre of the investigation and have to be informed of, and given reasons for, every step or decision taken by the coroner. Verdicts are replaced with determinations or conclusions and a new standard form is completed at the end of the inquest to replace the old inquisition.

A chief coroner, who must be a judge of the High Court or a circuit judge under the age of 70,[6] now coordinates and supervises the coronial system aiming to improve the quality of performance and to standardise procedure and training.

---

[2] SI 1984/552.
[3] SI 2013/1629.
[4] SI 2013/1616.
[5] SI 2013/1615.
[6] CJA 2009, Sch 8, para 1.

The original intention to give interested parties a right of appeal to the chief coroner, although contained in the Act,[7] have not, however, been implemented. The chief coroner may request information from a coroner in relation to an inquest and the coroner concerned must respond,[8] so it may well be worthwhile making representations to the chief coroner if communication with a coroner about a particular inquest falls on deaf ears. A system of medical examiners to assist in vetting death certificates is to be implemented shortly.[9]

5.1.3 Office

Nowadays the coroner still retains his independence as an independent judicial officer under the Crown appointed and paid for the by the local council or group of councils.[10] To qualify for the office of coroner in the future the candidate must be a qualified lawyer with five years or more experience.[11]

5.2 JURISDICTION

Section 1(2) of the Act sets out the jurisdiction for the holding by a coroner of an inquest. The coroner has compulsory jurisdiction if there is reasonable cause to suspect that the deceased died:

(a)   a violent or unnatural death

(b)   a sudden death whose cause is unknown

(c)   in custody or otherwise in state detention.

A death which appears to be due to natural causes can still be one in which the coroner's jurisdiction is invoked. In *Touche*[12] an unnatural death was described as 'where it was wholly unexpected and it would not have occurred but for some culpable human failing' where death resulting from inadequate monitoring of the deceased's blood pressure after giving birth was an unnatural death for the purposes of s 8(1)(a). 'An inquest should be held whenever a wholly unexpected death, albeit from natural causes, resulted from some culpable human failure, or, more strictly, whenever the coroner had reasonable grounds to suspect that such was the case.'

In other words a death may be unnatural for the purposes of the coroner's jurisdiction even though the determination or conclusion whether medical, legal or both may well be one of natural causes. Neglect or human failing may well be an issue in such cases as indeed might the unexpectedness of the death. To persuade a coroner that he has jurisdiction requires 'reasonable cause' to be

---

7   CJA 2009, s 40.

8   Coroners (Investigations) Regulations 2013, SI 2013/1629, reg 25.

9   CJA 2009, ss 19–20.

10   CJA 2009, Sch 2.

11   CJA 2008, Sch 3, Pt 2(3).

12   *R v H M Coroner Inner London ex parte Touche* [2001] QB 1206.

demonstrated but that refers to the suspicious circumstances of the death and not proof of a confirmed causative link between any act complained of and the death.[13]

Somewhat oddly there is still currently no statutory duty on anyone to report a death to the coroner.[14] There is, however, a common law duty which applies to everyone. This means that anyone can report a death to the coroner. If instructed by a family whose relative is dying or has died in circumstances which it is believed warrant investigation no coroner will object to being contacted and warned of the death or impending death. This may indeed spur the coroner to appoint a truly independent pathologist or indeed to call for more information to be provided to the pathologist than would otherwise be the case.

In the medico-legal context deaths will be reported to the coroner if a doctor cannot give a cause of death, the death occurred unexpectedly or if the death occurred after an operation.

When a case is first reported to a coroner more usually by a GP or a hospital doctor the first decision for the coroner is whether to investigate the death at all. If he decides that one of the criteria for his involvement is invoked he will first of all order a post-mortem.

5.3   THE POST-MORTEM

When a coroner accepts jurisdiction over a body he can insist on a post-mortem being carried out.[15] Relatives may need this to be explained to them as they may not wish the body to be 'cut up' but the coroner has the absolute power if he has decided that the death comes within his jurisdiction. These days, however, coroners and pathologists should be sensitive to the family's wishes and will aim to carry out their investigations with a minimum of intervention and with as much respect for relatives' views and religious and cultural sensitivities as the law and their professional judgment allows them.

The coroner has a duty to inform any person who has notified him of his or her interest that there is to be a post-mortem.[16] Interested parties will include relatives; the deceased's regular medical practitioner and hospital doctor; an enforcing panel or government department in any relevant case and the Chief of Police. Any of these interested parties can be represented at the post-mortem but (apart from the Chief Constable[17] who can be represented by a police officer) only by a qualified medical practitioner.[18] That medical practitioner

---

[13]   *Bicknell v HM Coroner for Birmingham* [2007] EWHC 2547.
[14]   The Government is consulting on the introduction of a statutory duty at least for public service personnel. Ministry of Justice Consultation Paper CP (L) 12/07.
[15]   *R v H M C Greater Manchester ex parte Worch* [1987] QB 627.
[16]   Coroners (Investigations) Regulations 2013, SI 2013/1629, reg 13.
[17]   SI 2013/1629, reg 13(5).
[18]   SI 2013/1629, reg 13(4).

must not interfere in the post-mortem. He or she is there merely as an observer. Any other person may attend with the permission of the coroner but a person complained of giving improper or negligent treatment cannot attend the post-mortem personally but can be represented.[19] The coroner's control over a body arises as soon as he decides to hold an inquest and lasts at common law until the inquest itself is determined.[20] But the body must be released as soon as practicable and if it cannot be released within 28 days the next of kin must be notified and the reason for the delay explained to them.[21] The body must be released when it is no longer required for the investigation.[22]

5.3.1 The pathologist

It is the coroner who appoints the pathologist. He must be what is termed 'a suitable practitioner'; that is a registered medical practitioner of a kind designated by the Chief Coroner as suitable to make examinations of the kind required in the individual case.[23]

He is employed or engaged for this purpose by the coroner even though he may be employed elsewhere by the NHS. The pathologist will be independent (and relatives can insist on this); must have suitable facilities for the conduct of a post-mortem and in order to be 'suitable' be of an appropriate discipline. A paediatric pathologist would therefore be appropriate in the case of the death of a child.

It is custom and practice therefore that if a death has occurred in a hospital in which it is suspected that the failure of treatment may have contributed to the death, the coroner should select a pathologist from another hospital or area. If he does not do so urgent representations should be made to the coroner.

5.3.2 A second post-mortem?

Whilst relatives cannot refuse a coroner's decision to hold a post-mortem, they are in turn entitled, as of right, to a second post-mortem.[24]

Because the coroner's pathologist is supposed to have the appropriate specialist knowledge and to be independent, it is rare that a second post-mortem can be justified. Once the independence of the coronial system and the coroner's pathologist has been explained, most relatives' desire for a second post-mortem disappears.

It may however be useful to ask the coroner for permission to talk to his pathologist or indeed if funding permits to ask your own pathologist or

---

[19]   Coroners and Justice Act 2009, s 14(4).
[20]   *R v Bristol Coroner ex p Kerr* [1974] 2 All ER 719.
[21]   Coroners (Investigations) Regulations 2013, SI 2013/1629, reg 20.
[22]   SI 2013/1629, reg 21.
[23]   SI 2013/1629, reg 11; CJA 2009, s 14.
[24]   *R v HM Coroner Greater London ex p Ridley* [1985] 1 WLR 1347.

histo-pathologist to review slides or test results. The reporting of deaths in hospitals tends to be delegated to junior doctors who may not in fact have knowledge of all the relevant circumstances. All too often the pathologist has lacked vital information of the patient's history; failed to carry out appropriate tests or simply failed to examine areas that may turn out to be highly relevant. It is a breach of Art 2 of the European Convention on Human Rights (ECHR) for the state to fail to provide an adequate post-mortem.[25]

5.3.3   Releasing the body

When the pathologist has finished the coroner will usually authorise the release of the body. The pathologist has authority to remove from the body and preserve material that has a bearing upon the cause of death but must notify the coroner that he has done so and indicate the length of time that the material will be needed. The coroner must then notify the next of kin.[26] The Human Tissue Act 2004 requires that the consent of relatives be obtained if organs or tissue are to be retained after the coroner has concluded his investigation. Following the Alder Hay and Bristol heart scandals many relatives now demand that all body tissues are restored to the body. It is not usual for blood samples to be returned but it is worth considering with the relatives and the pathologist whether it is worth retaining some samples in case further testing becomes relevant at a later stage in the inquiry.

Relatives may well need help in deciding whether to arrange the funeral without access to all the material which the pathologist may retain until the coroner's inquiry has been concluded. A balance has to be struck between the relatives' natural desire for the funeral to take place as soon as possible and their wish that all avenues be explored to find out how the deceased died. Some relatives prefer an early burial or cremation. Others will be happy to delay such ceremonies until they are reassured that no more testing will be required so they can have all slides, etc returned to them with the body.

When the materials taken by the pathologist are released they may be buried or cremated or otherwise lawfully disposed of by the pathologist, returned to the relatives or retained with the consent of the relatives for medical research or other purposes in accordance with the Human Tissue Act.[27] In any event the pathologist must keep a record of what happened to the material.[28]

In the unfortunate event of there being a dispute between relatives or relatives and executors as to the disposal of the body the hospital trust which following release of the body by the coroner will be left in possession of it, will have the right and duty to make disposal arrangements.[29]

---

[25]   *Kakouli v Turkey Fourth Section* [2005] ECHR 38595/97, (2005) 45 EHRR 355, paras 125-8.
[26]   Coroners (Investigations) Regulations 2013, SI 2013/1629, reg 14.
[27]   SI 2013/1629, reg 14.
[28]   SI 2013/1629, reg 15.
[29]   *Lewisham Hospital v Hamuth* [2006] EWHC 1609.

5.3.4 The post-mortem report

The post-mortem report itself is a confidential document which is supplied by the pathologist as soon as practicable after the examination to the coroner and to no-one else.[30] Any interested party can apply to the coroner for a copy of the post-mortem report.[31] The form of the post-mortem report will generally follow the form recommended by the World Health Organisation with an analysis of the body as seen on dissection followed by a conclusion, part one of which sets out the sequence of disease or conditions leading to death and part two listing other disease processes contributory to death but not directly involved.

A typical format for a cause of death is illustrated below for a patient suffering from Alzheimer's disease who died from pneumonia after an operation to set a fractured femur.

> Cause of death
> 1. –
>   (a) Broncho-pneumonia
>   (b) Alzheimer's disease
> 2. Fractured femur (operated)

If the coroner decides as a result of the post-mortem not to proceed with the investigation he must notify the next of kin and if requested give a written explanation.[32] The coroner must discontinue the investigation if the cause of death is revealed by the post-mortem and there is no necessity to investigate the cause of death further unless the death was violent or unnatural or took place in custody or detention.[33]

5.4 THE INQUEST

5.4.1 The issues

There are only four questions for the coroner to consider at an inquest.[34]

(1) **Who** the deceased was?

(2) **How** the deceased came by his death?

(3) **When** the deceased came by his death?

(4) **Where** the deceased came by his death?

---

[30] Coroners (Investigations) Regulations 2013, SI 2013/1629, reg 16.
[31] Coroners (Inquests) Rules 2013, SI 2013/1616, r 13.
[32] Coroners (Investigations) Regulations 2013, SI 2013/1629, reg 17.
[33] CJA 2009, s 4.
[34] CJA 2009, s 5.

The inquest is a fact-finding, non-adversarial inquiry. The coroner is expressly forbidden to consider criminal liability on the part of a named individual or civil responsibility.[35]

5.4.2   Opening

The coroner must inform the next of kin of the decision to begin an investigation[36] and must open the inquest in public as soon as is practicable.[37] At the opening of the inquest, which normally takes place a few days after the death, formal evidence of identification is given – often through the Coroner's Officer, and an interim certificate of the fact of death[38] is issued so that the relatives can get on with the administration of the deceased's estate. The coroner can then give an order for disposal of the body, authorising cremation or burial as appropriate, although that might take place some days or weeks later and can take place without the coroner actually opening an inquest. There is little or no point in the family instructing you to appear on that occasion. Indeed many coroners arrange things so that the family is excused attendance. The opening should be recorded and the coroner should set the date for the final inquest hearing or for a pre-inquest review hearing (PIR) and require statements to be provided by potential witnesses within six weeks.[39]

5.4.3   The pre-inquest review hearing

With the event of more complex inquest hearings particularly as the Human Rights Act increasingly affects the coroner's role, more and more coroners are adopting the practice of holding pre-inquest meetings of representatives of interested parties to plan the procedure for the inquest itself. This procedure is for the first time recognised in the legislation. The new r 6 provides that a pre-inquest hearing can take place at any time and like the inquest itself should be in public and recorded.[40] Items to be discussed can include the documents to be relied on; the calling of a jury and which witnesses should give oral evidence and which statements might be read. As we will see all the items are for the coroner alone but the interest of a fair and impartial inquiry demand these days that the coroner takes into account the views of interested parties before exercising his authority. What is important to realise, however, is that decisions or agreements made at such a hearing are binding and may restrict later challenges if the particular tactical decision is then regretted.[41] Guidance on good practice at pre–inquest hearings has been given by the Chief Coroner HH

---

[35]   CJA 2009, s 10.
[36]   Coroners (Investigations) Regulations 2013, SI 2013/1629, reg 6.
[37]   Coroners (Inquests) Rules 2013, SI 2013/1616, r 5.
[38]   Coroners (Investigations) Regulations 2013, SI 2013/1629, reg 9.
[39]   Chief Coroner's Guidance No 9.
[40]   Coroners (Inquests) Rules 2013, SI 2013/1616, rr 6, 11 and 26.
[41]   See eg *R (on the application of Shaw) v HM Coroner and Assistant Deputy Coroner for Leicester City and South Leicestershire* [2013] EWHC 386 (Admin).

Judge Peter Thornton QC when giving judgment in the High Court on a recent challenge to a coroner's inquest verdict.[42]

5.4.4 The resumed hearing

Once the coroner is satisfied he has gathered together all the material and witnesses he requires for his inquiry he will fix a date for the inquest to be resumed. It must be held on a working day[43] and on at least seven days' notice to the next of kin.[44] For the first time coroners have been given targets with the Chief Coroner to be notified if the investigation has not been concluded in 12 months and an explanation provided[45] while the inquest itself should be completed within six months or as soon as practicable.[46] The relationship of the terms investigation and inquiry and 12 months and six months is somewhat confusing but the aim of the new regime is clear. Coroners should have the resources to get on with these cases. However, it may be perfectly reasonable for a representative of bereaved relatives to seek time to prepare for the inquest once the results of the coroner's initial investigations are provided usually in the form of the inquest bundle. Provided that the relatives are fully informed of the reason for any delay and agree to it such a delay may be in their interests by ensuring that the inquest when held is comprehensive and answers their concerns. It must be born in mind by all parties that the bereaved are now at the centre of the coronial system and it is their wishes that should be given the greatest consideration.

There is no longer an absolute legal requirement for inquests to be held in a particular geographical area. In the reopened Hillsborough disaster inquest, for example, the coroner ruled that the inquest would take place in the north west (although not in Liverpool) explaining that: 'In the ordinary course of events, inquests can be expected to take place at a location which is most convenient to the bereaved and other interested persons and witnesses.'[47] The evidence to be given at the inquest is entirely within the control of the coroner. He decides which experts and which lay witnesses to call. He chooses the pathologist and decides whether or not to admit witness statements. He accepts hearsay evidence. The identification of child witnesses is banned.[48] Otherwise any witness called by a coroner is bound to attend and give evidence. If necessary evidence can be given by video link[49] or from behind a screen[50]

The coroner can require a witness by written notice to attend to give evidence, provide a statement and/or produce documents.[51] The witness can only refuse

---

[42] *Brown v HM Coroner for the County of Norfolk* [2014] EWHC 187 at para 36.
[43] Coroners (Inquests) Rules 2013, SI 2013/1616, r 7.
[44] SI 2013/1616, r 9.
[45] Coroners (Investigations) Regulations 2013, SI 2013/1629, reg 26.
[46] Coroners (Inquests) Rules 2013, SI 2013/1616, r 8.
[47] http://hillsboroughinquests.independent.gov.uk/documents-and-rulings.
[48] Children and Young Persons Act 1933, s 39(1).
[49] Coroners (Inquests) Rules 2013, SI 2013/1616, r 17.
[50] SI 2013/1616, r 18.
[51] CJA 2009, Sch 5.

to give evidence by attending and electing not to give evidence on the grounds of self-incrimination. In order to do so, there must be a real and appreciable risk of criminal offences and penalties.[52] There is however no complete immunity against questioning. The ability to refuse to give evidence only relates to those questions which would reflect the risk of criminal offences.

A coroner is charged with conducting an inquiry. The process is investigative not adversarial. Anyone with factual information which will assist the coroner and his pathologist with their inquiries is obliged to provide that information to the coroner. Once the coroner has decided that information is relevant he should share it in due course with all interested parties. There is no room in the system for information to be provided on the coroner's undertaking not to disclose it further, as has happened in the past.

5.4.5 Documents

Documentation for the inquest is likewise entirely controlled by the coroner. It is his decision whether or not documentary evidence should be admitted. Such evidence should be read aloud unless the coroner otherwise directs.

Written evidence can be admitted by the coroner if the maker cannot attend at all or within reasonable time or there is a good reason for his non-attendance but there is also provision for written evidence to be admitted if there is no good reason given by the maker. Otherwise the usual reason for admitting written evidence is that it is unlikely to be disputed.[53] This seems to relax the previous rule that interested parties had to consent before a written statement could be admitted.

The coroner can also admit written documents but must before doing so announce the nature of the document and its maker. The coroner may read aloud parts or all of the document but on this occasion an interested party can object to the documents admission.[54]

The full version of the post-mortem report is seldom read out. In any event, should an advocate be representing relatives at an inquest, it is recommended practice to ask the relatives whether they wish to hear the pathologist's evidence and suggest they leave the room whilst it is being given. Documentation used at the inquest however must be shown to interested parties who wish to see it at the time.[55]

The coroner can admit into evidence the findings of an inquiry and will often wait for such an inquiry to complete its work before listing the inquest. Before

---

[52] Coroners (Inquests) Rules 2013, SI 2013/1616, r 22(1).
[53] SI 2013/1616, r 23.
[54] SI 2013/1616, r 23.
[55] SI 2013/1616, r 23(2)(d).

admitting the inquiry findings the coroner must publicise the title, date of publication and give at least a brief account of its findings. Again any interested party is entitled to see a copy.[56]

Documents used in an inquest must be kept for 15 years and copies provided to any one considered by the coroner to be a proper person although a charge may be levied.[57] Fees for the production of documents are set out in the Coroners Allowances, Fees and Expenses Regulations 2013. A coroner cannot however charge for documents supplied before or during the inquest itself.[58]

5.4.6 Advance disclosure

Historically coroners have not been willing to disclose documentation to interested parties prior to the inquest hearing. Even now there is no automatic provision of documentation prior to an inquest. The new rules require interested parties to request them.[59] There is authority for the proposition that refusal to meet the reasonable requests by an interested party for advance disclosure of statements and experts reports may be grounds for overturning the inquest verdict.[60]

Sometimes advocates have available to them witness or documentary evidence which they may feel would assist the coroner in his inquiry. Indeed as indicated above there is a common law duty to assist the coroner with his inquiry. It is not possible for interested parties to call their own evidence. Instead, such evidence should be supplied to the coroner who can decide whether a particular witness or whether a particular item of evidence should be called during the course of the inquiry itself. It is now accepted that medical records should be supplied in advance of an inquest.[61] In an Art 2 inquest[62] the coroner is entitled to draw adverse inferences if the state fails to provide him with a satisfactory explanation[63] and the state has a duty to preserve relevant evidence.[64]

The only restriction on disclosure by a coroner to an interested party is if there is a statutory or legal prohibition on disclosure, the consent of the author or copyright holder of any document cannot be obtained, the request is considered unreasonable or relates to contemplated or commenced criminal action or the coroner considers that the document is irrelevant.[65]

---

[56] SI 2013/1616, r 24.
[57] Coroners (Investigations) Regulations 2013, SI 2013/1629, reg 27.
[58] Coroners (Inquests) Rules 2013, SI 2013/1616, r 16.
[59] SI 2013/1616, r 13.
[60] *R (Bentley) v HM Coroner for Avon* [2001] EWHC Admin 170.
[61] *Stobart v NHA* [1992] 3 Med LR 284.
[62] See para 5.4.12.
[63] *Timurtas v Turkey* (2002) 33 EHRR 121 para 66.
[64] *R (Rowley) v DPP* [2003] EWHC 693 (Admin) para 54.
[65] Coroners (Inquests) Rules 2013, SI 2013/1616, r 15.

5.4.7   Unused material

It may be the case that a coroner decides only to use during the inquest hearing itself part of the material which he has gathered in as part of his investigation.

Specific guidance is given to coroners in how to deal with unused material in an inquest into the death 'of a member of the public during or following contact with the police'.[66] There is no reason to suppose that unused documents in an inquest where relatives may be concerned that the death could have been caused as a result of clinical negligence should be treated any differently. The guidance from the Home Office is that:[67]

> 'where disclosure of material which is not likely to be called in evidence is contemplated, it may be preferable to arrange for interested parties to view the material in advance rather than the material being copied and provided directly to them, on the grounds that such material is generally not likely to be relevant.'

The same Home Office circular emphasises that pre-inquest disclosure 'may remove a source of friction between interested persons'.

There is every reason to suggest that such disclosure serves an equally important purpose in a death where clinical negligence may be in issue as bereaved relatives are often concerned at what they perceive to be a cover up by the 'medical mafia'. Certainly in an Article 2 inquest it appears that the state has a positive duty to disclose relevant information to the coroner and the coroner likewise has a duty to disclose such evidence to the deceased's family in advance unless it is privileged and such privilege has not been waived.[68]

Whenever documents are disclosed in advance of the inquest it should be made clear to relatives that save for medical records to which they are entitled anyway under the Access to Health Records Act 1990 such documents are confidential unless and until referred to in the inquest itself.

5.4.8   Briefing relatives

It is essential that relatives attending an inquest are briefed by the advocate representing them as interested parties as to what to expect.

It should be explained to them that a coroner's court is not like a Crown Court.

An inquest is an inquiry and not an adversarial proceeding. Although appearances may suggest otherwise there are in fact no parties. Everyone present is there to help the coroner. As seen above, the evidence is entirely within the control of the coroner. After the coroner has finished producing a witness and relevant documents and asked his own questions, only then may

---

[66]   Home Office Circular 31/2002.
[67]   Ibid, para 10(iv).
[68]   *R (D) v Home Secretary* [2006] EWCA Civ 143 para 46.

interested parties ask questions by way of examination but not by way of cross-examination. The order of questioning is now enshrined in the rules – first the coroner, then interested persons or their representatives and then the witness's representative if present.[69]

Relatives should also be reminded that the inquest is held in public so that the press may be there and are entitled to report the proceedings. Reporting restrictions in inquests (other than those by statute restricting the reporting of the identities of child witnesses) are rare as they would infringe the media's Art 10 ECHR rights to report the proceedings.[70]

There is nothing worse than bereaved relatives at a time when their feelings are likely to be particularly sore being surrounded by the media on the steps of the coroner's court. Before the inquest the relatives should be briefed on whether media attention is likely and if so how best to deal with it. Some relatives will wish to have nothing to do with the media. Others will make confident interviewees. Relatives should be offered the opportunity of giving interviews before the inquest, embargoed until its conclusion. In this way they can seize the agenda and speak at a time and at a location of their choosing when there is less pressure and an opportunity for several takes. The media will usually also look for a statement afterwards. Discuss with the relatives what might be said and whether you as solicitor or they themselves will make such a statement. If possible prepare in advance a short written statement with alternatives if necessary which can be read or handed out as appropriate.

Always ask the relatives to choose a photograph of their loved one which they would be happy for the world to see and ask them to bring it along with them. It could also be shown to the coroner. This helps personalise an inquiry which can at times seem horribly impersonal. There is nothing worse than media representatives door-stepping friends and relatives and publishing a far from flattering or inappropriate photograph. If TV is involved remember that it is a moving media so a DVD or video used sensitively may be chosen in advance and brought along.

5.4.9 Interested party

Only parties accepted by the coroner as being 'interested' can request to participate in an inquest and examine witnesses.[71]

An interested party is now defined under the Act.[72] The coroner may have to be asked to exercise his discretion[73] if remoter parties seek to participate. For example, a girlfriend who was not a partner may be excluded from the definition even though the parties may have intended to be married.

---

[69]   Coroners (Inquests) Rules 2013, SI 2013/1616, r 21.
[70]   *Re LM (Reporting Restrictions: Coroner's Inquest* [2007] EWHC 1902 (Fam).
[71]   Coroners (Inquests) Rules 2013, SI 2013/1616, r 19(1).
[72]   CJA 2009, s 47(2),
[73]   Under CJA 2009, s 47(2)(m).

5.4.10 Jury

A jury is mandatory in cases of deaths in custody or state detention where the death was violent, unnatural or the cause was unknown; where the death was due to an act or omission of the police in the execution of their duty or as a result of a notifiable accident, poisoning or disease.[74] In all other cases, whether or not the coroner holds an inquest with a jury depends on whether he considers there is sufficient reason to do so.

The coroner should first decide the scope of the inquiry he intends to conduct and then decide whether the criteria for him to summon a jury are satisfied. The views of the family as to whether there should be a jury should be taken into account.[75]

In the vast majority of cases the coroner will sit without a jury. If there is a jury the coroner must leave it to the jury to decide the facts which in clinical negligence cases will involve medical issues and in doing so they can choose not to accept an expert's opinion[76] providing they do so on a rational basis. The coroner must direct the jury as to the law and provide it with a summary of the evidence.[77]

5.4.11 The extent of the inquiry

The coroner will have to decide whether the death raises issues that would require that the inquest takes the form of an inquiry into a sudden death which is required to satisfy the state's obligations to the deceased's relatives under the ECHR. This Convention is incorporated into English law via the Human Rights Act 1998.

5.4.12 Article 2 ECHR

Article 2 of the ECHR provides that: 'Everyone's right to life shall be protected by law.' This gives rise to a duty on the state to investigate when deaths occur in circumstances where it owed such a duty to preserve life[78] based on the need to make the substantive protection provided by Art 2 effective in practice.

There must be:

---

[74] CJA 2009, s 7.

[75] Article 8 ECHR; *Jean Paul v Deputy Coroner of the Queens Household* [2007] EWHC 408 (Admin) para 44.

[76] *R v HM Coroner for North London ex p Diesa Koto* (1993) 157 JP 857.

[77] Coroners (Inquests) Rules 2013, SI 2013/1616, r 33.

[78] *Osman v UK* (1998) 5 BHRC 293, [1998] ECHR 23452/94.

'a full investigation of any death involving or possibly involving a violation of the state's substantive obligation to protect human life arising under Article 2 (essentially whenever state agents or bodies may bear responsibility for the death).'[79]

Although the European Court has ruled that that obligation is not confined to cases:

'where it was apparent that the state could have been responsible, either directly or through its positive obligations, for the death of an individual'

and indeed that:

'the obligations under Article 2 of the convention included the requirement for an effective independent system to be set up so that the cause of death of patients in the care of the medical profession, whether in the public or private sector, could be determined and those responsible made accountable.'[80]

The enquiries that a coroner has to make where Art 2 is engaged may be more extensive so that the question the coroner has to determine of 'how' the deceased came by his death is converted from 'by what means'[81] to 'by what means and in what broad circumstances did the deceased die'.[82] This may encourage the coroner to investigate overall or earlier failings in the health care system which may have contributed to the circumstances leading to the patient's death.

It is essential that an Art 2 inquiry conducted by the coroner is a full and effective inquiry otherwise deceased's relatives may have remedies to demand a full public inquiry.[83]

5.4.13 Criteria for compliance

The case of *Jordan*[84] sets out the criteria for such an investigation to be Art 2 compliant.

The inquiry must be:
(1) independent;
(2) effective;
(3) prompt;

---

[79] R (on the application of Hurst) v Commissioner of Police for the Metropolis [2007] 2 WLR 726, para 28.

[80] Silih v Slovenia 71463/01 ECHR 28 June 2007.

[81] R v HM Coroner N Humberside ex p Jamieson [1994] 3 All ER 972.

[82] R (Middleton) v West Somerset Coroner [2004] UKHL 10; R v WSC ex p Middlesex [2004] AC 182.

[83] See Arts 2 and 3 European Convention on Human Rights – McCann v UK [1996] 21 EHRR 97; Wright v Secretary of State for the Home Dept [2001] EWHC Admin 520.

[84] Jordan v UK [2001] ECHR 327, (2003) 37 EHRR 2 confirmed in R v Home Secretary ex p Amin [2004] 1 AC 653.

(4) involve a sufficient element of public scrutiny;

(5) involve the next of kin.

As Jackson J in that case reminded everyone:[85]

> 'steps should be taken to ensure that in every case where Article 2 of the Convention may be engaged, the coroner's inquest complies with the procedural obligations arising under that article.'

5.4.14 Conditions for engagement

It is difficult to discern when Art 2 may be engaged and indeed why there should be a difference between inquiries held into deaths related to medical treatment dependent on whether these factors are engaged. However, there is no doubt that Art 2 may be engaged when there has been a death in hospital.[86]

The conditions for engaging Art 2 have been explained[87] as follows:

(1) Simple negligence does not trigger the requirement for an inquiry into the state's obligation to protect life in that case.

(2) If there has been an effective civil action in negligence this may already have satisfied the obligation.

(3) The obligation may also have been satisfied if there have already been an inquiry or inquiries but only if the bereaved relatives have been able to participate effectively in them[88] and they have been carried out independently of the health care provider concerned.[89]

A police inquiry on its own will not usually be sufficient because the relatives play little active part in it. A civil action may be insufficient either because it has not yet taken place or because the defendant has already admitted liability so that there may not have been any inquiry into liability in which the relatives could participate.[90] As damages in fatal cases are often low it may not in fact be possible or cost effective for a civil trial to take place. In these cases the inquest becomes the obvious way in which the state discharges its Art 2 obligation to hold an inquiry. In any event it is for the state to conduct an inquiry not for the relatives to conduct one instead.

---

[85] Ibid at para 68. See also *R (on the application of Smith) v Oxfordshire Assistant Deputy Coroner* [2011] 1 AC 1.

[86] *Powell v UK* App No 45 395/99 (4 May 2000) (unreported); *Sieminska v Poland* app no 37602/97 (29 March 2001) (unreported); *Calvelli v Italy* [2002] ECHR 32967/96; *Vo v France* App no 53924/00 [2004] 40 EHRR 259; *Goodson v HM Coroner for Bedfordshire & Luton* [2004] EWHC 2931 (Admin); *R v HM Coroner for Inner London ex p Takoushis* [2006] 1 WLR 46.

[87] Per Richards J *Goodson v HM Coroner for Bedfordshire & Luton* [2004] EWHC 2931 (Admin); [2006] 1 WLR 432.

[88] *R v Secretary of State for Health ex p Khan* [2003] EWCA Civ 1129.

[89] *R (on the application of Amin) v Secretary of State for Home Dept* [2004] 1 AC 653 at para 20(7).

[90] *R v HM Coroner for Inner London ex p Takoushis* [2006] 1 WLR 46.

It appears therefore that in medico-legal cases Art 2 will be engaged whenever there is the potential for culpability or gross negligence or an abject failure of the health care system.

It is also arguable that the state's investigative duty extends to deaths in private hospitals but not now it appears in private care homes even those contracted to provide such a service by the local authority.[91] This appears to be at odds with the duty as explained by the European Court which considers that it extends to cover both public and private health care sector.[92]

5.5 Witnesses

The coroner may take evidence from any witness that he and he alone thinks is relevant to his inquiry although a verdict can be challenged on the basis that the coroner failed to call a witness who had obviously relevant information which should have helped the coroner's inquiry.[93]

5.5.1 Examination

The questioning of witnesses during the coroner's inquiry is entirely controlled by the coroner who will bear in mind the four questions which he is there to consider. In many inquests the interested parties have a much wider agenda than the coroner. Only if the coroner believes that it is in the public interest that the inquiry be widened is he likely to allow detailed examination of witnesses outside the strict limits of the four questions he has to answer. It is entirely his discretion whether to admit those questions and the inquiry will be stopped if the coroner considers the question is not relevant[94] or is a cross examination rather than an examination.[95]

Questions of those witnesses giving oral evidence can only be asked by an interested party or his representative.[96] First the coroner will lead the witness through his evidence sometimes simply reading his statement to him and then asking his own subsidiary questions. Only when the coroner has exhausted his own questions will he turn to the representatives of interested parties. Unless the witness concerned is a relative of the deceased the coroner will usually ask the bereaved relatives representative to go first with the hospital's representative or the representative for the individual doctor or nurse if separately represented going last.[97]

---

91 *Johnson v Havering London Borough Council* [2007] UKHL 27.
92 *Silih v Slovenia* Application ECHR 71463/01 (28 June 2007), (2009) 49 EHRR 996.
93 *R (Stanley) v HM Coroner Inner North London* [2003] EWHC Admin 1180.
94 Coroners (Inquests) Rules 2013, SI 2013/1616, r 19(2).
95 *R v South London Coroner ex p Thompson* (1982) 126 SJ 625.
96 Coroners (Inquests) Rules 2013, SI 2013/1616, r 19(1).
97 Coroners (Inquests) Rules 2013, SI 2013/1616, r 21.

As we have seen the coroner can seek to put a written statement into evidence[98] but only if the evidence is seen in advance by interested parties After it has been admitted it is too late to challenge such a statement.[99]

If a witness in providing an answer to any question put to him is likely to incriminate himself in potential criminal proceedings, the coroner should warn the witness that he may refuse to answer such a question. If this happens interested parties still have the right to put questions to the witness, but to each question the witness will be informed that he does not have to answer the question. However the right not to answer only applies to the specific questions whose answers may incriminate and not to his evidence generally and there must be an appreciable risk of criminal charges. There is thus no complete immunity against questioning.[100]

5.6 EXPERTS

Often in clinical negligence cases the issue faced by the coroner is whether to engage an expert witness.

Some coroners adopt the unsatisfactory practice of calling the consultant in charge of the relevant treating doctors who may not have had direct involvement in that patient's care in order for him to provide his view on the treatment given. This should be resisted although it is for the coroner to call witnesses and to decide which ones are appropriate. The courts have held[101] that whether a coroner calls an expert witness depends on the circumstances of the individual case including the issues being investigated and the coroner's own expertise as well as the availability of other evidence.

If a coroner decides not to call independent expert evidence there is nothing to stop an interested party surrendering his own expert evidence to the coroner. If the coroner decides that the evidence will help his inquiry he can decide to adopt the witness in which case that expert becomes the coroner's expert.

In preparing for an inquest, and if funds allow, it is often extremely useful either to have a provisional report from an expert or at least guidance on the likely issues and questions to raise with the various witnesses. Some coroners believe that if an interested party has an expert's report this should be surrendered to the coroner as he is conducting an inquiry and anyone with information likely to assist him should provide that information to him before the inquest resumes so that he can decide himself whether to call that witness to give evidence. This is to misunderstand the nature of advice given by experts to interested parties. There may be cases where tactically it makes sense for the coroner to be appraised of an expert's differing view but that report is privileged for the use of the commissioning party usually in preparation for a later adversarial case

---

[98] Coroners (Inquests) Rules 2013, SI 2013/1616, r 23.

[99] *R (Mulholland) v HM Coroner for St Pancras* [2003] EWHC Admin 2612.

[100] Coroners (Inquests) Rules 2013, SI 2013/1616, r 22(1).

[101] *Goodson v HM Coroner for Bedfordshire & Luton* [2006] 1 WLR 432.

and should only be handed over to the coroner if both the interested party and the expert consent. Otherwise an expert's provisional report should only be surrendered to the coroner if the evidence provides additional factual information.

If a coroner becomes aware of the existence of a medical report in the hands of an interested party he cannot force that party or his representative to disclose it to him although as seen above it may of course be volunteered. If the report was prepared for an anticipated civil action it is privileged in the hands of the interested party on whose behalf the report was commissioned. If the report is in essence advice to the interested party's solicitor on the medical issues arising at the inquest or questions to be asked then that advice attracts legal advice privilege in the hands of the interested party. It is of course that client's privilege not that of the instructed solicitor so must be communicated to the client in order to attract that privilege.[102]

5.7 THE DETERMINATION

At the conclusion of the evidence, the coroner or the jury must decide on the determination – which may include a short form conclusion previously known as the verdict.[103] Before doing so, it is open to the representatives of interested parties to make submissions. Those submissions however can only relate to the determination. They can only be made on behalf of an interested party; have to be made to the coroner in the absence of the jury and not to the jury and must be made prior to his summing up. The submissions must be of law and not as to the facts of the inquiry.

The determination involves the coroner (or the jury) completing Form 2,[104] which is a record of the inquest replacing the old inquisition and containing the answers to the four questions the coroner (or the jury) is required to decide.

As seen above, the coroner cannot be involved in determining criminal or civil liability.[105] The determination therefore cannot be framed to determine criminal liability on the part of a named person or civil liability on behalf of any person or organisation.

Conclusions that may be considered in a medico-legal case are likely to be as follows:
–   natural causes;
–   want of attention at birth;
–   suicide;
–   accidental or misadventure;

---

[102]   *Three Rivers District Council v Bank of England (No 6)* [2005] 1 AC 610 (see para 115).
[103]   Coroners (Inquests) Rules 2013, SI 2013/1616, r 34.
[104]   Coroners (Inquests) Rules 2013, SI 2013/1616, Sch 2.
[105]   CJA 2009, s 10.

–   unlawful killing;
–   open verdict;
–   still birth.

A coroner who sits with a jury is obliged to leave to the jury only those conclusions which are properly available to them in the circumstances heard on evidence. The coroner has to decide (without of course deciding the facts which have to be left to the jury) whether it would be safe for the jury to reach any of the conclusions which he wished to leave them to consider and where he has doubts he has to exercise his discretion only to leave the conclusions which he believes would be reasonable for the jury to arrive at.[106]

These conclusions in medical legal inquests are most often these days replaced by narrative verdicts that can be used as an alternative or in addition to the short form conclusions.

5.7.1   Unlawful killing

An unlawful killing conclusion is unlikely unless criminal proceedings are out of the question – for example because the perpetrator is already dead. Such a conclusion can cover murder, reckless manslaughter or gross negligence manslaughter. The most difficult area is probably in relation to the latter. In gross negligence manslaughter the evidence has to demonstrate the existence of a duty of care; a breach of that duty and gross negligence such as that the inattention or failure to advert to a serious risk whether beyond mere inadvertence in relation to the obvious and important matter which the duty demanded the individual should address.[107] The standard of proof is the criminal standard.[108] A breach of duty should only be categorised as gross when it involves 'such disregard for the life and safety of others as to amount to a crime against the state'. In a medical inquest 'mistakes, even very serious mistakes, and errors of judgment, even very serious errors of judgment, and the like, are nowhere near enough for a crime as serious as manslaughter to be committed'.[109]

If a perpetrator has already been convicted it is unlikely that a coroner will feel obliged to resume a full inquest. The test is whether there is sufficient cause for the inquest to be resumed after the criminal trial.

In the rare circumstances in which a health care provider, whether medical staff or institution, has already been tried the coroner may well decide to resume the inquest in order to ensure that he explores the areas of preventing re-occurrence

---

[106] *R v Galbraith* [1981] 1 WLR 1039; *R v HM Coroner for Exeter and East Devon ex p Palmer* [2000] Inquest LR 78; *R v Inner South London Coroner ex p Douglas Williams* [1999] 1 All ER 344; *R (Bennett) v HM Coroner for Inner South London* [2007] EWCA Civ 617.

[107] *R v Adomako* [1995] AC 171 (HL) and *R v Adomako, Prentice and Sulman* [1994] QB 302 CA.

[108] *R v West London Coroner ex p Gray* [1988] 1 QB 467.

[109] *R v Misra* [2005] 1 Cr App Rep 21 [25] (CA).

and improvement that involve his role as a guardian of the public's safety. Other reasons for resumption may be where there are issues as to the actual cause of death and the necessity for there to be an inquiry which complies with the bereaved relatives' Art 2 rights which a criminal trial may well not have satisfied.

It is likely that in such a case any conclusion would be narrative in form and may well be tied into the Coroners Rules recommendations.[110] It is theoretically possible for an unlawful killing conclusion to be returned even after a criminal trial has led to acquittal because a criminal court jury considers the criminal liability of a named individual whereas a coroner's jury cannot frame its conclusion to suggest that a named individual was criminally responsible but can do so to suggest that someone was. Otherwise a coroner's conclusion should not be inconsistent with the criminal verdict.[111]

In all other conclusions to be reviewed the requisite standard of proof required is the civil standard – a balance of probabilities.

5.7.2 Accidental death

Accidental death and misadventure are the same. Sometimes accidental death is used to denote the activities of the deceased whilst misadventure is used where the death was caused by a third party. Traditionally a death following an operation would result in a conclusion of misadventure. However, neither accidental nor misadventure conclusions do justice to the cause of deaths of many patients. Even before the advent of the Human Rights Act some enlightened coroners had started to reflect this in the use of narrative verdicts. An alternative is to describe the conclusion as an Accidental Adverse Healthcare Event.

5.7.3 Neglect

Conclusions of natural causes and want of attention at birth can carry the rider 'aggravated' or 'contributed to' by 'lack of care' or 'neglect'. This rider does not describe carelessness or negligence. Lack of care denotes neglect – the opposite of self-neglect.

If an advocate is considering representing parties at an inquest, the one case he should read is Jamieson[112] which contains a comprehensive review of the verdicts (now conclusions) open to a coroner with specific reference to the use of the verdict of lack of care or neglect.

---

[110] See below.
[111] CA 1988, s 16(7).
[112] *R v HM Coroner N Humberside ex p Jamieson* [1994] 3 All ER 972.

Neglect therefore is not the same as negligence and must amount to a continuous or systemic failure to provide treatment.[113]

A single error of clinical judgment is unlikely to amount to neglect.[114] It arises only where there has been a gross failure to provide basic medical care and there is a clear causal link between that failure and the death.[115]

A failure to take account of clear medical signs and therefore to provide treatment may amount to neglect.[116] This is not the same as making an incorrect medical judgment. That may of course amount to negligence if the Bolam criteria are satisfied in subsequent civil proceedings but it does not amount to neglect. So if a doctor had actually considered the patient and had taken a decision to treat or not to treat that cannot amount to neglect[117] unless the judgment made not to provide any treatment was grossly erroneous[118] or was arrived at from a grossly inadequate review of the patient.

As with any medico-legal judgment hindsight is a wonderful thing. Neglect will not arise as a potential verdict if there were on reflection a number of steps that could have been taken but in the exercise of reasonable clinical assessment at the time were not carried out. However, if no assessment took place, or such assessment as took place was grossly lacking, a conclusion including neglect may well have to be considered.

Examples of gross failure amounting to neglect in the medico-legal context are:

(1) a serious underestimate of the patient's condition;[119]

(2) a failure to follow routine procedures;[120]

(3) a failure to provide effective medical treatment.[121]

It is not clear whether the requirement for there to be a clear causal connection between the act of neglect and the death obliges a coroner to find that the death would have been avoided on a balance of probabilities or simply might have been.[122] The test is probably whether an opportunity to give potentially life saving treatment or care was missed[123] or that measures may have been taken which arguably would have prevented the death.[124]

---

[113] *R v Surrey Coroner ex p Wright* [1997] QB 786.
[114] *R (Metropolitan Police Comr) v HM Coroner Greater London* [2003] ACD 48.
[115] *R v HM Coroner N Humberside ex p Jamieson* [1994] 3 All ER 972.
[116] *R (Touche) v Inner London Coroner* [2001] QB 1206.
[117] *R (Mumford) v Reading Coroner* [2002] EWHC 2184.
[118] *R (Davies) v HM Deputy Coroner for Birmingham* [2003] EWHC 618.
[119] *R (Marshall) v Coventry Coroner* [2001] EWHC Admin 804.
[120] *R (Touche) v Inner London Coroner* [2001] QB 1206.
[121] *Clegg* [1996] EWHC Admin 307.
[122] *R (Khan) v HM Coroner West Hertfordshire* [2002] EWHC Admin 302 suggests 'would' but in Human Rights cases it is arguable that only 'might' is required. In Sacker Pill LJ suggested that the test was 'measures may well have been taken ... which arguably would have prevented the death'.
[123] *R v HM Coroner Coventry ex p Chief Constable of Staffs* (2000) 164 JP 665.
[124] *R (Sacker) v West Yorkshire Coroner* [2003] 3 All ER 278.

The questions to address are probably:

(1) could something have been done?

(2) if it had been done might it have made a difference?[125]

The neglect need not be the sole cause of the death[126] provided that the contribution was more than minimal[127] and therefore death at the time it happened might have been avoided altogether or at least delayed.

In an Article 2 inquest the coroner is entitled to find a breach of Art 2 where a failure increased the risk of death to a material extent[128] even if the failure did not cause the particular death being investigated.[129]

The following questions help build up a submission that the conclusion should include a finding of neglect:

(1) Was the deceased's condition known to the medical staff and if not should it have been known?

(2) Did the deceased's condition require that treatment be given?

(3) Was there a complete and total failure to provide the appropriate treatment?

(4) Had it been provided might this treatment have changed the outcome?

5.7.4 Narrative verdict

There is no requirement to return a determination that includes one of the standard conclusions listed above. The determination could simply incorporate a brief neutral and factual statement.[130] This applies whether or not the inquest is Art 2 compliant.[131]

Narrative statements come in all shapes and sizes. There is no guidance in the rules as to how a coroner should deal with a narrative verdict either by himself or when directing a jury. Sometimes a coroner will ask the advocates for interested parties to suggest draft forms of narrative statement. Others will supply a draft for discussion. The use of these narrative conclusions makes it impossible for an advocate to comply with the rule that submissions should relate only to law and not to fact, but the involvement of interested parties in the drafting of the outcome is a development which is usually to be welcomed. However, the danger for representatives of the bereaved relatives is not to agree a form of narrative conclusion which also rules out a causative link between

---

[125] *R (Dawson) v East Riding and Hull Coroner* [2001] EWHC Admin 352.

[126] *R v Cato* [1976] 1 WLR 110.

[127] *R v HM Coroner for Exeter and East Devon ex p Palmer* [2000] Inquest LR 78.

[128] *Van Colle v Chief Constable of Hertfordshire* [2007] EWCA Civ 325 paras 78–83.

[129] *R v HM Coroner for Coventry ex parte Chief Constable for Staffordshire* [2000] 164 JP 665; *R (Scott) v HM Coroner for Inner West London* (2001) 61 BMLR 222.

[130] *R (Middleton) v West Somerset Coroner* [2004] 2 AC 182.

[131] *R (on the application of Longfield Care Homes) v HM Coroner for Blackburn* [2004] EWHC 2467 (Admin) para 28–32.

any suggested default in medical procedure and the sad outcome unless there has been clear independent medical evidence denying any such link.

In complex cases of which clinical negligence deaths would be examples written guidance to a jury will undoubtedly be of assistance to their understanding of the medical issues. Such guidance could be by way of agreed written questions but it is essential in order for the state's Art 2 obligations to be met that framing those questions involve the participation of the relatives' advocate and that the questions themselves leave plenty of discretion in the way the jury could answer them.[132]

5.8   CONTENT OF DETERMINATION

However the coroner decides to formulate his determination he or the jury must provide a conclusion on relevant disputed factual issues.[133] The determination or conclusion and any commentary by the coroner must be framed in such a way as to ensure that 'those who have lost a relative may at least have the satisfaction of knowing that lessons learned from his death may save the lives of others'.[134] An incomplete factual conclusion will also hinder the coroner's ability to make Coroners Rules recommendations (see below).

The coroner's or the jury's conclusions can be judgmental without breaching the prohibition of rulings which pertain to civil or criminal responsibility. A critical factual conclusion that, for example, the condition from which the deceased dies was 'diagnosable' or 'treatable' is a perfectly acceptable conclusion on the facts if so warranted by the evidence. Words such as 'inappropriate'; 'inadequate'; 'proper precautions were not taken'; 'did not take' or 'failed to take' or 'failed to attend' are all words one may expect to find in a narrative conclusion following clinical negligence without the prohibition of dealing with civil or criminal issues being offended.

5.8.1   Recommendations

A coroner, who believes that action should be taken to prevent further fatalities similar to that in respect of which the inquest is being held is under a duty[135] to make a report to prevent other deaths.[136] After hearing all the evidence and considering all the documents the coroner can announce at the inquest that he is going to report the matter in writing, to a person or authority who in his opinion should receive it supplying the Chief Coroner with a copy at the same time.

---

[132] *R (Middleton) v West Somerset Coroner* [2004] 2 AC 182.
[133] Ibid.
[134] *R (Amin) v Secretary of State for the Home Department* [2004] 1 AC 653 at para 31; Middleton at para 18.
[135] CJA 2009, Sch 5, para 7(1).
[136] Coroners (Investigations) Regulations 2013, SI 2013/1629, reg 28.

The Chief Coroner can then send the report to anyone he believes will find it useful or of interest. The same applies to the response which must be supplied within 56 days[137] and must contain details of any action taken or proposed, a timetable for implementation or an explanation as to why no action is being taken. The respondent can also make representations about the release and publication of the response, which the coroner must pass on to the Chief Coroner who decides whether or not to publish any recommendation and response. The Chief Coroner has issued guidance to coroners on the use of recommendations, which is worth a read as this is something many relatives in potential clinical negligence cases find of value in assuring them that the death of their loved one has not been in vain.[138]

It has been suggested that the use of recommendations now forms part of the means by which the state discharges its Art 2 obligation.[139]

5.9 FUNDING

Asking relatives to pay to find out how their loved one died has always been a difficult exercise for a solicitor instructed by an interested party at an inquest. Asking relatives to pay to find out how their loved one died when that death was possibly caused by medical treatment provided by the state is even more difficult for them to understand.

5.9.1 Public funding

Legal aid is no longer generally available for clinical negligence claims but legal help is still available for advice and assistance for inquests into a death of a member of the family and exceptional funding is available for advocacy at an inquest.

The limits of this funding are set out in the guide to the Lord Chancellor's Exceptional Funding.

- Even if the client is financially eligible for legal help it only covers preparatory work. Advocacy at inquests is excluded so advocacy at the inquest can only be funded by legal aid under exceptional funding;
- If the inquest is to be the way in which the state complies with its Art 2 obligation[140] then in cases of serious misconduct/gross negligence by an employee of the state exceptional funding may be available from the scheme administered for the Ministry of Justice by the Legal Aid Agency if there is a significant wider public interest. This is rarely satisfied in clinical negligence inquests unless it can be shown that representation at the inquest produced wider benefits such as changes in procedure which

---

[137] SI 2013/1629, reg 29.
[138] Chief Coroner's Guidance No 5, 4 September 2013.
[139] *R (Lewis) v HM Coroner for the Mid & North Division of Shropshire* [2010] 1 WLR 1836.
[140] See *R (Gentle) v Prime Minister* [2008] 1 AC 1356.

improved future patient safety. Exceptional funding is available even if the traditional legal aid funding eligibility tests are not satisfied.[141]

The provision of exceptional funding was triggered by the case of *Khan*[142] in which the Court of Appeal held:

(1) that the state's obligation to investigate the death had not been fulfilled by the combination of the police investigation, the admission of liability and the trust's internal inquiry. The more serious the events, the more intensive the process of scrutiny had to be. The natural occasion for an effective judicial inquiry into the cause of death satisfying Art 2 was the inquest; and

(2) the inquest would not be an effective one unless the deceased's parents could play an effective part in it. The trust and its doctors and nurses would have the benefit of legal representation at public expense, so should the family.

The Court of Appeal then addressed the question as to whether, in the light of its judgment, the Secretary of state for Health had power to make the necessary funds available. In their Lordships' judgment, either reasonable funding had to be made available at an inquest to ensure that the family was represented, or the state had to set up some other type of inquiry at which such funding would be possible. They ordered a further hearing to take place at which they requested assistance of counsel instructed by the Lord Chancellor and the Attorney General so that the possibilities of funding could be considered.

Subsequent to the judgment and thereby avoiding a return to the Court of Appeal for that further hearing, the government elected to treat the inquest as the Art 2 inquiry and not to hold an independent inquiry. It required the Legal Services Commission (LSC) to provide appropriate funding. This was achieved by the passage of a statutory instrument[143] providing authority for the waiving of the financial eligibility requirements for representation at an inquest in these circumstances.

---

[141] Access to Justice Act 1999, s 6(8)(b).

[142] *Khan v Secretary of State* [2003] EWCA Civ 1129.

[143] Community Legal Service (Financial) (Amendment No 2) Regulations 2003, SI 2003/2838:
'3. After regulation 5B (Waiver of eligibility limit in Multi-Party actions of wider public interest), insert:
"**Waiver of eligibility limit in certain inquests**
5C. (1) This regulation applies to an application for the funding of legal representation to provide advocacy at an inquest into the death of a member of the immediate family of the client.
(2) Where this regulation applies, the Commission may, if it considers it equitable to do so, request the Secretary of State to disapply the eligibility limits in regulations 5(6) and 5A.
(3) In considering whether to make such a request, the Commission shall have regard in particular to any applicable Convention rights under Article 2 of Schedule 1 to the Human Rights Act 1998.
(4) On receipt of a request under paragraph (2) the Secretary of State may, if he thinks fit, disapply the eligibility limits.".'

The discretion to waive the financial eligibility criteria involves a consideration of:

(1) whether it is reasonable to expect the bereaved family to bear the full costs of representation;

(2) the nature and seriousness of the issues under investigation; and

(3) the view of the coroner.

Some coroners are willing to help bereaved relatives achieve effective representation. The coroner should certainly be approached if his view is likely to help achieve funding. Other coroners are less willing to be involved in funding matters which they believe to be outside their remit.

The position of granting legal aid in Art 2 inquests was reviewed by the courts in *Humberstone*:[144]

> 'Article 2 will be engaged in the much narrower range of cases where there is at least an arguable case that the state has been in breach of its substantive duty to protect life; in such cases the obligation is proactively to initiate a thorough investigation into the circumstances of the death.'[145]

5.9.2 Obtaining exceptional funding

Applications are submitted on forms CIV ECF 1 completing pages 1, 2, 9–12 and 14 only, together with CIV APP1 pages 1, 2 and 13 together with the appropriate means form and a schedule of anticipated costs. The Meansform must be completed for every interested relative. All forms are sent to the ECF Team DX161440 Westminster 8.

The Minister of Justice/Lord Chancellor interprets the criteria for the provision of exceptional funding slightly differently from the criteria laid down in the *Khan* case from that seemingly required by the Human Rights Act (HRA) as the following comparisons show:

Exceptional funding should be provided:

LC: to give relatives a reasonable opportunity to participate

Khan/HRA: To enable relatives to participate effectively

in cases which are of:

LC: significant wider public interest

HRA: importance to the relatives

where it is:

LC: necessary to enable the coroner to carry out an effective Art 2 investigation

---

[144] *R (Claire Humberstone) v LSC* [2010] EWCA Civ 1479.
[145] Ibid at para 67.

HRA: necessary to involve the relatives

Certainly key considerations will be where there have been:

- allegations of gross negligence, criminal conduct or attempts to conceal facts;
- issues of medical, legal or factual complexity;
- no family involvement in other investigations;
- doubts whether the family could effectively participate without representation;
- other represented agencies which might be able to present the same point of view as that of the relatives.[146]

In respect of the last point it is worth quoting Keith J at first instance in the *Main* case:[147]

> 'An effective Article 2 inquiry must ensure that dangerous practices and procedures are identified and rectified and the risk of future like deaths minimised.'

Funding should therefore be granted to ensure that the bereaved relatives

> 'may at least have the satisfaction of knowing that lessons learnt from the death ... may save the lives of others'.[148]

The LC's guidance is that the granting of exceptional funding legal aid for advocacy at inquests would be extremely unusual because the inquest is considered to be inquisitorial not adversarial and it is only in adversarial processes that lawyers may be of assistance. Legal Help may be available for preparation work and the financial eligibility criteria waived without exceptional funding being granted.[149]

The LC's approach does not place too much weight on how actively the family could participate in the inquest without representation. It accepts that without representation it is almost inconceivable that any grieving family can take an active role in the proceedings. Its view, however, is that Art 2 creates no general right to cross examination by the family and that is the responsibility of the coroner. This appears to be a blinkered and impractical approach in the more complex cases at least which should certainly be challenged.

The application for funding is a two stage process. The initial recommendation is made by the LC but the final decision is made by the Minister of Justice.

---

146 See Funding Code Guidance in Vol 3 LSC Manual 27.2 paras 8–11 issued pursuant to s 23 Access to Justice Act 1999.

147 *R v Minister for Legal Aid ex p Main* [2007] EWHC 742; decision overruled by Court of Appeal [2007] EWCA Civ 1147.

148 *R v Minister for Legal Aid ex p Main* at first instance [2007] EWHC 742, paras 49–50.

149 As explained in *R v Minister for Legal Aid ex p Main* in the Court of Appeal [2007] EWCA Civ 1147.

If funding is refused there is a right to ask for reconsideration by an LAA Funding Policy Adviser after which a challenge can be mounted by way of judicial review although the courts have made it clear that, just as in issues surrounding the provision of medical treatment, they are very reluctant to intervene in discretionary spending decisions particularly when the granting of exceptional funding for representation at inquests would 'risk imposing an unjustified burden on the funding system'.[150]

The tension between human rights and the public purse illustrated by the Court of Appeal in the *Main* case may be lessened in a clinical negligence inquest if the death was in a NHS hospital or resulted from action or inaction by a NHS doctor as the death in the *Main* case (a railway accident) was not triggered by a state employee but by the activities of a member of the public.

5.9.3 Extent of funding

Funding is for inquest advocacy against a budget contained in a schedule of costs submitted by the interested party's solicitor with the exceptional funding application. The budget should cover advocacy and immediate inquest preparation only. Other investigative work has to be financed separately possibly under the Legal Help Scheme.

An exceptional funding legal aid certificate can be retrospective if a decision has not been made before the inquest starts. Payment is made on submission by letter setting out the finalised details of the costs claim and is paid as a one-off grant less whatever contribution has been assessed from relatives. That contribution is for the solicitor to collect from the interested party or the relatives concerned.

5.9.4 Funding limitations

Although the *Khan* case led to a change in the law, the decision and consequent provision of exceptional funding only applies to Art 2 cases involving potential allegations of gross negligence. Even in those cases two significant handicaps still remain to relatives in such a position.

5.9.4.1 The statutory charge

The Statutory Charge applies. If a compensation claim follows the inquest, the costs of representation at the inquest will be clawed back from the damages unless legal liability was admitted prior to the inquest or the costs disallowed against the tortfeasor purely relate to the formalities of the inquest as opposed to the investigation of the evidence given.

---

[150] *R v Minister for Legal Aid ex p Main* in the Court of Appeal [2007] EWCA Civ 1147 at paras 42 and 52.

5.9.4.2 *Contribution*

Although the financial eligibility requirements have been removed, the contribution requirements have not. The LSC is required by the Legal Aid Regulations to obtain a contribution towards representation costs from relatives. Their means would need to be disclosed to the LSC who could require them to contribute to the costs of representation. This could for some families defeat the impact of the *Khan* judgment and make the removal of the financial eligibility test almost irrelevant. The contribution requirement can however be waived by the LSC

The factors influencing whether or not the contribution requirement will be waived are the:

- expenses already incurred;
- applicants financial circumstances;
- level of the proposed contribution;
- hardship to applicant;
- identity and interests of the relatives.

The LAA often requires remote relatives and even partners of those relatives to complete Means forms. Some of these people will be uninterested in the death and unwilling to participate. The Funding Code gives a wide discretion to the LSC as to what financial means to take into account.

The guidance uses words such as 'sometimes necessary' to provide means of others and 'generally expect' to receive certain information. This suggests that there is plenty of room for not applying the guidance in appropriate cases.

There is a strong argument to say that if the strict application by the LAA of the regulations leads to a stalemate because a partner will not co-operate, then the LAA should consider its wide discretion to decide what information it requires to do justice in the circumstances of the case and one important factor may well be that refusal may lead to the state being in breach of Art 2.

If a contribution is required it is collected by the interested party's solicitor and not the LAA and is deducted from the payment to that solicitor made by the LAA. This means of course that it is always open to the solicitor himself to waive the contribution although that of course further reduces the cost recovery and of course the economic viability of conducting this work.

The LAA will generally disregard home equity and will not normally expect more than one month's contribution from income. Hence the issue is usually restricted to whether the level of disposable capital is such that it is not appropriate for public funds to cover the full costs of representation at the inquest.

5.9.5 Recovering inquest costs

It is now clear that the costs of representing the relatives of a deceased patient are recoverable from the tortfeasor as costs of a subsequent successful civil action.[151]

Items on the bill of costs of the civil action are:

- recoverable against the health care provider at fault if the inquest is used to obtain evidence for a civil claim;
- recoverable if the submissions related to the factual evidence (although formal submissions on the facts are not usually allowed in an inquest). This would typically apply when the evidence is being reviewed as part of a narrative verdict;
- not recoverable if related to submissions on procedure and verdict;
- not recoverable if related to an expert witness providing advice for use at the inquest at the inquest whose evidence is unrelated to and not used in the civil claim.

The position is therefore that if:

- liability is admitted before the inquest – the statutory charge should not apply because the inquest is not used to gather evidence for the civil claim and the costs cannot be claimed against the health care provider;
- liability is admitted after the inquest – costs should be recoverable from the losing party save for pure inquest costs such as those incurred on submissions on procedure and verdict which should not attract the statutory charge because they relate to pure inquest work and have nothing to do with the civil process. This exclusion from the statutory charge may however only apply if exceptional inquest funding is obtained rather than funding simply for the clinical negligence claim.

Costs are not recoverable for submissions on the verdict to be returned because the coroner's verdict should be framed in such a way as to avoid determining civil liability[152] so it is suggested that such work cannot be said to have been preparatory for the civil claim.

It should still be open to argument that in a death which invokes Art 2 the costs of representation at the inquest if not otherwise paid for by the state should be indemnified in the civil action even if liability was admitted prior to the inquest because it is the state's obligation to ensure that there is a proper inquiry at which the deceased's relatives can effectively participate. Such an inquiry clearly flows from the admitted act of negligence. Presumably such expenditure would have to be claimed as special damages rather than as costs of the civil action.

---

[151] *King v Milton Keynes General NHS Trust* 13 May 2004 Gage J; *Stewart v Medway NHS Trust* 2004 EWHC 9013 (costs). See also *The Bowbelle* (Note) [1997] 2 Lloyd's Rep 196 (QB).

[152] Coroners (Inquests) Rules 2013, SI 2013/1616, r 42; *R v West Somerset Coroner ex p Middleton* [2004] UKHL 10.

5.10   AFTER THE INQUEST

The verdict given at the inquest is not determinative of any civil issues but the evidence given at the inquest, particularly if it has been thoroughly forensically scrutinised, may be a powerful influence on the outcome of any subsequent civil claim. Indeed the ability to recover costs in such an action is testament to the usefulness of the evidence garnered at an inquest as is the potential for huge savings in costs when cases are resolved as a result of the evidence given at an inquest without civil proceedings having been commenced.

The coroner is obliged to make and keep a recording of every inquest hearing including the pre-inquest review The coroner may on request of any interested party supply a transcript of the evidence either in the form of a copy tape or disc for which no charge should be made or in an actual transcript the fees of which are specified.[153]

The coroner will issue the final death certificate at which stage the relatives will finally be able to register the death.

5.10.1   Complaining

If the subject matter of a complaint relates to the personal conduct of a coroner, an affected party has the right to complain to the Office for Judicial Complaints (OJC). Examples of matters which can be the subject of a valid complaint include unreasonable delay in holding an inquest or in replying to correspondence. Such a complaint should first have been taken up with the coroner concerned and as has been seen the coroner is required to report such a delay to the Chief Coroner and to provide the relatives with an explanation.

A complaint to the OJC should be made within 12 months and may in turn be referred by the OJC to the Minister of Justice or the Lord Chief Justice who can order disciplinary action to be taken against the coroner even though technically he is employed by the local authority.[154] This includes the removal from office of a coroner for misbehaviour or inability in the course of his duties or lesser forms of disciplinary action such as suspension or admonishment.

If the complaint is not dealt with properly a further complaint lies to the Judicial Appointments and Conduct Ombudsman within 28 days.[155]

5.10.2   Challenging the coroner

There is no right of appeal from an inquest.

However, the coroner's decision may be challenged either by:

---

[153] Coroners Allowances, Fees and Expenses Regulations 2013, SI 2013/1615, reg 12(5).
[154] CJA 2009, Sch 3.
[155] See www.judicialombudsman.gov.uk.

(a) judicial review;

(b) an application to the Divisional Court under s 13 of the Coroners Act 1988;[156] or

(c) an application to the High Court under the Human Rights Act 1988.

The proposed introduction of a right of appeal to the Chief Coroner[157] has not been brought into force and has now been repealed.

In February 2014 the Ministry of Justice under s 24 of the Coroners and Justice Act 2009 published a *Guide to Coroner Services,* which provides information about the coroner's service and sets out standards which coroners should meet. It provides information about challenging a coroner's decision and how to complain about conduct and standards of service of coroners and pathologists.

5.10.3 Judicial review

The High Court may review the coroner's decision and decide whether it should be quashed and a new inquest ordered. Some examples of circumstances where the court may be prepared to order a new inquest include where there has been an inadequate investigation, relevant evidence has been rejected, a refusal to call expert evidence; a refusal to allow representatives to make submissions on law; and putting improper pressure on a jury to return a particular verdict or misdirecting the jury on the law.

Judicial review is a discretionary remedy. One of the relevant aspects that the court will consider is whether it is possible that a new inquest would furnish a different verdict. An application for judicial review should be made within three months of the decision being challenged. It would be unusual to make an application in the middle of an inquest. One such exceptional circumstance would be when the coroner refuses to put a possible verdict to a jury as otherwise the jury's deliberations may be flawed and the whole inquest would have to be heard again.[158]

---

[156] Although the Coroners Act 1988 was repealed by the 2009 Act that repeal has not been brought into force in its entirety. Section 13 is preserved in the Coroners and Justice Act 2009 (Commencement No. 15, Consequential and Transitory Provisions) Order 2013, SI 2013/1869 and the Coroners and Justice Act 2009 (Consequential Provisions) Order 2013, SI 2013/1874 and is still operating!

[157] Enacted as s 40, CJA 2009.

[158] *HM Coroner for Exeter and East Devon ex p Palmer*, CA (unreported) 10 December 1997: 'I finish by saying that it must be exceptional for there to be an application (for judicial review) to the courts during the course of a Coroner's inquisition. It means that the courts have to deal with the matter with great expedition as we have sought to do in the case of the present application. I would say, however, that, exceptionally, I regard this as a situation where the application was appropriately made at the end of the evidence of the inquest. It was important that the court's rulings on these matters should be given because, if the Coroner had gone wrong in deciding to withdraw a verdict of unlawful killing from the jury, that would have made the deliberations of the jury flawed and the whole inquest would have had to be heard again. But because the matter has been dealt with expeditiously, the jury will have the benefit of a summing-up by the Coroner which deals with the correct issues.'

5.10.4 Section 13 applications

An alternative route by which to challenge a coroner's decision is under s 13 of the Coroners Act 1988.

This provides that an application can be made by or on the authority of the Attorney General to the High Court on the grounds that the coroner refuses or neglects to hold an inquest which ought to be held or, where an inquest has been held, that whether by reason of fraud, rejection of evidence, irregularity of proceedings, insufficiency of inquiry, the discovery of new facts or evidence or otherwise, it is necessary in the interests of justice that another inquest be held.

An application must first be made to the Attorney-General for his or her permission (Fiat) to make an application to the Divisional Court. If a Fiat has been granted, the application proceeds to a full hearing by a Divisional Court. The procedure may be used in conjunction with judicial review proceedings.

The High Court may order an inquest, or a new inquest, to be held into the death.[159]

5.10.5 Human Rights Act 1998

If the coroner makes a decision that is inconsistent with the ECHR then any individual affected by that decision may seek a remedy before the High Court.

5.10.6 Costs of a challenge

A decision of the Court of Appeal[160] conveniently reviews the law and practice on the costs[161] of a challenge to the coroner as follows:

'(i) The established practice of the courts was to make no order for costs against an inferior court or tribunal which did not appear before it except when there was a flagrant instance of improper behaviour or when the inferior court or tribunal unreasonably declined or neglected to sign a consent order disposing of the proceedings;

(ii) The established practice of the courts was to treat an inferior court or tribunal which resisted an application actively by way of argument in such a way that it made itself an active party to the litigation, as if it was such a party, so that in the normal course of things costs would follow the event;

(iii) If, however, an inferior court or tribunal appeared in the proceedings in order to assist the court neutrally on questions of jurisdiction, procedure, specialist case law and suchlike, the established practice of the courts was to treat it as a neutral party, so that it would not make an order for costs in its favour or an order for costs against it whatever the outcome of the application;

(iv) There are, however, a number of important considerations which might tend to make the courts exercise their discretion in a different way today in cases

---

[159] A recent example is *Brown v HM Coroner for the County of Norfolk* [2014] EWHC 187.

[160] *R (Davies) v Birmingham Deputy Coroner (No 2)* [2004] EWCA Civ 207.

[161] CPR r 44.2 sets out the general costs rule.

in category (iii) above, so that a successful applicant, like Mr. Touche, who has to finance his own litigation without external funding, may be fairly compensated out of a source of public funds and not be put to irrecoverable expense in asserting his rights after a coroner (or other inferior tribunal) has gone wrong in law, and there is no other very obvious candidate available to pay his costs ...

Needless to say, if a coroner, in the light of this judgment, contents himself with signing a witness statement in which he sets out all the relevant facts surrounding the inquest and responds factually to any specific points made by the claimant in an attitude of strict neutrality, he will not be at risk of an adverse order for costs except in the circumstances set out above. In those circumstances the court may be obliged to request the assistance of an advocate to the court, as Simon Brown LJ suggested in Touche.'

As any interested party can intervene in the proceedings and it may not be known in advance whether the intervenor is adopting a neutral stance or one of opposition it may be wise if the case is being conducted on a conditional fee basis to ensure that any insurance covers both the coroner and all interested parties in whose favour costs orders may be made if the application is unsuccessful.

5.10.7 Protective costs order

It may also be possible to apply for a protective costs order in advance in order to clarify what the financial repercussions might be. In *Khan* the application for judicial review was lost before the High Court leading to a costs order potentially being made against the applicant who was uninsured. This was bargained away in a deal which saw the Court of Appeal application being fought *pro bono* on the basis that no order for costs would be sought by either side whatever the outcome.

An attempt to secure a pre-emptive protective costs order in a challenge against a coroner failed on the grounds that such orders are only granted by the court if there is no private interest involved.[162] However that decision raises issues as to whether the court's application of costs orders itself may infringe the bereaved relatives' rights under the ECHR where the challenge to the coroner relates to an inability to secure Art 2 investigation rights.[163]

TOP TIPS

* A natural cause death can still be one in which the coroner's jurisdiction is invoked.
* Ask the coroner for permission to talk to his pathologist.
* There is little or no point in appearing at the opening of the inquest.

---

[162] *Goodson v HM Coroner for Bedfordshire* [2005] EWCA Civ 1172.
[163] ECHR Art 6 guarantees a right of access to justice.

- The views of the family as to whether there should be a jury should be taken into account.
- It is essential that relatives attending an inquest are briefed as to what to expect.
- Consider briefing the media in advance and ask the relatives to bring a photograph.
- Article 2 will be engaged whenever there is the potential for culpability or gross negligence or an abject failure of the health care system.
- Ask the relatives whether they wish to hear the pathologist's evidence.
- Expert's advice must be communicated to the client in order to attract privilege.
- Submissions must be of law and not as to the facts of the inquiry.
- Read *R v HM Coroner N Humberside ex p Jamieson* [1994] 3 All ER 972.
- Study the new Form 2 – Record of Inquest.

CHAPTER 6

MEDICAL TREATMENT AND HUMAN RIGHTS

In this chapter barristers Philip Havers QC, Jeremy Hyam and Claire McGregor set out the legal principles governing the enforcement of human rights in relation to obtaining and receiving treatment on the NHS covering the rights of inviolability of person; to medical treatment and to life itself.

6.1   THE RIGHT OF INVIOLABILITY OF PERSON

The fundamental principle at the heart of medical law and ethics is that every person's body is inviolate.[1] The importance of this principle has been repeatedly emphasised.[2] It is explained by Lord Goff in *Re F:*[3]

> 'It is well established that the performance of a medical operation upon a person without his or her consent is unlawful, as constituting both the crime of battery and the tort of trespass to the person.'

This principle is an embodiment of the libertarian principle of self-determination or autonomy. That concept of autonomy is succinctly crystallised in the often recited words of Cardozo J in *Scholendorff v Society of New York Hospital:*[4]

> 'Every human being of adult years and sound mind has a right to determine what shall be done with his own body.'

Cardozo J here speaks of a 'right' to autonomy the content of which is described by Lord Scarman in *Sidaway v Board of Governors of the Bethlem Hospital and the Maudsley Hospital* as being:[5]

> '... what is no more and no less than the right of a patient to determine for himself whether he will or will not accept the doctor's advice.'

He added:

---

[1]   See, per Lord Goff of Chieveley in *Re F (Mental Patient: Sterilisation)* [1990] 2 AC 1 at 72E.
[2]   See Lord Reid in *S v McC and M (D S Intervener)*; *W v W* [1972] AC 24, 43; and Ward LJ in *Re A (Children) (Conjoined Twins: Surgical Separation)* [2001] 1 Fam 176.
[3]   [1990] 2 AC 1 at 71.
[4]   (1914) 105 NE 92, 93.
[5]   [1985] AC 871.

'... the patient's right to make his own decision ... may be seen as a basic human right protected by the common law.'

The right is, however, not absolute and may be overridden.

The difficulty is in ascertaining in what circumstances that freedom of choice may be lawfully overridden by a competing or countervailing interest. In *Re T (Adult: Refusal of Treatment)*[6] the President, Butler-Sloss LJ, recognising the qualified nature of the right, quoted with approval the following passage from Robins JA in *Malette v Shulman*:[7]

> '... the right to determine what shall be done with one's own body is a fundamental right in our society. The concepts inherent in this right are the bedrock upon which the principles of self-determination and individual autonomy are based. Free individual choice in matters affecting this right, should, in my opinion, be accorded very high priority.'

This right of inviolability of person, or autonomy, is thus a right to be accorded a very high priority by doctors and the courts.

It imposes both positive and negative obligations. The negative obligation is not to interfere with a person's autonomy or right of self-determination save where there is an overriding or competing countervailing interest. The positive obligation is to ensure that the right of autonomy is properly respected. As we shall see, the positive obligations inherent in the fundamental basic right of autonomy form the background to the procedures now enshrined in the Mental Capacity Act 2005 for ensuring that a person who may have capacity to consent/refuse treatment, is able to communicate his wish.[8]

Medical treatment disputes between doctors and patients, or relatives of patients – and in particular whether a particular form or course of treatment is in the best interests of an incapacitated patient or child can frequently arise. When they do, it may be necessary to apply to the court for declaratory relief as to whether a particular form of treatment is or is not lawful and appropriate. In the vast majority of cases the treating hospital or doctor will apply to the court. That court will then have to decide on the medical and other evidence made available to it, how the treatment dispute should be resolved. The court's approach is informed by the core principles discussed below.

6.1.1   ECHR and autonomy

While the right to autonomy is not expressly protected by the articles of the ECHR, it is clearly implicit in the interpretation of the guarantees provided by Art 3 and Art 8.

---

[6]   [1993] Fam 95 at 116.

[7]   (1990) 67 DLR (4th) 321 at 336.

[8]   See, in particular, MCA 2005, s 4.

For example, with respect to Art 3, the Commission in *X v Denmark*[9] held that medical treatment of an experimental character and without the consent of the person involved may under certain circumstances be regarded as prohibited under Art 3.

More striking is the court's analysis of Art 8 in *Pretty v United Kingdom*:[10]

' ... the concept of "private life" is a broad term not susceptible to exhaustive definition. It covers the physical and psychological integrity of a person. It can sometimes embrace aspects of an individual's physical and social identity ... Article 8 also protects a right to personal development, and the right to establish and develop relationships with other human beings and the outside world. Though no previous case has established as such any right to self-determination as being contained in Article 8 of the Convention, the court considers that the notion of personal autonomy is an important principle underlying the interpretation of its guarantees.'

And at para [65] the court added:

'The very essence of the Convention is respect for human dignity and human freedom.'

6.1.2   Application of the right of autonomy

As indicated above, the difficult problem with regard to autonomy is not so much the content of the right (a right to choose), nor the positive or negative obligations inherent in that right (some of which are now on a statutory footing), but rather understanding the circumstances when the right may be overridden.

The problem has been considered in a number of judgments of the Court of Appeal and House of Lords. A good example is *St Georges Healthcare ex p S*[11] which concerned a woman who was 36 weeks pregnant and suffering pre-eclampsia. Despite having been properly informed of the risks she wished to have her baby born naturally and refused the hospital's advice that she should undergo Caesarean section. She was then detained for assessment under s 2 of the Mental Health Act 1983, and a Caesarean was performed (after a declaration had been obtained from Hogg J as to the lawfulness of the treatment).

Although a baby girl was safely delivered to the mother, she challenged the lawfulness of the declaration, in particular arguing that she had had capacity to refuse the treatment and that her capacitated refusal should have been respected. Her arguments were accepted. The Court of Appeal holding at 953:

---

[9]   (1988) 32 DR 282 at 283.
[10]   (2002) 35 EHRR 1 at para 61.
[11]   [1998] 3 WLR 936.

'In the present case there was no conflict between the interests of the mother and the foetus: no one was faced with the awful dilemma of deciding on one form of treatment which risked one of their lives in order to save the other. Medically the procedures to be adopted to preserve the mother and her unborn child did not involve a preference for one rather than the other. The crucial issue can be identified by expressing the problem in different ways. If human life is sacred, why is a mother entitled to refuse to undergo treatment if this would preserve the life of the foetus without damaging her own? In the United States where such treatment has on occasions been forced on an unwilling mother this question has been described as "the unborn child's right to live" and "the state's compelling interest in preserving the life of the foetus" (*Jefferson v Griffin Spalding County Hospital Authority* (1981) 274 S.E.2d 457) or "the potentiality of human life" (*In Re Madyun* (1986) 573 A.2d 1259). In *Winnipeg Child and Family Services (Northwest Area) v G* [1997] 3 BHRC 611, a decision which will need further examination, in his dissenting judgment Major J commented, "where the harm is so great and the temporary remedy so slight, the law is compelled to act ... Someone must speak for those who cannot speak for themselves." That said, however, how can a forced invasion of a competent adult's body against her will even for the most laudable of motives (the preservation of life) be ordered without irremediably damaging the principle of self-determination? When human life is at stake the pressure to provide an affirmative answer authorising unwanted medical intervention is very powerful. Nevertheless the autonomy of each individual requires continuing protection even, perhaps particularly, when the motive for interfering with it is readily understandable, and indeed to many would appear commendable: hence the importance of remembering Lord Reid's warning against making "even minor concessions." If it has not already done so medical science will no doubt one day advance to the stage when a very minor procedure undergone by an adult would save the life of his or her child, or perhaps the life of a child of a complete stranger. The refusal would rightly be described as unreasonable, the benefit to another human life would be beyond value, and the motives of the doctors admirable. If, however, the adult were compelled to agree, or rendered helpless to resist, the principle of autonomy would be extinguished.'

Another striking application of the principle and one which emphasises its almost absolute nature, is the case of *Re MB (Medical Treatment)*.[12] MB was 40 weeks pregnant when it was discovered that her baby was lying in the breech position. She was told that a vaginal delivery would pose serious risks to the child (assessed at 50%) and that a Caesarean would substantially improve the child's chances of survival. MB had consented on more than one occasion to the operation but had subsequently withdrawn her consent on each occasion due to her irrational fear of needles, which became apparent at the anaesthetic stage of the procedure. The patient was in labour and was not responding to those in charge of her care. The health authority sought a declaration that it would be lawful for the doctors to operate on her and use reasonable force if necessary to effect such operation.

A declaration was made that the treatment was in the claimant's best interests and that her irrational fear of needles and ensuing panic meant that she was

---

12   [1997] 2 FLR 426.

deprived of the necessary capacity for the treatment in question. Butler-Sloss LJ stated the position as to autonomy thus:

> 'A competent woman, who has the capacity to decide, may, for religious reasons, other reasons, for rational or irrational reasons or for no reason at all, choose not to have medical intervention, even though the consequence may be the death or serious handicap of the child she bears, or her own death. In that event the courts do not have the jurisdiction to declare medical intervention lawful and the question of her own best interests objectively considered does not arise.'[13]

This statement of the law can be traced back to *Sidaway v Board of Governors of the Bethlem Royal Hospital*[14] where Lord Templeman said:

> '... the doctor is not entitled to make the final decision with regard to treatment which may have disadvantages or dangers. Where the patient's health and future are at stake, the patient must make the final decision. The patient is free to decide whether or not to submit to treatment recommended by the doctor and therefore the doctor impliedly contracts to provide information which is adequate to enable the patient to reach a balanced judgment, subject always to the doctor's own obligation to say and do nothing which the doctor is satisfied will be harmful to the patient ... If the doctor making a balanced judgment advises the patient to submit to the operation, the patient is entitled to reject that advice for reasons which are rational, or irrational, or for no reason. The duty of the doctor in these circumstances, subject to his overriding duty to have regard to the best interests of the patient, is to provide the patient with information which will enable the patient to make a balanced judgment if the patient chooses to make a balanced judgment.'

Further examples of the clash between the right of autonomy and the principle of sanctity of life may be seen in the prison and mental health context. In *Home Secretary v Robb*,[15] the court granted a declaration that the Home Secretary could lawfully abide by the decision of a prisoner who was competent to refuse nutrition and hydration so long as he had capacity to do so.

A similar view had been reached by Lord Keith in *Airedale Trust v Bland*,[16] namely that the principle of sanctity of human life did not authorise the forcible feeding of prisoners on hunger strike.

Different considerations of course apply, if (but only if) the patient is found to lack capacity. Thus in *R v Collins and Ashworth Hospital ex p Brady*,[17] the question was the legality of the force feeding of Ian Brady, the convicted murderer, who was detained in Ashworth Hospital. The court held that the force feeding was justified under emergency powers under the Mental Health

---

[13] The point here about jurisdiction is an important one. The court's jurisdiction to hear best interests cases is based (historically) on the *parens patriae* or inherent jurisdiction. The trigger for the exercise of the jurisdiction is the lack of capacity. Unless lack of capacity is demonstrated the court has no jurisdiction and no role to play.

[14] [1985] AC 871 at 904.

[15] [1995] 1 FLR 412.

[16] [1993] AC 789 at 859.

[17] [2000] Lloyds's Rep Med 355.

Act 1983 (s 63) because the hunger strike on which he was then engaged was a manifestation of his personality disorder. Of note in that judgment however is the observation by Maurice Kay J (as he then was) that the state might have power to prevent suicide by hunger strike on the part of prisoners by reference to the American case of *Thor v Superior Court*.[18]

Even where the law is clear, there may yet be disputes as to its application to the particular facts where the principles of autonomy and sanctity of life are in conflict.

This can be seen clearly in a case such as *Ms B v An NHS Hospital Trust*[19] where the claimant sought declarations under the inherent jurisdiction that she had capacity to accept or refuse medical treatment in circumstances in which refusal would almost inevitably lead to her death. Butler-Sloss (P) recognised the two fundamental principles in conflict, namely autonomy and sanctity of life and emphasised the importance of not confusing the question of capacity with the nature of the decision in question, however grave the consequences.

6.1.3 Sanctity of life, autonomy, and reconciliation of conflicting moral principles

As may be seen from the above, there may, on occasion arise a conflict between two competing moral principles, namely the sanctity of life, and the autonomy of the individual. In the ultimate, one must yield to the other. The point is recognised by Lord Donaldson in *Re T (Adult: Refusal of Treatment)*[20] where the issue was the state of competence of a pregnant young woman who had been injured in a car crash and was refusing a blood transfusion. He said:

> 'The situation gives rise to a conflict between two interests, that of the patient and that of the society in which he lives. The patient's interest consists in his right to self-determination – his right to live his own life how he wishes, even if it will damage his health or lead to his premature death. Society's interest is in upholding the concept that human life is sacred and that it should be preserved if at all possible. It is well established that in the ultimate the right of the individual is paramount.'

While it seems tolerably clear that the autonomy of the individual is 'in the ultimate' paramount, that does not appear to be the case where the individual cannot exercise that right himself and requires the assistance of another.

Thus in the case of *R (Pretty) v DPP*,[21] the House of Lords had to consider the legality of the Director of Public Prosecutions' refusal to give an undertaking not to prosecute the claimant's husband if he were to assist his wife to commit suicide. The House of Lords held that it was not unlawful, that the claimant's

---

[18]   (1993) 5 Cal. 4th 725.
[19]   [2002] 1 FLR 1090.
[20]   [1993] Fam 95 at 112.
[21]   [2001] UKHL 61.

rights under Art 3 were not infringed and that her rights under Art 8 were not engaged at all. In the European Court of Human Rights (ECtHR), it was held that Art 8 was engaged but that the interference with autonomy was justified. The ECtHR held as follows:[22]

> '... in agreement with the House of Lords and the majority of the Canadian Supreme Court in the Rodriguez case, that States are entitled to regulate through the operation of the general criminal law activities which are detrimental to the life and safety of other individuals (see also the above-mentioned Laskey, Jaggard and Brown case, § 43). The more serious the harm involved the more heavily will weigh in the balance considerations of public health and safety against the countervailing principle of personal autonomy. The law in issue in this case, section 2 of the 1961 Act, was designed to safeguard life by protecting the weak and vulnerable and especially those who are not in a condition to take informed decisions against acts intended to end life or to assist in ending life. Doubtless the condition of terminally ill individuals will vary. But many will be vulnerable and it is the vulnerability of the class which provides the rationale for the law in question. It is primarily for States to assess the risk and the likely incidence of abuse if the general prohibition on assisted suicides were relaxed or if exceptions were to be created. Clear risks of abuse do exist, notwithstanding arguments as to the possibility of safeguards and protective procedures.'

As this case graphically demonstrates, where the two key competing principles of sanctity of life and respect for personal autonomy and human dignity come into conflict an accommodation between the two has to be reached. In such a process the court must take into account the public policy considerations of coming down on one side or the other.

There is no necessarily right moral answer. The relevance of morals, or deeply held personal convictions, to a process such as this is explained most clearly in Hoffmann LJ's decision in *Bland* in the Court of Appeal:

> 'Our belief in the sanctity of life explains why we think it is almost always wrong to cause the death of another human being, even one who is terminally ill or so disabled that we think that if we were in his position we would rather be dead. Still less do we tolerate laws such as existed in Nazi Germany, by which handicapped people or inferior races could be put to death because someone else thought that their lives were useless.

> But the sanctity of life is only one of a cluster of ethical principles which we apply to decisions about how we should live. Another is respect for the individual human being and in particular for his right to choose how he should live his own life. We call this individual autonomy or the right of self-determination. And another principle, closely connected, is respect for the dignity of the individual human being: our belief that quite irrespective of what the person concerned may think about it, it is wrong for someone to be humiliated or treated without respect for his value as a person. The fact that the dignity of an individual is an intrinsic value is shown by the fact that we feel embarrassed and think it wrong when someone

---

22 At para 74.

behaves in a way which we think demeaning to himself, which does not show sufficient respect for himself as a person.

No one, I think, would quarrel with these deeply rooted ethical principles. But what is not always realised, and what is critical in this case, is that they are not always compatible with each other. Take, for example, the sanctity of life and the right of self-determination. We all believe in them and yet we cannot always have them both. The patient who refuses medical treatment which is necessary to save his life is exercising his right to self-determination. But allowing him, in effect, to choose to die, is something which many people will believe offends the principle of the sanctity of life. Suicide is no longer a crime, but its decriminalisation was a recognition that the principle of self-determination should in that case prevail over the sanctity of life ...

... A conflict between the principles of the sanctity of life and the individual's right of self-determination may therefore require a painful compromise to be made. In the case of the person who refuses an operation without which he will certainly die, one or other principle must be sacrificed. We may adopt a paternalist view, deny that his autonomy can be allowed to prevail in so extreme a case, and uphold the sanctity of life. Sometimes this looks an attractive solution, but it can have disturbing implications. Do we insist upon patients accepting life-saving treatment which is contrary to their strongly held religious beliefs? Should one force-feed prisoners on hunger strike? English law is, as one would expect, paternalist towards minors. But it upholds the autonomy of adults. A person of full age may refuse treatment for any reason or no reason at all, even if it appears certain that the result will be his death.

I do not suggest that the position which English law has taken is the only morally correct solution. Some might think that in cases of life and death, the law should be more paternalist even to adults. The point to be emphasised is that there is no morally correct solution which can be deduced from a single ethical principle like the sanctity of life or the right of self-determination. There must be an accommodation between principles, both of which seem rational and good, but which have come into conflict with each other.'

6.2   CAPACITY, NECESSITY AND BEST INTERESTS

As may be seen from *Re MB* above, and from the force-feeding cases, the right of autonomy vests in a person who has capacity.

6.2.1   Capacity

The presence or absence of capacity may make a fundamental difference to the rights of the individual in respect of a health care decision. It has the (some might think odd) consequence, that in the case of a capacitated refusal for say, a blood transfusion, or in the case of a hunger strike, the power to act in the best interests of the patient only arises when that patient has lost his capacity.

If a refusing patient makes a binding advance directive as to how he wishes to be treated (or not treated) after he loses capacity he can lawfully effect his own death by insisting on a refusal of resuscitative procedures.

However, if such a patient fails to make a valid advance directive then he will be treated and resuscitated in his 'best interests' since it is never going to be in his 'best interests' to be allowed to die – save in circumstances where clinically there is no purpose to continuing treatment.

The heart of the problem lies in preserving the individual's right to choose in respect of a period after which he has lost his capacity to consent or refuse treatment. This problem is sought to be resolved in the new Mental Capacity Act 2005 by the creation of statutory advance decisions, and the creation of a new form of Lasting Power of Attorney.

6.2.2 Necessity

First, however, it is useful to consider the doctrine of necessity and the associated concept of best interests. Perhaps surprisingly it was not until the House of Lords decision in *Re F (Patient Sterilisation)*[23] that the principle of necessity justifying intervention in a medical treatment case was established.

Lord Goff derived the principle from the agency of necessity in mercantile cases, in particular the advice of the Privy Council delivered by Sir Montague Smith in *Australasian Steam Navigation Co v Morse*,[24] in which he said:

> '... when by the force of circumstances a man has the duty cast upon him of taking some action for another, and under that obligation, adopts the course which, to the judgment of a wise and prudent man, is apparently the best for the interest of the persons for whom he acts in a given emergency, it may properly be said of the course so taken, that it was, in a mercantile sense, necessary to take it.'

Lord Brandon at 55, in the same case said:

> 'The operation or other treatment will be in their best interests if, but only if, it is carried out in order either to save their lives, or to ensure improvement or prevent deterioration in their physical or mental health.'

Re F therefore established a duty in principle to provide that treatment to an incompetent adult which is in his or her 'best interests'.

In this context best interests had a specific meaning. Perhaps the key insight into understanding what is meant by best interests in this context is Butler-Sloss LJ in *Re MB (Medical Treatment)*[25] when she said:

---

[23]   [1990] 2 AC 1.
[24]   (1872) LR 4 PC 222, 230.
[25]   [1997] 2 FLR 426 at 439.

'Best interests are not limited to best medical interests.'

In other words it encapsulates a wide range of other considerations including ethical, moral, emotional and welfare considerations.[26]

Moreover that which is acceptable to a responsible body of medical opinion, viz the *Bolam* test,[27] is not determinative of what a patient's best interests are.

The doctor's duty is not merely to act in accordance with a responsible and competent body of relevant professional opinion: his duty is to act in accordance with the patient's *best* interests.

Thus it follows that the question of best interests is not, or at least not solely, a question for the doctor, but rather, if the case comes before the court, the judge.

This insight is recognised most clearly by Hoffmann LJ in *Bland:*[28]

> 'It seems to me that the medical profession can tell the court about the patient's condition and prognosis and about the probable consequences of giving or not giving certain kinds of treatment or care, including the provision of artificial feeding. But whether in those circumstances it would be lawful to provide or withhold the treatment or care is a matter for the law and must be decided with regard to the general moral considerations of which I have spoken. As to these matters, the medical profession will no doubt have views which are entitled to great respect, but I would expect medical ethics to be formed by the law rather than the reverse.'

6.2.3   Capacity at common law

As may be seen from the above, determining whether or not a patient lacks capacity can have profound consequences for the patient's rights in respect of treatment proposed to be given.

The question whether or not a particular patient has or lacks capacity in respect of a particular decision is determined by the application of a threefold test as framed by Thorpe J in *Re C*[29] and the subsequent development of that test in *Re MB.*[30]

Re C concerned a schizophrenic detained under the Mental Health Act who, in the opinion of his treating doctors required the amputation of his foot to avoid the development of gangrene. C disagreed, and objected to the treatment. He sought injunctive relief under the inherent jurisdiction restraining the hospital from amputating his right leg without his express written consent. Thorpe J

---

26   See *A v A Health Authority, In Re J (A Child), R (S) v Secretary of State for the Home Department* [2002] EWHC 18 (Fam/Admin), [2002] Fam 213, at para 43.

27   See *Bolam v Friern Hospital Management Committee* [1957] 1 WLR 582.

28   At 834.

29   [1994] 1 All ER 819 (Fam).

30   (1997) 38 BMLR 175 (CA).

granted the injunction sought and adopted a three-stage test for establishing a patient's capacity or competence to decide:

- could the patient comprehend and retain the necessary information;
- was he able to believe it; and
- was he able to weigh the information, balancing risks and needs, so as to arrive at an informed choice.

In *Re MB* the court adopted the approach in *Re C* (although formulated slightly differently) and enunciated the following principles:

- Every person is presumed to have the capacity to consent or to refuse medical treatment unless and until that presumption is rebutted.
- Irrationality is used to connote a decision which is so outrageous in its defiance of logic, or of accepted moral standards, that no sensible person, who had applied his mind to the question to be decided could have arrived at it.
- Although it may be thought that irrationality sits uneasily with competence to decide, panic, indecisiveness and irrationality, in themselves, do not as such amount to incompetence.
- The graver the consequences of the decision, the commensurately greater the level of competence is required to take the decision.
- A person lacks capacity if some impairment or disturbance of mental functioning renders the person unable to make a decision whether to consent to, or to refuse, treatment. That inability to make a decision will occur when:
  (a) the patient is unable to comprehend and retain the material which is material to the decision, especially as to the likely consequences of having, or not having, the treatment in question;
  (b) the patient is unable to use the information and weigh it in the balance as part of the process of arriving at the decision.

6.2.4 Capacity and the Mental Capacity Act 2005

The position at common law now must be considered in the light of the light of the Mental Capacity Act 2005 (MCA 2005).

The Act provides a comprehensive statutory framework for assisting those lacking capacity to make decisions for themselves. The MCA 2005 takes precedence over the common law where issues overlap, but clearly the common law will inform the proper interpretation of the Act.

Significantly, the Act only applies to persons aged 16 or over and the treatment of children under 16 will continue to be governed by common-law principles under the inherent jurisdiction of the court.

In addition, the Act only applies to adults who have lost capacity by reason of 'an impairment of, or a disturbance in the functioning of, the mind or brain', per s 2(1) of the Act. The High Court retains its inherent jurisdiction for the protection of adults in relation to any individual who loses capacity for any other reason, such as because they are under constraint, subject to coercion or undue influence, or for some other reason deprived of the capacity to make the relevant decision, or incapacitated or disabled from expressing a genuine consent, ie by matters other than those covered by the 2005 Act.[31]

Section 1 of MCA 2005 sets out the key principles applying to decisions and actions taken under the Act. The starting point is a presumption of capacity. A person must also be supported to make his own decision, as far it is practicable to do so. The Act requires 'all practicable steps' to be taken to help the person. This could include, for example, making sure that the person is in an environment in which he is comfortable or involving an expert in helping him express his views.

It is expressly provided that a person is not to be treated as lacking capacity to make a decision simply because he makes an unwise decision. This means that a person who has the necessary ability to make the decision has the right to make irrational or eccentric decisions that others may not judge to be in his best interests.

The concept of best interests is also put on a statutory footing. The Act provides that everything done, or any decision made, under the Act for a person who lacks capacity must be done in that person's best interests.

In an attempt to ensure that all such decisions are also proportionate, the Act requires that the 'least restrictive option' principle must always be considered. In other words, the person making the decision or acting must think whether it is possible to decide or act in a way that would interfere less with the rights and freedom of action of the person who lacks capacity.

Section 2 of MCA 2005 specifies what amounts to a lack of capacity. Essentially it is an inability to make the relevant decision which is caused by an impairment of or disturbance in the functioning of the mind or brain. This is the so-called 'diagnostic test'. This could cover a range of problems, such as psychiatric illness, learning disability, dementia, brain damage or even a toxic confusional state, as long as it has the necessary effect on the functioning of the mind or brain, causing the person to be unable to make the decision. The test is functional in nature and looks at the decision-making process itself.

To make a decision, a person must first be able to:

- comprehend the information relevant to the decision;
- retain this information;[32]

---

[31] *DL v A Local Authority* [2012] EWCA Civ 253.

[32] The second-stage test in *Re C* included a requirement that the patient 'believe' the information. By saying this it is not considered that Thorpe J was intending to indicate that a person must believe the correctness of their doctor's advice, ie that without amputation the leg would

- use and weigh that information as part of the process of making the decision; or

- communicate his decision (whether by talking, using sign language or any other means).

6.2.5 Best interests under MCA 2005

The best interests principle is a core principle under the Act and is said to 'build *on the common law*' while offering further guidance.[33] Best interests under the Act is not a test of 'substituted judgement' (what the person would have wanted), but rather it requires a determination to be made by applying an objective test as to what would be in the person's 'best interests'.

The process as to how those best interests are to be ascertained is set out at ss 4(1)–(8) of MCA 2005 and an accompanying Code of Practice. The process includes a requirement that the decision maker must consider whether the individual concerned is likely to have capacity at some future date.[34] This is in case the decision can be put off until the person can make it himself. Even if the decision cannot be put off, the decision is likely to be influenced by whether the person will always lack capacity or is likely to regain capacity. It also includes a requirement that the decision maker must, so far as reasonably practicable, permit and encourage the person to participate, or to improve his ability to participate, as fully as possible, in any act done for him and any decision affecting him.

In *Aintree University Hospitals NHS Foundation Trust v James*,[35] the first case dealing with the Act to come before it, the Supreme Court emphasised the wide range of the factors to be weighed up in applying the 'best interest' test:

> 'in considering the best interests of this particular patient at this particular time, decision-makers must look at his welfare in the widest sense, not just medical but social and psychological; they must consider the nature of the medical treatment in question, what it involves and its prospects of success; they must consider what the outcome of that treatment for the patient is likely to be; they must try and put themselves in the place of the individual patient and ask what his attitude to the treatment is or would be likely to be; and they must consult others who are looking after him or interested in his welfare, in particular for their view of what his attitude would be.'[36]

Section 4(5) of MCA 2005 provides that 'where the determination relates to life-sustaining treatment he must not, in considering whether the treatment is in the best interests of the person concerned be motivated by a desire to bring about his death'.

---

succumb to gangrene and the patient would die, but rather that the person must believe, in the sense of comprehend, understand and retain the content of the advice.

[33] See the explanatory note to the Act.
[34] See MCA 2005, s 4(3).
[35] [2013] UKSC 67.
[36] [2013] UKSC 67 per Lady Hale DP at para 39.

This provision was inserted at the Committee stage in the House of Lords in an attempt to respond to the concern of those who considered that decisions concerning life-sustaining treatment could lead to euthanasia by omission. This insertion is unnecessary and unhelpful. The withdrawal of artificial ventilation and hydration to a person who requires such treatment to remain alive (life-sustaining treatment) will have the virtually certain consequence of causing the patient's death. It may nonetheless be in his or her best interests because continued treatment is futile and contrary to the patient's best interests. This is not killing or murder for the reasons explained in the *Bland* case but rather letting die. The doctors in *Bland* did, conscientiously, wish to bring about Anthony Bland's death because continued treatment was no longer in his best interests. To import as a relevant consideration what the respective doctors' or carers' 'motivations' are for a particular cause of action seems to cause unnecessary confusion and uncertainty and may mean that perfectly proper decisions to omit treatment in a patient's best interests will not be pursued.

The Mental Capacity Act Code attempts to clarify the scope of s 4(5) by indicating that it 'cannot be interpreted to mean that doctors are under an obligation to provide, or to continue to provide, life-sustaining treatment where that treatment is not in the best interests of the person, even where the person's death is foreseen'.[37]

However, in attempting to clarify s 4(5) and the relevant considerations when dealing with decisions about life-sustaining treatment, the Mental Capacity Act Code raised further issues, and in particular the proper interpretation of its guidance that

> 'There will be a limited number of cases where treatment is futile, overly burdensome to the patient or where there is no prospect of recovery.'[38]

In *Aintree*, the Supreme Court grappled with two interpretations of what amounted to 'futile' treatment and 'recovery'. At first instance, the judge considered that 'recovery does not mean a return to full health, but that the resumption of a quality of life which [the patient] would regard as worthwhile'. By contrast, the Court of Appeal found that treatment was futile unless it had 'a real prospect of curing or at least palliating the life-threatening disease or illness from which the patient is suffering'.

The Supreme Court unanimously endorsed the reasoning of the first instance judge and disagreed with the Court of Appeal, finding that its interpretation 'set the goal too high'. Rather:

> 'where a patient is suffering from an incurable illness, disease or disability, it is not very helpful to talk of recovering a state of "good health". The patient's life may still be very well worth living. Resuming a quality of life which the patient would regard as worthwhile is more readily applicable, particularly in the case of a

---

37   Mental Capacity Act 2005 Code of Practice, para 5.33.
38   Mental Capacity Act 2005 Code of Practice, para 5.31.

patient with permanent disabilities. As was emphasised in *Re J* (1991), it is not for others to say that a life which the patient would regard as worthwhile is not worth living'.[39]

6.2.6   Section 5: acts in connection with care or treatment

Section 5 provides statutory protection against liability for certain acts done in connection with the care or treatment of another person. If an act qualifies as a 'Section 5 act' then a carer can be confident that he will not face civil liability or criminal prosecution. Civil liability could involve being sued for committing a tort such as battery, false imprisonment or breach of confidence. Criminal prosecution might be for an offence against the person (assault or causing actual bodily harm) or for an offence against property (theft).

A qualifying 'Section 5 act' may be performed by a wide range of people. The key requirements are that the person (D) acts in connection with the care or treatment of another person (P) and that D has formed a reasonable belief as to P's lack of capacity and best interests. This section offers protection against liability where P is unable to give a valid consent, as long as the step is taken in connection with caring for him and is in his best interests.

It may thus be seen that best interests are at the heart of MCA 2005 and provided that acts are carried out in the best interests of the person lacking capacity then, in the normal run of cases, no civil or criminal liability should arise. Essentially, for the person who lacks capacity this amounts to a right to be treated in his best interests as properly considered by those caring for him.

6.3   THE RIGHT TO MEDICAL TREATMENT ON THE NHS

The National Health Service Act 2006 (NHSA 2006) imposes a statutory duty upon the Secretary of State for Health to provide, in essence, a National Health Service. The core duty to ensure the provision of a health service is laid upon the Secretary of State in extremely broad terms:

'(1) The Secretary of State must continue the promotion in England of a comprehensive health service designed to secure improvement –

(a)   in the physical and mental health of the people of England, and
(b)   in the prevention, diagnosis and treatment of physical and mental illness.

(2) For that purpose, the Secretary of State must exercise the functions conferred by this Act so as to secure that services are provided in accordance with this Act.'

The functional duty has since the Lansley reforms in the Health and Social Care Act 2012 been delegated to Clinical Commissioning Groups (CCGs) operating under the overall control of NHS England – the NHS Commissioning Board. It is not the place in this chapter to analyse the far-reaching effects of these sections other than to observe that generally speaking what were formerly PCT

---

[39]   *Aintree University Hospitals NHS Foundation Trust v James* [2013] UKSC 67, at 44.

commissioning decisions are now taken by CCGs, with a degree of oversight from NHS England and the Secretary of State in the form of the issue of Standing Rules.

What was formerly the Secretary of State's duty under s 3 of the NHS Act to arrange for services now falls to CCG's for the area for which they have responsibility. That s 3 duty remains subject to two qualifications:

(a)   that the obligation is limited to providing the services identified to the extent that the CCG considers they are necessary to meet all reasonable requirements; and

(b)   as to the facilities referred to in s 3, eg 'facilities for the prevention of illness', there is a qualification in that the CCG has to consider whether they are appropriate to be provided 'as part of the Health Service'.

The effect of these provisions is that in domestic law a person in receipt of treatment will often be without effective remedy[40] because:

- s 1 of NHSA 2006 does not oblige the Secretary of State to provide a comprehensive health service but to continue to promote such a service; and

- s 3 of NHSA 2006 limits the CCG's duty regards the provision of services to do so 'to such extent as the CCG considers necessary to meet all reasonable requirements' for the area for which it has responsibility and in the case of the provision of facilities referred to in s 3(1)(e) to provide those 'the CCG considers are appropriate as part of the health service'.

In summary, ss 1 and 3 do not impose an *absolute* duty to provide the specified services with the result that a CCG can in the course of performing its functions determine that it will provide no treatment at all for a particular condition, even if the condition is medically recognised as an illness requiring intervention that is categorised as medical and curative, rather than merely cosmetic or a matter of convenience or lifestyle, only subject to the qualification that such decisions must be taken in accordance with the well known principles of public law – illegality, irrationality and procedural impropriety. Those principles must now be read subject to the functions of NICE to give recommendations as to appropriate treatment that ought to be offered. Certainly in relation to technology appraisal recommendations, and arguably in relation to other NICE recommendations, CCGs have a duty to fund those treatments which are recommended by NICE.

Those public law principles include a requirement that the decisions are *rationally based*, upon a *proper consideration of the facts* and that an NHS patient will not be deprived of an *expectation founded on a reasonable basis* that his or her request for treatment would be dealt with in a particular way. Such decisions, if challenged, will be subject to anxious scrutiny by the courts where interference with the citizen's rights is involved. Essentially, the more

---

40   See *R v Cambridge Health Authority ex p B* [1995] 1 WLR 898 and *R v North West Lancashire Health Authority ex p A* [2000] 1 WLR 977.

important the interest of the citizen that the decision affects, the greater will be the degree of consideration that is required of the decision-maker and the greater the degree of scrutiny of that decision by the court.

A different sort of dispute may arise when a patient, or group of patients, considers that they ought to be able to obtain certain treatments from the NHS free at the point delivery. In these circumstances, the basis of the application for the treatment in question is not by way of contractual claim – there is no contract between a patient and the NHS – neither by reference to inherent jurisdiction, or the Court of Protection, as discussed above, but rather by way of public law challenge to the hospital, or care provider on traditional public law principles of irrationality, illegality and procedural impropriety. Such cases must be brought promptly and in any event within 3 months of the decision under challenge. It is also usually necessary to exhaust alternative remedies (eg internal appeal with the hospital) before a legal challenge is brought.

One example of such a claim is *R (Booker) v NHS Oldham*.[41] Ms Booker had been cared for by her local PCT after sustaining injuries in a road traffic accident, and had been assessed as being eligible for future healthcare. However, the PCT decided to withdraw nursing care on the basis that she had the means to fund a privately provided care package by reason of damages received from an insurance company, a decision that Ms Booker challenged. The decision was found to be contrary to the principle in the National Health Service Act 2006 s 1(3), as well as irrational. A claimant who was successful in recovering damages was entitled to do with the damages as he or she pleased. To refuse treatment by reference to the means of the patient would be contrary to the principle that the NHS was not a means-tested service and was provided to patients on the basis of their medical needs without reference to their financial position.

6.3.1 Public law 'rights' to treatment – exceptional circumstances

As indicated above because of the absence of any enforceable private law 'right' to treatment under the NHS Act, a patient is often without effective remedy if a particular treatment is denied on the ground of lack of resources. However, there are cases where it has been possible for a patient to obtain treatment which is at first denied by the relevant health care body on the basis that the refusal to provide it is irrational, or that, properly viewed, the patient falls within the health body's exceptionality criteria.

Nearly all CCGs, whose delegated function it is to commission health services within each CCG area, operate a system of what are sometimes described as 'exceptional treatment panels' whose role is to determine the provision in exceptional circumstances of certain treatment or services not usually provided by the CCG.

---

[41] [2010] EWHC 2593 (Admin).

It is common for a CCG to have its own local guidance on the approach to the funding of specific drugs and/or treatments that may be controversial; for example, newly available, but expensive cancer drugs, or say, weight loss (bariatric) surgery. In such circumstances any judicial review challenge will either be to the policy operated by the CCG itself, or, of a failure properly to apply it, or perhaps a failure to follow a recommendation in NICE Guidance. The most usual circumstances in which such policies are impugned is in respect of a failure properly to delineate what amounts to exceptional circumstances or a failure to apply the exceptional circumstances policy to the facts.

In *R v North West Lancashire Health Authority ex p A, D and G*,[42] the respondents were transsexuals who wanted to undergo gender reassignment treatment. The appellant authority refused to fund such treatment save in the event of overriding clinical need, or exceptional circumstances, on the basis that it was low in the list of priorities for public funding.

Auld LJ, giving the leading judgment, held that a policy of refusal of funding save for in undefined exceptional circumstances was unlawful. His analysis is illuminating:

'As illustrated in the Cambridge Health Authority case [1999] 1 WLR 898 and Coughlan's case [2000] 2 WLR 622, it is an unhappy but unavoidable feature of state funded health care that regional health authorities have to establish certain priorities in funding different treatments from their finite resources. It is natural that each authority, in establishing its own priorities, will give greater priority to life-threatening and other grave illnesses than to others obviously less demanding of medical intervention. The precise allocation and weighting of priorities is clearly a matter of judgment for each authority, keeping well in mind its statutory obligations to meet the reasonable requirements of all those within its area for which it is responsible. It makes sense to have a policy for the purpose – indeed, it might well be irrational not to have one – and it makes sense too that, in settling on such a policy, an authority would normally place treatment of transsexualism lower in its scale of priorities than, say, cancer or heart disease or kidney failure. Authorities might reasonably differ as to precisely where in the scale transsexualism should be placed and as to the criteria for determining the appropriateness and need for treatment of it in individual cases. It is proper for an authority to adopt a general policy for the exercise of such an administrative discretion, to allow for exceptions from it in 'exceptional circumstances' and to leave those circumstances undefined: see *Re Findlay* [1985] AC 318, 335-336, per Lord Scarman. In my view, a policy to place transsexualism low in an order of priorities of illnesses for treatment and to deny it treatment save in exceptional circumstances such as overriding clinical need is not in principle irrational, provided that the policy genuinely recognises the possibility of there being an overriding clinical need and requires each request for treatment to be considered on its individual merits.'

A more recent challenge to a PCT's decision properly to apply an exceptional circumstances policy, is *R (Rogers) v Swindon Primary Care Trust*.[43] The

---

42   [2000] 1 WLR 977.
43   [2006] EWCA Civ 392.

claimant challenged the refusal by her PCT to fund Herceptin treatment for her breast cancer. At first instance her claim for judicial review was dismissed, the court considering that the PCT was justified in refusing the treatment on the ground that there were not exceptional circumstances in her case. Allowing her appeal the Court of Appeal considered that the defendant's exceptional circumstances policy was irrational because it was not possible to envisage any circumstances in which the exceptional circumstances policy would obtain.

Another example is *R (Otley) v Barking and Dagenham NHS Primary Care Trust*,[44] where the claimant applied for judicial review of a decision of the defendant NHS Trust not to provide funding for treatment with Avastin, a cancer drug which, acting in concert with standard second-line chemotherapy had been reported to show some evidence of benefit, albeit not such as to be recommended by National Institute for Health and Clinical Excellence for routine funding. The claimant had initially sought and obtained Avastin on a private basis and reported subjective improvement. The PCT's funding panel refused treatment on the NHS because it did not consider that it would significantly prolong the claimant's life or be cost effective.

Granting the application for judicial review, the judge held that in the panel's own opinion there were no other treatments available to the claimant which were likely to have any benefit, and that the panel had failed to take into account the slim, but nonetheless important chance that treatment including Avastin could prolong the claimant's life by more than a few months. On the facts therefore, the claimant's case was exceptional by reference to the PCT's own criteria, and at least five cycles of treatment were ordered to be funded by the PCT, it being held that the availability of scarce resources was not in that case the decisive factor against such funding.

In *R (Condliff) v North Staffordshire PCT*,[45] the claimant was morbidly obese and failed to qualify for gastric by-pass surgery under the trust's relevant policy but made an individual funding request ('IFR') on the grounds of exceptionality. The PCT's IFR policy stated that when determining exceptionality 'social factors', which were non-clinical factors, would not be taken into account. The claimant sought judicial review, on the basis that the PCT's policy breached his rights under art 8 of the ECHR. This was dismissed at first instance, and by the Court of Appeal. The policy of allocating scarce medical resources on a basis of the comparative assessment of clinical needs was intentionally non-discriminatory. Any attempts made to impose a positive obligation on the state to provide support for an individual under art 8 had been unsuccessful.

6.3.2   Challenges to government guidance

The National Institute for Clinical Excellence, was set up in 1999 and on 1 April 2005 joined with the Health Development Agency to become the new

---

[44]   [2007] EWHC 1927 (Admin).
[45]   [2011] EWCA Civ 910.

'National Institute for Health and Clinical Excellence' (NICE). The purpose of NICE is to publish clinical appraisals and guidelines as to whether particular treatments should be considered worthwhile by the NHS.

In December 2001, a Direction was made by the Secretary of State that NHS trusts should make the necessary funding available in respect of any treatment that is recommended by NICE. In 2005, the Secretary of State published amended Directions and Consolidating Directions to NICE ('the NICE Directions') which provide that a function of NICE is to produce guidelines for the NHS covering all aspects of NHS health care.

Paragraph 2(1) of the NICE Directions provides:

'(1) the Secretary of State directs the Institute to exercise the following functions in connection with the promotion of clinical excellence and the effective use of available resources in the health service:
(a)   to appraise the clinical benefits and the costs of such health care interventions as may be notified by the Secretary of State and to make recommendations;
(b)   to develop guidelines providing advice on good practice in the management of such diseases and conditions as may be notified by the Secretary of State ...'

Paragraph 2(4) of the NICE Directions directs NICE as to how to exercise the above functions, including the production of guidelines, in these terms:

'(4) In exercising the functions described in paragraphs (1)(a)–(d) and (3) above the Institute shall have regard to the following factors –
(a)   the broad balance of clinical benefits and costs;
(b)   the degree of clinical need of patients with the Condition or disease under consideration.'

The guidelines and appraisals produced by NICE are, as may be seen from the above, based primarily on cost effectiveness. Such Guidelines were introduced in an attempt to meet the perceived problem of 'postcode lottery' availability treatment – the problem that the range of treatments available to patients depends on the differing resources of local PCTs. For this reason NHS trusts are expected to implement all sets of NICE guidelines and when a PCT is allocating and weighting priorities in funding different treatments from finite resources, it must have regard to NICE guidelines. The guidelines themselves can therefore be highly controversial and may be subject to challenge by judicial review.

In *R (Eisai) v NICE*,[46] the claimant, a pharmaceutical company and other interested parties including the Alzheimer's Society, sought judicial review of guidance issued by NICE in respect of the use of acetylcholinesterase inhibitors to treat sufferers from Alzheimers on the basis that the guidance was irrational and discriminatory. The claim failed on irrationality but succeeded in demonstrating the Guidance to be discriminatory because NICE's adherence to

---

[46]   [2007] EWHC 1941 (Admin).

a mini mental state examination (MMSE) score as the exclusive test of defining the severity of the disease discriminated unfairly against certain atypical groups whose condition was severe but which would not be revealed by a MMSE.

In *R (Servier Laboratories Ltd) v NICE*,[47] the claimant challenged NICE's reasons for putting forward an alternative drug over one of its own drugs for the treatment of osteoporosis. On appeal, it was held that NICE had failed to give adequate reasons and was required to make a fresh decision.

6.3.3 Other sources of guidance

There are of course other sources of guidance which prescribe, or appear to prescribe, how and when particular treatments will be given or withdrawn. These too may be subject to challenge.

A good example, and which is referred under the heading 'right to life' below, is *R (Leslie Burke) v General Medical Council*.[48] In that case the claimant sought judicial review of guidance contained in the General Medical Council's 'Withholding and Withdrawing Life-prolonging Treatments: Good Practice in Decision Making'. The claimant specifically sought to challenge that part of the guidance which stated that it was the doctor's responsibility to decide on the withdrawal of treatment taking into account the patient's views.

The judge at first instance (Munby J) held that the guidance was open to criticism as its emphasis was on the right of the patient to refuse treatment. It failed to acknowledge that it was the duty of the doctor who was unwilling to treat a patient to find another doctor who would do so; failed to acknowledge the heavy presumption in favour of life-prolonging treatment, and failed to detail the legal requirement to obtain prior judicial sanction before withdrawing artificial nutrition and hydration.

On appeal however, the Court of Appeal[49] considered that the questions sought to be raised by the claimant were not properly justiciable before the court and emphasised the dangers of the court attempting to grapple with issues such as those addressed at first instance by the judge when detached from the factual context that required their determination. Within the limited factual context of the dispute, there was no basis for declaring any part of the Guidance unlawful. In particular the judge was wrong to consider that there was a legal duty to obtain court approval to the withdrawal of artificial nutrition and hydration in the circumstances he identified. The true position being that the court did not 'authorise' treatment that would otherwise be unlawful.

---

[47] [2010] EWCA Civ 346.
[48] [2005] 2 WLR 431.
[49] [2005] 3 WLR 1132.

6.3.4 Summary

Strictly speaking a patient on the NHS has no 'right' to any particular treatment at any particular time. A right to particular treatment may in exceptional circumstances be established on traditional public law principles by the use of judicial review challenge either to the funding decision of a CCG, or to the Guidance which prescribes or strongly influences how that discretion is to be exercised. Examples of successful judicial reviews resulting in the obtaining of treatment which had been initially been refused, are however, relatively rare. It is for this reason that some patients have been forced to seek appropriate treatment for their specific clinical needs either privately or abroad. A new dimension to such cases is the impact of European law and the right to be reimbursed for treatment obtained abroad which could or should have been provided in the UK within a reasonable time but was not.

6.3.5 A right to treatment abroad

In order to understand the basis of a claim for a right to reimbursement for treatment obtained abroad, one has first to understand (at least in general terms) the specific features of the provision of health care under the NHS system. The following helpful summary is adapted from the Secretary of State's submissions to the European Court of Justice in *R (Watts) v Bedford Primary Care Trust (1) Secretary of State for Health (2)*:[50]

> 'National Health Service bodies provide hospital care free of charge at the point of delivery to all persons ordinarily resident in the United Kingdom. Such treatment is funded directly by the State almost entirely from general taxation revenue which is apportioned by central government to the various NHS bodies according to population size.
>
> There is no system of employee or employer contributions to sickness insurance schemes and no system of patient co-payments for such treatment. There are nevertheless payments made between NHS bodies as a method of distributing State funding between them.
>
> NHS hospitals provide healthcare to all persons ordinarily resident in the United Kingdom on a non-profit making basis. An NHS patient does not make direct payment for hospital treatment provided by the NHS and is not reimbursed in respect of any such treatment. NHS patients are not able to obtain hospital treatment in the private sector in England and claim reimbursement from the NHS. NHS bodies have a discretion to determine the allocation and weighting of clinical priorities within national guidelines.
>
> An NHS patient has no contract with, and therefore no contractual entitlement to, any specific treatment or the funding of any specific treatment by the NHS, such enforceable right to treatment as an NHS patient has, being based on principles of public law.

---

[50] Case C-372/04.

Under the NHS system the type, location and timing of hospital treatment are determined on the basis of clinical priority and the availability of resources by the relevant NHS body, and not at the choice of the patient. The management of waiting lists is intended to ensure the provision of hospital care in accordance with appropriate priorities and decisions made by the relevant NHS bodies as to the use of resources and to maintain fairness between patients who require hospital treatment for differing conditions and with different degrees of urgency.

The possibility exists for an NHS patient ordinarily resident in the United Kingdom to receive hospital treatment in another Member State pursuant to Article 22(1)(c) of Regulation 1408/71 (the E112 system), in which case reimbursement is made in accordance with that Regulation directly to the competent institution in the Member State in which the treatment was obtained at the rate of reimbursement normally applicable in the Member State of treatment, and not to the patient.

There is no United Kingdom legislation implementing Article 22(1)(c) of Regulation 1408/71. The Regulation is directly applicable in all Member States including the United Kingdom.

The financial resources available to the NHS are decided each year by Parliament and then apportioned amongst various health bodies by central government. Funding is allocated to local Primary Care Trusts (PCTs) on the basis of the relative needs of the populations in the geographical areas for which they are responsible.

PCTs are funded by the Secretary of State. In each financial year, a PCT is paid an amount allotted to it by the Secretary of State designed to cover expenditure on hospital care and administration costs. (The funding for non-hospital care, namely that provided by General Practitioners, dentists, opthalmists and pharmacists is dealt with separately). The amount made available to PCTs in respect of hospital care is subject to a cash-limit.

"NHS trusts" are separate legal bodies which were set up under the National Health Service and Community Care Act 1990 to assume responsibility for the ownership and management of hospitals or other establishments or facilities previously managed or provided by a Health Authority, or to provide and manage hospitals or other establishments or facilities which were not previously so managed or provided. Nearly all hospitals are run by NHS trusts, although increasingly, smaller "community" hospitals are being run by PCTs. Generally speaking, NHS trusts do not have money paid to them directly by the Secretary of State, but instead receive their funding through payments made by PCTs for the treatments and healthcare commissioned by them from the NHS trusts.

The nature of the arrangements between PCTs and NHS trusts is not that of an ordinary contract enforceable at law. Instead, the 2006 Act provides for a system of "NHS contracts" which are explicitly not contracts enforceable at law but which have attaching to them a special form of internal dispute resolution by the Secretary of State. The contracts are usually on the basis of a service level agreement which specifies x amount of treatment for y amount of money.

While NHS contracts are not contracts enforceable by the courts, the courts may, nevertheless, be called upon in certain circumstances to consider (or take account of) their terms. All the potential parties to an NHS contract are public bodies and, as a consequence, are amenable to judicial review if they exceed their statutory powers.

Since its inception, the NHS has been funded mainly from general taxation, (ie provided directly by the Government from general tax revenue). A small proportion comes from that element of National Insurance contributions allocated to the NHS and the remaining portion of NHS expenditure comes from charges and receipts by certain health bodies, including hospitals, of money raised through income generating powers (e.g. from hospital shops and car parks and making facilities available to private patients).'

6.3.5.1 The case for treatment abroad under Article 56 TFEU (formerly Article 49 EC)

It was against the above background that Mrs Watts sought treatment abroad for a hip replacement operation. Essentially her case was that she could not get the treatment she needed within a reasonable time on the NHS and was therefore entitled, under the principles of Art 49 (now Art 56 TFEU and/or Article 20 of Regulation EC 883/2004 (formerly EC Regulation 1408/71), to seek treatment abroad and claim reimbursement for that treatment.

She initially sought support from her local PCT (now it would be a CCG) for an E112 application (now called an S2 route application) for treatment abroad. The PCT refused to support it on the grounds that Mrs Watts would only have to wait between 3 and 4 months for treatment locally and repeated its reliance on NHS treatment plan targets as being determinative of the question of whether there was 'undue delay' in the claimant's case.

The claimant sought judicial review of this refusal arguing in particular that NHS treatment plan targets (being essentially purely economic criteria) could not be determinative of whether there was 'undue delay' in the treatment of her condition, which had to be considered objectively, and that, objectively the period she had had to wait was 'undue'.

At first instance the judge accepted the claimant's argument that the medical services provided to the claimant in France and paid for by her there did not cease to fall within the scope of the freedom to provide services guaranteed by the EC treaty – ie did not fall outside the ambit of Art 49 – merely because reimbursement of the costs of the treatment involved is applied for under the NHS.

However, he dismissed the claim on the facts. Although he held that any national authority properly directing itself in accordance with the principles laid down by the ECJ[51] would have been bound to conclude in October–November 2002 that the anticipated delay of approximately one year was on any view 'undue', and thus such as to trigger the claimant's right under Art 49 to reimbursement of the costs of obtaining more timely treatment in another member state, the judge considered that Mrs Watts had in fact not had to face 'undue delay' after her case was reassessed.

The Secretary of State for Health and Mrs Watts both appealed to the Court of Appeal. By its judgment of 20 February 2004 the Court of Appeal decided to make a reference to the Court of Justice. The Grand Chamber delivered its decision on the reference on 16 May 2006 holding that:

(1) the principles in Art 49 EC applied to the NHS just as much as it did to an insurance–based system such as that in France;

(2) it was justifiable for a state to operate a system of prior authorisation provided that: (a) it was based on objective non-discriminatory criteria; (b) could not be based on the existence of waiting lists intended to enable hospital care to be planned and managed on the basis of predetermined general clinical priorities without carrying out in each individual case an assessment of the patient's medical condition, the history and probable course of his illness, the degree of pain he was in, and the nature of his disability at the time of the request for authorisation; and

(3) that the NHS was obliged to provide mechanisms for the reimbursement of the cost of hospital treatment in another member state to patients to whom it was not able to provide the treatment required in a medically acceptable time.

The impact of this judgment is far-reaching and has already profoundly affected the delivery of health care in the UK as well as prompting discussion of a new EU Directive to codify the decision effectively Art 56 (formerly Art 49) will continue to be a route by which a patient who cannot obtain the treatment he needs within a reasonable time on the NHS, can obtain that treatment free of charge abroad and claim reimbursement of the costs from the NHS. The effect of *Watts* has been put on a statutory footing in the NHS Act 2006 with the consequence that the claimant now needs to demonstrate:[52]

'(a) that the requested service is necessary to treat or diagnose a medical condition of the patient,

(b) that the requested service is the same as or equivalent to a service that the Secretary of State, the Board or a responsible authority would make available to the patient in the circumstances of the patient's case, and

(c) that the Secretary or State, the Board or a responsible authority cannot provide to the patient a service that is the same as or equivalent to the requested service within a period of time that is acceptable on the basis of medical evidence as to the

---

[51] In particular *Geraets-Smits v Stichting VGZ* (Case C-157/99) [2002] QB 409 and *Muller-Fauré v Canderlinge Waarborgmaatschappij OZ Zoorgverzekeringen UA* (Case C-385/99) [2004] QB 1081.

[52] Section 6B(4) and (5) of the NHS Act 2006.

patient's clinical needs, taking into account the patient's state of health at the time the decision under this section is made and the probable course of the medical condition to which the service relates.'

6.3.6   Overseas visitors – rights to treatment

The NHS (Charges to Overseas Visitors) Regulations 1989[53] as amended provide for the making and recovery of charges for NHS treatment provided to an 'overseas visitor' (defined as a person not ordinarily resident in the UK). The Regulations provide for exemptions in certain circumstances; for example, accident and emergency treatment, and to reflect the rights of Community nationals. Such charges are collected by the NHS body providing treatment and these are retained. A PCT which provides treatment to an 'overseas visitor' has no discretion not to charge for such treatment unless that patient satisfies any of the exemption criteria in the Regulations. In certain circumstances payment may be requested in advance.

In *R v Hammersmith Hospitals NHS Trust ex p Reffell*[54] the claimant, an overseas visitor from Nigeria, was refused non-emergency kidney dialysis treatment unless he paid for such treatment in advance. The trust contended that it had no discretion to waive such charges in such a case and was entitled to require prior payment. His application for judicial review of this decision was dismissed. On appeal, the court confirmed that the under the Regulations the trust was bound to 'charge and recover' the costs of the treatment. There was a discretion as to whether to seek payment in advance. The court commented that the case for irrationality would have been a strong one if continuation of the type of treatment were to be refused without there being any alternative, simply on the basis that payment in advance could not be secured. The fact that the alternative treatment was available in Nigeria, did not make the trust's decision irrational.

The application of the Regulations is not well understood. This has the consequence that frequently treatment is provided without charge that ought not to have been; and conversely that treatment that ought to be provided free of charge, such as maternity services (which NHS Guidance on entitlement defines as immediately necessary treatment), is not. This can give rise to potential claims of negligence, if treatment is wrongly refused, and/or judicial review.

In such cases the Human Rights Act 1998, in particular Art 2 and Art 3 of the ECHR, may have a role to play if high threshold for the invocation of those articles is crossed. One such case was *D v UK*[55] where the claimant, a failed asylum seeker was subject to removal directions to St Kitts which would entail the loss of the HIV treatment he was then receiving thereby shortening his life expectancy. The Court held that the state may not take direct action in relation

53   SI 1989/306.
54   (2000) 55 BMLR 743.
55   [1997] 24 EHRR 423.

to an individual which would inevitably involve the infliction of treatment proscribed by Arts 2 and 3 of the Convention.

In *R (YA) v Secretary of State for Health*,[56] the claimant who was a failed asylum seeker failed to persuade the Court of Appeal that he was 'ordinarily resident' for the purpose of the NHSA 2006. The Court found that the aim of the Act was to provide a service for the people of England and that did not include those who ought not to be in England such as failed asylum seekers. However, the claimant succeeded in arguing that the National Health Service (Charges to Overseas Visitors) Regulations 1989, advising NHS trusts to charge failed asylum seekers for NHS services, was unlawful in so far as it failed to make clear how the discretion to withhold or allow treatment in certain circumstances, particularly where the treatment was urgent and the failed asylum seeker was unable to pay for the treatment, should be exercised.

6.4   RIGHT TO LIFE – THE COMMON LAW AND HUMAN RIGHTS ACT 1998

Life, or the right to it, is legally protected by the law of murder;[57] the law prohibiting assisted suicide,[58] and the prohibition from intentional taking of life under Art 2 of the ECHR.

The Suicide Act 1961 abrogated the rule against suicide (literally self-killing) but retained the offence of assisting suicide.

Section 2 of the Suicide Act 1961 provides:

> '(1) A person who aids, abets, counsels or procures the suicide of another, or an attempt by another to commit suicide, shall be liable on conviction on indictment to imprisonment for a term not exceeding fourteen years.
>
> ...
>
> (4) no proceedings shall be instituted for an offence under this section except by or with the consent of the Director of Public Prosecutions.'

Schedule 1 to the Human Rights Act 1998 incorporates the main provisions of the ECHR into domestic law. Article 2 of the ECHR provides:

> '1. Everyone's right to life shall be protected by law. No one shall be deprived of his life intentionally save in the execution of a sentence of a court following his conviction of a crime for which this penalty is provided by law.

---

[56]   [2009] EWCA Civ 225.
[57]   Homicide Act 1957.
[58]   Suicide Act 1961.

2. Deprivation of life shall not be regarded as inflicted in contravention of this Article when it results from the use of force which is no more than absolutely necessary:

(a)   in defence of any person from unlawful violence;

(b)   in order to effect a lawful arrest or to prevent the escape of a person lawfully detained;

(c)   in action lawfully taken for the purpose of quelling a riot or insurrection.'

End of life decisions will almost always require the involvement of the Official Solicitor whose experience in this field in assisting the court is a key part of ensuring decisions are made lawfully. The Official Solicitor will usually be invited to act on a particular patient's behalf and will then be appointed by the court to look after the best interests of an incapacitated adult. Anyone bringing an end of life case is well advised to begin by making at least an informal inquiry of the Official Solicitor as to the necessity for, and preferred means of bringing such proceedings. The Official Solicitor's website contains useful and up-to-date guidance on specific applications.[59]

In *W v M*,[60] M was a patient who had been in a coma for the previous eight years. Her mother, W, and other family members sought a declaration that the doctors might lawfully discontinue and withhold all life-sustaining treatment, including artificial nutrition and hydration ('ANH'). Evidence was brought forward by a care professional who opposed the declaration that M was in a minimally conscious state ('MSC'), a level of consciousness above that of vegetative state ('VS'). In its wide-ranging judgment exemplifying the complexities of end-of-life decisions, the Court of Protection rehearsed some of the key points to be born in mind in this area:

• The factor which carried substantial weight was the preservation of life. Although not an absolute rule, the law regarded the preservation of life as a fundamental principle.

• The burden of establishing that discontinuance of treatment was in a person's best interests was always on those who asserted that life-sustaining treatment be withdrawn.

• In determining the best interests of an incapacitated adult, the courts relied on the use of a 'balance sheet' approach, as explained in *Re A (Medical Treatment: Male Sterilisation)*,[61] which weighs up benefits and losses to the incapacitated person of following a particular course of action.

• A decision by the court, applying the principles laid down in *Bland* and subsequent cases, including the use of the balance-sheet approach, that it would be in a patient's best interests to withhold or withdraw life-sustaining treatment, did not give rise to any breach of Articles 2, 3 or 8 of the ECHR. A best interests assessment, properly conducted under English law, in accordance with established principles, was fully compliant with the ECHR.

---

[59]   At www.officialsolicitor.gov.uk.

[60]   W *(by her litigation friend, B) v* M *(by her litigation friend, the Official Solicitor)* [2011] EWHC 2443 (Fam).

[61]   [2000] 1 FCR 193.

6.4.1 The value and sanctity of life

It has been said that the wrongness of killing another person is chiefly the wrongness of permanently depriving that person of whatever it is that makes it possible for him to value his own life. So that even although each person may find different and unique value in his own life, each is equally wronged by being deprived of a life, the continuation of which he values.[62]

It is obvious that all lives have value, and the principle of sanctity of life reflects this. It is not however absolute. As Lord Goff said in *Airedale Trust v Bland:*[63]

> '... the fundamental principle ... of the sanctity of human life [is] ... a principle long recognised not only in our own society but also in most, if not all, civilised societies throughout the modern world, as is indeed evidenced by its recognition both in art 2 of the European Convention on Human Rights and Fundamental Freedoms ... But this principle, fundamental though it is, is not an absolute. Indeed there are circumstances in which it is lawful to take another man's life for example by a lawful act of self-defence, or, (in the days when capital punishment was acceptable in our society) by lawful execution.'

As a principle it is also on occasion in conflict with the principle of personal autonomy. As the passage cited below from Hoffmann LJ's judgment in *Bland* in the Court of Appeal demonstrates, where there is a stark conflict between the two principles, personal autonomy will prevail:[64]

> 'A conflict between the principles of the sanctity of life and the individual's right of self-determination may therefore require a painful compromise to be made. In the case of the person who refuses an operation without which he will certainly die, one or other principle must be sacrificed. We may adopt a paternalist view, deny that his autonomy can be allowed to prevail in so extreme a case, and uphold the sanctity of life. Sometimes this looks an attractive solution, but it can have disturbing implications. Do we insist upon patients accepting life-saving treatment which is contrary to their strongly held religious beliefs? Should one force-feed prisoners on hunger strike? English law is, as one would expect, paternalist towards minors. But it upholds the autonomy of adults. A person of full age may refuse treatment for any reason or no reason at all, even if it appears certain that the result will be his death.'

It follows that once a person of full age and capacity has determined that he no longer values his own life, nor the continuation of it, personal autonomy requires the wishes of that person to be respected to the extent that his death may come about in consequence.

This point is clearly demonstrated by *Ms B v An NHS Trust.*[65] In that case Ms B, suffered from tetraplegia following an operation to her spine. She was kept alive by artificial ventilation. She had been offered rehabilitation and had

---

[62] See John Harris, *The Value of Life, An Introduction to Medical Ethics* (Routledge, 1985) 17.
[63] [1993] AC 789.
[64] [1993] 1 All ER 821 at 854.
[65] [2002] 2 All ER 449.

considered it carefully, but was not happy to continue living as she was. However, she did not want to commit suicide and even if she did was, by reason of her tetraplegia, deprived of the means of doing so. She wanted to end her life by having the artificial ventilation withdrawn. Her death would then come about by letting nature take its course.

Although the law was clear that a patient with the mental capacity to take decisions has an absolute right to refuse treatment, Ms B was deprived of the facility to exercise that right because no doctor within the NHS Trust caring for her was willing to carry out her wishes and the trust had failed to take steps to find a doctor outside the trust who was prepared to do so.

Dame Elizabeth Butler-Sloss highlighted the 'serious danger, exemplified in this case of a benevolent paternalism which does not embrace recognition of the personal autonomy of the severely disabled patient'. As a result of the case, a doctor was found, outside the trust who was willing to withdraw the artificial ventilation, and she died some days later, having been administered appropriate palliative care to ease her suffering and allow her to die with dignity.

However, the legal tussle between the two competing principles of sanctity of life and the right of autonomy remains live. In contrast with Hoffmann LJ's formulation in *Bland*, the Court of Appeal in the case of Tony Nicklinson (discussed further below) seemed to give precedence to the sanctity of life over the right of autonomy:

> '... there are circumstances when rights of autonomy and dignity may have to yield to other rights or interests. That is manifestly correct and the question is whether they should do so here. In that context it is important to bear in mind that the argument based on these rights is not simply advancing a claim why the individual should be permitted to take his or her own life; it is seeking to require positive action by the state to protect third parties who are willing to give effect to those rights. [...] the sanctity of life is if anything an even more fundamental principle of the common law, reflected in the unqualified right to life found in art 2 of the Convention. In *R (on the application of Pretty) v DPP* Lord Hobhouse commented that it was "probably the most fundamental of the human ... values" ((2001) 63 BMLR 1 at [109], [2002] 1 AC 800 at [109]). There is no self-evident reason why it should give way to the values of autonomy or dignity and there are cogent reasons why sensible people might properly think that it should not. So the mere fact that there may be rights to autonomy and to be treated with dignity does no more than raise the question whether they should be given priority in circumstances like this; it does not of itself carry the day.'

It appears therefore what which of the two principles is to prevail may not depend on the merit of the principles themselves, but on the circumstances of their application, ie the practical moral dilemma being faced. For an individual choosing to let themselves die, the right of autonomy prevails. Whereas, for an individual seeking assistance from another to hasten death, the sanctity of life is given greater weight, as can be seen in the section below.

6.4.2   Assisted suicide

The case of Ms B may usefully be contrasted with that of Diane Pretty. In that case, the claimant, who suffered from motor neurone disease, sought the assurance of the Director of Public Prosecutions (the DPP) that her husband would not be prosecuted if he assisted her to commit suicide. The DPP refused to give such an undertaking. The claimant therefore applied for a declaration that the refusal to give the undertaking was incompatible with Arts 2, 3, 8, 9 and 14 of the ECHR. Both the Divisional Court and the House of Lords held that the DPP had no power to give such an undertaking and was not in any event obliged to do so in order to comply with his obligations under the ECHR. The claimant then complained to the European Court of Human Rights in the first case to come before that court which had already been adjudicated in the national court under the Human Rights Act 1998. The ECtHR held in *Pretty v UK*,[66] that:

- The right to die could not be read into the right to life protected by Art 2.

- The state's obligation to prevent ill-treatment pursuant to Art 3 could not be considered to include permitting actions designed to cause death. The state was not required to undertake not to prosecute the applicant's husband if he helped her to commit suicide.

- The right to refuse treatment was within the ambit of Art 8(1).

- The failure of English Law to allow Mrs Pretty the assistance of her husband to end her life constituted an interference with her private life and it was necessary therefore to consider whether the interference was in accordance with Art 8(2).

- It was clear that the interference was prescribed by law and pursued a legitimate aim.

- A blanket ban on assisted suicide was not disproportionate. The interference complained of was necessary in a democratic society.

- The state had a reasonable and objective justification for not distinguishing in law between individuals who were not capable of committing suicide.

- There had been no violation of Art 14.

However assisted suicide is not unlawful in all countries. In particular, in Switzerland and Canada. This leads to the slightly complicated situation where a person may, with the assistance of another seek to undergo assisted suicide abroad.

In *Local Authority v Mr Z and the Official Solicitor*,[67] the claimant local authority sought clarification from the court as to whether it was obliged to seek to continue an injunction to prevent a husband from removing his wife from England to Switzerland. The wife, who suffered from cerebellar ataxia,

---

[66]   (2002) 35 EHRR 1.
[67]   [2005] 1 WLR 959.

whose condition was deteriorating and irreversible and who had previously attempted suicide wished to arrange an assisted suicide in Switzerland, where it is not unlawful.

The court held that although assisted suicide was not criminal under the law of Switzerland, the husband would contravene s 2 of the Suicide Act by making arrangements and taking steps in the UK to assist his wife to travel to Switzerland for that purpose. However, the duty of the local authority did not extend beyond giving appropriate advice and assistance and informing the police if it considered that a criminal offence might be involved (which it had done). Absent any attempt by the DPP or the police to restrain the husband and wife from leaving for Switzerland, the court would not of its own motion continue the injunction.

The House of Lords revisited its decision in *Pretty* subsequent to the ECtHR ruling in the case of Debbie Purdy.[68] Ms Purdy applied for judicial review in respect of the Director of Public Prosecution's ('DPP') failure to set out guidance as to when a prosecution for aiding and abetting suicide might be brought under s 2(1) of the Suicide Act 1961.

The key factual differences between the *Pretty* and *Purdy* cases are as follows:
- Ms Pretty sought a undertaking that her husband would be immune from prosecution under s 2(1), whereas Ms Purdy sought a clarification from the DPP of the circumstances in which prosecution would or would not be brought under s 2(1).
- Ms Purdy was contemplating travelling to another country where assisted suicide was lawful, with her husband assisting with travel arrangements, whereas Ms Pretty contemplated her husband assisting her in the very act of suicide.
- Ms Purdy was concerned that she may be forced by lack of information about prosecution policy to choose between ending her life earlier than she would otherwise have wished while she was still able to do this without her husband's assistance, which was not the case of Ms Pretty.

In its last judgment as the House of Lords before its reincarnation as the Supreme Court, the House reversed its decision in *Pretty* that art 8(1) was not engaged by a person's decision on the manner in which she wished to die. The requirements of art 8(2) that the law be sufficiently accessible and precise were not satisfied by the developments relied on by the DPP as setting out his position on which factors were likely to be taken into account in the case of a person with a severe and incurable disability who was likely to need assistance in travelling to a country where assisted suicide was lawful. As such the DPP was required to promulgate an offence-specific policy identifying the facts and circumstances that he would take into account in deciding in a case such as that which the claimant's case exemplified, whether or not to consent to a prosecution under s 2(1) of the Suicide Act 1961.

---

[68] *R (on the application of Purdy) v Director of Public Prosecutions* [2009] UKHL 45.

In February 2010, the DPP duly released the *Policy for Prosecutors in Respect of Cases of Encouraging or Assisting Suicide*. It lays out a list of those factors which would tend against prosecution under s 2(1), including:

'1.   the victim had reached a voluntary, clear, settled and informed decision to commit suicide;

2.   the suspect was wholly motivated by compassion;

3.   the actions of the suspect, although sufficient to come within the definition of the offence, were of only minor encouragement or assistance;

4.   the suspect had sought to dissuade the victim from taking the course of action which resulted in his or her suicide;

5.   the actions of the suspect may be characterised as reluctant encouragement or assistance in the face of a determined wish on the part of the victim to commit suicide;

6.   the suspect reported the victim's suicide to the police and fully assisted them in their enquiries into the circumstances of the suicide or the attempt and his or her part in providing encouragement or assistance.'

That guidance came under scrutiny in the case of Tony Nicklinson, carried forward to the Court of Appeal after his death by his wife.[69] Ms Nicklinson sought greater detail in the guidance set out by the DPP to make the law in this area more accessible and foreseeable. The Court of Appeal agreed to a limited extent in finding that the guidance was not sufficiently clear to satisfy the requirements of art 8(2) in relation to the likelihood of prosecutions of healthcare professionals when providing assistance in dying. A further clarification of the *Policy for Prosecutors in Respect of Cases of Encouraging or Assisting Suicide* should therefore be expected.

Ms Nicklinson also sought a declaration that there existed a defence of necessity in the common law to the charge of euthanasia and assisted suicide where certain conditions were met. This was roundly dismissed by the Court of Appeal, finding that it was a matter for Parliament to attempt to fashion a defence in this complex and controversial field. The Court of Appeal also dismissed the argument that the blanket legal prohibition on providing assistance to those wishing to die constituted a disproportionate interference with art 8, relying on the Supreme Court's decisions in *Pretty* and *Purdy*.

In the light of the above, the current position in law therefore appears to be that an adult of full age and capacity may:

•   refuse medical treatment without which his death will come about as a virtually certain consequence;

•   commit suicide;

•   dictate (by way of advance directive – see below) that treatment is to be refused when he loses capacity;

---

[69]   R *(on the application of Nicklinson) v Ministry of Justice (Director of Public Prosecutions and another, interested parties) (CNK Alliance Ltd and another, intervening); R (on the application of AM) v Director of Public Prosecutions (A Primary Care Trust, interested party) (CNK Alliance Ltd and another, intervening)* [2013] EWCA Civ 961.

- travel abroad to a country where assisted suicide is not unlawful;
- in certain circumstances, obtain the assistance of another to commit suicide, albeit there is no guarantee that such a person would not face criminal prosecution.

But it remains unlawful for a person (whether a doctor or another) to assist suicide, at least in circumstances where the assistance given cannot be covered by the principle of double effect.

6.4.2.1   Doctor assisted suicide and double effect

There may however be circumstances in which the treatment which the patient seeks from a third party (often a doctor) is such that if provided, death although not primarily intended, will be the likely result. The commonest example of such treatment is in the final stages of treatment for incurable cancer. Is such treatment lawful?

First, whether or not a particular treatment does amount to euthanasia or assisting suicide is a question not of medical ethics but one of law, with the law informing the morality of a particular action rather than the reverse.[70] This can be seen strikingly in Hoffmann LJ's decision in *Bland* in the Court of Appeal:[71]

> 'It seems to me that the medical profession can tell the court about the patient's condition and prognosis and about the probable consequences of giving or not giving certain kinds of treatment or care; including the provision of artificial feeding. But whether in those circumstances it would be lawful to provide or withhold the treatment or care is a matter for the law and must be decided with regard to the general moral considerations of which I have spoken. As to these matters, the medical profession will no doubt have views which are entitled to great respect, but I would expect medical ethics to be formed by the law rather than the reverse.'

The legality of the giving of treatment which had the effect (if not the intention) of bringing about death, is often determined by the application of the principle of double effect. See, for example, *R v Adams*,[72] where Devlin J commented:

> 'If the first purpose of medicine – the restoration of health – can no longer be achieved, there is still much a doctor to do, and he is entitled to do all that is proper and necessary to relieve pain and suffering, even if the measures he takes may incidentally shorten life.'

This principle (which has its origins in Catholic theology) has been considered judicially in *Re J*;[73] and *Airedale NHS Trust v Bland*.[74]

---

[70]   See for example the discussion of euthanasia and assisted Suicide in *R (Pretty) v DPP* [2001] 3 WLR 1623.

[71]   At [1993] AC 834D.

[72]   [1957] Crim LR 365 at 375.

[73]   [1991] Fam 33.

[74]   [1993] AC 789, 867D, per Lord Goff.

It can be very difficult to apply in practice as may be seen by Ward LJ's observations in the conjoined twins case:[75]

> 'The principle of Double Effect. This teaches us that an act which produces a bad effect is nevertheless morally permissible if the action is good in itself, the intention is solely to produce the good effect, the good effect is not produced through the bad effect and there is sufficient reason to permit the bad effect. It may be difficult to reconcile with *R v Woollin*. Nevertheless it seems to enjoy some approval from Lord Donaldson of Lymington MR: see *In Re J* [1991] Fam 33, 46C and Lord Goff in *Bland's* case [1993] AC 789, 867C-D. I can readily see how the doctrine works when doctors are treating one patient administering pain-killing drugs for the sole good purpose of relieving pain, yet appreciating the bad side effect that it will hasten the patient's death. I simply fail to see how it can apply here where the side effect to the good cure for Jodie is another patient's, Mary's, death, and when the treatment cannot have been undertaken to effect any benefit for Mary.'

The difficulty referred to above, of reconciling the case of *R v Woollin*[76] is the criminal law approach to certainty of intention. In that case, the appellant lost his temper and threw his 3-year-old son onto a hard surface. The child sustained a fractured skull and died. The jury found that W had the necessary intention and rejected his defence of provocation. The House of Lords considered the relevant direction as to intention, and concluded that the critical direction was that from *R v Nedrick*:[77]

> 'Where the charge is murder and in the rare cases where the simple direction is not enough, the jury should be directed that they are not entitled to infer the necessary intention, unless they feel sure that death or serious bodily injury was a virtual certainty as a result of the defendant's actions and the defendant appreciated that such was the case.'

W's conviction for murder was quashed and a verdict for manslaughter substituted.

In end-of-life cases involving doctors it will often be possible to say that:

(1) death was a virtually certain consequence of the pain relieving treatment; and

(2) that the doctor giving the treatment would have appreciated this fact.

Thus, the question is raised whether there is such thing as a special defence for doctors to a charge of murder, even in circumstances where death is a virtual certainty.

There is some reason for thinking that such a special defence does exist and survives *R v Woollin*. See in particular, Professor JC Smith's comment[78] that:

---

[75] At [2001] 1 Fam 199.

[76] [1999] 1 AC 82.

[77] [1986] 1 WLR 1025.

[78] In *A Comment on Moor's case* [2000] Crim LR 41 at 44.

'The question whether the doctor has a special defence has already been answered; according to Moor, at least, he has: although he knows his act will accelerate death significantly, the jury is not entitled to convict him of murder if his purpose is to give treatment which he believes, in the circumstances as he understands them, to be proper treatment to relieve pain.'

Professor Smith goes on to observe, that it was commented by an expert medical witness at the GMC hearing in Cox's case[79] that his mistake was to give potassium chloride. Had he given a large dose of sedative causing B to lapse into a coma his actions would have fallen on the right side of the law. Dr Cox could then have truthfully said that his purpose was not to kill but to prevent pain, even if the effect on the patient would not have been materially different.

6.4.3   Advance directives/decisions – refusals

The Mental Capacity Act 2005 has put on a statutory footing the availability of advance decisions or directives by which a person of full age and capacity can stipulate what he wishes to happen when he lacks capacity to consent to the carrying out or continuation of treatment. Where such advance decisions amount to refusals as opposed to requests for specific treatment, then they must be respected.[80]

Advance directives had already been considered by the courts before MCA 2005, in particular by Hughes J in *AK (Adult Patient) (Medical Treatment: Consent)*;[81] and by Munby J in *HE v A Hospital NHS Trust*[82] which sets out the criteria for testing their validity.

MCA 2005 now provides its own criteria for the assessment of whether an advance decision is effective and binding. Section 25(2)–(5) sets out the circumstances in which such a decision will not be valid. The terms of these sections are very wide, and will certainly give rise to argument in disputed cases.

In particular, an advance directive will not be valid if the person making the decision, P, has done anything else 'clearly inconsistent with the advance decision remaining his fixed decision'; or if 'there are reasonable grounds for believing that circumstances exist which P did not anticipate at the time of the advance decision and which would have affected his decision had he anticipated them'.

These conditions will make advance decisions (i) very difficult to draft, and (ii) difficult to implement in practice. However, the Act also allows persons to

---

[79]   *R v Cox* (1994) 12 BMLR 38.
[80]   See MCA 2005, s 24.
[81]   [2001] 1 FLR 129.
[82]   [2003] EWHC 1017.

create lasting powers of attorney[83] which have the effect of authorising a person to take health care decisions on their behalf when they have lost capacity. This represents a significant change to the existing law.

In an appropriately worded instrument, the donee of a lasting power of attorney now has the power to refuse medical treatment on behalf of the patient subject to any advance decision made by the patient. This represents a significant change in the doctor/patient relationship because a non-medical donee can now override the doctor's clinical judgment as to what is or is not in the patient's best interest. Any person wishing to let his relatives rather than the medical profession choose how best he is to be treated following the loss of capacity would be well advised both to make an advance decision specifying the type of treatment he seeks (or refuses) and to confer a lasting power of attorney on an appropriate donee.

6.4.3.1 Advance decisions – requests

The case of *R (Burke) v General Medical Council*,[84] considered the question of when a patient might lawfully request (as opposed to refuse) specific treatment in advance.

The claimant was suffering from a degenerative brain illness that would eventually result in an inability to swallow. In the future he would almost certainly require artificial nutrition and hydration (ANH). He sought clarification of when such treatment might lawfully be withdrawn. From his point of view he wanted it to continue as long as possible. Munby J at first instance held that the previous position that prohibited advance directives from being used to require treatment against the doctor's clinical judgment would have to be modified in the light of Art 3 and Art 8, saying that:

> 'Article 8 means that in principle it is for the competent patient, not his doctor, to decide what treatment should or should not be given in order to achieve what the patient believes concluded to his dignity and in order to avoid what the patient would find distressing.'

On appeal the Court of Appeal overturned this decision, considering that where life depended upon the continued provision of ANH there could be no question of the supply of ANH not being clinically indicated unless a clinical decision had been taken that the life in question should come to an end. Mr Burke's concerns seemed to be his fears of withdrawal of treatment while still competent. This would not just be a breach of Arts 3 and 8 but would be a breach of Art 2 and murder. The difficult issue, namely whether or not the withdrawal of ANH treatment would be in the patient's best interests when he had lost capacity, was not a matter that could be determined by a simple test at a stage well in advance. The application for declaratory relief in that respect was not justiciable and was premature.

---

[83] See MCA 2005, s 11.
[84] [2004] 2 FLR 1121.

6.4.4   Conclusions

Medico-legal ethics is perhaps most problematic when it comes to end-of-life decision making. The high value given by the law to the sanctity of life has the necessary consequence that patients whose own perception of the value or quality of their own lives is such that they wish their suffering would be at an end are effectively precluded on public policy grounds from seeking doctor assisted suicide.

The clash between the sanctity of life and the autonomy of the person leads to great difficulties in resolving hard cases. The tendency of the courts is to value life as a thing intrinsically good in itself, without regard to that life's quality but as has been commented by the philosopher, A C Grayling in respect of Diane Pretty's case:

> '"Life" in the phrase "the right to life" is not mere existence. It is existence with at least a minimum degree of quality and value. It means a life in which an individual is protected from arbitrary power and threat, is free to seek opportunities and to exercise choices, to enjoy the rewards of endeavours in peace, and to seek and foster personal relationships – and which to the degree reasonably possible for anyone in this world, is free from distress and pain. As this implies, mere existence is not automatically a good. If it were no life-support machine would ever be switched off and contraception would be outlawed ... people oppose contraception and euthanasia on the ground that they value quantity over quality of life. But it takes only a moment's thought to see the spuriousness of this view. The judges in Mrs Pretty's case, alas, failed to see that this was the tendency of their argument.'

Set against this is the salutary warning from Lord Reid in *S v McC; W v W*:[85]

> 'English law goes to great lengths to protect a person of full age and capacity from interference with his personal liberty. We have too often seen freedom disappear in other countries not only by *coups d'état* but by gradual erosion: and often it is the first step that counts. So it would be unwise to make even minor concessions.'

With the advent of MCA 2005, and lasting powers of attorney, there are likely to be some hard cases where it is necessary for the courts again to attempt to reconcile the conflict between these two core principles.

TOP TIPS

- The fundamental principle is that every person's body is inviolate.
- Different considerations apply if the patient is found to lack capacity.
- A doctor's duty is not merely to act in accordance with a responsible and competent body of relevant professional opinion but to act in accordance with the patient's *best* interests.
- It is important not to confuse the question of capacity with the nature of the treatment decision in question.

---

[85]   [1972] AC 24.

- The power to act in the best interests of the patient only arises when that patient has lost his capacity.

- If a patient makes a binding advance directive as to how he wishes to be treated (or not treated) after he loses capacity he can lawfully effect his own death by insisting on a refusal of resuscitative procedures.

- MCA 2005 takes precedence over the common law where issues overlap but the Act only applies to persons aged 16 or over so the treatment of children under 16 will continue to be governed by common-law principles under the inherent jurisdiction of the court.

- Whatever the NHS constitution may say, a patient on the NHS has in law no 'right' to any particular treatment at any particular time save that which can be insisted upon by way of public law principles of legitimate expectation, or, in respect of funding decisions, irrational decision-making by reference to published policy.

- MCA 2005 allows a patient to create a lasting power of attorney which has the effect of authorising a third party rather than doctors to take health care decisions on his behalf when he has lost capacity.

- An adult of full age and capacity may lawfully refuse medical treatment without which his death will come about as a virtually certain consequence.

CHAPTER 7

THE DUTY OF CARE, STANDARD OF CARE AND ESTABLISHING BREACH OF DUTY

In this chapter barristers Adrian Hopkins QC, Simon Cridland, Sarah Simcock, and Suzanne Staunton review the first hurdle a claimant needs to overcome; that of establishing that the medical provider concerned has been in breach of duty.

7.1 DUTY

When referring to the duty a doctor or health care provider may owe his patients, the law imposes a minimum standard. A breach of this minimum standard gives rise to an enforceable legal liability. A doctor's duties to his patient, in terms of his ethical and professional responsibilities – including those enshrined within the General Medical Council's (GMC) expectation that the medical profession follows its issued guidance – may be wider than the duty simply to exercise reasonable care and skill. A failure to follow such guidance, in principle, may not automatically give rise to civil liability. However, it may give rise to Fitness to Practise proceedings being brought against the doctor before the GMC.

7.1.1 Clinician

The duty of care owed by a physician to a patient is, in practice, unlikely to be disputed; it clearly arises out of the relationship between the two. The legal rationale for the duty is that there is an assumption of responsibility by the doctor for his patient. Implicit in this relationship is that a lack of care by the doctor may give rise to harm to the patient. Therefore, nowadays, it is not necessary to plead foreseeability of harm – at least not in cases where the injured party is the patient. Once this relationship is established, there is a duty to take reasonable care once acting, but also a duty to take some action. Thus, a doctor may be liable for a negligent omission to act.

7.1.2 Institutional health care provider

An institutional health care provider, such as a hospital trust, owes a duty of care to their patients in respect of the acts and omissions of its employees, servants or agents. They also owe a direct duty of care, which is the same as that owed by its staff. This duty may also be relevant where, for example, they have failed adequately to supervise or train their clinicians, or where hygiene standards have not been maintained properly.[1]

7.1.3   Joint liability and contribution

Where there is more than one party responsible for the same damage, they will be entitled to claim a contribution from one another under the Civil Liability (Contribution) Act 1978, where each party owes a duty to the claimant. The Act allows apportionment between the defendants. It does not act as a defence to the claim. A judgment against one defendant does not bar the action against the others, and if the judgment remains unsatisfied, the claimant is free to pursue the others, subject only to possible costs implications. The claimant need not sue all parties he believes to be responsible for the damage. If any particular defendant wishes, he may bring in another defendant in Part 20 proceedings.

However, if the claimant's claim is settled in full, or judgment is satisfied in full by one defendant, a subsequent claim against other defendants is barred; if such a claim was allowed, this could lead to double recovery on the claimant's part.[2] However, this is only the case where the claimant has recovered, or is to be treated as having recovered, the full measure of his loss from that defendant.[3] Whether he has done so, or not, will depend upon the proper construction of the relevant compromise agreement.

7.1.4   Contract

In practice, the vast majority of claims concerning unsatisfactory medical treatment will be brought in tort, if only on the basis that they concern treatment provided under the NHS. Although in the past there have been attempts to argue that, in certain circumstances, NHS care can give rise to a liability in contract, it seems extremely unlikely to be the case. If, however, the patient received private treatment, there will be a contract, whether written or by conduct.

All doctors owe to their patients a duty to exercise that degree of skill and care that is ordinarily incidental to their professional calling when carrying out their professional skills of diagnosis, advice and treatment. Normally, any contractual duty will be concurrent with this tortious duty. In principle, it is possible for the contractual obligation to be wider in scope than the tortious obligation. This is rare in practice, and in the absence of express provision in the contract, the courts are likely to be reluctant to conclude that the patient and doctor contracted on terms which imposed a greater duty on the treating

---

[1]   *Wilsher v Essex Area Health Authority* [1986] 3 All ER 801, at 833H–J.
[2]   See, for example, *Rawlinson v North Essex Health Authority* [2000] Lloyd's Rep Med 54.
[3]   *Jameson v Central Electricity Generating Board and Others* [2000] 1 AC 455.

clinician than that imposed by the common law. For example, in sterilisation cases, attempts to argue that the surgeon guaranteed that the procedure would be successful have failed in the past.

An argument that the treating clinician or surgeon has guaranteed a particular result is most likely, in principle, to succeed in the fields of elective cosmetic surgery or dentistry. For example, this argument is strong in cases where the patient may have been shown a computer generated image of the result the surgery was intended to achieve. Nevertheless, even in cases such as these, the courts are still likely to require strong evidence before they are prepared to infer that the operating surgeon or dentist guaranteed or warranted a particular cosmetic result.[4]

Vicarious liability for a doctor's actions is unlikely to be established where the care is private care, provided in a private hospital. Normally a private doctor will be self-employed and issues of vicarious liability will not arise. Where the patient is treated in a private hospital, it is very unlikely that doctors of consultant status will be employees or agents of the hospital. Rather, they are likely to have 'admission privileges', whereby the consultant can make use of the hospital's facilities and nursing staff when providing treatment.

7.1.5   Duty to third parties

Are there circumstances where a doctor owes a duty to someone who is not his patient?

In *Palmer v Tees Health Authority*,[5] a mother claimed compensation for psychiatric injury, as a result of the murder of her young daughter by a mentally disordered patient. The court held that the defendant owed no duty to the general public in respect of the care given to such patients. The situation may be different where there is someone who has specifically been identified as being at risk from a particular patient. Similarly, a surgeon carrying out a vasectomy does not owe a duty to all the potential sexual partners of the patient.[6]

What duty does a clinician owe to the family of a patient diagnosed with a genetic condition where the identity of any potential claimants is within the knowledge of the doctor?

There is the potential for a duty to be found to pass on the information, and to advise that other family members potentially affected are tested. There is, as yet, no decided English case, although the duty was established in the American case of *Safer v Pack*.[7]

---

4   *Thake v Maurice* [1986] 1 All ER 497.
5   [1998] Lloyd's Rep Med 447.
6   See *Goodwill v British Pregnancy Advisory Service* [1996] 1 WLR 1397 (CA).
7   (1996) 677 A 2d 1188 (NJ Sup Ct, App Div).

Where the courts are dealing with financial matters in relation to third parties, they have been reluctant to find a duty of care extending beyond the doctor and patient relationship. This was the case even where loss to a third party was reasonably foreseeable as a result of negligence by the defendant. In the case of *West Bromwich Albion Football Club v El Safty*,[8] a football club whose player had been negligently treated by an orthopaedic surgeon argued that a duty was owed by the surgeon to them as a third party as they were covered by insurance for players' medical treatment, to which the players themselves were not a party. The surgeon gave negligent advice to the player who never recovered fully from knee injuries he sustained, resulting in his retirement from professional football. The club and the insurance company had not paid fees to the surgeon to give advice or treatment to the club. The club sought damages from the surgeon for the financial losses it suffered in consequence of his negligence. The Court of Appeal held that the surgeon owed no duty of care in tort to the club in respect of foreseeable economic loss. There was no assumption of responsibility by the surgeon to the club for financial loss. Moreover, the question of conflict of interest emphasised that the surgeon's exclusive concern was, or should have been, his patient's well-being, not the club's finances. So, even though it was reasonably foreseeable by the surgeon that the club would suffer financial loss if his medical treatment was negligent, and there was proximity of a sort between him and the club, it was not such that it would be fair, just or reasonable to impose such a duty on the surgeon.

7.1.6 Provision of health care abroad and NHS care in private institutions

Today, NHS patients may not have their care provided by NHS institutions. Broadly, a patient can encounter three situations:

- treatment by overseas teams flown in to use NHS facilities;
- treatment in private UK hospitals; and
- treatment overseas.

Where in such circumstances does the duty of care lie?

As has already been explained, hospitals owe patients admitted into their care a direct and non-delegable duty; 'those conducting a hospital are under a direct duty of care to those admitted as patients'.[9]

However, this is an institutional liability, and the scope of the duty owed extends only to those matters within the institution's control. There would be no such control if the NHS hospital contracted the duty out, or, if the patient never entered the NHS system, but instead simply had his care paid for by the relevant NHS trust.

---

8   [2006] EWCA Civ 1299.
9   See Lord Browne–Wilkinson in *X (Minors) v Bedfordshire County Council* [1995] AC 633.

In these cases, the issue that arises is whether the NHS trust owes a non-delegable duty to the patient to ensure the provision of treatment to its patient. At first blush, one might think the answer to this question has to be 'yes'; after all, the patient is an NHS patient, the treatment – wherever it is provided – is provided at the request of the NHS Trust, and is, of course, paid for by the Trust. In *M v Calderdale & Kirklees Health Authority*,[10] HHJ Garner (in the county court) considered such a duty did exist in a case which concerned a failed termination. However, in *A v Ministry of Defence*,[11] the Court of Appeal was clear that *M* did not correctly reflect English law. Following *A*, it seems very unlikely that an NHS Trust will owe a patient who has his treatment under the auspices of the NHS, but in a private institution, a non-delegable duty to ensure that the treatment is provided with reasonable skill and care. The potential injustice to patients created by the decision in *A* is obvious and is an issue to which we will return below.

To some extent, the potential injustice will be ameliorated by the principle that hospitals owe an organisational duty to use reasonable skill and care to ensure that staff, facilities and administration are appropriate so that a satisfactory medical service is provided.[12] Therefore, a commissioning trust will likely be liable if it fails to exercise reasonable skill and care in its selection of private facilities.

Where foreign teams of doctors are flown in, the members of the foreign team will have a contract with the commissioning NHS Trust, and the trust will probably have vicarious liability in respect of their acts or omissions.

Where the treatment is NHS treatment in a private hospital, the appropriate defendants are likely to be the doctor providing the treatment, or the private hospital. Having said that, there would now appear to be (at least in England) a pragmatic approach to avoiding the injustice that *A* creates.

NHS indemnity is provided under the NHS (Clinical Negligence Scheme) Regulations 1996[13] as periodically amended. In 2002, the Regulations were further amended[14] to cover negligence on the part of independent contractors of members of the Clinical Negligence Scheme for Trusts. The Scheme was further extended[15] so as to provide that, where an independent contractor is engaged to perform functions that had been performed by a member of a Primary Care Trust, any liability of the independent contractor would be treated for the purposes of the Scheme as a liability of the PCT.

The National Health Service Litigation Authority (NHSLA) has indicated (on its website) that:

---

[10] [1998] Lloyd's Rep Med 157.
[11] [2004] Lloyd's Rep Med 351.
[12] *Bull v Devon Area Health Authority* [1994] 4 Med LR 117 and *Robertson v Nottingham Health Authority* [1997] 8 Med LR 1.
[13] SI 1996/251.
[14] By SI 2002/1073.
[15] By SI 2006/3087.

- as long as Independent Sector Treatment Centres are treating NHS patients, the same benefits of the Clinical Negligence Scheme for Trusts will apply as they do where the treatment is provided in an NHS hospital;
- the Independent Sector Treatment Centres agree to comply with the Scheme's rules, and to allow the NHSLA to handle claims; and
- the Independent Sector Treatment Centres' risk management systems must mirror those of the NHS.

Therefore, although in such circumstances the commissioning NHS Trust may not, as a matter of law, owe a non-delegable duty of care to ensure the services were provided by the private body with reasonable skill and care, it will still be possible, for the time being at least, for an injured patient to bring his claim against the commissioning NHS trust. The situation is likely to be similar where the NHS treatment is provided overseas.

7.1.7   Normally, in practice, identifying the appropriate defendant should not cause difficulties. Where the care is provided by a general practitioner or privately, early correspondence should advise the doctor to confirm the identity of his defence organisation and to pass the correspondence to the defence organisation. Similarly, correspondence with the risk manager, or other appropriate individual, at the hospital which provided the care will normally identify the trust responsible. Claims against NHS trusts will, normally, be taken over by the NHSLA.

7.1.8   Expert witnesses

Expert witnesses are not immune from suit in civil,[16] or disciplinary, regulatory or fitness to practise proceedings.[17] In *Jones v Kaney*,[18] the Supreme Court found that there is an actionable duty to provide services to their client, but there is an overriding duty to the court and the public. There exists a contractual duty to exercise reasonable skill and care.

The Supreme Court found that experts owe a duty to the court to give full and candid evidence, even in situations where the evidence is contrary to their client's case or interests. However, expert witnesses do not owe a duty of care not to defame in relation to statements made in the course of proceedings.

It is envisaged that a successful claim will be in the 'rare case where the witness behaves in an egregious manner ... or otherwise causes his client loss by adopting or adhering to an opinion outside the permissible range of reasonable expert opinions'. Lord Brown considered that successful claims against expert witnesses would be 'highly exceptional'.

---

[16]   *Jones v Kaney* [2011] UKSC 13.
[17]   *Meadow v GMC* [2006] EWCA Civ 1390.
[18]   [2011] UKSC 13.

7.1.9   Scope of the duty of care

Traditionally in medical cases, in contrast to commercial claims, the courts have not often resorted to the concept of the scope of the duty of care in order to limit potential liability. Nevertheless, in *South Australia Asset Management Corp v York Montague Ltd*,[19] a case that did not concern medical malpractice, Lord Hoffmann used an example of a doctor who negligently advised a patient that his knee was fit. As a result the mountaineer patient embarked upon an expedition he would not otherwise have undertaken. Lord Hoffmann considered that, if the mountaineer suffered an injury as a result of mountaineering but it had nothing to do with the knee, the doctor would not be liable on the basis that the injury sustained was outside of the scope of the duty of care, which only extended to advice in respect of the patient's knee.

There now exists a duty of care in respect to sperm,[20] and so, potentially, human tissue. In the case of *Yearworth v North Bristol NHS Trust*,[21] it was found that men have ownership of their sperm in circumstances where the male's ejaculation was for the purposes of potential fertilisation treatment.

This shows that when a medical professional undertakes to take possession of sperm, or human tissue, in circumstances when they assume a responsibility of special skill (in this case, in preserving sperm), there is a duty to handle the sperm with that heightened skill. Failure to do so will result in a breach of duty in negligence, and also bailment surrounding loss or damage, or psychiatric injury sustained by the claimant.

7.2   WHAT IS THE APPROPRIATE STANDARD OF CARE?

7.2.1   *Bolam*

In medical cases, the appropriate standard of care is authoritatively set out in the direction of McNair J to the jury in the case of *Bolam v Friern Hospital Management Committee*:[22]

> 'A doctor is not guilty of negligence if he has acted in accordance with a practice accepted as proper by a responsible body of medical men skilled in that particular art ... Putting it the other way round, a doctor is not negligent, if he is acting in accordance with such a practice, merely because there is a body of opinion which takes a contrary view.'

This is so, even where the body of opinion holding the contrary view is a minority one. A doctor need not, therefore, possess the highest expert skill but merely that of an ordinary competent doctor exercising that particular skill.

---

[19]   [1997] AC 213–214.
[20]   *Yearworth & Ors v North Bristol NHS Trust* [2009] 2 All ER 986.
[21]   [2009] 2 All ER 986.
[22]   [1957] 2 All ER 118 at 122.

The standard of care is to be applied given the conditions and practice employed at the material time. One might expect a different standard of care from a centre of excellence than from a district general hospital. A hospital besieged by casualties during a disaster may be judged differently than on a quiet day. Equally, advances are made in medicine as time moves on and one must be careful not to look at practices employed with the benefit of hindsight or new and improved practices or techniques introduced later.

7.2.2 Bolitho

The test was reviewed by the House of Lords in *Bolitho v City and Hackney Health Authority*.[23] The facts of that case were as follows. A 2-year-old child was admitted to hospital suffering from respiratory difficulties. The following day, his breathing suddenly deteriorated. A nurse summoned the doctor in charge by telephone. The doctor did not attend. In the event the child recovered. Later, he suffered a second episode of difficulty which the nurse again reported to the doctor. Again, the child apparently recovered without the doctor having attended. Shortly afterwards, the child collapsed owing to failure of his respiratory system, and as a result of this, he suffered a cardiac arrest. By the time his respiratory and cardiac functions were restored, he had sustained severe brain damage. Proceedings were brought against the defendant health authority for damages for negligence. Expert evidence was adduced that any competent doctor attending the child after the second episode would have arranged for prophylactic intubation so as to provide an airway. Such procedure would have avoided the cardiac arrest and subsequent injury. The defendant's expert evidence was that intubation would not have been appropriate, and therefore, the judge held that a decision not to intubate was in accordance with a body of responsible professional opinion and the claimant therefore failed. Appeals to the Court of Appeal and House of Lords were unsuccessful.

Lord Browne–Wilkinson (with whom the other Lords agreed) stated that the court is not bound to hold that a defendant doctor escapes liability for negligent treatment or diagnosis just because he leads evidence from a number of medical experts who are genuinely of the opinion that the defendant's treatment or diagnosis accorded with sound medical practice. He went on to make the following significant comment:

> 'McNair J stated that the defendant had to have acted in accordance with the practice accepted as proper by a "responsible body of medical men". Later, he referred to "a standard of practice recognised as proper by a competent reasonable body of opinion." Again,[24] Lord Scarman refers to a "respectable" body of professional opinion. The use of these adjectives – responsible, reasonable and respectable – all show that the court has to be satisfied that the exponents of the body of opinion relied upon can demonstrate that such opinion has a logical basis. In particular in cases involving, as they so often do, the weighing of risks against

---

[23] [1997] 4 All ER 771.
[24] In *Maynard v West Midlands Regional Health Authority* [1985] 1 All ER 635.

benefits, the judge before accepting a body of opinion as being responsible, reasonable or respectable, will need to be satisfied that, in forming their views, the experts have directed their minds to the question of comparative risks and benefits and have reached a defensible conclusion on the matter.'

In most cases, the very fact that there are experts in the field who agree with the doctor's action will serve to demonstrate its reasonableness. But, there will be rare cases where the professional opinion is not capable of withstanding logical analysis. This may present conceptual difficulties due to the fact that many medical decisions are not based upon logic but on a judgment call.

It seems that in reality the question to be asked is whether the decision was properly considered, rational and reasonable. Where a judge is minded to reject expert opinion by applying the rationale in *Bolitho*, he should not do so until the parties' experts have had a proper opportunity to explain the logical rationale for their approach.[25]

A judge may reject the defendant's expert evidence that a responsible body of medical opinion would have found the conduct acceptable for a variety of reasons; for example, by finding that the expert does not speak for such a responsible body of opinion but only for himself; the expert is unreliable or partisan, or has not considered all the appropriate factors.

The judge may take the view that the defendant's expert is wrong when he says that he would have done the same as the doctor in fact did in the circumstances.

It is important to recognise that reasonable skill and care does not amount to best practice, and that there will not be a finding of negligence if the care provided accords with a responsible body of relevant opinion. The practitioner is to be judged by the standards of the ordinary competent practitioner in the relevant specialty and no more unless he holds himself out as possessing a particular excellence of skill or contracts with the patient on that basis. Either scenario would be highly unusual.

7.2.3 Specialist

It goes without saying that inherent in the *Bolam* test is the principle that a specialist must display the degree of care and skill of a specialist, and not a more general practitioner.[26] The higher the level of skill, the higher the standard to be expected. However, he or she does not have to display the highest degree of skill or competence, merely a reasonable level within that specialist field.

---

[25]   *S R Burne v A* [2006] EWCA Civ 24.
[26]   *Sidaway v Governors of the Bethlem Royal Hospital* [1985] 1 All ER 643, at 660F–G.

7.2.4   Inexperience

Inexperience does not found a defence to an allegation of negligence. In *Wilsher v Essex Area Health Authority*,[27] a junior doctor who was training in an intensive care neonatal unit inserted a catheter into a vein rather than an artery causing serious injury to the infant patient's sight. The registrar also failed to check, and then made the same error. The Court of Appeal by a majority held them to have been negligent (the case was subsequently reversed in the House of Lords on grounds relating to the issue of causation).[28] Mustill LJ stated:

> 'To my mind, this notion of a duty tailored to the actor, rather than the act which he elects to perform, has no place in the law of tort ... it would be a false step to subordinate the legitimate expectation of the patient that he will receive from each person concerned with his care a degree of skill appropriate to the task which he undertakes to an understandable wish to minimise the psychological and financial pressures on hard-pressed young doctors.'

7.2.5   Limits to *Bolam*

Where there is a dispute of fact, whether it is actual or hypothetical, the *Bolam* test should not come into play. A judge must decide on the balance of probabilities which is the more likely factual scenario on the evidence. For example, whether an injury was caused by one mechanism or another (a question of past fact), or whether a course of treatment would have had one outcome or another (a question of hypothetical fact).

In considering this question, a judge is entitled to prefer the evidence of one witness to another, or one expert to the other as to what happened, or as to what would have happened. The judge may then go on to consider whether any *Bolam* question arises. For example, having found as a matter of fact that a clinician carried out a particular action, he may consider whether that action was one a responsible body of medical opinion would have carried out, and whether it withstands logical analysis.

Many, if not the majority, of clinical negligence cases will turn, not on whether the care provided was in accordance with a responsible body of opinion, but on competing expert theories as to what occurred and how things went wrong. In such cases, the court will determine that question of fact on the basis of usual principles, without the application of the *Bolam* test. For example, in *Fallows v Randle*[29] the question upon which the issue of breach of duty turned was how a sterilisation operation could have failed. Stuart-Smith LJ stated that:

> '[*Bolam*] has really no application where what the judge has to decide is, on balance, which of two explanations – for something which has undoubtedly occurred which shows that the operation has been unsuccessful – is to be

---

[27]   [1987] 1 QB 730, 750F–751A.
[28]   [1988] 1 AC 1074.
[29]   [1997] 8 Med LR 160, 165.

preferred. That is a question of fact which the judge has to determine on the ordinary balance of probability. It is not a question of saying whether there was a respectable body of opinion here which says this can happen by chance without any negligence, it is a question for the judge to weigh up the evidence on both sides, and he is, in my judgment, entitled in a situation like this, to prefer the evidence of one expert witness to that of the other.'

In preferring the expert evidence of one expert over that of another, the judge should give reasons why, and it will not be sufficient simply to state that preference, nor to state that the preferred expert was representative of a responsible body of medical opinion and therefore the treatment was not negligent.[30]

7.2.6   Prevention of self-harm

Where a patient should be identified as at risk of suicide or self-harm, the duty of the clinicians caring for the patient extends to a duty to avoid, or prevent actions, by the patient himself which are reasonably foreseeable and cause self-inflicted harm. In *Drake v Pontefract Health Authority*,[31] a claim succeeded against the defendant health authority where the claimant had jumped from a footbridge and been very seriously injured. The court made extensive findings against the clinicians, including that there had been a failure in their duty to evaluate the claimant as a suicide risk, to make an adequate psychiatric assessment, to arrive at a proper diagnosis, and thereafter properly to treat her. It was also held that she should have been observed on a one-to-one basis.

7.2.7   Disclosure of risks

In *Sidaway v Board of Governors of the Bethlem Royal Hospital*,[32] the claimant suffered paralysis following an operation upon her cervical vertebrae. The operation carried a 2% risk of damage to a nerve root or the spinal cord. Damage to the cord would be far more serious and the risk of that was less than 1%. The surgeon warned of the risk to the nerve root but not of the risk to the spinal cord. The trial judge found that the patient had not been told of all the material risks so as to be able to give informed consent. However, as the surgeon had acted in accordance with standard practice at the time as supported by a responsible body of medical opinion the claimant failed. The Court of Appeal endorsed the decision. The House of Lords, by a bare majority, also endorsed the medical test with the following proviso: that a judge might come to the conclusion, depending upon the circumstances, that disclosure of a particular risk was so necessary to the ability of the patient to make an informed choice that no reasonably careful and competent clinician could fail to make such disclosure.

---

[30] See *Smith v Southampton University Hospital NHS Trust* [2007] EWCA Civ 387.
[31] [1999] Lloyd's Rep Med 425.
[32] [1985] 1 All ER 643.

Therefore, following *Sidaway*, the *Bolam* test remained the cornerstone for establishing liability in consent cases. However, there is still the possibility that the court could hold a doctor liable for not disclosing a risk notwithstanding the existence of a responsible body of opinion in favour of not providing a warning.

In the Australian case of *Rogers v Whittaker*,[33] the patient, who was already almost entirely blind in her right eye, was not warned of the risk of becoming blind in her left eye as a result of the proposed operative procedure. The evidence was that there was a responsible body of medical opinion which would not in these circumstances advise the patient of the risk of blindness. The High Court of Australia found for the patient holding that the law should recognise that a doctor has a duty to warn a patient of a material risk inherent in proposed treatment if a reasonable person in the patient's position, if warned of the risk, would be likely to attach significance to it, or if the medical practitioner is, or should reasonably be aware, that the particular patient, if warned of the risk, would be likely to attach significance to it.

In *Pearce v United Bristol Health Care Trust*[34] Lord Woolf MR, in reviewing the impact of *Bolitho* on *Sidaway* considered that where there was a significant risk which would affect the judgment of a reasonable patient, the doctor should inform his patient of that significant risk if the information was needed so that the patient could determine for themselves what course to adopt. This approach was comparable to that adopted in *Rogers v Whittaker*.

In *Chester v Afshar*,[35] the defendant neurosurgeon recommended that the claimant undergo a procedure to her spine which carried with it a small risk of cauda equine syndrome developing even when performed non-negligently. The claimant reluctantly agreed to the procedure. The surgery was performed and she subsequently developed cauda equine syndrome. The trial judge held that the defendant had negligently failed to warn the claimant of the risk of cauda equine syndrome and that, had the claimant been so warned, she would have sought alternative surgical advice and the procedure would not have taken place when it in fact did. The trial judge therefore held the defendant liable. The defendant's subsequent appeals were dismissed by the Court of Appeal and also the House of Lords.

Much of the speeches in the House of Lords are taken up with the issue of causation. However, Lord Steyn, giving the leading speech of the majority, gave the following guidance in relation to the issue of adequate consent:[36]

> 'The starting point is that every individual of adult years and sound mind has a right to decide what may or may not be done with his or her body. Individuals have a right to make important medical decisions affecting their lives for

---

[33] (1992) 109 ALR 625.
[34] (1998) 48 BMLR 118.
[35] [2005] 1 AC 134.
[36] [2005] 1 AC 134, 143C–D.

themselves: they have the right to make decisions which doctors regard as ill advised. Surgery performed without the informed consent of the patient is unlawful. The court is the final arbiter of what constitutes informed consent. Usually, informed consent will presuppose a general warning by the surgeon of a significant risk of the surgery.'

Having quoted from the observations of Lord Woolf MR in *Pearce*, Lord Steyn went on to state:

'A surgeon owes a legal duty to a patient to warn him or her in general terms of possible serious risks involved in the procedure. The only qualification is that there may be wholly exceptional cases where objectively in the best interests of the patient the surgeon may be excused from giving a warning ... In modern law medical paternalism no longer rules and a patient has a prima facie right to be informed by a surgeon of a small, but well established, risk of serious injury.'[37]

It would appear following *Pearce* and *Chester*, therefore, that the *Bolam* test has been superseded in relation to the issue of consent, with a rights based approach which reflects the importance placed in modern society on patient autonomy. Breach of duty will therefore now be established where a patient has not been informed of a serious risk of the procedure notwithstanding that the risk may be small, provided it is well established.

Where the patient has not consented to the procedure, in contrast to the situation where he has consented following inadequate counselling, the medical treatment will constitute a battery and damages will in principle be recoverable. In considering consent cases, issues in relation to a particular patient's capacity to consent to medical treatment may arise which are outside the scope of this chapter.

7.3 PSYCHIATRIC INJURY

To what extent can a doctor who negligently treats a patient be liable for psychiatric injury to the patient or his relatives, where that psychiatric injury is the *only* injury suffered by the patient or relative? The answer is to be found in four House of Lords decisions.[38]

The distinction between primary and secondary victims is important.

Where the patient has been exposed to a risk or danger the patient is entitled to claim for pure psychiatric injury as a primary victim.

---

[37] [2005] 1 AC 134, 143H.
[38] *McLoughlin v O'Brian* [1983] 1 AC 410; *Alcock v Chief Constable of South Yorkshire Police* [1992] 1 AC 310; *Page v Smith* [1996] AC 155; *White v Chief Constable of South Yorkshire Police* [1999] 1 All ER 1.

A relative would be classed as a secondary victim whose ability to recover compensation is subject to the test laid out by the House of Lords, namely that the claimant has to prove that:

(1)   there was a recognised psychiatric injury and not merely grief;

(2)   this resulted from shock, ie the sudden and direct appreciation by sight or sound of a horrifying event or events;

(3)   there was propinquity in time or space from the causative event or its immediate aftermath;

(4)   the injury was reasonably foreseeable;

(5)   the relationship between the claimant and defendant was sufficiently proximate.

In the leading clinical negligence case of *Sion v Hampstead HA*,[39] Peter Gibson LJ made clear that a claim of this sort would not fail simply on the basis that there is no 'unexpected' or 'shocking' event. What is crucial is the unexpected or shocking nature of the discovery by the claimant.

However, there remains the distinction between a gradual onset of psychiatric harm and a psychiatric injury which flows from a sudden 'shock'. A more flexible approach to this criterion is illustrated by the case of *Walters v North Glamorgan NHS Trust*,[40] where a baby was negligently misdiagnosed leading to his death from acute hepatitis, and his mother recovered compensation for the psychiatric harm she suffered in circumstances where the baby died 36 hours after the mother's initial appreciation that her son was seriously ill. Thomas J held that the period of 36 hours from when the mother first saw her son having an epileptic fit through to the time of the baby's death was a horrifying event. The initial witnessing of the fit was not such an event in its own right but the court should look realistically at all the events which happened over the period until death. Also, the psychiatric evidence meant that it was not possible to isolate the causative effect of each incident within the 36-hour period. The accumulation of all events had contributed to the injury.

The Court of Appeal affirmed the ruling stating that the court should take a realistic view of the word 'event' and should not be overly restrictive in its interpretation, so that a series of events may satisfy the test, depending upon the individual circumstances of the case.

7.4   ECONOMIC LOSS

Pure economic loss, that is economic loss not consequent upon physical injury or the threat of it, is not, as a general rule, recoverable in tort. However, it is recoverable where it arises from careless statements where there is a duty on the person making the statement to take care, such as where there is a fiduciary relationship. The courts have more recently allowed recovery where there is a

---

[39]   [1994] 5 Med LR 170 (CA).

[40]   [2002] Lloyd's Rep Med 227.

relationship of sufficient proximity between the parties such that there is an inference that the defendant has voluntarily assumed responsibility for the negligently carried out activity.

For example, a doctor may be liable for the economic loss suffered by a patient as a result of a negligently prepared medical report. In *Hughes v Lloyds Bank plc*[41] the claimant argued that her claim for personal injury had been settled too early on the basis of a negligent prognosis of her condition in a medical report, which stated that her injuries would improve with time. The Court of Appeal held that it was arguable that the doctor did owe a duty to take reasonable care to describe the claimant's conditions accurately.

The courts have otherwise used public policy grounds to prevent recovery where there has been no physical damage. Following *McFarlane v Tayside Health Board*,[42] the parents of a healthy child may not recover for economic loss suffered as a result of bringing up a child, where the birth of that child was caused by the negligence of the defendant. Further, in *Rees v Darlington Memorial Hospital NHS Trust*[43] the House of Lords by a majority held that a disabled mother who gives birth to a healthy child may not recover the additional costs of rearing the child consequent on her disability. However, as she had been the victim of a legal wrong she was entitled to a 'conventional lump sum' award of £15,000. Previously the Court of Appeal in *Parkinson v St James and Seacroft University Hospital NHS Trust*[44] had held that the parents of a disabled child may recover the additional costs consequent on the disability in similar circumstances as in *McFarlane*. It seems that *Parkinson* remains good law, as any comments made in *Rees* by the Law Lords are obiter.

7.5 COMMUNICATION NEGLIGENCE

In principle, it seems that *Bolam* will apply to cases which involve allegations of negligence in communicating information to patients. However, difficulties may arise as to the proper approach to be adopted in such cases by the courts where there is no respectable body of opinion on the matter.

An example of this type of problem arose in *AB v Tameside and Glossop Health Authority*.[45] In this case, a health worker was diagnosed as being HIV positive. The defendant health authority wrote to patients informing them that there was a remote risk they could have contracted the virus as a result of being treated. A claim was subsequently brought by a group of patients in respect of psychological injury suffered as a result of how they were notified of matters by the health authority. The authority admitted that a duty of care in respect of the communication was owed in the circumstances. The Court of Appeal reversed the decision of French J that the authority was in breach of its duty of care. In

---

[41] [1998] PIQR P98.
[42] [2000] 2 AC 59.
[43] [2004] 1 AC 309.
[44] [2001] EWCA Civ 530.
[45] [1997] 8 Med LR 91.

doing so, it rejected the contention that the health authority's duty was to use the best possible means of communication. In principle, *Bolam* still applied, but in practice on the facts of the case the *Bolam* test did not provide assistance because the problem had not previously arisen in comparable circumstances and there was no general practice. Once the authority had decided to provide the information to patients, its duty was to take all such steps to implement that decision which were reasonable, having regard to the foreseeable risk of psychiatric injury. In an unusual example of how the benefit of hindsight was brought to bear upon the issue of breach of duty, the Court of Appeal was influenced in its decision by virtue of the fact that subsequent Department of Health Guidelines advised that the approach adopted by the health authority in this case should be followed.

In *Allin v City and Hackney Health Authority,*[46] the claimant had undergone a very difficult labour and was subsequently incorrectly told by hospital staff that her baby had died. The existence of a duty of care in respect of the provision of information was conceded and the defendant was held liable for its breach.

It is also arguable that a practitioner will be under a legal duty to inform a patient when something has gone wrong with his treatment. In *Naylor v Preston Area Health Authority*[47] Sir John Donaldson MR stated: 'In medical negligence cases there is a duty of candour resting on the professional man.' However, although a Department of Health Consultation paper in 2003 recommended that there should be a statutory duty of candour on a medical professional with protection from disciplinary action when reporting potentially negligent acts, the recommendation was not taken further. Both the British Medical Association (BMA) and GMC support the proposition that a doctor should use his clinical judgment and where appropriate report all adverse outcomes to the patient affected, whether or not negligence might be involved. There remains, however, no binding legal authority on the point.

A failure to give adequate instructions to a patient can, in principle, give rise to liability. Many procedures will require the patient's cooperation, and in such circumstances, a doctor will need to give instructions to a patient in comprehensible terms so that the patient follows them. This duty extends not only to the giving of instructions to a patient pre- or post-procedure, but can also extend to the provision of advice in respect of his lifestyle. For example, in *Hutchinson v Epson & St Helier NHS Trust*[48] there was a duty to advise a patient who had cirrhosis of their liver to stop drinking.

Similarly, doctors are under a duty to warn patients of the side effects of drugs and of the action or precautions they should take should such side effects manifest themselves.

---

[46]   [1996] 7 Med LR 167.
[47]   [1987] 2 All ER 353, 360.
[48]   [2002] EWHC 2363.

Doctors will also be liable for a failure adequately to communicate with other health care professionals, and hospitals will be liable if they do not have adequate systems of communication in place. For example, in *Bull v Devon Area Health Authority*,[49] the health authority had an inadequate system for the summoning of expert obstetric assistance.

Prescriptions need to be written carefully and legibly. In *Prendergast v Sam and Dee Ltd*,[50] the claimant's GP issued a prescription for the ubiquitous antibiotic Amoxil. The pharmacist misread the prescription and issued another drug, Daonil, used in the control of diabetes. The claimant developed hypoglycaemia as a result of taking the incorrect drug and suffered brain damage. Both GP and pharmacist were held liable. The GP was held liable on the basis that the prescription could reasonably have been read incorrectly.

7.6   DEFENCES

Relevant specific defences are contributory negligence, *volenti non fit injuria* and illegality, although they are comparatively rare, with the latter two particularly so. In practice, the most frequent defence will be that primary limitation has expired under the Limitation Act 1980.

7.6.1   Contributory negligence

A patient's cooperation is often needed by the doctor; for example, an accurate history may be vital in order to make a diagnosis. Also, his cooperation is often necessary for treatment to be effective or for a condition to be monitored adequately. Although a defence of contributory negligence may apply to clinical negligence cases in the same way as any other type of case, in practice such a defence is rarely successful. Indeed the defence is not often pleaded, perhaps due to an inherent reluctance on the part of a defendant to assert that a claimant injured by the defendant's negligence is also partly responsible for his own injury.

The case of *Pidgeon v Doncaster Health Authority*,[51] concerned a claimant who had developed cervical cancer. She had undergone a cervical smear test which she was told was negative. She failed to undergo further repeat tests despite frequent reminders to do so. She was held to be two-thirds contributory negligent. A doctor is not, however, entitled to delegate his own professional responsibility to the patient himself. There remains a duty upon the doctor to give clear instructions to the patient and to ensure that their importance is adequately understood.

A claimant may also be found to be contributory negligent where he has made a suicide attempt (whether successful or not) and a claim is brought against

---

[49]   [1993] 4 Med LR 117.
[50]   [1989] 1 Med LR 36.
[51]   [2002] Lloyd's Rep Med 130.

medical staff for a negligent failure to prevent it. A similar type of claim succeeded in *Reeves v Commissioner of Police of the Metropolis*,[52] where the police failed to protect the prisoner, who was a known suicide risk, from his own decision to commit suicide.

7.6.2 *Volenti non fit injuria*

This essentially involves a waiver by the claimant. The claimant agrees to waive liability in respect of the consequences of an unreasonable risk of harm created by the defendant where the claimant has full knowledge of both the nature and extent of the risk. This is not to be confused with consent, where but for the claimant's consent treatment would constitute a battery. A situation where this defence is likely to be considered is in a suicide where the defendant was under a duty to take reasonable precautions to prevent an attempt. However, in *Reeves*, mentioned above, the House of Lords held that this did not arise where the claimant's act was the very subject of the defendant's duty.

A case which raises another situation in which the defence of *volenti* is potentially relevant is *Watson v British Boxing Board of Control*,[53] which is of interest when looking at the nature of the risk accepted by the claimant. In that case, the claimant boxer claimed for damages for personal injury sustained in a professional boxing match held under the control of the Board. As a result of a blow to the head sustained during the bout, the claimant suffered a subdural haemorrhage and was rendered an invalid. In substance, the claimant claimed that the Board owed him a duty of care to provide appropriate medical assistance, in particular resuscitation equipment and a person or persons qualified to use such equipment at the ringside in the event of such injuries being sustained, and the Board had failed to do so, and in consequence a largely remediable condition had become irremediable. The Board denied that it owed the claimant the duty of care alleged. All professional boxing contests held in Great Britain took place under the aegis of the Board, which required the promoters of those contests to comply with safety arrangements laid down by it. Those arrangements included a requirement that three approved doctors should be in attendance at the ringside, as indeed they were in the instant case. However, no resuscitation equipment was available and none of the doctors in attendance possessed the skills necessary to use such equipment.

The main issue in the case was as to the nature of the duty of care between the Board and the claimant, and as to whether causation was in fact established. However, as to *volenti*, the court held that although the claimant clearly consented to the risk of injury at the hands of his opponent, he did not consent to the risk of injury flowing from the Board's failure to ensure that its safety arrangements were as carefully worked out as they might have been. Although the Board appealed this point, the Court of Appeal decided the case on other grounds and did not discuss *volenti* in their judgments.

---

[52] [2000] 1 AC 360.
[53] [2001] QB 1134.

7.6.3   Illegality

This principle is traditionally expressed by the maxim *ex turpi causa non oritur actio* (no right of action arises from a shameful cause). In the case of *Clunis v Camden and Islington Health Authority*,[54] the claimant claimed that, had he been given appropriate care subsequent to his release from detention under the Mental Health Act 1983, he would not have gone on to kill someone, and thereafter have been convicted of manslaughter after a plea of diminished responsibility and detained in a special hospital. The claim was struck out by the Court of Appeal as being based upon the claimant's own illegal act. However, the Court's reasoning centred upon public policy grounds and that the claimant knew the nature and quality of his act, and that it was wrong. If this was not the case, arguably the defence would not apply.

The principle of public policy will also be invoked even in those cases where there has been no criminal conviction. In the non-clinical negligence case of *Hewison v Meridian Shipping Services Pte Ltd*,[55] the Court of Appeal agreed with the ruling of the first instance judge that the claimant could not rely on an unlawful act to enable recovery in tortious damages. The courts, however, have also recognised that injustice may result from always allowing a defendant to raise illegality as a complete defence. Judges have accepted that it is in the interests of justice on occasions to evaluate the relative culpability of the parties to an action or to make a distinction between those cases where the claim arises directly from the unlawful act and those where the unlawful conduct is merely incidental.[56]

Another situation where this arises is in fertility treatment cases where the claimant cannot recover the costs of surrogacy procedures if those procedures are in breach of the Surrogacy Arrangements Act 1985.[57] However, although commercial surrogacy arrangements are unlawful in this country, it is lawful for a surrogate mother to be paid expenses in return for agreeing to carry and hand over the child.

7.7   ESTABLISHING BREACH

The burden of establishing breach of duty resulting in injury on the balance of probabilities is on the claimant. It is not for the defendant to prove that he exercised appropriate skill and care, and where there are two equally likely possibilities for the injury, one negligent and one not, it must follow logically that the claim will fail.

However, the importance of the burden of proof should not be overstated. Normally, the judge should make appropriate findings of fact. Only in an

---

[54]   [1998] QB 978.
[55]   [2002] EWCA Civ 1821.
[56]   Cf *Saunders v Edwards* [1987] 2 All ER 651.
[57]   Cf *Briody v St Helen's and Knowsley Area Health Authority* [2002] QB 856.

exceptional case should he determine the action in the defendant's favour on the basis that he could not determine where the truth lay. As to the potential relevance of *res ipsa loquitur* in such cases, see below.[58]

There may also be occasions when, although there may not be direct evidence of a breach of duty, the claimant can legitimately invite the judge to infer one from known facts. There are, however, limits to such an approach. By way of example, the fact that, negligently, an x-ray was not taken prior to the decision to undergo surgery, does not of itself prove that intra-operative complications suffered which themselves could have a negligent or non-negligent cause were caused by the surgeon's breach of duty. Although, it may be argued that the negligent omission to take a pre-operative radiograph is indicative of a generalised lack of care.

The case of *Maynard v West Midlands Regional Health Authority*[59] makes clear that it is for the judge to determine whether the defendant acted as a reasonable doctor in the circumstances, by relying on and evaluating the expert evidence and applying the *Bolam* test.

However, as Lord Scarman noted, the judge must not give effect to its own preference for one responsible body over another where he is satisfied that both bodies are indeed to be classed as responsible. In considering that question the judge will weigh all the circumstances, for example, the difficulty of making a diagnosis, the techniques reasonably available used to determine a diagnosis and the risks associated with any other differential diagnosis.

In *Maynard*, a consultant physician and a consultant surgeon were treating the claimant. They recognised that the most likely diagnosis of the claimant's illness was tuberculosis. But they took the view that Hodgkin's disease, carcinoma and sarcoidosis were also possible diagnoses. As Hodgkin's disease was fatal unless remedial steps were taken in its early stages, they decided that, rather than await the result of a sputum test, which would involve some weeks' delay, an operation should be performed to provide them with a biopsy. The operation involved a risk of damage to the left laryngeal recurrent nerve even if properly performed. Although the surgeon carried out the operation correctly, that damage in fact occurred. The biopsy proved negative. It was subsequently confirmed that the claimant was suffering from tuberculosis and not Hodgkin's disease. The claimant alleged that the defendant health authority was negligent as the decision to carry out the operation rather than await the result of the sputum test had been wrong. At trial, a distinguished body of expert medical opinion was called approving of the action of the clinicians. The judge, however, preferred the evidence of an expert witness called by the claimant, who had stated that the case had almost certainly been one of tuberculosis from the outset and should have been diagnosed accordingly. The judge found that it had been wrong and dangerous to undertake the operation and held for the

---

[58] At 7.7.3.
[59] [1984] 1 WLR 634.

claimant, but the Court of Appeal reversed his decision and the Court of Appeal's decision was upheld by the House of Lords.

7.7.1 Absence of practice

What is the effect of a situation where there is simply no adequate well of professional experience on which the court can draw?

In *AB v Tameside and Glossop Health Authority*,[60] discussed above in relation to communication negligence, Brooke LJ looked at all the relevant circumstances, in what was a novel situation, and then set the appropriate legal standard. He stated that the judge must 'perform the familiar role of considering the factual evidence carefully, listening to the expert evidence, and forming a view' on what should reasonably have been done in the circumstances.

Increasingly, modern practice within the NHS is to have written guidelines and protocols concerning proper advice, diagnosis and treatment. The GMC also issues written guidance as to a doctor's duties to his patient. There are also often written publications, from, for example, the Royal Colleges or the National Institute for Clinical Excellence. Where there are such documents available, the court is not bound to accept them as definitive evidence of the appropriate standard, but it is likely that they will have considerable persuasive force.

7.7.2 Departure from usual practice

Reasonable practice may not necessarily be common or accepted practice. Departure from usual practice is not of itself indicative of negligence. A claimant must show that the course taken was one that no doctor of ordinary skill would have taken if exercising reasonable care. In other words, the departure from usual practice must have been justified in the circumstances.

In *Wilsher v Essex Area Health Authority*[61] Mustill LJ said:

> '... where the doctor embarks on a form of treatment which is still comparatively untried, with techniques and safeguards which are still in the course of development, or where the treatment is of particular technical difficulty ... if the decision to embark on the treatment was at all justifiable and was taken with the informed consent of the patient, the court should ... be particularly careful not to impute negligence simply because something has gone wrong.'

7.7.3 *Res ipsa loquitur*

The doctrine of *res ipsa loquitur*, or the matter speaks for itself, may be relied upon by a claimant alleging negligent medical treatment as was set out by

---

[60] [1997] 8 Med LR 91 (CA).
[61] [1987] QB 730 (CA).

Lord Denning in *Cassidy v Ministry of Health*.[62] The claimant had undergone treatment for Dupuytren's contracture of the hand which had left it in a worse state. Lord Denning stated as follows:

> 'If the plaintiff had to prove that some particular doctor or nurse is negligent, he would not be able to do it. But he was not put to that impossible task: he says, "I went into the hospital to be cured of two stiff fingers. I have come out with four stiff fingers, and my hand is useless. That should not have happened if due care had been used. Explain it, if you can."'

In practice, the doctrine is unlikely to be of much assistance to the claimant in all but the starkest of cases, which are in any event unlikely to proceed to a contested hearing, as was noted by Brooke LJ in *Ratcliffe v Plymouth & Torbay HA*:[63]

> '... although in very simple situations the res may speak for itself at the end of the lay evidence adduced on behalf of the plaintiff, in practice the inference is then buttressed by expert evidence adduced on his behalf, and if the defendant were to call no evidence, the judge would be deciding the case on inferences he was entitled to draw from the whole of the evidence (including expert evidence), and not on the application of the maxim in its purest form.'

In practice very few clinical negligence cases will involve a true application of the doctrine of *res ipsa loquitur*, as there are usually alternative explanations for the condition about which complaint is made and which the judge will need to consider.

7.7.4   Errors of judgment

The question is always whether the clinician has exercised appropriate care and skill. Where there is an issue of clinical judgment, it may be more difficult for a claimant to show that the doctor was negligent. Not every mistake or adverse outcome will found liability. In *Hucks v Cole*,[64] Lord Denning MR said:

> 'With the best will in the world, things sometimes go amiss in surgical operations or medical treatment. A doctor is not to be held negligent simply because something has gone wrong. He is not liable for mischance or misadventure; or for an error of judgement. He is not liable for taking one choice out of two or favouring one school rather than another. He is only liable when he falls below the standard of a reasonably competent practitioner in his field so much that his conduct may be deserving of censure or inexcusable.'

So, a mere error of clinical judgment will not necessarily amount to negligence, provided the doctor concerned has acted reasonably and put himself in a reasonable position to make that judgment, even if that judgment subsequently proved to be wrong.

---

[62]   [1951] 2 KB 343.
[63]   [1998] Lloyd's Rep Med 162 at 172, para 48.
[64]   [1993] 4 Med L R 393 (CA).

The key to establishing breach of duty or indeed a defence to it is the expert evidence. When dealing with experts, it is probably unhelpful to use expressions such as an 'error of judgement'. Liability will depend upon the circumstances and whether a doctor acting with reasonable care would have done what the defendant did. One error of judgment may be negligent whereas another may not. A distinguished surgeon of immense skill and expertise may on one occasion fall below an acceptable standard for whatever reason.

TOP TIPS

- Establishing the existence of a duty of care owed by a health care professional to a patient is unlikely to be controversial.

- When the treatment is carried out privately, the existence of a contract and in particular a specific guarantee or warranty given should be considered.

- Where specific risk has been identified, a health care professional arguably owes a duty to a known third party who is the subject of that risk.

- In law, no duty is owed by a commissioning NHS trust for treatment provided privately to a patient (whether overseas or in the UK) other than to exercise reasonable skill and care in its choice of provider, but in practice, a patient is able to recover due to the NHS (Clinical Negligence Scheme) Regulations 1996, as amended.

- Where a responsible or reasonable body of medical opinion supports the action taken by a clinician, even where the body is in the minority in the profession, there will be no breach of duty (the *Bolam* test).

- Such a professional opinion must, however, be capable of withstanding logical analysis (*Bolitho*).

- Past facts are to be judged on the balance of probabilities in the usual way and the trial judge is entitled to prefer the opinion of one expert over that of another.

- A patient may have a claim where there has been a failure to warn him of recognised risks of treatment, but in practice, will face several hurdles in proving such a claim.

- A failure to communicate or to give adequate instructions may give rise to liability in particular situations.

- The burden of establishing breach of duty on the balance of probabilities remains on the claimant.

- Where there is an absence of practice, the court is likely to consider (even in hindsight) any professional guidelines or publications to assist in deciding when breach has been established, although such guidance is not, in law, determinative.

- In practical terms, many cases are more likely to turn on disputed evidence of fact, in which expert evidence will be important, than on a rigid application of the *Bolam* test.

- Expert evidence will be crucial in determining issues of past or hypothetical fact as well as issues of whether there has been a breach of duty.

CHAPTER 8

CAUSATION

The true battle ground in many clinical negligence cases is not breach of duty at all but the vexed question of causation. In this chapter barristers Christopher Gibson QC and Robert Dickason explore this medical and legal hurdle.

8.1 STANDARD OF PROOF AND CAUSATION OF LOSS IN DAMAGES ASSESSMENT

In many clinical negligence cases the issues of standard of proof and causation do not cause difficulties; but it is necessary to approach the facts of each case with care and to be careful not to miss any possible complication. Difficult cases and exceptions from general rules are considered below. The correct answer can often be seen as a matter of common sense, but it is vital to approach a causation problem by principled analysis.

Most clinical negligence cases, unless they arise out of elective cosmetic surgery or family planning, involve claimants who by definition were ill or injured before the treatment was given or sought and by the very nature of their complaint are ill or injured at the end of the process. Demonstrating the causation of the particular injury or illness complained of to the requisite legal standard can be of the utmost medical and legal complexity.

It is convenient to address the topics of standard of proof and causation in relation to damages assessment together, because the two principles are often interrelated and have to be considered together in an analysis of causation.

8.2 TOUCHSTONE PRINCIPLES

With an appropriate degree of caution, it is perhaps helpful to set out some basic or 'touchstone' principles to try to assist with the different strands of analysis, although it has to be recognised that they would not necessarily be accepted by all lawyers in the form in which they are set out.

- The burden of proof of establishing a causal connection between the breach of duty and damage lies on the claimant.
- Questions of what did happen (past fact) are judged on the balance of probabilities (at least where such questions relate to liability).

- Once a finding is made as to past fact the finding is treated as certain, even though there is anything up to a 49% chance of it being incorrect.

- A finding as to a future event[1] is not judged as a matter of probability but one of chance, at the quantification stage.

- Issues of liability concern past fact, or hypothetical past fact, but not future events.

- Issues of liability, when they are concerned with hypothetical events such as whether the same injury would have been suffered but for the tort, are judged on the balance of probabilities.[2]

- Causation of primary injury at the liability stage may take a number of forms: classical 'but for' causation, material contribution, and causation in the rare claims where the analysis of the causation of damage departs from a strict approach which would leave a claimant unable to prove damage.[3]

- Where 'but for' causation is invoked, it must be shown that it is more probable than not that the primary injury would have been avoided if the negligence had not occurred. The mere possibility of avoidance of injury is not enough.[4]

- Where the claimant establishes 'material contribution' causation of the primary injury for liability purposes, then at the quantification of damages stage, arguably 'but for' causation does not apply.

  The rule in such circumstances can be stated as follows: where a primary injury has more than one concurrent or consecutive cause which combine to produce the injury and scientific knowledge does not permit a finding whether the injury would have been avoided but for the tortious contributory cause, the claimant's cause of action is complete provided the defendant's tort was a material contributory cause to that primary injury, even though the non-tortious causes may also have contributed.

  The claimant recovers in full where the primary injury is indivisible.

---

[1]   It is to be borne in mind that a distinction can and should be drawn between a past event with future effects and a future event when considering whether there is liability for the event. This is most clearly illustrated by *Gregg v Scott* [2005] 2 AC 176.

[2]   The first principle is incontrovertible: *Pickford v ICI* [1998] 1 WLR 1189, *Newman v Laver* [2006] EWCA Civ 1135 at [125]-128]. The second to sixth principles are also uncontroversial: *Mallett v McMonagle* [1970] AC 166, *Davies v Taylor* [1974] AC 207. The sixth principle is also supported and illustrated by *Bright v Barnsley District Hospital* [2005] Lloyds Rep Med 449 at [37–41]; see also *Gregg v Scott* [2005] 2 AC 176 at [10-14].

[3]   See for example *Chester v Afshar* [2005] 1 AC 134 where the neurosurgeon's failure to obtain informed consent did not increase the independent risk associated with the operation the claimant then underwent, but merely exposed her to the same risk she would have been at on some other date had she postponed surgery in the event of informed consent. There was explicit relaxation of ordinary causation principles because otherwise it was found by the majority of the House of Lords that the duty to obtain informed consent would be drained of content: see at [8], [24–25], [31–32], [84], [87], [101]. It should be noted that this exceptional approach to causation has not been applied as yet to other fields: *Beary v Pall Mall Investments* [2005] EWCA Civ 415 at [38]; see also *White v Paul Davidson & Taylor* [2004] EWCA Civ 1511 at [40–42].

[4]   *Gregg v Scott* [2005] 2 AC 176. The Court of Appeal has confirmed that it considers *Gregg v Scott* effectively to have foreclosed clinical negligence claims being run on a lost chance basis, and that it would be for the Supreme Court to revisit the issue: *Wright (A Child) v Cambridge Medical Group* [2011] EWCA Civ 669.

Where the primary injury is divisible, the claimant recovers to the extent the defendant contributed to that primary injury, and the damages are apportioned.

Where the defendant is exceptionally found to be liable to the claimant for materially increasing the risk of a primary injury which has occurred, but it cannot be established that the defendant materially contributed to the resultant injury, the defendant is liable only to the extent to which it is found it contributed to the risk of injury and the damages are apportioned. This is so whether the injury is divisible or not.[5]

- Subject to the qualifications already made, once it has been shown that 'primary injury' has been caused by the negligence, the question of causation of losses ('secondary damage') attributed to that primary injury belongs in the realm of assessment of damages and the claimant may recover for the past and *future* consequences of the injury caused by the breach of duty.

- Issues of quantification of loss embrace not only issues about what happened and would have happened, but also future events. The events should be judged as possibilities or chances, provided the secondary damage itself (such as *the fact* of diminished prospects of survival, capacity to work or to care for oneself in distinction to the effects or consequences of such damage) has been caused on the balance of probabilities by the primary injury.[6]

This list of principles is not exhaustive, and not all lawyers would set out them in this way. There are some real problems in making such general statements which do not necessarily fit the analysis of some of the difficult cases. It is necessary to examine the application of these propositions further, as the law in this regard is complex and not always consistent.

8.3 STANDARD OF PROOF: THE BALANCE OF PROBABILITIES TEST

That the standard of proof applicable to findings in a civil action is a balance of probabilities should be a statement of the obvious. However, this standard of proof is not applied in all circumstances to all issues of assessment of loss. This is not always appreciated in practice and can lead to complications. The law permits in certain circumstances the *im*probable but *possible* loss or avoidance of loss to be taken into account in assessing causation of loss and the quantification of damages. Not all losses are required to be proved on the balance of probability to result in an award of damages.

---

[5]   *Fairchild v Glenhaven Funeral Services Ltd* [2003] 1 AC 32; *Barker v Corus (UK) Plc* [2006] 2 AC 572 at [31], [35–36], [43], [48], [50], [53], [57], [59], [62], [64], [103], [113], [126], [129]; *Holtby v Brigham & Cowan (Hull) Ltd* [2000] PIQR Q293 at [32]. Note the reversal of the position in mesothelioma cases pursuant to s 3 of the Compensation Act 2006.

[6]   *Gregg v Scott* [2005] 2 AC 176. As will be seen, questions of causal connection between primary injury and secondary damage must be established on balance of probability.

The threshold to be crossed is not always the magic 51% chance to convert a possibility into probability, and then into certainty. A straitjacket of probability in this area of causation and quantification is not always imposed by the law. It is sometimes difficult to identify the occasions when a claimant is required to cross the high hurdle of probability or the lower hurdle of possibility or chance to recover damages for a particular head of pecuniary loss, and it can be just as difficult to identify coherent principles to reconcile difficult cases.

8.4   CAUSATION AND THE APPLICATION OF THE BALANCE OF PROBABILITIES TEST

At first sight, this sub-heading would appear to conflate two separate issues:

(1) what is the standard of proof which is required to establish loss; and

(2) when does the law treat that loss as *caused* by the defendant's wrongdoing?

The issues are distinct but closely interrelated. So far as is possible, the two issues are treated separately below, but because of their interrelationship they are considered together here.

Traditionally, it is said that in relation to past loss, because the court is concerned with a past event, the question of causation and proof of the fact of loss is a balance of probabilities question, whereas in relation to future loss, evidentially the issue is one of chance.

Lord Reid analysed the different approaches to past and future events in the following way in *Davies v Taylor*:[7]

> 'When the question is whether a certain thing is or is not true – whether a certain event did or did not happen – then the court must decide one way or the other. There is no question of chance or probability. Either it did or it did not happen. But the standard of civil proof is a balance of probabilities. If the evidence shows a balance in favour of it having happened then it is proved that it did in fact happen ... You can prove that a past event happened, but you cannot prove that a future event will happen and I do not think that the law is so foolish as to suppose that you can. All you can do is to evaluate the chance. Sometimes it is virtually 100 per cent: sometimes virtually nil. But often it is somewhere in between. And if it is somewhere in between I do not see much difference between a probability of 51 per cent. and a probability of 49 per cent.'

In *Mallet v McMonagle*, Lord Diplock expressed the distinction between past and future events in similar vein as follows:[8]

> 'The role of the court in making an assessment of damages which depends on its view as to what will be and what would have been is to be contrasted with its

7   [1974] AC 207 at 212–213.
8   [1970] AC 166 at 176E–176G (HL).

ordinary function in civil actions of determining what was. In determining what did happen in the past a court decides on the balance of probabilities. Anything that is more probable than not it treats as certain. But in assessing damages which depend on its view as to what will happen in the future or would have happened in the future if something had not happened in the past, the court must make an estimate as to what are the chances that a particular thing will or would have happened and reflect those chances, whether they are more or less than even, in the amount of damages which it awards.'

These statements from such distinguished judges, whilst accurate insofar as they go, do not sufficiently distinguish between the application of the balance of probabilities test at the liability and quantification stages, and do not resolve all questions of standard of proof in causation at the quantification stage in practice, in particular in areas where personal injury lawyers are becoming ever more dependent on the Ogden Tables, and the information published in Facts and Figures.

For instance, in relation to future loss, how is causality to be judged and what is being assessed as a chance – the fact of loss, or its extent?

In relation to past loss, are contingencies to be ignored where they did not meet the balance of probabilities test?

The following deliberately simple hypothetical example can be considered:

A, aged 19, suffers catastrophic brain injuries during an operation as a result of the negligence of an anaesthetist. She can no longer work and her life expectancy is compromised. At trial the judge assesses her past loss of earnings, both the fact of loss and its causation on the balance of probabilities (that is, was the loss due to the negligence and would she have not worked anyway because say she would have gone to degree level study?). The judge concludes she could not have worked because of the operation. However, the judge also concludes that, while there was a chance she would have worked, on balance of probability she would not have worked anyway in the pre-trial period. The question immediately arises whether there is or is not a past loss of earnings claim. Many lawyers would cite the passages quoted above and say there is no loss, and therefore no recovery because all questions of fact relate to past events. However, if there was a chance she would have worked which is greater than *de minimis* (a term considered further below), why should the claimant not recover damages to reflect the loss of that chance? This is arguably not truly a question relating to a past actual event, but one relating to a hypothetical past event. It is a 'what if' question relating to secondary damage, which should be assessed as a matter of chance. Alternatively, it could be described as an assessment of the hypothetical chance or effect of the proven probable secondary damage (the inability to work).

The House of Lords in *Gregg v Scott* were unable to agree what the answer would be in this situation and there is genuine uncertainty as to how the law would be applied in this context. This probably results more from an inability to agree about the conclusions to be drawn from the evidence in *Gregg v Scott*, the unsatisfactory nature of the evidence and the differing formulations of 'primary injury' and 'secondary damage', than a fundamental dispute as to the relevant causation principles, at least as between four of their Lordships.[9]

With a degree of caution and uncertainty, given the difficulty of drawing firm conclusions from the case, it seems that the majority of their Lordships (excepting Lord Nicholls, who took a more radical approach to causation)[10] agreed with the basic proposition that if the primary injury caused the secondary damage (the inability to work), then the claimant can recover for the chance that she would have earned during the relevant period, but not otherwise. The following passage from Lord Hope's minority opinion probably represents the law on this question:[11]

> 'An analogy may be drawn with cases where it is proved that a person's employment prospects, or his prospects of promotion, have been adversely affected by a physical injury. The claimant is not required, in a case of that kind, to prove on a balance of probabilities what his employment record would have been or that he would in fact have been promoted but for his injury. It is enough for him to prove that there was a prospect immediately before he was injured which he has lost due to the wrongdoer's negligence. The claim is for the loss of prospects assessed as at that date, not for the loss of a certainty. Some evidence is, of course, needed to enable the court to assess those prospects. Without that evidence the claim would be speculative, as any decision would be based on pure guesswork. But the law does not insist on proof that events would in fact have taken the course that the prospects relied upon have indicated.'

It is arguable in the example given that a finding that the claimant's inability to work was caused (the secondary damage) by the brain injury (the primary injury) on the balance of probability is sufficient to allow the claimant to recover damages for the chance that she may have worked if she had not been injured, and the judge should not be asked to assess that chance on the basis of the balance of probability.

It is suggested that such a situation is to be sharply distinguished from the situation in *Gregg v Scott* where the claimant could not establish that the negligent delay in the diagnosis of his cancer had caused any measurable diminution in his life expectancy (arguably a past event, although its effects lay in the future) and he sought to recover damages for the chance that it might do, which by the majority the House of Lords declined to do.[12] The majority of the House of Lords found that Mr Gregg must establish that there was (or, more

---

9   [2005] 2 *AC 176* at [13]–[14], [17], [57]–[58], per Lord Nicholls; [67]–[68], [71], [82]–[84], per Lord Hoffmann; [117]–[121], per Lord Hope; [175], [187], per Lord Phillips; [194]–[196], [200], per Baroness Hale.

10   [2005] 2 AC 176 at [57]–[58].

11   [2005] 2 AC 176 at [67]–[68], [71], per Lord Hoffmann; [117]–[121], per Lord Hope; [175], [187], per Lord Phillips; but see [200], per Baroness Hale. It is suggested that Baroness Hale's example fails to identify the nature of the secondary damage which is the inability to work, not the failure to obtain to work or promotion or a different job. It is suggested that the difference between her position and that of the other three Law Lords is probably more apparent than real on this issue.

12   [2005] 2 AC 176. See J Stapleton (2005) 68(6) MLR 996.

accurately, had been) a diminution in his life expectancy as a result of the negligent delay as a fact on the balance of probabilities.

It is suggested that the approach set out by Lord Hope accords more with day-to-day practice in the courts and is consistent with the true ratio of *Gregg v Scott*. However, this is by no means free from doubt.

In the example given the consideration of the extent of A's past loss must take account of all the different prospects, including the chance that if she had worked it might have only been on a part-time basis, or she might have done something with a higher or lower remuneration than claimed, or she would only have worked remuneratively for part of the pre-trial period whilst doing something else with the rest of her time.

If the balance of probabilities test applies to the question of whether there is any past loss of earnings at all, then it ought to follow that all chances of the loss of earnings being reduced or increased in any event (reflecting the possibilities identified) are ignored where they fall below 51%, but are fully taken into account where they are greater than 51%.

The reality is judges do take such chances into account, although it is the experience of all practitioners that when they do, the decision is often expressed as a decision on the balance of probabilities indicating an assessed figure for lost earnings rather than an assessed figure for the loss of the chance to earn. It is suggested when doing so they are usually making 'chance' not 'balance of probability' assessments despite the occasional use of language that sometimes implies the balance of probability.

It is submitted that consistency demands that all chances are taken into account once the basic causal connection between the primary injury (the brain damage) and the secondary damage (the inability to work) is established on balance of probability.

Taking the example further, in considering A's future loss of earnings, should the judge be invited to award the claimant damages for the loss of the chance of working to a certain age at different rates, or to conclude on the balance of probabilities that the claimant would have worked to age 65, or some other age, in a particular job at a particular level of remuneration?

In practice, judges are often invited to follow the latter path, even though it runs counter to principle as to proof of future events, and they do indeed express themselves and make findings as to such future events on the balance of probabilities, thereby treating the loss as certain, and discount down (and sometimes, although rarely, upwards) for contingencies, both in relation to the multiplier and the multiplicand.[13] This may achieve practical justice where

---

[13] *Brown v MOD* [2006] EWCA Civ 546 at [19], [24], applied in *Leesmith v Evans* [2008] EWHC 134 (QB). See explanation in *Smee v Adye* (unreported) 19 April 2000 at [6]–[7] (CA). See *R (on the application of Soper) v Criminal Injuries Compensation Appeals Panel* [2002]

computation is necessarily educated guesswork rather than scientific calculation, but the basis in principle for such an approach is difficult to identify. A more nuanced and arguably more principled stance has begun to be worked through in relation to future loss of earnings.[14]

The approach in principle to proof becomes even more difficult to discern when considering A's life expectancy in the example given. Assume in the same example that the judge finds in the quantification of the future care claim that A will probably live a further 36 years to the age of 55 as opposed to her projected life expectancy of a further 68 years. The judge is forecasting a future event[15] and apparently ignoring the chances of either earlier or later death. The judicial prediction of the date of death is treated for calculation purposes as certain, when in truth it is a judicial guess informed by a mixture of statistical evidence based on life expectancy data, clinical evidence, and (although diminishingly) expert intuition. This may or may not be statistically most unsatisfactory, but the court in this context is seeking to ensure that the claimant's damages do not run out:[16]

> 'There is no room for any discount in the case of a whole life multiplier with an agreed expectation of life. In the case of life expectancy the contingency can work in either direction. The plaintiff may exceed his normal expectation of life or he may fall short of it. There is no purpose in the Courts making as accurate a prediction as they can of the plaintiff's future needs if the resulting sum is arbitrarily reduced for no better reason than the prediction might be wrong. A prediction remains a prediction.'

Perhaps this is more of a problem of expression than substance. When the judge finds a future life expectancy of 36 years, even if it is expressed as a finding that that the claimant is going to die in 36 years' time, there may be no difference in substance if it was expressed differently – to the effect that taking all of the significant chances into account a figure of a further 36 years would be a fair reflection of the claimant's future life expectancy.

In *Gregg v Scott*, the claimant sought to recover for a reduction in his life expectancy as a result of a delayed diagnosis of his cancer, but to do so on the basis not of life expectancy data but on the basis of survival for a disease-free interval and equating that with cure. This raised peculiar problems of proof specific to that class of case because it could not be said that the claimant had suffered a reduction in life expectancy by reference to life tables in the usual

---

EWCA Civ 1803 at [21]–[30]. See *Daw v Intel Corp (UK) Ltd* [2006] EWHC 1097 (QB) at [211-214] where exactly this approach was taken.

[14] *Langford v Hebran* [2001] EWCA Civ 361, applied in *Clarke v Maltby* [2010] EWHC 1201 (QB), although rejected as excessively complicated and no more likely to produce an accurate result in the field of share valuation in *Law Debenture Trust Corp Plc v Elektrim SA* [2010] EWCA Civ 1142.

[15] Albeit it can be said that the diminution in survival is a past fact caused by the primary injury, but its effects will be felt in the future; and it is the magnitude of this effect that the judge is required to *forecast*.

[16] *Wells v Wells* [1999] 1 AC 345 at 378D–378E, per Lord Lloyd; *Royal Victoria Infirmary v B* [2002] EWCA Civ 348 at [25], [40].

way. The claimant ultimately failed (in the absence of a pure loss of chance case being accepted) because according to the majority, the claimant could not prove on balance of probabilities that the primary injury (the increased size of his tumour and its 'upstaging' as a result of a negligent delay) caused the secondary damage (an actual diminution in his life expectancy, as a matter of past fact) on the balance of probabilities. According to the majority of their Lordships he could only establish it had reduced his *chance* of a disease-free survival for a fixed period of time. Further and more problematically, it was still unresolved post-trial what his actual chance of disease free survival was and would have been but for the negligence.[17]

Had the claimant been able to convert disease-free survival data into a reduced life expectancy or had sought provisional damages, he might have succeeded, provided the reduction in life expectancy or the recurrence of the disease (when seeking a further award) was caused by the primary injury on the balance of probability.[18]

It is suggested that the correct analysis is that the reason for Mr Gregg's failure was ultimately not a legal one, but an evidential one.

It is also the case that it is widely believed that the Court was reluctant to award or to appear to award damages in a clinical negligence case for the mere loss of a chance of a better result that was less than 50% because to do so might have changed the entire approach to proof in clinical negligence cases. Certainly the Court of Appeal has expressed the view that it would be for the Supreme Court to revisit the issue of lost chance claims in this context: *Wright (A Child) v Cambridge Medical Group.*[19]

The decision in *Gregg v Scott* may be contrasted with *Judge v Huntingdon Health Authority*[20] where the deputy High Court Judge found that the negligence of the doctor in failing to detect that the claimant had a lump in her breast caused a 9-month delay in diagnosis of breast cancer which probably caused involvement of the lymph nodes. The injury complained of was the spread of the tumour into the lymph nodes, but not the tumour itself. Therefore, the judge found as a question of past fact, as a matter of probability, that the undiagnosed tumour 9 months earlier had not spread into the lymph nodes. The failure to diagnose constituted the breach of duty. The judge then had to determine hypothetically what the consequence would have been had the diagnosis been 9 months earlier.

---

[17] J Stapleton (2005) 68(6) MLR 996 at 997.

[18] [2005] 2 AC 176 at [70]–[71], per Lord Hoffmann; [159], [169], [176], [183]–[186], [191], per Lord Phillips; [207]–[208], per Baroness Hale.

[19] [2011] EWCA Civ 669, per Lord Neuberger [82], [84], with whom Elias LJ agreed on the point.

[20] [1995] 6 Med LR 223.

The consequence of that was the loss in the future of a chance of cure that the evidence demonstrated was 80%. The claimant was entitled to damages representing 80% of her losses caused by the loss of a cure.

This decision does not rest easily with *Gregg v Scott*. It is not clear that the case would now be decided the same way. If the secondary damage was loss of a chance of cure, then if the lost chance of cure was 80% and applying the reasoning of the majority of their Lordships in *Gregg v Scott*, arguably the claimant was entitled to recover in full because but for the negligence the probability was that the claimant would have been cured. Mrs Judge had lost more than a chance of being cured. On balance of probabilities she would have been cured.

It is suggested that this approach gives rise to further problems and highlights the peculiar difficulty raised by claims for a diminished prospect or chance of survival. Applying the reasoning in *Gregg v Scott*, the claimant was entitled to be treated as having a normal life expectancy but for the negligence because she had lost an 80% chance of cure.

This introduces another layer of difficulty into such a case. This is because the claimant would in order to unlock the key to a lost years claim then have to show what her life expectancy was now in contrast to what it would have been for an unimpaired woman of her age who had been 'cured'.

As a matter of convention (derived from the literature) oncologists speak of a disease-free interval of 5 or 10 years and sometimes longer. In the absence of being able to convert such data into life expectancy, the claimant would still have failed to prove what her loss was in *Judge*. In that sense the decision in *Judge* can be understood as a pragmatic solution to a difficult problem of proof.

It is suggested that the preferable approach in such cases is to seek provisional damages where it can be established on the expert evidence that if the cancer recurs, the recurrence is the result of the negligence on the balance of probabilities, and invite the court initially to treat the claimant as having no reduction in life expectancy.[21]

8.5   MATERIAL CONTRIBUTION CAUSATION AND QUANTIFICATION OF DAMAGES

In dealing with the concept of material contribution, it should be noted that it is a rare thing in life for an injury or an event to have only one cause. Industrial disease, product liability, environmental exposure and clinical negligence claims all exemplify this problem.

---

[21]   See *Rothwell v Chemical & Insulating Co Ltd* [2006] EWCA Civ 27 per Lord Phillips of Worth Matravers CJ at [130], unaffected by the decision of the House of Lords upholding the Court of Appeal.

In the rare single cause case, the application of causation principles at the liability stage may be simply a question of assessment of the available factual and expert evidence on a balance of probability test, applying the well-understood 'but for' test: but for the breach of duty of care would the claimant have suffered the injury?

However, potential multiple cause cases bristle with legal and evidential difficulty. A given disease or injury may have several possible causes, including the identified breach of duty. Those causes may be true alternative causes, or they may combine cumulatively to produce the disease or injury, or the state of scientific knowledge may be insufficient to say whether or to what extent the negligent cause contributed to an injury, or which causation category the injury falls within.[22]

The starting point in every case is the 'but for' test, and in the vast majority of cases it is determinative. If the claimant can establish on the balance of probabilities that the injury would not have occurred but for the defendant's negligence, causation will be made out. Conversely, if the evidence demonstrates that the injury would probably have occurred as a result of non-tortious causes, the claim will fail. The classic example of such a case is *Hotson v East Berkshire Area Health Authority*,[23] in which the claimant's avascular necrosis was 75% likely to have developed regardless of the defendant's negligence, and so it could not be said that the negligence probably caused the injury.

In cases where there are multiple possible causative factors at play, it may be impossible to prove that but for the negligence the injury would not have been suffered. It is sufficient then for the claimant to show that the negligent cause made a more than minimal contribution to the injury.

The principle is probably best summarised in the following passage in *McGhee v National Coal Board*:[24]

> 'But *Bonnington Castings Ltd v Wardlaw* [1956] AC 613 and *Nicholson v Atlas Steel Foundry and Engineering Co Ltd* [1957] 1 WLR 613 establish, in my view, that where an injury is caused by two (or more) factors operating *cumulatively*, one (or more) of which factors is a breach of duty and one (or more) is not so, in such a way that it is impossible to ascertain the proportion in which the factors were effective in producing the injury or which factor was decisive, the law does not require a pursuer or a plaintiff to prove the impossible, but holds that he is entitled to damages for the injury if he proves on a balance of probabilities that the breach or breaches of duty contributed substantially to causing the injury. If such

---

[22] Examples of claimants failing on the latter ground – see *Loveday v Renton* [1990] 1 Med LR 117; *Dingley v Strathclyde Police* (2000) 55 BMLR 1; *Vadera v Shaw* (1998) 45 BMLR 162; *Reay and Hope v British Nuclear Fuels plc* [1994] 5 Med LR 1. A rare contrary example is *Huxley v Elvicta* (unreported) 19 April 2000.

[23] [1987] AC 750.

[24] [1973] 1 WLR at 8C–8D (HL).

factors so operate cumulatively, it is in my judgment, immaterial whether they do so concurrently or successively' (per Lord Simon, *emphasis added*).

Waller LJ in *Bailey v Ministry of Defence* has affirmed this approach to cumulative cause cases as good law:[25]

> 'In my view one cannot draw a distinction between medical negligence cases and others. I would summarise the position in relation to cumulative cause cases as follows. If the evidence demonstrates on a balance of probabilities that the injury would have occurred as a result of the non-tortious cause or causes in any event, the claimant will have failed to establish that the tortious cause contributed. Hotson's case exemplifies such a situation. If the evidence demonstrates that "but for" the contribution of the tortious cause the injury would probably not have occurred, the claimant will (obviously) have discharged the burden. In a case where medical science cannot establish the probability that "but for" an act of negligence the injury would not have happened but can establish that the contribution of the negligent cause was more than negligible, the "but for" test is modified, and the claimant will succeed.'

The approach in *Bailey* has since recurred throughout clinical negligence judgments.[26] However, it is important to understand the limits of this doctrine.

First, the negligence must contribute to the injury itself. Contribution to the *risk* of injury is not enough (outside exceptional *Fairchild* circumstances).[27] In *Hussain v Bradford Teaching Hospital NHS Foundation Trust*,[28] the claimant developed Cauda Equina Syndrome but could not establish that 48-hour negligent delay in surgery caused or made a material contribution to his injury. It was not sufficient to show that the delay materially increased the risk of injury, or that delay is generally capable of causing injury without also proving that it did in fact cause measurable damage.

Second, the contribution must be 'material', which means more than *de minimis*.[29]

---

[25] [2008] EWCA Civ 883, para 46.

[26] *Canning-Kishver v Sandwell and West Birmingham Hospitals NHS Trust* [2008] EWHC 2384 (QB); *Mugweni v NHS London* [2012] EWCA Civ 20; *Popple v Birmingham Women's NHS Foundation Trust* [2012] EWCA Civ 1628 at [79]; *Leigh v London Ambulance Service NHS Trust* [2014] EWHC 286 (QB).

[27] *Fairchild v Glenhaven Funeral Services Ltd* [2003] 1 AC 32. It is beyond the scope of this chapter to define the precise circumstances in which the *Fairchild* exception can be invoked, but see at [2], [34], [61], [63], [67] and [168]–[170] for an analysis of the circumstances in which the exception was thought to apply by a majority of their Lordships. The extent to which the exception might be widened was left open for decision by the House of Lords: [34], [43], [74], [118], [170]. It is reasonably clear that the *Fairchild* exception has very limited application. See *Barker v Corus (UK) Plc* [2006] 2 AC 572 at [5], [22-4], [48], [57], [64], [103], [114], [129]. See also *Clough v First Choice Holidays and Flights Ltd* [2006] EWCA Civ 15 at [43]–[44], decided before *Barker*. For a critical evaluation of the decision in *Fairchild*, see J Stapleton (2003) 10 Tort LJ 276.

[28] [2011] EWHC 2914 (QB).

[29] *Bonnington*, per Lord Reid at 621.

Third, there must be no alternative complete cause of the injury. That is because, if there is an alternative cause that could have been solely causative of the injury, the claimant will necessarily be unable to prove that the negligence in fact made any contribution at all. This is the classic *Wilsher v Essex Area Health Authority* situation.[30] The defendant's negligence had led to the provision of excess oxygen, but this was only one of five possible causes, each of which could alone have caused the child's blindness. It therefore could not be established that the negligence had any causative effect.

Another way of stating this third restriction is that material contribution will only apply to genuine cumulative cause cases, where the final injury has been contributed to by a number of factors including negligence. These are to be contrasted with alternative cause cases, where the final injury could have been caused without the negligence making any contribution.

It can often be very difficult to determine whether a particular case involves genuine cumulative causes or not. Very similar cases can yield different answers. Take the intraventricular haemorrhage suffered by the prematurely born claimant in *Boustead v North West Strategic Health Authority*.[31] The expert evidence was that the IVH was cumulatively caused by the claimant's prematurity, respiratory illness due to lung immaturity, and the (negligently caused) hypoxia at birth. But it would not be at all surprising for a case with the same essential facts to produce expert evidence to the effect that the prematurity and/or respiratory illness ought properly to be regarded as sufficient, alternative causes of IVH. Material contribution would then not be available.

8.6 APPORTIONMENT OF DAMAGES FOR MATERIAL CONTRIBUTION

Where material contribution is available and proved, the claimant is entitled to recover in full just as if 'but for' causation had been made out. As Lord Bridge stated in *Hotson* at page 783:

> 'But if the plaintiff had proved on a balance of probabilities that the authority's negligent failure to diagnose and treat his injury promptly had materially contributed to the development of avascular necrosis, I know of no principle of English law which would have entitled the authority to a discount from the full measure of damage to reflect the chance that, even given prompt treatment, avascular necrosis might well still have developed. The decisions of this House in and McGhee v National Coal Board [1973] 1 WLR 1 give no support to such a view.'

Full recovery is therefore permitted in circumstances where the claimant cannot establish what proportion of his injury is attributable to the negligence. This

---

[30] [1988] AC 1074, HL, at 1090–1.
[31] [2008] EWHC 2375.

can be contrasted with the position in *Fairchild* cases, whereby a defendant's liability for materially increasing the risk of injury is proportionate to its contribution to the risk.[32]

However, if the evidence does permit an assessment to be made of the tortious contribution to injury, the courts will seek to do justice to the defendant and make a best estimate of its proportion of liability. This approach is neatly summarised in *Rugby Joinery Ltd v Whitfield*:[33]

'In this case, as in almost any case where only part of the claimant's medical condition can be attributed to the defendant's negligence, questions of causation and apportionment are difficult. The topic, albeit not in connection with VWF, was discussed by Mustill J in *Thompson v Smiths Ship Repairers (North Shields) Ltd* [1984] QB 405 at 437–448, where he said this at 438D:

"The defendants as well as the plaintiffs are entitled to a just result. If we know ... that a substantial part of the impairment took place before the defendants were in breach, why in fairness should they be made to pay for it? The fact that precise quantification is impossible should not alter the position ... what justice does demand, to my mind, is that the courts should make the best estimate which it can, in the light of the evidence, making the fullest allowance in favour of the plaintiffs of the uncertainties known to be involved in any apportionment. In the end, notwithstanding all the care lavished on it by the scientists and by counsel I believe that it has to be regarded as a jury question, and I propose to approach it as such."

In *Holtby v Brigham & Cowan (Hull) Ltd* [2000] 3 All ER 421, Stuart-Smith LJ approved the approach of Mustill J, and said this in paragraph 20:

"In reality I do not think that these cases should be determined on onus of proof. The question should be whether at the end of the day and on consideration of all the evidence the claimant has proved that the defendants are responsible for the whole or a quantifiable part of his disability. The question of quantification may be difficult and the court only has to do the best it can using its common sense ..."

The touchstone is therefore whether a quantifiable part of the injury can be attributed to the defendant's negligence. Often this is turned on its head, to ask whether a quantifiable part of the injury would have occurred in any event.

In *Telles v South West Strategic Health Authority*,[34] the newborn claimant suffered damaging hypoxia in the first week of life due in part to a negligent cardiac shunt procedure. The expert evidence was that, although some damaging hypoxia would have occurred prior to the operation (ie without negligence), there was no way in which that amount of damage could be calculated or quantified separately to the whole period, and it was unlikely that the damage would have occurred equally over the whole period. Saunders J

---

[32]   Except as reserved in mesothelioma cases by the Compensation Act 2006.
[33]   [2005] EWCA Civ 561, per Neuberger LJ as he then was at paras [35]–[36].
[34]   [2008] EWHC 292 (QB).

found, with the agreement of the parties, that the claimant was entitled to recover in full where the portion of damage which would have occurred without negligence was unquantifiable. The same approach can be seen in the context of psychiatric injury in *Hartman v South Essex Mental Health & Community Care NHS Trust*.[35]

The question whether a quantifiable part of the injury can be identified leads directly to a consideration of the divisibility or indivisibility of injury. That is because, where an injury is divisible, there is likely to be a quantifiable proportion that can be attributed to the breach of duty, and that will be the only amount for which the defendant can be justly held liable.

The application of this 'jury question' to discount damages to reflect the non-tortious element(s) of damage can be seen in the industrial disease,[36] occupational stress,[37] and sexual abuse contexts.[38]

Examples in the clinical negligence context from recent years include *Ingram v Williams* and *Wright (A Child) v Cambridge Medical Group*.[39] *Ingram* was a cerebral palsy case brought against the claimant's GP for failing to identify a rupture of the membranes and refer accordingly. The claim failed on its facts but HHJ Walker went on to address (*obiter* and expressly briefly) the position on causation. The expert evidence was that several cumulative factors (prematurity, birth outside hospital, neonatal infection) made unquantifiable contributions to the injury. The injury was not divisible on the evidence and recovery would in principle have been in full. By contrast, the delayed GP referral in *Wright* led to avoidable pain and suffering during the period of delay, but this was divisible from the permanent hip injury which the claimant went on to suffer following further negligence at hospital. The negligent hospital treatment was not so egregious as to break the chain of causation, but the injury which the GP had caused could be separately quantified.

The courts' attempts to do justice in cases of material contribution to a divisible injury may fairly be seen to reflect the approach adopted in the *Fairchild*-type cases. There, following *Barker v Corus Plc* and subject to the statutory reversal in mesothelioma cases,[40] the defendant who has materially contributed to the risk of harm will only be liable to the extent of his contribution. In both

---

[35] [2005] EWCA Civ 6.
[36] *Thompson v Smiths Ship Repairers (North Shields) Ltd* [1984] QB 405; *Holtby v Brigham & Cowan (Hull) Ltd* [2000] 3 All ER 421; *Rugby Joinery Ltd v Whitfield* [2005] EWCA Civ 561; *Gerard-Reynolds v Brent LBC* [2006] CLY 2921.
[37] *Hatton v Sutherland* [2002] 2 All ER 1 at [35]–[42]. This aspect of the Court of Appeal decision is unaffected by the House of Lords decision in *Barber v Somerset County Council* [2004] UKHL 13. This approach was applied in *Garrod v North Devon NHS PCT* [2006] EWHC 850 (QB).
[38] *C v D* [2006] EWHC 166 (QB) at 1020.
[39] [2010] EWHC 758 (QB) and [2011] EWCA Civ 669 respectively.
[40] [2006] 2 AC 572. See s 3 of the Compensation Act 2006.

circumstances, the common law does not hold a defendant liable for the totality of injury or risk where the breach of duty relates only to an identifiable portion of that injury or risk.

8.7   THE EGGSHELL SKULL PRINCIPLE AND SECOND TORTS

It is a well-established principle that the defendant must take the claimant as he finds him. Therefore, if the claimant is particularly vulnerable to injury, this will not absolve the defendant of liability, except in relation to psychiatric injury where he is treated as a 'secondary victim'.[41]

It follows therefore that where the claimant is susceptible to psychiatric injury but is a 'primary victim' he can recover provided the accident made a material contribution to the injury, notwithstanding the susceptibility.[42]

However, when it comes to the assessment of damages, the physical or psychological frailties of the claimant are relevant and will be taken into account by the court.[43]

This rule becomes problematic where there is a second tortious event and there is then a question of whether the second tortfeasor's action eclipses the responsibility of the first tortfeasor.

The rules in this context can be stated as follows:

*   Where an indivisible injury has been caused by two concurrent tortfeasors, the claimant may elect to sue only one tortfeasor and recover all damages from that tortfeasor.[44]

*   Where a divisible injury is caused by two concurrent or consecutive tortfeasors, each is only liable for the damage each has caused. Where the torts are consecutive, apportionment will be determined on the basis of what the two tortfeasors should be justly held responsible for, having

---

[41]   See *Alcock v South Yorkshire Chief Constable* [1992] 1 AC 310 where Lord Oliver introduced the concepts of 'primary' and 'secondary' victim, and laid down control mechanisms for limiting the ability of secondary victims to recover for psychiatric illness.

[42]   See *Page v Smith* where Otton J [as he then was] invoked the accident as a material contributor to the causation of the claimant's chronic fatigue syndrome. This sits uncomfortably with the approach of the Court of Appeal in other psychiatric damage cases: *Page v Smith (No 2)* [1996] 1 WLR 855 at 857H–858F. It is to be wondered how one can have a material contribution to a recrudescence of pre-existing pathology where the other factors (underlying pathology and other life events) stood as alternative causes, unless they operated in combination. It is too wondered why the but for test was not applied in these circumstances. For a similar approach, see the judgment of Evans LJ in *Vernon v Bosley (No 1)* [1997] 1 All ER 577 at 604E–605A; *Farrell v Merton, Sutton and Wandsworth Health Authority* (2000) 57 BMLR 158; *Donachie v Chief Constable of Greater Manchester Police* [2004] EWCA Civ 405.

[43]   See n 37 above in relation to psychiatric injury cases. In relation to physical injury cases: see *Kenth v Heimdale Hotel Investment Ltd* [2001] EWCA Civ 1283 at [36]–[41], applied in *Smithurst v Sealant Construction Services Ltd* [2011] EWCA Civ 1277 at [11], [13]–[16], [22]–[23].

[44]   See *Clerk and Lindsell on Torts* (Sweet & Maxwell, 20th edition at para 4-02.

regard to the nature of the duty of care. Gross supervening negligence will break the chain of causation, but not otherwise.[45]

Difficult questions of causation arise where there are successive torts causing a divisible injury, or different injuries that causally interact. The claimant in such a circumstance would be well advised to sue both defendants on the ground that he can only recover for that part of the injury and consequential damage for which each defendant is liable.

If it were an indivisible injury, he ought to be able to sue one defendant, leaving that defendant to its rights under the Civil Liability (Contribution) Act 1978.

In *Rahman*,[46] the Court of Appeal was confronted with a claimant who had been injured as a result of his employer's negligence suffering an eye injury and a psychological injury. Both injuries were then compounded by the hospital's subsequent negligence which resulted in the claimant being rendered blind in one eye. The court concluded that both defendants were liable for different damage and the 1978 Act did not apply.

The employer could not treat the negligence of the hospital as an intervening event (in the absence of gross negligence) and the hospital's liability could not be enlarged on the basis that by the time the claimant reached the hospital he had an eggshell personality.

Each defendant could only be made liable for that which the court considered it was justly held to be responsible.

How such an assessment is to be made is not clear from the judgment.[47] In *Webb v Barclays Bank*, the Court of Appeal specifically concluded that where a second tort causes further injury affecting the consequences of the original tort, the chain of causation will only be broken where that second tort amounts to gross negligence.[48] The court was there concerned with clinical negligence following on from an employer negligence case.

---

[45] *Rahman v Arearose Ltd* [2001] QB 351 at [26]–[33]. Similarly, different causal rules may apply where further secondary damage is caused by the independent act of the claimant. The issue will then arise whether that has been caused by the primary injury in law and in fact: *Corr v IBC Vehicles Ltd* [2006] EWCA Civ 331 at [45–49], [77], upheld by the House of Lords at [2008] UKHL 13. Where two separate successive claims are made because the two torts happen at different points in time, the court trying the second claim will be most reluctant to make an award on a basis inconsistent with the first claim where this allows for double recovery, but where matters have taken a turn for the worse since the first claim, the court may have regard to the fact in assessing damages against the second defendant: *Murrell v Healy* [2001] EWCA Civ 486 at [18]–[23].

[46] *Rahman Ibid.*

[47] *Rahman Ibid*, at [26]–[33]. See also the related discussion in *Heil v Rankin (No 2)* [2001] QB 272.

[48] *Webb v Barclays Bank* [2001] EWCA Civ 1141 at [53]–[56].

A typical example of clinical negligence following on from clinical negligence is *Wright (A Child) v Cambridge Medical Group*.[49] The claimant's GP partnership was liable for a delayed referral to hospital, and the hospital for negligent treatment. The claim was brought only against the GP partnership. The claimant argued that, once it was established that the GP's negligence had caused some injury, damages could be recovered in full. The Court of Appeal, following *Rahman*, held that the hospital's negligence was not so egregious as to break the chain of causation, but the pain and suffering caused by the delayed referral was divisible from the permanent hip injury finally sustained. The GP was only liable for the former.

However, it is plain, subject to issues of remoteness, that where as a result of a primary injury for which the defendant is liable the claimant has to undergo medical treatment which non-negligently goes disastrously wrong resulting in devastating secondary damage, the defendant remains liable for all the consequences of the primary injury.[50]

TOP TIPS

- It is vital to approach a causation problem by principled analysis.
- Questions of what did happen (past fact) are judged on the balance of probabilities.
- A finding as to a future event is not judged as a matter of probability but one of chance.
- Once it has been shown that 'primary injury' has been caused by the negligence, the question of causation of losses attributed to that primary injury belongs in the realm of assessment of damages. Not all losses are required to be proved on the balance of probability to result in an award of damages.
- Where there are cumulative causes of injury and it is impossible to quantify the probability of injury in the absence of negligence, it is sufficient to prove a material contribution to injury. The claimant will then recover in full unless a divisible and quantifiable proportion of the injury attributable to negligence can be ascertained.
- Where the claimant is susceptible to psychiatric injury but is a 'primary victim', he can recover provided the accident made a material contribution to the injury, notwithstanding the susceptibility.

---

[49] [2011] EWCA Civ 669.
[50] See *Robinson v Post Office* [1974] 1 WLR 1176 where the claimant suffered a minor injury as a result of the negligence of the defendant. He required an anti-tetanus injection, which resulted in a serious reaction and secondary brain damage. The defendant was liable for the brain damage.

CHAPTER 9

LIMITATION

In this chapter Michael Mylonas QC, Fiona Neale and Tim Meakin, all experienced clinical negligence counsel, explore the law, practice and pitfalls of limitation: one of the key areas of uncertainty and a potential trap in any clinical negligence investigation. First, Michael Mylonas QC explores the law; then Fiona Neale reviews date of knowledge and, finally, Tim Meakin considers how the primary limitation period may be extended using s 33 discretion. The chapter has been updated by junior counsel, Aaron Rathmell.

9.1 LIMITATION AND CLAIMS INVOLVING PERSONAL INJURY

The Limitation Act 1980 sets up the statutory framework within which limitation issues are adjudicated. By s 2 of the Act the limitation period in claims founded in tort is 6 years from the date on which the cause of action accrues. However, in actions which include a claim for personal injuries, s 11 halves that period to 3 years.

Ascertaining the point in time when the limitation clock starts to run is dealt with elsewhere in this chapter.[1] However, once a claim includes an element of recompense for personal injury the shorter 3-year period applies to the entirety of the claim.

Consideration of limitation issues is a critical part of the assessment of any claim. In actions alleging personal injury the position is significantly more flexible than in most other areas both because of the arguments that can be raised about date of knowledge and because of the availability of the discretionary remedy under s 33 of the Limitation Act 1980 to disapply the debarring provisions of the Act.

On a practical basis there are several good reasons for analysing limitation issues very carefully from the outset.

---

[1] See **9.8**.

9.1.1 Litigation risk

In an environment where proceedings are generally funded by conditional fee agreements (CFAs) an early and informed assessment of risk will be a critical part of the decision as to whether a case should be accepted. A carefully documented analysis of risk will be useful support against any attacks that might subsequently be made on high success fees.

9.1.2 Case planning for claimants

For those instructed on behalf of claimants an early awareness of the risks raised by potential limitation arguments will allow proper collation of evidence and case preparation so as to minimise those risks and perhaps result in the defendant formally dropping a limitation defence.

Where limitation is in issue then all facts and matters relevant to the arguments should be investigated and the claimant's case on limitation should be clearly and forcefully advanced in the pre-action protocol correspondence and the particulars of claim. A defendant is significantly more likely to give up a limitation defence if it appreciates early on that the chances of successfully running such a case are small.

9.1.3 Case planning for defendants

Raising a successful limitation defence is often significantly harder than it is for a claimant to overcome such a defence. Even if the defendant establishes that the claim has been issued outside the primary limitation period the courts are often willing to exercise the s 33 discretion. Once again, early attention to all relevant evidential matters will pay dividends.

The establishment of prejudice (forensic, rather than financial)[2] is often the defendant's strongest argument once the s 33 discretion has been invoked. The court will not be sympathetic to a defendant who alleges prejudice but has delayed investigation despite notification of a claim.

At the same time, once all facts and matters relevant to both date of knowledge and discretion arguments have been obtained they should be advanced clearly in the protocol correspondence and defence. Even if this does not succeed in dissuading a claimant from continuing further it is likely to result in the claimant's advisers allowing a significantly larger discount for the litigation risks associated with such arguments.

---

[2]   *Cain v Francis, McKay v Hamlani* [2008] EWCA Civ 1451, [2009] QB 754, [2009] 3 WLR 551, [2009] 2 All ER 579, [2009] CP Rep 19, [2009] LS Law Medical 82.

9.2 DISABILITY – MEANING AND EFFECT

Where a claimant is acting under a 'disability' as defined by the Limitation Act then important consequences flow for limitation purposes. The relevant sections of the Act are set out below:

Section 28(1) of the Act provides that:

> 'Subject to the following provisions of this section, if on the date when any right of action accrued for which a period of limitation is prescribed by this Act, the person to whom it accrued was under a disability, the action may be brought at any time before the expiration of six years from the date when he ceased to be under a disability or died (whichever first occurred) notwithstanding that the period of limitation has expired.'

Section 28(6) provides that:

> 'If the action is one to which section 11 or 12(2) of this Act applies, subsection (1) above shall have effect as if for the words "six years" there were substituted the words "three years".'

Finally, s 38(2) states:

> 'For the purposes of this Act a person shall be treated as under a disability while he is an infant, or lacks capacity (within the meaning of the Mental Capacity Act 2005) to conduct legal proceedings.'

9.2.1 Minors

Where a claim is brought on behalf of a minor the limitation period does not run until his 18th birthday, unless he or she lacks capacity for some other reason.

9.2.2 Mental incapacity

Where a claimant lacks capacity for the purposes of legal proceedings then limitation will not start to run until capacity is recovered. This question is determined by reference to the Mental Capacity Act 2005 (MCA 2005).

Persons are presumed by s 1 of the MCA 2005 to have capacity, unless it is established otherwise. Section 2 provides:

> 'For the purposes of this Act, a person lacks capacity in relation to a matter if at the material time he is unable to make a decision for himself in relation to the matter because of an impairment of, or a disturbance in the functioning of, the mind or brain.'

In the case of a severely brain injured claimant or one suffering from an untreatable mental illness then it is unlikely that capacity will ever be recovered and limitation issues are unlikely to trouble the parties. However, where the mental state of the claimant is not so clearly defined then early commission of a psychiatric review would be advised together with continuing reviews if it is thought that the claimant's mental capacity is likely to alter in the future.

Practitioners will therefore have to apply the correct legal test under MCA 2005 with the benefit of supportive expert evidence in order to argue successfully that the claimant lacks mental capacity to litigate and is therefore a protected party against whom the limitation period does not run.

9.3   ASSAULT AND TRESPASS CASES

In *Stubbings v Webb*[3] the House of Lords held that claims in respect of deliberate assault or trespass to the person were not included within the definition of an 'action for damages for negligence, nuisance or breach of duty'. Instead they lay as simple claims in tort.

That finding had three important ramifications:
- the limitation period was covered by s 2 of the Act;
- the primary limitation period was 6 years as opposed to the 3 years applicable to personal injury claims under ss 11–14; and
- since the discretion to disapply the limitation period provided by s 33 (see below) did not apply to s 2, the 6-year period was not extendable in any circumstances.

Stubbings v Webb confirmed, in effect, an arguably unjust and prejudicial interpretation of the legislation which often affected those who most justified the exercise of a discretion to disapply the limitation period.

The class of victims whose claims were therefore caught by s 2 included both minors and adults who had been subject to physical and emotional abuse. Often those claimants were victims of a serial assailant or abuser. There is a readily understandable reluctance on the part of some victims to make disclosures unless and until they are made aware of disclosures by others against the perpetrator. In those circumstances a significant number of claimants who only brought their claims outside the 6-year limitation period found themselves debarred.

In 1995 the Law Commission was tasked with reviewing the position.[4] Its report was not made public until 2001 and recommended[5] that the problems described above could be avoided by a simple reform which provided the trial judge with a discretion similar to that provided by s 33.

---

[3]   [1993] AC 498.
[4]   The Law Commission's Sixth Programme of Law Reform (1995), Law Com No 234.
[5]   Limitation of Actions (2001) Law Com No 270.

On 16 July 2002 the Lord Chancellor indicated in a parliamentary written answer that the government accepted the recommendation. In February 2003 the Court of Appeal endorsed the proposed reform when, in the course of *KR v Bryn Alyn Community Ltd*[6] Auld LJ noted the Law Commission's recommendation:

> '... that claims for personal injuries, including those of child abuse, whether in trespass to the person or in negligence, should be subject to the same core regime of an extendable three years limitation period with discretion to disapply ... For what it is worth, we warmly commend such a proposal. Early statutory implementation of it would obviate much arid and highly wasteful litigation turning on a distinction of no apparent principle or other merit.'

However, in the case of *A v Hoare*[7] (a series of conjoined appeals) the House of Lords held that their earlier decision in *Stubbings v Webb* was wrong insofar as it asserted that s 11 of the Limitation Act 1980 applied only to cases of accidentally caused personal injury. Lord Hoffmann commented that the focus placed by the decision in *Stubbings* upon the division between accidental and intentional injury had led to increasingly artificial attempts to try to circumvent its effects. Their Lordships departed from the previous decision[8] and allowed claims brought substantially outside the limitation period.

The effect of this decision is that claimants can bring cases for compensation as a result of intentional injury such as sexual and physical abuse many years after the events, provided that a court considers that a fair trial is still possible. It will now be possible for claimants to rely upon the discretion given to the court under s 33 of the Limitation Act 1980 in order to persuade the court to disapply the provisions of that Act. There remains, however, a considerable degree of uncertainty as to how the courts will treat cases brought many years after the event where there is no relevant conviction and where defendants have real difficulties in mounting a defence because of the passage of time.

9.4 LIMITATION AND THE HUMAN RIGHTS ACT 1998

9.4.1 Time-limits for applications

The general procedural expectation is that a litigant will bring a claim based on existing remedies in order to enforce a European Convention on Human Rights ('the Convention') right in a UK court. However, a free-standing claim can be brought under s 7 of the Human Rights Act 1998 (HRA 1998). As to the time-limit for bringing such claims s 7(5) of HRA 1998 states that the

---

[6] [2003] EWCA Civ 85, [2003] QB 1441 at para 100.

[7] *A v Hoare, C (FC) v Middlesbrough Council, X (FC) and another (FC) v London Borough of Wandsworth (Conjoined Appeals), H (FC) v Suffolk County Council, Young (FC) v Catholic Care (Diocese of Leeds)* [2008] UKHL 6; [2008] 1 AC 844; [2008] 2 WLR 311; [2008] 2 All ER 1.

[8] In accordance with the *Practice Statement (Judicial Precedent)* [1966] 1 WLR 1234.

limitation period against a public body is initially set at one year from the date of the act(s) or omission(s) founding the complaint in question, but that the court has the power to extend time:

> 'Proceedings under subs (1)(a) must be brought before the end of –
> (a)   the period of one year beginning with the date on which the act complained of took place; or
> (b)   such longer period as the court or tribunal considers equitable having regard to all the circumstances.'

In the case of *Rabone v Pennine Care NHS Trust* the Supreme Court held:[9]

> 'The court has a wide discretion in determining whether it is equitable to extend time in the particular circumstances of the case. It will often be appropriate to take into account factors of the type listed in section 33(3) of the Limitation Act 1980 as being relevant when deciding whether to extend time for a domestic law action in respect of personal injury or death ... However, I agree with what the Court of Appeal said in *Dunn v Parole Board* [2009] 1 WLR 728, paras 31, 43 and 48 that the words of section 7(5)(b) of the HRA mean what they say and the court should not attempt to rewrite them. There can be no question of interpreting section 7(5)(b) as if it contained the language of section 33(3) of the Limitation Act 1980.'

(See the discussion of s 33 of the Limitation Act 1980 below.)

If an application is made to the European Court of Human Rights after domestic legal processes have been exhausted the time-limits are different to those under HRA 1998 stated above.

Assuming that a domestic remedy exists for a party to the litigation, an application to the European Court of Human Rights has to be made within a strictly defined period: within 6 months of the date of the judgment, or notification of the same (known as 'the 6 month rule') which has the effect of exhausting the final domestic remedy.

Time starts running on the date of final judgment (or notification to the applicant) and will only stop running when notification of the application is made to the court. This time-limit cannot be waived by the court or the other party to the application. However the rule will not apply where:

(a)   the applicant has used an ineffective remedy; or

(b)   where the alleged breach is continuing.

9.4.2   Article 6 and the Limitation Act 1980

By s 3 of HRA 1998 primary legislation and subordinate legislation must be read and given effect in a way which is compatible with the Convention rights. Section 3 therefore in principle entitles a court to reappraise the interpretation

---

9   [2012] UKSC 2, [2012] 2 AC 72, per Lord Dyson JSC at para 75.

of Limitation Act 1980 so that it is compliant with Convention rights. Against that background the issue is whether the imposition of time-limits for personal injury claims (and in particular ss 2 and 11 of the Limitation Act) offend against Convention rights. In short, the case-law and analysis set out below demonstrates that, to date, the Limitation Act 1980 has been held to be compliant with the Convention.

The main application of human rights law in the context of limitation is Art 6,[10] which states that:

> 'In the determination of his civil rights and obligations ... everyone is entitled to a fair and public hearing within a reasonable time by an independent and impartial tribunal established by law.'

Essentially the entitlement under Art 6 is a right of access to the court.[11] It has been argued that to deny a favourable exercise of the discretion under s 33 would be to adopt an unfair and disproportionate approach. This argument has failed to find success with the courts (both domestic and the European Court). It was specifically rejected in the context of a claim under the Fatal Accidents Act 1976 which considered the application of s 12 of the Limitation Act 1980 in the context of HRA 1998, s 3.[12]

The rationale for upholding the Limitation Act 1980 was based on *Stubbings v UK*.[13] As we have seen[14] the House of Lords in *Stubbings v Webb*[15] had held that in the case of deliberate assaults (including sexual assaults) any civil action fell outside of the ambit of s 11 of the Limitation Act 1980 and so was governed by the 6-year limitation period under s 2. The limitation period in such cases could not be extended under s 14 irrespective of a claimant's knowledge of injury and there was no discretion under s 33 to extend the limitation period. On appeal to the Strasbourg Court it was argued on behalf of the appellant that this ruling violated Art 6 as the 6-year limitation period did not pursue a legitimate aim and/or was disproportionate. That was rejected and it was held that the 6-year limitation period did not violate Art 6. The immediate problem caused by the judgment in *Stubbings* has of course now been alleviated by the judgment in *Hoare*.[16]

In *Ashingdane v United Kingdom*[17] the Court ruled, in summary, as follows:

(1) The right to institute proceedings is not absolute and can be subject to limitations.

---

10 Article 8 (respect for private life) has been relied upon but is probably, at best, of tangential relevance.
11 *Ashingdane v United Kingdom* (1985) 7 EHRR 528.
12 See *Thompson et al v Arnold* [2007] EWHC 1875.
13 (1997) 23 EHRR 213.
14 See **9.3.**
15 [1999] 3 AC 498.
16 See **9.3.**
17 (1985) 7 EHRR 528.

(2) The right of access can be regulated by the state and the contracting states enjoy a certain margin of appreciation.

(3) As long as the limitations do not restrict or reduce access left to the individual in such a way that the right is impaired then the Convention's requirements are observed.

(4) In addition limitation is not incompatible with Art 6(1) if it pursues a legitimate aim and there is a reasonable relationship of proportionality between the means employed and the aim achieved.

(5) Limitation periods in personal injury actions are a common feature of domestic legal systems of contracting states and they serve important purposes. In particular they provide finality and certainty in litigation.

There is therefore no necessary incompatibility between domestic law under the Limitation Act 1980 and Convention rights.

9.5   PRODUCTS: CONSUMER PROTECTION ACT 1987[18]

A claim may be brought for a defective product under the Consumer Protection Act 1987 (the 1987 Act). Under s 1(1) of the 1987 Act various persons are potentially liable for the damage (including injury: s 5(1)) caused wholly or partly by a defect in the product and this includes producers of the product. Liability is strict but subject to a number of defences set out in s 4 of the 1987 Act. The 1987 Act is therefore of particular relevance to the clinical negligence practitioner in relation to claims brought for defective medical products (for example, breast implants) and claims against pharmaceutical companies in relation to drugs and vaccines.

Conventional limitation periods apply to claims for defective products, namely the claimant has 3 years to bring a claim, based on the accrual of the cause of action, or if later, then his or her knowledge of it. In the case of a personal injury action based on defective products, the court has a discretion to override the 3-year limitation period. Section 6(6) of the 1987 Act amends the Limitation Act 1980 and it inserts a new s 11A which in turn amends ss 12(1), 14, 28, 32 and 33 of the 1980 Act.

However, in addition, s 11A(1) of the 1980 Act applies exclusively to an action for damages by virtue of Part 1 of the 1987 Act and under that section any claim is extinguished 10 years from the time the product was put into circulation whether or not the cause of action has accrued. In contrast to the 3-year limitation period, the 10-year ('long stop') period even applies if the claimant is under a disability (s 11A(3)). Furthermore, the 10-year period cannot be disapplied under s 33. This reform was necessitated by Art 11 of Council Directive 85/374/EEC on the approximation of the laws, regulations and administrative provisions of the Member States concerning liability for defective products.

---

[18]   See Chapter 10.

9.6 AMENDMENTS OUTSIDE THE LIMITATION PERIOD

A claimant may commence an action against a party only subsequently to discover, out of time, that another party is the proper defendant. In seeking to rectify such an error, reference must be made to the provisions of the Civil Procedure Rules and the Limitation Act 1980 as to the strict criteria to be applied.

Under the 1980 Act there is a power to amend statements of case to add and/or substitute parties outside the limitation period. Where the wrong defendant has been sued and the limitation period has expired then the court has a discretionary power to correct the mistake under CPR 19.5 and s 35 of the 1980 Act.

Where the limitation period was current at the commencement of proceedings, but has since expired, then genuine mistakes (ie where the identity of the defendant was not in question) will usually be rectified if deemed necessary for the proceedings to continue.[19] However, once outside the limitation period any such order is discretionary and so proper grounds must be demonstrated applying the criteria contained in s 33 of the 1980 Act.

Again, the position in relation to Consumer Protection Act 1987 claims against producers of defective products warrants special consideration, in light of Art 11 of Directive 85/374/EEC.

In *O'Byrne v Aventis Pasteur MSD Ltd*[20] the claimant was initially successful in substituting a UK vaccine distributor (which he had mistakenly sued first) for its French parent company producer (who was sued out of time). On appeal to the Supreme Court however the appellant was successful in resisting substitution. In accordance with the case-law of the Court of Justice of the European Union on Art 11 of the Directive, the Supreme Court held that substitution of parties could not be made after the expiry of the 10-year limitation. The only way the claimant could have succeeded was if the parent company had directed when the subsidiary (sued within the time-limit) put the product in question into circulation. The fact that the existing defendant was a wholly owned subsidiary of the proposed defendant did not determine that question.

9.7 LIMITATION AND THE FATAL ACCIDENTS ACT 1976

The 1980 Act also places limitations upon claimants seeking to make a claim under the Fatal Accidents Act 1976 (FAA 1976). Section 12(1) provides:

---

[19] *Sion v Hampstead Health Authority* [1994] 5 Med LR 170; *Welsh Development Agency v Redpath Dorman Long Ltd* [1994] 1 WLR 1409.
[20] [2010] UKSC 23, [2010] 1 WLR 1412.

'An action under the Fatal Accidents Act 1976 shall not be brought if the death occurred when the person injured could no longer maintain an action and recover damages in respect of the injury (whether because of a time limit in this Act or in any other Act, or for any other reason). Where any such action by the injured person would have been barred by the time limit in section 11 or 11A of this Act, no account shall be taken of the possibility of that time limit being overridden under section 33 of this Act.'

Section 12(1) therefore ensures that a defendant will be in no worse a position as against a dependant or other person suing under FAA 1976 than would have been the case if the original victim was still alive. In fact a defendant is likely to be in a significantly stronger position under a FAA 1976 claim because the dependants cannot ask the court to exercise the s 33 discretion and disapply the limitation period.

Section 12(2) of the Act provides:

'None of the time limits given in the preceding provisions of this Act shall apply to an action under the Fatal Accidents Act 1976, but no such action shall be brought after the expiration of three years from –
(a)   the date of death; or
(b)   the date of knowledge of the person for whose benefit the action is brought;

whichever is the later.'

Section 12(2) introduces a two-fold test for establishing the latest time by which a claim may be brought on behalf of a dependant. If the deceased passed away prior to the expiration of limitation, the three-year period for the claim by their dependant starts from the date of death or the date of knowledge of the dependant. It is particularly interesting to note the way in which the second limb of the test allows a dependant to rely upon his own date of knowledge.

9.8   DATE OF KNOWLEDGE

The commencement of the 3-year limitation period for a personal injury action is either the date of the accrual of the cause of action, or, if later, the date of knowledge of the injured person.[21]

9.8.1   The statutory provisions

Section 14 of the Limitation Act 1980 defines the date of knowledge as follows:

'(1) ... in sections 11 and 12 of this Act references to a person's date of knowledge are references to the date on which he first had knowledge of the following facts –

(a)   that the injury in question was significant; and
(b)   that the injury was attributable in whole or in part to the act or omission which is alleged to constitute negligence, nuisance or breach of duty; and

---

[21]   Limitation Act 1980, s 11(4).

(c) the identity of the defendant; and

(d) if it is alleged that the act or omission was that of a person other than the defendant, the identity of that person and the additional facts supporting the bringing of an action against the defendant;

and knowledge that any acts or omissions did or did not, as a matter of law, involve negligence, nuisance or breach of duty is irrelevant.

(2) For the purposes of this section an injury is significant if the person whose date of knowledge is in question would reasonably have considered it sufficiently serious to justify his instituting proceedings for damages against a defendant who did not dispute liability and was able to satisfy a judgment.

(3) For the purposes of this section a person's knowledge includes knowledge which he might reasonably have been expected to acquire –

(a) from facts observable or ascertainable by him; or

(b) from facts ascertainable by him with the help of medical or other appropriate expert advice which it is reasonable for him to seek;

but a person shall not be fixed under this subsection with knowledge of a fact ascertainable only with the help of expert advice so long as he has taken all reasonable steps to obtain (and, where appropriate, to act on) that advice.'

Section 14(1) describes what is conventionally termed 'actual knowledge'.

Section 14(3) describes 'constructive knowledge'.

9.8.2 Utility of these provisions

A claimant who can bring himself within the provisions of s 11(4), by satisfying the requirements of s 14, can start his claim outside the 3-year primary limitation period as of right.

This is useful in particular in the following situations:

- where a claimant has been injured by exposure to a dangerous substance (eg chemicals, radioactive materials) but the consequences have not been apparent until much later;

- where a claimant has had a poor outcome from medical treatment, but has not known why this was so;

- where a claimant has not known which of several candidates was responsible for injuring him.

9.8.3 Approach to these provisions

It is never safe to assume that, because a claimant is genuine when he says, 'I didn't know I had a claim', s 14 will assist him.

Case-law has been gradually moving against a laxer, more claimant-friendly approach, in favour of a stricter construction.[22]

The Court of Appeal in *McCoubrey v Ministry of Defence*,[23] considering a claim involving s 14(2), held:

> 'Given that a claimant who can successfully invoke sections 11(1)(b) and 14 is able to extend his limitation period, possibly by many years ... as of right, it seems to me that it should be relatively narrowly construed, bearing in mind that such a claimant will always have the possibility of a fall-back position in the form of section 33 ... I would have thought that a construction of section 14 which minimises the number of cases would be more likely to be correct than one which carried with it the implication of many such cases.'

9.8.4   Burden of proof

Following the adage, 'he who asserts must prove', the onus is on the claimant to plead and prove the date of knowledge he contends for. If the defendant contends for an earlier date, the onus is on him to prove this.

It is for the defendant to prove constructive knowledge.[24]

Litigants should urge trial judges to address and make findings on all of the elements that arise under s 14. The importance of this was made clear by the Court of Appeal in *Furniss v Firth Brown Tools Ltd*.[25] The claimant alleged noise-induced hearing loss against his former employer. Because of the progressive nature of that condition, and the fact that it overlapped with an ear wax problem and the claimant's advancing age, there was real uncertainty as to when the claimant realised the significance of his injury.

That plainly worked to the disadvantage of the defendant, as Smith LJ was forced to hold:

> '[27] If I were asked to consider whether there was a date by which I could properly hold that the appellant had knowledge that his injury was significant (as defined by section 14(2)), I would say that it would be difficult to reach any firm conclusion; the point was not sufficiently explored in evidence. Accordingly, because the burden of proof under section 14 lies on the respondent, I conclude that that burden has not been discharged. The defence under sections 11 and 14 has not been made out.'

---

22   See *Forbes v Wandsworth Health Authority* [1997] QB 402; *Adams v Bracewell Forest Borough Council* [2004] UKHL 29.

23   [2007] EWCA Civ 17, judgment of Neuberger LJ, Ward LJ and Tugendhat J concurring.

24   *Nash v Eli Lilly & Co* [1993] 1 WLR 782 (CA); *Forbes v Wandsworth Health Authority* [1997] QB 402.

25   *Furniss v Firth Brown Tools Ltd* [2008] EWCA Civ 182.

9.9 COMPONENTS OF KNOWLEDGE

9.9.1 Knowledge of what?

Section 14(1) clearly lists the matters in respect of which knowledge is required:
- that the injury in question was significant;
- that it was attributable to the act or omission alleged to constitute negligence;
- the identity of the defendant (including, if appropriate, such facts as make him vicariously liable for the acts or omissions of another person).

No other knowledge is required. In particular, it cannot be stressed too much, knowledge that any acts or omissions did or did not constitute negligence, nuisance or breach of duty is irrelevant.

9.9.2 Significant injury

9.9.2.1 *The injury*

Sometimes, the injury is obvious from the start. It may, however present more insidiously. In *Roberts v Winbow*[26] the Court of Appeal considered the case where the main injury complained of (an oesophageal stricture) was preceded by a short period of severe illness. It was held that the latter on its own constituted a significant injury sufficient to start the clock.

A claimant may not discount what would objectively be considered as an injury, in the belief that it is normal, or properly caused.[27] This can pose particular problems where the 'injury' masquerades as the inevitable after-effect of necessary medical treatment, but in considering this component of knowledge, it is important to remember that it is not knowledge of the cause which is in issue.

In *Briggs v Pitt Payne*[28] the claimant argued that he had no knowledge of significant injury (serious side-effects from valium prescriptions) until he knew that the side-effects were not justified by a positive therapeutic corollary. The Court of Appeal declined to differentiate misprescription cases from others, and held that there was no justification for the benefit-deficit equation for which the claimant contended.

---

[26] [1999] Lloyd's LR Med 31 (CA).
[27] *Dobbie v Medway Health Authority* [1994] 1 WLR 1234 (CA).
[28] [1999] Lloyd's LR Med 1 (CA).

9.9.2.2 'Significant'

The word significant is, 'directed solely to the quantum of the injury, and not to the plaintiff's evaluation of its cause, nature or usualness ...'.[29]

The value of the claim does not need to be very high to qualify as significant. In *Roberts v Winbow*,[30] the Court of Appeal was, in late 1998, prepared to assume that a claim where general damages were worth less than £2,000 would be significant.

It is the injury itself which is to be considered, and not its effect, or perceived effect, on a claimant's private life or career.[31] As in the case of *Furniss v Firth Brown Tools Ltd* discussed above, this may not be simple in the case of progressive conditions, which simply bother a claimant at first, but acquire significance with time.

9.9.2.3 An objective test

For some years the question of knowledge of significant injury was perceived as a part-subjective, part-objective test:[32]

'Taking that plaintiff, with that plaintiff's intelligence, would he have been reasonable in considering the injury not sufficiently serious to justify instituting proceedings for damages?'

This approach was adopted in a number of subsequent cases, including *KR v Bryn Alyn Community (Holdings) Ltd*,[33] where the test was described as 'partly subjective'.

However, in 2004, the House of Lords in *Adams v Bracknell Forest BC*[34] held that the test in respect of constructive knowledge under s 14(3) was an objective one.

In *Catholic Care (Diocese of Leeds) v Young*[35] the Court of Appeal held that the part-subjective approach to s 14(2) could not survive after the decision in *Adams*: logic and consistency required the same approach to be taken in both. Dyson LJ summarised the result:

'... the claimant is to be assumed to be a person who has suffered the injury in question, but in all other respects he is to be assumed simply to be a reasonable person. In determining whether a claimant had knowledge which he might reasonably be expected to acquire, the court has to consider how a reasonable

---

29 *Dobbie v Medway Health Authority* [1994] 1 WLR 1234 (CA).
30 [1999] Lloyd's LR Med 31 (CA).
31 *McCoubrey v Ministry of Defence* [2007] EWCA Civ 17.
32 *McCafferty v Metropolitan Police District Receiver* [1977] 1 WLR 1073 (CA).
33 [2003] EWCA Civ 85.
34 [2004] UKHL 29.
35 [2006] EWCA Civ 1534.

person in the situation of the claimant would have acted, save that ... aspects of character or intelligence peculiar to the claimant are to be disregarded. On the other hand, if the injury affects the claimant's ability to acquire knowledge or to seek expert advice, these are matters that can be taken into account. But in all other respects, the claimant is to be regarded simply as a reasonable person. Thus, his personal characteristics, such as shyness, embarrassment, his intelligence and his general circumstances are irrelevant so far as section 14(3) is concerned.'

The Court of Appeal in *McCoubrey v Ministry of Defence*[36] endorsed this, with the refinement that:

'... the person contemplated by sections 14(2) and 14(3) is a person who is in the same position, in objective terms, as the claimant. Thus in the present case, he would be a serving soldier aged 18 at the time that he suffered the injury.'

The House of Lords[37] has now confirmed that the test is purely objective. Lord Hoffmann pointed out[38] that:

'The test for imputing knowledge in section 14(3) is by reference to what the claimant ought reasonably to have *done*. It asks whether he ought reasonably to have acquired certain knowledge from observable or ascertainable facts or to have obtained expert advice. But section 14(2) is simply a standard of seriousness applied to what the claimant knew or must be treated as having known. It involves no inquiry into what the claimant ought to have done. A conclusion that the injury would reasonably have been considered sufficiently serious to justify the issue of proceedings implies no finding that the claimant ought reasonably to have issued proceedings. He may have had perfectly good reasons for not doing so. It is a standard to determine one thing and one thing only, namely whether the injury was sufficiently serious to count as significant.

The difference between section 14(2) and 14(3) emerges very clearly if one considers the relevance in each case of the claimant's injury. Because section 14(3) turns on what the claimant ought reasonably to have done, one must take into account the injury which the claimant has suffered. You do not assume that a person who has been blinded could reasonably have acquired knowledge by seeing things. In section 14(2), on the other hand, the test is external to the claimant and involves no inquiry into what he ought reasonably to have done. It is applied to what the claimant knew or was deemed to have known but the standard itself is impersonal. The effect of the claimant's injuries upon what he could reasonably have been expected to do is therefore irrelevant.'

---

[36] [2007] EWCA Civ 17.

[37] *A v Hoare, C (FC) v Middlesbrough Council, X (FC) and another (FC) v London Borough of Wandsworth (Conjoined Appeals), H (FC) v Suffolk County Council, Young (FC) v Catholic Care (Diocese of Leeds)* [2008] UKHL 6, [2008] 1 AC 844, [2008] 2 WLR 311, [2008] 2 All ER 1.

[38] At paras 38 and 39.

9.9.3 Attributability

9.9.3.1 The meaning of 'attributable to'

'Attributable to' means 'capable of being attributed to', not 'caused by'.[39] The Court of Appeal in *Nash v Eli Lilly* rejected a suggestion that the test should be 'reasonably' attributable, and endorsed the approach that:

> 'The act or omission of the defendant must be a possible cause as opposed to a probable cause of the injury.'

For years the way in which this requirement was to be applied was litigated with some frequency, the crux of the dispute being, what detail and degree of certainty of knowledge was required.

In 1997 some relief was afforded by the decision of the Court of Appeal in *North Essex CHA v Spargo*,[40] in which, after a reference to the gross overload of reported authorities, the following principles were set out by Brooke LJ:

> '(1) The knowledge required to satisfy section 14(1)(b) is a broad knowledge of the essence of the causally relevant act or omission to which the injury is attributable;
>
> (2) "Attributable" in this context means "capable of being attributed to", in the sense of being a real possibility.
>
> (3) A plaintiff has the requisite knowledge when she knows enough to make it reasonable for her to begin to investigate whether or not she has a case against the defendant. Another way of putting this is to say that she will have such knowledge if she so firmly believes that her condition is capable of being attributed to an act or omission which she can identify (in broad terms) that she goes to a solicitor to seek advice about making a claim for compensation.
>
> (4) On the other hand she will not have the requisite knowledge if she thinks she knows the acts or omissions she should investigate but in fact is barking up the wrong tree; or if her knowledge of what the defendant did or did not do is so vague or general that she cannot fairly be expected to know what she should investigate; or if her state of mind is such that she thinks her condition is capable of being attributed to the act or omission alleged to constitute negligence, but is not sure about this, and would need to check with an expert before she could be properly said to know that it was.'

Brooke LJ went on to consider the difference between attributability and proof:

> '... the judge had spoken of the solicitor's perception that he needed confirmation that there *was* the relevant causal connection, and a little later he added that the question will, in certain circumstances, be whether a particular injury *was* caused by an operation or was caused by something else. In my judgment, in all these passages the judge is substituting the much tougher test of proof of causation for

---

[39] *Davies v City and Hackney Health Authority* [1989] 2 Med LR 366 (CA); *Nash v Eli Lilly & Co* [1993] 1 WLR 782 (CA).

[40] [1997] 8 Med LR 125.

the much less vigorous statutory test of attributability, in the sense that the identified injury was capable of being attributed to the identified omission. The test is a subjective one …'.

9.9.3.2 Identifying a relevant act

The first of Brooke LJ's four principles was derived from a string of previous decisions. In *Hallam-Eames v Merrett Syndicates Ltd*[41] Hoffmann LJ has said:

'If all that was necessary was that a plaintiff should have known that the damage was attributable to an act or omission of the defendant, the statute would have said so. Instead, it speaks of the damage being attributable to "the act or omission which is alleged to constitute negligence." In other words, the act or omission of which the plaintiff must have knowledge must be that which is causally relevant for the purposes of an allegation of negligence.'

This is not to say that the claimant's knowledge needs to be of a degree sufficient to plead particulars of negligence: as set out above, it is a 'broad knowledge' of 'the essence of the causally relevant act or omission'.

9.9.3.3 Identifying a relevant omission

Omissions pose particular problems. In *Forbes v Wandsworth Health Authority*[42] the Court of Appeal pointed out that a claimant cannot know of an omission without knowing what it is that is omitted. This approach was followed in *Smith v Leicestershire Health Authority*,[43] where it was held that the claimant could only have gained the requisite knowledge (that there was a lost opportunity to prevent her tetraplegia) with the aid of expert advice.

It should not, however, be assumed that because omissions are pleaded as particulars of negligence, that the requisite knowledge could only have been acquired with expert advice. Some omissions are, when more carefully looked at, in fact part of a case which is essentially about both acts and omissions. Some omissions are capable of being immediately appreciated by the layman, eg those involving obvious delays in treatment.

9.9.3.4 The acquisition of knowledge without expert advice

Once knowledge is acquired, the clock starts: subsequent medical views which support or do not support such 'knowledge' do not negate this.[44]

The case of *AB v Ministry of Defence*,[45] while unusual, demonstrates this starkly. The claimants were representative of a pool of 1,011 ex-servicemen

---

[41] [1995] 7 Med LR 122 (CA).
[42] [1997] QB 402 (CA).
[43] [1998] Lloyd's Rep Med 77 (CA).
[44] *Roberts v Winbow* [1999] Lloyd's Rep Med 31; *Sniezek v Bundy (Letchworth) Ltd* [2000] PIQR P213.
[45] [2012] UKSC 9, [2013] 1 AC.

alleging injury (including death) caused by exposure to radiation during military testing between 1952 and 1958.

By a 4:3 majority the Supreme Court confirmed that the standard is as follows: a claimant is 'likely to have acquired knowledge of the facts specified in section 14 when he first came reasonably to believe them'.[46]

Mere suspicion is not knowledge in this sense, but a sufficiently confident belief in the attributability of significant injury is. In *AB* the claimants had voiced firm confidence in public statements and campaigns more than three years before (most) of the claims were issued; time had run, and expired.

Lord Kerr encapsulated the dissenting view at para 206: s 14 should invite consideration of 'what the claimant knew as a fact or, at least, on what he knew was a possible fact – and not on what he believed'. In other words, 'confidence' in attributability should not amount to knowledge for the purposes of ss 11 and 14, until it acquired some basis in some objective evidence.

But Lord Walker for the majority emphasised a crucial distinction in this respect:

> '[58] ... there is a distinction in principle between a claimant's knowledge (actual or constructive) that he has a real possibility of a claim (Brooke LJ's second point in *Spargo*), and the assembly by the claimant and his legal team, with the help of experts, of material justifying the commencement of proceedings with a reasonable prospect of success. Of all the difficulties in this anxious appeal, the biggest difficulty of all, to my mind, is in the practical application of this abstract distinction between knowledge of the "essence" of a claim and the evidence necessary to prove it to the requisite legal standard.'

Most of the claimants in *AB* had knowledge of the 'essence' of their claims more than three years prior to commencement, albeit that they had not received what they considered to be the objective expert evidence until later. Indeed it would be odd if the later, more compelling, expert evidence were held to be the trigger for knowledge in the s 14 sense for the *AB* claimants who had issued their claims before receipt of the relevant report: Lord Wilson JSC in the majority was clear that it was a 'legal impossibility for a claimant to lack knowledge of attributability for the purposes of s 14(1) at a time after he had issued his claim'.[47]

9.9.3.5   Expert advice

In those cases which do necessitate expert advice, this would generally be specialist advice, rather than legal advice[48] but there are few absolutes in this

---

[46]   Lord Wilson JSC.
[47]   For instance, Lord Wilson JSC at para 3.
[48]   *Henderson v Temple Pier Co Ltd* [1998] 1 WLR 1540.

area of the law, and there are many solicitors capable of filling gaps in a claimant's knowledge by virtue of their own special expertise.

9.9.4 Identity of the defendant

This piece of knowledge is unique in that it has given rise to no issues of note. It is a simple question of fact. It seems unlikely that the knowledge required would go so far as knowing with exactness the full legal title of a defendant; or if it did, that requirement would be met by the inference of constructive knowledge. The Court of Appeal in *Nash v Eli Lilly & Co*[49] remarked that:

> 'It is a clear requirement of section 14(1)(c) that the plaintiff must have knowledge of the identity of the defendant. However, in the case of a corporate entity, such as those with which these appeals are concerned, the laws applicable to the operation of such corporations may be expected to provide, and do provide that the true position of the individual members of the corporate structure are ascertainable. These details as facts would therefore fall within section 14(3)(a).'

9.10 THE QUALITY OF KNOWLEDGE

9.10.1 Knowing or believing?

As can be seen from *Roberts v Winbow*[50] a claimant who is clear in his belief about the cause of his injury may end up much worse off than the muddled thinker who wants someone else to make up his mind. See also the discussion of *AB v Ministry of Defence*, above.

Discussion in *Sniezek v Bundy (Letchworth) Ltd*[51] might suggest that there is a distinction between:

- a claimant who believes he has a significant injury connected to his working conditions, and who maintains that belief despite negative medical advice: he has 'knowledge';
- a claimant who thinks he probably has an injury attributable to his working conditions, but who is not certain, particularly in the absence of expert medical advice: he does not have 'knowledge'.

It is perhaps hard to see why the different mindsets of the two hypothetical claimants should lead to a different outcome; difficult also to understand why the second hypothetical claimant requires so high a degree of certainty, rather than just a sufficient degree of confidence to take him to see a solicitor.

---

[49] [1993] 1 WLR 782 (CA).
[50] [1999] Lloyd's LR Med 31.
[51] [2000] PIQR P213.

9.10.2　Knowledge is not lost

Knowledge once acquired cannot be 'lost': once the limitation clock starts, there are no intermissions save by reason of death or loss of capacity.

9.10.3　Whose knowledge?

A child may acquire knowledge, albeit this is of no significance until he reaches majority. However, a child is not deemed to have knowledge possessed by his parent.[52]

9.11　CONSTRUCTIVE KNOWLEDGE

9.11.1　Section 14(3) sets out an objective test

That s 14(3) is an objective rather than a part-subjective test was clearly set out in *Forbes v Wandsworth Health Authority*.[53] Nevertheless, a debate continued for a while as to whether the individual characteristics of the claimant were to be taken into account, until the House of Lords resolved the matter in *Adams v Bracknell Forrest Borough Council*.[54]

It is to be noted that the Court of Appeal has twice indicated that the ratio of that case is to be taken from the first three speeches.[55]

In *Adams*, Lord Scott referred to the phrase, 'knowledge which he might reasonably have been expected to acquire', in s 14(3) as being:

> '... [a] reference to knowledge which a person in the situation of the claimant i.e. an adult who knows he is illiterate, could reasonably be expected to acquire. Personal characteristics such as shyness and embarrassment, which may have inhibited the claimant from seeking advice about his illiteracy problems but which would not be expected to have inhibited others with a like disability, should be left out of the equation.'

9.11.2　The reasonable claimant

In *Forbes v Wandsworth Health Authority*[56] it is made plain that the defendant does not have to show that the claimant who fails to investigate his claim may be fixed with constructive knowledge. Stuart-Smith LJ said:

> 'Turning to the words of section 14(3), it is clear that the deceased could reasonably have been expected to acquire the relevant knowledge with the help of

---

[52]　*Appleby v Walsall Health Authority* [1991] 2 Med LR 346.
[53]　[1997] QB 402.
[54]　[2004] UKHL 29.
[55]　In *Catholic Care (Diocese of Leeds) v Young* [2006] EWCA Civ 1534, and *McCoubrey v Ministry of Defence* [2007] EWCA Civ 17.
[56]　[1997] QB 402.

suitable medical advice. The real question is whether it was reasonable for him to seek that advice. If it was, he took no steps at all to do so. One of the problems with the language of section 14(3)(b) is that two alternative courses of action may be perfectly reasonable. Thus, it may be perfectly reasonable for a person who is not cured when he hoped to be to say, "Oh well, it is just one of those things. I expect the doctors did their best." Alternatively, the explanation for the lack of success may be due to want of care on the part of those in whose charge he was, in which case it would be perfectly reasonable to take a second opinion. And I do not think that the person who adopts the first alternative can necessarily be said to be acting unreasonably. But he is in effect making a choice, either consciously by deciding to do nothing, or unconsciously by in fact doing nothing. Can a person who has effectively made this choice, many years later, and without any alteration of circumstances, change his mind and then seek advice which reveals that all along he had a claim? I think not. It seems to me that where, as here, the deceased expected, or at least hoped, that the operation would be successful and it manifestly was not, with the result that he sustained a major injury, a reasonable man of moderate intelligence, such as the deceased, if he thought about the matter, would say that the lack of success was "either just one of those things, a risk of the operation, or something may have gone wrong and there may have been a want of care; I do not know which, but if I am ever to make a claim, I must find out."

In my judgment, any other construction would make the Act unworkable since a plaintiff could delay indefinitely before seeking expert advice and say, as the deceased did in this case, "I had no occasion to seek it earlier." He would therefore be able, as of right, to bring the action, no matter how many years had elapsed. This is contrary to the whole purpose of the Act which is to prevent defendants being vexed by stale claims which it is no longer possible to contest'.

See also the brief discussion of the case of *Adams* above. In *Whiston v London Strategic Health Authority*[57] the Court of Appeal applied 'the "tightened up" approach as to degree of curiosity that is expected of a reasonable claimant' following *Adams*. The claimant who suffered cerebral palsy was deemed to have constructive knowledge for the purposes of s 14(1), (3) sufficient to trigger investigation, more than three years before he issued the claim, which was therefore time barred.

However while the subjective knowledge of the claimant is irrelevant for the purposes of considering the triggering of the primary limitation period where constructive knowledge has been established, it may remain important for consideration in a s 33 application (discussed in detail below). Indeed in *Whiston* the Court of Appeal exercised the s 33 discretion in favour of the claimant because, while a 'borderline case',[58] a fair trial was still possible.

---

[57] [2010] EWCA Civ 195, [2010] 1 WLR 1582.
[58] Longmore LJ at para 91.

9.12   APPLICATIONS UNDER S 33 OF THE LIMITATION ACT 1980

9.12.1   Overview

Section 33[59] of the Limitation Act 1980 gives the court a discretion to disapply the limitation period in defined circumstances. The 3-year period in which to commence a claim imposed by s 11 is set aside and a claim can proceed.

It is an equitable remedy based on the balance of prejudice between the parties. The court has a wide discretion which by s 33(3) includes an assessment of 'all the circumstances of the case', in addition to the checklist of factors under that subsection.

It is this subsection that should be the focus for the assessment of the merits of an application under s 33.

Section 33(1) of the Limitation Act 1980 states:

'(1) If it appears to the court that it would be equitable to allow an action to proceed having regard to the degree to which –

(a)   the provisions of section 11 or 11A or 12 of this Act prejudice the plaintiff or any person whom he represents; and

(b)   any decision of the court under this subsection would prejudice the defendant or any person whom he represents;

the court may direct that those provisions shall not apply to the action, or shall not apply to any specified cause of action to which the action relates.'

It has been emphasised frequently that, as an order under s 33 effectively deprives a defendant of its limitation defence, then an order should not be made lightly. As the exercise of the discretion to a claimant has been described as 'an exceptional indulgence' then a claimant has a challenging task in order to secure an order disapplying the limitation period.[60]

The burden of proof lies on the claimant.[61]

9.12.2   The discretion under s 33

The court has a wide-ranging discretion in deciding cases under s 33. This is to be contrasted with the more narrow approach under s 14 of the 1980 Act.

The assumption under s 33 is that the limitation period has expired, whereas that is not the case in relation to s 14. Accordingly, where it is conceded that a case is statute barred the issues under s 14 may nevertheless still be relevant to

---

[59]   The section is drawn from ss 2A and 2D of the Limitation Act 1939.
[60]   *KR v Bryn Alyn Community Ltd* [2003] QB 1441.
[61]   *Adams v Bracknell Forest Borough Council* [2005] 1 AC 76.

assess precisely when the limitation period expired, which in turn will determine the period of delay by the claimant in commencing the claim.

The interrelationship between s 14 and s 33 therefore has to be considered carefully in deciding the precise nature of the application to be made and the remedy sought.

The over-arching general discretion under s 33 is that it is unfettered and takes account of 'all the circumstances of the case' in deciding whether to disapply the limitation period.[62]

In *Horton v Sadler*[63] it was stated:[64]

> '... the question for the court under section 33 is always whether it is equitable or inequitable as between the parties to override the time bar which, if relied on by the defendant, will, unless disapplied by order of the court, defeat the action which the plaintiff has ex hypothesi brought out of time ... the court must be guided by what appears to it to be equitable, which I take to mean no more (but no less) than fair and it must have regard to all the circumstances of the case and in particular the six matters listed in sub-section 33(3) ...'

This case is notable because the House of Lords overruled *Walkley v Precision Forgings Ltd*[65] and held that courts could exercise their s 33 discretion, even where a claimant previously brought an action before expiry of the limitation period but that claim had been aborted for any reason.

Section 33 provides an equitable remedy based on the prejudice caused to the parties, either by granting or not granting the application. It is not exclusively determined by a comparative balance of hardship test.[66]

Proportionality is also a relevant consideration in the exercise of the discretion.

Specifically, for a court to exercise its discretion in favour of a claimant there should be medical evidence that demonstrates 'a serious effect on the claimant's health or enjoyment of life and employability'.[67]

In terms of an appeal, if the 'unfettered' discretion is exercised judicially with all relevant factors being considered and further that a judge was not 'plainly wrong' then the Court of Appeal will be reluctant to interfere.[68]

---

[62] *Thompson v Brown Construction (Ebbw Vale) Ltd* [1981] 2 All ER 296 (HL).
[63] [2006] UKHL 27, [2007] 1 AC 307.
[64] At para 32.
[65] [1979] 1 WLR 606.
[66] *Whitfield v North Durham Health Authority.*
[67] *Adams v Bracknell Forest Borough Council* [2005] 1 AC 76 at para 54; *Robinson v St Helens MBC* [2003] PIQR 128.
[68] *Nash v Eli Lilly & Co* [1993] 4 All ER 383, *Horton v Sadler* [2006] UKHL 27 at para 33, *Bryn Alyn Community (Holdings) Ltd* [2003] EWCA Civ 85 at para 69.

Whilst the discretion of the court is wide-ranging, it is required to have regard to the particular factors under s 33(3) in determining whether it would be equitable to disapply the limitation period.[69] These factors are 'exemplary but not definitive'.[70]

The court will assess an application by considering and exercising its discretion under s 33(3). The weight accorded to each factor is a matter for the judge.[71] Each of the following subsections is considered below:

> '(3) In acting under this section the court shall have regard to all the circumstances of the case and in particular to –
> (a)   the length of, and the reasons for, the delay on the part of the plaintiff;
> (b)   the extent to which, having regard to the delay, the evidence adduced or likely to be adduced by the plaintiff or the defendant is or is likely to be less cogent than if the action had been brought within the time allowed by section 11, by section 11A or (as the case may be) by section 12;
> (c)   the conduct of the defendant after the cause of action arose, including the extent (if any) to which he responded to requests reasonably made by the plaintiff for information or inspection for the purpose of ascertaining facts which were or might be relevant to the plaintiff's cause of action against the defendant;
> (d)   the duration of any disability of the plaintiff arising after the date of the accrual of the cause of action;
> (e)   the extent to which the plaintiff acted promptly and reasonably once he knew whether or not the act or omission of the defendant, to which the injury was attributable, might be capable at that time of giving rise to an action for damages;
> (f)   the steps, if any, taken by the plaintiff to obtain medical, legal or other expert advice and the nature of any such advice he may have received.'

In relation to all these factors keep in mind that the discretion of the court is broad and unfettered. The burden of proof, or at least the burden of persuasion as regards matters of judgment, is on the claimant. The Court of Appeal said in *Sayers v Hunters (a firm)* that this burden is not necessarily a heavy one; rather, 'How difficult or easy it is for the claimant to discharge the burden will depend upon the facts of the particular case'.[72]

9.12.3   Section 33(3)(a): delay

First, it is emphasised that under 'all the circumstances of the case' the court can consider the whole period of delay since accrual of the cause of action,[73] though usually under this subsection subsection the focus is on any delay

---

[69]   *Nash v Eli Lilly & Co* [1993] 4 All ER 383 CA.

[70]   *Barrand v British Cellophane Plc* (1995) *The Times*, February 16.

[71]   *Halford v Brookes* [1991] 3 All ER 559, although subsequent cases have applied a different emphasis: *KR v Bryn Alyn (Holdings) Ltd* [2003] EWCA Civ 85 at para 81.

[72]   [2012] EWCA Civ 1715, [2013] 1 WLR 1695.

[73]   In particular see *Donovan v Gwentoys* [1990] 1 All ER 1018: where the claimant is statute-barred the court can consider all periods of delay relating to the claim.

between the expiry of the limitation period and the date of issue of proceedings. In *Collins v Secretary of State for Business Innovation and Skills*[74] Jackson LJ reviewed the authorities and held:

> '[66] Construing s 33(3) as best I can in the light of the authorities, my conclusions are:
>
> i) The period of time which elapses between a tortfeasor's breach of duty and the commencement of the limitation period must be part of "the circumstances of the case" within the meaning of s 33(3).
>
> ii) The primary factors to which the court must have regard are those set out in s 33(3)(a)–(f). Parliament has singled those factors out for special mention.
>
> iii) Therefore, although the court will have regard to time elapsed before the claimant's date of knowledge, the court will accord less weight to this factor. It will treat pre-limitation period effluxion of time as merely one of the relevant factors to take into account.
>
> iv) Both parties may rely upon that factor for different purposes. The claimant may rely upon the earlier passage of time in order to buttress his case under s 33(3)(b). The claimant may argue that recent delay has had little or no impact on the cogency of the evidence. The damage was done before the claimant started being dilatory. The defendant may rely upon the earlier passage of time, in order to show that it already faced massive difficulties in defending the action; therefore any additional problems caused by the claimant's recent delay are a serious matter. It is for the court to assess these and similar considerations, then decide on which side of the scales to place this particular factor.'

Secondly, the issues are (i) length of the delay, and (ii) the reasons (as opposed to excuses) for it. The test is subjective and so the court will hear the reasons and then assess them, as opposed to applying a test of reasonableness.[75]

A short delay will usually not be a sufficient basis to refuse to disapply the limitation period. Examples of potentially excusable delay include:

(1) *Hartley v Birmingham City Council*:[76] 1 day;

(2) *Thompson v Brown*:[77] 37 days;

(3) *Horton v Sadler*:[78] 5 months (which covered a situation where the first claim, brought within the limitation period was discontinued and a second one was brought outside the limitation period);[79]

(4) *A v Hoare*:[80] 13 years and 10 months.

---

[74] [2014] EWCA Civ 717.

[75] *Adams v Bracknell Forest BC* [2005] 1 AC 76 at paras 44–45. Note there is a mismatch in that the test under s 14(1) is objective.

[76] [1992] 2 All ER 213.

[77] [1981] 1 WLR 744.

[78] [2006] UKHL 27.

[79] This decision overruled *Walkley v Precision Forgings* [1979] 1 WLR 606, which held such cases were statute-barred.

[80] [2008] EWHC 1573. This followed the House of Lords ruling by the same name, referred to above, which remitted the exercise of the s 33 discretion on the facts to the Queen's Bench Division.

Plainly these cases turn on their facts. But in *Cain v Francis* Smith LJ in the Court of Appeal demanded at least consistency of approach:

> 'In my view, there should be consistency of approach between judges on an issue as fundamental as whether the loss of a limitation defence amounts to real prejudice in a case where the defendant has no defence to liability on the merits. It is said that judges have an unfettered discretion on applications under section 33 but, if judges as experienced as these two take diametrically opposed views on the kind of issue which has arisen here, applications under section 33 will be a lottery for litigants.'[81]

The essence of this subsection is whether the reason is a good one or not and in particular whether the claimant is to blame in material respects for the relevant delay. There is no tariff on the period of delay, but the longer the delay the more likely that prejudice may have been caused to the defendant.[82]

A good example of this (and of the balancing exercise involved in the s 33 discretion generally) is *McDonnell v Walker*.[83] Following a road traffic accident the claimant solicitors issued in time, but served the claim one day late and were refused an extension. New solicitors then issued and served a second claim based on the same facts, outside the limitation period, following the decision in *Horton v Sadler*[84] which provided hope for disapplication of the limitation period.

The inexcusable nature of the delay took centre stage in the Court of Appeal, together with some forensic prejudice because the second claim was for greater quantum:

> '36 The delay which is relevant is the whole period since the accident occurred. Each period of delay needs separate consideration as to whether it was excusable. First there is the delay of three years or so up to service of the first proceedings; this was the fault either of the claimants themselves or their solicitors. No excuse has been provided for that delay. The failure to serve on time was negligent and the claimants will have a claim for that negligence. There is then a period of 17 months until *Horton* was decided in June 2006; it may have been excusable from the claimants' point of view but this was certainly not a period where the defendant was at fault. There is finally the period of 22 months until the issue of the second set of proceedings; there is no excuse for that period. The solicitors discussing how that claim should be funded provides no excuse for the non-issue of the second proceedings vis-à-vis the defendant.'

It is necessary to provide realistic and persuasive explanations as opposed to excuses for inaction. The explanations for delay are multiple and varied.

---

[81]　[2008] EWCA Civ 1451, [2009] QB 754, [2009] 3 WLR 551, [2009] 2 All ER 579, [2009] CP Rep 19, [2009] LS Law Medical 82, at para 39.

[82]　*KR v Bryn Alyn Community Holdings Ltd* [2003] EWCA Civ 85, [2003] QB 1441.

[83]　[2009] EWCA Civ 1257, [2010] CP Rep 14.

[84]　[2007] 1 AC 307.

A summary of some of the explanations that have found favour with the court is as follows:

(1)   a belief that the claimant could not claim damages if she actually returned to work after the accident;[85]

(2)   impecuniosity[86] and a claimant's disabilities;[87]

(3)   trying to maintain good working relations with the claimant's employer[88] and a fear of losing one's job;

(4)   ignorance of the law.[89]

Whilst the fact a claimant was blameless will not automatically result in the disapplication of the limitation period, it is a factor that is weighted strongly in the claimant's favour.[90]

Where no blame attaches to the claimant for the passage of time then this must be considered by the court.[91]

Each case is assessed on its individual facts but in general the longer the delay the more difficult it will be to succeed under this subsection. Consideration needs to be given as to whether permission should be sought to call the claimant to explain the delay, although the Court of Appeal has indicated that most applications would be dealt with on paper.[92]

In *Berry v Calderdale Health Authority*,[93] the claimant suffered an injury but delayed 15 months from the time of taking advice from her medical practitioners and the commencement of proceedings. The application under s 33 failed as the period of delay, combined with the failure to explain the delay, meant the defendant was significantly prejudiced although there did not have to be actual prejudice as the same can prima facie be inferred from expiry of the limitation period.

9.12.4   Section 33(3)(b): cogency of the evidence

The issue of delay discussed above is particularly important as regards the impact. In *Cain v Francis* Smith LJ reviewed the authorities:

'[57] It appears to me that there is now a long line of authority to support the proposition that, in a case where the defendant has had early notice of the claim, the accrual of a limitation defence should be regarded as a windfall and the

---

[85]   *Coad v Cornwall and Isles of Scilly Health Authority* [1997] 1 WLR 189, [1997] PIQR P 12.

[86]   *Lye v Marks and Spencer plc* [1988] *The Times*, February 15.

[87]   *Pearse v Barnet Health Authority* [1998] PIQR 39.

[88]   *McCafferty v Metropolitan Police Receiver* [1977] 1 WLR 1073.

[89]   *Halford v Brookes* [1991] 3 All ER 559, [1991] 1 WLR 428, CA.

[90]   *Bates v Leicester Health Authority* [1998] 3 Lloyd's Law Rep Med 93; a delay of 5 years.

[91]   *Smith v Leicester Health Authority* [1998] 3 Lloyd's Law Rep Med 77 at 91.

[92]   See *Bryn Alyn*, although there is nothing to prevent an application for such permission at the interim stage of the case.

[93]   [1998] 5 Lloyd's Law Rep 179.

prospect of its loss, by the exercise of the section 33 discretion, should be regarded as either no prejudice at all (see *Firman v Ellis* [1978] QB 886) or only a slight degree of prejudice: see *Donovan v Gwentoys Ltd* [1990] 1 WLR 472. It is true that, in *Thompson v Brown* [1981] 1 WLR 744, Lord Diplock said that the accrual of the defence might be regarded as a windfall only where the delay in issuing proceedings was short. However, with great respect, it does not seem to me that the length of the delay can be, of itself, a deciding factor. It is whether the defendant has suffered any evidential or other forensic prejudice which should make the difference.'

The Court of Appeal also indicated that the key concern of s 33(3)(b) is with forensic prejudice to the defendant, rather than financial prejudice:

'70 ... although on a literal construction of section 33(1), it appears to be relevant to the exercise of the discretion that the defendant would suffer the financial prejudice of having to pay damages if the arbitrary time limit were to be disapplied, Parliament cannot have intended that that financial prejudice, as such, should be taken into account. That is because, in fairness and justice, the defendant ought to pay the damages if, having had a fair opportunity to defend himself, he is found liable. If having to pay the damages is not a relevant prejudice under section 33(1), it cannot be relevant either as one of the circumstances of the case.

71 I accept that some judges appear to have thought that this financial prejudice, as such, was relevant to the exercise of the discretion. In particular, Lord Diplock appears to have thought so and the rest of the House agreed with him. I must say, with hesitation and great respect, that I think he was wrong. I comfort myself with the knowledge that his remarks were not essential to the ratio of the decision in *Thompson v Brown* [1981] 1 WLR 744. Apart from Lord Diplock's, all the other judicial utterances are broadly consistent with the reasoning I have advanced.

72 A claimant's position is different. He has a substantive right, his cause of action, but he cannot proceed with it because of the operation of section 11. He has therefore been prejudiced by the loss of the right to enforce his cause of action. That prejudice is greatly reduced if he has a good claim over against his solicitor. In a case where the defendant has suffered some forensic or procedural prejudice, which will diminish his ability to defend himself, it will be relevant to consider that the claimant has another remedy. But the fact that the claimant has a claim over will not necessarily mean that the direction should be refused. It might still be fair and just that the defendant remains in the frame. It is the defendant who has, ex hypothesi, committed the tort and, as Lord Denning MR pointed out in *Firman v Ellis* [1978] QB 886, 906, it is his insurer who has received the premiums in respect of the relevant risk. So the fact that the claimant will not suffer financially in the end is relevant but not determinative.

73 It seems to me that, in the exercise of the discretion, the basic question to be asked is whether it is fair and just in all the circumstances to expect the defendant to meet this claim on the merits, notwithstanding the delay in commencement. The length of the delay will be important, not so much for itself as to the effect it has had. To what extent has the defendant been disadvantaged in his investigation of the claim and/or the assembly of evidence, in respect of the issues of both liability and quantum? But it will also be important to consider the reasons for the delay.

Thus, there may be some unfairness to the defendant due to the delay in issue but the delay may have arisen for so excusable a reason, that, looking at the matter in the round, on balance, it is fair and just that the action should proceed. On the other hand, the balance may go in the opposite direction, partly because the delay has caused procedural disadvantage and unfairness to the defendant and partly because the reasons for the delay (or its length) are not good ones.'

In terms of forensic prejudice the court will assess whether and to what extent the cogency of the evidence as relied upon by the parties has been adversely affected by the delay. 'Cogency' is defined as the ability or otherwise of a party to present its case at trial, based on the delay from the date of the accrual of the cause of action or date of knowledge, which in turn has affected the quantity and quality of the evidence.[94]

This subsection is based on the two main areas: first, witness evidence and second, documentary evidence. Essentially, the greater the loss of cogency of the evidence the stronger will be a defendant's position under this subsection in arguing it cannot properly defend the claim.[95]

9.12.4.1   Cogency issues: witness evidence

The court will consider all aspects of an alleged loss of cogency relating to witness evidence. This encompasses not only the inability of the defendant to trace and call witnesses to give evidence at trial, but also the extent to which the recollection of witnesses has been adversely affected by the passing of time. Each case will have to be assessed on its facts and an initial assessment should be made on:

(1)   What are the central evidential issues in the case to which the question of cogency will be applied?

(2)   Who are the central witnesses in the case and could they have been available in the limitation period in any event?

(3)   What evidence would that witness have been likely to provide if he or she had been available in the limitation period in any event?[96]

Witness evidence has heightened importance on the balance of prejudice where there are critical disputes of fact. If the case in question will turn on what can be recollected by witnesses at a particular time then the inability to trace relevant witnesses, or the loss of recollection of that witness if traced, will usually be fatal to any claim.

Examples include the advice given by a clinician to a patient at a consultation, consent to treatment issues, and the basis of a contentious clinical decision in the treatment of a patient.[97]

---

[94]   *Pratima Rani Das v Dr Durga Ganju* [1999] 6 Lloyd's Rep Med 198.
[95]   *Kelly v Bastible* [1997] 8 Med LR 15.
[96]   *Pearse v Barnet Health Authority* [1998] PIQR 39.
[97]   *Baig v Hackney Health Authority* [1994] 5 Med LR 22.

In *Smith v Hampshire County Council,*[98] the claimant claimed damages for alleged educational neglect by the defendant local authority. The claimant left school in 1994 at 15 years of age and commenced proceedings at the age of 23 years. The defendant alleged prejudice based on a loss of cogency of the evidence and the Court of Appeal agreed. The defendant was strongly prejudiced in that it had searched for the relevant documents which could not be located and which as a matter of policy would have been destroyed in 1999 in any event. Moreover, few teachers had any recollection of the claimant and the combination of these two factors rendered it inequitable to disapply the limitation period.

Whilst whether a witness can be traced by date of trial is an important factor, that factor depends in part on the defendant's system to maintain contact with, or knowledge of, the whereabouts of relevant witnesses. Hospitals, for example, with a high turnover of clinical staff, require a system to be in place for tracing potential witnesses. A failure to maintain a system to locate both staff and relevant documentation can lead a court to conclude that any subsequent evidential difficulties were substantially self-inflicted.[99]

Assuming the witness could have been traced and given evidence in the limitation period, what would have been the quality of that evidence? Would that witness have provided valuable evidence on central issues in the case? For example, *Farthing v NE Essex Health Authority*[100] held that even if a clinical negligence action was heard within the limitation period the relevant medical staff would have been unlikely to have provided beneficial evidence on the central issues.

Likewise, even if witnesses are untraceable, it may be that that disadvantage can be surmounted by extensive documentary evidence still in existence (eg medical notes).[101]

9.12.4.2 Cogency issues: documentary evidence

Where relevant documentary evidence can no longer be traced outside the limitation period then a defendant's ability to defend the claim will probably be significantly reduced.[102]

Statement evidence from an authorised employee of the defendant (or insurer) will be essential to support this contention at a limitation hearing.

First, the documentation must be identified on which the issues of liability turn and whether this documentation would have been available in the limitation

---

[98] [2007] EWCA Civ 246.
[99] *Hind v York* [1997] 8 Med LR 377.
[100] [1998] 2 Lloyd's Rep Med 37.
[101] [1999] 2 Lloyd's Rep Med 31.
[102] *Adams v Bracknell Forest Borough Council* [2005] 1 AC 76 (HL).

period. Secondly, the defendant must demonstrate that it has a system for the retention of important documentation (eg clinical notes) and that it has undertaken a proper search.

The inability to trace documentation must not be self-inflicted through its failure to maintain a proper records system.[103]

It may be that a judge can be persuaded to disapply the limitation period under s 33, notwithstanding *some* risk of prejudice to a defendant caused by the absence of potentially relevant documentation, on the basis that the risk can be confronted and managed, if and when it arises at trial. For instance, in *Bedford v Bedfordshire County Council*,[104] in the analogous context of the exercise of discretion under s 7(5) of HRA 1998, Jay J said 'in the absence of documentary evidence which might have been available at an earlier stage I should be very slow to draw inferences adverse to the defendant' and, later, 'I will not draw inferences adverse to the defendant in areas where I consider that a timeous claim might have supplied me with relevant evidence.'

9.12.5   Section 33(3)(c): the defendant's conduct

Section 33(3)(c) requires the court to consider inter alia the defendant's conduct after the accrual of the cause of action.[105]

Conduct arising before the accrual of the cause of action is not usually taken into account. The conduct in question will have to be shown to have a material bearing on any delay in the case, the cogency of the evidence, or a factor that comes within the broad category of 'all the circumstances of the case'.

The subsection is intended to cover deliberate or reckless conduct of a defendant that aims to delay or undermine proceedings. For example, where a defendant has prolonged the negotiation period giving the claimant the prospect of a settlement, whereas in fact it was stringing the claimant along in bad faith until the limitation period expires, then a court could take such conduct into account.

9.12.6   Section 33(3)(d): the duration of any disability of the claimant

Section 33(3)(d) relates to a claimant who is under a disability, as defined in s 38(2)(3) of the Act. The relevant period is since the accrual of the cause of action.[106] The definition covers only children and patients and not a claimant's psychological illness which does not render him a protected party/patient under the Mental Health Act 1983.

---

[103] *Hammond West Lancashire Health Authority* [1998] 4 Lloyds Rep Med 146, *Drury v Grimsby Health Authority* [1997] 8 Med LR 38.
[104] [2013] EWHC 1717 (QB), [2014] Med LR 89, [90]–[94].
[105] *Halford v Brookes* [1991] 1 WLR 428.
[106] See s 28 of the Act.

Whilst a mental disorder may not be sufficiently serious to come within the disability under s 38(2)(3) a court can still take account of an illness of the claimant within the over-arching factor of 'all the circumstances of the case'.[107]

9.12.7   Section 33(3)(e): prompt and reasonable action by the claimant

Section 33(3)(e) relates to whether a claimant has acted promptly and reasonably once he knew whether or not the act or omission of the defendant, to which the injury was attributable, might be capable of giving rise to an action for damages.

A distinction must be made between the knowledge of an injury under s 14(1) (which can trigger the limitation period) and knowledge of a claim in negligence (which is covered by s 33(3)(e)).

There is also an overlap with delay as assessed under s 33(3)(a). There is no definition of 'prompt and reasonable' but it will be widely construed on an objective basis. It covers the entire period of a claimant's knowledge of a cause of action and so that must be identified to establish the period of delay.

The thrust of the section is to identify those claims where a claimant has discovered, or in any event knows, there is a cause of action but has taken no steps to advance the claim. The burden of proof is on the claimant to explain any inaction.

Once a court finds that there has been culpable and material delay then the burden will be a heavy one to discharge. A claimant will have to give a full account under this subsection.[108] Where the fault for any material delay lies with the solicitors of a blameless claimant then the court can exonerate the claimant.[109]

The fact that a claimant may or may not have a right against his insured lawyers (eg who were responsible for inexcusable delay), or may have some other alternative remedy, is a relevant factor that can be taken into account under s 33 and this overlaps with prejudice and consideration of 'all the circumstances of the case' generally.[110]

If a claimant alleges that he had no knowledge of the legal rights available then this can be an acceptable explanation for delay. However, a claimant must provide persuasive evidence on the point and the general approach of the courts

---

[107]   *Davis v Jacobs and Camden/Islington Health Authority* [1999] Lloyd's Rep Med 72.

[108]   *Berry v Calderdale Health Authority* [1998] 5 Lloyd's Rep Med 179, *McCafferty v Metropolitan Police Receiver* [1977] 1 WLR 1073 (CA).

[109]   *Pratima Rani Das v Dr Durga Ganju* [1999] Lloyd's Rep Med 198, *Roberts v Winbow* [1999] Lloyd's Rep Med 31.

[110]   *Horton v Sadler* [2006] UKHL 27 at para 32, *Thompson v Brown Construction (Ebbw Vale) Ltd* [1981] 2 All ER 296, [1981] 1 WLR 744.

is that a claimant who knows he has a cause of action, but who fails to progress it will have a difficult task in persuading a court to exercise its discretion in his favour.[111]

9.12.8 Section 33(3)(f): steps taken by the claimant to obtain expert evidence

Section 33(3)(f) requires the court to consider:

> 'the steps, if any taken by the plaintiff to obtain medical, legal or other expert advice and the nature of any such advice he may have received.'

The court can exercise its discretion where a claimant demonstrates the reason for delay was negative legal or medical advice. There must obviously be a connection between the advice given and the material delay in the case and the issue of waiver of privilege has to be carefully considered.[112]

Where, however, a claimant was presented with the opportunity to take advice but did not do so, then it is unlikely that any consequent delay will be easily explained.

In *Skitt v Khan*,[113] by proceedings issued in 1993, the claimant alleged a negligent omission to diagnose cancer by the defendant in 1986. Limitation was not disapplied as the claimant had knowledge of a negligence claim in 1986 but had not pursued the case at that stage. The resultant delay was such that the balance of prejudice lay in the defendant's favour and the court did not exercise its discretion to disapply the limitation period.

9.12.9 Additional Factors: the merits and value of the claim

The court may consider the size, complexity and merits of the case within the over-arching discretion afforded by 'all the circumstances of the case'.

In broad terms the stronger the case on the merits the more weight the court will give to disapplying the limitation period.[114]

In *Bates v Leicester Health Authority* it was stated:[115]

> '... it is always prejudicial to a defendant to be deprived of a limitation defence, but it is less inequitable or unfair where, as here, the plaintiff has a strong case than where he has a weak one.'

---

[111] *Halford v Brookes* [1991] 1 WLR 428; *Johnson v Busfield (Deceased)* (1998) 38 BMLR 29.
[112] *Das v Ganju* (1998) 42 BMLR 28.
[113] [1997] 8 Med LR 105, *Jones v Liverpool Health Authority* [1996] PIQR 251.
[114] *Nash v Eli Lilly & Co* [1993] 4 All ER 383.
[115] [1998] 3 Lloyd's Rep Med 93, relying on *Forbes v Wandsworth Health Authority* [1996] 3 WLR 1108 at 1120G.

The court must have evidence available at the hearing on which to make that assessment and so a claimant has to demonstrate that there was more than a mere chance of success.[116]

Courts are naturally cautious about making such an assessment when it is likely that not all the evidence is available to it. Any such assessment would have to be based on taking an overall view of the prospects of success.

In *Smith v Hampshire County Council*[117] it was stated that:[118]

> '... the court must resist the natural temptation on any s 33 application to try the action which would take place if one disapplied the limitation period.'

Evidence in support of an application under s 33 therefore has to be carefully assessed to ensure that the merits of a strong claim are properly but succinctly presented before the court.

Likewise the complexity and value of a claim is a material factor within the consideration of proportionality under s 33.

In *Robinson v St Helens Metropolitan Borough Council*[119] it was held (at paras 33 and 37):[120]

> 'Courts should be slow to exercise their discretion in favour of a claimant in the absence of cogent evidence showing a serious effect on the claimant's health or enjoyment of life and employability. The likely amount of an award is an important factor to consider, especially if, as is usual in these cases they are likely to take a considerable time to try.'

In *Bettamix Ltd v Tarmac Ltd*,[121] Leveson LJ developed the point further as follows:

> 'It is not that there is a specific financial hurdle which must be overcome for any claim of this nature to succeed, but rather a consideration both of the benefits to the claimant in terms of strength and value of the claim and the potential cost both legal and in manpower or otherwise to the organization of the proposed defendant.'

In *Bedford v Bedfordshire County Council*,[122] again in the analogous context of the exercise of discretion under s 7(5) of HRA 1998, Jay J considered proportionality, practicality and the public interest:

---

[116] As to the problems encountered on the merits and CFA insurance in the context of limitation cases see *Kew v Bettamix Ltd* [2006] EWCA Civ 1535.

[117] [2007] EWCA Civ 246.

[118] At para 37.

[119] [2003] PIQR 128.

[120] See also *Adams v Bracknell Forest Borough Council, McGhie v British Telecommunications PLC* [2005] EWCA Civ 48.

[121] [2006] EWCA Civ 1535.

[122] [2013] EWHC 1717 (QB), [2014] Med LR 89, [90]–[94].

'76 As would be the case if this were an application under section 33 of the Limitation Act 1980 in a common law action for personal injuries, I have an untrammelled discretion. I must take into account the fact that the limitation period under the HRA is one year, not three years, and that it is clearly the policy of the legislature that HRA claims should be dealt with both swiftly and economically. All such claims are, by definition, brought against public authorities, and there is no public interest in these being burdened by expensive, time consuming and tardy claims brought years after the event ...

92 ... Proceedings of this nature are extremely expensive to mount and advance, and difficult to prove. The defendant has had to obtain three detailed witness statements from its employees and complex expert evidence, and expend a considerable amount of managerial time in defending this case.'

That kind of analysis (compelling, with respect, on the facts of that case) underscores that 'all the circumstances of the case' means what it says and that judges have a broad discretion.

TOP TIPS

- Early awareness of the risks raised by potential limitation arguments will allow proper collation of evidence and case preparation.
- Commencement of the 3-year limitation period for a personal injury action is either the date of the accrual of the cause of action, or, if later, the date of knowledge of the injured person.
- It is never safe to assume that simply because a claimant is genuine when he says, 'I didn't know I had a claim', s 14 will assist him.
- Knowledge whether any particular acts or omissions did or did not constitute negligence or breach of duty is irrelevant.
- The test in respect of constructive knowledge under s 14(3) is an objective one.
- The act or omission of which the claimant must have knowledge must be that which is causally relevant for the purposes of an allegation of negligence.
- Once knowledge is acquired, the clock starts and is not stopped by subsequent medical views which do not support such 'knowledge'.
- A claimant who delays once he knows he has a case in negligence, then fails to commence within the limitation period, will usually fail.
- Disapplying the limitation period is a discretionary remedy and is based on the balance of prejudice.
- A court can take 'all the circumstances of the case' into account.
- Delay in issuing proceedings has to be explained. The longer the delay the heavier the burden on the claimant.

- In considering alleged prejudice to a defendant courts tend to give great weight to the fact that medical records are still in existence.
- Proportionality of a claim is now an additional consideration so evidence must be submitted in support of that issue.

CHAPTER 10

CLAIMS INVOLVING MEDICAL PRODUCTS

In this chapter Jalil Asif QC explains how to use product liability law to bring claims involving medical products without having to prove fault.

10.1 INTRODUCTION

Whilst claims relating to the conduct of medical practitioners are usually advanced on the basis of negligence of some kind, if a patient is injured by a medical product he may have a more easily proved claim framed in terms of a producer's or supplier's liability under product safety legislation or in private medicine in contract or consumer credit.

10.1.1 Product liability

The real attraction for a claimant is that this is a form of strict liability (subject to a limited range of defences) so that there is no need to prove fault on the part of the defendant, eliminating an issue which is often extremely troublesome for a claimant to establish in negligence-based claims.

The major developments in product safety and liability law over the past 40 years have mainly originated in European Directives which the UK government has then introduced into UK law. The relevant UK legislation therefore has to be understood, construed and applied in light of the Directives in question, against a European law background, and with a view to achieving reasonable consistency in the implementation of those Directives across Europe. The result is that this is one area where the law in other European jurisdictions may be highly material to the UK courts' approach.

Currently, there are two main legal regimes in place. The General Product Safety Directive[1] ensures that all products available to consumers in the EU are 'safe', ie that they present the minimum acceptable risks compatible with their use. If producers, importers or distributers discover that their products are not safe they must take prompt steps to disseminate information or warnings, or to organise replacements and/or product recalls, and they face criminal penalties if they do not.

---

[1]   2001/95/EC [2002] OJ L11/4.

As indicated by its name, the General Product Safety Directive is of general application to products of all kinds. In addition, medicinal products and medical devices are subject to their own licensing and safety regimes, including a number of specific European Directives.

The purpose of the General Product Safety Directive and of the various Directives relating to medicinal products and devices is to prevent dangerous products from getting into circulation, rather than to provide redress for those who are injured by a dangerous or unsafe product. This chapter therefore does not deal any further with this area of the law.

The second legal regime, which is the one that provides the necessary right of redress for individuals injured by unsafe products, is that of the Product Liability Directive,[2] implemented in the UK by Part 1 of the Consumer Protection Act 1987. This chapter deals with bringing a claim under the Consumer Protection Act 1987 and the Product Liability Directive.

10.2 SOURCES OF LAW

The Consumer Protection Act 1987 (CPA 1987) and Product Liability Directive (the Directive) impose strict liability on producers to consumers for damage caused by their products (subject to a limited range of defences). The liability is entirely artificial, and was created for public policy reasons. The statutory cause of action is separate and distinct from the usual English law of obligations; it does not depend on any nexus or duty relationship between the producer of the product and the person who suffers damage.

The legal test is simply that: (a) the product in question is not as safe as people generally are entitled to expect; and (b) the product caused the damage in question. Recourse to concepts associated with negligence or contract law is therefore of limited help in understanding or applying this area of law, other than to test what product liability is not.

10.2.1 The Consumer Protection Act 1987

The legal cause of action in the UK is created by Part 1 of CPA 1987. There are some significant differences between the wording of CPA 1987 and the Directive.[3] However, it is generally accepted that the Directive takes precedence over CPA 1987. The usual practice is therefore to focus on the terms of the Directive except for the purpose of pleading the claim.[4]

---

2   85/374/EEC [1985] OJ L210/29.
3   These were sufficient to cause the Commission to bring enforcement proceedings against the UK, arguing that the UK had not properly complied with its treaty obligation faithfully to enact the Product Liability Directive: *Commission v UK* (Case C-300/95) [1997] All ER (EC) 481. However, the ECJ accepted the UK's argument that although CPA 1987 used different terminology from the Directive, the UK courts would ensure that they applied CPA 1987 consistently with the Directive.
4   The Directive is not directly enforceable in England and Wales. However, s 1(1) of CPA 1987

10.2.2   The Product Liability Directive

European Directives must always be construed in a purposive manner rather than using the traditional UK approach to statutory construction. It is therefore essential to understand the background and purposes of the Directive.

The origin of the Directive was the Thalidomide scandal in the late 1960s. Thalidomide (Contergan) was made and supplied by Distillers as an anti-morning sickness medicine for pregnant women, but after being put on the market it was then found to be severely teratogenic causing a range of physical abnormalities in developing fetuses. Legal actions against Distillers failed in England and Germany (and elsewhere) on the ground that Distillers had not been negligent in putting the medicine on the market. This outcome generated public dissatisfaction with the state of the law, particularly in mainland Europe. In 1969/70 the European Commission therefore started work on developing a new Community-wide law for consumer protection, and the Directive was finally agreed and adopted on 25 July 1985.

The intended purposes of the Directive appear from its recitals. The main purpose is, for public policy reasons, to impose liability on producers to achieve the fair redistribution of risk between consumers and producers of products. In other words, the intention of the Directive is to move the burden of damage from the individual victim, who would otherwise be unable to recover compensation in the absence of proof of fault, to the producer, who can redistribute the burden on society as a whole by insuring or self-insuring (or can simply stop producing the product and thereby can avoid liability, but more importantly will prevent his products from causing damage to others). In some cases it is necessary to have regard to this underlying philosophy in order to understand how the Directive should be interpreted and applied.

Subsidiary purposes include making it easier for injured consumers within the EU to obtain compensation by removing the need for them to have to prove fault as an element of liability, whilst at the same time providing the producer with a limited range of defences and achieving harmonisation of national laws on product liability within the EU.[5]

---

provides that:
'This Part shall have effect for the purpose of making such provision as is necessary in order to comply with the Product Liability Directive and shall be construed accordingly.'
In addition, it is well established in European law that national courts must interpret the terms of domestic legislation implementing a Community Directive in the light of the wording and purpose of that directive, so as to achieve its result and to comply with the terms of the third paragraph of Art 249 of the EC Treaty (Art 189 in the old numbering), which provides:
'A directive shall be binding, as to the result to be achieved, upon each Member State to which it is addressed, but shall leave to the national authorities the choice of form and methods.'
If there are discrepancies between the directive and the domestic legislation, the former must prevail and the domestic legislation must be interpreted in the light of the Directive's language, aims and purposes: see *Marleasing SA v La Commercial Internacional de Alimentation SA* (Case C-106/89) [1990] ECR I-4135.
[5] See *Commission of the European Communities v France* (C-52/00) [2002] ECR I-3827, *Commission of the European Communities v Greece* (C-154/00) [2002] ECR I-3879, *Skov*

It follows that as well as the wording of the Directive itself, the following are all useful additional legal sources:

(1)   other official language versions of the Directive;[6]

(2)   other EU national implementations of the Directive;

(3)   judgments of the UK courts;

(4)   judgments of the European Court of Justice;[7] and

(5)   decisions of other EU national courts.

10.3   APPLICABLE LAW

10.3.1   Essential features

The essential features of liability under the Directive (and CPA 1987) are as follows:

(1)   'Product' means any moveable goods (or electricity), including items incorporated into something else (whether a moveable or not), either as components or as raw materials.

(2)   A 'producer' is a person who manufactured the product or any raw material or component part, any person who holds himself out as its producer (for example by putting his name on it), or the first importer of the product into the EU if the product was produced outside the EU. It is possible for there to be more than one 'producer' of a product.

(3)   A product is 'defective' (or contains a defect)[8] if it does not provide the safety which persons generally are entitled to expect, taking into account all the (relevant) circumstances.

(4)   The producer's liability is to *any* person damaged by the product, whoever that might be. There is no limitation of such liability, for example, to the person to whom the product was originally supplied.

(5)   Because fault is irrelevant, the focus should be on the safety of the product, not on the conduct of the producer.

(6)   The construction given to the Directive must be capable of being applied with equal validity to the whole range of products in circulation; ie it must work not just in relation to medical products but for all types of consumer products.

(7)   If the claimant is unable to identify the producer/importer, he may require anyone in the supply chain to identify the producer/importer or the next supplier up the chain, until they are able to identify the producer/importer.

AEG v Bilka Lavprisvarehus A/S (C-402/03) [2006] ECR I-199, [2006] 2 CMLR 16; and *Centre hospitalier universitaire de Besançon v Dutrueux* (Case C-495/10) [2012] 2 CMLR 1.

[6]   European Directives are routinely produced in each of the official Community languages. These are of equal legal validity to the English language version and sometimes shed additional light on its intended meaning.

[7]   Including the opinions of the Advocate General, although they are of lesser weight.

[8]   See further *Is the product 'defective'?* below (**10.3.5**).

If any supplier fails to provide that information within a reasonable time, the claimant is entitled to sue that supplier instead.

(8) Limited statutory defences are provided, the most important of which is that the state of scientific and technical knowledge did not permit the lack of safety to be discovered at the time when the product was put into circulation.

Although the Directive (and CPA 1987) imposes strict liability on the defendant (subject to the available defences), the claimant bears the burden of proving:

(1) the item in question is a 'product';

(2) the product does not provide the safety which persons generally are entitled to expect in all the circumstances – ie the claimant must prove any particular circumstances said to be relevant, and the expectation of safety which persons generally were entitled to have in respect of the product having regard to the relevant circumstances;

(3) the lack of safety in the product caused the damage suffered by the claimant.

To the extent that the defendant seeks to raise one of the statutory defences the burden of proof is on the defendant.

10.3.2   What is a product?

'Product' is defined by Art 2 of the Directive and s 1(2) of CPA 1987 in very broad terms. Some colour is given to its meaning by CPA 1987, which includes (as part of its definition of 'producer') a requirement that the product must have been 'manufactured', 'won' or 'abstracted', or that its essential characteristics must be attributable to an industrial or other process having been carried out on it.

Medicines and medical devices are clearly 'products'. It is generally accepted that human blood and blood products are also 'products'.[9] There is no decision whether human tissue or organs for transplantation are 'products', although it is easy to see the argument that they have been 'abstracted' or 'won' when harvested.[10]

---

[9]   This was conceded by the National Blood Authority in *A & Others v NBA* [2001] 3 All ER 289, [2001] Lloyd's Rep Med 187, (2001) 60 BMLR 1.

[10]   *Veedfald v Arhus Regional Authority* (Case C-203/99) (2002) 66 BMLR 1 indirectly suggests that the ECJ would treat an organ as a product. A kidney harvested for transplantation was treated with a flushing fluid prior to implant. The fluid was contaminated, ruining the kidney. The claim was made in relation to the fluid, rather than the kidney, and concerned whether use of the fluid within the local medical service without putting it into circulation in the market excluded it from the product liability regime (it did not). The ECJ considered that the harvested kidney was 'property' damaged by the fluid; it would seem to follow that the kidney would be a product.

10.3.3 The producer and intermediate supplier liability

'Producer' is defined in Art 3 of the Directive, as summarised above. The approach in CPA 1987 is slightly different and more complex, but achieves the same result (see ss 1(2) and 2(2) of CPA 1987).

The Directive clearly envisages that there may be more than one person liable as producer of a particular product, and provides in Art 5 for joint and several liability in such cases, without prejudice to any national law rights of contribution between the producers.

Unless the producer (or importer, in a case where the product was produced outside the EU) has clearly labelled the product, packaging or leaflets with his name and the claimant has had an opportunity to read such labelling or has retained it, the claimant will probably not know by whom the product was produced or imported.

The Directive (and CPA) therefore provides a mechanism for the claimant to find that information, by enquiring of any intermediate supplier. The CPA requires a notice to be served by the claimant, for which there is no specified form, although this is not a requirement of the Directive.

If, but only if, the intermediate supplier fails to inform the claimant within a reasonable time of the name of the producer/importer or of another supplier higher up the supply chain, the claimant is entitled to bring the claim against that intermediate supplier instead of against the producer/importer.

Unless the claimant already knows the identity of the producer/importer, the claimant will therefore have to trace the chain of supply back to its origin. Usually, the claimant has to start with the person who supplied the product to him, since this is the only information he will have.

The Directive (and CPA) permits the supplier 'a reasonable period' to provide a name in response to a prospective claimant's enquiry. Assuming the next supplier up the line is identified, the claimant must then repeat the process in turn against each supplier up the chain. In the light of the limitation issues discussed below, it is prudent to start this task long before the limitation period appears likely to run out.

10.3.4 Is the product 'defective'?

The terms 'defect' and 'defectiveness' are often used interchangeably when discussing product liability issues. However, it is important to understand that they do not bear their everyday English language meaning in this context; instead they are legal short-hand for the statutory test of whether the product:

'... does not provide the safety which a person [ie persons generally[11]] is entitled to expect, taking all circumstances into account ...'

It is important not to fall into the trap of trying to decide whether and why the product in question justifies the epithet 'defective' or contains a 'defect' as those terms are usually used in everyday English.

Given that the UK courts will be applying the Directive in the national context, and that the aim of the Directive is the harmonisation of laws, 'persons generally' will probably be treated by the courts as meaning the UK population.[12] In other words, the judge will have to decide what expectation of safety regarding the product society in the UK as a whole is entitled to have. This may differ from the expectation in other parts of the EU, some of which have a more relaxed approach to safety issues.

Article 6 of the Directive (s 3 of CPA 1987) refers to three particular circumstances as being relevant to the issue, namely:

(a)   the presentation of the product;

(b)   the use to which it could reasonably be expected that the product would be put; and

(c)   the time when the product was put into circulation.

It also provides that a product shall not be considered defective for the sole reason that a better product is subsequently put into circulation.

The Directive is unhelpful in clarifying what is intended in relation to 'presentation', and CPA 1987 again adds some colour in s 3(2) by paraphrasing this requirement as:

'... the manner in which, and purposes for which, the product has been marketed, its get-up, the use of any mark in relation to the product and any instructions for, or warnings with respect to, doing or refraining from doing anything with or in relation to the product.'

However, the elaboration in CPA 1987 can cause difficulty in that it sometimes leads claimants to advance their claim on the basis that the labelling or product information was defective, which then becomes difficult to reconcile with the overall structure of liability under the Directive.

The better view is that it is the presentation of the product to persons generally which is relevant rather than the presentation to the individual claimant.

---

[11]   This is a good example of the importance of the other language versions of the Directive: the English language version uses 'a person' which is ambiguous, but the French version uses '*on*', and the German, '*Mann*' – following this approach, CPA 1987 expressly refers to 'persons generally'.

[12]   There are arguments that it should connote a wider geographical area (eg the EU community as a whole), and equally a smaller one (eg the area of an administrative region within a country), but this issue has not been expressly addressed in any of the cases.

In addition, allowing the content of labelling or product information to affect the question of the product's lack of safety is difficult to reconcile with Art 12, which forbids a producer from attempting to limit or exclude his liability under the Directive.[13]

On the other hand the purpose and time of supply do not usually create any difficulty.

In *A & Others v NBA*[14] Burton J concluded that 'all circumstances' does not mean *all* circumstances, but only those which are relevant to the purposes of the Directive, in particular the intention to move away from a fault-based system to a strict liability regime in order to make it easier for victims to obtain compensation.

According to Burton J the conduct of the producer is therefore *not* relevant and neither is cost/benefit or cost/utility considerations, since allowing these in would be to reintroduce negligence by the back door.

Two other areas often raised by defendants in relation to medical products are the fact that the product complied with the licensing regime, and that it was only available on medical advice. It is suggested that neither of these matters are relevant circumstances. If the first were relevant, it would have the effect of substituting a test of regulatory compliance to establish liability, which is clearly contrary to the intention of the Directive. The effect of the second argument would be to reintroduce considerations of cost/benefit or cost/utility through the medium of the medical practitioner which Burton J concluded was forbidden.

The need to take into account all the relevant circumstances may, however, make it very difficult to decide whether or not a particular product is likely to be held not to provide the necessary level of safety.

The difficulties can be illustrated by the following example:

(1)   Cytotoxic drugs used in the treatment of cancer are well known to be very dangerous and to have very serious effects on the body.

(2)   Nevertheless their use is justified in order to treat the particular disease which is itself very serious and has potentially fatal consequences.

(3)   If the drug is subsequently discovered to have harmful side-effects other than the known effect on cancer tissue does that make it unsafe?

(4)   This can only be answered by considering the expectation of safety which persons generally are entitled to have in relation to the product. But is this to be determined having regard to the expectation of the average patient with similar characteristics to the damaged patient, or the public at large?

---

[13]   In relation to this, however, see the judgment of Ebsworth J in *Worsley v Tambrands* [2000] PIQR P95, although this must now be read subject to *A & Others v NBA* [2001] 3 All ER 289, [2001] Lloyd's Rep Med 187, (2001) 60 BMLR 1.

[14]   [2001] 3 All ER 289, [2001] Lloyd's Rep Med 187, (2001) 60 BMLR 1.

(5)   What is the nature of the expectation such people are entitled to have? For example, that treatment with the product will be no less safe than no treatment at all, or that it will carry the least possible risk of side-effects, or no side-effects at all?

(6)   Is the practicality, reliability or cost of methods of avoiding the harmful side effects relevant as a circumstance?

There is no reason why the court cannot in an appropriate case conclude that the expectation of safety regarding a particular product is that it will be 100% safe. Two examples illustrate this.

In a German case,[15] the German Federal Supreme Court[16] allowed the claimant's appeal and held the defendant liable for the explosion of a mineral water bottle even though it was the result of a hairline crack in the bottle that it was not technically possible to detect (and the bottle had gone through seven different inspections in the course of its manufacture), because people generally were entitled to expect that such a bottle would not have any damage whether obvious or microscopic that might cause it to explode.

In *A & Others v NBA*, Burton J concluded that persons generally were entitled to expect that blood and blood products for transfusion would be 100% safe, so that recipients of blood transfusions and blood products contaminated with the hepatitis C virus were entitled to recover damages.

Although this has been criticised by some commentators, Burton J helpfully suggested in *A & Others v NBA* that the most useful approach to the question of liability is to ask the following questions:

(1)   What is the harmful characteristic? This may or may not equate to the lack of safety as defined in Art 6 of the Directive and s 3(1) of CPA 1987.

(2)   Is the product 'standard' or 'non-standard', ie was the offending product that caused the damage the same as all other products in the series or different from them in some identifiable way? This distinction is not founded on the Directive (or CPA 1987), but it is a useful forensic tool which indicates the nature of the comparison to be carried out when assessing the level of safety that persons generally are entitled to expect, ie is the offending product to be compared against other products in the same series or against other similar products on the market?

(3)   If the product is 'non-standard', is it the quality of the product making it non-standard that caused the damage, and if so does that have the result that the product is not as safe as persons generally are entitled to expect? Comparison with other instances of the product in the series is likely to be crucial.

(4)   If the product is 'standard', does comparison with any comparable products on the market shed light on whether the product is as safe as persons generally are entitled to expect? In particular, when considering a

---

15   Usually simply known as the *German Bottle case* 9 May 1995, NJW 1995, 2162.
16   The Bundesgerichtshof.

'standard' product side-effects will generally only be socially acceptable if their existence is made widely known, but even then the court will not sanction a form of Russian roulette.

Finally, it is worth pointing out that the expectation of society will usually be broad and unsophisticated. As Burton J said in *A & Others v NBA*:[17]

'... it is impossible to inject into the consumer's legitimate expectation matters which would not by any stretch of the imagination be in his actual expectation.'

10.3.5 Causation

Although the Directive and CPA 1987 introduce a wholly new system of liability, there is no change to the normal requirement that the claimant must prove the causal link between the lack of safety in the product and the damage. The Directive does not attempt to lay down a European approach to determining causation so national laws apply in each jurisdiction. Causation may therefore still present a claimant with a difficult hurdle to overcome. Causation in medical claims is dealt with in Chapter 8 and is therefore not considered separately here.

10.3.6 Damage

Damage is a necessary requirement for liability under the Directive and CPA 1987. The usual triggers for liability under the Directive are the occurrence of personal injury or death. In addition, compensation can be claimed for damage to other property of a type intended for and used or consumed for private purposes. Damage does not include pure economic loss,[18] damage to the product itself[19] or damage to any other property not usually for private use and used for that purpose.[20] In addition, there is a financial threshold for pursuing a claim if the only damage suffered is damage to property. Other than this, neither the Directive nor CPA 1987 affects the usual approach to the heads of loss potentially recoverable and their quantification, as in any other kind of medical claim. These aspects are dealt with in Chapter 16 and are therefore not considered separately here.

---

[17] At [56].
[18] Neither the definition of damage in the Directive nor that in CPA 1987 includes pure economic loss.
[19] The cost of a damaged medical device cannot be recovered therefore but the cost of replacement can – see *Hems v Poly Implants Prostheses* (2006) MLC 1454.
[20] See also *Société Moteurs Leroy Somer v Société Dalkia France* (C-285/08) [2009] ECR I-4733 where a fire in a hospital caused by a faulty alternator caused damage to property intended to be and used for professional purposes, but was held not to give rise to liability under the Directive.

10.3.7 Defences

Article 7 of the Directive provides a producer with six specific defences, which are implemented in s 4(1) of CPA 1987. These are now considered individually.

10.3.7.1 He did not put the product into circulation

Whilst the Directive generally contemplates that the product in question must have been put into circulation in some way (ie it must have been made available to consumers), this statement must be qualified in two respects.

First, in *Veedfald v Arhus Regional Authority* (Case C-203/99)[21] the ECJ held that use within the local health service of a fluid to preserve an organ for transplantation, which it had manufactured, was sufficient for the fluid to be considered to have been put 'into circulation'. It therefore appears that this defence will be construed very narrowly.

Secondly, in its two judgments in *O'Byrne v Aventis Pasteur MSD Ltd* (Case C-127/04) and (Case C-358/08)[22] the ECJ indicated that a product is put into circulation when it completes the production process and commences the marketing or distribution process in the form in which it is offered to the public in order to be used or consumed, although as a matter of fact, for example, where a manufacturer and distributor subsidiary are so closely involved in the distribution and supply that they can both be treated as a 'producer', the product can be treated as being put into circulation when it is supplied to a third party rather than when the manufacturer supplies to the distributor.

10.3.7.2 The defect did not exist when he put the product into circulation

Richardson v LRC[23] provides an example of this defence. The claimant was using a condom, which split during intercourse. The judge concluded that the defect causing it to do so was not present when the condom was put into circulation.

However, the availability of the defence is particularly sensitive to the way in which the lack of safety is characterised. For example, it may be possible to avoid an outcome similar to that in *Richardson* by adopting a 'latent defect' approach to characterisation of the relevant lack of safety.

---

[21] (2002) 66 BMLR 1.
[22] [2006] All ER (EC) 674, (2006) 91 BMLR 175, [2010] 1 WLR 1375.
[23] [2000] Lloyd's Rep Med 280, (2001) 59 BMLR 185.

10.3.7.3   The product was not made or distributed for a commercial or economic purpose

This defence relaxes the impact of the product liability regime for those not engaged in a commercial activity, ie where the product was not made for sale or distribution for an economic purpose and was not made in the course of the producer's business.

However, in *Veedfald v Arhus Regional Authority* (Case C-203/99)[24] the ECJ held that the fact that a preservative fluid for use with organs for transplantation was made by a publicly funded health service and used within the hospital it operated did not detract from the economic and business character of the manufacture; the activity in issue was not a charitable one covered by this defence.

10.3.7.4   The defect is due to regulatory compliance

There are no cases known to the author where this has been argued. Note that the defence is not that the product complied with the appropriate regulations, but that the *defect* is the result of such compliance. It therefore seems inherently unlikely to arise in practice.

10.3.7.5   The state of scientific and technical knowledge did not enable the defect to be discovered

This defence, often called the 'state of the art' or 'development risks' defence, is the most common to be argued by a defendant. The intention of the Directive is to protect the producer from liability for the unknown (the *inconnu*). The producer must prove that the state of scientific and technical knowledge at the time when he put the product into circulation was not such as to enable the existence of the defect to be discovered.

This does not mean proving that the producer's own scientific and technical knowledge did not enable him to discover the lack of safety, but that the whole body of scientific and technical knowledge did not enable him do so. However, this is qualified to the extent that the relevant scientific and technical knowledge must be *accessible*. This qualification originates in the following passage from the opinion of Advocate General Tesauro in *European Commission v UK* (Case C-300/95),[25] which was implicitly approved by the ECJ:

> '22. Where in the whole gamut of scientific opinion at a particular time there is also one isolated opinion (which, as the history of science shows, might become, with the passage of time, *opinio communis*) as to the potentially defective and/or

---

[24]   (2002) 66 BMLR 1.
[25]   [1997] All ER (EC) 481 at 490.

hazardous nature of the product, the manufacturer is no longer faced with an unforeseeable risk, since, as such, it is outside the scope of the rules imposed by the directive.

23. The aspect which I have just been discussing is closely linked with the question of the availability of scientific and technical knowledge, in the sense of the accessibility of the sum of knowledge at a given time to interested persons. It is undeniable that the circulation of information is affected by objective factors, such as, for example, its place of origin, the language in which it is given and the circulation of the journals in which it is published. To be plain, there exist quite major differences in point of the speed in which it gets into circulation and the scale of its dissemination between a study of a researcher in a university in the United States published in an international English-language journal and, to take an example given by the Commission, similar research carried out by an academic in Manchuria published in the local scientific journal in Chinese which does not go outside the boundaries of the region.

24. In such a situation, it would be unrealistic, I would say unreasonable, to take the view that the study published in Chinese has the same chances as the other of being known to a European product manufacturer. So, I do not consider that in such a case a producer could be held liable on the ground that at the time at which he put the product into circulation the brilliant Asian researcher had discovered the defect in it. More generally, the "state of knowledge" must be construed so as to include all data in the information circuit of the scientific community as a whole, bearing in mind, however, on the basis of a reasonableness test the actual opportunities for the information to circulate.'

In *A & Others v NBA*[26] Burton J quoted this passage and then pointed out that it cannot be taken too literally. For example, the area of scientific study in question might be a Manchurian speciality to which the rest of the world pays attention. He suggested that it was better to treat as inaccessible an unpublished document or unpublished research, not available to the general public, retained within the laboratory or research department of a particular company, and he implied that anything else would be treated as being accessible to the producer.

Having regard to the wording, 'to enable the existence of the defect to be discovered' and the purpose of the Directive, Burton J concluded that as soon as it is known that there is a risk that the defect might be present in the product the producer loses the benefit of this defence, even if the state of scientific and technical knowledge does not allow the producer to identify which particular instances of the product contain the defect.[27]

There remain, however, other unanswered questions regarding the scope of the defence. For example:

(1) Where the defence requires consideration of the state of scientific and technical knowledge at the time the product was put into circulation, does this mean when the particular defective instance of the product was distributed or when the product generally was first put into circulation?

---

[26] At [49].
[27] At [74]–[77].

For products with a long life on the market but where the state of scientific and technical knowledge is advancing, this may be an important question.

(2)   Does the defence cease to be available when it is possible to identify at a general level that there is or might be a safety issue of some kind with some of the products in question, or does it continue to be available until it is possible to identify precisely what that problem is?

(3)   Is the availability of the defence affected by the practicality for the producer of discovering the knowledge in question? This appears to be contrary to the intention of the Directive, the approach of the ECJ in *European Commission v UK* and of Burton J in *A & Others v NBA*, but was recognised by MacKay J in *XYZ v Schering Health Care Limited (the Oral Contraception litigation)*[28] as being a relevant issue to be argued (in the event it was not decided due to the collapse of the litigation).

(4)   Similarly, is the availability of the defence affected by the reliability or cost of the possible methods of detecting the defect?

It is useful to bear in mind that the overall purpose of the Directive is to make it easier for consumers to obtain redress, so it is suggested that the defences are intended to be construed narrowly.

10.3.7.6   Producer of components not liable for defect of product as a whole

This defence is only available in the case of a producer of component parts where the lack of safety is attributable to the design of the product in which the component has been fitted, to a different (and distinguishable) part of the product, or to the instructions given by the manufacturer of the product. In other words, the producer of such a component part will be liable if it is his component which causes the product not to provide the requisite safety, but will escape liability if not.

10.3.8   Contributory negligence

Because liability is founded on the expectation as to the safety of the product of persons generally, the knowledge of the particular user or recipient of the product is not relevant. However, it is conceivable that in some cases his own knowledge of the relevant lack of safety and continued use of the product nonetheless could amount to contributory negligence. The Directive makes clear in Art 8 that the fault of the consumer can allow contributory negligence to be raised.

---

[28]   [2002] EWHC 1420, (2002) 70 BMLR 88.

10.3.9   Claims for contribution

A claimant is unlikely to be interested in the allocation of liability between multiple defendants, but it may occasionally be of strategic value to be aware that the Directive and CPA 1987 preserve the right of a defendant to seek contribution from others. In the UK, such a claim will be made under the Civil Liability (Contribution) Act 1978 so long as the other party is liable for the same damage. Such a claim might therefore be made against someone else who also qualifies as a producer in relation to the product, or possibly against the medical staff involved if they were guilty of negligence, for example in relation to the prescription, supply or administration of the product.

10.4   LIMITATION

Limitation in relation to product liability claims is similar to limitation in relation to clinical negligence claims, but has the important difference of the 10-year long-stop provision. The relevant UK statutory provisions are contained in CPA 1987 and in s 11A of the Limitation Act 1980.

10.4.1   Primary limitation period

The primary limitation period for a product liability claim under CPA 1987 is, in effect, the same as that for any other personal injury claim, namely 3 years from the accrual of the claimant's cause of action or date of knowledge, whichever is the later.

The claimant's cause of action accrues when damage is suffered, which should be easy to determine. The familiar provisions of s 14 of the Limitation Act apply in order to determine the claimant's date of knowledge, if different.[29] They are dealt with in detail in Chapter 9 and are not considered further here.

10.4.2   Suspension, interruption and discretionary extension of the limitation period

As with a claim in negligence, time will not run whilst the claimant is under a disability, ie he is a minor or lacks capacity, or as a result of fraud, deliberate concealment or mistake. The court has the general power under s 33 of the Limitation Act to disapply the primary limitation period in an appropriate case. These provisions are dealt with in detail in Chapter 9. However, all of these are subject to the 10-year long-stop which cannot be extended.

---

[29]   With minor adjustment to focus on knowledge of the product's lack of safety rather than the fault of the producer, since fault is irrelevant: see Limitation Act 1980, s 14(1A).

10.4.3   Law reform and Fatal Accidents Act claims

Where the person injured by the product has died, claims can be brought in the normal way on behalf of his or her estate and on behalf of the dependants, but must be commenced within 3 years of death or of the date of knowledge of the person's executors or dependants, as appropriate, again subject to the long-stop.

10.4.4   The long-stop

The Directive and CPA 1987 impose a 10-year long-stop in relation to product liability claims, as a counter-balance to the breadth of the producer's potential liability. The long-stop is different from most UK limitation provisions in that it does not bar the remedy, but expressly extinguishes the right of action under CPA 1987. There is no means of avoiding this: the long-stop overrides all of the provisions permitting extension of the limitation period for disability, fraud, concealment or mistake and the discretionary power in s 33, and the court has *no* power to disapply the 10-year long-stop period.[30] For example, the long-stop runs even against a child during his minority.

The second important feature is that the 10-year period in relation to the long-stop starts to run from an earlier date than the accrual of the claimant's cause of action. By a combination of s 11A(3) of the Limitation Act and s 4(2) of CPA 1987, the long-stop starts to run on the date when the product left the producer and was put into the supply chain. Where the person being sued is a producer, the relevant date is when he first supplied the product to someone else[31]; where the claim is brought against an intermediate supplier,[32] the relevant date is when the product was last supplied to someone else by someone who is a producer.

---

[30]   After a short period of uncertainty, this has been confirmed by the Supreme Court in *O'Byrne v Aventis Pasteur MSD Ltd* [2010] UKSC 23 following a second reference of the case to the European Court of Justice. C commenced an action against D in relation to a vaccine he was given, allegedly causing him brain damage. D was the UK distributor and subsidiary of the French producer, and raised that point in its defence. C commenced an action against the French producer, which by then was outside the 10-year long-stop. C therefore sought to substitute the French producer for the UK subsidiary in the first action. The High Court referred the case for guidance from ECJ, which appeared to indicate that whether substitution was permissible would be for national law: *O'Byrne v Sanofi Pasteur MSD Ltd* (Case C-127/04) [2006] 1 WLR 1606. The High Court and Court of Appeal therefore permitted the substitution. On appeal to the House of Lords, the case was referred to the ECJ again, which explained its previous decision and clarified that the Directive precluded substitution to allow a producer to be sued after the long-stop had expired in any circumstances: *O'Byrne v Aventis Pasteur SA* (Case C-358/08) [2010] 1 WLR 1375. The House of Lords therefore allowed the appeal and refused to allow substitution: *O'Byrne v Aventis Pasteur MSD Ltd* [2010] UKSC 23.

[31]   However, the ECJ in *O'Byrne v Sanofi Pasteur MSD Ltd* (Case C-127/04) [2006] 1 WLR 1606 indicated that where the distributor was a subsidiary of the producer and forms part of the manufacturing process, it is possible to say that any transfer between the two does not amount to putting the product into the supply chain, and that that occurs only when the distributor

Thus, the 10-year long-stop may not even run from the date of supply to the end user. It may do, if there is no intermediary in the supply chain. But whenever there is such an intermediary, the 10-year period will run from the date of supply to an intermediary by the producer, rather than the date of supply by the last intermediary to the end user.

Where the product has a short shelf life, or the producer operates a 'just-in-time' supply/distribution system, this may be of lesser significance, although even being one day outside the 10-year long-stop will be fatal to the claim.

But where the product has a long shelf life, it will be impossible for the claimant (or his lawyers) to know in advance when the 10-year period commences, and hence when the long-stop period expires, until the defendant producer informs them. This can be a major problem in relation to claims concerning vaccines or medical devices. For example, in the MMR litigation, the vaccines in question had a shelf life approaching 2 years.

10.5 PLEADING THE CASE

10.5.1 The particulars of claim

As a result of the strict liability nature of product liability claims it should usually be possible to plead a claim quite simply. Having identified the parties and, if necessary, the capacities in which they sue or are sued, and having set out the factual background needed to understand the claim, the important matters to plead are:

(1) a factual description of the complaint made about the product, for example that it was contaminated with a particular virus or chemical;

(2) the item was a product within the meaning of CPA 1987;

(3) the expectation of safety which persons generally were entitled to have in relation to the product, including any circumstances said to be relevant when determining that expectation;

(4) the effect of the harmful characteristic in the item was that the product failed to provide the safety that persons generally were entitled to expect (ie there was a 'defect' in the product or it was 'defective') within the meaning of CPA 1987;

(5) the item was produced by the producer, within the meaning of CPA 1987;

(6) the chain of supply from the producer to the claimant (if known);

(7) the case on causation;

---

passes it to a third party. This was confirmed by the ECJ in *O'Byrne v Aventis Pasteur SA* (Case C-358/08) [2010] 1 WLR 1375 and applied by the House of Lords in *O'Byrne v Aventis Pasteur MSD Ltd* [2010] UKSC 23.

[32] This should only be the case if the supplier has failed to provide the claimant with details of the producer/importer or of another supplier higher up the supply chain.

(8) loss and damage.

If the claim is brought outside the 3-year primary limitation period and before the expiry of the 10-year long-stop it is good practice to plead why the claim is not already statute-barred or why the court should exercise its discretion under s 33 to disapply the three-year primary limitation period.

10.5.2 The defence

In many cases, there will be no dispute whether the item in question was a product, and an appropriate admission should be made.

On the other hand, it is likely that there will be a real argument as to whether a medical product which causes side effects or has some untoward effect on the patient is not as safe as people are entitled to expect (ie 'defective').

A defendant who wishes to put this in issue must set out what his case is on the following points:
(1) whether it is accepted the allegedly harmful characteristic was present in the product at all; and
(2) whether it is accepted the allegedly harmful characteristic amounted to a failure to provide the safety which people are entitled to expect.

The defendant will have to identify any circumstances said to be relevant to that issue, and will have to set out the expectation of safety which he says persons generally were entitled to have in respect of the product, assuming the defendant formulates that safety expectation differently from the claimant.

If the defendant also wishes to rely on one of the statutory defences he must plead it. More particularly, if the defendant intends to rely on the state of scientific and technical knowledge defence he will have to identify what he says was the state of accessible scientific and technical knowledge at the time. This may require particulars to be provided of articles in scientific textbooks or journals upon which reliance is placed. If so, it is helpful to include copies of such articles annexed to the defence.

The primary focus of the defence is often on the issue of causation. Most defendants wish to do more than simply deny that causation is established, and to put forward a positive case on the point. Any such positive case must be pleaded; even where a positive case in the strict sense is not advanced, but the defendant wishes to rely on particular matters to support its position that the claimant has failed to prove causation, the better practice is for the defendant to specify all such matters in its defence.

Equally, if the defendant wishes to take a limitation defence or to raise contributory negligence those points must be pleaded specifically.

10.5.3   The reply

Responding to a defendant's reliance upon one of the statutory defences or addressing the defendant's position on causation provide two of the rare situations where a claimant is likely really to need to plead a reply. In the example of a defendant relying on the state of scientific and technical knowledge defence, the claimant may wish to assert that the state of scientific and technical knowledge at the time did allow the lack of safety to be discovered, and will have to set out what he says was the state of knowledge. Again, this may require the claimant to provide particulars of scientific articles or papers relied upon, which it can be useful to annex to the reply.

Where the claimant is responding on causation, he may need expressly to address and rebut the defendant's arguments in its defence.

10.6   ALTERNATIVE CAUSES OF ACTION IN PRIVATE MEDICINE

Sometimes the product liability remedy is not available to a claimant, for example when the liable manufacturer, importer or supplier is in liquidation or fails to have sufficient if any insurance.

Here a patient may wish to investigate causes of action for breach of contract or under the Supply of Goods and Services Act 1982 for supplying an unsatisfactory product. The advantage of such a cause of action is that again there is no need to prove fault. The only test is whether the product or service supplied was satisfactory.

In addition if payment for the private treatment was made by the patient wholly or in part by a credit card then there is coterminous liability under s 75 Consumer Credit Act on the part of the credit supplier providing that the credit card was issued to the patient as only then will the necessary debtor-creditor–supplier relationship have been established.

These alternative claims became particularly important in the PIP breast implant litigation in which the French manufacturers were bankrupt and uninsured, leaving these the only remedies available to the patients. In some instances clinics and surgeons also became insolvent or were uninsured leaving the credit card suppliers as the only solvent defendants.

TOP TIPS

- Where injury is caused by a medical product a claim based on product liability law may be much easier to bring than a traditional negligence claim.

- It is essential to be aware of the importance of European law principles and European comparative law in this area.

- A Consumer Protection Act claim should be made against the producer of the product, anyone who holds themselves out as a producer, or the first importer if the product originates outside the EU.

- If the claimant does not know the producer/importer he can approach anyone in the supply chain to provide that information.

- A supplier who fails to identify the producer/importer or someone higher up the supply chain within a reasonable time can then be sued as if he were the producer/importer.

- Liability arises whenever the safety of the product is not such as persons generally are entitled to expect in all the circumstances, unless the defendant can establish one of the limited available defences.

- The claimant must still prove causation.

- Apart from challenging causation, the most usual defence to be run is that the state of scientific and technical knowledge did not enable the existence of the defect (ie the lack of safety) to be discovered.

- The primary limitation period for bringing a claim is 3 years from when the claimant suffers damage or from the date of knowledge subject to the 10-year long-stop.

- The 10-year long-stop runs from the date when the product was first put into circulation and may be significantly earlier than when the product reaches (or injures) the claimant.

- The 10-year long-stop applies in Consumer Protection Act cases and cannot be suspended or disapplied.

- Private patients may have additional causes of action against clinics or surgeons under the Supply of Goods and Services Act 1982 or against credit providers under s 75 of the Consumer Credit Act 1974.

CHAPTER 11

THE CLINICAL NEGLIGENCE PRE-ACTION PROTOCOL

The early stages of a clinical negligence investigation are governed by the Pre-Action Protocol for the Resolution of Clinical Disputes.[1] In this chapter the full wording of the protocol is set out with commentary.[2]

11.1 GENERAL COMMENTARY

The introduction of this Protocol represented a very significant step forward in the conduct of this area of litigation. As noted in the introductory remarks to the protocol, it was the product of a collaborative effort by parties involved on both sides on the clinical negligence litigation equation and was designed to lay down minimum standards for cooperation between the parties.

The Protocol has been widely disseminated across all areas of clinical practice including NHS Trusts and other health care providers so all interested parties should have full knowledge of its scope and operation.

With the advent of the Jackson CPR amendments in April 2013, there will be renewed focus upon the parties complying with the spirit as well as the letter of pre-action protocols.

'Executive Summary

1 The Clinical Disputes Forum is a multi-disciplinary body which was formed in 1997, as a result of Lord Woolf's "Access to Justice" inquiry. One of the aims of the Forum is to find less adversarial and more cost effective ways of resolving disputes about healthcare and medical treatment. The names and addresses of the Chairman and Secretary of the Forum can be found at Annex E.

2 This protocol is the Forum's first major initiative. It has been drawn up carefully, including extensive consultations with most of the key stakeholders in the medico-legal system.

3 The protocol:

---

[1]   Original commencement date: 26 April 1999 (published January 1999).
[2]   Even though some of the expressions are now out of date.

- encourages a climate of openness when something has "gone wrong" with a patient's treatment or the patient is dissatisfied with that treatment and/or the outcome. This reflects the new and developing requirements for clinical governance within healthcare;
- provides **general guidance** on how this more open culture might be achieved when disputes arise;
- recommends **a timed sequence** of steps for patients and healthcare providers, and their advisers, to follow when a dispute arises. This should facilitate and speed up exchanging relevant information and increase the prospects that disputes can be resolved without resort to legal action.

4 This Protocol has been prepared by a working party of the Clinical Disputes Forum. It has the support of the Lord Chancellor's Department, the Department of Health and NHS Executive, the Law Society, the Legal Aid Board and many other key organisations.

1 Why this Protocol?

Mistrust in Healthcare Disputes

1.1 The number of complaints and claims against hospitals, GPs, dentists and private healthcare providers is growing as patients become more prepared to question the treatment they are given, to seek explanations of what happened, and to seek appropriate redress. Patients may require further treatment, an apology, assurances about future action or compensation. These trends are unlikely to change. The Patients' Charter encourages patients to have high expectations, and a revised NHS Complaints Procedure was implemented in 1996. The civil justice reforms and new Rules of Court should make litigation quicker, more user friendly and less expensive.

1.2 It is clearly in the interests of patients, healthcare professionals and providers that patients' concerns, complaints and claims arising from their treatment are resolved as quickly, efficiently and professionally as possible. A climate of mistrust and lack of openness can seriously damage the patient/clinician relationship, unnecessarily prolong disputes (especially litigation), and reduce the resources available for treating patients. It may also cause additional work for, and lower the morale of, healthcare professionals.

1.3 At present there is often mistrust by both sides. This can mean that patients fail to raise their concerns with the healthcare provider as early as possible. Sometimes patients may pursue a complaint or claim which has little merit, due to a lack of sufficient information and understanding. It can also mean that patients become reluctant, once advice has been taken on a potential claim, to disclose sufficient information to enable the provider to investigate that claim efficiently and, where appropriate, resolve it.

1.4 On the side of the healthcare provider this mistrust can be shown in a reluctance to be honest with patients, a failure to provide prompt clear explanations, especially of adverse outcomes (whether or not there may have been negligence) and a tendency to "close ranks" once a claim is made.

What Needs to Change

1.5 If that mistrust is to be removed, and a more co-operative culture is to develop:
* healthcare professionals and providers need to adopt a constructive approach to complaints and claims. They should accept that concerned patients are entitled to an explanation and an apology, if warranted, and to appropriate redress in the event of negligence. An overly defensive approach is not in the long-term interest of their main goal: patient care;
* patients should recognise that unintended and/or unfortunate consequences of medical treatment can only be rectified if they are brought to the attention of the healthcare provider as soon as possible.

1.6 A protocol which sets out 'ground rules' for the handling of disputes at their early stages should, if it is to be subscribed to, and followed –
* encourage greater openness between the parties;
* encourage parties to find the most appropriate way of resolving the particular dispute;
* reduce delay and costs;
* reduce the need for litigation.

Why this Protocol Now?

1.7 Lord Woolf in his Access to Justice Report in July 1996, concluded that major causes of costs and delay in medical negligence litigation occur at the pre-action stage. He recommended that patients, their advisers and healthcare providers, should work more closely together to try to resolve disputes co-operatively, rather than proceed to litigation. He specifically recommended a pre-action protocol for medical negligence cases.

1.8 A fuller summary of Lord Woolf's recommendations is at Annex D.

Where the Protocol Fits in

1.9 Protocols serve the needs of litigation and pre-litigation practice, especially:
* predictability in the time needed for steps pre-proceedings;
* standardisation of relevant information, including records and documents to be disclosed.

1.10 Building upon Lord Woolf's recommendations, the Lord Chancellor's Department is now promoting the adoption of protocols in specific areas, including medical negligence.

1.11 It is recognised that contexts differ significantly. For example, patients tend to have an ongoing relationship with a GP, more so than with a hospital; clinical staff in the National Health Service are often employees, while those in the private sector may be contractors; providing records quickly may be relatively easy for GPs and dentists, but can be a complicated procedure in a large multi-department hospital. The protocol which follows is intended to be sufficiently broadly based, and flexible, to apply to all aspects of the health service: primary and secondary; public and private sectors.

Enforcement of the Protocol and Sanctions

1.12 The civil justice reforms were implemented in April 1999. One new set of Court Rules and procedures have replaced the existing rules for both the High Court and county courts. This and the personal injury protocol are being published with the Rules, Practice Directions and key court forms. The courts are able to treat the standards set in protocols as the normal reasonable approach to pre-action conduct.

1.13 If proceedings are issued it is for the court to decide whether non-compliance with a protocol should merit sanctions. Guidance on the court's likely approach will be given from time to time in practice directions.

1.14 If the court has to consider the question of compliance after proceedings have begun it will not be concerned with minor infringements, eg failure by a short period to provide relevant information. One minor breach does not entitle the "innocent" party to abandon following the protocol. The court will look at the effect of non-compliance on the other party when deciding whether to impose sanctions.

2 The Aims of the Protocol

2.1 The *general* aims of the protocol are:
* to maintain/restore the patient/healthcare provider relationship;
* to resolve as many disputes as possible without litigation.

2.2 The *specific* objectives are:

Openness
* to encourage early communication of the perceived problem between patients and healthcare providers;
* to encourage patients to voice any concerns or dissatisfaction with their treatment as soon as practicable;
* to encourage healthcare providers to develop systems of early reporting and investigation for serious adverse treatment outcomes and to provide full and prompt explanations to dissatisfied patients;
* to ensure that sufficient information is disclosed by both parties to enable each to understand the other's perspective and case, and to encourage early resolution.

Timeliness
* to provide an early opportunity for healthcare providers to identify cases where an investigation is required and to carry out that investigation promptly;
* to encourage primary and private healthcare providers to involve their defence organisations or insurers at an early stage;
* to ensure that all relevant medical records are provided to patients or their appointed representatives on request, to a realistic timetable by any healthcare provider;
* to ensure that relevant records which are not in a healthcare providers' possession are made available to them by patients and their advisers at an appropriate stage;

- where a resolution is not achievable to lay the ground to enable litigation to proceed on a reasonable timetable, at a reasonable and proportionate cost and to limit the matters in contention;
- to discourage the prolonged pursuit of unmeritorious claims and the prolonged defence of meritorious claims.

Awareness of Options

- To ensure that patients and healthcare providers are made aware of the available options to pursue and resolve disputes and what each might involve.

2.3 This protocol does not attempt to be prescriptive about a number of related clinical governance issues which will have a bearing on healthcare providers' ability to meet the standards within the protocol. Good clinical governance requires the following to be considered:

(a) **Clinical risk management:** the protocol does not provide any detailed guidance to healthcare providers on clinical risk management or the adoption of risk management systems and procedures. This must be a matter for the NHS Executive, the National Health Service Litigation Authority, individual trusts and providers, including GPs, dentists and the private sector. However, effective co-ordinated, focused clinical risk management strategies and procedures can help in managing risk and in the early identification and investigation of adverse outcomes.

(b) **Adverse outcome reporting:** the protocol does not provide any detailed guidance on which adverse outcomes should trigger an investigation. However, healthcare providers should have in place procedures for such investigations, including recording of statements of key witnesses. These procedures should also cover when and how to inform patients that an adverse outcome has occurred.

(c) **The professional's duty to report:** the protocol does not recommend changes to the codes of conduct of professionals in healthcare, or attempt to impose a specific duty on those professionals to report known adverse outcomes or untoward incidents. Lord Woolf in his final report suggested that the professional bodies might consider this. The General Medical Council is preparing guidance to doctors about their duty to report adverse incidents and to co-operate with inquiries.

3 The Protocol

3.1 This Protocol is not a comprehensive code governing all the steps in clinical disputes. Rather it attempts to set out **a code of good practice** which parties should follow when litigation might be a possibility.

3.2 The **commitments** section of the Protocol summarises the guiding principles which healthcare providers and patients and their advisers are invited to endorse when dealing with patient dissatisfaction with treatment and its outcome, and with potential complaints and claims.

3.3 The **steps** section sets out in a more prescriptive form, a recommended sequence of actions to be followed if litigation is a prospect.

Good Practice Commitments

3.4 Healthcare providers should:

(i)　ensure that **key staff**, including claims and litigation managers, are appropriately trained and have some knowledge of healthcare law, and of complaints procedures and civil litigation practice and procedure;

(ii)　develop an approach to **clinical governance** that ensures that clinical practice is delivered to commonly accepted standards and that this is routinely monitored through a system of clinical audit and clinical risk management (particularly adverse outcome investigation);

(iii)　set up **adverse outcome reporting systems** in all specialties to record and investigate unexpected serious adverse outcomes as soon as possible. Such systems can enable evidence to be gathered quickly, which makes it easier to provide an accurate explanation of what happened and to defend or settle any subsequent claims;

(iv)　use the results of **adverse incidents and complaints positively** as a guide to how to improve services to patients in the future;

(v)　ensure **that patients receive clear and comprehensible information** in an accessible form about how to raise their concerns or complaints;

(vi)　establish **efficient and effective systems of recording and storing patient records**, notes, diagnostic reports and x-rays, and to retain these in accordance with Department of Health guidance (currently for a minimum of eight years in the case of adults, and all obstetric and paediatric notes for children until they reach the age of 25);

(vii)　**advise patients** of a serious adverse outcome and provide on request to the patient or the patient's representative an oral or written explanation of what happened, information on further steps open to the patient, including where appropriate an offer of future treatment to rectify the problem, an apology, changes in procedure which will benefit patients and/or compensation.

3.5 Patients and their advisers should:

(i)　**report any concerns and dissatisfaction** to the healthcare provider as soon as is reasonable to enable that provider to offer clinical advice where possible, to advise the patient if anything has gone wrong and take appropriate action;

(ii)　consider the **full range of options** available following an adverse outcome with which a patient is dissatisfied, including a request for an explanation, a meeting, a complaint, and other appropriate dispute resolution methods (including mediation) and negotiation, not only litigation;

(iii)　**inform the healthcare provider when the patient is satisfied** that the matter has been concluded: legal advisers should notify the provider when they are no longer acting for the patient, particularly if proceedings have not started.

Protocol Steps

3.6 The steps of this Protocol which follow have been kept deliberately simple. An illustration of the likely sequence of events in a number of healthcare situations is at Annex A.

Obtaining the Health Records

3.7 Any request for records by the patient or their adviser should:

- **provide sufficient information** to alert the healthcare provider where an adverse outcome has been serious or had serious consequences;

- be as **specific as possible** about the records which are required.

3.8 Requests for copies of the patient's clinical records should be made using the Law Society and Department of Health approved **standard forms** (enclosed at Annex B), adapted as necessary.

3.9 The copy records should be provided **within 40 days** of the request and for a cost not exceeding the charges permissible under the Access to Health Records Act 1990 (currently a maximum of £10 plus photocopying and postage).

3.10 In the rare circumstances that the healthcare provider is in difficulty in complying with the request within 40 days, the **problem should be explained** quickly and details given of what is being done to resolve it.

3.11 It will not be practicable for healthcare providers to investigate in detail each case when records are requested. But healthcare providers should **adopt a policy on which cases will be investigated** (see paragraph 3.5 on clinical governance and adverse outcome reporting).

3.12 If the healthcare provider fails to provide the health records within 40 days, the patient or their adviser can then apply to the court for an **order for pre-action disclosure**. The new Civil Procedure Rules should make pre-action applications to the court easier. The court will also have the power to impose costs sanctions for unreasonable delay in providing records.

3.13 If either the patient or the healthcare provider considers **additional health records are required from a third party**, in the first instance these should be requested by or through the patient. Third party healthcare providers are expected to co-operate. The Civil Procedure Rules will enable patients and healthcare providers to apply to the court for pre-action disclosure by third parties.'

11.2 MEDICAL RECORDS – COMMENTARY

The disclosure of records envisaged by the protocol is not intended to be restricted to those records disclosable under the Access to Health Records Act 1990, Data Protection Act 1998, Senior Courts Act 1981, ss 33, 34 and County Courts Act 1984, ss 52, 53.

Instead the protocol envisages that both an intended party to proceedings and a non-party should, upon proper request as outlined above, provide copies of all records relevant to the case.

'Records' has a wide interpretation and will include all clinical documents, scans, test results and correspondence.

The intention is that the parties should have available all documentation necessary to enable a detailed investigation of the case.

11.2.1 'Within 40 days' (paras 3.9 and 3.12)

This time-limit was deemed reasonable to permit a health care provider to assemble and copy the relevant records.

In general terms, no application to court under CPR, r 31.16 should be made within this time-limit. Consistent with the overriding objective flexibility maybe required; for example, in the context of a case where the limitation period is due to expire imminently, a shortened timescale maybe appropriate, or in a case where access to records is difficult because of ongoing treatment, more time may be necessary.

11.2.2 Access to Health Records Act 1990

This legislation has now been repealed except for sections dealing with requests for access to records relating to a deceased person. Requests for access to records of deceased persons will continue to be made under that Act but requests for access to health records relating to living individuals will now fall within the scope of the Data Protection Act 1998. This Act was implemented on 1 March 2000 and governs both manual and automated records.[3]

11.2.3 Data Protection Act 1998

A guidance note on the operation of the Act was issued by the Office of the Data Protection Commissioner in August 2000 and provides helpful information on the applicability of the legislation to the subject of access to health records. It is important to note that the Data Protection Act 1998 defines a 'health record' as being any record which consists of information relating to the physical or mental health or condition of an individual and has been made by or on behalf of a health professional in connection with the care of that individual. The guidance note makes clear that this definition has a wide interpretation and will, for example, include radiographic material.[4]

11.2.4 Cost

This has been a vexed issue in the past with wide discrepancies around the country. The protocol intended that a reasonable limit should be imposed in line with the charging structure described in the Access to Health Records Act 1990. The position has been significantly clarified by the Data Protection Act 1998 and is as follows:

(a) A maximum fee of £10 for granting access to health records which are automatically processed or are recorded with the intention that they be so processed.

---

[3] See Chapter 2.
[4] See Chapter 2.

(b)   A maximum fee of £50 for granting access to manual records, or a mixture of manual and automated records.

(c)   There is no provision for there to be any separate or additional charge for copying or postage.

(d)   There is no charge for allowing an individual to inspect records, where the request relates to recently created records, ie where at least some of the records were made within the period of 40 days prior to the date of request (thus replicating the previous provision of the Access to Health Records Act 1990).

(e)   Note the position regarding records of a deceased person remains governed by the Access to Health Records Act 1990.

This statutory regulation of charging now provides consistency and eliminates the variation of charges being requested, for example, by GPs.[5]

11.2.5   Health records from a third party (para 3.13)

Whilst CPR, r 31.16 limits disclosure before proceedings start to documents from those respondents likely to be a party to proceedings, the Protocol is wider and requires third party disclosure. This may be highly relevant in clinical negligence cases to help determine issues such as causation. Hence, note the requirement for third party cooperation.

Two points arise:

(a)   query whether the wide power of CPR, r 31.18 may be applied to support the protocol intent and, thus, in the event of non cooperation by a third party, permit a pre-action application to court; or

(b)   in the alternative, if a post commencement of proceedings application for third party disclosure is made, that third party may bear a costs penalty for failure to cooperate with a Protocol request.

'Letter of Claim

3.14 Annex C1 to this Protocol provides **a template for the recommended contents of a letter of claim**: the level of detail will need to be varied to suit the particular circumstances.

3.15 If, following the receipt and analysis of the records, and the receipt of any further advice (including from experts if necessary – see Section 4), the patient/adviser decides that there are grounds for a claim, they should then send, as soon as practicable, to the healthcare provider/potential defendant, a **letter of claim**. [Any letter of claim sent to an NHS trust or Independent Sector Treatment Centre should be copied to the National Health Service Litigation Authority,][6]

---

5   See Chapter 2.
6   Amendment: Words inserted: Supplement 53 (issued July 2010), with effect from 1 October 2010.

3.16 This letter should contain a **clear summary of the facts** on which the claim is based, including the alleged adverse outcome, and the **main allegations of negligence.** It should also describe the **patient's injuries,** and present condition and prognosis. The **financial loss** incurred by the plaintiff should be outlined with an indication of the heads of damage to be claimed and the scale of the loss, unless this is impracticable.

3.17 In more complex cases a **chronology** of the relevant events should be provided, particularly if the patient has been treated by a number of different healthcare providers.

3.18 The letter of claim **should refer to any relevant documents,** including health records, and if possible enclose copies of any of those which will not already be in the potential defendant's possession, eg any relevant general practitioner records if the plaintiff's claim is against a hospital.

3.19 **Sufficient information** must be given to enable the healthcare provider defendant to **commence investigations** and to put an initial valuation on the claim.

3.20 Letters of claim are **not** intended to have the same formal status as a **pleading,** nor should any sanctions necessarily apply if the letter of claim and any subsequent statement of claim in the proceedings differ.

3.21 **Proceedings should not be issued until after [four]**[7] *months from the letter of claim,* unless there is a limitation problem and/or the patient's position needs to be protected by early issue.

3.22 The patient or their adviser may want to make an **offer to settle** the claim at this early stage by putting forward an amount of compensation which would be satisfactory (possibly including any costs incurred to date). If an offer to settle is made, generally this should be supported by a medical report which deals with the injuries, condition and prognosis, and by a schedule of loss and supporting documentation. The level of detail necessary will depend on the value of the claim. Medical reports may not be necessary where there is no significant continuing injury, and a detailed schedule may not be necessary in a low value case. The Civil Procedure Rules are expected to set out the legal and procedural requirements for making offers to settle.'

11.3   LETTER OF CLAIM – COMMENTARY

11.3.1   Recommended contents (para 3.19)

Note paras 3.14 and 3.16 which should be read in the context of para 3.19.

The level of detail to be provided will vary depending upon the complexity of the case. The Protocol is not intended to be overly prescriptive; disclosure of a report on condition and prognosis is not mandated; a comprehensive schedule of financial loss is not required (in a smaller case an analysis of the financial

---

7   Amendment: Test substituted: Supplement 55 (issued February 2011), with effect from 6 April 2011.

losses maybe appropriate; in a major injury case, which will require expert analysis of quantum issues, a summary of the main heads of claim maybe sufficient). The intention is not to create a welter of case-law interpreting whether a letter of claim is protocol compliant but rather to instil a sensible level of exchange of information consistent with the overall aim of the Protocol.

Recoverability of additional liabilities (success fees and after the event insurance premiums) was generally abolished by the Legal Aid, Sentencing and Punishment of Offenders Act 2012 (LASPO) with effect from 1 April 2013, except for 'pre-commencement funding arrangements' (see chapter 3). It follows therefore that with regard to cases where the funding arrangement post-dates 1 April 2013 the letter of claim does not need to give details of the conditional fee agreement as the success fee is payable by the client and not by the opponent. However, because part of the after the event insurance premium in clinical negligence cases is still recoverable under s 46 of LASPO as an additional liability, should notice of the after the event insurance premium still be given in the letter of claim or, if taken out later, within seven days of taking it out? Technically the answer is not straightforward, but practically it is submitted that notice should be given where possible.

Section 4 of Practice Direction 48 – Part 2 of the Legal Aid, Sentencing and Punishment of Offenders Act 2012 Relating to Civil Litigation Funding and Costs: Transitional Provision and Exceptions states:

'4.1 Section 46 of the 2012 Act enables the Lord Chancellor by regulations to provide that a costs order may include provision requiring the payment of an amount in respect of all or part of the premium of a costs insurance policy, where –

(a) the order is made in favour of a party to clinical negligence proceedings of a prescribed description;

(b) the party has taken out a costs insurance policy insuring against the risk of incurring a liability to pay for one or more expert reports in respect of clinical negligence in connection with the proceedings (or against that risk and other risks);

(c) the policy is of a prescribed description;

(d) the policy states how much of the premium relates to the liability to pay for such an expert report or reports, and the amount to be paid is in respect of that part of the premium.

4.2 The regulations made under the power are the Recovery of Costs Insurance Premiums in Clinical Negligence Proceedings Regulations 2013 (SI 2013/92). The regulations relate only to clinical negligence cases where a costs insurance policy is taken out on or after 1 April 2013, so the provisions in force in the CPR prior to 1 April 2013 relating to funding arrangements will not apply.'

It will be noted that this provision expressly states that the old notice provisions do not apply, but does not then provide for any new notice provisions.

The old relevant provision was para 9.3 of Section IV to the Practice Direction (Pre-action Conduct) which read:

'Where a party enters into a funding arrangement within the meaning of rule 43.2(1)(k), that party must inform the other parties about this arrangement as soon as possible and in any event either within 7 days of entering into the funding arrangement concerned or, where a claimant enters into a funding arrangement before sending a letter before claim, in the letter before claim.'

Notice of Funding in Form N251 then had to be given on commencement of proceedings (or on subsequently taking out or varying a funding arrangement).

Furthermore, CPR PD 44 para 19.4 specified that the relevant information about an after the event insurance premium was:

'Where the funding arrangement is an insurance policy, the party must:
a) state the name and address of the insurer, the policy number and the date of the policy and identify the claim or claims to which it relates (including Part 20 claims if any);
b) state the level of cover provided by the insurance;
c) state whether the insurance premiums are staged and, if so, the points at which an increased premium is payable.'

Section 9.3 of Section IV to the Practice Direction (Pre-action Conduct) and CPR PD 44.19 para 19.4 have both been revoked. They are only expressed to apply to 'pre-commencement funding arrangements' by way of transitional provisions. A clinical negligence after the event insurance policy taken out after 1 April 2013 does have a partial additional liability payable by the opponent, but is obviously not a 'pre-commencement funding arrangement'.

However, it is submitted that, as the greater risk is of non-recovery of the additional liability if notice and information about the premium is not given to the opponent, but the rules are somehow interpreted that it should be, best practice would be to continue to give notice of the after the event insurance premium as the rules provided prior to 1 April 2013. However, it is unclear whether or not failure to do so would in fact be a breach of the rules.

11.3.2 'Not intended to have ... formal status' (para 3.20)

This is important.

The letter of claim is intended to provide adequate information to enable a respondent to understand, in general terms, the nature of the case it has to meet.

It is recognised that after the submission of that letter the claimant's position may vary, for example, because of the impact of the letter of response, receipt of further information or expert advice. Hence, whilst sanctions are not expressly ruled out by para 3.20, it is intended that they should be applied only in the most appropriate of cases.

11.3.3 'Four months' (para 3.21)

This period is intended to dovetail with the time for response – see below. This period was extended from three months in 2010 (53rd Update to the CPR). It is recognised that, for example, limitation difficulties may require earlier issue. Where this arises, then consistent with both the aim of the protocol and the overriding objective, flexibility will be required so that, for example, it may be appropriate to extend the time for delivery of full particulars of claim until after the response letter has been received; a stay may be sensible to permit the sending of a response letter and to enable the parties to discuss the case.

11.3.4 'Offer to settle' (para 3.22)

This provision is intended to dovetail with Part 36.

Note that in the context of a clinical negligence case, a claimant wishing to make an offer before proceedings have been commenced should generally provide information in support of quantum, eg a report on condition and prognosis.

'The Response

3.23 Attached at Annex C2 is a template for the suggested contents of the **letter of response**.

3.24 The healthcare provider should **acknowledge** the letter of claim **within 14 days of receipt** and should identify who will be dealing with the matter.

3.25 The healthcare provider should, **within [four][8]** *months* of the letter of claim, provide a **reasoned answer:**
- if the **claim is admitted** the healthcare provider should say so in clear terms;
- if only **part of the claim is admitted** the healthcare provider should make clear which issues of breach of duty and/or causation are admitted and which are denied and why;
- if it is intended that any **admissions will be binding;**
- if the claim is denied, this should include specific comments on the allegations of negligence, and if a synopsis or chronology of relevant events has been provided and is disputed, the healthcare provider's version of those events;
- where additional documents are relied upon, eg an internal protocol, copies should be provided.

3.26 If the patient has made an offer to settle, the healthcare provider should **respond to that offer** in the response letter, preferably with reasons. The provider may make its own offer to settle at this stage, either as a counter-offer to the patient's, or of its own accord, but should accompany any offer by any supporting medical evidence, and/or by any other evidence in relation to the value of the claim which is in the healthcare provider's possession.

---

[8] Amendment: Words substituted: Supplement 53 (issued July 2010), with effect from 1 October 2010.

3.27 If the parties reach agreement on liability, but time is needed to resolve the value of the claim, they should aim to agree a reasonable period.'

11.4   THE RESPONSE – COMMENTARY

11.4.1   'Letter of response' (para 3.23)

The response should reciprocate the intention of the letter of claim and thus provide a detailed answer to the claim sufficient to enable the patient/patient's adviser to understand the position.

A bare denial is unacceptable. Hence, note the detail required by para 3.25 and envisaged by the template letter at Annex C2.

11.4.2   'Within four months' (para 3.25)

Several points arise:
(a)   This time-limit starts to run from the date of receipt of the letter of claim. Thus, the 14-day period for acknowledgement of receipt falls within the 4 months.
(b)   The time-limit was felt to be reasonable for the following reasons:
   (i)   It balances the patient's desire for a speedy response against the healthcare provider's need for time to investigate and consult with those involved.
   (ii)   Consistent with the Good Practice Commitments, a healthcare provider is expected proactively to identify adverse outcomes, report them and tell the patient. Hence, there may well be and possibly should be a level of awareness before even the request for records is received.
   (iii) The receipt of the request for records should alert as to the possibility of a claim and possibly prompt investigation.
   (iv)   There may well be knowledge of the position because of an internal investigation or pursuit of a formal complaint, eg under the NHS complaints system.

11.4.3   'Admissions will be binding' (para 3.25)

This is a fundamental point.

It is not intended that there should be any facility to resile from an admission. This contrasts with CPR, r 14.1(5) (the facility given there is not intended to apply in the protocol situation). An admission made under the protocol will be binding when proceedings are later commenced.

The issue was tested to some extent in the Queen's Bench Division case of *Basildon and Thurrock University NHS Trust v Braybrook*.[9] The applicant trust sought permission under CPR, r 14.1(5) to withdraw an admission made by letter. It was held that in exercising its discretion the court would consider all the circumstances of the case and seek to give effect to the overriding objective of the CPR. The nearer any application was to a final hearing, the less chance of success it would have even if the party making the application could establish clear prejudice. In this case, the balance of prejudice weighed heavily in the respondent's favour, as did the need to uphold the overriding objective.

11.4.4 'Respond to that offer' (para 3.26)

Note the requirement to respond to an offer to settle in this situation (not something required by Part 36) and note the obligation, if making a counter offer, to provide documentation in support.

'4 Experts

4.1 In clinical negligence disputes expert opinions may be needed:
- on breach of duty and causation;
- on the patient's condition and prognosis;
- to assist in valuing aspects of the claim.

4.2 The civil justice reforms and the new **Civil Procedure Rules** will encourage economy in the use of experts and a **less adversarial expert culture**. It is recognised that in clinical negligence disputes, the parties and their advisers will require flexibility in their approach to expert evidence. Decisions on whether experts might be instructed jointly, and on whether reports might be disclosed sequentially or by exchange, should rest with the parties and their advisers. Sharing expert evidence may be appropriate on issues relating to the value of the claim. However, this protocol does not attempt to be prescriptive on issues in relation to expert evidence.

4.3 Obtaining expert evidence will often be an expensive step and may take time, especially in specialised areas of medicine where there are limited numbers of suitable experts. Patients and healthcare providers, and their advisers, will therefore need to consider carefully how best to obtain any necessary expert help quickly and cost-effectively. Assistance with locating a suitable expert is available from a number of sources.'

11.5 EXPERTS – COMMENTARY

The Protocol deliberately does not prescribe any procedures with regard to the use of experts in contrast to the Pre-Action Protocol for Personal Injury Claims.

It was recognised that clinical negligence litigation involved special or unusual areas of difficulty and that, particularly on issues of breach of duty and causation, each party should be able to access experts of their own choosing.

---

[9]   [2004] EWHC 3352 (QB).

Consistent with this approach, there is no requirement to identify experts to be instructed in advance to the other side and no need to tender names.

11.5.1   Use of experts (para 4.2)

The court's discretion is wide. Any exercise of the court's discretion will be subject to the provisions of the overriding objective in CPR, r 1.1 and the court's duty to manage cases under CPR, r 1.4.

In clinical negligence cases, it will be exceptional for joint experts to be used on issues relating to breach of duty. In the context of quantum issues, occasionally joint experts may be used to deal with non-controversial or low value heads of claim.[10]

In *Oxley v Penwarden*[11] the judge at first instance felt there was apparently a conflict between para 4.2 of the Protocol and CPR, r 35.7(1). The latter gives power to the court to direct that evidence on a particular issue be given by just one expert. The judge saw no reason to treat a clinical negligence claim differently from any other claim and imposed an order for a single expert to be used on the issue of causation. The case went to the Court of Appeal which allowed the appeal and restored an original order permitting each side to use its own expert. The Court made clear there was no presumption in favour of a single joint expert. Mantell LJ felt this was eminently a case for each side to have its own expert evidence.

11.6   ALTERNATIVE DISPUTE RESOLUTION – COMMENTARY

11.6.1   ADR is defined in the glossary to the CPR as a 'collective description of methods of resolving disputes otherwise than through the normal trial process'.[12]

> **'5 Alternative Dispute Resolution**
>
> 5.1 The parties should consider whether some form of alternative dispute resolution procedure would be more suitable than litigation, and if so, endeavour to agree which form to adopt. Both the claimant and defendant may be required by the court to provide evidence that alternative means of resolving their dispute were considered. The Courts take the view that litigation should be a last resort, and that claims should not be issued prematurely when a settlement is still actively being explored. Parties are warned that if the protocol is not followed (including this paragraph) then the court must have regard to such conduct when determining costs.

---

[10]   See Chapters 12 and 15.
[11]   [2001] Lloyd's Rep Med 347.
[12]   See Chapter 16.

5.2 It is not practicable in this Protocol to address in detail how the parties might decide which method to adopt to resolve their particular dispute. However, summarised below are some of the options for resolving disputes without litigation:

- Discussion and negotiation. Parties should bear in mind that carefully planned face-to-face meetings may be particularly helpful in exploring further treatment for the patient, in reaching understandings about what happened, and on both parties' positions, in narrowing the issues in dispute and, if the timing is right, in helping to settle the whole matter especially if the patient wants an apology, explanation, or assurances about how other patients will be affected.
- Early neutral evaluation by an independent third party (for example, a lawyer experienced in the field of clinical negligence or an individual experienced in the subject matter of the claim).
- Mediation – a form of facilitated negotiation assisted by an independent neutral party. The Clinical Disputes Forum has published a Guide to Mediation which will assist – available on the Clinical Disputes Forum website at www.clinicaldisputesforum.org.uk.
- The NHS Complaints Procedure is designed to provide patients with an explanation of what happened and an apology if appropriate. It is not designed to provide compensation for cases of negligence. However, patients might choose to use the procedure if their only, or main, goal is to obtain an explanation, or to obtain more information to help them decide what other action might be appropriate.

5.3 The Legal Services Commission has published a booklet on "Alternatives to Court", CLS Direct Information Leaflet 23 (www.clsdirect.org.uk/legalhelp/leaflet23.1sp), which lists a number of organisations that provide alternative dispute resolution services.

5.4 It is expressly recognised that no party can or should be forced to mediate or enter into any form of ADR.'[13]

There has been an increasing emphasis on the importance of ADR, and judicial support for its usage. It is now common for case management directions, particularly those issued by the Central Registry, to incorporate a request that parties shall consider the use of ADR. The government's commitment to supporting the use of ADR was emphasised in its pledge, announced by the Lord Chancellor in March 2001, that ADR will be considered and used in all suitable cases wherever the other party accepts it. The introduction of the CPR has seen a significant increase in the use of ADR and further encouragement and publicity is one of the key recommendations in the Final Report by Jackson, LJ into costs and case management in civil cases.

---

[13] Amendment: Paragraphs substituted: Supplement 41 (issued January 2006), with effect from 6 April 2006.

The best known and most definitive decision of the Court of Appeal concerning the approach that litigating parties should adopt when considering mediation is *Halsey v Milton Keynes General NHS Trust*,[14] which is discussed in detail at 16.4.3.

Annex A
Illustrative Flowchart

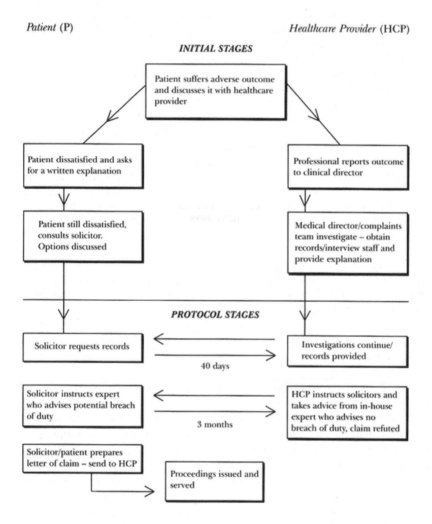

Patient (P)   *Healthcare Provider* (HCP)

INITIAL STAGES

Patient suffers adverse outcome and discusses it with healthcare provider

Patient dissatisfied and asks for a written explanation

Professional reports outcome to clinical director

Patient still dissatisfied, consults solicitor. Options discussed

Medical director/complaints team investigate – obtain records/interview staff and provide explanation

PROTOCOL STAGES

Solicitor requests records

Investigations continue/ records provided

40 days

Solicitor instructs expert who advises potential breach of duty

HCP instructs solicitors and takes advice from in-house expert who advises no breach of duty, claim refuted

3 months

Solicitor/patient prepares letter of claim – send to HCP

Proceedings issued and served

---

14   [2004] 1 WLR 3002.

Annex B
Protocol for Obtaining Hospital Medical Records

(Revised Edition (June 1998); Civil Litigation Committee, The Law Society)

Application on Behalf of a Patient for Hospital Medical Records for Use When Court Proceedings are Contemplated

Purpose of the Forms

This application form and response forms have been prepared by a working party of the Law Society's Civil Litigation Committee and approved by the Department of Health for use in NHS and Trust hospitals.

The purpose of the forms is to standardise and streamline the disclosure of medical records to a patient's solicitors, who are investigating pursuing a personal injury claim against a third party, or a medical negligence claim against the hospital to which the application is addressed and/or other hospitals or general practitioners.

Use of the Forms

Use of the forms is entirely voluntary and does not prejudice any party's right under the Access to Health Records Act 1990, the Data Protection Act 1984, or ss 33 and 34 of the Supreme Court Act 1981. However, it is the Department of Health policy that patients be permitted to see what has been written about them, and that healthcare providers should make arrangements to allow patients to see all their records, not only those covered by the Access to Health Records Act 1990. The aim of the forms is to save time and costs for all concerned for the benefit of the patient and the hospital and in the interests of justice. Use of the forms should make it unnecessary in most cases for there to be exchanges of letters or other enquiries. If there is any unusual matter not covered by the form, the patient's solicitor may write a separate letter at the outset.

Charges for Records

The Access to Health Records Act 1990 prescribes a maximum fee of £10. Photocopying and postage costs can be charged in addition. No other charges may be made.

The NHS Executive guidance makes it clear to healthcare providers that "it is a perfectly proper use" of the 1990 Act to request records in that framework for the purpose of potential or actual litigation, whether against a third party or against the hospital or trust.

The 1990 Act does not permit differential rates of charges to be levied if the application is made by the patient, or by a solicitor on his or her behalf, or whether the response to the application is made by the healthcare provider directly (the medical records manager or a claims manager) or by a solicitor.

The NHS Executive guidance recommends that the same practice should be followed with regard to charges when the records are provided under a voluntary agreement as under the 1990 Act, except that in those circumstances the £10 access fee will not be appropriate.

The NHS Executive also advises;
- that the cost of photocopying may include "the cost of staff time in making copies" and the costs of running the copier (but not costs of locating and sifting records);
- that the common practice of setting a standard rate for an application or charging an administration fee is not acceptable because there will be cases when this fails to comply with the 1990 Act.

Records: What Might be Included

X-rays and test results form part of the patient's records. Additional charges for copying X-rays are permissible. If there are large numbers of X-rays, the records officer should check with the patient/solicitor before arranging copying.

Reports on an "adverse incident" and reports on the patient made for risk management and audit purposes may form part of the records and be discloseable: the exception will be any specific record or report made solely or mainly in connection with an actual or potential claim.

Records: Quality Standards

When copying records healthcare providers should ensure:
1   All documents are legible, and complete, if necessary by photocopying at less than 100% size.
2   Documents larger than A4 in the original, eg ITU charts, should be reproduced in A3, or reduced to A4 where this retains readability.
3   Documents are only copied on one side of paper, unless the original is two sided.
4   Documents should not be unnecessarily shuffled or bound and holes should not be made in the copied papers.

Enquiries/Further Information

Any enquiries about the forms should be made initially to the solicitors making the request. Comments on the use and content of the forms should be made to the Secretary, Civil Litigation Committee, The Law Society, 113 Chancery Lane, London WC2A 1PL, telephone 0171 320 5739, or to the NHS Management Executive, Quarry House, Quarry Hill, Leeds LS2 7UE.

The Law Society

May 1998

Application on Behalf of a Patient for Hospital Medical Records for Use when Court Proceedings are Contemplated

This should be completed as fully as possible.

Insert Hospital Name and Address	TO: Medical Records Officer Hospital	
1 (a)	Full name of patient (including previous surnames)	
(b)	Address now	
(c)	Address at start of treatment	
(d)	Date of birth (and death, if applicable)	
(e)	Hospital ref no if available	
(f)	N.I. number, if available	
2	This application is made because the patient is considering	
(a)	a claim against your hospital as detailed in para 7 overleaf	YES/NO
(b)	pursuing an action against some one else	YES/NO
3	Department(s) where treatment was received	
4	Name(s) of consultant(s) at your hospital in charge of the treatment	
5	Whether treatment at your hospital was private or NHS, wholly or in part	

6	A description of the treatment received, with approximate dates	
7	If the answer to Q2(a) is 'Yes' details of	
	(a) the likely nature of the claim	
	(b) grounds for the claim	
	(c) approximate dates of the events involved	
8	If the answer to Q2(b) is 'Yes' insert	
	(a) the names of the proposed defendants	
	(b) whether legal proceedings yet begun	YES/NO
	(c) if appropriate, details of the claim and action number	
9	We confirm we will pay reasonable copying charges	
10	We request prior details of	YES/NO
	(a) photocopying and administration charges for medical records	
	(b) number of and cost of copying x-ray and scan films	YES/NO
11	Any other relevant information, particular requirements, or any particular documents not required (eg copies of computerised records)	
	Signature of Solicitor	

	Name
	Address
	Ref.
	Telephone number	
	Fax number	

	Please print name beneath each signature. Signature by child over 12 but under 18 years also requires signature by parent
Signature of patient Signature of parent or next friend if appropriate	

Signature of personal representative where patient has died

First Response to Application for Hospital Records

	NAME OF PATIENT Our ref Your ref	
1	Date of receipt of patient's application	
2	We intend that copy medical records will be dispatched within 6 weeks of that date	YES/NO
3	We require pre-payment of photocopying charges	YES/NO
4	If estimate of photocopying charges requested or pre-payment required the amount will be	£ / notified to you
5	The cost of x-ray and scan films will be	£ / notified to you
6	If there is any problem, we shall write to you within those 6 weeks	YES/NO

7	Any other information	
	Please address further correspondence to	
	Signed	
	Direct telephone number	
	Direct fax number	
	Dated	

Second Response Enclosing Patient's Hospital Medical Records

Address		Our Ref Your Ref	
1	**NAME OF PATIENT:** We confirm that the enclosed copy medical records are all those within the control of the hospital, relevant to the application which you have made to the best of our knowledge and belief, subject to paras 2–5 below	YES/NO	
2	Details of any other documents which have not yet been located	
3	Date by when it is expected that these will be supplied	
4	Details of any records which we are not producing	
5	The reasons for not doing so	

6	An invoice for copying and administration charges is attached	YES/NO
	Signed	
	Date	

Annex C
Templates for Letters of Claim and Response

C1 Letter of Claim

Essential Contents

1 Client's name, address, date of birth, etc

2 Dates of allegedly negligent treatment

3 Events giving rise to the claim:
- an outline of what happened, including details of other relevant treatments to the client by other healthcare providers.

4 Allegation of negligence and causal link with injuries:
- an outline of the allegations or a more detailed list in a complex case;
- an outline of the causal link between allegations and the injuries complained of.

5 The client's injuries, condition and future prognosis

6 Request for clinical records (if not previously provided)
- use the Law Society form if appropriate or adapt;
- specify the records required;
- if other records are held by other providers, and may be relevant, say so;
- State what investigations have been carried out to date, eg information from client and witnesses, any complaint and the outcome, if any clinical records have been seen or expert's advice obtained.

7 The likely value of the claim
- an outline of the main heads of damage, or, in straightforward cases, the details of loss.

Optional Information

What investigations have been carried out

An offer to settle without supporting evidence

Suggestions for obtaining expert evidence

Suggestions for meetings, negotiations, discussion or mediation

Possible Enclosures

Chronology

Clinical records request form and client's authorisation

Expert report(s)

Schedules of loss and supporting evidence

C2 Letter of Response

Essential Contents

1 Provide **requested records** and invoice for copying:
- explain if records are incomplete or extensive records are held and ask for further instructions;
- request additional records from third parties.

2 Comments on events and/or chronology:
- if events are disputed or the healthcare provider has further information or documents on which they wish to rely, these should be provided, eg internal protocol;
- details of any further information needed from the patient or a third party should be provided.

3 If breach of duty and causation are accepted:
- suggestions might be made for resolving the claim and/or requests for further information;
- a response should be made to any offer to settle.

4 If breach of duty and/or causation are denied:
- a bare denial will not be sufficient. If the healthcare provider has other explanations for what happened, these should be given at least in outline;
- suggestions might be made for the next steps, eg further investigations, obtaining expert evidence, meetings/negotiations or mediation, or an invitation to issue proceedings.

Optional Matters

An offer to settle if the patient has not made one, or a counter offer to the patient's with supporting evidence

Possible Enclosures

Clinical records

Annotated chronology

Expert reports

Annex D
Lord Woolf's Recommendations

1 Lord Woolf in his Access to Justice Report in July 1996, following a detailed review of the problems of medical negligence claims, identified that one of the major sources of **costs and delay** is **at the pre-litigation stage** because –

(a) Inadequate incident reporting and record keeping in hospitals, and mobility of staff, make it difficult to establish facts, often several years after the event.

(b) Claimants must incur the cost of an expert in order to establish whether they have a viable claim.

(c) There is often a long delay before a claim is made.

(d) Defendants do not have sufficient resources to carry out a full investigation of every incident, and do not consider it worthwhile to start an investigation as soon as they receive a request for records, because many cases do not proceed beyond that stage.

(e) Patients often give the defendant little or no notice of a firm intention to pursue a claim. Consequently, many incidents are not investigated by the defendants until after proceedings have started.

(f) Doctors and other clinical staff are traditionally reluctant to admit negligence or apologise to, or negotiate with, claimants for fear of damage to their professional reputations or career prospects.

2 Lord Woolf acknowledged that under the present arrangements **healthcare providers**, faced with possible medical negligence claims, have a number of **practical problems** to contend with –

(a) Difficulties of finding patients' records and tracing former staff, which can be exacerbated by late notification and by the health-care provider's own failure to identify adverse incidents.

(b) The healthcare provider may have only treated the patient for a limited time or for a specific complaint: the patient's previous history may be relevant but the records may be in the possession of one of several other healthcare providers.

(c) The large number of potential claims do not proceed beyond the stage of a request for medical records, or an explanation; and that it is difficult for healthcare providers to investigate fully every case whenever a patient asks to see the records.

Annex E
How to Contact the Forum

The Clinical Disputes Forum

Chairman

Dr Alastair Scotland

[Medical Director and Chief Officer

National Clinical Assessment Authority

9th Floor, Market Towers

London

SW8 5NQ]   Telephone : [0207 273 0850]
Secretary
Sarah Leigh
c/o Margaret Dangoor
3 Clydesdale Gardens
Richmond
Surrey
TW10 5EG   Telephone: [0208][15] 408 1012

---

[15] Amendment: Text in square brackets substituted: Supplement 24 (issued 7 September 2001), with effect from 15 October 2001.

CHAPTER 12

CASE MANAGEMENT DIRECTIONS

In this chapter solicitor Jon Nicholson looks at case management directions in clinical negligence cases. The chapter assumes knowledge of general civil procedure and directions and considers the respects in which directions in clinical negligence cases may differ from those used in other types of litigation. The chapter covers directions questionnaires, the detail of the standard directions, areas of particular difficulty in clinical negligence case management and pre-trial checklists.

12.1 DIRECTIONS QUESTIONNAIRES

The new directions questionnaire (court form N181) replaced the old allocation questionnaire with effect from 1 April 2013 and will be familiar to all civil litigation practitioners. In clinical negligence matters, it is worth taking the time to complete this fully.

Part A gives the parties an opportunity to request a one-month stay to attempt to settle the claim. This is rarely appropriate in clinical negligence cases.

If the pre-action protocol has been followed, proceedings will not have been commenced unless liability is denied or negotiations have broken down. Having taken the decision to issue, the claimant is unlikely to benefit from a further month's delay before the claim progresses towards resolution.

If liability is formally denied, the defendant is unlikely to request a stay of proceedings for negotiations on settlement, as this would betray a lack of confidence in its pleaded defence which the claimant would want to exploit during any such negotiations.

Consequently, a stay of proceedings is only likely to be attractive to the parties if the defence contains an admission of liability for the first time, which should only happen if the pre-action protocol has not been followed (for example because of an impending limitation deadline).

Part B of the directions questionnaire gives the parties an opportunity to state whether the claim needs to be heard at a particular court and, if so, why. This may be an opportunity to request that the claim issued in the county court be transferred to the High Court on the grounds of its importance or complexity or because the sum claimed is significantly greater than appeared likely at the time when protective proceedings were issued.

Most clinical negligence claims include a claim for damages in respect of personal injuries and so cannot be started in the High Court unless the value of the claim is £25,000 or more.[1] It may be argued that many clinical negligence cases valued at less than £25,000 are appropriate for the High Court because of their complexity and because they involve allegations against a professional whose reputation and livelihood may be affected by the outcome. However, in practice, most county court district judges do not take kindly to the suggestion that a claim is too complicated or important for their court and such requests normally succeed only in alienating the district judge from the party making the request. Consequently, requesting a transfer to the High Court is a high risk strategy which should only be embarked upon in the most clear-cut cases.

More realistically, there may be a possibility of transferring a case to a court in another part of the country which is closer to one or both parties or the witnesses or where the events complained of took place. If this is a possibility, then practitioners may wish to request such a transfer or anticipate their opponent making such a request and set out reasons why the action should remain in the court in which it was issued.

Following the implementation of the Jackson reforms in April 2013, the Masters at the Royal Courts of Justice have indicated that they will be transferring lower value clinical negligence cases to a county court and that claimants are discouraged from issuing such cases in the High Court. This policy appears to have been prompted by concern about the Masters' workloads as a result of the reforms. Therefore, if a lower value claim has been issued in the High Court, the directions questionnaire is an opportunity to explain why it should remain in that court.

Good reasons for an action to be heard in a particular court include the convenience of the claimant (particularly a disabled claimant) and the convenience of witnesses (particularly busy medical practitioners working for the NHS who are either witnesses of fact or experts). If the claimant's address on the claim form is some distance from the court, it may be worth explaining that he works nearby. The location where the events took place is of limited relevance and it is unlikely that any weight will be attached to the convenience of solicitors or counsel. Obviously, the judiciary sitting at a particular court may be a factor influencing a party's preference, but cannot be given as a reason.

Part C of the directions questionnaire asks whether a pre-action protocol applies to the claim and whether it has been complied with. If the party completing the directions questionnaire has not complied with the clinical negligence pre-action protocol, it is now essential to explain the reasons fully. If

---

[1]   Para 4A of High Court and County Courts Jurisdiction Order 1991, 1991/724 as amended on
       6 April 2009.

the other party has failed to comply with the protocol without obvious reason, it may be appropriate to draw this to the court's attention in the directions questionnaire.

Part D of the directions questionnaire requests various case management information including matters relating to disclosure, which is not normally a major issue in clinical negligence. This part of the directions questionnaire also asks which track is considered most suitable for the claim and this is dealt with at **12.2.3**.

Part E of the directions questionnaire seeks details of the expert evidence required, including the experts' names, field of expertise, the justification for such expert evidence and an estimate of the associated costs. The latter two requirements are new and have been added as part of the Jackson reforms. Many procedural judges will expect a full justification for the use of an expert, rather than a single word, such as 'causation'.

The requirement to give the names of experts upon whom the party wishes to rely is a potential problem. In clinical negligence cases, the identity of the opposing experts is always of interest, but it is probably not wise for a party to disclose the name of an expert whom they intend to instruct, but whose opinion they have not yet received. The danger is that if that opinion proves to be unfavourable and a report from another expert in the same discipline is subsequently obtained and relied upon, the opposing party will know that the expert relied upon is different from the one named in the directions questionnaire and, in the absence of any other explanation, will infer that the named expert gave an unwelcome opinion. This knowledge obviously weakens the position of the party who has had to change experts for this reason. Moreover, it is now possible for the opposing party to ask the court to make permission to rely upon the new expert conditional on disclosing the unsupportive report of the previous expert.[2]

The problem is wholly avoidable, because the directions questionnaire only requires a party to name experts upon whom they wish to rely, not experts whom they propose to instruct. If the party completing the directions questionnaire has not yet received the opinion of a particular expert, he does not yet know whether he wishes to rely on this expert and so he is not required to name that expert in the directions questionnaire. It is suggested that a party should only name experts whose opinions have already been received and whom are known to support the case. Otherwise, experts should be identified by their field of expertise only with the name 'to be advised'.

However, the new CPR 35.4 provides that parties seeking permission to rely upon an expert must provide the expert's name 'where practicable' and the standard directions now envisage that experts will be named in the order. As a result, opportunities to avoid the naming of experts have considerably reduced. This is further discussed at **12.2.9.1**.

---

[2] *Edwards-Tubb v JD Wetherspoon Plc* [2011] 1 WLR 1373, [2011] PIQR P16.

Part H of the directions questionnaire refers to the requirement to file a costs budget by a date to be directed by the court or, if no such date has been specified, seven days before the first case management conference. Costs budgeting and costs management orders are covered in the new edition of *APIL Guide to Costs and Funding*.[3]

Part J of the directions questionnaire invites the parties to set out any further information to assist the judge with case management. This is a valuable opportunity to communicate directly with the court about these issues and to, for example, explain any unusual directions sought.

Part K of the directions questionnaire allows the parties to attach draft directions which they consider appropriate for the management of the claim. Doing so is not mandatory, but is normally good practice. The drafting of such directions is considered at **12.2**.

12.2　DIRECTIONS

Although directions orders are made by the court, they are usually drafted by the parties. Paragraph 2.3(2) of the Practice Direction supplementing CPR Part 26 states that the parties 'must try to agree the case management directions which they will invite the court to make'. If appropriate agreed directions are filed with the directions questionnaires, the court may approve them without a hearing and make an order in the terms proposed.[4]

If the parties cannot reach agreement or if the agreed directions are not suitable, the court will give directions, usually at a case management conference. However, the court will normally be working from a draft prepared by one of the parties and amending this as appropriate. This section deals in detail with issues relating to the drafting of directions in clinical negligence cases.

Some courts, particularly those where there are proactive district judges or where there are delays in listing case management hearings, adopt the practice of sending out initial case management directions leaving it to the parties to apply to vary them. Some may be confined to disclosure but whatever they contain such orders merit close attendance and observance as a district judge is now very unlikely to be sympathetic to a party who has simply ignored such an order.

12.2.1　Deadlines in directions

When drafting directions, it is vital to be realistic about the dates by which steps must be taken. Although the parties may wish to see the case resolved as soon as possible, an unrealistic timetable can become a rod for their own backs. Since 1 April 2013, enforcing compliance with directions orders has been part

---

3　Jordan Publishing (March 2014).
4　CPR 29.4.

of the overriding objective[5] and the judiciary have indicated that it will now be more difficult to obtain orders extending deadlines.[6] Most directions involve a sanction for failure to comply and it is now difficult to apply successfully for relief from sanctions.[7] It is very important to consult with other members of the team such as experts and counsel about their availability and the time that they will require for the work which they will need to undertake (for example finalising a report for exchange in the light of the defendant's witness evidence).

It is good practice to avoid deadlines falling on a Friday, so that if a party fails to comply with a deadline, it is possible for the other party to apply to the court for a consequential order the following day if appropriate.

12.2.2 Standard directions

All clinical negligence cases issued at the Royal Courts of Justice (RCJ) in London are assigned to one of two Masters who deal with clinical negligence case management. The Masters currently undertaking this role are Master Roberts and Master Cook.

The clinical negligence masters at the RCJ published suggested model directions which were updated periodically. The first model directions were published in March 2002 after consultation with various parties including a committee of the Clinical Disputes Forum.

The model directions consisted of specimen paragraphs which could be used to prepare a draft directions order. The introductory note stated that they 'need not be slavishly followed' and were guidelines only. Nevertheless, parties were expected to use this format for clinical negligence directions at the RCJ and the model directions were also used all over the country at both High Court and county court level. This practice was encouraged by Lord Justice Brooke in *Wardlaw v Farrar*, when he made the following point about the model directions in the context of a case where medical literature had been disclosed late:

> 'Now that so many relatively heavy clinical negligence actions in the multi-track are being conducted in county courts, in addition to district registries of the High Court, it is essential that best practice should be followed throughout the country in relation to case management directions in the multi-track in this specialist field. If these directions had been made in the present case, the medical literature would have been handled in a more orderly manner.'[8]

---

5   CPR 1.1(f).
6   See speech delivered by the Master of the Rolls, Lord Justice Dyson, to the District Judges Annual Seminar on 22 March 2013.
7   *Mitchell v News Group Newspapers Ltd* [2014] 1 WLR 795; *Denton v TH White Ltd* [2014] EWCA Civ 906.
8   [2003] 4 All ER 1358, [2004] Lloyd's Rep Med 1998, (2003) *The Times*, December 5 at para 24.

In March 2013, the Ministry of Justice published specimen directions for various categories of case, which have been allocated to the multi-track. These are available on the Justice website.[9] These include two sets of standard directions for clinical negligence; one for cases being litigated at the RCJ and the other for cases outside the RCJ. The two standard orders are very similar and are both based closely on the old model directions. They can be found at Appendix 3.

The remainder of this section will deal with clinical negligence directions under the same headings and in the same order as they appear in the standard directions.

12.2.3   Allocation

Clinical negligence actions are almost invariably allocated to the multi-track. Even if a claim has a financial value of no more than the current fast-track limit of £25,000, a case will only be allocated to the fast-track if the trial is likely to last for no longer than one day,[10] which is taken to be 5 hours.[11] Very few clinical negligence claims where liability is disputed are capable of being tried within such a short time. Moreover, CPR 35.5(2) provides that the court will not normally permit an expert to attend a fast-track trial and, as explained at **12.2.9.5**, oral evidence from experts is normally required in any clinical negligence claim where liability is in dispute.

Consequently, clinical negligence claims will generally be allocated to the multi-track even if their value is £25,000 or less. The only such cases likely to be suitable for the fast-track are those where liability is wholly admitted and quantum is unlikely to exceed £25,000. The notes to the new standard directions for use outside the RCJ go so far as to say that all claims alleging clinical negligence 'must' be allocated to the multi-track.

In the standard directions for use outside the RCJ, the paragraph dealing with allocation also states that the action is assigned to a particular district judge for case management. This implements Jackson LJ's recommendation that 'docketing' be introduced for all clinical negligence claims, as was already occurring at the RCJ (on issue) and at some other courts.[12] This means that there should be a single specialist judge who is dealing with all case management issues in a particular action throughout its lifetime.

---

[9]   www.justice.gov.uk/courts/procedure-rules/civil/standard-directions/general/list-of-cases-of-
     common-occurance.
[10] CPR 26.6(5)(a).
[11] Para 9.1(3)(a) of the Practice Direction to CPR Part 26.
[12] Paragraph 5.3 of Chapter 23 of Jackson LJ's 'Review of Civil Litigation Costs' ('the Jackson
     Report'), published December 2009.

12.2.4 Preservation of evidence

The standard directions include a sub-paragraph requiring the defendant to 'retain the original clinical notes relating to issues in this claim' and to give facilities for inspection of those original notes by the claimant, their lawyers and experts, upon seven days' written notice.

12.2.5 Maintenance of records and reports

The standard directions contain a sub-paragraph requiring that all references in expert reports to records should be made by reference to the relevant page number(s) in a paginated bundle to be prepared and maintained by the claimant's solicitor. The intention is that both parties should be using the same pagination so that the other side and the court can easily identify the record to which an expert is referring. Previously, it was not uncommon for each side to paginate the records differently and sometimes it was necessary to have available at trial two sets of copies of the same records, differently paginated, with each side referring to a different copy.

12.2.6 Trial of preliminary issue

Although there can be trials on other preliminary issues (such as limitation), the usual candidates for a trial of a preliminary issue in a disputed clinical negligence matter are breach of duty and causation. This is normally referred to as a 'split trial', although the standard directions suggest a longer form of wording to make it clear precisely what issues should be determined at a 'liability trial'. Whether there should be a split trial is often a contentious case management question.

The issue arises in cases where the quantification of damages involves further expert evidence and substantial costs. In such cases the claimant may seek a split trial in order to avoid incurring those costs needlessly if the claim is not successful on liability. Many clinical negligence claimants are still proceeding with the benefit of public funding (although new certificates are now only granted in a very limited category of cases) and, as a matter of policy, the Legal Aid Agency expects practitioners to apply for breach of duty and causation to be tried as a preliminary issue in cases where this would result in a substantial saving if the claim is unsuccessful.

Claimants' lawyers acting under conditional fee agreements may also be looking for an early resolution of breach of duty and causation before undertaking substantial work on quantum which would be unremunerated if the claim fails. In large cases, the claimant can also gain a tactical advantage in relation to quantum if breach of duty and causation have been dealt with first and interim payments are obtained to fund a care regime which the defendant may then find it difficult to attack.

Split trials are more attractive to claimants who believe that their case on breach of duty and causation is strong even though the case is defended. In cases which are less strong, the disadvantage of split trials is that they tend to discourage settlement. They make it cheaper for the defendant to fight the case to trial. They also make it more difficult for the defendant to settle on a global basis, because the claim has not been properly quantified.

If a defendant wishes to settle in these circumstances, it must either offer to concede a percentage of liability (without knowing how much this will cost them) or guess the value of the claim with limited information and make a global offer based on that estimate. Neither is an attractive option. Many claimants' solicitors therefore have reservations about applying for a split trial in every case where breach of duty and/or causation are disputed, but in publicly funded cases the Legal Aid Agency will normally require such an application to be made.

Split trials are not popular with defendants unless they are very confident of success (and such cases are rarely brought). If a claim is proceeding on the basis that breach of duty and causation will be tried as a preliminary issue, it is very difficult for the defendant to estimate the claim's realistic value for the purposes of both financial planning and settlement. Typically, a claimant seeking a split trial will serve only a preliminary outline schedule,[13] which contains limited information. If a split trial is ordered, disclosure will normally be limited to documents relevant to breach of duty and causation, and obviously the claimant's witness and expert evidence will only address these issues. The claimant's legal team may be reluctant to allow the defendants' quantum experts to assess the claimant in circumstances where the claimant's funders are not allowing them to do any work to be done on quantum. Consequently, it is common for defendants to oppose applications for split trials.

The attitude of procedural judges to an application for a split trial varies. However, as a general rule, in cases where breach of duty and causation are disputed dealing with these matters as a preliminary issue will give effect to the overriding objective[14] by saving court time and expense. Once breach of duty and causation have been dealt with, either the case will be over or settlement is much more likely than it was when these matters were in issue.

Particular factors which are likely to influence the court's decision one way or the other are as follows:

- Is there any reason why the claim cannot be quantified now? If breach of duty and causation are in dispute and quantification of the claim is not possible at this stage (for example because of uncertainty regarding the claimant's medical prognosis), then this would be a good reason to order a split trial.

---

[13]   See **12.2.11.1**.
[14]   CPR 1.1.

- Are breach of duty and causation wholly in dispute? If the defendant admits some negligence which caused some damage, then the court is unlikely to agree to a split trial even if other allegations of breach of duty and causation are disputed. The fact that some part of the claim has been admitted means that the court will have to consider some element of quantum at some point and dealing with breach of duty and causation first is unlikely to result in any significant saving of court time or expense.

- What is the likely cost of assessing quantum? The more complex the quantum issues and the greater the number of experts required to assist the court on quantum, the more likely it is that a split trial will be ordered.

- Are any of the same experts required in relation to both breach of duty/causation and quantum? It is not uncommon for the area of specialism of the expert dealing with causation also to be the discipline required to deal with condition and prognosis. In these circumstances, the experts in this discipline may potentially be required to give evidence at the trials of both breach of duty/causation and quantum, which would be more expensive than those experts giving evidence at just one trial. The fact that the same expert is required for both breach of duty/causation and quantum is a reason not to have a split trial, unless this inconvenience is outweighed by the substantial number of experts who would be required to deal only with quantum.

12.2.7 Disclosure and inspection

Practice relating to disclosure in clinical negligence matters is not significantly different from any other type of civil litigation.

Pursuant to CPR 31.15(c), a party requesting copies of documents disclosed by the opposing party must 'undertake to pay reasonable copying costs'. This has been an area of recent difficulty, because some claimant solicitors are now seeking to charge up to 35p per page for such photocopying, whereas the NHS Litigation Authority appears to have instructed panel firms to pay no more than 25p per page. This is a separate issue from seeking to recover internal photocopying charges as a disbursement at detailed assessment, which is not normally possible. The issue has been argued before the Queen's Bench masters in a couple of cases where photocopying charges of 35p per page have been upheld as reasonable,[15] but there is no higher authority on the point.

The standard directions require the parties to serve and file with the court a list of issues relevant to the search for and disclosure of electronically stored documents or to confirm that there are no such issues, following Practice Direction 31B. However, most hospital records are still paper-based and the disclosure and management of electronic documents is therefore less likely to be an issue in clinical negligence than in many other types of claim. Jackson LJ recommended that personal injury and clinical negligence claims be excluded

---

[15] *Coveney v P&O Ferries Ltd* LTL 20/5/11 and *DH v South Devon Healthcare NHS Foundation Trust*, unreported but summarised in October 2011 *APIL PI Focus*.

from his 'menu' of options for electronic disclosure 'as standard disclosure usually works satisfactorily in these cases'.[16]

12.2.8   Witness statements

If breach of duty and/or causation are in dispute and are to be decided at the same time as quantum, in larger cases it is often helpful to provide for witness statements on breach of duty and causation to be exchanged separately and before witness statements on quantum. The model directions order recognises this by providing for two different dates for the exchange of statements, depending on the issues to which the witness evidence is directed.

This is helpful in cases where the parties are able to proceed to an early exchange of witness statements on breach of duty and causation, but where the claimant needs more time to prepare witness statements on quantum. The statements of the clinicians being criticised and their colleagues are important evidence on breach of duty and causation which the claimant's experts will not normally have seen. If statements on these issues can be exchanged early, the experts can begin preparing their final reports on breach of duty and causation without waiting until the claimant's solicitor has finished preparing quantum witness statements.

In some cases, there are likely to be further developments relevant to quantum taking place after the date for exchange of statements and before trial. For example, it may be that interim payments are being used to fund a care regime and evidence is required at trial on what has been done and how this has worked in practice. In these circumstances, it is necessary for the directions to provide for service of supplementary witness statements dealing only with matters arising since the date for exchange with such statements to be served, say, no less than six weeks before trial or the commencement of any trial period. Following the implementation of the Jackson reforms, such a direction is needed because CPR 32.10 imposes a sanction for failure to serve a witness statement within the time specified by the court, namely that the witness may not then be called to give oral evidence unless the court gives permission. It is now difficult to obtain relief from sanctions. The need for a specific direction for updated witness statements was highlighted by Turner J in *Karbhari v Ahmed*.[17]

12.2.8.1   *Statements of treating doctors*

The standard direction for the exchange of witness statements provides that 'For the avoidance of doubt statements of all concerned with the relevant treatment and care of the claimant must be included'.

---

[16]   Paragraph 6.6 of the Executive Summary to the Jackson Report.
[17]   LTL 19/12/2013: [2014] 1 Costs LR 151.

This clearly includes the statements of the clinicians alleged to have been negligent and, if applicable, any other clinicians employed by the defendant whose evidence is to be relied upon. However, the wording also requires the defendant to produce statements of treating clinicians whose evidence is not relied upon, for example because it adds nothing or because it actually supports the claimant's case. In an adversarial system, in very unusual for the court to order a party to obtain and serve witness statements upon which it does not rely and which in fact favour the opposing party, but that is the effect of this order. The consequence is that some defendants may overlook the requirement to obtain and serve such statements and claimants should be alert to this possibility.

It may also be necessary for either party to obtain and serve statements from other treating clinicians unconnected with the defendant, who might be able to give evidence on the background to the alleged negligence or its consequences and whom either the claimant or the defendant propose to call as witnesses of fact. If necessary, the defendant can obtain a direction requiring that the claimant provide an authority to enable the defendant to interview other treating doctors, although any such authority should be limited to information relevant to the issues in the case.[18]

The difficulty with the statements of doctors in clinical negligence cases is that it is sometimes difficult to distinguish between factual evidence in such statements and matters of expert opinion, which should normally be dealt with only by expert witnesses upon whose evidence the parties require permission to rely.

Not all evidence of medical practice on the part of treating doctors is expert evidence. In *Kirkman v Euro Exide Corporation*,[19] the Court of Appeal held that the evidence of a treating doctor as to what he himself would have done in hypothetical circumstances (if a particular event had not happened), was evidence of fact and not an expert opinion on what most competent surgeons would have done in the same situation.

Moreover, a medical practitioner whose actions are being criticised is permitted to give some opinion evidence in his own defence. In *ES (By her Mother and Litigation Friend, DS) v Chesterfield and North Derbyshire Royal Hospital NHS Trust*[20] (discussed more fully at **12.2.9.3**), the Court of Appeal endorsed the following comment made by Master Ungley (emphasis added):[21]

> 'It is inevitable that a witness who happens to be a professional will give evidence *of his actions* based upon his or her professional experience and expertise ...'

---

[18] *Nicholson v Halton General Hospital NHS Trust* [1999] PIQR P310. See also *Shaw v Skeet Aung Sooriakumaran* [1996] 7 Med LR 371.
[19] (2007) *The Times*, February 6.
[20] [2004] Lloyd's Rep Med 90.
[21] Ibid paras 23 and 31.

The Court of Appeal held that such evidence could seek to explain or justify such actions and to touch upon the question of whether they fell short of the required standard.

This dictum is clearly limited to a professional witness giving evidence of his own actions. It does not extend to such a witness commenting on the actions of colleagues or on matters of causation. The claimant is normally only able to call upon opinion evidence from one expert in the relevant field. The defendant will also have an independent expert witness in that field and if the defendant is also able to rely upon the opinions of medical practitioners called as witnesses of fact, the parties will not be on an equal footing, as required by the overriding objective. Claimants' representatives therefore need to be alert to inadmissable opinion evidence in the defendant's witness statements and to take appropriate action if necessary. Such action would normally involve an application for an order striking out the offending passages from the witness statement or putting the defendant to its election as to whether to remove those passages or to rely upon the witness as its sole expert in the relevant field.

12.2.9   Experts

Expert evidence forms a vital part of any clinical negligence case and it is unsurprising that the standard directions deal with this in some detail.[22]

12.2.9.1   *Permission to adduce expert evidence*

CPR 35.1 states:

> 'Expert evidence shall be restricted to that which is reasonably required to resolve the proceedings.'

CPR 35.4 provides:

> '(1) No party may call an expert or put in evidence an expert's report without the court's permission.
>
> (2) When parties apply for permission they must provide an estimate of the costs of the proposed expert evidence.'

The combined effect of these rules is that in order to rely upon expert evidence at trial, it is necessary to persuade the court that such evidence is reasonably required and that the cost is proportionate. The difficulty or otherwise of obtaining the necessary permission will depend on the usual factors, including the nature and complexity of the issues involved, the value of the claim and the nature of the expert evidence sought, but also on the cost.

It is easier to obtain permission to rely upon expert evidence in some disciplines than in others. For example, before the introduction of the CPR, it was

---

[22]   Instructing experts is dealt with in Chapter 13.

common for parties to rely upon expert evidence from employment consultants regarding a claimant's likely earnings if the injury had not occurred and the extent of any residual earning capacity. Such evidence was usually based on an analysis of published earnings and employment statistics rather than the employment consultant's personal experience. Since the introduction of the CPR, reliance upon employment consultants has been discouraged and it is now very difficult to obtain the necessary permission even in problematic and unusual cases.[23]

In catastrophic claims, such as those involving cerebral palsy, the number of expert disciplines required to assist the court in the quantification of the claim is potentially very large. This is often a point of dispute between the parties, with the defendants being conscious that each additional expert discipline not only adds to the costs, but also potentially introduces another head of loss.

In some cases, it may be appropriate to try and tackle this problem by early exchange of the reports of the core quantum experts and possibly even an early discussion between these experts to establish what other expert disciplines are necessary to enable the court to assess quantum. However, in most cases, postponing the instruction of such further quantum experts until this step has been taken is likely to delay the overall resolution of the claim.

It should be noted that permission is required to call an expert or to put in evidence an expert's report. Permission is not required to instruct an expert. If a party has difficulty in obtaining permission to rely upon expert evidence in a particular field, one possible course of action is to obtain such an expert opinion without permission and to then put the report before the court in the hope that its value will then be self-evident and permission will be granted. Although such an approach is often successful, the disadvantage is that if permission is still refused, the party which has obtained expert evidence without permission may have difficulty recovering the cost from the other party at the end of the litigation.

CPR 35.4 goes on to say:

'(2) When parties apply for permission they must ... identify –

(a)   The field in which expert evidence is required and the issues which the expert evidence will address; and

(b)   Where practicable, the name of the proposed expert.

(3) If permission is granted, it shall be in relation only to the expert named or the field identified under paragraph (2). The order granting permission may specify the issues which the expert evidence should address.'

The danger of naming an expert whose opinion has not yet been received is discussed at **12.1**. However, the standard directions now envisage that the names of experts for whom permission is granted will be stated, not their disciplines. Nevertheless, it is suggested that practitioners should if possible

---

[23]   See, for example, the decision in *Turner v Walsall Hospital* LTL 11/4/2013.

resist the naming of experts in the directions order, because it would then be necessary to apply for the permission of the court to rely upon a different expert. Such permission will normally only be granted on terms that the report of the previous expert be disclosed,[24] which is an outcome which the applicant is usually seeking to avoid. No such permission is required if the expert is not named in the order.[25]

The standard clinical negligence directions now include provision for the court to specify the issues that the expert evidence can address.

12.2.9.2   Choice between separately or jointly instructed experts

CPR 35.7(1) empowers the court to direct that evidence be given by a single joint expert. The standard directions therefore include suggested wording for paragraphs giving permission for evidence from both separate experts and joint single experts.

Although the standard directions appear to allow for this, it is not appropriate for issues of breach of duty and/or causation to be addressed by joint single experts. When the Civil Procedure Rules were first introduced in 1999, there were some orders made for joint single experts on these matters, but these were generally overturned on appeal.[26] The reason is that the expert evidence on these questions in clinical negligence cases is largely determinative of the issue and for the court to have access to only a single expert opinion on breach of duty and/or causation would amount to 'trial by expert'.

A view then developed that medical experts should generally be separately instructed and non-medical experts who are concerned only with quantum should be jointly instructed. This approach can be seen in the judgment of Lord Woolf in *MP v Mid Kent Healthcare NHS Trust*,[27] in which it was suggested that non-medical expert evidence should be given by single experts 'in the vast majority of cases'. However, these remarks were obiter. The appeal did not relate to the direction that all seven non-medical quantum experts be jointly instructed (including the care expert), but rather to a subsequent direction relating to the proposed attendance of a single joint expert at a consultation with counsel.

Another view is that the issue of whether experts in a particular discipline should be separately or jointly instructed depends on whether the parties are able to agree on a mutually acceptable expert in that discipline. This is a pragmatic approach, but it puts the cart before the horse. If a particular issue requiring expert evidence is suitable for a joint report, then it is incumbent on

---

[24]   *Beck v Ministry of Defence* [2005] 1 WLR 2206, (2003) *The Times*, July 21 and *Edwards-Tubb v JD Wetherspoon Plc* [2011] 1 WLR 1373, [2011] PIQR P16.

[25]   *Hajigeordiou v Vasiliou* [2005] 1 WLR 2195, [2005] 3 All ER 17, (2005) *The Times*, March 22.

[26]   See, for example, *Simms v Birmingham Health Authority* [2001] Lloyd's Rep Med 382.

[27]   [2001] 1 WLR 210, [2002] 3 All ER 688, (2001) *The Times*, November 19.

the parties to compromise on the choice of expert, rather than deciding that in fact the issue requires separate experts because they cannot easily agree on a joint choice.

It is suggested that the proper approach is to consider the importance of the particular expert discipline to the issues in the case and the cost and to then reach a decision on whether it is proportionate for the parties to instruct separate experts in that discipline. Medical experts dealing with breach of duty and causation should invariably be separately instructed. A medical expert dealing only with a minor aspect of quantum might be jointly instructed.

Non-medical experts dealing with highly contentious and valuable aspects of quantum should be separately instructed, because otherwise a large proportion of damages will be assessed by a single expert whose evidence is not tested at trial, rather than having the damages assessed by the court. Care experts will therefore normally be separately instructed in any substantial case, because a very large proportion of damages will normally relate to care and because there are very few experts in this field who have the confidence of both claimants and defendants. Assessing what level of care is 'reasonable' is partly a subjective exercise on which the views of different experts can vary greatly. Other non-medical quantum disciplines where separate experts may be appropriate will depend on the facts of the case, but often include accommodation experts and psychologists, whereas therapists whose reports make relatively little difference to the overall quantum are commonly jointly instructed.

Where there is a direction for a joint single expert, there can be difficulties in agreeing the identity of that expert. The standard directions provide that if no joint expert is instructed by a certain date, the claimant is to apply to the court by 4pm the following day for further directions. The old model directions suggested that at such a hearing 'the parties are to provide details of the CVs, availability and estimated fee of the expert they propose and reasonable objections to any other proposed'. This would still seem to be a sensible approach.

As stated, the most important experts should be separately instructed, but difficulties can still arise if one party or the other is unhappy with a jointly instructed expert's conclusions. The proper approach to take in these circumstances was first considered by the Court of Appeal in the personal injury case of *Daniels v Walker*.[28] Lord Woolf's judgment in that case suggests the following:

- The first step is normally for the party dissatisfied with the joint expert's opinion to ask questions of that expert pursuant to CPR 35.6.

- If the joint expert's answers to these questions do not resolve the matter, the dissatisfied party can investigate the issue further, normally by obtaining its own report from another expert in the same discipline. As stated at **12.2.9**, obtaining an expert's report does not require the court's

---

[28] [2000] 1 WLR 1382, (2000) *The Times*, May 17.

permission. However, it is appropriate to let the other party know that this step is being taken, so that he can consider whether he also wishes to obtain his own expert opinion on the issue. If the cooperation of the other party is required in order for the dissatisfied party to obtain his own expert report, then such cooperation should normally be given, as long as the dissatisfied party has provided full information about his intentions. For example, in *Daniels v Walker* the Court of Appeal ruled that the defendant should have facilities to have the claimant examined by his own care expert when he was dissatisfied with the report of the jointly instructed care expert and without permission having been given at that time to adduce evidence from separate care experts.

- If the dissatisfied party then wishes to rely upon the evidence of his separately instructed expert, rather than the jointly instructed expert, he must apply to the court for permission to do so.

In the boundary dispute case of *Cosgrove v Pattison*,[29] Neuberger J listed the following factors to be taken into account by the court when considering an application by a party to rely upon his own expert evidence in respect of an issue upon which a jointly instructed expert had already reported:

- the nature of the issue or issues;
- the number of issues between the parties;
- the reason the new expert is wanted. In *Cosgrove*, the reason was that the applicants had received a report from a new expert which called into question some of the conclusions reached by the jointly instructed expert;
- the amount of damages depending on the expert evidence in question;
- the effect of permitting one party to call further expert evidence on the conduct of the trial;
- the delay, if any, in making the application. It would appear from *Daniels v Walker*, that a delay in order to obtain a second expert opinion is permissible (although the other party should be informed that this is being done). However, once this opinion has been received, any application for permission to rely upon it should be made promptly;
- any delay that the instructing and calling of the new expert will cause;
- any other special features of the case;
- the overall justice to the parties in the context of the litigation.

The judge said that 'it would be wrong to pretend that this is an exhaustive list', but it is difficult to identify what might have been omitted. It would be sensible for an application of this type to be accompanied by a witness statement addressing each of these factors.

---

[29]   (2001) *The Times*, February 13.

12.2.9.3 *Number of experts per specialism*

The general rule is that where experts are separately instructed, the parties are limited to one expert in each discipline. This is consistent with the court's duty to restrict expert evidence to that which is reasonably required.[30] However, there are two situations where this approach can cause difficulty.

One such situation is that which arose in *ES v Chesterfield and North Derbyshire Royal Hospital NHS Trust*.[31] As discussed at **12.2.8.1**, in this case the Court of Appeal recognised that in clinical negligence cases professional witnesses will inevitably give expert opinion evidence to explain or justify their actions. In *ES* there were two such witnesses who were both consultant obstetricians by the time of the litigation. The claimant's expert was therefore faced with three opposing consultants (two 'witnesses of fact' plus the defendant's expert witness). The Court of Appeal overturned the Master's refusal to allow the claimant to instruct a second obstetric expert, so as to put the parties on an equal footing.

The Court of Appeal in *ES* referred to the complexity and value of the claim. The judgments emphasise that the case was 'exceptional' and that 'in the vast majority of cases there should be no more than one expert in any one speciality' and that the judges were not giving 'any sort of green light to the calling of two experts in a single discipline in any case which does not have exceptional features'. However, it is difficult to identify what made the case so exceptional. It was a cerebral palsy claim with an estimated value of £1.5m (very modest by today's standards). The only unusual feature was that two of the clinicians facing criticism had since attained consultant status, but that is not exceptional bearing in mind the time which sometimes elapses between a birth and the matter becoming the subject of litigation.

Nevertheless, the *ES* decision is interpreted very restrictively in practice and it is extremely unusual for a claimant to obtain a direction permitting reliance on two experts in the same discipline. For example, in *Beaumont v Ministry of Defence*,[32] the claimant failed in an application for permission to rely upon two obstetric experts in circumstances where the defendant obstetrician was an experienced medico-legal expert who would rely upon his own expertise when giving factual evidence in addition to calling an independent obstetric expert.

The other situation where the 'one expert per discipline' rule may give rise to difficulties is where there is a clinical negligence claim against two or more separately represented defendants. On issues where separate experts are appropriate but where the defendants have a commonality of interest (such as quantum), the court will direct that the defendants act jointly in instructing an expert to represent their interests. The suggested paragraph in the standard directions for quantum expert evidence makes provision for this.

---

[30] CPR 35.1.
[31] [2004] Lloyd's Rep Med 90.
[32] [2009] EWHC 1258 (QB), LTL 18/6/2009.

However, in such cases there may be a conflict of interest between the defendants in relation to issues of breach of duty and causation, so that it is appropriate for each defendant to have a separately instructed expert dealing with these matters. In these cases, it is important that the directions prevent the defendants' experts in a particular discipline 'ganging up' on the claimant's sole expert in that discipline by each commenting adversely on the claimant's case against the other defendant as well as against the defendant on whose behalf they are instructed. This can be avoided by a direction that each expert instructed on behalf of a defendant deals only with the claimant's allegations against that defendant and not with the allegations against the co-defendant.

In cases where an expert of the same discipline is also qualified to comment on an issue where the defendants have a common interest (perhaps causation for example), it may be appropriate that the directions require the defendants to nominate one of their experts to deal with that aspect, with the evidence of the expert(s) in the same discipline instructed on behalf of the other defendant(s) being limited to liability issues in respect of the defendant on whose behalf they are instructed.

12.2.9.4 Exchange of expert evidence

The normal direction for disclosure of expert reports on breach of duty and causation is that these are exchanged simultaneously. Although each side will have set out its case in the particulars of claim and defence, it is correctly considered that sequential exchange of reports on breach of duty and causation would give an unfair advantage to the party whose expert has had an opportunity to see the opposing expert's opinion before finalising his own report.

However, simultaneous exchange is no longer the norm in relation to separate expert evidence on quantum. The normal direction is now that the claimant's quantum expert evidence is served first and the defendant's evidence is served about 3 months later. This practice gives the defendant an advantage, but is normally justified on the following grounds:

- The rules require that the claimant serve a medical report dealing with his injuries with the proceedings and so the principle of simultaneous exchange in relation to quantum expert evidence is departed from at the outset.
- The defendant needs to know the case which he has to meet before obtaining his own quantum expert evidence (but the injuries and losses contended for will have been pleaded in the particulars of claim and detailed in the accompanying medical report and schedule).
- Once the claimant's quantum expert evidence has been disclosed, the defendant may be able to agree the reports in one or more disciplines, thereby saving the expense of the defendant obtaining his own reports in these disciplines (but in practice defendants very commonly request

facilities for their experts in all quantum disciplines to assess the claimant at an early stage, long before the service of the claimant's quantum reports).

- Quantum expert evidence is normally less contentious than breach of duty and causation and therefore the principle of simultaneous exchange is less important in relation to quantum.

As can be seen, some of these arguments are weak and it would not be unreasonable for the claimant to seek a direction for simultaneous exchange of quantum expert evidence in an appropriate case, particularly where a full schedule was served with the proceedings and the defendant has already requested facilities for the claimant to be assessed by his quantum experts.

Certainly, in a case where the defendant has had the claimant assessed by a quantum expert before the case management conference (CMC), the claimant can and should seek a direction that this report be disclosed at a very early stage, before service of quantum evidence which has yet to be obtained by the claimant. The principle of 'cards on the table' in relation to quantum expert evidence should operate in both directions and it may be helpful for the claimant's quantum experts or jointly instructed quantum experts to see all of the available quantum evidence before preparing their own reports and that includes any quantum expert evidence already obtained on behalf of the defendant.

12.2.9.5 *Permission to call experts at trial*

CPR 35.5(1) provides that:

> 'Expert evidence is to be given in a written report unless the court directs otherwise.'

This means that the permission of the court is required in order to rely upon oral expert evidence at trial.

In clinical negligence cases where separately instructed experts have not reached agreement, it is normally essential that the court hears their oral evidence. As previously stated, this evidence is likely to be determinative of issues of breach of duty and causation and of important matters relating to quantum. It is only by hearing the evidence tested through cross-examination that the court can reach a view as to which opinion is to be preferred.

By contrast, permission is not normally given for a joint single expert to attend trial to be cross-examined.[33]

---

[33] Obiter remarks in *MP v Mid Kent Healthcare NHS Trust* [2002] 1 WLR 210, [2002] 3 All ER 688, [2002] Lloyd's Rep Med 33, (2001) *The Times*, November 19, applied in *Popek v National Westminster Bank plc* [2002] EWCA Civ 42, [2002] CPLR 370 and in *Austen v Oxford City Council* (unreported) 14 June 2002, QBD.

The standard clinical negligence directions give two options regarding permission to call oral evidence of experts. One is to give such permission at the outset in specified disciplines. The alternative is to require a party seeking to call oral expert evidence at trial to apply for permission to do so before pre-trial checklists are filed. The latter approach is preferred by some county courts.

12.2.9.6   Medical literature

The standard directions include the following:

> 'Any unpublished literature upon which any expert witness proposes to rely shall be served at the same time as service of his report together with a list of published literature. Any supplementary literature upon which any expert witness relies must be notified to all parties at least one month before trial. No expert witness may rely upon any publications that have not been disclosed in accordance with this order without the permission of the trial judge subject to costs as appropriate.'

This is the direction which found favour with Lord Justice Brooke in *Wardlaw v Farrar*,[34] a clinical negligence case in which serious difficulties were caused by experts producing literature during the course of the trial which the other party had not seen beforehand.

12.2.9.7   Conflicts of interest

The standard directions provide that each expert should, at the time of producing their reports 'incorporate details of any employment or activity which raises a possible conflict of interest'. This implements a recommendation made by Sir Michael Potter when giving the judgment of the Court of Appeal in *Toth v Jarman*,[35] where it transpired that one of the defendant's experts was a member of the cases committee of the Medical Defence Union, who acted for the defendant. If the expert discloses a material or significant conflict of interest, the court is likely to decline to act on the expert's evidence or to give permission for such evidence to be adduced.

12.2.10   Experts' discussions

The standard directions contain the following provisions:

> 'Unless the reports are agreed, there must be a without prejudice discussion between the experts of like discipline by 4pm on xxxx.

However, the following direction from the old model order is given as an alternative:

---

[34]   [2003] 4 All ER 158, [2004] Lloyd's Rep Med 98, (2003) *The Times*, December 5.
[35]   [2006] 4 All ER 1276, [2006] Lloyd's Rep Med 397, (2006) *The Times*, August 17.

'Discussions between experts are not mandatory. The parties should consider, with their expert, whether there is likely to be any useful purpose in holding a discussion and should be prepared to agree that no discussion is in fact needed.'

This paragraph was introduced to the model directions in June 2007 because of concerns that experts' discussions were routinely held even in cases where there was no real benefit in having such a discussion, either because there were no material differences of opinion between the experts, or because they were poles apart, or perhaps because the two experts in question had given evidence on opposing sides on the same point on many previous occasions and so have nothing more to say to each other.

It is not normally possible to determine whether an experts' discussion will be beneficial until after exchange of expert evidence in the relevant field and so the old model directions left it to the parties and experts to decide at that time whether a discussion is appropriate, rather than incurring the expense of a further case management conference at this stage. The new standard directions appear to go back requiring expert discussions in every case where reports are not agreed, with the previous approach being an optional alternative that the court may order instead.

The power to order experts' discussions is bestowed on the court by CPR 35.12(1) which reads (emphasis added):

'The court *may*, at any stage, direct a discussion between experts.'

The practice of routinely directing an experts' discussion in every clinical negligence matter unless all parties agree otherwise was challenged by the claimants in the Court of Appeal case of *Hubbard v Lambeth Southwark and Lewisham Health Authority*.[36] In this case, the claimants were concerned that the doctors being criticised included an eminent professor who was well known to their experts and who their experts had said they would feel inhibited in criticising during such a discussion.

In the lead judgment, Lord Justice Tuckey said:[37]

'I see nothing wrong with a general approach that an order for such discussions to take place will usually be made where there has been an exchange of expert reports.'

The Court held that an objection by one party would not be sufficient to prevent such a discussion unless he could show a 'very good reason' for this. In the instant case, the claimants had not done so because their experts had already committed themselves to paper in criticising the professor in the knowledge that those views would have to be defended at trial and

---

[36] [2002] Lloyd's Rep 8, (2001) *The Times*, October 8.
[37] Ibid para 17.

consequently there was no good reason why those views should not also be defended in a discussion with the opposing experts.

12.2.10.1 Purpose of experts' discussions

The standard directions simply state that in their discussions 'the experts will identify the issues between them and reach agreement if possible'. However, the following wording from the old model directions is provided as an alternative for use 'where it is necessary to identify more specifically the areas of discussion':

> 'The purpose of the discussions is to identify:
> (i)   The extent of the agreement between the experts;
> (ii) The points of disagreement and short reasons for disagreement;
> (iii) Action, if any, which may be taken to resolve the outstanding points of disagreement;
> (iv) Any further material points not raised in the agenda and the extent to which these are agreed.'

The standard directions provide that the experts 'will prepare for the court and sign a statement of the issues on which they agree and on which they disagree with a summary of their reasons ... no later than 7 days after the discussion'. In practice, 14 days is more realistic. The standard directions also provide that 'For the avoidance of doubt, experts do not require the authorisation of solicitor or counsel before signing a joint statement'. A note to the old model directions confirmed that this does not affect CPR 35.12(5) which provides that an agreement between experts during discussions 'shall not bind the parties unless the parties expressly agree to be bound by the agreement'.

12.2.10.2 Attendance by solicitors at experts' discussions

The old model directions included the following:

> '**Unless otherwise ordered by the court, or unless agreed by all parties, including the experts,** the parties' solicitors shall not attend such discussions ... where solicitors do attend, they should not normally intervene, save to answer questions put to them by the experts or to advise them upon the law.'

This wording also appears in the *Protocol for the Instruction of Experts* published by the Civil Justice Council.[38] It is not in the new standard directions, but there is no doubt this remains the view of the judiciary, defendants' representatives and most experts. However, this approach is controversial and claimants' groups such as AvMA and many claimants' lawyers believe that in many cases solicitors should attend experts' discussions. Their point is that the joint statement arising from such discussions frequently determines the outcome of the litigation. If the claimant's expert changes his view or makes crucial concessions, the case may be lost at the experts' discussion, rather than at trial.

---

[38]   Ibid para 18.8.

Although this may result in a considerable saving of public money, the process lacks transparency. Lay clients struggle to understand how a case which appeared to be on course has been lost at a meeting or telephone discussion which neither they nor their solicitors attended and in respect of which only the outcome has been recorded.

In *Hubbard*, the claimants went so far as to suggest that the provisions for experts' meetings in the CPR might breach Art 6 of the European Convention on Human Rights, which guarantees the right to a fair trial. This argument was rejected by the Court of Appeal on the grounds that the judge giving the case management directions has discretion not to order an experts' discussion if the particular circumstances of the case would make it unfair to do so.

The argument for attendance by solicitors (either in person or by telephone) at an experts' discussion is therefore that this will at least enable them to witness and understand why an expert has changed his mind on a crucial point and thrown the case away. They will then be able to report this to their client, thereby making the process more transparent.

Attendance by solicitors would also ensure that the experts deal with the discussions in a principled manner and do not seek to 'trade' concessions or make the mistake of believing that the purpose of the discussion is to reach agreement, rather than to identify the areas of agreement and disagreement. Moreover, as suggested in the old model directions, solicitors attending experts' discussions would be able to assist the experts with any points of law or other queries arising from the agenda. In addition, such an attendance may encourage settlement by enabling solicitors to judge the quality of the opposing expert in advance of trial.

It was the claimant's fall-back position in *Hubbard* that if the court ordered that there should be an experts' discussion, the claimant's solicitors should be able to attend, notwithstanding the defendants' objections.

The Court of Appeal upheld the practice of ordering that solicitors should not normally attend the experts' discussions. The reasons given included the fact that the parties had agreed that the discussions should be tape recorded and the fact that the experts would be using agendas prepared by experienced solicitors. Lady Justice Hale suggested that the parties could also follow the practice of the Family Courts in children cases by having the experts' discussion chaired by an independent neutral person, who would probably be legally qualified and have experience of clinical negligence litigation. Unfortunately, this suggestion is rarely taken up in practice and is not popular with experts.

Applications for orders allowing solicitors to attend experts' discussions can still be made, but are very rare, because the perception is that they are unlikely to succeed.

The problem of experts' discussions determining cases in a way which is not transparent therefore remains. A very limited safeguard is provided by the following paragraph included in the standard directions:

> 'If an expert radically alters his or her opinion, the joint statement should include a note or addendum by that expert explaining the change of opinion.'

An alternative would be to follow the example of the parties in *Hubbard* and arrange for the discussions to be recorded. Again, this is not popular with experts, but that should not be the only consideration. In some cases, it may be appropriate to seek a direction that the experts' discussions be recorded.

12.2.10.3   *Agendas for experts' discussions*

The use of agendas in experts' discussions is endorsed by the *Protocol for the Instruction of Experts*.[39] In the new standard directions all of the provisions relating agendas are optional. They include the following:

> '**Unless otherwise agreed by all parties' solicitors,** after consulting with the experts, a draft agenda ... shall be prepared.'

The optional provisions of the standard directions go on to stipulate that the agenda should be drafted jointly by the claimant's solicitors and experts and sent to the defendant's solicitors at least 35 days before the date of the experts' discussion. The defendant then has 21 days in which to agree the agenda or propose amendments and 7 days thereafter both parties 'shall use their best endeavours to agree'. In default of agreement, both versions are to be used, with the numbering of the questions in the second agenda following on consecutively from the first. The agendas are to be provided to the experts at least 7 days before the discussion is due to take place.

Many experts comment that agendas for their discussions are often excessively lengthy, cumbersome and even oppressive. It is common for the parties to fail to reach agreement on a single agenda and for there to be two agendas, each with questions covering the same points in different ways, in the hope of getting an answer favourable to the case of the party represented by that agenda's author.

Consequently, the optional provisions of the standard directions include the following:

> 'The use of agendas is not mandatory. Solicitors should consult with the experts to ensure that agendas are necessary and, if used, are reasonable in scope.'

The following also now appears in the section on agreeing agendas:

> 'Points of disagreement should be on matters of real substance and not semantics or on matters the experts could resolve of their own accord at the discussion.'

---

[39] Published by the Civil Justice Council, at paras 18.5 and 18.6.

Agendas do have a place in complex clinical negligence cases. They can be used to ensure that the experts address all of the relevant issues and apply the correct legal tests when doing so. An experts' discussion is an expensive exercise for the parties and in order to obtain value for money, it is necessary to ensure that the experts correctly address all of the outstanding issues on which their assistance is required.

It is the responsibility of the parties' representatives to ensure that agendas are not excessively lengthy and are not used as a means for one party or the other to argue its case. In order to achieve this, it is essential that experts are consulted on the content of agendas. The parties' representatives also need to exercise some restraint and self-discipline in ensuring that the agenda questions are no more than is necessary to ensure that the experts' discussion serves its purpose.

The optional provisions of the standard directions give some guidance by suggesting that each agenda should include the following:

- a preamble indicating the form of joint statement, stating the standard of proof and the *Bolam* test, and reminding the experts not to attempt to determine factual issues or to stray outside their field of expertise;
- a list of outstanding issues relevant to the experts' discipline. Although the standard directions suggest that this list be included in the preamble, it might be more appropriate for such a list to form the substance of the questions themselves. In some cases, this may be all that is required;
- the agenda should assist the experts and should not be in the form of leading questions or hostile in tone. Early versions of the old model directions stated that the questions should be capable, as far as possible, of being answered 'yes' or 'no'. Although this promoted clarity, it also substantially increased the number of questions necessary to cover adequately the various aspects of each issue and consequently that wording is no longer recommended;
- it is also helpful to provide a comprehensive list of the materials which the experts have seen (or should have seen), perhaps in the form of an agreed supplementary bundle (or an appendix to the agenda). This enables experts to prepare for the discussion by checking that they have seen all of the material available to their counterpart and it gives them an opportunity to remedy the situation before the discussion if this is not the case.

12.2.10.4 *Requirement to advise experts of the timetable*

The old model directions included the following:

> 'Experts instructed by the parties in accordance with this and any subsequent order shall be provided with a copy of the order within 7 days after it is sealed, or at the time of instruction, whichever is the later.'

This was introduced following feedback from experts that they would commonly hear nothing about a case for years and then suddenly receive a request to finalise their report for exchange or to take part in a discussion with a looming court deadline about which they knew nothing at a time when they are extremely busy with other commitments. The direction ensures that busy clinicians receive prompt notification of the timetable and of the deadlines with which they are expected to comply.

After this paragraph was introduced into the model directions, the Practice Direction to Part 35 was amended to include a new paragraph (currently para 8) requiring those instructing experts in litigation to serve on their experts copies of orders affecting them and clarifying that, in the case of jointly instructed experts, it is the claimant's responsibility to serve the order. However, the Practice Direction does not give any deadline by which the order must be provided to the experts and so the paragraph in the model directions still served a purpose.

The wording in the new standard directions is as follows:

> 'A copy of this order must be served on each expert by the Claimant with the expert's instructions.'

This wording is odd, because in the case of separately instructed experts it appears only to relate to those instructed on behalf of the claimant. Nor does it appear to cover experts instructed before the directions order was made, which is most liability experts in a clinical negligence case. It may be better to continue to use the old wording.

As mentioned at **12.2.1**, it is recommended that solicitors actually consult their experts about a realistic timetable before the directions order is made, rather than merely inform their experts of the timetable after it has been set. However, a further reason to send a copy of the court order to an expert is that if the expert then fails to comply with a deadline ordered by the court and upon which they were previously consulted and the instructing party's case is lost or diminished as a result (following a failure to obtain relief from sanctions), then that party may have a remedy against the expert. In these circumstances, it would be essential to show that the expert was aware of the deadlines that had been ordered by the court and sending the expert a copy of the relevant order is a means of achieving this.

12.2.11 Schedules

The standard directions provide for service of an 'updated' schedule of loss and, 'in the event of challenge' for service of an 'updated' counter-schedule. A note encourages the parties to serve their schedules electronically on disk or as an email attachment, so as to enable the counter-schedule to follow the format of the claimant's schedule for ease of comparison.

12.2.11.1 *Preliminary outline schedule*

The general rule is where a claimant claims damages for personal injury he 'must attach to his particulars of claim a schedule of details of any past and future expenses and losses which he claims'.[40] In some cases this will be a full schedule which only requires minimal updating before trial. Examples of cases where this might apply would include modest claims where all of the financial losses claimed are in the past or readily identified or in cases where liability was admitted at the pre-action stage and proceedings have only been issued because it has not been possible for the parties to agree a settlement following full quantification of the claim.

However, often it is not possible or appropriate for the claimant to serve a full schedule with the proceedings. The most common reason for this is there has been no admission of liability at the pre-action stage and the claimant proposes to apply for breach of duty and causation to be determined as a preliminary issue, either because this is what the claimant's advisers recommend or because the claimant's funder requires such an approach. The object of dealing with breach of duty and causation as a preliminary issue is to avoid the cost of obtaining evidence on the quantification of damages in circumstances where the claim may be unsuccessful and that object would be defeated if the claimant served a full schedule with the proceedings.

Other circumstances where a full schedule might not be served are cases where there has been insufficient time to obtain quantification evidence before expiry of the limitation period or where it is not possible to quantify the claim accurately because of uncertainty about the claimant's condition, prognosis or needs, or cases where proceedings have only been issued in order to obtain court approval for an interim payment on behalf of a child or protected party in circumstances where liability has been admitted but the claim has not yet been quantified.

In all of these circumstances, the claimant may be tempted not to serve any form of schedule with the proceedings and to ask the court to dispense with this requirement. However, such a request is invariably opposed by the defendant, who wishes to have the case quantified as soon as possible, in order to put a reserve on the claim or to seek protection on costs by making a Part 36 offer at the earliest opportunity. This is therefore frequently an issue at the hearing at which directions are given.

The recommended practice is to serve a preliminary outline schedule with the proceedings or alternatively to expect to be ordered to serve one at the CMC. The purpose of a preliminary outline schedule is to give the defendant a rough idea of the potential value of the claim to enable a reserve to be fixed and possibly an offer to be made, whilst at the same time not requiring the claimant to provide a full quantification at a time when this may not be possible or appropriate.

---

[40] Para 4.2 of the Practice Direction to CPR Part 16.

The usual guidance is that a preliminary outline schedule should be no more than a couple of pages, setting out the heads of loss and an idea of the quantum of each head (for example whether the claimant requires 24-hour care and, if so, whether one or two carers are required). The recommendation is that the preliminary outline schedule should include figures, but such sums will, of necessity, be broad estimates only and the claimant should reserve the right to depart substantially from these figures once the claim has been fully quantified and the updated schedule is served. It is also prudent to reserve the right to add additional heads of loss at that stage.

12.2.11.2   *Service of schedules*

If a full schedule of past and future financial loss was served with the proceedings, the general rule is that the defence must be accompanied by a counter-schedule.[41] If this is not practical because the defendant has not yet had an opportunity to investigate quantum, then the timing of service of the counter-schedule will need to be dealt with in the directions and will be determined by the time which the defendant reasonably requires in order to obtain the necessary evidence.

However, the more common scenario is where the proceedings are not accompanied by a full schedule and the directions need to deal with timing of both the schedule and the counter-schedule.

There are two schools of thought on this:

- Most directions provide for the schedule to be served with the claimant's quantum expert evidence and for the counter-schedule to be served with the equivalent evidence on behalf of the defendant, usually after an interval of 3 months, to allow the defendant sufficient time to obtain the necessary expert evidence. Discussions between quantum experts then take place following service of the counter-schedule.

- The alternative approach is for service of the schedule to be delayed until after discussions between quantum experts, with service of the counter-schedule a short time thereafter giving sufficient time for the defendant's legal team to consider the schedule and to draft the counter-schedule based on the quantum expert evidence which the defendant will already have obtained by that stage.

The alternative approach enables the schedule and counter-schedule to take account of the concessions which quantum experts on both sides invariably make during the course of experts' discussions and which mean that the figures in their reports need to be changed. Serving the schedule and counter-schedule later in the process also means that they are less likely to require substantial amendments to take account of changes in the claimant's needs or expenditure or in prices in the period before trial.

---

[41]   Para 12.2 of the Practice Direction to CPR Part 16.

The alternative approach can therefore result in a substantial saving in costs, but nevertheless does not find favour with defendants, who will argue that they need to know the case which they have to meet and that their quantum experts need to see the schedule before finalising their reports.

There are, of course, obvious benefits in claimants serving meaningful schedules as early as possible, but in most cases the outline schedule and the claimant's quantum expert evidence is sufficient to enable the defendants to put an accurate reserve on the claim and to protect themselves on costs by means of a realistic Part 36 offer. The defendants' quantum experts are not lawyers and do not need to see a schedule in order to respond to recommendations made in the reports of their counter-parts on the claimant's side.

12.2.12 Trial directions

The directions will normally provide for a trial window, although in some cases the fixing of a trial window will be deferred until a second CMC (see **12.2.14**).

It is important that there is sufficient time between the last step in the directions and the opening of the trial window. This is required to allow for negotiations and effective Part 36 offers after all of the evidence is available and before briefs are delivered. As a general rule, it is appropriate to leave a gap of about two months.

Many clinical negligence cases involve large numbers of experts, some of whom are in great demand for medico-legal work and many of whom are also very busy with clinical and other commitments. The complexity of clinical negligence claims also means that it is desirable and cost-effective to retain the same barrister for trial as has advised earlier in the case. As a result of these considerations, it is desirable to fix the trial date, or at least a trial period within the trial window, at the earliest possible stage, so that this commitment can be entered into the diaries of the relevant experts and counsel.

As stated, there are now two sets of standard directions for clinical negligence litigation; one for use at the RCJ and the other for use elsewhere. The two documents are virtually identical, but directions for trial are one of the few points on which they differ.

The standard directions for use at the RCJ require the claimant to apply to Queen's Bench Judges' Listing for a listing appointment for a trial with a specified time estimate to be heard within a specified window. The notes to the directions suggest that there be a deadline for making such an application which is usually 6 weeks after the CMC. Pre-trial checklists are then filed as directed by Queen's Bench Judges' Listing, which means that they are normally filed a month or two before trial and are limited to confirming the time estimate and whether further directions are required.

The standard directions for use outside the RCJ specify the trial window and time estimate, and require the parties to 'file with the court their availability for trial, preferably agreed and with a nominated single point of contact.' The notes to the standard order suggest that the deadline for filing this may be 28 days after the directions order. The court will then list the trial and notify the parties, with pre-trial checklists to be filed at a later date.

This means that both standard orders allow the trial to be fixed at an early stage when there is still sufficient availability in the diaries of experts and counsel.

12.2.13   Alternative dispute resolution

The use of mediation and ADR in clinical negligence cases is considered in Chapter 15. The standard directions contain the following provisions to encourage this:

> 'At all stages the parties must consider settling this case by any means of Alternative Dispute Resolution (including round table conferences, early neutral evaluation, mediation and arbitration); any party not engaging in any means proposed by another is to serve a witness statement giving reasons within 21 days of receipt of that proposal. That witness statement must not be shown to the trial judge until questions of costs arise.'

A very similar provision appeared in the old model directions and was commended by the Court of Appeal in *Halsey v Milton Keynes General Hospital NHS Trust*[42] as being 'particularly valuable'. The court commented:

> 'We can see no reason why such an order should not also routinely be made at least in general personal injury litigation, and perhaps in other litigation too.'

The use of this order resulted in earlier settlements in clinical negligence cases, with fewer cases being settled 'at the doors of the court'.

However, the previous version of this paragraph specified a date by which the use of ADR was to be considered, with the notes suggesting that this would usually be about three months before the trial window opens. The new version requires ADR to be considered 'at all stages'. The standard order includes an optional provision that any form of ADR used should be concluded at least 35 days before trial.

The terms of the standard order make it clear that ADR does not just mean mediation and encompasses other forms of dispute resolution, including a roundtable meeting of the parties' representatives. In practice, such meetings are the norm, as they are cheaper than mediation and frequently just as effective.

---

[42]   [2004] EWCA Civ 576, [2004] 1 WLR 3002, [2004] 4 All ER 920, (2004) *The Times*, May 27 at paras 32 and 33.

12.2.14   Review CMC/pre-trial review

The standard directions provide for a further hearing to take place four weeks before the trial window starts to review the readiness of the case and to make any further directions that may be necessary. In the directions for use at the RCJ, this is referred to as a 'review case management conference' and outside the RCJ it is a 'pre-trial review', but the directions are otherwise identical. A note to the standard directions for the RCJ states that if all directions have been complied with and no further order is required, the review CMC can be vacated by consent, but there is no such note to the directions for use outside the RCJ. It is not clear whether this is intentional.

In fact, current practice at the RCJ is no longer to list matters for a review CMC and this paragraph of the standard directions is no longer included in orders made. The reason is lack of judicial time as a result of the burden of costs budgeting. The parties now have to wait up to six months for the first CMC in a clinical negligence action and if there were a review CMC in every case, this would compound the problem.

12.3   PROBLEM AREAS IN DIRECTIONS

There are a number of areas in clinical negligence directions where problems can arise. These mainly relate to matters where the law has recently developed and the parties are unsure how to deal with these issues within the framework of a 'traditional' directions order.

12.3.1   Variation by agreement

The decision in *Mitchell v News Group Newspapers Ltd*[43] confirming the new tough approach to applications for relief from sanctions has inevitably focused attention on those provisions in the CPR that provide for automatic sanctions for failure to comply with various directions. As discussed at **12.2.8,** CPR 32.10 incorporates a sanction if witness statements are not served within the time specified by the court. CPR 35.13 provides that the party who fails to disclose an expert's report may not use the report at trial or call the expert to give evidence. Although this rule does not include the phrase 'within the time specified by the court', there are authorities that a party who wishes to rely upon an expert report served late must apply for relief from sanctions (see, for example, *Dass v Dass*[44]). CPR 31.21 provides that a party may not rely on any document that he fails to disclose or in respect of which he fails to permit inspection unless the court gives permission. By analogy with the cases concerning expert evidence, this situation arises whenever disclosure or inspection is given late, after the deadline specified by the court.

---

[43]   [2014] 1 WLR 795.
[44]   [2013] EWHC 2520 (QB).

This means that there are sanctions built into the CPR for failure to give disclosure, serve witness statements or serve expert reports by the dates specified in a directions order. This creates an additional problem because CPR 3.8(3) provided that the parties were not able to agree to extend time for doing an act where a rule specifies the consequence of a failure to do so in time. In other words, following *Mitchell*, it appeared that the parties could not validly extend time by agreement for disclosure or exchange of witness statements or exchange of expert evidence without the court's approval.

This resulted in a flood of applications to procedural judges seeking approval for perfectly sensible extensions of time agreed by the parties which had no effect on the trial date or on the overall progress of the litigation, but which were only valid if judicial approval was given. In an attempt to reduce the number of such applications, the clinical negligence masters at the RCJ added the following paragraph to the end of the standard directions (at para 25):

> 'The parties may, by prior agreement in writing, extend the time for directions, in the Order dated xxxxxx, by up to 28 days and without the need to apply to Court. Beyond that 28 day period, any agreed extension of time must be submitted to the Court by email including a brief explanation of the reasons, confirmation that it will not prejudice any hearing date and with a draft Consent Order in word format. The Court will then consider whether a formal Application and Hearing is necessary.'

This paragraph was largely superseded by a new CPR 3.8(4), which came into effect on 5 June 2014. This provides that where the rules include an automatic sanction for failing to comply with a direction, the time for compliance may nevertheless 'be extended by prior written agreement of the parties for up to a maximum of 28 days, provided always that such extension does not put at risk any hearing date'.

Nevertheless, it is suggested that para 25 of the standard directions is still useful because it provides a mechanism whereby the parties can obtain court approval of an extension beyond 28 days by way of a simple email, without the need for a formal application and hearing and associated costs.

12.3.2   The claimant's case manager

In cases involving a severely injured claimant, a clinical case manager is often appointed, usually by the claimant's solicitors and funded by an interim payment. Such a case manager's role will be to co-ordinate and manage a package of rehabilitation and care/support relevant to the claimant's needs. The case manager's first step is normally to visit the claimant and prepare an assessment report setting out costed proposals for approval by the claimant and/or their litigation friend/financial deputy/the Court of Protection. Experienced case managers will often act as expert witnesses in other cases.

Defendants sometimes think of the case manager as an expert witness, particularly after disclosure of the case management assessment, which resembles an expert report. Complaint is made that the directions do not provide for such an expert. It is sometimes suggested that the case manager should be jointly instructed.

These issues were considered by the Court of Appeal in the personal injury case of *Wright v Sullivan*.[45] In this case, the Court of Appeal held that a case manager owed duties to the claimant alone and acted in the claimant's best interest, which was incompatible with a joint instruction. If a case manager is called to give evidence, he does so as a witness of fact and would not and should not be giving evidence of expert opinion.

Case managers are therefore covered by the standard directions and do not normally need to be dealt with specifically in the directions order. A party wishing to call a case manager to give evidence should serve a statement in the same way as with other witnesses of fact. Communications between the case manager and the claimant's legal team or experts regarding the claim may be covered by legal privilege, but otherwise documents produced by the case manager are subject to the same rules of disclosure as other relevant documents. Any case management assessment will therefore be sent to the defendants' representatives as part of the claimant's disclosure, but it does not thereby become an expert report requiring permission to adduce. Similarly, a case management assessment can be shown to experts advising the court in the same way as those experts can be shown the assessments of other treating clinicians, but the relevant experts must formulate their own opinions as to what case management and care/support the claimant reasonably requires.

12.3.3 Statutory services provision

As reviewed in Chapter 19 in *Sowden v Lodge*,[46] the Court of Appeal held that the availability of local authority residential care may be taken into account when assessing damages, so that the defendant may be required only to pay any top-up required to ensure that the claimant's reasonable needs are met. In *Crofton v NHSLA*,[47] the Court of Appeal held that a local authority's direct payments to the claimant towards the cost of private carers could be taken into account when assessing damages, but appropriately discounted to reflect the uncertainties regarding the future funding of such payments. The result of these decisions was to make defendants very interested in what community care provision the claimant was receiving or might be entitled to receive.

Most claimants and their advisers are anxious to avoid any reduction in the award to take account of community care provision, not because they wish to recover 'double compensation', but because of concerns about the reliability and security of statutory provision (particularly in the current economic and

---

[45] [2006] 1 WLR 172, [2006] PIQR Q4, (2005) 84 BMLR 196, (2005) *The Times*, June 24.
[46] [2005] 1 WLR 2129, [2005] 1 All ER 581, [2005] Lloyds Rep Med 86.
[47] [2007] 1 WLR 923, (2007) *The Times*, February 15.

political climate) and because of the belief that the full cost of providing for the claimant's needs should be met by the tortfeasor.

The judgments in *Sowden* made it clear that the burden was on the defendant to plead a positive case in relation to statutory provision and to adduce evidence concerning what is actually available. Moreover, in *Crofton* it was made clear that any such evidence should be served at an early stage and not at the last minute. The case management difficulty arose because the evidence which the defendant required was largely within the control of the claimant. There were potentially three areas where the defendant might be looking for the claimant's assistance in the hope of reducing the damages award:

- the disclosure of documents held by the local authority relating to the claimant;
- the interviewing of local authority employees concerning statutory provision available to the claimant;
- assessment of the claimant's needs by the local authority under s 47 of the National Health Service and Community Care Act 1990.

Since the introduction of the CPR, there has been much greater voluntary cooperation between opposing parties, but to what extent could the court directions require a reluctant claimant to assist in these matters?

The provisions of the Data Protection Act 1998 give claimants the right to inspect and to obtain copies of documents held about them by a local authority. Such documents are therefore within the claimant's control and potentially disclosable under CPR Part 31.[48] The claimant should therefore obtain and disclose such documents if it becomes clear that the defendant proposes to raise community care issues (thereby making the documents relevant). In case of difficulty, it is likely that the court has a jurisdiction to order a claimant to provide the defendant with a signed form of consent to enable the defendant to obtain such documents directly from the local authority,[49] but the better practice is for the claimant to retain control of the process by obtaining and disclosing these documents if the defendant so requests.

If a defendant wishes to interview local authority employees regarding the statutory provision available to the claimant, confidentiality issues may arise and the local authority is likely to want to be satisfied that the claimant consents to such an interview. Again, the court probably has jurisdiction to order the claimant to provide a signed consent to enable such interviews to take place, although the consent can be limited to information relevant to the issues in the case. As mentioned at **12.2.8.1**, there are authorities to this effect in relation to interviewing treating doctors[50] and, by analogy, these must also apply to interviews with local authority employees who are concerned about

---

[48] CPR 31.8(2)(c).
[49] By analogy with *Bennett v Compass Group UK* [2002] ICR 1177 which concerns medical records.
[50] *Shaw v Skeet Aung Sooriakumaran* [1996] 7 Med LR 371 and *Nicholson v Halton General Hospital NHS Trust* [1999] PIQR P310.

disclosing confidential information regarding the claimant. Again, it may be prudent for the claimant's representatives to seek to retain control of the process by interviewing the relevant local authority employees themselves as soon as they receive a request for the claimant's consent to the defendant's representatives carrying out any such interviews.

In practical terms, the first step before the claimant receives any statutory provision is for an assessment to be carried out under s 47 of the National Health Service and Community Care Act 1990. If no such assessment has been carried out, the defendant may invite the claimant to request one.

Such a request should not be necessary, because the local authority is under a duty to carry out an assessment in any case where it appears that there may be a need for community care services, whether or not the potential service-user has requested one. It should be sufficient for the defendant merely to draw the situation to the local authority's attention. If the local authority insists that a request for an assessment is actually made by the claimant, this may reveal something about their willingness or ability to provide care or services.

Whether or not a claimant can be required to request an assessment for services which they may not wish to use, it is clear that claimants are required to cooperate with the assessment process if it is taking place.

In *Sowden v Lodge*, Lord Justice Pill stated that 'claimants, and those advising them, must be expected to co-operate with local authorities discharging their statutory duties'.[51] In *X v Y Health Authority*,[52] Mr Justice Langstaff accepted the principle that the court could order a stay of proceedings in circumstances where a claimant refused to cooperate with a s 47 assessment. This was based on an analogy with the situation where a claimant refused to be examined by an expert instructed by the defendant. However, the judge indicated that a stay would only be ordered if the proposed assessment was on balance not a disproportionate interference with the private life of the claimant and his family, as might apply if the assessment involved a series of lengthy visits to the family home.

It is important to appreciate that in *X v Y Health Authority*, the judge made it clear that he was not holding that the claimant was under a duty to mitigate his losses by taking advantage of whatever state-funded provision was available. Since then, the Court of Appeal has held that claimants are fully entitled to opt to claim the cost of all future needs from the tortfeasor and in these circumstances there can be no reduction in damages to reflect the availability of statutory provision.[53] This means that the above points are now of very limited applicability and would only arise in a case where it was clear that the claimant wished to rely in part on statutory funding. Such cases must be extremely rare.

---

[51] [2004] EWCA Civ 1370, [2005] 1 WLR 2129, [2005] 1 All ER 581, [2005] Lloyds Rep Med 86 at para 63.
[52] (2007) *Clinical Risk* 248.
[53] *Peters v East Midlands Strategic Health Authority* [2009] WLR 737, [2009] PIQR Q1.

12.3.4   Periodical payments

As seen in Chapters 16 and 18 the rules relating to periodical payments under the Damages Act 1996 came into force on 1 April 2005. As a result CPR 41.6 provides:

> 'The court shall consider and indicate to the parties as soon as practicable whether periodical payments or a lump sum is likely to be the more appropriate form for all or part of an award of damages.'

CPR 41.5 permits the parties to specify their preferred form of award in their statements of case, providing particulars of the circumstances which are relied upon in coming to that preference. CPR 41.5 also empowers the court to order a party to state his preferred form of award or to provide further particulars of the circumstances relied upon in stating such a preference.

These rules appear to envisage that consideration of the appropriate form of award would take place during the case management stage of the proceedings. However, in practice it is frequently not possible to say what form of award is appropriate in the early stages of a case. The issue of periodical payments really only arises in substantial cases and in those cases it is unusual for the claim to have been fully quantified at the time of the first CMC. Moreover, there may be issues of liability which will affect the appropriate form of award. Consequently, the notes to the old model directions stated only that:

> 'Parties should, at the first CMC, be prepared to give their provisional view as to whether the case is one in which a periodical payments order might be appropriate.'

The standard directions contain a paragraph requiring the parties to set out their respective positions on the issue of periodical payments in the schedule and counter-schedule.

12.3.4.1   Financial advisers

Financial advisers play an important part in the consideration of periodical payments. One of the factors which the court must take into account when considering whether periodical payments or a lump sum is the more appropriate form of award is 'the nature of any financial advice received by the claimant'.[54] Moreover, the rules dealing with the approval of settlements on behalf of a child or protected party require the court to be satisfied that the parties have considered periodical payments in cases involving damages for future financial loss[55] and require the parties to provide the court with a copy of any financial advice relating to the proposed settlement.[56] In practice, the court will expect to see a financial advice in cases where the proposed

---

[54]   Para 1 of the Practice Direction to CPR Part 41.
[55]   Paras 5.3, 5.4 and 6.2 of the Practice Direction to CPR Part 21.
[56]   Paras 5.1 and 6.4 of the Practice Direction to CPR Part 21.

settlement includes periodical payments and in cases where the settlement is purely for a lump sum but it appears that periodical payments might have been appropriate.

A difficulty which sometimes arises at the directions stage is whether the claimant needs the court's permission to obtain financial advice on the appropriateness or otherwise of periodical payments.

The answer is that the court's permission is only required if the financial adviser is going to be giving expert evidence on this issue, as has occurred in some cases where there was a dispute between the parties as to whether or not periodical payments were appropriate.[57] In these circumstances, CPR Part 35 applies.

However, if a financial advice is being obtained only for the claimant's benefit to assist in deciding whether to seek periodical payments, it is not an expert opinion and Part 35 does not apply, even though the advice may be put before the court when seeking approval of a settlement or may be referred to in argument as a factor in relation to the question of whether periodical payments should be awarded.

The cost of a claimant obtaining financial advice in managing his award is not recoverable as part of his damages,[58] but the cost of properly obtaining financial advice on the appropriateness of periodical payments can form part of the claimant's recoverable legal costs, even though that advice will have been obtained without the permission of the court and will not have been disclosed to the defendant. In this respect, obtaining financial advice is analogous to obtaining counsel's opinion on a particular aspect of a case.

12.4 PRE-TRIAL CHECKLISTS

In most civil litigation, the directions will provide for the court to send out a pre-trial checklist (listing questionnaire) to each party, to be completed and returned by a date specified in the directions order. The checklist is Form N170, with which all civil litigation practitioners will be familiar. However, as discussed at **12.2.12**, the large number of experts and other professionals involved in clinical negligence litigation means that it is usually desirable to fix trial dates long in advance, at an early stage, and before the end of the directions timetable. Consequently, both versions of the standard directions provide for the trial dates to be fixed soon after the directions order is made and for pre-trial checklists to be filed at a later date as directed by Queen's Bench Judges' Listing (in the RCJ) or as specified in the order (Outside the RCJ). In both circumstances the court is likely to dispense with those questions which relate only to the fixing of the trial date.

---

[57] See, for example, *A v B Hospitals NHS Trust* [2007] LS Law Medical 303, (2007) 95 BMLR 240.

[58] *Eagle v Chambers* [2004] 1 WLR 3081, [2005] 1 All ER 136, [2005] PIQR Q2, [2004] Lloyd's Rep Med 413, (2005) 82 BMLR 22, (2004) *The Times*, August 30.

Section A of the pre-trial checklist invites the parties to confirm that they have complied with the directions and, if they are unable to give such confirmation, to specify the directions which are outstanding and the date by which they will be complied with. The parties are also invited to apply for any additional directions which they consider necessary.

If the procedural judge is not satisfied with the compliance with the directions to date or the proposals to remedy this, or if the directions sought are controversial, then this can be dealt with at a review CMC (in the RCJ) or pre-trial review (outside the RCJ), which may have already been listed if the standard directions have been used.

Section C of the pre-trial checklist draws attention to the fact that permission is required for experts to give oral evidence at trial. If the standard directions have been used, such permission will either have already been given or the parties will have been directed to apply for permission **before** pre-trial checklists are filed. As stated at **12.2.9.5**, it is normally essential that separately instructed experts who disagree are permitted to give oral evidence.

12.4.1   Timetable for trial

The pre-trial checklist encourages the parties to agree and file a timetable for trial. In theory, if this is not done, the court will set a trial timetable in consultation with the parties,[59] normally at a pre-trial review. However, in practice few courts are proactive enough to do this.

Nevertheless, the large number of experts involved in clinical negligence trials makes it essential for the parties to try and agree a timetable. The expense involved in having all experts at court throughout the trial is usually prohibitive. Moreover, many experts will have commitments such as clinics which they do not wish to break and which mean that they are only able to be at court on certain days. It is important that the parties try and accommodate these preferences, rather than risk alienating their experts.

It is therefore essential to try and agree with the other party which experts will be giving evidence on which days and in which order. If experts are initially committed to attend court throughout the trial, it is preferable to agree the dates when they will actually be required sufficiently early to avoid any cancellation fees which might arise if an expert is given short notice that he is no longer required on a particular day.

Traditionally, the order of evidence in a civil action is the claimant's lay and expert witnesses followed by the defendant's lay and expert witnesses. However, this is not appropriate for a clinical negligence trial. For example, the claimant's experts on breach of duty will need to hear the factual evidence of the defendant's clinicians upon whose standard of care the liability experts are

---

[59]   See CPR 29.8 and para 39.4 of the Practice Direction to CPR Part 39.

commenting. It is also helpful for the judge to hear the evidence of experts in a particular discipline 'back to back', in order to make comparison easier and to gain a better understanding of the issues. Some judges now favour 'concurrent expert evidence' or 'hot tubbing', which is now provided for in paragraph 11 of the Practice Direction to Part 35. This is a practice imported from Australia, whereby experts in the same discipline give evidence at the same time, answering questions put by the judge, as well as by the opposing parties.

Therefore, the normal order of evidence in a clinical negligence trial will be the claimant's factual witnesses, followed by the defendant's factual witnesses, followed by the experts in each discipline, either consecutively or concurrently or a mixture of the two. The order of the expert disciplines is normally those dealing with breach of duty followed by causation, followed by quantum (assuming that all issues are being tried together). However, sometimes a party may wish to vary this order. For example, the claimant's case on breach of duty may depend on the evidence as to the cause of an adverse outcome, which may mean that the claimant wants the court to consider causation before breach of duty. The defendant may well disagree. Although it is possible to ask the judge to rule on the timetable at the commencement of trial, the need for forward planning and to avoid cancellation fees means that it is preferable for any timetable disputes to be dealt with by the court at an earlier stage and this normally involves one or both parties raising the issue at a review CMC or pre-trial review.

TOP TIPS

- Avoid naming in a directions questionnaire or order an expert whom it is proposed to instruct, but whose opinion has not yet been received.
- Consult experts before proposing or agreeing a timetable and ensure that they are provided with the timetable ordered.
- Use the appropriate form of clinical negligence standard directions in all cases.
- Request a split trial if this would be to the advantage of the client or the funder.
- Even if there is no split trial, consider exchanging witness statements relevant to liability separately and before exchanging statements relevant to quantum.
- Check that statements of treating doctors served by your opponent do not include inadmissible opinion evidence.
- Apply for early disclosure of any quantum report known to have been obtained by the other party before directions are given.
- Keep agendas for experts' discussions short and focused on the issues and consult experts on their content.
- Fix the trial date or period at the earliest opportunity.

- Ensure that there is sufficient time between the last step in the directions and the opening of the trial window to allow for slippage and reflection.
- Agree a trial timetable at an early stage and before any expert cancellation fees take effect.

CHAPTER 13

EXPERTS

In this chapter solicitor Claire Fazan, addresses the issues relating to obtaining expert evidence including the choice and instruction of experts, expert reports, expert discussions and expert evidence at trial.

13.1 INTRODUCTION

Throughout a case, from initial instruction to trial or final settlement, the lawyer must clearly understand and keep under review what the potential/pleaded issues are in the case and which of these may be or are in dispute.

Clarity about the potential issues relating to breach of duty and causation is essential for the selection of which experts should be instructed to advise in the case. The court will restrict expert evidence to that which is reasonably required to resolve the proceedings (CPR 35.1).

Understanding of that medical advice and the identified issues in the case and continuous critical review of them will be fundamental to how the case is pleaded, how it is litigated, what expert and other witness evidence is sought and/or served, whether experts meet, the agendas for such meetings, approach to settlement and trial. It will also be central to cost budgeting.

Many of the difficulties that are encountered in cases arise as a consequence of a failure adequately to understand or to communicate what the issues are to which expert evidence needs to be directed, which issues remain in dispute and the litigation consequences of those issues.

13.2 CHOICE OF EXPERTS

From the first instruction by the client it is essential to have in mind the expertise potentially required by way of expert evidence on issues of breach of duty, causation and quantification. Given the relatively small number of experts who take on medico-legal work and the demands litigation makes upon their time, it is advisable to approach the experts it is proposed to instruct at a very early stage in order to ascertain whether they can in fact advise in the particular case and within an acceptable timescale. This early approach is particularly important in the case of a client who instructs solicitors close to the expiry of the limitation period.

Early identification of what expert evidence will be necessary is not just important in terms of securing the expert required, but also in order to be able to give cost and time estimates to the client and to potential funders such as the Legal Aid Authority or Legal Expense Insurers. It will also enable the solicitor to predict probable demands on cash flow if it is intended that the firm will fund disbursements under a conditional fee agreement (CFA). As the case progresses and is approaching the first case and costs management (CMC) hearing, much greater clarity as to what particular expert opinion is needed and why together with the projected cost of that for the entire case will be required.

This chapter will focus to a significant extent on liability expert evidence. However, identification of the expert advice likely to be required in order to quantify the claim is also necessary. This is because as well as ensuring the appropriate expertise is lined up, undertaking this exercise at the outset enables the lawyer to identify and advise the client and potential funder of any costs risks consequent upon the number of experts required to prove and value the claim.

Expert evidence needs to be kept under review throughout a case. Throughout the case the solicitor has to have in mind four questions: (1) what are the issues in dispute in the case? (2) what expert evidence is required in relation to elucidating and proving those issues ? (3) how is the proposed expert evidence of relevance to the particular issue/s in dispute? and (4) what is the cost of that particular expert evidence and is it proportionate to the potential quantum?

Following initial instruction by the client, the next key stage at which it is advisable to review choice of specialty, the order in which experts are to be instructed and the need for particular expert opinion will be on receipt and review of the medical records. For example, on review of the records it may become apparent that the client's condition, its history or manner of onset is not one typically caused by the suspected breach of duty and thus early examination and advice on condition will be fundamental to subsequent causation advice. In such a case the instruction of expert(s) on condition and prognosis and causation may be the priority rather than obtaining initial advice on breach of duty.

The choice of expert will be dictated by a number of factors. The first and most obvious factor will be relevant experience in the field of medicine which is the subject of criticism and review. Thus, for example, if the breach of duty relates to the management of labour, expert evidence will be required from an obstetrician. If the labour was managed by a midwife and the failings appear to lie in that care it will also be necessary to instruct a midwife. Similarly, if the care relates to the management of a diabetic, expertise will be required from a physician who specialises in diabetic medicine.

As far as causation is concerned it will be necessary to identify what medical expertise will be required to advise on the consequences of any identified breach of duty including the probable cause and timing of the injury. Expert evidence on causation in the obstetric case will need to be drawn from those disciplines which can cast light on the timing and cause of injury and thus from paediatric neurology, neonatology and neuro-radiology. In the diabetic case and other cases in which there is a pre-existing and evolving condition, evidence will be required from those specialists who can advise on the probable normal (non-negligently caused or enhanced) progression of the condition as well as those who can advise on timing and cause of the injury suffered in the particular case. Thus, in the diabetic case it may be necessary to seek advice from a vascular surgeon or an ophthalmic expert as well as a physician specialising in diabetes.

If possible, the expert commenting on breach of duty should be from a similar type of hospital. Criticisms of care in a district general hospital made by an expert working out of a teaching hospital may be open to critical cross-examination on the basis that his view is a counsel of perfection rather than being based on a reasonable standard of care.

At the time of drafting it is understood that the Civil Justice Council Protocol for the Instruction of Experts may be under review and may be revised. However, the current Protocol states:[1]

> '6.1 Those intending to instruct experts to give or prepare evidence for the purpose of civil proceedings should consider whether expert evidence is appropriate, taking account of the principles set out in CPR Parts 1 and 35, and in particular whether:
> (a)   it is relevant to a matter which is in dispute between the parties;
> (b)   it is reasonably required to resolve the proceedings (CPR 35.1);
> (c)   the expert has expertise relevant to the issue on which an opinion is sought;
> (d)   the expert has the experience, expertise and training appropriate to the value, complexity and importance of the case; and whether
> (e)   these objects can be achieved by the appointment of a single joint expert ...
>
> 6.2 Although the court's permission is not generally required to instruct an expert, the court's permission is required before experts can be called to give evidence or their evidence can be put in (CPR 35.4).'

13.3   THE NUMBER OF EXPERTS

Throughout the case, an eye needs to be kept on the number of experts. Under the provisions of CPR 35.1, the court has a duty to restrict expert evidence 'to that which is reasonably required to resolve the proceedings'. The application of this was reviewed in *Turner v Walsall NHS Trust*.[2]

---

[1]   June 2005 (amended October 2009).
[2]   [2013] EWHC 1221 (QB).

Thus, generally, if there is to be separate (not joint) instruction of an expert the court will only permit one expert per party as will funders.

There are cases in which more than one expert per specialty may be required and permission should be sought. It is not the case that a party will never be permitted to call more than one expert per area of specialism. The issue was reviewed in detail by the Court of Appeal in the case of *ES v Chesterfield and North Derbyshire Royal Hospitals NHS Trust*.[3] In that case, the Court of Appeal indicated that:

> 'The governing rule, therefore, limits expert evidence to that which is reasonably required to resolve the proceedings in issue. What is reasonable in any particular context will inevitably be fact sensitive. It would be wrong to approach this question with the predetermined belief that to instruct more than one expert in the same discipline will always be excessive. In addition to considering the facts, the court will need to remind itself in any contentious case of the principles underlying the overriding objective in CPR 1.1. In the present context the most important of the considerations set out in CPR 1.1.(2) appear to be:
> (a)   ensuring that the parties are on an equal footing;
> (b)   dealing with the case in ways which are proportionate –
>   (i)   to the amount of money involved;
>   (ii)   to the importance of the case;
>   (iii) to the complexity of the issues;
>   (iv)   to the financial position of each party.
>
> Anybody watching the trial would be bound to be impressed by the fact that there was only one consultant obstetrician giving evidence for the claimant, while there would be three giving evidence for the defendant hospital trust, and those three would cover a much wider spectrum of personal experience than the single expert permitted to the claimant ... I do not moreover consider that the extra time and expense that would be introduced into the trial by the calling of a second expert for the claimant would be disproportionate in a case of this monetary value and importance.'

However, it was made clear that permission for more than one expert per discipline was to be the exception:

> 'Nothing in this judgment must be taken to give any sort of green light to the calling of two experts in a single discipline in any case which does not have exceptional features. On this appeal the presence of three consultants on the defendants' side constitutes such an exceptional feature ...'

The issue was revisited in *Beaumont v Ministry of Defence*.[4] It was not appropriate for a claimant in clinical negligence proceedings to engage a second expert witness where no exceptional circumstances existed so as to take the case away from the usual rule of one expert on each side.

---

3   [2003] EWCA Civ 1284, see also **12.2.9.3**.
4   (Unreported) 3 October 2008, QBD.

Thought thus needs to be given to whether the specific case should be an exception. It may not be apparent at the outset, but by close of pleadings and allocation questionnaire time it probably will be. By the time of the first case management conference (CMC) identification as to which and how many professional witnesses of fact the defendant/s propose to call is important. Where there is more than one defendant it will be important to ascertain whether each defendant proposes to instruct its own experts or whether experts will be jointly instructed by them. If the claimant wishes to call more than one expert per discipline specific permission for this will have to be sought from the court.[5] Previous decisions were made prior to the introduction of the revision of the over-riding objective to include proportionality and cost management orders in April 2013 and will now have to be argued and determined in the light of the cost and proportionality.

If two experts per discipline are to be instructed and retained, funder authority for this will be necessary. This should be possible in cases in which the court has given permission to do so, although in the very few cases conducted with the benefit of public funding the challenge will be to persuade the LAA to authorise instruction of a second expert at realistic fee rates.

The sheer number of experts is not necessarily the key to winning a case. Successful cross-examination can drive a wedge between experts instructed for the same party and in such cases it can be a weakness rather than a strength to call a large number of experts. If it is proposed that more than one expert in a discipline be instructed, it will be essential to test the extent of agreement or disagreement between them in conference before pleading the case and before reports are served. If there is a difference of opinion which could be used to the defendant's advantage it may be tactically prudent to rely on only one expert. If funding is not an issue, thought can be given to retaining the second expert in an advisory only capacity. The costs of doing so, however, will probably not be recoverable from the other party.

13.4   FINDING AND APPROACHING NEW EXPERTS

The majority of lawyers experienced in the field will have a large pool of experts from whom they can draw for expert opinion in a specific case. Where this is not the case, there are a variety of ways to locate and identify whom to instruct. AvMA and APIL can be approached for recommendations. Other experts are often a source of useful recommendations and contacts. Review of recently decided cases can prove a helpful method of assessing the impression an expert has made on the court. Other lawyers who specialise in the field will frequently be able to make recommendations. However the new expert is located, it will be essential to check that the case comes within his particular field of specialism both by asking him this and by asking for a CV.

---

[5]   See Chapter 12.

Many experts new to the field of medico-legal work are given little indication by those instructing them as to the very high demands that may be made upon their time as the case progresses. For many, their experience of medico-legal litigation will be limited to producing a report and they may be unprepared for the demands of attending not just one but several conferences, relatively short court imposed deadlines once a case has been issued, reviewing material and commenting on this (often at short notice in the run up to trial), preparing for and participating in expert discussions and making sufficient time available to attend trial not just to give evidence, but also to listen to the evidence of others. When instructing an expert for the first time the instructing solicitor should ensure that the expert understands the potential for such demands.

With the decrease in number of trials, relatively few experts have experience of giving oral evidence at trial and the intensity of the preparation work in the period which immediately precedes a trial.

All experts (new or experienced) should be asked to confirm fees for reports, conferences and trial and for estimated timescale for reporting from receipt of instructions. With the introduction of cost budgeting, experts now need to be informed about the probable work at all stages of the case that they will be instructed to undertake and they will need to give fee estimates for each piece of work from the outset of the case. Those fee estimates will need to be reviewed and if necessary refined prior to the cost budget being prepared and lodged. By that time experts who have already been instructed to advise on liability issues will have a clearer sense of the volume of records, the complexities of the issues and the issues that are in dispute between the parties (all of which will determine the amount of expert time which is likely to be dedicated to the case).

Once the court has given directions, set the litigation timetable and set the budget for the case, the experts should be advised of deadlines, including trial date. The Model Directions require the parties to provide experts with a copy of the Order for Directions. Experts will also need to be notified of the budget that the court has set and the importance of advising the solicitor in advance of going over the budget for their work if there is a risk of doing so and why in order to enable the solicitor to seek an increase in the budget. General reasons such as 'it took me longer than anticipated' will be insufficient to achieve an increase in the budget. Reasons particular to the facts of the case as to why it took longer than could have been anticipated at the time of the fee estimate will have to be given.

13.5 JOINT OR SINGLE EXPERTS

The court has the power[6] to direct that where two or more parties wish to submit expert evidence on a particular issue this should be provided by a single joint expert.

---

6   CPR 35.7.

The parties should try to agree the joint instructions and agree the documents that the expert is to be given, but in default each party may give instructions.[7] Where an expert is instructed jointly any party instructing that expert must provide a copy of those instructions to the other party/ies.

A single joint expert should copy correspondence to all those instructing him and should serve his report on all instructing parties simultaneously. He should not attend a conference or meeting which is not joint unless all the parties have agreed this in writing or the court has directed it.[8] In *Peet v Mid-Kent Healthcare Trust*[9] the Court of Appeal refused the claimant's request that a single joint expert attend a conference with counsel in the absence of the other party on the basis that all contact with a single joint expert must be transparent.

Whether experts are to be jointly instructed or whether each party is to singly instruct his own expert will be determined on a case-by-case basis. In a low value case it may not be proportionate to have separate experts instructed on all issues. Consequently, with the introduction of costs budgeting the court may not permit it. Prior to the introduction of costs budgeting it was rarely if ever considered to be appropriate to instruct an expert on a joint basis to advise on breach of duty or causation. Time will tell whether cost arguments and the new definition of the over-riding objective will persuade a court that advice so fundamental to the success of a claim should be commissioned on a joint basis. It will be inappropriate to instruct an expert to advise on life expectation on a joint basis when the difference of a couple of years on a lifetime multiplier may amount to thousands or hundreds of thousands of pounds.

It is often said that instructing an expert jointly leads to a saving of costs. For this reason, the joint instruction of experts (especially in relation to quantum) is going to be looked at far more closely by the court when giving case management directions and setting cost budgets. It is not necessarily the case that joint instruction of experts leads to a saving in costs. Given the time that can be involved in agreeing which expert should be instructed and/or the terms of those instructions, the cost of putting questions of clarification to the jointly instructed expert and the added costs caused by having to have separate conferences with those jointly instructed it can be no less costly than single instruction. Further, the benefit of consecutive rather than simultaneous exchange of quantum evidence enables the defendant to review whether in fact it wishes or needs to instruct an expert in a particular field. Thorough review of served evidence coupled with carefully constructed questions[10] to experts will often enable the defendant to prepare its case properly without the additional costs of either a jointly or a singly instructed expert being required.

---

7   Civil Justice Council Protocol for the Instruction of Experts, para 17.

8   Ibid.

9   [2002] 1 WLR 210 (CA).

10   CPR 35.6.

Where an expert is instructed on a joint basis, CPR Part 35.8(5) provides that unless the court otherwise directs the parties will be jointly and severally liable for the expert's fees.

On occasions it may be necessary for a party to instruct a single expert after an expert of similar discipline has been instructed on a joint basis. For example, it may be considered that the jointly instructed quantum expert has failed to give reasonable and proper regard to key issues which are fundamental to the appropriate quantification of the case. It will be necessary to obtain the permission of the court to rely on the new expert's evidence.

13.6   INSTRUCTING THE EXPERT

13.6.1   Documents

It will be essential that any expert instructed to advise is provided with all of the information and documentation relevant to the issues upon which he is asked to advise.

Thus, obviously, an expert advising on breach of duty and causation is going to require all relevant medical records.

Where there are other experts giving an opinion which will be of relevance they should also be provided with that expert's opinion at the most appropriate stage.

An expert advising on causation will, obviously, need to see the expert report on breach of duty before finalising his own advice since he will need to know the nature and time of the breach of duty and what and when different care should have been given. A causation expert is likely to need the reports dealing with condition and prognosis and imaging (such as neuroradiology) before advising. It may be appropriate not to provide reports from other causation experts where there is an overlap in order to ensure the expert reviews the issues with a fresh eye. If this approach is taken the expert should be made aware of the instruction of the other expert.

Where matters have progressed to a letter of claim, letter of response or formal pleadings, the expert, should, of course, be provided with that documentation.

Experts should also be provided with all factual witness statements: those prepared on behalf of the claimant or for the defendant if witness evidence has already been served or those disclosed by way of pre-action discovery (for example witness statements taken as part of a hospital's adverse incident enquiry procedure).

It will be important to identify and obtain from the relevant defendant any protocols or guidelines for treatment/medical management of the type given in the particular case. Such documents should be provided to the relevant expert. For example, in an obstetric case where labour has been induced, the hospital's labour ward protocols for the management of induction of labour should be obtained and provided to the obstetric and midwifery experts.

The Civil Justice Protocol for the Instruction of Experts sets out a useful checklist of documentation to be sent to experts.

13.6.2 The letter of instruction

The letter of instruction should:

- identify the party on whose behalf the expert is instructed (or parties if jointly instructed);
- itemise the documentation being sent to the expert;
- contain a summary of the case;
- set out the currently identified/pleaded issues in the case and those which remain in dispute;
- explain the aspects upon which the expert is instructed to advise;
- specify the timeframe within which the expert is asked to advise, including any court imposed deadline or limitation date;
- refer to the expert's duties under CPR Part 35 and the requirements in terms of the contents of the report. A copy of PD 35, para 3.2 may be of assistance to new experts;
- request that the expert indicates if he believes that there are missing records or further documentation or investigations may be available which will assist in clarifying advice/issues or whether further expert evidence is required in order to do so;
- request that where there are differing factual scenarios on the face of the records and/or witness evidence that the expert gives advice on the basis of both alternatives, but indicates (if appropriate) whether there are clinical reasons why one alternative is less likely;
- refer in the context of cost budgeting the importance of accurate fee estimates, continuing review of those estimates as against the budget and the need to warn if the budget is in danger of being exceeded and why.

13.7 REVIEW OF EXPERT EVIDENCE

13.7.1 Initial review of expert evidence

Clinical negligence cases are generally won or lost on expert evidence. Review of expert evidence both pre-action and throughout the litigation is, therefore, an essential exercise. Too often the temptation to 'cut corners' and therefore limit costs results in crucial issues which are fundamental to the success of a claim being identified late in the process. This is exceptionally hard and disappointing for the claimant and potentially very costly.

There will be occasions, even in the most well prepared of cases, when perhaps because of new evidence, new medical research or the natural deterioration or improvement in the claimant's condition, it may be necessary to advise a client late into the case that the claim no longer has a reasonable prospect of success or to accept a very low offer. Clients must be advised that expert evidence and the merits of the claim have to be continually reviewed throughout the case and should be advised from the outset and after the review of expert evidence about 'vulnerable' parts of the case which might impact on the merits or quantum.

Thorough pre-action review of the expert evidence and testing of that evidence in conference should result in a clearly, concisely and properly pleaded case and to the identification of potential gaps in expert evidence that require opinion from a further field of expertise and/or issues that may be pleaded on behalf of the defendant and used to defend the claim.

It is not always necessary for the expert to attend a conference in person. It is frequently more time and cost efficient for the expert to participate via telephone link. That said, it is probably inadvisable to proceed to a trial without ever having had a face-to-face conference with the expert.

If the instruction and review of expert evidence has taken place prior to the drafting of the letter of claim, the letter of response from the defendant should be forwarded to the experts for comment. The experts should be asked to confirm whether the contents of the letter of response causes them to alter their advice and if so, why and/or whether the response indicates a need for further expert advice and, if so of what kind.

13.7.2 Directions in relation to expert evidence

The directions to be sought in a clinical negligence case are addressed elsewhere. However, so far as expert evidence is concerned it should be noted that the court will consider and direct what expert evidence will be permitted. As indicated above, under CPR 35.1 it will restrict the expert evidence to that which is reasonably required to resolve the proceedings.

Under CPR 35.4(2) 'when the Parties apply for permission they must provide an estimate of the costs of the proposed expert evidence and identify (a) the field in which expert evidence is required; and (b) where practicable, the name of the proposed expert.'

If permission is granted by the court the permission may specify the issues which the expert evidence should address (CPR 35.4(3)). PD35 sets out the sort of issues the court will consider in this regard. Under CPR 35.4(4) the court may limit the amount of a party's expert fees and expenses that can be recovered from any other party.

13.7.3 Review of pleadings by experts

Once the particulars of claim are drafted these should be sent to the experts in order to ensure that the pleadings accurately reflect their expert opinion prior to them being served. This approach is equally important with the preparation of the schedule of loss which should be approved by those experts whose advice is relevant to quantification.

An ideal opportunity to review the pleadings is in conference. Any instruction for a first conference to review the evidence in a case with clearly supportive expert evidence should include an instruction to counsel to prepare draft pleadings for review and discussion at the conference. By doing this not only can the pleadings be drafted so that they accurately reflect the views of the experts as expressed in conference, but it will also ensure that a letter of claim (which can even attach proposed draft particulars of claim) is sent out immediately following the conference thereby limiting any delay.

When the defence is served the claimants' experts should be asked to review and comment upon it including whether there are pleaded issues which lead them to change their opinions and if so, how and why.

If there are pleaded issues in the defence not previously identified by an expert the relevance and merits of those points need to be discussed with the expert. Within the context of that discussion, thought will need to be given to whether the pleadings require amendment, if additional expert advice is required and whether the merits of the claim have changed. The client and funder will need to be advised accordingly and the approach to the budget (which will probably not have been set at this point) revised.

13.7.4 Review of expert evidence in the context of exchanged factual evidence

The exchange of factual witness evidence and receipt of the witness statements of those involved in the claimant's care is a key stage in any litigation. Not infrequently it is a stage at which experts will reconsider the opinions expressed in preliminary pre-action reports which are likely to have been based upon the claimant's medical records and witness evidence alone.

Factual evidence served on behalf of all parties should be sent to the experts. They should be asked whether the contents lead them to alter their previously expressed views and if they do in what way.

Where the exchanged factual evidence demonstrates differing accounts of what happened and when, the expert should be asked whether there are clinical reasons why one account is less likely than another.

However, experts should be cautioned about making determinations about what are essentially factual issues as that is the function of the judge. The role of the expert is limited to indicating whether there is a scientific or medical reason why it is more probable than not that something occurred. For example, the accuracy of a witness account of a defence witness who claims that observations were taken and were normal (uncorroborated by any note in the medical records) may be called into question if the expert explains that the aetiology and normal progression of the condition cannot support such an observation.

Since exchange of factual evidence occurs immediately prior to the exchange of expert evidence on liability issues, it is prudent to arrange a further conference with the experts in order to carry out a rigorous review of all the material relied upon by all of the parties: records, pleadings, factual witness evidence and the claimant's preliminary expert evidence on liability issues.

Ideally such conferences should be pre-arranged to take place promptly after exchange of factual witness evidence. This is in order to ensure that there is sufficient time before exchange of expert evidence to take any necessary further steps. The conference should explore with the relevant experts whether a request for clarification or additional information from a witness should be sought,[11] or whether further witnesses need to be tracked down and proofed or pleadings need to be amended.

In preparation for this review the experts should be asked to confirm:
- how, if at all, their advice is altered by the contents of the defence, exchanged witness statements and any other relevant new documentation received since they first reported;
- if it has altered why it has altered and why this was not identifiable when they first reported;
- what implications the change in opinion has in terms of the nature and extent of injury caused by all and any of the remaining allegations of negligence;
- what, if any, further information, documents, literature or investigations are required to clarify issues in dispute which are relevant to the claim.

Experts should be provided with the comments of other liability experts instructed on behalf of the claimant.

Where there appear to be tensions or differences between the opinions of experts instructed on behalf of the claimant these should be explored in discussion with all the experts concerned in order to identify whether there is in fact a difference of opinion or whether one or more aspects of one expert's opinion means that there is a fatal flaw in the logic of either another expert's opinion or the pleaded case. If there is, the claimant will have to be advised what implications this has for the merits and value of the claim and how this can be addressed within the litigation, if at all.

---

[11]   Under the provisions of CPR Part 18.

13.8 EXCHANGE OF EXPERT EVIDENCE

13.8.1 The expert report

After the review of factual evidence the experts should be instructed to put their reports into final form for disclosure. Experts should ensure that the report complies with CPR 35.10.

Not infrequently expert reports fail to refer to material disclosed within the litigation process. Reports which are served within the proceedings should identify the documentation reviewed and relied upon by the expert and should therefore list the pleadings and exchanged factual statements as well as records, protocols, and documentation arising from a complaint or adverse incident investigation provided to and read by the expert. It is good practice for the expert to identify in the report any pleaded issues that have been admitted which are relevant to his expert opinion.

Experts should be reminded of their duties under CPR 35.3.

The expert's evidence should be the independent product of that expert uninfluenced by the pressures of litigation. However, reports must be capable of being understood by the court; should where relevant apply the appropriate tests (*Bolam/Bolitho* and balance of probabilities not scientific certainty); should give details of the literature or other material which the expert has relied upon in making the report but should not set out privileged material;[12] and should comply with CPR Part 35. For this reason it is perfectly proper for lawyers to review an expert's evidence before it is served and indicate to the expert if his report needs adjusting to comply with the rules and the appropriate legal tests.

13.8.2 Review of the exchanged expert evidence

On receipt of the defendant's expert evidence the pleaded issues in the case should be reviewed.

Experts should be sent all the exchanged expert evidence.

The lawyers, with the assistance of the experts, should identify what pleaded issues remain in dispute, which are agreed and what if any new issues appear to be being raised which may lead to an amendment of a pleading. This should be done initially on paper and then in conference.

If the results of the review have the potential implications for the costs budget, this will need to be identified urgently and if an increased budget is required this will need to be sought.

---

[12] *Lucas v Barking, Havering and Redbridge Hospitals NHS Trust* [2004] 1 WLR 220.

13.9 CLARIFICATION OF EXPERT EVIDENCE UNDER THE PROVISIONS OF CPR PART 35.6

CPR 35.6 permits a party to put questions to an expert for the purpose of clarifying his report. Such questions must be put in writing and sent direct to the expert no later than 28 days after service of the report. The questions must be 'proportionate'. A copy of the questions should be provided to the other party. The response to the questions should be sent within 28 days.

This procedure is a relatively under-used one. It can be invaluable in honing down the number of issues that truly remain in dispute. In some cases CPR 35.6 questions can avoid the need for expert discussion.

In deciding whether to put questions to an expert thought needs to be given as to whether the questions are truly ones intended to clarify the report or whether they are really ones of cross-examination which should be left for trial. There is also a tactical decision to be made as to whether asking a specific question will alert the other party to an issue or deficiency in its case which it may not previously have identified and inadvertently help it tighten up its case.

The Practice Direction to CPR Part 35 makes it clear that the party instructing the expert must pay the fees charged by that expert for answering questions put under r 35.6.

13.10 EXPERT DISCUSSIONS

13.10.1 CPR 35.12

Rule 35.12 provides that the court can direct discussions between experts for the purpose of requiring the experts to:

> '(a) identify and discuss the expert issues in the proceedings; and
> (b) where possible, reach an agreed opinion on those issues.'

The parties may also agree that discussions take place between experts.

Anecdotal evidence suggests that the wording of Part 35 may have led some experts to conclude that they have a duty to endeavour to reach agreement. This is, of course, not the case.

Practice Direction 35, para 9.2 helpfully sets out that the:

> 'purpose of discussions between experts is not for experts to settle cases but to agree and narrow issues and in particular to identify:
> (i) the extent of agreement between them;
> (ii) the points of and short reasons for disagreement;
> (iii) action if any to be taken to resolve any outstanding points of disagreement ...'

13.10.2 When should expert discussions take place?

There has perhaps been a tendency since the introduction of CPR to assume that expert discussions must take place and that the parties will be criticised by the court at trial if they have not done so. This is not so. PD 35, para 9 1 makes it clear that they are not mandatory, but rather that the parties should consider whether there is any useful purpose in having a discussion between experts. By contrast the New Model Directions issued after April 2013 state that 'Unless the reports are agreed, there must be a without prejudice discussion between the experts of like discipline'. The writer's opinion is the current Model Directions require revision in this regard to make them consistent with the Practice Direction.

Expert discussions are a costly part of the litigation process. They are also enormously burdensome for the experts concerned. The intention of expert discussions is to assist the court and to limit the amount of court time required in relation to expert evidence. If a discussion will add nothing to this process it is hard to see how the cost of a discussion can be justified or proportionate.

If it is evident from the reports of the experts in one particular discipline that the expert issues are in fact agreed between them, no purpose can be served by requiring them to meet. If the document that is likely to be produced from an expert discussion is one that is so long and so complex that it is unlikely to assist the court or limit time spent on those expert issues, it is again hard to see what purpose can be served by requiring those experts to meet.

The first step in identifying whether experts should be asked to meet in a particular case is when the exchanged expert evidence is reviewed in conference. The purpose of that review should be to identify and record in a succinct way what pleaded issues are agreed and what remains in dispute and, if issues remain in dispute, whether they are issues to which specific expert evidence relates. Having done so, further consideration should be given to whether a discussion of the relevant experts is required.

The lawyers should then incorporate that record of agreed and disputed issues into a preamble to any expert agenda that is drafted.

In some cases, it may be more appropriate to produce a note of agreed issues which is signed by the parties and included in a trial bundle rather than requiring experts to meet and produce a joint statement.

Careful thought needs to be given to whether a discussion between quantum experts is likely to assist the court since very considerable costs, minimal agreement, lengthy and complex joint statements and significant delay can result from some quantum discussions such as those between care experts.

Discussions between those experts addressing condition, prognosis and life expectation are likely both to assist the court and to be required.

Given that, typically, a defendant's quantum expert will incorporate into his/her report comments on the claimant's expert recommendations, a less costly and more helpful approach may be to replace the quantum expert discussion with provision in the directions that the defendant's expert should identify in their report the extent to which the evidence served on behalf of the claimant is agreed and that the claimant's expert serve a supplementary report within 28 days of service of the defendant's evidence, limited to identifying the extent of agreement or disagreement with the defendant's expert.

13.10.3   Model directions

Over the years since the Woolf reforms, the Masters assigned to the clinical negligence work in the High Court in London produced and refined suggested model directions for use in the High Court.[13] Those directions have been replaced since April 2013 with the New Model Directions which it is understood are intended to be applied nationally and to other types of litigation.

It is understood at the time of drafting that there may be some revision to the new 2013 Model Directions. It is hoped by the writer that they will be amended because some of the well tried and tested and very practical directions from the High Court Model Clinical Negligence Directions have been lost.

In the meantime, when drafting directions thought should be given as to whether it would be helpful in the individual case to import some of the old model directions in to the order being sought for the particular case. For this reason, copies of both the old High Court Model Directions (version 4) and the New Model Directions (2013) are included in the appendices to this chapter.

13.10.4   Format and timing of expert discussions

The case management directions in the case will have provided a timetable for expert discussions. Experts should have been made aware of this. If the timetable is tight it may be prudent to fix provisional dates for discussions at an earlier stage of the case, in particular if the case is one in which a discussion between one set of experts and their joint statement really needs to be completed before another expert discussion takes place.

Expert discussions can be held either face to face or via telephone. Sometimes the location of the respective experts and their other commitments means that a telephone discussion is the only feasible option. Arrangements should be proportionate to the case and thus in relatively low value cases a telephone discussion may be the preferred option.

Whatever the format of the discussion, it needs to be agreed in advance how and when the joint statement is to be produced. If the experts are having their

---

[13]   See **12.2.9**.

discussion via telephone and one or both have the agenda in electronic format, the joint statement can be produced during the discussion and sent electronically for checking and signature.

What is essential is that, whatever arrangement is made, it provides sufficient time both for the discussion itself and for the individual expert to prepare for the discussion. This requires the agenda for the discussion to be finalised and sent to the expert well ahead of the discussion.

It is also essential that experts ensure that they have the bundle of relevant documentation in front of them and available to refer to during the discussion.

13.10.5   The agenda

In some cases, the preparation of agendas for expert discussion has become one of the most contentious parts of the litigation.

All too often agendas (and thus expert discussions) have become too complicated, the process has become expensive, time consuming and slow and, in turn in some cases, is adding to rather than reducing the length of trial. There has been a prevalence of dual agendas or multiple questions. This probably stems from a number of causes:

- failure on the part of the lawyers to understand what the issues are and whether they are (or remain) in dispute;
- failure on the part of the lawyers or those instructing them to accommodate within an agenda the case being put by the other side;
- an attempt by parties to use expert discussions either to cross-examine experts by agenda or to see if advantage can be gained in some way;
- an overly rigid adherence to questions proposed by counsel/client leading to duplication of questions or questions that are so complex that they are incomprehensible.

The post-exchange review of expert evidence in conference with the experts should not only have led to the identification of the issues which are agreed and those which remain in dispute, but should also seek to identify the questions that need to be included in any agenda for discussion between the relevant experts. In this way the expert and, if appropriate counsel, can be involved in the preparation of the agenda in the most efficient way.

Agendas should focus on the pleaded issues in the case that are relevant to the particular discipline of expert evidence for which the agenda is drafted. This focus and clarity should be assisted if the issues which are agreed and those which remain in dispute are set out in the preamble to the agenda.

The preamble to the agenda should list the documents which the experts have seen, including medical records, pleadings, itemised witness statements, expert reports and other relevant documentation. Good practice is to produce an indexed bundle specifically for the discussion which is agreed between the parties and sent to the experts.

The preamble should also remind the experts of the legal test applied by the court in determining the case.

The questions on the agenda should follow the pleadings. Thus, for example, if there are five allegations of obstetric negligence, in principle there should only need to be five principle questions for the obstetric experts. That said, an allegation of 'the D was negligent in failing to act on the CTG abnormalities between 10.00 am and 11.00 am', would probably require the following:

- Is it agreed that there were abnormalities on the CTG trace between 10.00 am and 11.00 am?
- If there were, what were they?
- Did these abnormalities require intervention?
- If so, what intervention was required and by what time?

So far as is possible and sensible questions should be closed questions, unless such an approach would lead to an excessive number of questions or a lack of clarity of response.

For example, it is more sensible to ask 'By what time should the claimant have been delivered?' rather than going through a series of times for each minute of the allegedly negligent delay.

There should not be a rigid approach to the issue of whether a question is open or closed. It may be that breach of duty questions can more easily be reduced to 'yes' or 'no' than causation.

Questions of fact should not be included in an agenda, save where they bear directly on a pleaded issue. For example, if there are differing factual accounts that will require determination by the court it may be appropriate to include a question or questions for the experts which address the medical issues relevant to that evidence.

Thus, if the normal progression of a condition prior to collapse calls into question the accuracy of a witness account that observations were taken and were normal prior to collapse a question addressing this can be included as long as it is worded in such a way that the experts are not required to make a finding of fact. They should be cautioned within the agenda that they should avoid doing so.

Questions designed to go to the credit of an expert should not be included. Thus, 'What experience do the experts have of this condition?' is not an appropriate question for inclusion on an agenda.

It is not always easy to draft clear questions for quantum issue agendas or for the experts to draft clear joint statements from those discussions. Very considerable costs, minimal agreement, lengthy and complex joint statements and significant delay can result from these discussions.

The model directions provide the following in relation to agendas:

> '(b) **Unless otherwise agreed by all parties' solicitors, after consulting with the experts,** a draft Agenda which directs the experts to the remaining issues relevant to the experts' discipline, as identified in the statements of case shall be prepared jointly by the Claimant's solicitors and experts and sent to the Defendant's solicitors for comment at least 35 days before the agreed date for the experts' discussions.
>
> The use of agendas is not mandatory. Solicitors should consult with the experts to ensure that agendas are necessary and, if used, are reasonable in scope. The agenda should assist the experts and should not be in the form of leading questions or hostile in tone. An agenda must include a list of the outstanding issues in the preamble.
>
> (c) The Defendants shall within 21 days of receipt agree the Agenda, or propose amendments.
>
> (d) Seven days thereafter all solicitors shall use their best endeavours to agree the Agenda. Points of disagreement should be on matters of real substance and not semantics or on matters the experts could resolve of their own accord at the discussion. In default of agreement, both versions shall be considered at the discussions. Agendas, when used, shall be provided to the experts not less than 7 days before the date fixed for discussions.

13.10.6   Expert preparation for discussion

It is essential that experts prepare for their discussion with the degree of attention to detail and with reference to all the relevant documentation just as they would do for giving evidence at trial. This means that an expert needs to ensure that time is allocated in his diary for this preparation. Obviously, it also requires that the agenda is provided sufficiently far in advance for him to prepare.

Arrangements whereby expert discussions take place via mobile telephone when one expert is travelling or when both experts are attending a professional engagement such as a conference are not conducive to clarity of thought or communication, neither are they likely to ensure adequate pre-discussion preparation.

13.10.7   The joint statement

One of the problems that not infrequently arises is a failure by one or more experts to ensure that the joint statement is signed and circulated promptly to the parties' lawyers.

Sometimes this occurs because an expert does not agree that a response to a question has been accurately recorded. Sometimes it occurs because an expert goes away before the document is sent for signature.

Sometimes it occurs because an expert wishes to change a response and this leads in effect to a continuation of the discussion. Whilst this is not ideal, it is not necessarily inappropriate. For example, a point recorded in the medical records relevant to the pleaded issues in dispute may be raised during the discussion which has not previously been raised or highlighted in evidence and this may lead one expert to want time to consider the point in more detail than the discussion allows.

What is not appropriate is for the parties' lawyers to seek to influence the final version of the joint statement. The expert's duty is to the court and that obligation overrides any obligation to the person from whom he has received instructions. The Civil Justice Council protocol makes it clear that those instructing experts should not instruct experts to avoid reaching agreement (or to defer doing so) on any matter within the experts competence and experts should not accept instructions to do so.

PD 35, para 9. 6 provides for the preparation and delivery to the parties of the Joint statement. It says:

> 'The experts will prepare for the court and sign a statement of the issues on which they agree and on which they disagree with a summary of their reasons in accordance with Rule 35.12 Civil Procedure Rules, and each statement must be sent to the parties to be received by 4pm on xxxx and in any event no later than 7 days after the discussion.'

Thought should be given as to whether such a provision should be inserted in to the Order.

CPR 35.12 provides that where experts reach agreement on an issue during their discussions, the agreement shall not bind the parties unless the parties expressly agree to be bound by the agreement.

If an expert radically alters his or her opinion, the joint statement should include a note or addendum by that expert explaining the change of opinion (PD 35, para 9.8).

The benefit of the lawyers listening to the discussion is that it can be agreed by the experts and parties alike that one of the lawyers will, but only on the experts dictation, record and type the answers to the questions on the agenda so that that typed record can be circulated via email to the experts for checking and signature immediately upon the conclusion of the discussion.

13.10.8   Lawyers at expert discussions

There has been much debate since the introduction of CPR as to whether lawyers should be present at expert discussions. In a judicial system which prides itself on justice being seen to be done, it is very difficult for the injured claimant to understand why, following a discussion behind closed doors between experts at which no lawyer has been present, a case that had had good prospects of success suddenly has to be abandoned. For lawyers, clients and experts alike there is a real concern that closed discussions can create an environment in which one expert can pressurise another or in which two colleagues who respect each other professionally find it hard to disagree and thus endeavour to find common ground and compromise.

In addition there are occasions when the experts believe that they have reached agreement or answered a question in one way only for legal analysis to produce a different and unintended consequence or interpretation.

Reasons usually given for suggesting that lawyers should not be present at meetings of experts are that experts are likely to feel inhibited in their discussion or intimidated by the presence of lawyers and that the presence of lawyers increases costs.

If an expert has prepared his/her report in accordance with the requirements of Part 35 and that evidence has been tested and reviewed in conference throughout the litigation there should be nothing relevant to the evidence in the case that the expert has not already communicated to the instructing solicitor. In a case that has been well prepared by lawyer and expert alike, it is difficult to understand how the presence of lawyers inhibits discussion between experts, neither anecdotally does there appear to be evidence that it does so.

There is a misapprehension that lawyers being present means that the discussion has to be held as a face-to-face one. This is not the case. In these days of easy telephone linking lawyers can listen in to a telephone discussion and the experts can be at different corners of the country.

The new model directions make no provision in terms of the presence of lawyers at the expert discussion, whereas the old version 4 made express provision as follows:

> 'Unless otherwise ordered by the Court, or unless agreed by all parties, including the experts, the parties' solicitors shall not attend such discussions, if solicitors do attend, the experts may if they so request, hold a part of their discussions in the absence of the solicitors. Where solicitors do attend, they should not normally intervene, save to answer questions put to them by the experts or to advise them upon the law.'

This is mirrored in PD 35, paras 9.4 and 9.5. Again, thought will need to be given as to whether to include provision for this in the Order itself.

The issue of the presence of lawyers at an expert discussion was the subject of an appeal in the case of *Hubbard v Lambeth, Southwark and Lewisham Health Authority*.[14] In that case (which was one in which it had been agreed that there should be a recording of the discussion), the court ordered that they should not be present. Lady Justice Hale invited the parties to consider the possibility of appointing a neutral and independent chairperson.

It seems unlikely that the listening to and transcription of a recording of an expert discussion or the appointment, instruction and preparation of an independent chairperson will result in lower costs than the cost of two solicitors already familiar with all the issues in the case listening to the discussion via a telephone link.

Experience suggests that solicitors should attend any meeting involving experts from more than one discipline or two agendas because these are just the sort of meetings at which the experts are likely to require clarification/assistance from lawyers, which in turn is likely to lead to a substantial saving of costs and a greater prospect of resolution of issues.

13.11   REVIEW OF OUTCOME OF EXPERT DISCUSSIONS

It will be necessary to review the joint statements and identify how, if at all, these impact upon merits and quantum. Where necessary, for example where there has been a concession by an expert, this review may need to be done in conference with the expert in order to prepare for any settlement discussions, for preparation for trial and in order to be able to advise the client.

Thought will also have to be given as to how, if at all, the outcome impacts upon the costs budget and whether an application for an increase will need to be made.

13.12   PRE-TRIAL PREPARATION WITH EXPERTS

If the case is going to proceed to a trial it will be necessary to have pre-trial conferences with those experts who will give evidence. It is always sensible to have these pre-trial conferences booked well ahead so that there is no difficulty with fitting them into everyone's diaries.

13.13   CONSECUTIVE EXPERT EVIDENCE: 'HOT TUBBING'

There is a new provision whereby the Court can direct that expert evidence is heard concurrently. This is set out in PD 35, para 11 which states:

---

[14]   [2002] Lloyd's Rep Med 8.

'11.1 At any stage in the proceedings the court may direct that some or all of the experts from like disciplines shall give their evidence concurrently. The following procedure shall then apply.

11.2 The court may direct that the parties agree an agenda for the taking of concurrent evidence, based upon the areas of disagreement identified in the experts' joint statements made pursuant to rule 35.12.

11.3 At the appropriate time the relevant experts will each take the oath or affirm. Unless the court orders otherwise, the experts will then address the items on the agenda in the manner set out in paragraph 11.4.

11.4 In relation to each issue on the agenda, and subject to the judge's discretion to modify the procedure –
(1) the judge may initiate the discussion by asking the experts, in turn, for their views. Once an expert has expressed a view the judge may ask questions about it. At one or more appropriate stages when questioning a particular expert, the judge may invite the other expert to comment or to ask that expert's own questions of the first expert;
(2) after the process set out in (1) has been completed for all the experts, the parties' representatives may ask questions of them. While such questioning may be designed to test the correctness of an expert's view, or seek clarification of it, it should not cover ground which has been fully explored already. In general a full cross-examination or re-examination is neither necessary nor appropriate; and
(3) after the process set out in (2) has been completed, the judge may summarise the experts' different positions on the issue and ask them to confirm or correct that summary.'

At the time of drafting it is not known whether it has yet been used in a clinical negligence case, but readers should be aware of it and consider whether an application for evidence to be heard in this way should be made/opposed.

13.14 TRIAL

It is important to ensure that from the point that the trial date is fixed experts are notified and reminded of the trial fixture. It is also prudent to serve each expert with a witness summons in order to ensure their attendance at court but it is only polite that this should be done only after the rationale for serving the summons has been explained to each expert concerned.

As the trial date looms closer it is sensible to try to reach agreement with the other party over the order of witnesses so that the experts can be given an indication as to when their attendance at court is likely to be required. Some experts will need to attend not just to give their own evidence, but also to hear that of some or all factual witnesses and the evidence of their opposite number.

Experts need to be aware that once a matter goes to trial nothing is certain, including the timetable for evidence. They need to be prepared for the fact that so far as possible their clinical and other professional commitments will be taken into account, but that the exact time of day or actual days on which they will be required cannot be guaranteed. It is not unusual for the evidence and cross-examination of one or two witnesses to take longer than anticipated and this in turn can impact upon the timetable of the entire trial.

Experts also need to be prepared for the fact that they may be required to participate in conferences at very short notice during the trial or to undertake further research or review of material during it.

TOP TIPS

- Understand and review the medical issues from the first instruction and then at every stage of the case.

- Approach the experts it is proposed to instruct at a very early stage.

- It is the quality of expert evidence and not necessarily the number of experts which is the key to winning a case.

- When instructing an expert for the first time ensure that the expert understands the demands of the litigation process.

- If an experts' meeting is unlikely to clarify issues which remain in dispute, do not organise one.

- Solicitors should consider attending any expert meeting involving experts from more than one discipline or two agendas.

- Seek agreement with the other party over the order of witnesses at trial.

CHAPTER 14

INSTRUCTING AN EXPERT: A MEDIC'S PERSPECTIVE

In this chapter Dr Tom Boyd looks at the instruction of experts from the viewpoint of the expert witness.

14.1 INTRODUCTION

This section is written from the perspective of an expert in general practice. The diagnostic process in general practice is more dependent on history-taking and less dependent on special investigations than that in hospital. The therapeutic process is less complex, relying mainly on the prescription of oral medications. These differences influence my task as an expert and the recommendations I make, but I believe that they are of general application and should assist lawyers instructing experts in all branches of medicine.

14.2 WHICH EXPERT?

It is frequently easy to identify the specialism from which your expert should be drawn. In some cases, however, this may cause difficulty. It may not be obvious whether a medical or surgical opinion is required: neurologist or neurosurgeon; cardiologist or cardiothoracic surgeon; rheumatologist or orthopaedic surgeon and so on.

In the case of rare diseases there may be few doctors in the UK who deal with the condition under scrutiny and fewer still who are prepared to be medico-legal experts. In some specialties – microbiology, for example – some consultants may have little or no direct contact with patients, whilst others are frequently at the bedside.

A reasonable expert will always be happy to discuss a potential instruction in advance and tell you honestly whether or not he is the most appropriate kind of person to instruct. You might ask, 'Is this kind of patient referred to you as a routine or would someone else more often deal with this problem?'.

You will wish to have an expert whose views stand up to scrutiny and who will be able to hold his own in a meeting of experts and in court. Your client will not be well-served by an expert who provides a positive liability or causation report only instantly to change his mind when confronted by a colleague or, worse, when he enters the witness box and is subject to cross-examination.

However, you should also beware of the rigid expert: I heard one such boast that he had never changed his mind. Beware also the expert – there are some – who asks for your views or guidance on liability and appears to want to please you by providing the kind of report you expect. For the same reason I believe that it is better to avoid attempting to influence your expert with statements such as, 'I don't think there's much in this, but I'd be grateful if you could have a look at it,' or, 'I've done my own research and I'm sure the treatment was negligent'.

The best way to select an expert is to use one with whom you have worked before and who served you well. Your firm might consider – if it does not already have one – keeping a database of relevant experts and, more importantly, updating it regularly with comments on the experts' performance. Alternatively you may wish to ask the views of other lawyers or of doctors whose judgment you regard as sound. Experienced experts will have views about their colleagues. Experienced experts in general practice will have met experts in most specialties and consultants will often know an appropriate expert in related disciplines.

There are some bodies of experts which doctors may join and whose sole criterion for membership is the payment of a fee. These should not be relied upon as a source of expertise, because membership no more guarantees expertise than does membership of the Royal Horticultural Society ensure that the member can identify a daffodil. Some experts indulge in constant self-promotion, I recommend that you avoid them: a good expert will be too busy to advertise.

Eminence in the appropriate specialty may be an advantage to an expert but can also be a hindrance. Does your expert have his feet sufficiently on the ground to be able to give an opinion about reasonable and responsible practice or is he now so eminent that he has lost touch with his colleagues practising at the coal-face? A colleague of mine was delighted to hear a judge list the many achievements of his illustrious opposite number in his judgment only then to say, 'Dr X, on the other hand, has his finger on the pulse of modern general practice'. My colleague's views were preferred.

My own view is that you should usually use an expert who is in active clinical practice. Medicine changes so rapidly that a doctor who has retired or whose sole practice is a medico-legal one will find it very difficult to give an authoritative opinion concerning standard practice. Distance from the hurly-burly of medicine may cause an expert to have idealised or unrealistic views about his colleagues' standards of care. For cases in which the events under scrutiny took place many years ago you might have to instruct an expert who has retired. General practice can be a rather solitary specialty and there is a wider variation in the standard of practice than is usual in hospital practice. I would recommend that you instruct a general practice expert who has frequent contact with the clinical practice of his colleagues, perhaps through teaching or examining.

An expert needs to have accumulated sufficient clinical experience to be aware of the range of practice and expertise within his own specialty and of the common pitfalls of practice. He is unlikely to have done so until he has been a principal in general practice or a consultant in hospital practice for, say, 10 to 15 years.

A medico-legal expert needs, to a certain degree, to be obsessive. To provide an adequate opinion he needs to examine the chronology in detail and hunt through the records to find material which might bear on his opinion. In the case of a patient who is managed by his general practitioner and is eventually admitted to hospital, for example, important material often exists in the medical records made on admission or may lurk in the comments made in the nursing 'Kardex'. I am often impressed by the fact that effective lawyers, amongst their other qualities, pay great attention to detail. This is something you should seek in an expert.

Experts' views should be uninfluenced by the source of their instructions. Some lawyers prefer to instruct experts who receive instructions from both claimants and defendants but I do not think that this is any guarantee that the expert does not 'lean' one way or the other. The medical defence organisations often instruct experts who are on their advisory or management boards. This has been the subject of adverse comment by some judges, because it gives the appearance of a conflict of interest.

14.3　THE LETTER OF APPROACH

Having identified an appropriate expert, you should write a letter of approach. This should include:

- the name(s) and place of practice of any doctor(s) who are potentially the subject of criticism (in order for your expert to identify any conflict of interest);
- a brief chronology of the case;
- a summary of the issues you wish your expert to address;
- details of any deadlines, such as those imposed by limitation or a planned conference;
- the number of pages or lever-arch files of documents you wish the expert to consider;
- whether, and under what conditions, you need your expert to see and/or examine the claimant (this is not usually required for liability reports);
- any special circumstances or conditions applying to the case;
- a request for your expert to state what his hourly and maximum fees are;

- a request for your expert to give you an estimate of the amount of time he will require to prepare his report after receipt of the records and your final letter of instruction.

I do not like letters which are full of legalese or which consist of pages of standard documents 'topped and tailed' with a few details relevant to the case. If there are standard rules you wish your experts to follow (they are likely to disregard them anyway if they are not included in CPR Part 35) it is better to enclose them as a separate document. If your expert needs that kind of guidance, perhaps you should be considering instructing one with more experience.

Some instructing solicitors include a witness statement with the letter of approach to give detailed information and more of the flavour of the case. This can be useful but is not a substitute for the information I have described above.

A good expert will tell you if the case clearly has no merit on the information you have supplied, or if liability is so clear that you should attempt to request an admission of liability without a report.

14.4 'BRIEF PRELIMINARY' REPORTS

I am sometimes approached to write brief preliminary reports and nearly always refuse such requests. When doctors are considering an intervention for a patient they sometimes consider whether or not it is one they would happily accept for themselves. I doubt that, had I suffered a medical misadventure, I would be satisfied by a medical expert who considered my case under great pressure of time and furnished me with a partially argued opinion.

Brief preliminary reports may cause meritorious claims to be prematurely abandoned and ultimately hopeless cases to be pursued. If the case is so straightforward or trivial that the issues can be identified, considered and reported upon in little more than an hour then an expert may not be required at all. 'Preliminary' implies that the expert might reach a different opinion after more detailed consideration. Such reports are a false economy. Some issues are very straightforward and can be considered briefly. An expert you instruct more than very occasionally should, I think, be prepared to give 'free' advice on such issues by telephone or email or explain why the issue is too complex to be dealt with in that way.

14.5 THE WITNESS STATEMENT(S)

Most cases centre on one main witness statement: usually that made by the injured party or a surviving relative. This is the cornerstone of the evidence on which the expert should base his opinion. A well-drafted witness statement makes an expert's task much easier. A superficial or inaccurate one complicates the expert's work and may fatally damage the case.

Solicitors are to some extent at the mercy of the client's powers of recall but I have sometimes noticed in conference that probing by skilled counsel or questioning by medical experts may elicit vital details when insufficient time has been expended on the first witness statement. As memories fade with time, you are likely to be able to get the best information early on.

It is very frustrating for an expert if the chronology in the witness statement bears little resemblance to that revealed by the medical records. This will cause the expert to write a much longer report based on the alternative scenarios which may be accepted by a court. Unless there is good reason to believe that the records have been altered or are not contemporaneous (both unusual, but not unheard of), I suggest that the client should be asked to compare his or her recollection with the notes. It should be made clear within the statement that memories have been aided by the records or that the accuracy of the records is disputed.

The best witness statements contain detailed accounts of the development of symptoms and the encounters with doctors and others. Objective data are far more useful than subjective ones: it is much more meaningful to say, for example, 'On Wednesday she ate only one slice of toast and a few grapes and was so weak that she required the assistance of two people to climb the stairs, to use the toilet and to wash', than to state, 'We didn't like the look of her, she was grey and pasty'. The descriptions of consultations should ideally include information amounting to a verbatim transcript of the conversation between the patient and the doctor and a detailed description of the examination performed, the explanation offered by the doctor and recommendations about treatment and follow-up.

14.6 THE DOCUMENTS AND THE FINAL LETTER OF INSTRUCTION

In order for the expert to concentrate on the liability or causation issues to be addressed, he should be provided with well-sorted, catalogued and paginated records. I am not infrequently sent unpaginated records, which I always paginate or return. Poorly sorted or unpaginated records cause experts to suspect that they are dealing with a sloppy lawyer.

I would rather receive too many medical notes than too few. If the hospital fluid balance charts or prescribing records are irrelevant to me, it is easy to disregard them if they are properly sorted. If I do not see the hospital microbiology report which reveals the nature of the infection previously treated in general practice then I may be deprived of information vital to my consideration of the case.

Many solicitors employ nurses or others to prepare detailed chronologies of the records. I am afraid that I rarely find these helpful. Occasionally they assist me in preparing my own chronology, but only when they contain references to the pagination, which frequently they do not.

Some solicitors send large bundles of papers secured by treasury tags or rubber bands. These are impossible to work with, so I always put them in lever-arch files.

If you have written a comprehensive letter of approach then the letter accompanying the documents can usually be succinct and refer back to it. It can be irksome to the expert if you raise a new set of issues or identify a multitude of questions to which you seek answers at this stage. This is especially so if you have already imposed restrictive conditions relating to time and payment.

If you have already obtained other reports about the case you will need to consider whether to include these in the bundle sent to the expert. Whilst it may be appropriate to include a liability report to an expert instructed to deal with causation, I believe that it is generally inappropriate for an expert on liability to see other liability reports before he has reached and recorded his own conclusion. I do not want to have my opinion skewed by the approach of other experts, so I almost always leave their reports unread and make this explicit within my report.

14.7   ON RECEIPT OF THE REPORT

If the right expert has been instructed, you will receive a well-argued report which addresses the questions you posed and which does so in a way which enables you to communicate the reasoning and conclusions to your client. A good expert will attempt to come to fairly unambiguous conclusions and will, where appropriate, support his conclusions by reference to relevant literature.

If you need to write a long letter seeking clarification of the report you may well have instructed the wrong expert.

14.8   DEADLINES

You are entitled to expect your expert to produce his report at least approximately on time. If there are compelling reasons, such as limitation, to impose a specific deadline please be explicit about this from the outset. Experts in active clinical practice with a substantial medico-legal commitment may, for good reasons, sometimes underestimate their workload and may then sometimes be slightly late in delivering reports. You should feel free to send them gentle reminders. You may choose not to instruct an expert who is consistently causing you and your client difficulties by his tardiness.

An experienced expert will have a good idea of the time it takes the Legal Services Commission, for example, to reimburse your firm for his fees. Prompt payment of fees is a delight to experts. Having to write letters of reminder concerning unpaid fees and to follow these up with telephone calls is a considerable irritation to many experts. I decline instructions from firms who have been especially difficult in this respect. Experts also talk about this issue when they meet each other; you do not want your firm to be labelled as a late payer.

14.9 CONFERENCE WITH COUNSEL

Once the requisite reports have been obtained, you may wish to instruct counsel and consider a conference. It is, in my experience, much more efficient to gather experts together with a well-constructed agenda than to indulge in protracted multi-directional correspondence. I am not a fan of telephone conferences. Experts on communication skills estimate that as much as 90% of communication is non-verbal. Although this may be an exaggeration, most of this is lost on the telephone.

A conference is most productive if your experts are well-prepared. It is probably best to prepare a conference file of the most important documents and send this to the experts a week or two ahead of the conference. I am surprised at how few experts bring the original medical records to conferences when these often need to be referred to. Were I a lawyer, I would instruct my experts to bring the records to the conference. If there are a few critical pages, you may wish to include these in the conference file.

14.10 AVAILABILITY OF EXPERTS

An expert who is in active clinical practice is unlikely to be able to free himself at very short notice. Experts in general practice are likely to have a particularly onerous clinical commitment on Mondays. An expert in hospital practice may have a regular clinic or operating session which is difficult to cancel or postpone. However, you have the right to expect an expert to be sufficiently committed to his medico-legal work to be reasonably available to attend conferences with counsel and court. Your expert should appreciate the logistical difficulty of arranging a conference involving you, your client, counsel and perhaps several other experts and should give you the impression that his commitment to your case is high in his sense of priorities. If this is the case, then it is irritating if you cancel or change such arrangements for what appear to be avoidable reasons. My own experience is that late changes in arrangements are usually caused by other experts.

14.11 TEAMWORK

In the *Pertussis* vaccine litigation Stuart-Smith LJ said:[1]

> 'The Court has to evaluate the witness and the soundness of his opinion. Most importantly this involves an examination of the reasons given for his opinions and the extent to which they are supported by the evidence. The Judge also has to

---

[1] [1990] 1 Med LR 117.

decide what weight to attach to a witness's opinion by examining the internal consistency and logic of his evidence; the care with which he has considered the subject and presented his evidence; his precision and accuracy of thought as demonstrated by his answers; how he responds to searching and informed cross-examination and in particular the extent to which a witness faces up to and accepts the logic of a proposition put in cross-examination or is prepared to concede points that are seen to be correct; the extent to which a witness has conceived an opinion and is reluctant to re-examine it in the light of later evidence, or demonstrates a flexibility of mind which may involve changing or modifying opinions previously held; whether or not a witness is biased or lacks independence.'

You should be able to judge whether your expert is likely to be able to satisfy these criteria by reading his reports and meeting him in conference. Ultimately the test of whether an expert is suitable for your case depends on whether or not you and he can work well together and become part of an effective team, without sacrificing any of his independence or impartiality.

14.12   IMMUNITY FROM SUIT

In 2011 the Supreme Court (*Jones v Kaney*[2]) decided, by a majority of five to two, to remove the immunity that prevented a client from suing an expert he has retained. The case concerned a clinical psychologist who had prepared a report for a road traffic accident victim. She subsequently signed a joint statement after a meeting of experts which was damaging to the claim. It transpired that she had not seen the reports of the opposing expert at the time of the experts' meeting and that the joint statement she had signed did not reflect her views.

In his leading judgement, Lord Phillips compared the role of experts with that of barristers, who had had their immunity from liability in negligence removed by the House of Lords in 2000:

> 'Thus the expert witness has this in common with the advocate. Each undertakes a duty to provide services to the client. In each case they services include a paramount duty to the court and the public, which may require the advocate or the witness to act in a way which does not advance the client's case. The advocate must disclose to the court authorities that are unfavourable to his client. The expert witness must give his evidence honestly, even if this involves concessions that are contrary to his client's interests. The expert witness has far more in common with the advocate then he does with the witness of fact.'

I do not believe that a conscientious expert should be deterred from his task by the fear of being sued. I am not aware that there has been a flood of such cases and he should, in any case, be indemnified by his medical defence organisation. A greater fear, especially among experts giving evidence in cases of alleged child abuse, might be that of disciplinary action by the General Medical Council. In 2005 Professor Sir Roy Meadow was struck off the medical register after

---

[2]   [2011] UKSC 13.

stating incorrectly in court that the odds against two cot deaths occurring in the same family were 73 million to 1. The GMC's decision was subsequently reversed after appeals to the High Court and the Court of Appeal.

TOP TIPS

- Membership of a body of experts does not guarantee expertise.
- Eminence can be a hindrance as well as a benefit.
- A well-drafted witness statement makes the expert's task easier.
- Chronologies are only helpful if cross-referenced to the records.
- Provide the expert with a conference file including critical pages from the medical records.

CHAPTER 15

PART 36 OFFERS

Originally perceived as the defendant's friend over the years Part 36 offers have become an increasingly powerful tool in the claimant's armoury. In this chapter solicitor John McQuater explains the law and tactics involved in striving to achieve a settlement using CPR Part 36 procedure.

15.1 INTRODUCTION

CPR Part 36 provides a formal framework for negotiations which operates as a self-contained code where the terms of the rule prevail over the general law of contract, in particular with offer and acceptance.

15.2 GENERAL PRINCIPLES

There are a number of general principles applicable to Part 36 Offers.

15.2.1 The forensic approach

The correct forensic approach to Part 36 is dictated by that rule being drafted,[1] as a 'self-contained code'. Consequently, it is the terms of Part 36 itself that, at least in the first instance, the practitioner must look when deciding: whether it is available for the purposes of an offer; making an offer intended to have the consequences of Part 36; if reviewing if and considering the consequences of an offer which refers to the rule; whenever withdrawing or changing such an offer; and when accepting a Part 36 offer.

15.2.2 Scope of Part 36 offers

CPR 36.A1 confirms the rule comprises Section I and Section II, but as Section II relates only to offers made in non-clinical negligence protocols any Part 36 offers made in clinical negligence claims will be under Section I.

---

[1]   As Moore-Bick LJ observed in *Gibbon v Manchester City Council* [2010] EWCA Civ 726, [2011] 2 All ER 258, [2010] 1 WLR 2081, [2010] All ER (D) 218 (Jun).

CPR 36.3(2)(a) confirms that a Part 36 offer may be made at any time, including before the commencement of proceedings.[2]

15.2.3 Offers on issues

CPR 36.2(2)(d) recognises that an offer may relate to the whole of the claim, part of the claim or an issue in the claim. It is, of course, a requirement of form and content to state what the offer does relate to. CPR 36.2(5) expressly provides that an offeror may make a Part 36 offer solely in relation to liability, a tactic that can be very effective for claimants.

15.2.4 Offers in appeals

CPR 36.3(2)(b) confirms that a Part 36 offer may be made in appeal proceedings. That is important as CPR 36.3(4) provides a Part 36 offer will only have Part 36 costs consequences in relation to the costs of the proceedings in respect of which it is made and not in relation to the costs of any appeal from the final decision in those proceedings. If appeal proceedings are subject to the CPR then a Part 36 offer may be made even if that would not have been possible in the original proceedings to which the appeal relates.

15.2.5 Offers in costs proceedings

The phrase 'any time' might be considered wide enough to encompass offers in costs proceedings after the substantive claim has been dealt with.[3] Where detailed assessment proceedings are commenced after 1 April 2013, CPR 47.21(4) expressly provides that the provisions of Part 36 will, with appropriate modifications, apply to the costs of those detailed assessment proceedings.

15.3　MAKING A PART 36 OFFER

The general requirements as to the form and content of a Part 36 offer are found in CPR 36.2(2). This rule applies to every offer that is intended to be made in accordance with Part 36 and requires such an offer:

- by CPR 36.2(2)(a) to be in writing;[4]
- by CPR 36.2(2)(b) to state on its face that it is intended to have the consequences of Section I of Part 36;[5]

---

[2]　See *Thompson v Bruce* [2011] EWHC 2228 (QB) and *Solomon v Cromwell Group plc* [2011] EWCA Civ 1584, [2012] 1 WLR 1048, [2012] 2 All ER 825, [2012] CP Rep 14, [2012] 2 Costs LR 314, [2012] RTR 24, [2012] PIQR P9.

[3]　*Howell v Lees-Millais* [2011] EWCA Civ 786, [2011] WTLR 1795, [2011] 4 Costs LR 456, [2011] All ER (D) 48 (Jul).

[4]　CPR 36.2(2)(a).

[5]　CPR 36.2(2)(b).

- by CPR 36.2(2)(c) to specify a period of not less than 21 days within which the defendant will be liable for the claimant's costs in accordance with CPR 36.10 if the offer is accepted;[6]
- by CPR 36.2(2)(d) to state whether it relates to the whole of the claim or to part of it or to an issue that arises in it and if so to which part or issue;[7] and
- by CPR 36.2(2)(e) to state whether it takes into account any counterclaim.[8]

The period stated in the offer, necessary to comply with CPR 36.2(2)(c), is defined by CPR 36.3(1)(c) as 'the relevant period'.

Where an offer is made less than 21 days before trial the relevant period will be the period up to the end of the trial or such other period as the court has determined. Thus, the rule itself provides a specific exception to the usually applicable minimum of 21 days, as defined in CPR 36.2. Moreover, this provision is the exception to the general rule that the court has no discretion to dispense with the rules on form and content found in Part 36.2. That allows the court to stipulate a relevant period of less than 21 days, so a late offer may be effective against the costs of trial. The court may also, if demanded by the justice of the case, make such an order even before the offer has been made.

Where a late offer is made the offeree will still need permission from the court to accept once the trial has started but, if permission is given, the deemed costs order under CPR 36.10(1) will be applicable, as acceptance will then have been within the relevant period.

Save for the exception provided for in CPR 36.3(1)(c), when an offer is made not less than 21 days before trial, the requirement for a relevant period of at least 21 days, in accordance with CPR 36.2(2)(c), is obligatory. In practice it has been this requirement to specify a period of not less than 21 days, within which the defendant will be liable for the claimant's costs in accordance with CPR 36.10 if the offer is accepted, that has proved most problematic so far as compliance with the rules on form and content are concerned. Particular difficulties have been caused by offerors adopting the pre-2007 terms of the rule by expressing the offer to remain open for 21 days.

While the court will try to give effect to an offer which described itself as a Part 36 offer that does not allow the court to circumvent the mandatory requirement for the offer to contain a relevant period of not less than 21 days.[9]

---

6   CPR 36.2(2)(c).
7   CPR 36.2(2)(d).
8   CPR 36.2(2)(e).
9   *C v D* [2011] EWCA Civ 646, [2012] 1 WLR 1962, [2012] 1 All ER 302, [2011] CP Rep 38, [2011] 2 EGLR 95, [2011] 23 EG 86, [2011] 5 Costs LR 773, 136 Con LR 109.

Hence in *PHI Group Ltd v Robert West Consulting Ltd*,[10] where the offer was expressed as being intended to have the consequences of Part 36 but as to time simply stated 'our client would be grateful if your client's response to this offer could be provided within the next 7 days', Lloyd LJ emphasised, as the offer letter failed to specify a period of not less than 21 days, that: 'The judge considered in those circumstances this was fatal, and I agree with him.'

Lloyd LJ did go on to observe:

> 'it is ... not part of the mandatory requirements of the rule, once the period has been specified, to state expressly that this is the period "within which the defendant will be liable for the claimant's costs in accordance with rule 36.10 if the offer is accepted". But this letter did not specify any period for the purposes of the rule.'

Whilst the offer in that case also failed to refer, specifically, to Section I of Part 36, as now required by CPR 36.2, that, of itself, would not have meant the offer failed to meet the requirements as to form and content, because there was nothing in Section II that could have been of relevance to the offer and hence no doubt which section of Part 36 was intended to apply.

The importance of the rules on form and content was again stressed by the Court of Appeal in *F & C Alternative Investments (Holdings) Ltd v Barthelemy*[11] where Davis LJ held:

> '... there is no reason or justification, in my view, for indirectly extending Part 36 beyond its expressed ambit. Indeed to do so would tend to undermine the requirements of Part 36 ... Part 36 is highly prescriptive with regard to both procedures and sanctions.'

Davis LJ also observed:

> 'Perhaps there can be de minimis errors or obvious slips which mislead no one: but the general rule, in my opinion, is that for an offer to be a Part 36 offer it must strictly comply with the requirements.'

CPR 36.2(4) provides that, in appropriate circumstances, further provisions relating to form and content will apply namely. The requirements of CPR 36.5 will be applicable where there is a claim for future pecuniary loss. CPR 36.5 will apply where there is a claim for provisional damages. CPR 36.15 provides for additional rules on form and content applicable to a defendant's Part 36 offer to deal with CRU. CPR 36.5 (future pecuniary loss); CPR 36.5 (provisional damages); and CPR 36.15 (CRU).

With multiple defendants the claimant's approach to making offers will depend upon whether those defendants are joint tortfeasors (or perhaps more

---

[10]   [2012] EWCA Civ 588, [2012] All ER (D) 34 (Jun).
[11]   [2011] EWCA Civ 843.

frequently separate tortfeasors but responsible for the same damage) or separate tortfeasors responsible for separate damage.

If the defendants are alleged to be responsible for the same damage, whether or not joint tortfeasors, the claimant should be able to make a Part 36 offer in the same terms to each of those defendants, given that the value of the claim against every defendant will be identical (any apportionment being an issue between those defendants). If only one of the defendants accepts the offer the claimant will need to argue the 'costs of the proceedings', for the purposes of CPR 36.10, include costs of joining some or all of the other defendants.

If separate damage has been caused by defendants who are not joint tortfeasors the claimant may need to value the claim against each defendant and make Part 36 offers to each reflecting that assessment. The claimant should make clear any such offer is to settle only the issue of the claim against that defendant rather than the claim as a whole so that, if accepted, the claimant is able to pursue claims against other defendants.

Should the claimant not be able to value the separate claims against each defendant, but can value the claim overall, there is nothing to stop the claimant making an offer on that basis because, if accepted, adequate damages will have been recovered. Such an offer is less likely to have the potential of attracting the costs consequences found in CPR 36.14, against an individual defendant, but the focus of the claimant may be more on resolving the claim than trying to secure those benefits.

15.3.1 Service

CPR 36.7 confirms a Part 36 offer is made when served. CPR 6.20 to 6.29, found in Section III of Part 6, deal with service of documents other than the claim form and so apply to the making of a Part 36 offer. CPR 6.20 sets out available methods of service, CPR 6.26 confirms the deemed date of service, according to the method adopted, whilst CPR 6.23 deals with, at least once the claim form has been served, the requirement for any party to the proceedings to give an address for service. Additionally, para 1.2 of the Practice Direction to Part 36 confirms that where there is a legal representative a Part 36 offer must be served on that representative. This may be particularly relevant pre-issue of court proceedings. If, at that stage, a party is legally represented any Part 36 offer must be sent to that legal representative. There is, however, no requirement, as there is prior to service of the claim form, for the address of that legal representative to be given as the address for service.

The rules relating to service are important under Part 36 as it may be critical for a party to establish the fact and/or precise timing of a Part 36 offer being made, changed or withdrawn.

The relationship between Part 6 and Part 36 was illustrated in *Sutton Jigsaw Transport Ltd v Croydon London Borough Council*.[12]

The defendant made a Part 36 offer that was not withdrawn after the 21-day period referred to in the offer had elapsed.

At court, on the first day of the trial, the claimant sought orally to accept the offer. The defendant stated that oral acceptance was insufficient under Part 36 following which the claimant handed over a handwritten note purporting to accept the offer. The defendant then promptly sent a fax to the office of the claimant's solicitors withdrawing the offer.

The judge held that Part 36 provided a mechanism by which parties were able to settle claims and provided clear rules, being in effect a code to ensure the parties were on a level playing field. CPR 36.9(1) provided that a Part 36 offer was accepted by serving written notice on the offeror. While CPR 6.22(2)(a) did allow for personal service of documents an exception was where a party had given an address for service. The defendant had given the address of the solicitors acting as the address for service.

The judge concluded that to dispense with service or retrospectively order substituted service would give the claimant an unfair advantage over the defendant who had complied with the rules. Consequently, there had been no valid acceptance of the offer prior to that offer being withdrawn.

15.3.2 How to make a Part 36 offer

Problems in complying with the rules as to form and content under Part 36 can be avoided if Practice Form N242A is used when making offers.

Use of Form N242A is encouraged by the terms of para 1.1 of Practice Direction 36A, which expressly refers to that form. There has also been judicial encouragement to utilise this form.[13]

Any covering letter, and indeed any letter containing what is intended to be a Part 36 offer, should be headed as a Part 36 offer and, to err on the side of caution, also expressed to be 'without prejudice except as to costs'. The offer must, of course, be duly served on the offeree, in accordance with Part 6, to ensure it is 'made' for the purposes of CPR 36.7.

15.3.3 Failure to comply with form and content

CPR 36.1(2) provides that if an offer is not made in accordance with CPR 36.2 it will not have the consequences specified in CPR 36.10, 36.11 and 36.14.

---

[12] [2013] EWHC 874 (QB).
[13] *Shah v Elliott* [2011] EW Misc 8.

That may be significant for a claimant who wishes to rely on an offer made as being effective under Part 36. In particular:

- if the claimant seeks to rely on the costs provisions found in CPR 36.10 in the event of acceptance within the relevant period; and/or

- if the claimant needs to rely on other provisions contained within Part 36 such as timescale for payment; and/or

- if the claimant later obtains judgment against the defendant in terms that are at least as advantageous to the claimant as the offer and the claimant wishes to obtain the benefits conferred by CPR 36.14(3).

The rules on form and content, and hence whether an offer is an effective Part 36 offer, will also be significant if any party wishes to accept an offer made by another party once the relevant period has expired, as such acceptance will usually be effective where Part 36 applies but otherwise the general law of contract will determine whether or not an agreement has been reached.

Where an offer is made by a defendant the effectiveness of that offer, for the purposes of Part 36, may be important if the claimant fails to obtain judgment which is at least as advantageous as that offer and the defendant seeks the benefits conferred by CPR 36.14(2). Consequently, the rules on form and content of Part 36 offers are just as important to the claimant at the stage of reviewing an offer received as they are when making an offer.

15.3.4 Reviewing a Part 36 offer

The rules about form and content of Part 36 offers are as important to the offeree as the offeror, because the offeree needs to know whether or not the offer is subject to the provisions of Part 36 for a number of reasons.

First, if an offer is subject to the terms of Part 36 this will give the claimant the potential benefits of the deemed costs order in CPR 36.10, if accepted within the relevant period, and the possibility of late acceptance along with a degree of certainty on the costs consequences in that eventuality, even where acceptance would not be permitted under the general law of contract (unless the offer is changed or withdrawn meanwhile).

Secondly, if there has been an effective Part 36 offer the offeree faces the potential detriment of the adverse consequences provided for in CPR 36.14.

Consequently, the first consideration for the offeree is to assess the status of an offer that purports to be made under Part 36. If the offer is indeed a Part 36 offer then, depending on the circumstances, some other tactical considerations may arise.

15.3.5 Costs inclusive offers

An offer that is made inclusive of costs is unlikely to be a valid Part 36 offer.[14] That is principally because the costs consequences provided for under Part 36 are inconsistent with a term as to costs being part of an offer made under that rule.

The same approach, from the courts, seems likely if the usual costs provisions found in Part 36 are otherwise excluded. For example, an offer which is purported to be made under Part 36 but proposes terms that there be no order as to costs or that costs be dealt with other than by assessment on the standard basis, would be inconsistent with the terms of CPR 36.10 and hence be at odds with that fundamental aspect of the rule.[15]

If the defendant does make a costs-inclusive offer it will usually be reasonable for the claimant to ask that this be broken down between damages and costs except, perhaps, where a figure for damages has already been identified or agreed. Indeed, without such a breakdown it may be very difficult, if not impossible, to identify whether the offer was more advantageous to the claimant than the judgment eventually obtained.

15.3.6 'Total capitulation' offers

A defendant might propose the claimant simply discontinue the claim (although such an offer might well be ineffective in any event if, as is likely, it seeks to exclude the provisions of Part 36.10 that the defendant pay the claimant's costs if the offer is accepted within the relevant period). A claimant might offer to accept 100% on liability (with a view to arguing later that judgment in such terms is 'at least as advantageous' as the offer for the purposes of CPR 36.14(1A)). The effectiveness of which might be regarded as a 'total capitulation' offer, for the purposes of Part 36, was considered in *AB v CD*[16] where Henderson J held:

> 'The concept of an "offer to settle" is nowhere defined in Part 36. I think it clear, however, that a request to a defendant to submit to judgment for the entirety of the relief sought by the claimant cannot be an "offer to settle" within the meaning of Part 36. If it were otherwise, any claimant could obtain the favourable consequences of a successful Part 36 offer, including the award of indemnity costs, by the simple expedient of making an "offer" which required total capitulation by

---

[14] *Mitchell v James* [2002] EWCA Civ 997, [2004] 1 WLR 158, [2003] 2 All ER 1064, [2002] CP Rep 72, [2002] CPLR 764, (2002) 99(36) LSG 38, (2002) 146 SJLB 202, (2002) *The Times*, 20 July, (2002) *The Independent*, 18 July; *L G Blower Specialist Bricklayer Ltd v Reeves* [2010] EWCA Civ 726, [2010] 1 WLR 2081, [2011] 2 All ER 258, [2010] CP Rep 40, [2010] 5 Costs LR 828, [2010] PIQR P16, [2010] 3 EGLR 85, [2010] 36 EG 120, [2010] 27 EG 84 (CS); *French v Groupama Insurance Company Ltd* [2011] EWCA Civ 1119, [2012] CP Rep 2, [2011] 4 Costs LO 547.

[15] *Howell v Lees-Millais* [2011] EWCA Civ 786, [2011] WTLR 1795, [2011] 4 Costs LR 456, [2011] All ER (D) 48 (Jul).

[16] [2011] EWHC 602 (Ch), [2011] All ER (D) 25 (Apr).

the defendant. In my judgment the offer must contain some genuine element of concession on the part of the claimant, to which a significant value can be attached in the context of the litigation. The basic policy of Part 36 is to encourage the sensible settlement of claims before trial, or even before the issue of proceedings (see rule 36.3(2)(a) which provides that a Part 36 offer may be made at any time, including before the commencement of proceedings). The concept of a settlement must, by its very nature, involve an element of give and take. A so-called "settlement" which was all take and no give would in my view be a contradiction in terms.'

The words 'significant value' should, perhaps, be viewed with caution given the guidance now provided for comparing offer and judgment in CPR 36.14(1A). Additionally, and certainly in the context of an appeal, there is support for the view a party may make an offer, effective under Part 36, for exactly that which the party is entitled to.

Consequently, a better way for the court to approach such an offer might perhaps be to conclude that it would be 'unjust' for the consequences found in CPR 36.14 to apply. That was very much the approach taken by the Court of Appeal in *Huck v Robson*[17] when contrasting an offer of 95% on liability, which was held to be valid for the purposes of Part 36, and a notional offer of 99.9%, which the court appeared to doubt would be effective for costs purposes under the rule.

15.3.7 Offers without adequate CRU information

Because the terms of CPR 36.15 are prescriptive, and by CPR 36.2 incorporated into the rules relating to form and content, a failure by the defendant to comply with the requirements of this provision may also mean, whether or not the offer is expressed as intending to have the consequences of Part 36, the terms of CPR 36.10, 36.11 and 36.14 will not apply.[18] Despite the introduction of CPR 36.15, in 2007, it is still not unusual to see offers that fail to comply with the terms of that rule. For example, offers made 'net of CRU', hence failing to identify whether the gross offer does or does not include any deductible benefits, or 'gross of CRU', hence failing to identify the information required by CPR 36.15(6) and the net offer after allowing for any deductible benefits.

15.3.8 Other ineffective offers

The failure in other circumstances to comply with the rules on form and content, or the imposition of an express term inconsistent with a fundamental precept of the rule, is likely to render an offer ineffective under Part 36.

---

[17] [2002] EWCA Civ 398, [2002] 3 All ER 263, [2003] 1 WLR 1340, [2002] CP Rep 38, [2002] CPLR 345, [2003] 1 Costs LR 19, [2002] PIQR P31.
[18] *Williams v Devon County Council* [2003] EWCA Civ 365, [2003] CP Rep 47, [2003] PIQR Q4, (2003) *The Times*, 26 March.

15.3.9   Clarification

Part 36.8 provides that the offeree may, within seven days of a Part 36 offer being made, request the offeror to clarify that offer. If clarification is not provided the offeree may apply to the court for an order the clarification be given. Furthermore, the absence of clarification might be relevant when the court determines whether it is 'unjust' for the usual costs consequences to apply in relation to that offer. The court may decide the costs implications in Part 36, even if otherwise applicable, should not take effect until such time as clarification is given. It would seem appropriate, at the very least, for there to be clarification of matters required by the terms of Part 36 itself such as, in an offer that includes deductible benefits, the information identified in CPR 36.15(6) are not given. There is no definitive definition of the appropriate scope of a request for clarification though guidance can be drawn from the provisions of the CPR and case-law. In *R v Secretary of State for Transport ex p Factortame Ltd*[19] the court held that a party might ask for clarification in order to understand the basis of an offer but could not interrogate the other party as to the thinking behind the making of the offer, for example what view was taken on the chances of success for the purposes of the offer. However, the court also held that, distinct from the issue of clarification, was the question whether documents or other information should have been provided by the offeror to apply proper consideration of the offer and, if not, the justice of Part 36 costs consequences applying to the offer.

In *Johnson v Deer*[20] it was held that, to further the aim of the overriding objective of dealing with the case justly and expeditiously, it was appropriate to order clarification, in a personal injury claim, so that the defendant had to specify either the approximate division of the offer between general and special damages or the approximate percentage on liability on which the offer was based.

Nevertheless, the overriding objective, and the general philosophy of the CPR, encourages the parties to assist each other. That would suggest, generally, clarification ought to be given, or at least appropriate information provided to allow proper evaluation of the offer. Paragraph 3.21 of the Protocol appears to endorse this view and confirms that general approach should apply pre-action.

Evidence which will allow the recipient to properly judge the offer should normally be disclosed. Accordingly, clarification of such matters might to be allowed.

The judgment will be compared with any relevant offer on a 'like-for-like' basis, so interest will need to be taken into account. Accordingly, that will mean excluding further interest, between the date of offer and date of judgment, so it

---

[19]   [2002] EWCA Civ 22, [2002] 1 WLR 2438, [2002] 2 All ER 838, [2002] CPLR 385, (2002) 152 NLJ 171.
[20]   [2001] CLY 619.

may be necessary to seek clarification of the interest element of any offer which excludes interest (though under CPR 36.3(3) interest is deemed to be included unless expressly excluded).

If clarification is not given the offeree may either:

- apply to the court for an order there be clarification under CPR 36.8(2); or
- reserve the right to argue, if necessary at a later stage, it would be unjust, for the purposes of CPR 36.14 for the offer to carry the costs consequences found in that rule in the absence of the clarification requested.

If a court order is obtained that will determine the need for clarification though a party may prefer not to run the risk that the court will rule against clarification and rely on the opportunity to argue, at a later stage if necessary, costs consequences under Part 36 would be unjust without the clarification, even though no order was made that it be provided.

It would not seem necessary for a party to obtain an order for clarification before arguing, if necessary at a later stage, it would be unjust, with particular reference to the information available to (or perhaps more accurately absent from) the parties for the purposes of CPR 36.14(4)(c), for the usual costs consequences under CPR 36.14 to apply.[21]

15.3.10 Multiple defendants

Care is necessary when reviewing a Part 36 offer if there are multiple defendants. If a Part 36 offer is made by all the defendants that may be accepted without the need for court permission (unless that permission is required for any of the other reasons identified in CPR 36.9(3)). Where, however, a Part 36 offer is made by one or more, but not all, of a number of defendants the claimant must be more cautious.

- CPR 36.12(2) provides that if the defendants are sued jointly or in the alternative the claimant may accept the offer only if the claim is discontinued against those defendants who have not made the offer and those defendants give written consent to the acceptance of the offer.
- CPR 36.12(3) provides that if the claimant alleges the defendants have a several liability the claimant may accept the offer and continue with the claims against the other defendants if entitled to do so.
- CPR 36.12(4) requires the claimant, in all other cases, to apply to the court for an order permitting acceptance of the Part 36 offer.

Consequently, when this is not made clear at the time of the offer, the claimant may wish to seek confirmation that the offer is made on behalf of all defendants and, if not, to try and agree terms, in relation to the costs of those other

---

[21] *Mehjoo v Harben* [2013] EWHC 1669 (QB), [2013] 5 Costs LR 645.

defendants, as a preliminary to acceptance. If that is not done the claimant may be at risk in relation to the costs of the other defendants by simply accepting the offer.

The claimant may, alternatively, apply to the court for an order in accordance with CPR 36.12(4) permitting acceptance of the Part 36 offer but may wish, in these circumstances, to make clear any agreement to accept the offer is conditional upon appropriate provision as to costs. Without any such provision any deemed costs order in favour of the claimant for the 'costs of the proceedings' is likely to be limited to the costs of the proceedings, concerning the defendant against whom the deemed order has been made: *Haynes v Department for Business Innovation and Skills.*[22]

15.3.11 Single sum of money

CPR 36.4 requires a Part 36 offer by a defendant to pay a sum of money in settlement of a claim be an offer to pay a single sum of money (unless the offer includes periodical payments and/or provisional damages).

The offeree does, however, have the option of treating the offer as effective under Part 36 by accepting the offer. Sometimes the disadvantage to a claimant, of not receiving damages as a single sum of money, may be outweighed by the advantages of Part 36, in particular the costs consequences where a Part 36 offer is accepted within the relevant period.

15.3.12 Format

The offeror will, ideally, have used Form N242A or, at least, given in any letter making the offer all the information in that form. If that is not done the offeree will need to carefully review the offer and, if there is any ambiguity, indicate whether the offer is treated as a Part 36 offer and, if not, certainly where the offer refers expressly to Part 36, explaining the reasons for that stance.

If the status of the offer is unclear the offeree might also be invited to clarify any issues, and perhaps to remake the offer using Form N242A if that has not already been done, to avoid any ambiguity and, perhaps, issues arising in the future as to the status of the offer.

15.4   WITHDRAWING AND CHANGING A PART 36 OFFER

CPR 36.3(5) restricts an offeror from withdrawing or changing the terms of an offer, to be less advantageous to the offeree, prior to expiry of the 'relevant period' unless the court gives permission. Paragraph 2.2 of the Practice Direction to Part 36 confirms application for such an order must be made in accordance with Part 23 of the CPR.

---

[22]   [2014] EWHC 643 (QB).

The 'relevant period' is the period specified in the offer within which the defendant will be liable for the claimant's costs if the offer is accepted or, if the offer is made less than 21 days before trial, the period up to the end of the trial or such other period as the court determines. Once the relevant period has elapsed then, unless accepted meanwhile, the offeree may either withdraw the offer or change the offer so that it is less advantageous to the offeree without needing permission from the court.

It is, accordingly, important that the offeree understands the risk that an offer, once made, may not remain open for acceptance because that offer may be withdrawn or changed by the offeror unless accepted meanwhile.

15.4.1 Withdrawing a Part 36 offer

CPR 36.3(6) allows the offeror, after expiry of the relevant period and provided the offeree has not previously served notice of acceptance, to withdraw the offer without permission of the court.

CPR 36.3(7) requires the withdrawal of a Part 36 offer to be effected by serving a 'written notice' on the offeree. There is no practice form for use when withdrawing an offer (unlike when making an offer) but the Court of Appeal in *Gibbon v Manchester City Council*[23] gave some guidance on what will be required effectively to withdraw a Part 36 offer. Moore-Bick LJ observed:

> 'Rule 36.3(7) provides that an offer is withdrawn by serving written notice on the offeree. In my view that leaves no room for the concept of implied withdrawal; it requires express notice in writing in terms which bring home to the offeree that the offer has been withdrawn. If justification for that requirement is sought, it can be found once again in the need for clarity and certainty in the operation of the Part 36 procedure. Although the rule does not prescribe any particular form of notice, in order to avoid uncertainty it should include an express reference to the date of the offer and its terms, together with some words making it clear that it is withdrawn.'

The need to 'bring home to the offeree that the offer has been withdrawn' suggests use of words in the notice such as 'withdrawn' or 'withdrawal'.

Excluding the concept of an implied withdrawal means that, for example, the making of a further Part 36 offer will not, of itself, amount to a withdrawal of an earlier Part 36 offer. On the facts in *Gibbon* a letter from the claimant's solicitors, rejecting the defendant's offer, was not only irrelevant, in the sense that rejection itself could not affect the status of the Part 36 offer, but could not amount to notice of withdrawal of the kind required by CPR 36.3(7).

The requirement to serve written notice of withdrawal, under CPR 36.6(7), and to do so after expiry of the relevant period, in accordance with CPR 36.6(6),

---

[23] [2010] EWCA Civ 726, [2011] 2 All ER 258, [2010] 1 WLR 2081, [2010] All ER (D) 218 (Jun).

prevents a party expressing a Part 36 offer in a way that prospectively, and automatically, withdraws the offer at the end of the relevant period. Depending on the precise words used such a term seems likely to either to be ineffective (so that there will be an extant Part 36 offer unless and until it is withdrawn or changed) or to create a time-limited offer (which by definition is not a Part 36 offer at all).

CPR 36.9(2) provides that once notice of withdrawal has been served the offer may no longer be accepted.

It is important to note that CPR 36.14(6) confirms that the costs consequences otherwise provided for in that rule do not apply to a Part 36 offer that has been withdrawn, or changed so that its terms are less advantageous to the offeree (provided the offeree has beaten that less advantageous offer).

15.4.2 Changing a Part 36 offer

CPR 36.3(5) also restricts an offeror from changing the terms of an offer, to be less advantageous to the offeree, prior to the expiry of the 'relevant period' unless the court gives permission.

CPR 36.6(6) confirms that once the relevant period has expired, provided the offeree has not previously served notice of acceptance, the offeror may then change the offer, so the terms are less advantageous to the offeree, without permission of the court.

An offer must be changed, in accordance with CPR 36.3(7), by giving written notice of the change of terms to the offeree.

There is, once again, no scope for impliedly changing an offer, whether by making a subsequent Part 36 offer in different terms or otherwise.[24] For the avoidance of any doubt, the offeror may wish expressly to identify both the offer which is being changed and precisely how that offer has been changed. That might be by serving an amended version of the original N242A denoting the changes (assuming that form has been used to make the original offer).

15.4.3 Tactics on withdrawing or changing a Part 36 offer

Practical and tactical considerations will determine whether the offeror withdraws a Part 36 offer, changes a Part 36 offer or makes a further Part 36 offer.

---

[24] *LG Blower Specialist Bricklayer Ltd v Reeves* [2010] EWCA Civ 726, [2010] 1 WLR 2081, [2011] 2 All ER 258, [2010] CP Rep 40, [2010] 5 Costs LR 828, [2010] PIQR P16, [2010] 3 EGLR 85, [2010] 36 EG 120, [2010] 27 EG 84 (CS).

15.4.4 When to withdraw an offer

When the offeror considers an earlier offer is now too advantageous to the offeror but cannot identify terms that would be acceptable, the safest course will be to withdraw the earlier offer despite the loss of potential costs consequences under CPR 36.14.

15.4.5 When to change an offer

When the offeror considers an earlier offer is now too advantageous to the offeror but can identify new terms which would be appropriate for agreeing the relevant issue or the claim as a whole, there may be advantages in changing the earlier offer rather than withdrawing any such offer and making a new offer.

That is because when a Part 36 offer is changed the original offer retains potential costs consequences, for the purposes of CPR 36.14, at a later stage (though it will then be necessary to compare the offer as changed with the judgment entered given the terms of CPR 36.14(6)). Hence an offer, once changed, effectively continues to stand for the purposes of Part 36, though in its varied form, as from the date it was originally made.

Changing an earlier offer in this way will be crucial, if the terms are now less advantageous to the offeree, otherwise that offeree may simply accept the earlier offer.

15.4.6 When to make a new offer

The ability to make more than one Part 36 offer at any time allows the offeror, rather than withdrawing or changing an offer, just to make a new offer. Where the offeror chooses to make a new offer that, in the absence of any implied withdrawal or change of earlier offers, will leave any earlier offers open for acceptance (subject to the terms of CPR 36.9(3)).

That does not present any difficulty where the new offer is more advantageous to the offeree, as will often be the case. Indeed, in such circumstances, it would not be appropriate, or necessary, to either change or withdraw the earlier offer, as the offeror will wish to retain any potential costs consequences of such an offer. Furthermore, even if the offeree decided to accept such an offer, which seems most unlikely, that would not prejudice the offeror.

The making of a new offer by the offeror, which is more advantageous to the offeree, does not impliedly withdraw any earlier offer hence any such offer will retain the potential for costs consequences under CPR 36.14.[25]

---

[25] *Mahmood v Elmi* [2010] EWHC 1933 (QB).

15.4.7 How to withdraw or change a Part 36 offer

The rules require written notice to either withdraw or change an offer. The absence of a practice form makes clarity on the part of the offeror essential but provided an offeror serves something in writing which would be understood by any reasonable offeree as withdrawing a Part 36 offer that should suffice: *Supergroup plc v Justenough Software Corp Inc.*[26]

The written notice must be served on the offeree. Once again, as when making a Part 36 offer, service will need to be in accordance with Part 6. The correct method of service, at the appropriate address for service, may be critical if the offeror seeks to withdraw or change an offer before the offeree can serve notice of acceptance as occurred.[27]

15.5 ACCEPTING A PART 36 OFFER

Part 36.9(3) provides that the permission of the court is required to accept a Part 36 offer only where:

- the claimant wishes to accept a Part 36 offer made by one or more, but not all, of a number of defendants unless:
- in accordance with CPR 36.12(2), the defendants are sued jointly or in the alternative, the claimant discontinues the claim against those defendants who have not made the offer and those defendants give written consent to the acceptance of the offer; or
- in accordance with CPR 36.12(3), the claimant alleges the defendants have a several liability, in which case the claimant may accept the offer and continue with the claims against all other defendants if entitled to do so; or
- the offer includes deductible benefits, the 'relevant period' has expired and further deductible benefits have been paid since the date of the offer; or
- the court needs to apportion money in a fatal claim; or
- the trial has started.

Additionally, CPR 21.10 provides that where a claim is made by or on behalf of a child or protected party or against a child or protected party, no settlement will be valid, so far as it relates to the claim by or against the child or protected party, without the approval of the court.

Different considerations may be applicable depending on the circumstances in which permission from the court is required to accept a Part 36 offer.

---

[26] (Unreported) 27 June 2014, QBD.
[27] *Sutton Jigsaw Transport Ltd v Croydon London Borough Council* [2013] EWHC 874 (QB).

15.5.1 Multiple defendants

Where the claimant wishes to accept a Part 36 offer made by one or more, but not all, of a number of defendants the court, if granting permission, may need to reflect, if the costs are not agreed, what seems appropriate on the basis of general principles applicable to cases where there are successful defendants and unsuccessful defendants. Subject to that costs point if the offer is 'on the table' it would seem likely permission to accept will be given.

15.5.2 CRU

If the claimant is accepting an offer inclusive of deductible benefits, where further benefits have been paid since the offer, the court may wish to consider granting permission in a way that does not prejudice the defendant. Subject to that consideration then, once again, it would seem appropriate to allow acceptance of an offer which remains 'on the table'.

15.5.3 Fatal claims

In a fatal claim the court will apportion damages in a way that protects, and reflects, the interests of all concerned. Once again where the offer is 'on the table' it seems likely the court will give permission.

15.5.4 During the trial

Where a party wishes to accept an offer after the trial has started the court is likely to be more reluctant than in the other situations covered by CPR 36.9(3) to give permission for acceptance even though that offer remains 'on the table' because the complexion of, and risks associated with, a case can quickly change as soon as a trial starts.

A trial is likely to have 'started' for the purposes of Part 36 at the same point as, under Part 45, the 100% success fee, where success fees are fixed under the rule, is triggered. For these purposes there is no distinction between the commencement of a hearing and the commencement of a contested hearing. Even if the final hearing only opens for the purpose of one party seeking an adjournment this is likely to be regarded as the commencement of the 'trial'.

Once a trial has started the offeree will need permission from the court to accept a Part 36 offer.

In *Sampla v Rushmoor Borough Council*[28] the principal issue was whether a Part 36 offer could be accepted after the trial had started. The judge noted there was no implied term an offer could not be accepted once the trial had started, as that would inconsistent with the terms of CPR 36.9(3), which makes plain the court can give permission to accept an offer after the trial has started. The

---

[28]   [2008] EWHC 2616 (TCC), [2008] All ER (D) 335 (Oct).

judge held that whenever exercising the discretion to give permission to accept an offer once the trial had started the relevant test was that set out in *Flynn v Scougall*,[29] namely whether there had been a sufficient change of circumstances such that it would now be just to refuse permission.

A change in the perception of the parties on the likely outcome of the trial would be a material change of circumstance. However, it was not necessary for there to be a 'knock-out blow'.[30]

The words 'the trial had started' in CPR 36.9(3)(d) have been held to include the trial of any preliminary issue. Consequently, where a Part 36 offer to settle the whole claim was made prior to the trial of a preliminary issue the offeree could not accept, at least in the absence of permission from the court, that offer once the trial of a preliminary issue had commenced.

Once such a trial has started, let alone concluded, it is likely a 'knock-out blow' will occur. In any event, once the trial has ended but before judgment is handed down CPR 36.9(5) prevents a Part 36 offer being accepted unless this is agreed by the parties (and without that agreement the court no longer has discretion to allow acceptance). Once judgment has been given that will, of itself, prevent acceptance of a relevant Part 36 offer.

In such circumstances the offeror may be in the unusual position of having made a Part 36 offer that can no longer be accepted but, as not withdrawn, continues to have potential costs consequences. Ultimately, so far as costs are concerned, much may depend on whether the offeree subsequently makes an appropriate offer to settle and it is possible more than one party could be in a position to argue judgment is entered on terms 'more advantageous' or 'at least as advantageous' as a Part 36 offer.[31]

15.5.5 After the trial

Once the trial has ended but prior to judgment being handed down CPR 36.9(5) prevents a Part 36 offer being accepted at all, unless the parties agree. Once judgment has been handed down, and even when a draft judgment has been circulated, it is unlikely a Part 36 offer could be accepted.

15.5.6 Approval

Although CPR 21.10(2) infers agreement will be reached before approval is sought, given the approach in cases such as *Drinkall v Whitwood*[32] it would seem that there is no valid acceptance, which would amount to a binding

---

29 [2004] EWCA Civ 873, [2004] 3 All ER 609, [2004] 1 WLR 3069.
30 *Nulty v Milton Keynes Borough Council* [2012] EWHC 730 (QB); *Wilson v Ministry of Defence* [2013] CP Rep 33.
31 *Pankhurst v White & MIB* [2010] EWCA Civ 1445, [2010] All ER (D) 184 (Dec).
32 [2003] EWCA Civ 1547, [2004] 4 All ER 378, [2004] 1 WLR 462.

compromise, until the court has approved the proposed settlement. This may be significant if the offeror, as in *Drinkall*, withdraws, or changes so that it is less advantageous, the offer meanwhile.

15.5.7 Exercise of discretion for permission

The need for permission, where CPR 36.9(3) applies, clearly gives the court a discretion as to whether permission should be granted. Usually on an application under subparagraphs (a), (b) or (c) of CPR 36.9(3) it seems likely, as already noted, the court will follow the approach in *Gibbon*,[33] namely that a Part 36 offer should be treated as 'on the table' until changed or withdrawn, and hence be open for acceptance.

However, if there has been a 'knock-out blow' or a sufficient change of circumstances (applying the test in *Flynn*[34] from the days when permission to accept a payment into court late was required), so that it would be just to refuse permission to accept, even before trial, the court might so rule. Ultimately, as ever, exercise of discretion will be shaped by the overriding objective.

15.5.8 When permission to accept is not required

If the court's permission to accept an offer is not required then, unless notice of withdrawal has been served, an offer, if changed in that amended form, may be accepted at any time, whether or not the 'relevant period' has expired.

Even if a claim has been stayed an extant Part 36 offer can be accepted during the currency of that stay.

A number of cases have illustrated how there may be valid acceptance of a Part 36 offer after that offer has been rejected or a considerable amount of time has elapsed, so the offer could not have been accepted outside of Part 36 under the general law of contract.[35]

For reasons explained by Moore-Bick LJ in *Gibbon*[36] the general law of contract will not apply to Part 36 offers so as to restrict the ability of the offeree to accept an offer, unless and until that offer has been changed or withdrawn, but it seems likely the court retains a discretion which allows some principles from the law of contract to be applied by analogy.

---

[33] [2010] EWCA Civ 726, [2011] 2 All ER 258, [2010] 1 WLR 2081, [2010] All ER (D) 218 (Jun).

[34] [2004] EWCA Civ 873, [2004] 3 All ER 609, [2004] 1 WLR 3069.

[35] *J Murphy & Sons Ltd v Johnston Precast Ltd* [2008] EWHC 3104 (TCC), [2009] 5 Costs LR 745; *Fitzpatrick Contractors Ltd v Tyco Fire & Integrated Solutions (UK) Ltd (No 3)* [2009] EWHC 274 (TCC), [2009] BLR 144, 123 Con LR 69, [2009] CILL 2700, [2009] All ER (D) 70 (Mar); and *Lumb v Hampsey* [2011] EWHC 2808 (QB), [2012] All ER (D) 18 (Feb).

[36] [2010] EWCA Civ 726, [2011] 2 All ER 258, [2010] 1 WLR 2081, [2010] All ER (D) 218 (Jun).

15.5.9   Acceptance with multiple defendants

Difficulties can arise where one of a number of defendants makes a Part 36 offer which is then accepted by the claimant, in reliance on CPR 36.12, without court permission or the claimant otherwise reaches terms with one defendant that involves discontinuing against any other defendants.

In *Messih v McMillan Williams*[37] the claimant settled the claim with one defendant and then discontinued against the other defendant. The issue of the costs of that other defendant then arose. At first instance, the claimant was successful in an application that the other defendant should not recover costs. The Court of Appeal, reversing that decision, concluded that there must be some reason to make it just to depart from the normal rule, found in CPR 38.6, that a claimant who discontinues a claim should pay the costs of the defendant concerned.

If several defendants make a collective offer this problem will not arise. Otherwise, however, the claimant may need to seek agreement the offer is made on behalf of all the defendants, or aim to agree terms in relation to the costs of those other defendants, as a preliminary to acceptance. If that is not done the claimant is likely to recover the 'costs of the proceedings' only against the defendant who made the offer: *Haynes v Department for Business Innovation and Skills.*[38]

In clinical negligence claims where there is more than one defendant those defendants may be joint tortfeasors, or more likely separate tortfeasors but responsible for the same damage, so there is a reasonable prospect those defendants will confer and make a joint offer, combined offers or an offer by one defendant that acknowledges responsibility for costs of other defendants in the event of acceptance.

15.5.10   Acceptance with multiple offers

Where the offeror has made a number of Part 36 offers then, unless earlier offers are expressly withdrawn or changed, the offeree may choose which offer to accept.[39] That is so even if an offer to settle an issue in the claim happens to coincide with an offer to settle the whole claim.

Where, however, an offer to settle the whole claim is accepted that has the effect of extinguishing the claim preventing the offeree then accepting any other offers that may have been extant up to that point.[40] If, however, the offers do not all deal with the whole of the claim, or identical issues in the claim, they can be accepted individually.

---

[37]   [2010] EWCA Civ 844, [2010] CP Rep 41, [2010] 6 Costs LR 914.
[38]   [2014] EWHC 643 (QB).
[39]   *Gibbon v Manchester City Council* [2010] EWCA Civ 726, [2011] 2 All ER 258, [2010] 1 WLR 2081, [2010] All ER (D) 218 (Jun).
[40]   *Mahmood v Elmi* [2010] EWHC 1933 (QB).

15.5.11   Acceptance after earlier rejection

Whilst CPR 36.9(2) expressly states that a different offer by the offeree (in other words a counter-offer) will not preclude acceptance of a Part 36 offer case-law confirms that this is just an example of how Part 36 operates differently to offers made outside the rule.[41] The general law of contract, relating to offer and acceptance, does not apply where inconsistent with the terms of Part 36. There is a clear distinction between the effect of offers to settle made under Part 36 and other offers to settle which may be subject to the usual law of contract. That distinction is crucial to the acceptance of offers, as well as the costs consequences of those offers, with Part 36 offers, unlike non-Part 36 offers, remaining 'on the table' for acceptance unless and until withdrawn or changed (subject to the need for court permission only where the terms of CPR 36.9(3) apply).

Part 36 is a statutory schemes not simply based on the law of contract. Whilst rejection of a Part 36 offer will not have any bearing on the ability of the offeree later to accept that offer, unless withdrawn or changed by the offeror meanwhile, the fact of rejection may be very relevant if the claimant, having accepted the offer after expiry of the relevant period, seeks to argue that the usual costs consequences provided for by CPR 36.10(5) would be 'unjust'. That is because, in such circumstances, the court may more readily conclude the claimant viewed the offer as inadequate rather than being unable, on the information then available, to reach a decision on whether to accept that offer within the relevant period.

15.5.12   How to accept a Part 36 offer

CPR 36.9(1) provides that a Part 36 offer is accepted by serving written notice of acceptance on the offeror.

There is no practice form for the acceptance of a Part 36 offer so, just as when withdrawing or changing an offer, precision is important. The offeree may be wise to use words such as 'accept' or 'accepted'.

Particular care is required by the offeree if there is more than one Part 36 offer from the offeree open for acceptance at the relevant time (given that a further Part 36 offer will not be taken, of itself, to withdraw or change an earlier offer). In these circumstances the offeree should clearly identify the offer which is being accepted.

Even if there is only a single Part 36 offer open at the time the offeree wishes to accept precision is essential. If the intentions of the offeror are not made clear it may be necessary for the court to determine whether there has been acceptance

---

[41]   *Gibbon v Manchester City Council* [2010] EWCA Civ 726, [2011] 2 All ER 258, [2010] 1 WLR 2081, [2010] All ER (D) 218 (Jun).

or a counter offer, which may lead on to the further question of whether the original offeror has then accepted that counter offer.

It may be prudent for the offeree to recite the terms of the offer being accepted to avoid any ambiguity and the risk of the court finding that, rather than accepting the offer as a whole, the offeree is offering to agree an issue or a part of the claim.[42]

The requirement to serve notice of acceptance means that, once more, the terms of Part 6 are significant. Acceptance must be served by a prescribed method at the appropriate address for service. Failure to comply with the requirements of Part 6 may give the offeror the opportunity of changing or withdrawing the offer, if appropriate notice is duly served first, before the offeree has served notice of acceptance.[43]

15.5.13   Ineffective acceptance

Despite the terms of CPR 36.9(2), that a Part 36 offer may be accepted at any time unless the offeror serves notice of withdrawal, and the relatively limited circumstances in which permission to accept will be required under CPR 36.9(3) there remain a number of circumstances in which purported acceptance of an apparently extant Part 36 offer will be ineffective.

15.5.14   Agreement or agreement to agree?

For there to be effective acceptance there must be an agreement, rather than merely an agreement to agree.

An agreement will require a consensus between the parties on all necessary terms. Part 36, once again, will assist the parties in reaching agreement because, by definition, both offer and acceptance will have been in writing. Moreover, reference to Part 36 will carry with it a number of important consequences provided for under the rule, even if not expressly spelt out by the parties, which should ensure agreement is implied, if not expressly spelt out, on all terms which are likely to be material.

For an agreement, rather than an agreement to agree, there will need to be a sufficient consensus coupled with an intention to create legal relations. Consequently, the court may have to analyse the dealings between the parties, even where Part 36 has been invoked in the course of those dealings, if there is a dispute about whether the parties have reached the stage of concluding an agreement.

---

[42]   As occurred, for example, in *Rosario v Nadell Patisserie Ltd* [2010] EWHC 1886 (QB), [2010] All ER (D) 288 (Jul).
[43]   As occurred, for example, in *Sutton Jigsaw Transport Ltd v Croydon London Borough Council* [2013] EWHC 874 (QB).

15.5.15   Acceptance or counter offer?

An offeree, even when purporting to accept an offer, who adds terms or otherwise suggests there is not a consensus between the parties may be treated as having made a counter offer. Where a counter offer, even implicitly, is made questions may then arise as to whether the original offeror has, by subsequent dealings, accepted that counter offer.[44]

15.5.16   Strike out

Where a claim has been struck out any Part 36 offer can no longer be accepted, even if relief from sanctions is subsequently given and the action reinstated, as the claim had in substance then been brought to an end.[45]

15.5.17   Judgment

For the same reason that it would be inappropriate for a Part 36 offer to be accepted after strike out, the unsuccessful party will not be able to accept a Part 36 offer, made by the successful party, following judgment.

If an issue, such as liability, is dealt with at a preliminary trial, judgment on that issue would, on this basis, prevent subsequent acceptance of the offer even though the claim, as a whole, remains extant.[46]

Once again, as such an offer would not have been withdrawn, there seems no reason why it could not continue to carry costs consequences though there might, ultimately, be offers by both parties which, to them, are more advantageous or at least as advantageous as the judgment entered. Under the current version of Part 36 the court may need to resolve that tension by deciding the extent to which costs consequences in favour of each party, on judgment, would be 'unjust' for the purposes of CPR 36.14(2) or (3).

Where there has been a trial CPR 36.9(5) prevents acceptance of a Part 36 offer before judgment is handed down, unless the parties otherwise agree. This rule does not deal with the situation where there has been a hearing which will be determinative of the claim, or a relevant issue, but that hearing is not a trial. The offeror needs to be mindful that the offeree may be able to accept during, and even after, such a hearing and hence weigh up the advantages and disadvantages of withdrawing or changing the relevant offer. Once a draft judgment has been circulated, whether or not there has been a trial, acceptance of a Part 36 offer by the offeree, to pre-empt an adverse decision, might amount to a contempt of court. That is because para 2.4(b) of Practice Direction 40E provides that no action is to be taken in response to a draft judgment before it

[44] *Rosario v Nadell Patisserie Ltd* [2010] EWHC 1886 (QB), [2010] All ER (D) 288 (Jul); *Mahmood v Elmi* [2010] EWHC 1933 (QB); *Howell v Lees-Millais* [2011] EWCA Civ 786, [2011] WTLR 1795, [2011] 4 Costs LR 456, [2011] All ER (D) 48 (Jul).

[45] *Joyce v West Bus Coach Services Ltd* [2012] EWHC 404 (QB), [2012] 3 Costs LR 540.

[46] *Pankhurst v White & MIB* [2010] EWCA Civ 1445, [2010] All ER (D) 184 (Dec).

is formally handed down, while para 2.8 expressly provides that any breach of para 2.4 may be treated as a contempt of court.

15.5.18 Compromise

If the parties reach agreement on the claim as a whole then a prior Part 36 offer cannot be accepted as the settlement distinguishes the cause of action.[47]

15.5.19 General discretion and mistake

It does seem that the court has a residual general discretion, for use in appropriate circumstances, to control whether acceptance of a Part 36 offer is effective. That discretion might be used, for example, where the offeror makes what must have been to the offeree an obvious mistake in the offer.[48]

Where, however, there is nothing to alert the offeree to an obvious mistake it is likely that acceptance of the offer will create a binding compromise that the court will recognise.[49] The same principles ought to apply if the offeree makes what must have been to the offeror an obvious mistake when accepting an offer.

When distinguishing an obvious mistake, which would prevent valid acceptance, from a mistaken offer that nevertheless can give rise to a binding compromise the court may also take account of the duties of legal representatives in this context.

In addition to mistake the general law of contract may also apply to vitiate a purported agreement on grounds such as misrepresentation, duress, undue influence and illegality (as well as capacity where approval has not been sought).

15.5.20 Action following acceptance

When a Part 36 offer is accepted para 3.1 of Practice Direction 36A requires notice of acceptance to be both served on the offeree and filed with the court where the case is proceeding.

This is important to ensure the court is aware of the extent to which the issues have been narrowed, or the claim as a whole resolved, and also in the event of the defendant failing to honour the agreement, so that further steps can then be taken promptly. Accordingly, whether it is the claimant accepting the defendant's offer, or vice versa, the claimant may wish to ensure this part of the Practice Direction is complied with by filing relevant documentation at court. Moreover, because the acceptance will not always spell out the precise terms of

---

[47] As Cox J observed in *Mahmood v Elmi* [2010] EWHC 1933 (QB).

[48] *OT Africa Line Ltd v Vickers* [1996] 1 Lloyd's Rep 700, [1996] CLC 722, QBD.

[49] *Milton v Schlegal (2006) Ltd* (unreported) 31 October 2008, Cambridge Cty Ct.

the offer it will generally be necessary to file both the offer and the acceptance at court. Obviously, this provision is only applicable when court proceedings have been issued.

Additionally, there are two situations in which, on acceptance of a Part 36 offer, a further step will be necessary.

- If an offeree accepts a Part 36 offer which includes payment of any part of the damage in the form of periodical payments the claimant must, in accordance with CPR 36.5(7), within seven days of the date of acceptance apply to the court for an order that there be an award of damages in the form of periodical payments under CPR 41.8.

- If the offeree accepts a Part 36 offer that provides for an award of provisional damages the claimant, to comply with CPR 36.6(5), must within seven days of the date of acceptance apply to the court for an order for an award of provisional damages under CPR 41.2.

15.5.21   Effect of acceptance

CPR 36.11 provides that if a Part 36 offer is accepted the claim will be stayed, if the relevant offer relates to part only of the claim then the claim will be stayed as to that part on the terms of the offer.

Any stay arising under CPR 36.11 does not affect the power of the court to enforce the terms of a Part 36 offer or to deal with any question of costs relating to the proceedings. Furthermore, if approval of the court is required before a settlement can be binding any stay which would otherwise arise on acceptance of a Part 36 offer will take effect only when that approval has been given.

In *Jolly v Harsco Infrastructure Services Ltd*[50] the view was expressed that the stay imposed by CPR 36.11 prevented judgment being entered, which may have some significance for the costs consequences in the event of acceptance of a claimant's Part 36 offer by the defendant after expiry of the relevant period, although CPR 36.11(7) expressly provides that where a sum accepted is not paid within the appropriate timescale judgment may be entered. CPR 36.10 deals with the costs consequences on acceptance of a Part 36 offer.

15.5.22   Timescale for payment

CPR 36.11(6) requires the defendant when a Part 36 offer to pay a single sum of money is accepted, unless the parties agree otherwise in writing, to make payment within 14 days. In *Cave v Bulley Davey*[51] it was held that the terms of CPR 36.11(6) require payment of the accepted sum by the due date in full even when the claimant had accepted the relevant offer outside the relevant period and it was agreed there would be liability on the part of the claimant for costs

---

[50]   [2012] EWHC 3086 (QB), [2013] 1 Costs LR 115.
[51]   [2013] EWHC 4246 (QB).

from the end of the relevant period down to the date of acceptance. That was because the terms of the rule give no right to set off costs against damages in these circumstances.

Where the offer included deductible benefits the sum payable will be the net figure. If there is an appeal against the amount of recoverable benefits, following the conclusion of the claim, a further sum may then be payable to the claimant.

If payment of the full sum due is not made within 14 days the offeree may, under CPR 36.11(7), enter judgment for the unpaid sum. Whilst this rule talks only of the offeree making application the court may well entertain a request made by the claimant as offeror (when the defendant has accepted the claimant's Part 36 offer) to save the costs of an application that would otherwise be necessary, under Part 23, for judgment.

CPR 36.11(7) has no requirement for an application, simply allowing judgment to be entered, so a letter to the court should suffice, with no fee being payable, provided the relevant documentation evidencing the agreement has, in accordance with Practice Direction 36A, already been filed (and if not it will need to be filed with the request). If such a request is made the claimant may also wish to request that the judgment expressly record any deemed costs order to which the claimant is entitled, on acceptance of the offer, under CPR 36.10.

If a Part 36 offer is accepted before court proceedings have been commenced this procedure will not be open to the claimant who may, therefore, need to issue a Part 7 claim form seeking a declaration a binding compromise has been concluded on the basis of a Part 36 offer that has been accepted. If, however, any agreed damages are paid, the only issue being costs, a Part 8 claim may be the appropriate way of dealing with those costs.

15.5.23 Enforcement

Once the claimant has judgment, it may be enforced by any available and appropriate method.

15.5.24 Indemnity

Until 2007, when most offers to settle by a defendant required a payment into court, the claimant could be confident of receiving relevant funds on acceptance, as the monies would then be paid out of court.

It is now implicit that a party making a Part 36 offer is good for the money and will honour any agreement made by prompt payment. Where an insurer is involved on behalf of the defendant the claimant might have earlier sought confirmation that the insurer will indemnify the claim and may, at the stage of any Part 36 offer, wish to make clear that reliance will be placed on that insurer providing an indemnity and hence making prompt payment if the offer is accepted. That should help to mitigate the risk of having to take enforcement proceedings against the defendant following acceptance.

15.6 COSTS CONSEQUENCES OF PART 36 OFFERS

CPR 36.10 and 36.14 deal with the cost consequences of the rule. Whilst CPR 36.10 deals with the costs consequences on acceptance of an offer made under the rule, CPR 36.14 deals with the costs consequences of such an offer following judgment. Where an offer to settle the whole claim, or issue in the claim, is accepted within the relevant period, specific costs consequences are deemed to apply by CPR 36.10(1). In other circumstances, under both CPR 36.10 and 36.14, the court will be exercising a discretion as to costs, but a much more restricted discretion than that conferred by CPR 44.3 given the prescriptive nature of both CPR 36.10 and 36.14.

15.6.1 Preliminaries to costs consequences under Part 36

CPR 36.1(2) confirms that if an offer is not made in accordance with the terms of Part 36.2 it will not have the consequences specified in CPR 36.10 and 36.14. Accordingly, it is vital the rules on form and content are complied with if an offer is to carry costs consequences under Part 36.

More fundamentally there must, before this is clothed with potential costs consequences under the rule by reference to Part 36, be an 'offer'.

Consequently, a proposal which, in effect, seeks total capitulation on the part of the offeree may not be an offer at all.

Similarly, a proposal must have the necessary degree of finality, if accepted, to constitute an offer, so an interim payment would not suffice for these purposes.

Furthermore, a Part 36 offer carries costs consequences of CPR 36.10 and 36.14 only in relation to the costs of the proceedings in which that offer is made and, specifically, not to any appeal from a final decision in those proceedings.

This rule means it is essential, in the event of an appeal against a final order, that the parties consider whether any further Part 36 offer is appropriate in order to secure the potential consequences provided for under CPR 36.14(1), in relation to the appeal, whilst remaining mindful of the costs consequences in the event of such an offer being accepted within the relevant period.

A party may make a Part 36 offer in appeal proceedings which are subject to the CPR even if the decision being appealed was made in a forum, such as a tribunal, where Part 36 would not applicable.[52] If there is an offer, but not an

---

[52] See *Blue Sphere Global Ltd v Revenue & Customs Comrs* [2010] EWCA Civ 517, [2010] STC 1436, [2010] Lloyd's Rep FC 445, [2010] BVC 638.

effective Part 36 offer, acceptance will be governed by the general law of contract, rather than the terms of Part 36, and any costs consequences solely by the terms of CPR 44.3. If an offer is effective under Part 36 then the terms of that rule will prevail over the common law, so far as acceptance is concerned, and, crucially, provide for very specific costs consequences in relevant circumstances identified in the rule.

Finally, CPR 36.13 does prevent the court being referred to a Part 36 offer in certain circumstances, notably when the trial of preliminary issues has taken place but the claim as a whole is not resolved.

15.6.2 Costs consequences on acceptance of a Part 36 offer within the relevant period

Where a Part 36 offer is accepted within the relevant period there will be costs consequences in favour of the claimant.

Where the court's permission is required to accept a Part 36 offer, even though this may be sought within the relevant period, CPR 36.9(4) requires the court, unless this issue is agreed by the parties, to make an order dealing with costs. That rule also provides that the court may order the costs consequences set out in CPR 36.10 will apply, hence if application for permission to accept the offer is made within the relevant period the court might order the costs consequences provided for under CPR 36.10(1) may apply (or perhaps CPR 36.10(2) if the offer accepted related to part only of the claim and the claimant abandons the balance of the claim).

15.6.3 Costs consequences on acceptance of a Part 36 offer after the relevant period

CPR 36.10(4) deals with costs consequences on the acceptance of a Part 36 offer after expiry of the relevant period (as well as acceptance of any Part 36 offer made less than 21 days before the start of trial). This rule provides that if the parties do not agree the liability for costs then the court will make an order as to costs.

Once again the terms of CPR 36.9(4) will be applicable if permission to accept the offer is required by CPR 36.9(3). If costs are not agreed the court may order the consequences set out in CPR 36.10 will apply. In other words, where permission to accept an offer is required, the starting point for the court is likely to be the consequences applicable under CPR 36.10, depending upon whether or not the offer has been accepted within the relevant period. Where an offer is accepted within the relevant period CPR 36.10(1) will apply but otherwise the terms of CPR 36.10(5) will be relevant.

CPR 36.10(5) effectively creates a presumption that where a Part 36 offer is accepted after expiry of the relevant period the claimant will be entitled to the costs of the proceedings up to the date on which that relevant period expired and the offeree will be liable for the offeror's costs thereafter. In *Jopling v Leavesley*[53] the Court of Appeal recognised the importance of this presumption, recognising that if it did not apply a defendant, as an offeree, might conclude it was better to delay acceptance until after the relevant period, which was entirely inappropriate when, as Lewison LJ observed: 'the whole point of Part 36 is to encourage settlement and to minimise cost'.

This rule, at face value, suggests late acceptance will confer the costs benefits provided for under CPR 36.14(2) on a defendant, against a late accepting claimant, but not necessarily those set out in CPR 36.14(3) in favour of a claimant, against a late accepting defendant.

15.6.4 Claimant accepting late

The presumption created by the terms of CPR 36.10(5), although that rule does not expressly use this word, may result, by analogy with CPR 36.14, in the court applying this presumption unless that would be 'unjust'.

The defendant's conduct may have a bearing on whether the costs consequences set out in CPR 36.10(5) would be unjust when a claimant accepts a Part 36 offer late.

Consequently, where the claimant was a litigant in person and the defendant had not spelt out the costs consequences likely to follow in the event of late acceptance the presumption the claimant would have to meet the defendant's costs after the end of the relevant period was displaced.

In *Thompson v Bruce*[54] the court ruled that CPR 36.10 does apply prior to the issue of court proceedings so the presumption in CPR 36.10(5) was the appropriate starting point on late acceptance of a pre-issue offer. The judge emphasised, however, that this rule gives the court a discretion to displace when is in effect a presumption. On the facts of the case that presumption was displaced given that, in particular, the defendant had been granted extensions of time by the claimant to provide a response to the letter of claim, under the relevant pre-action protocol, and had never suggested the response, when it arrived, would be accompanied by a Part 36 offer. An argument by the defendant that the offer could have been assessed, when made, because the claim should have been valued before sending the letter of claim was rejected by the court as the relevant protocol does not envisage the claim will have been fully quantified before the letter of claim, requiring at that stage only an outline of the financial loss incurred and an indication of the heads of damage to be claimed. Consequently, the defendant was ordered to meet the claimant's costs down to and including the hearing which sought approval by late acceptance of the offer. Whilst recognising the claimant might have sought an extension of

---

[53] [2013] EWCA Civ 1605.
[54] (Unreported) 28 June 2011, QBD.

time to accept the offer the judge concluded that this was no more than an oversight and may well have arisen because of the cordial way the parties had been dealing with each other.

In *PGF II SA v OMFS Co*[55] the defendant's failure in responding to a suggestion of mediation was relevant, following the claimant's late acceptance of a Part 36 offer by the defendant, because the defendant had been unreasonable in refusing to mediate when there was a prospect that mediation would have been successful. Consequently, no order for costs between the parties was appropriate from the expiry date of the relevant period.

Whilst it will not be unjust for the presumption in CPR 36.10(5) to apply simply because the claimant is a child or protected party, and hence will need court approval of any settlement, the claimant's status is a factor the court must take into account when deciding whether applying the terms of CPR 36.10(5) would be unjust.[56]

Even where the presumption in CPR 36.10(5) is applicable if the case involves a child or protected party, the claimant ought still to recover the costs of seeking approval, given that this would have been required in any event.

Whilst the claimant can recover, as incidental, costs incurred in contemplation of proceedings the defendant is not necessarily able to do so. That is because the defendant, even though proceedings were subsequently issued, has been held to have been unable to recover costs of dealing with matters raised pre-issue but not pursued in the proceedings. Moreover, if no court proceedings are commenced the court does not usually have jurisdiction to make an order that a potential party pay the costs of another potential party.

These potential difficulties for the defendant are, therefore, a very relevant consideration in the event of the claimant accepting a Part 36 offer late but before court proceedings have been commenced.

The distinction between the position of a claimant, who may force the issue of costs by commencing court proceedings, and the defendant, who may at least not so readily be able to do so, might be significant if there is late acceptance by the claimant of a defendant's Part 36 offer at a stage when court proceedings have yet to be commenced. A defendant may not have instructed lawyers, and hence incurred costs, at that stage but even if costs have been generated these may simply not be recoverable in the absence of court proceedings.

Thus a claimant faced with a very early Part 36 offer, which cannot properly be assessed, may, rather than relying on the court later refusing to make an adverse costs order in the event of late acceptance, prefer to defer issuing proceedings until an assessment of the offer can be made given that, unless withdrawn or changed, a Part 36 offer will remain open for acceptance at any time.

---

[55]   [2013] EWCA Civ 1288.
[56]   *SG v Hewitt* [2012] EWCA Civ 1053.

If, of course, the claimant has commenced Part 7 proceedings the defendant will have a strong argument for recovering costs, even those incurred prior to issue of those proceedings. It is less clear whether Part 8 proceedings would generate the same entitlement. The point did not arise in *Thompson* and, in any event, would not have been determinative given the decision in that case.

15.6.5 Defendant accepting late

If a defendant accepts a claimant's Part 36 offer after the end of the relevant period that defendant will be the 'offeree' and the claimant 'offeror', so the presumption under CPR 35.10(5) is that the defendant will pay the claimant's costs up to acceptance. Once again, as effectively a presumption, such an outcome may be displaced by the court if that would be unjust.

In these circumstances, however, can the claimant obtain the benefits conferred by CPR 36.14(3), normally the reward where judgment is entered on terms which are at least as advantageous to the claimant as the claimant's own offer? A negative answer to this question was given in *Fitzpatrick Contractors Ltd v Tyco Fire & Integrated Solutions (UK) Ltd (No 3)*,[57] a case where the claimant's offer was accepted by the defendant a year after it was made.

This ruling was, perhaps, influenced by the basis on which submissions were made for the claimant, which focused upon what the costs position would have been under CPR 36.14 following 'trial'. Whilst the pre-2007 version of Part 36 did indeed use, in this context, the word 'trial', the current rule refers to 'judgment'. Thus there needs to be a 'judgment', but not necessarily a 'trial', to raise the presumption that the costs consequences, set out in CPR 36.14 will apply, unless that would be 'unjust'.

A different answer to the same question was given in *Bunch v The Scouts Association and Guides Association*[58] where the defendant accepted, again well outside the relevant period, a Part 36 offer on liability made by the claimant. Crucially, the court entered judgment for the claimant in the terms then agreed. The court then held that it was not 'unjust' for the claimant to receive the benefits provided for under CPR 36.14, rejecting an argument by the defendant that upon acceptance the claim was stayed, to the extent of the agreement reached, thereby precluding the entry of judgment.

Similarly, in *Andrews v Aylott*[59] the defendant accepted the claimant's offer on liability outside the relevant period but, again significantly, judgment was then entered in those terms. Rejecting the defendant's argument the claim was thereby stayed, the court gave, in principle, the claimant the benefits provided for under CPR 36.14(3), although subsequently it was ruled interest on

---

[57] [2009] EWHC 274 (TCC), [2009] BLR 144, 123 Con LR 69, [2009] CILL 2700, [2009] All ER (D) 70 (Mar).

[58] (Unreported) 3 December 2009, QBD.

[59] [2010] EWHC 597 (QB), [2010] 4 Costs LR 568, [2010] PIQR P13, [2010] All ER (D) 242 (Mar).

damages did not extend to the capitalised value of future periodical payments. Tactically, therefore, a claimant whose Part 36 offer is accepted late by the defendant might be advised to seek judgment and then argue the consequences of CPR 36.14, for indemnity costs and enhanced interest, are not unjust.

In *Jolly v Harsco Infrastructure Services Ltd*,[60] however, the court concluded the terms of CPR 36.11 precluded there being a judgment, with the costs consequences that would then follow under CPR 36.14, but accepted issues such as the basis of assessment should, in these circumstances, be held over to detailed assessment.

Even without a judgment ensuring parity between a late accepting claimant and a late accepting defendant would suggest that the consequences provided for, respectively, under CPR 36.14, when judgment is entered, ought to apply on late acceptance, unless this would be unjust.

The issue of parity between the parties is a relevant consideration given that the current version of Part 36 was drafted with that factor very much in mind. In the consultation paper, preceding the introduction of the new rule in 2007, the Department for Constitutional Affairs observed:

'Policy Objectives

6. The policy objectives behind these proposals are, while preserving the effectiveness of the system in encouraging early settlement of cases:
- to make it easier and more attractive to use Part 36 by removing unnecessary burdens/processes, in particular by:
  - allowing some categories of defendant to make written offers to settle without requiring a payment into court to support the offer, because it can be assumed that their offers are genuine and would be honoured if accepted;
  - allowing parties to accept offers after the initial time limit has expired without requiring the court's permission and, to balance that, allowing unaccepted offers and payments to be withdrawn after the time for acceptance has expired;
- to provide equal or equivalent treatment of claimants' and defendants' offers; ...'

On this analysis, a defendant who accepts the claimant's Part 36 offer late ought to do more than just show that this was a reasonable way of dealing with the matter.

Moreover, as the focus under CPR 36.14 is always on the terms of the judgment, with the claimant needing to establish this is 'more advantageous' than the defendant's offer or 'at least as advantageous' as the claimant's own offer, parity would suggest the claimant ought to be at liberty to seek judgment even if that involves the court lifting any stay imposed by CPR 36.11.

---

[60] [2012] EWHC 3086 (QB), [2013] 1 Costs LR 115.

15.7 COSTS CONSEQUENCES OF A PART 36 OFFER ON JUDGMENT (WHOLE CLAIM)

Rule 36.14 deals with the costs consequences of a Part 36 offer 'upon judgment being entered' where either:

- a claimant fails to obtain a judgment 'more advantageous' than a defendant's Part 36 offer; or
- judgment against the defendant is 'at least as advantageous' to the claimant as the proposals contained in a claimant's Part 36 offer.

The specific costs consequences are set out in CPR 36.14(2), where the claimant fails to obtain a judgment more advantageous than the defendant's Part 36 offer, and in CPR 36.14(3), where judgment against the defendant is at least as advantageous to the claimant as the claimant's own offer.

Those consequences will be applicable unless the court considers that would be 'unjust'. However, such consequences will not apply to a Part 36 offer that has been withdrawn or changed (unless the offeree beats the offer as changed) or to an offer made less than 21 days before trial (unless the court have abridged the relevant period for that offer).

The applicability of costs consequences set out in CPR 36.14 depends upon a number of issues.

There must, as a preliminary, be an offer against which any subsequent judgment can be compared. Moreover, as CPR 36.1(2) makes clear, an offer not made in accordance with the rules on form and content found in CPR 36.2 will not have the consequences specified in CPR 36.14.

15.7.1 JUDGMENT

If there is an effective Part 36 offer that must be compared with the terms of any judgment entered before deciding whether the consequences provided for under CPR 36.14 may be applicable.

The 2007 version of Part 36 provides for costs consequences of Part 36 offers to apply on 'judgment' rather than, as it was pre-2007, following 'trial'. Consequently, for example, a successful application for summary judgment would now bring the cost consequences found in CPR 36.14 into play. The court may enter judgment in other circumstances, without a trial,[61] although doubt has since been expressed on whether judgment can be entered when a stay is imposed by the acceptance of a Part 36 offer.

---

[61] As illustrated in both *Bunch v The Scouts Association and Guides Association* (2009) 3 December, QBD and *Andrews v Aylott* [2010] EWHC 597 (QB), [2010] 4 Costs LR 568, [2010] PIQR P13, [2010] All ER (D) 242 (Mar).

There must also be an 'offer' against which any subsequent judgment can be compared. That, given the terms of CPR 36.1(2), means an offer made in accordance with relevant provisions of the rule, including CPR 36.2 and, where applicable, CPR 36.4, 36.5, 36.6 and 36.15.

Consequently, an offer, even if referring to Part 36, which does not comply with the rule should not trigger the cost consequences of CPR 36.14. Anything that does not even amount to an offer cannot, by definition, suffice for these purposes.

15.7.2   Consequences for the defendant

CPR 36.14(1)(a) and 36.14(2) provide that (unless the court considers this would be unjust) where a claimant fails to obtain a judgment more advantageous than a defendant's Part 36 offer the defendant is entitled to:

- costs from the date on which the relevant period expired; and
- interest on those costs.

There is no provision under CPR 36.14(2), unlike CPR 36.14(3), for costs to be assessed on the indemnity basis. That may be appropriate, under Part 44, but does not follow automatically and will require some unusual feature that justifies such an order.

15.7.3   Consequences for the claimant

CPR 36.14(1)(b) and 36.14(3) provide that if judgment against the defendant is at least as advantageous to the claimant as the proposals contained in a claimant's Part 36 offer (unless the court considers this would be unjust) the claimant is entitled to:

- interest on the whole or part of any sum of money (excluding interest) awarded at a rate not exceeding 10% above base rate for some or all of the period starting with the date on which the relevant period expired;
- costs on the indemnity basis from the date on which the relevant period expired;
- interest on those costs at a rate not exceeding 10% above base rate; and (for offers made on or after 1 April 2013);
- an additional amount, namely 10% of the amount awarded up to £500,000 and 5% on any amount awarded above £500,000 up to £1,000,000, on the sum awarded to the claimant by the court, where the claim is or includes a money claim, or on the sum awarded to the claimant by the court in respect of costs, where the claim is only a non-monetary claim, subject to a maximum of £75,000.

The court has a discretion on the enhanced interest rate, and when this will apply. Case-law reflects the range of awards up to and including the maximum 10%.

No interest, under the terms of CPR 36.14(3), was awarded on that part of the judgment relating to future periodical payments in *Andrews v Aylott*.[62]

The court may conclude that it would be unjust for the claimant to recover some, but not all, of the consequences provided for under CPR 36.14(3). In *Davison v Leitch*[63] the claimant did not recover indemnity costs and only a small amount of enhanced interest but did recover the full additional amount under CPR 36.14(3)(d), even though the relevant offer was made at a very late stage. In similar circumstances, however, the claimant was not awarded an additional amount in *Feltam v Freer Bouskell*.[64] Similarly no additional amount under Part 36.14(3)(d) was allowed in *Elsevier Ltd v Munro*.[65]

15.7.4 Costs consequences of withdrawn or changed Part 36 offers

CPR 36.14(6) provides, significantly, that the costs benefits potentially available under CPR 36.14 do not apply to an offer that has been withdrawn or changed so that its terms are less advantageous to the offeree, provided in the latter case the offeree has beaten the less advantageous offer.

Thus rule means that:

- if an offer is withdrawn the costs consequences otherwise provided for under CPR 36.14 do not apply; and

- if an offer is changed so that the terms are less advantageous to the offeree, and the offeree fails to beat the less advantageous offer as changed, the original offer will be effective for costs purposes (presumably, therefore, back to the date when the 'relevant period' of that original offer expired); but

- if an offer is changed so the terms are less advantageous to the offeree, but the offeree beats the less advantageous offer as changed, the offer will not have the costs consequences otherwise provided for under CPR 36.14 (even if the offeree fails to beat the offer as originally made).

There may, unusually, be circumstances in which an offer has not been withdrawn or changed, cannot, be accepted yet may remain effective for the purposes of CPR 36.14.

In *Pankhurst v White*[66] there was a preliminary trial on the issue of liability at which the claimant obtained judgment at least as advantageous as his offer on that issue. The version of Part 36 then in force had no provision equivalent to that now dealing with the consequences of withdrawing an offer. The claimant's

---

[62] [2010] EWHC 597 (QB), [2010] 4 Costs LR 568, [2010] PIQR P13, [2010] All ER (D) 242 (Mar).

[63] [2013] EWHC 3092 (QB).

[64] [2013] EWHC 3086 (Ch).

[65] [2014] EWHC 2728 (QB).

[66] [2010] EWCA Civ 1445, [2010] All ER (D) 184 (Dec).

offer was held to still have 'costs potency' up to the time the defendant made a Part 36 offer to settle the whole claim, which offer the claimant ultimately failed to beat at the trial of quantum.

Under the current version of Part 36 the offer on liability could not have been accepted, at least without permission of the court, once trial of that issue started, and could not have been accepted once judgment on that issue given. However, without withdrawal or change that offer should have remained effective for costs purposes (though given the terms of the defendant's subsequent offer to settle the whole of the claim it might well have been 'unjust' for those consequences to have applied thereafter).

Tactically, rather than simply withdrawing an offer, it may be preferable to change that offer so that it is less advantageous to the offeree given that if the offeree ultimately fails to beat the offer as changed the original offer will remain effective for costs purposes but, once changed, is incapable of acceptance in its original form.

Where an offeror makes, as will more usually happen, offers which are increasingly more advantageous to the offeree the making of those further offers does not amount to a withdrawal of the earlier offers which therefore retain the potential for costs consequences. An argument to the contrary was rejected by Cox J in *Mahmood v Elmi*.[67]

The court can still take a withdrawn Part 36 offer into account when exercising the general discretion on costs found in CPR 44.2. On this basis withdrawn offers were held to be relevant to costs in *Rehill v Rider Holdings Ltd*[68] (though this decision may need to be treated with some caution as the Court of Appeal carried the concept of what would be 'unjust', specifically applicable where an offer is effective under Part 36, into the more general discretion conferred by Part 44, where there is no equivalent test).

15.7.5 'Unjust'?

The costs consequences on judgment provided for under CPR 36.14 are only presumptions but the court must order those consequences unless it would be unjust to do so.

When considering whether the usual costs consequences would be unjust, CPR 36.14(4) requires the court to take into account all the circumstances of the case. That rule also identifies some specific circumstances which, as with all similar rules in the CPR setting out a structured decision-making process, the court must take into account where applicable.

The specific circumstances identified in CPR 36.14(4) are:

---

[67] [2010] EWHC 1933 (QB).
[68] [2014] EWCA Civ 42.

- the terms of any Part 36 offer;
- the stage in the proceedings when any Part 36 offer was made;
- the information available to the parties at the time when the Part 36 offer was made; and
- the conduct of the parties with regard to the giving or refusing to give information for the purposes of enabling the offer to be made or evaluated.

There is, however, no limit to the type of circumstances that may, in any particular case, make it unjust the costs consequences set out in CPR 36.14 should follow.

A number of cases have illustrated how the court should approach the question of what would be unjust for the purposes of CPR 36.14 and which, by analogy, may well be relevant in deciding whether the presumption as to costs found in CPR 36.10(5) should prevail where there is late acceptance.[69]

Although the claimant's capacity is not a factor specifically identified in CPR 36.14 it is one of the 'circumstances' of the case and must, therefore, be a factor taken into account when deciding what will be unjust. Consequently, where the claimant accepted, late, a Part 36 offer for an injury that, crucially, had been caused by the defendant's breach of duty it was unjust for the costs consequences in CPR 36.14 to apply.

Given the terms of CPR 36.14(4), and in particular the significance of information which enables the offer to be evaluated, the absence of clarification, where requested, even without an order from the court this be provided, may be relevant in determining whether the costs consequences under CPR 36.14 would be unjust. For these purposes information has been held to mean factual information rather than the way an issue on the law is to be argued.

Even without a request for clarification where a party has withheld material relevant to the offer, thereby making a proper appraisal of that party's case more difficult, that may have the effect of making the costs consequences under CPR 36.14 unjust.

---

[69] *Kiam v MGN Ltd* [2002] EWCA Civ 66, [2002] 1 WLR 2810, [2002] 2 All ER 242, [2002] CP Rep 30, [2002] EMLR 26; *F & C Alternative Investments (Holdings) Ltd v Barthelemy* (2013) APIL 391; *Huck v Robson* [2002] EWCA Civ 398, [2002] 3 All ER 263, [2003] 1 WLR 1340, [2002] CP Rep 38, [2002] CPLR 345, [2003] 1 Costs LR 19, [2002] PIQR P31; *Matthews v Metal Improvements Co Inc* [2007] EWCA Civ 215, [2007] CP Rep 27, (2007) 151 SJLB 396; *Ford v GKR Construction Ltd* [2000] 1 All ER 802, [2000] 1 WLR 1397, [1999] CPLR 788, CA; *Walsh v Singh* [2011] EWCA Civ 80, [2011] 2 FLR 599, [2011] Fam Law 344; *Epsom College v Pierse Contracting Southern Ltd* [2011] EWCA Civ 1449, [2012] TCLR 2, [2012] 3 Costs LR 451, 142 Con LR 59; *Hutchinson v Neale* [2012] EWCA Civ 345, [2012] All ER (D) 151 (Mar); *Smith v Trafford Housing Trust* [2012] EWHC 3320 (Ch).

If there is a pre-action protocol which provides for exchange of information, such as disclosure, it may be unjust for the consequences of CPR 36.14 to apply when the exchange of information envisaged by the protocol had not taken place.

The court's approach reflects the need to conduct litigation, for the purposes of the overriding objective, in a way that allows other parties to know where they stand at the earliest possible stage and make informed decisions about the prospects and conduct of the case at the lowest practicable cost. Nevertheless, if the claimant has not complied with the timetable for case management directions the defendant may secure the normal costs consequences under Part 36 if there is a corresponding delay in disclosing surveillance evidence.

Generally, however, the courts are likely to take the view that, in the absence of some particularly relevant circumstances, it will not be unjust for the consequences provided for under CPR 36.14, where otherwise applicable, to prevail. That is because, under Part 36 as opposed to Part 44, indemnity costs are not to be seen as penal, or carrying any stigma, given that even on the indemnity basis a receiving party may only recover costs which have actually been incurred.

It is, therefore, wrong to characterise the benefits conferred on the claimant under CPR 36.14 as a windfall because the rules confer, in appropriate circumstances, that entitlement and unless relevant costs sanctions are imposed there would be no incentive on a defendant to take offers made by the claimant seriously.[70]

15.7.6 'Advantageous'?

Part 36.14 uses the word 'advantageous' in both sub-paras (2) and (3), for the purposes of comparing any judgment with a Part 36 offer made by either the claimant or the defendant.

For the purposes of CPR 36.14(2) the term 'more advantageous' means taking a broad view about whether the judgment, when compared with the relevant offer, was 'worth the fight'.[71] In most cases success in financial terms will be the governing consideration.

However, the approach taken in *Carver* has been considered as only appropriate where one party has engaged in ADR and the other has not and

---

[70] *Nixon v Chanceoption Developments Ltd* [2002] EWCA Civ 558, [2002] All ER (D) 14 (Apr); *Blue Sphere Global Ltd v Revenue & Customs Comrs* [2010] EWCA Civ 517, [2010] STC 1436, [2010] Lloyd's Rep FC 445, [2010] BVC 638; *Hemming v Westminster City Council* [2011] 4 Costs LO 44312, [2011] EWHC 1582 (Admin); *Crema v Cenkos Securities Plc* [2011] EWCA Civ 10, [2011] 4 Costs LR 552; *Seeff v Ho* [2011] EWCA Civ 401, [2011] 4 Costs LO 443.

[71] *Carver v BAA* [2008] EWCA Civ 412, [2008] 3 All ER 911, [2008] All ER (D) 295 (Apr), CA.

was not followed in *Morgan v UPS*,[72] even though the defendant's offer was only beaten 'by a whisker', because the claimant had engaged in reasonable negotiations.[73]

If, unusually, the court does take account of factors other than success in financial terms this approach will apply equally to a claimant, when deciding whether judgment is at least as advantageous as the claimant's own offer, as it does to a defendant.

The approach taken in recent case-law to the interpretation of CPR 36.14 has been endorsed by the Civil Procedure (Amendment No 2) Rules 2011,[74] which provide that after CPR 36.14(1) there shall be inserted:

> '(1A) For the purposes of (1), in relation to any money claim or money element of a claim, "more advantageous" means better in money terms by any amount, however small, and "at least as advantageous" shall be construed accordingly.'

Paragraph 1(4) of these rules confirms that the new rule applies to offers to settle made in accordance with CPR 36.2 on or after 1 October 2011. However, given case-law such as *Gibbon*, a court seems likely to adopt the same approach to pre-October 2011 offers. When comparing offer and judgment in a non-money claim, or on the non-money element of a claim, CPR 36.14(1A) will not apply but guidance on the correct approach can be obtained from earlier case-law.[75]

If a party seeks more than monetary damages that may be a factor in determining what is 'advantageous' but if the case really is 'all about money' then the comparison will be made on that basis alone. In this context, therefore, what the claimant has gained by pressing ahead will be just as relevant to answering the question of what is more 'advantageous' as it is to the, usually, anterior question of who has won.

The court must compare like with like when contrasting offer and judgment. Accordingly, when comparing the defendant's offer with the judgment entered any interest adding to the value of the judgment from the date of the offer must be disregarded. Similarly, when comparing a claimant's Part 36 offer with any judgment entered, interest must be calculated on the judgment sum up to the date the relevant period in the offer expired so as to make an accurate comparison.

---

[72] [2008] EWCA Civ 1476, [2008] All ER (D) 100 (Nov).

[73] See also *Fox v Foundation Piling Ltd* [2011] EWCA Civ 790, [2011] CP Rep 41, [2011] 6 Costs LR 961, [2011] All ER (D) 61 (Jul); *Gibbon v Manchester City Council* [2010] EWCA Civ 726, [2011] 2 All ER 258, [2010] 1 WLR 2081, [2010] All ER (D) 218 (Jun); *McGinty v Pipe* [2012] EWHC 506 (QB); *Blue Sphere Global Ltd v Revenue & Customs Comrs* [2010] EWCA Civ 517, [2010] STC 1436, [2010] Lloyd's Rep FC 445, [2010] BVC 638; *Acre 1127 Ltd (in liquidation) v De Montfort Fine Art Ltd* [2011] EWCA Civ 130.

[74] SI 2011/515.

[75] Such as *Huck v Robson* [2002] EWCA Civ 398, [2002] 3 All ER 263, [2003] 1 WLR 1340, [2002] CP Rep 38, [2002] CPLR 345, [2003] 1 Costs LR 19, [2002] PIQR P31.

Given the obligation under CPR 36.15 on a defendant who makes a Part 36 offer to deal with CRU that element of the claim may have an important bearing on whether or not any subsequently judgment is 'more advantageous' to the claimant than the offer.

Where the defendant elects to make a Part 36 offer that includes deductible benefits CPR 36.15(8) confirms that, when deciding what is 'more advantageous' the comparison must be made between the net amount of the offer and the net amount of the judgment, in each case after CRU deduction. That is why it is important any Part 36 offer by the defendant complies with the requirements of CPR 36.15(3) and, where deductible benefits are included in the offer, gives the information stipulated in CPR 36.15(6).

Where there is a change in the CRU certificate, reducing the amount of deductible benefits, between offer and judgment or if the court, when giving judgment, restricts the amount of deductible benefits, the claimant may recover less, gross, than the relevant offer but nevertheless obtain a judgment that is 'more advantageous' than the offer because the net sum payable has increased.

Where an offer is made without regard to any liability for recoverable benefits the notional gross amount of both offer and judgment, including any benefits, will be irrelevant, the comparison being made between the offer and net sum payable to the claimant.

If the defendant makes an offer including any deductible benefits and, following acceptance, either party appeals the deduction, any refund should go to the claimant as the claimant has effectively accepted the gross sum.

If the offer is made 'without regard to any liability for recoverable amounts' under CPR 36.15(3)(a), the claimant will have effectively accepted a net figure so in the event of an appeal any refund should be due to the defendant as that was never part of the offer. It is the significance of CRU on the issue of what is 'advantageous', as well as the implications of any subsequent CRU appeal, that makes it important the defendant's Part 36 offer does comply with the requirements of CPR 36.15 rather than, for example, being silent about CRU, stating the offer is 'net of CRU' or even 'gross of CRU'.

15.7.7 Costs consequences of a Part 36 offer after judgment on a preliminary issue

A Part 36 offer made on any issue tried as a preliminary is likely to be relevant to the costs of that issue, depending upon who made the offer and how the judgment compares with that offer.

However, given the terms of CPR 36.13, communication to the court of any relevant offer may be prohibited until such time as the claim as a whole has been determined.

Where there has been a Part 36 offer on an issue that may have a bearing on the costs of that issue, even when the claim as a whole is tried.

Where the only Part 36 offers are to settle the whole claim there is conflicting case-law about the costs consequences of such offers where the court deals with a preliminary issue. In *HSS*[76] the Court of Appeal held that where preliminary points have been decided by a court at first instance but there is a Part 36 offer of settlement, and quantum is still unknown, the best person ultimately to rule on costs will be the trial judge. In *Kew v Bettamix*,[77] however, there was a preliminary trial on the issue of limitation and, although succeeding in part, on that issue, the claimant was ordered to pay the defendant's costs for the issue on which the claimant did not succeed, despite the claimant having made a Part 36 offer to settle the whole claim which, of course, the claimant might ultimately have matched or bettered.

At face value it does seem curious if a claimant who has made a Part 36 offer of outright settlement and is unsuccessful on a preliminary issue should be ordered to pay the costs of that issue there and then whilst a defendant, in essentially the same situation, can defer determination of the costs issue until such time as the outcome of the case as a whole is known.

In these circumstances a party who has made a Part 36 offer of settlement can, at the very least, argue the costs of a preliminary issue, which goes against that party, might not be determined until all aspects of the case are concluded. If, however, the relevant issue is a discrete one, which can readily be seen to have added to the overall costs of the case, the court may feel able to make a costs ruling there and then, notwithstanding the offer of outright settlement.

A distinction can be drawn between costs following the trial of preliminary issues and costs orders made for interim hearings, whether case management hearing or the hearing of an application.[78]

Where there is a freestanding application the court may be more ready to conclude costs should follow the event in that application, certainly where it might be said one party has generated the need for that application and hence incurred costs that could otherwise have been avoided. It might be argued, even so, that where a party has made an offer to settle that ultimately proves to have been well-judged then any further costs, including costs of interim applications, are generated by the other party having not accepted the offer, unless the conduct of the offeror does merit a sanction in costs. With case management hearings, of course, costs will usually be in the case and, if anything, the prospect of Part 36 offers later having an impact on the incidence of such costs

---

[76] *HSS Hire Services Group PLC v (1) BMB Builders Merchants Ltd (2) Grafton Group (UK) PLC* [2005] EWCA Civ 626, [2005] 3 All ER 86, [2005] 1 WLR 3159; subsequently followed in *RTS Flexible Systems Ltd v Morkerei Alois Müller GmbH & Co KG* [2009] EWCA Civ 26, [2009] 2 All ER (Comm) 542, [2009] BLR 181, 123 Con LR 130.

[77] [2006] EWCA Civ 1535, [2007] PIQR P210, (2006) 150 SJLB 1534, (2006) 103(46) LSG 30, CA.

[78] *Jean Scene Ltd v Tesco Stores Ltd* [2012] EWHC 1275 (Ch).

only endorses the appropriateness of such an order in the vast majority of case management hearings even where it might be said one party or the other is, to a greater or lesser extent, successful or unsuccessful on particular issues.

15.7.8   2013 transitional provisions

The amendment to CPR 36.14(3), which implements the offers to settle in the Civil Proceedings Order 2013, does not apply to a claimant's Part 36 offer which was made before 1 April 2013.[79] That amendment provides for the claimant to recover an 'additional amount' if judgment is at least as advantageous to the claimant as the claimant's own Part 36 offer. Consequently, a claimant may wish to make a further Part 36 offer, in the terms of any earlier Part 36 offer the claimant stands by, after 1 April 2013 as, under Part 36, there is no prohibition on multiple offers.

TOP TIPS

- Make full use of Part 36 to encourage settlement and to give certainty about potential costs and other consequences including enhanced interest, indemnity costs and the award of an additional amount.

- Remember that so far as costs are assessed on the indemnity basis the claimant will not be limited to any costs budget set.

- Ensure any offers intended to be made under Part 36 comply precisely with the rules on form and content as otherwise technical challenges can be expected.

- Remember Part 36 offers can be made on issues, in particular liability.

- Seek clarification of Part 36 offers made on behalf of the defendant whenever necessary.

- Do not let the defendant make offers in terms such that it is not clear whether the terms of Part 36 will, or will not, apply.

---

[79]   Rule 22(7) of the Civil Procedure (Amendment) Rules 2013.

CHAPTER 16

MEDIATION AND ADR

In this chapter Paul Balen, who is a director of specialist personal injury and clinical negligence mediators Trust Mediation, examines alternative dispute resolution as a method of resolving clinical negligence claims. This chapter was originally written by Margaret Bowron QC who is also an experienced accredited mediator.

16.1 WHY HAVE MEDIATION AND ADR BECOME SO IMPORTANT?

It is an almost universal truth that litigants involved in clinical negligence claims want their claims to be resolved as quickly, cheaply and with as little anxiety as possible. At the forefront of such early resolution is the drive to get parties to mediate their claims or to undergo alternative dispute resolution (ADR) in one of its other guises.

Before explaining the practical impact and effect of mediation and ADR and the advantages and disadvantages of one form of ADR over another it is necessary to understand the historical context of the development of the drive for cases to be disposed of without a trial.

16.1.1 Historical context

In very general terms, the move for claims of all sorts to be resolved by agreement began in the early 1990s and was of particular importance for clinical negligence claims, perhaps more than many others, due to their not infrequent combination of high costs but relatively low damages. It was then, with the experience of mediation in other fields since the late 1980s in the UK, that academics, lawyers and judges began to appreciate more fully the real benefits to litigants of early resolution of the majority of claims by means of mediation and ADR. As Lord Woolf of Barnes undertook his extensive research and review of civil procedure which led to the production of the Civil Procedure Rules (CPR) so his personal enthusiasm for all forms of ADR increased whilst Jackson LJ was similarly enthusiastic when he produced his seminal review of the costs of civil litigation.[1]

---

[1] Jackson, *Review of civil litigation costs*, Final Report (March 2014), www.judiciary.gov.uk/publications/review-of-civil-litigation-costs/.

16.2 WHAT IS MEANT BY MEDIATION?

Mediation, as it has developed in the UK, is a private, voluntary (or largely so – see below), confidential, without prejudice and non-binding process in which a neutral third party helps the parties to resolve their differences in a manner which is acceptable to each of them. Unlike an arbitrator, a mediator is not expected to come to a formal determination on the issues. However, as is explored further below, as experience has grown, a mediator may increasingly be asked to provide informal input on the merits or aspects of them in so far as the necessary expertise to do so is held by him or her.

The process is not (but rarely may be) a straight alternative to the bringing of a claim in the court system and the usual situation is that litigation and mediation complement one another. The timing of mediation is very variable. The process may take place before the issuing of proceedings but, equally, appeals to the Court of Appeal are not infrequently resolved by this means.

16.3 WHAT OTHER FORMS OF ADR ARE THERE IN CLINICAL NEGLIGENCE CLAIMS?

In reality, and for practical purposes, in clinical negligence cases, the ADR method most likely to be employed is the round table meeting. Such a meeting necessarily and importantly imposes a greater degree of formality upon the resolution process than attempting to settle by correspondence or telephone calls between the respective legal advisers. Such meetings are dealt with in greater detail below.

Further, in cases involving a litigant in person, then the only real hope of the defendant resolving the claim other than by paying up in full or defeating the claim at an interlocutory stage is by such a formal form of ADR.

16.4 THE LEGAL FRAMEWORK

16.4.1 The government's stance in the drive for mediation and ADR

In 2001, the then Lord Chancellor, Lord Irvine, announced an ADR 'pledge' by which all government departments and agencies made a number of commitments including that: 'Alternative dispute resolution will be considered and used in *all* suitable cases wherever the other party accepts it.' That was followed by a Department of Constitutional Affairs report in July 2002 underlining the perceived effectiveness of that commitment and launching a mediation initiative on the part of the NHSLA as set out in the following paragraph.

Towards the end of 2000, discussions began between AvMA and the NHSLA about the use of mediation in clinical negligence claims. A pilot project was decided upon and CEDR (the Centre for Effective Dispute Resolution (CEDR) was invited to develop such a project. It took place between May and September 2002 and was funded in part by the Legal Services Commission (LSC). There was extensive discussion about developing qualified specialist clinical negligence mediators and for the provision of training to those taking part in mediations for the parties. A report on the initial phase of the project was published in late October 2002. It has to be observed that the impetus for mediation to expand in this field as envisaged by the hard work of the participants in this initial project has somewhat evaporated.

In the summer of 2001, the Clinical Disputes Forum's Guide to Mediating Clinical Negligence Claims[2] was published and it is a very useful reference point. It has a helpful and well set out table of the needs of parties to a claim and the ways in which those needs may or may not be met by different forms of resolution including, of course, mediation. It is suggested that that might form a good starting point for discussions in which a claimant's lawyer may be trying to persuade the other parties to a claim of the potential advantages of mediation over other methods of ADR.

The NHSLA remains committed to resolving cases wherever possible without recourse to a trial in court for obvious reasons of saving money, and a concern to avoid the distress that a trial imposes upon both the claimant and the clinicians involved. However, its enthusiasm for mediation has hitherto been less evident in practice than the public utterances of support by its leaders may lead one to believe. Instead, ADR in its most usual manifestation in these cases of an RTM will more commonly be agreed to. In the 4th edition[3] of its Reporting Guidelines published in January 2007 at paragraph 8.3, the shift of emphasis from mediation to ADR in all of its forms was seen as it stated:

> 'Mediation involves a trained mediator acting as a go-between to facilitate settlement. ADR can take one of a number of different forms, eg a time-limited discussion. Consider always the potential cost of such a step against the benefits which might be achieved. As a general guide, claims of relatively limited financial value, but possessing major emotional elements, e.g. the death of a child might be suitable candidates. All cases, however, may potentially benefit from mediation or ADR *at any stage*.'

Claimants' solicitors have complained for years that the NHSLA has paid lip service to promoting mediation and in practice suggestions for mediation from claimants' solicitors have more usually been rejected. The introduction of QOCS may well cause the NHSLA to review this and it is hoped that ADR and particularly earlier mediation may become more prevalent.

---

[2] To be found on the Forum's website, see www.clinical-disputes-forum.org.uk/.
[3] To be found on the NHSLA website, see www.nhsla.com.

16.4.2   The role of the judiciary

As mentioned above, Lord Woolf was an enthusiast of ADR and mediation when he pioneered the CPR. As a judge, in *Cowl v Plymouth City Council*,[4] he had said: 'Today, sufficient should be known about alternative dispute resolution to make the failure to adopt it, particularly when public money is involved, indefensible'.

The CPR state in r 1.4(1), in defining 'active case management' that that involves '... encouraging parties to use an alternative dispute resolution procedure if the court considers that appropriate and facilitating the use of such a procedure'.

Shortly after the decision in *Cowl*, Brooke LJ extolled the virtues of mediation in the well known case of *Dunnett v Railtrack plc*.[5] The background to the court's decision and his comments was that when granting permission to appeal the single Court of Appeal judge made it very clear that the parties should attempt to mediate or arbitrate to resolve their differences. The defendant, Railtrack, both the victor at trial and on appeal, did not follow that exhortation and was duly refused its costs of the appeal. In giving judgment Brooke LJ commented: 'Skilled mediators are now able to achieve results satisfactory to both parties in many cases which are quite beyond the power of lawyers and courts to achieve'.

It could be said that the outcome of this case was something of an invitation to the reluctant party who feels very strongly that the merits are on their side to 'go along' with mediation and pay lip service to the process. However, it may mark, in some respects, the high point of judicial enthusiasm for mediation as later decisions will show.

16.4.3   The decision in *Halsey v Milton Keynes General NHS Trust*

The best known and most definitive decision of the Court of Appeal is *Halsey v Milton Keynes General NHS Trust & another*.[6] The cases were (i) a clinical negligence action brought under the Fatal Accidents Act 1976 in which the claimant lost at trial and the defendant was awarded its costs regardless of its refusal of the claimant's invitation to mediate and (ii) a personal injury claim in which a Part 20 defendant was exonerated and awarded its costs against the defendant despite having refused to mediate.

The Court of Appeal dealt with oral submissions not only from the litigants themselves but also from the Law Society and the ADR Group as interested parties and with written submissions from the Civil Mediation Council and CEDR. To the marked disappointment of those who were advocating that the

---

4   [2002] 1 WLR 803.
5   [2002] 1 WLR 2434.
6   [2004] 1 WLR 3002.

courts should be able to order parties to mediate against their will, the court, in Dyson LJ's careful judgment, refused to go that far.

Interestingly in one of his last judgments before retiring as Master of the Rolls, Evans LJ who was a member of the Appeal Court in *Halsey*, seemed to regret the failure of that court to be more proactive in support of mediation.

16.4.3.1 What did the Court of Appeal lay down in terms of general principles?

These can be summarised as follows:

- Lawyers must actively consider ADR in every case and inform their clients about mediation etc and in particular the possibility of adverse costs orders.

- The advantages of mediation are that it is usually cheaper; it offers a wider range of possible solutions; there is the possibility of a business relationship continuing; it is flexible and available at short notice, usually lasts no more than a day, is informal, a forum for testing the merits and demerits of the case; the lay client can be actively involved and it can bring in protagonists that are not and may never be formal parties to the litigation.

- Most cases are suitable for mediation but some are not, for example, where a decision on a point of law is sought, injunctive relief is needed or where fraud is alleged.

- The decision to deny the successful party his costs if he refuses to mediate is an exception to the general rule on costs in CPR 44.3(2). It considered that the following factors (but the list is non-exhaustive) were to be taken into account in determining whether a refusal to mediate or to take part in ADR is reasonable: the nature of the dispute; the merits; the extent to which other methods of settlement have been attempted; whether the costs of ADR would be disproportionate; ADR delay which might have been prejudicial; and whether ADR had a reasonable prospect of success. No single point will be determinative and there is a wide discretion so lawyers will need to be able to cover all aspects and not rely, for example, on the strong merits alone.

The Court of Appeal encouraged interlocutory orders which promote mediation and particularly commented upon the Commercial Court practice which, at that time, required:

- the parties to exchange lists of 3 people who can conduct 'ADR procedures' and to endeavour to agree upon one of them;

- in the event the parties cannot agree, the court will facilitate agreement;

- if the case goes to trial, the parties must explain what ADR steps have been taken and why they have failed.

There is a tension between the obvious sense in trying to resolve cases quickly and as cheaply as possible without the need to recourse to a full blown trial, and the right of a party who believes strongly that he will win outright and wants to have the matter determined to be unfettered by an intermediate step perceived to be unnecessary and consequently wasteful of money.

The court recognised that and concluded that compulsion to mediate would be contrary to Art 6 ECHR jurisprudence and, even if such a jurisdiction existed stated: 'We find it difficult to conceive of circumstances in which it would be appropriate to exercise it'.[7]

16.4.4 The ADR/mediation case management orders made in clinical negligence cases

In *Halsey*, the Court of Appeal commented favourably upon the case management order for ADR made by the designated clinical negligence Masters.

This is reflected in the current standard directions on clinical negligence cases.[8]

16.4.5 Decisions post *Halsey*

What has happened since and how have the courts interpreted the *Halsey* guidance?

It is clear that individual judges have their own take on the interplay between mediation/ADR and the trial process. Some of the more instructive are:

- *Al-Khatib v Masry*[9] was a family appeal in which the Court of Appeal said all cases were potentially open to successful mediation. The Court of Appeal ADR scheme had been employed and a mediator appointed before the appeal was heard but he was a commercial mediator with no family experience and the process was abandoned. Against this background Thorpe J said that court supervision of the process was vital, that the selection of the appropriate mediator in a difficult case was crucial, and that the availability of the supervising judge to deal with 'crisis' is very important. This statement was reaffirmed by Baker J in *AI v MT*.[10] The court will encourage and permit the parties to participate fully in any process that will precipitate resolution by agreement.
- *Couwenbergh v Valkova*[11] was a Court of Appeal decision only two weeks after *Halsey*, in which the court seems to contradict that decision by saying that a case involving fraud was 'crying out for alternative dispute resolution'.

---

[7] [2004] 1 WLR 3002 at 3007F, para 9.
[8] See Chapter 12.
[9] [2005] 1 FLR 381.
[10] [2013] EWHC 100 (Fam).
[11] [2004] EWCA Civ 676.

- *Vahidi v Fairhouse School Trust Ltd.*[12] Here the Court of Appeal in dismissing a stress at work claim by a teacher said that as many of the principles of such claims had now been determined, the parties should seek to mediate and to do so pre-trial and not pre-appeal.

- *C v RHL*[13] Coleman J in a Commercial Court case seemingly without a request from either party in a labyrinthine action adjourned an application before him and gave the parties 28 days to appoint a mediator or panel of mediators and to conclude the meetings.

- *Lewis v Barnett*[14] in a long running battle (arising out of claim for less than £11,000 for feed and stabling fees which had theoretically been settled in 1992) the Court of Appeal in postponing the substantive appeal said that the parties had been told of the potential consequences of the refusal to mediate and that they needed to bear that in mind 'as well as the benefit of putting a negotiated end to this long running dispute without further financial and emotional blood letting'.

- *R (on the application of A) v East Sussex County Council*[15] was a judicial review case in which Munby J did not reduce the successful applicant's costs by reason of their failure to mediate. He considered the respondent's suggestion that mediation stood reasonable prospects of success as verging on the fanciful as every conceivable point of law and factual issue had been aired and because of 'the enthusiasm with which the forensic battle was apparently waged by all parties.' Further the respondent had sought to impose unreasonable conditions upon the agreement to mediate and the applicant was entitled to reject them.

- *Yorkshire Bank and Clydesdale Bank Asset Finance Ltd v RDM Finance Ltd and John Broadhurst*[16] in which HHJ Langan ordered the defendant to pay 65% and not 50% of the claimant's costs as it had refused to mediate.

- *Rolf v De Guerin*[17] in which the court commented 'this is an appeal solely about costs. It is also a sad case about lost opportunities for mediation'. As a result of his refusal to mediate or attend a round table meeting the winning party failed to recover his costs.

- *Wilkinson v Kerdene Ltd*[18] in which the judges expressed their regret that the parties had failed to resolve their dispute through mediation that the court had offered to them at the last hearing.

- *Frost v Wake Smith & Tofields Solicitors.*[19] In their judgment[20] the Appeal Court judges reaffirmed the notion that there is no case, however intractable, that is unsuitable for a mediated resolution. The court pointed

---

[12] [2005] EWCA Civ 765.
[13] [2005] EWHC 873 (Comm).
[14] [2004] EWCA Civ 807.
[15] [2005] EWHC 585 (Admin).
[16] (unreported) June 2004, Leeds Mercantile Court.
[17] [2011] EWCA Civ 78.
[18] [2013] EWCA Civ 44.
[19] [2013] EWCA Civ 772.
[20] Para 1.

out[21] that mediation had proved to be a flexible and immensely valuable process of dispute resolution that it 'would normally be part of a solicitor's duty to advise his client, especially a lay client as opposed to a professional litigator such as a liability insurer, of the nature of the process and of the status of any agreement reached as a result'.

It can be seen that there is no true uniformity of approach but it has to be said that a party is brave if not foolhardy to turn his face against mediation or ADR in some form as, particularly in the post-Jackson climate, sanctions could well follow. One such example was *PGF II SA v OMFS Co Ltd*[22] a case where the claimant accepted a Part 36 offer out of time but the judge at first instance refused to order the claimant to pay the costs incurred since the Pt 36 offer on the grounds that the defendant had failed to respond at all to offers to mediate. Per Briggs LJ:

> 51. I agree with the general thrust of Mr Fetherstonhaugh's submission, that a finding of unreasonable conduct constituted by a refusal to accept an invitation to participate in ADR or, which is more serious in my view, a refusal even to engage in discussion about ADR, produces no automatic results in terms of a costs penalty. It is simply an aspect of the parties' conduct which needs to be addressed in a wider balancing exercise. It is plain both from the Halsey case itself and from Arden LJ's reference to the wide discretion arising from such conduct in the Hewitt case, that the proper response in any particular case may range between the disallowing of the whole, or only a modest part of, the otherwise successful party's costs.

> 52. There appears no recognition in the Halsey case that the court might go further, and order the otherwise successful party to pay all or part of the unsuccessful party's costs. While in principle the court must have that power, it seems to me that a sanction that draconian should be reserved for only the most serious and flagrant failures to engage with ADR, for example where the court had taken it upon itself to encourage the parties to do so, and its encouragement had been ignored. In the present case the court did not address the issue at all. I therefore have no hesitation in rejecting Mr Seitler's submission that the judge did not go far enough in penalising the defendant's refusal to engage with ADR.

> ...

> 54. Had I been free to do so, I would have concluded that, notwithstanding a blameworthy failure to engage with a serious invitation to participate in ADR, and indeed an unreasonable refusal to do so, the overall responsibility for the expenditure of a further £500,000 odd in costs during the relevant period nonetheless still lay primarily with the claimant. While, viewed from the perspective of Part 36, the judge's order only deprived the defendant of half the benefits which would otherwise have accrued from its use of that procedure, I would nonetheless have concluded that this was a case in which only some proportion of its costs as the successful party, rather than the whole of them, should have been disallowed.

---

[21] Para 37.
[22] [2013] EWCA Civ 1288.

55. Nonetheless, the discretion is clearly that of the judge. He was plainly conscious throughout that he was exercising a broad discretion, and his approach to the basis upon which the court could properly depart from the otherwise automatic consequences of Part 36 was entirely correct. To deprive the defendant of the whole of its costs during the relevant period was within the range of proper responses to the seriously unreasonable conduct which the judge identified, and the lack of an express balancing exercise, after a lengthy analysis of the points put before him by counsel, by no means demonstrates that he did not in fact carry it out in his mind.

56. Finally, as is recognised by the weight placed on the judge's decision in the passage in the ADR Handbook to which I have referred, this case sends out an important message to civil litigants, requiring them to engage with a serious invitation to participate in ADR, even if they have reasons which might justify a refusal, or the undertaking of some other form of ADR, or ADR at some other time in the litigation. To allow the present appeal would, as it seems to me, blunt that message. The court's task in encouraging the more proportionate conduct of civil litigation is so important in current economic circumstances that it is appropriate to emphasise that message by a sanction which, even if a little more vigorous than I would have preferred, nonetheless operates pour encourager les autres.

16.4.6 Do the courts make ADR in some form inevitable?

In the vast majority of cases which are assigned to the multi track or issued in the High Court in the first place, it is highly likely that ADR in some form will be encouraged to a greater or lesser extent by the court if not agreed upon by the parties themselves. There is now reference to ADR on the front page of the allocation questionnaire as well as we have seen in the standard case management directions. Parties can now expect judges both at case management hearings, pre-trial reviews and indeed at trial to enquire why mediation has not been considered and, if it has, why it has been rejected. Although a court cannot order the parties to mediate failure to do so after a recommendation by a judge could well lead to a costs penalty against an otherwise successful party in exactly the same way as courts frequently take conduct, issues and proportionality into account when deciding the appropriate order for costs.

16.5 ADR BY MEANS OF A ROUND TABLE MEETING

16.5.1 Why a round table meeting?

In the clinical negligence field, the two main methods of face-to-face resolution short of a judicial determination are mediation and the round table meeting. The latter is usually attended by the lawyers on both sides, whether both solicitors and counsel or solicitors alone, and almost invariably by the claimant and/or his litigation friend. Less usually, the defendant is present in person or in a representative capacity in the form of a representative of the trust or of the NHSLA or of the defence organisation. Historically the opportunity for the claimant at such a meeting to express his views on what has happened to him to the person being held responsible may not have been seen to be a vital part of this process but many find it cathartic and more is said about this below.

Many cases are resolved in this manner and it is particularly well suited to cases where quantum alone is in issue. In such cases, the additional dynamic of a mediator can still be useful, particularly if, for some reason, feelings are unduly high or there are other barriers to useful face-to-face discussion, but it is likely that the parties' lawyers unaided by a third party mediator will be able to do a deal or vastly narrow the issues between them.

16.5.2   What happens at a round table meeting?

The meetings are usually, but not invariably, held at the offices or chambers of the claimant's representative. Understandably, that allows the claimant himself or herself to feel more comfortable and in charge of the process which can be of considerable importance. In all but the most modest of claims where costs limitations and constraints may demand that the solicitor for each party speak on the telephone and not even meet at all, the sense and need in having the client present to take instructions from and to feel involved in an important and potentially determinative process is obvious.

Practice varies enormously as to whether the claimant is present for some or all of the discussions which take place between the lawyers. For almost all claimants in these circumstances this will be a very important day as it may well mark the end of a long road starting at the time of the medical accident which affected them or a family member at least several years before, potentially many years earlier. They will have been subjected to questioning by their lawyers about an unhappy incident which has already led to physical and/or psychological harm, more questioning and examination by a number of medical experts and, in the more substantial cases, their homes will have been opened up to a large number of quantum experts for both sides.

It is therefore vitally important that claimants who have survived the above are not left alone in a room with the feeling that their lawyers are discussing them and compromising their claim and that they are being excluded from the process. This is particularly important in those cases where the round table meeting is convened to discuss overall settlement of both liability and quantum as any settlement will almost inevitably be on a discounted basis to a greater or lesser degree. Very careful handling will be needed when explaining the above to the claimant.

16.5.3   What needs to be done before such a meeting?

Managing the expectations of a claimant is always an important part of the lawyer's job and that is put into stark focus when a claim is resolved by agreement during a half day or full day meeting between the lawyers. This is not the same as being able to say to the client, 'Well that's what the judge has decided, there is nothing more to be said'.

It is perfectly acceptable to compile a Schedule of Loss which is high and includes heads of loss which are at best optimistic but it is vital that the client has been fully informed that the tactic is to ensure that the defendant's offer may be increased to an extent by the high overall figure claimed. Should that not be done in advance of the meeting, then an offer made at a round table meeting which reflects both a discount for the risk of the claim being lost altogether and the inevitable compromise on many, if not all, of the heads of loss could be seen by the lay client as derisory and insulting and be unwisely rejected. Alternatively, it may be grudgingly accepted on the day and then mulled over subsequently with an increasing feeling of grievance which may well be wholly misplaced. The time thereafter which may be taken up with dealing with queries, complaints or, even worse, proceedings, would be much more constructively spent in ensuring that the client is fully informed in advance.

16.5.4 The role of the lay client

There is much to be said for the claimant to be directly included in at least part of the face-to-face discussions. He may wish to say something direct to the other side if only to explain the impact that the events in issue have had upon him. No sensible defendant's representative will refuse to allow such an interchange to take place and the fact that this is an important and potentially life changing day for the claimant should be very much in everyone's mind.

On the other hand, if the point comes at which it is either necessary to discuss sensitive, personal medical issues and in particular, very significantly, the likely life expectation of the claimant, then the wise course may be to conduct such matters in the absence of the client. Whilst he will be fully aware that this is a live issue in the assessment of his loss, few people wish to hear such a matter being debated in the necessarily rather cold way in which it has to be approached in litigation. This may be the case equally for the parents of a young claimant with severe cerebral palsy whose life expectation may not exceed his late teens at best as for a middle aged patient with a delayed cancer diagnosis claim.

If it is decided that the claimant should not take part at all in any of the face-to-face encounters then it is almost invariably requested, or ought to be, by the defendant's lawyers that they meet and have a short conversation with the claimant either at the outset of the meeting or at its conclusion whether or not a settlement has been reached. There is much merit in such a course in all but those really very rare cases where tensions are so high that such a step could be counterproductive.

16.5.5   The possible perils of not being prepared

It almost goes without saying that preparation for such meetings is absolutely crucial as much will hang upon the outcome for the parties, be they the claimant or the defendant. Whilst, as far as is known, no case has yet been reported on the point, it has to be at least a possibility that a poorly prepared representative at such a meeting (or, of course, at a mediation) could expose the client to an adverse costs order were it to be argued at trial that this lack of preparation was symptomatic of that side's unwillingness to take part properly in the process. That would be hard to prove but not impossible and, as costs bills mount, parties will plainly look for ways to minimise their liabilities.

Experience shows that even the most inauspicious of cases in terms of the prospects of successfully achieving a resolution acceptable to both sides can be settled at a round table meeting. There may be factual evidential problems on one side of which the other is blissfully unaware or a concern that an apparently robust case on causation is based on somewhat rocky foundations. Such considerations play a vital part in the preparation for the meeting not least in ensuring that the claimant is fully aware of the strengths and weaknesses so that an offer of, say, 60% of full entitlement is received positively in a case where total loss at an eventual trial is a very real possibility.

16.6   MEDIATION – THE PRACTICAL EXPERIENCE

16.6.1   Setting the stage – why a mediation?

The agreement that there should be a mediation rather than a different type of ADR may take some time to reach. This needs to be factored into the timetable in advance to avoid rushed decisions. There may well be resistance to the idea at all or to the proposed venue or to the identity of the mediator or to all three.

Why does the case under consideration need to be formally mediated and not the subject of a round table meeting? The answer may be obvious to the claimant's solicitor but far from clear to the defendant's representative if it is related, for example, to a particular burning sense of grievance about, say, a non-negligent aspect of the care provided which has coloured the client's entire approach to the claim itself. Such a situation could legitimately tip the scales in favour of a mediation as the chosen form of resolution rather than a less formal method of ADR.

It must be stressed that many defendants will need to be persuaded that a case necessitates mediation because that will be viewed by them to be more costly than alternative methods of ADR. The perceived benefits of mediation need to be carefully considered and explained.

The possible benefits of having a formal mediation rather than a round table meeting will necessarily be very case and fact dependent. In difficult liability only or liability and quantum cases there can be a real benefit in having a mediator to help bring the parties together particularly one who has experience of clinical negligence claims.

In clinical negligence cases, some understanding not only of the law on breach of duty and causation (not always entirely obvious) and quantum but also the practicalities of life in the NHS or private medicine and the concerns of the dissatisfied patient claimant counts for a lot.

As Sir Henry Brooke, at the time Vice-President of the Court of Appeal but later a renowned and respected mediator himself, observed: 'skilled mediators are now able to achieve results satisfactory to both parties in many cases that are quite beyond the power of lawyers and courts to achieve.'[23]

16.6.2 What can such a mediator bring that is genuinely 'added value'?

Listed below are some of the possible advantages:

- Input on the merits if the parties want it as almost all do. Such input does not have to be to the exclusion of a caring approach to the claimant and his or her particular problems and concerns. A good mediator can and does marry the two and if asked can be persuaded to be evaluative. Indeed the parties could agree in advance that a neutral evaluation from a mediator with clinical negligence experience on all or a specific issue would be likely to aid eventual resolution of the case.

- The chance to allow the parties, usually the claimant but not inevitably, to focus on what really matters to them. This is often crucial in small value claims, for example a Fatal Accidents Act claim following the death of an elderly person or child. It is often also easier to place the claimant in particular in the centre of a mediation conducted by a third party than during the debates which often characterise a round table meeting. The claimant patient or a bereaved family can be encouraged to let off steam, unconstrained by formal witness statements or court issues. Having done so they may be more receptive to concentrate on the issues under scrutiny in the case and their legal resolution. It is wrong also to think that this advantage is restricted to patients or their relatives. Clinicians if present may find the process equally cathartic in a way that the formal court process could not provide.

- A degree of drive which might just tip the reluctant party to engage in the process when the alternative of attending a simple round table meeting would allow him to go through the motions with little chance of a resolution of the claim.

- The extra formality of a mediation over a round table meeting does, usually, lead to more focused preparation by the lawyers – although the need to prepare is obviously vital in all cases. Such focusing and the rather

---

[23]   *Dunnett v Railtrack* [2002] 1 WLR 2434.

more disciplined procedure of the mediation itself can often be conducive at least to a reduction in the number of issues at stake if not total agreement.

- The chance to bring a freshness of thought and approach to a case which may be both stale but also deeply contentious – an unhappy mix – that might engender a joint spirit by the parties of a desire to find a way through that which had seemed intractable.

- In cases involving multiple defendants, a mediator can bring a real extra dimension by cutting through the posturing that can creep into such cases.

16.6.3   Choosing your mediator

The first crucial question to consider before a date is set is whether the mediator should be an individual with experience in the field or not. The traditional view was that a mediator is a neutral facilitator who is there to assist the parties to find a resolution but without expressing his or her view on the merits of the claim in any way. He is neither arbitrator nor judge.

That approach has, in recent years, somewhat altered and many participants in mediations in the clinical negligence area consider that there is much value in having a practitioner in the field who can, if requested, provide some evaluation of the parties' respective prospects if the claim were to be litigated. Whilst in no way formally adjudicating upon any of the issues that arise in a case, a mediator with experience in clinical negligence will have a feel for the work and can highlight, for example, causation problems or give assistance on how a court might resolve a factual issue upon which the key question on breach of duty will turn. Such experience can be particularly useful if either or both parties are perceived as being intransigent as the other side may feel that the firm and informed hand of the mediator will make sense prevail.

Ultimately, the decision on the type of expertise and precise identity of the mediator is a matter for the parties to seek to agree upon. That is not always easy and a consideration that cannot be overlooked is cost. Those who contend that mediation has insufficient benefit over and above a round table meeting will cite the cost of the former as the main disadvantage to what otherwise might be the preferred course. In practice there are a growing number of specialist clinical negligence mediators whose charges are really very modest. Some mediation organisations now have panels of specialist clinical negligence mediators.

16.6.4   The lead up to a mediation

Having fixed upon the individual and set a date, certain steps need to be taken before the appointed day.

First, where is the mediation to take place? Many mediators can offer accommodation whether in their office or chambers and that is a consideration when deciding on the person to be the mediator as the cost of the necessary three rooms for a whole day can be high. If accommodation has to be found, that too needs to be discussed and agreed prospectively with the other side.

Secondly, the parties need to sign the mediation agreement. A model agreement is appended to this chapter. It is not infrequent for the signing to be done at the start of the mediation but that is best avoided in case, albeit that it would be highly unusual, there are any problems over its contents. The agreement appended is largely self-explanatory but the key points are:

- The representatives of the parties must have authority to negotiate and settle the claim. This could be important in the case of a protected person whose litigation friend must be appointed and present.

- The costs are assumed, unless otherwise stated, to be borne equally by the parties. This is plainly something that needs to be carefully agreed in advance.

- The parties must act in good faith.

- The mediation is confidential. This is explored a little further below.

- There is no binding settlement until the parties have signed a written agreement.

Some agreements also make express provision for the mediator to be entitled but not obliged to express a view in private to any party as to the reasonableness of proposals or arguments advanced by that party. It may also be expressly provided what documents will be exchanged and/or provided to the mediator alone.

Thirdly, papers need to be prepared and sent to the mediator, generally in the region of 7 days before the date fixed. Agreement should be sought as to what to include in that bundle, which should be kept as slim as is practicable.

Fourthly, the parties will be asked to provide position papers setting out in brief what their case is on the issues in dispute in a format that, almost invariably, can be disclosed to the other side. This is not meant to be a rehash of the pleadings as that will add nothing as the mediator is almost bound to be supplied with the pleadings. It should be a concise and focused document and, when well done, it can be very helpful indeed. A claimant can include within it particular matters which may be tangential to the pleaded allegations but of vital personal significance. For example, that reassurance from the head of the pathology laboratory that results will not be delayed as they were in the case of their dead relative even when that delay, whilst acknowledged to be in breach of duty, is accepted to be non causative. Parties should remember that the ADR process involved is designed to help resolution. Preparation by the parties including the documents supplied should have that in mind. A schedule of loss with TBA against every item is scarcely going to help any more than would an overtly adversarial approach.

Fifthly, a party can provide a further confidential position paper or documents, possibly some expert evidence which has not yet been exchanged, which is for use by the mediator and not the other side. This can be problematic but the fact that this is even possible marks out where a mediation with its confidentiality as between each party and the mediator can be very useful.

Sixthly, as for the round table meeting, good and full preparation is obviously vital. A sound knowledge of the factual background and of the real strength and weaknesses of the parties' respective cases is hugely important. The latter is inevitably bound to come into the spotlight at a mediation as the day unfolds.

16.7   THE MEDIATION ITSELF

16.7.1   The opening session

The usual and most helpful format is for the day to begin, once the documentary formalities are resolved, with a session at which all of those attending sit round a table. Conventionally, this is known as the plenary session and, when well conducted by all of those professionals taking part, it can be very useful.

The mediator will begin by introducing himself, explaining what will happen, largely but not exclusively for the lay participants but useful too as a reminder for the lawyers that they are not in court and that it is not intended to be an adversarial occasion. The confidential nature will be stressed. That is vital and needs to be spelt out. Not only will the mediator not pass on information divulged in private session to the opposition unless told that he may but also the whole process is confidential and may not be spoken of or referred to in a later court hearing or otherwise.

The parties then have the opportunity to speak. This again is not meant to be akin to a trial opening but rather an oral opportunity to put across what is in the position statement. Many let their representative speak for them but not infrequently a claimant will want to say something to the defendant face to face. It may be his only chance since the events giving rise to their claim to vent his views and concerns, because if the case does resolve, it will not happen at court and if it does not resolve some of the items concerning the claimant may not be ventilated in the trial. If not too distressing many claimants find it very helpful to read out something short which has been prepared by them. Often that can be emotional for all concerned as the clinicians themselves may well attend for the defendant and they, as caring doctors and nurses, can also be affected by the whole experience. The impact of a few chosen words by a patient or his relative should not be underestimated.

16.7.2 The private sessions

After the open session, the parties will return to their own rooms and the mediator will begin a process of what could be called shuttle diplomacy, going from room to room. Whom he starts with and what is talked about will necessarily vary from case to case. In this regard, the individual practice of the mediator will come into play. However when he is given information in these private sessions it is for the party making the disclosure to decide whether the mediator should be authorised to pass that information over to the other party.

The first few times that the mediator comes to speak to a party will be very much a fact finding exercise and an attempt by him to ascertain that party's real position. Whether a view is expressed by the mediator on the merits of a particular point will be something which is clarified by the mediator in advance. If the lay client is being obstinate on a point where his lawyers perceive difficulties which the client is reluctant to acknowledge, then an informed third party expressing a view is usually more of a help than a hindrance.

Where the mediation is concerned either with overall settlement or quantum alone, the time may well come when the mediator asks for a bottom line figure from the claimant's team. That is hardly surprising and it will be necessary to have prepared the client carefully for that eventuality. If a full Schedule of Loss has been prepared which claims, say, £750,000 then it is unwise to suggest for the first time at the mediation that a realistic valuation is actually £450,000. The claimant would have good cause for feeling disgruntled and the mediation may well founder or, at best, resolve on a sour note.

There will be times during what can be a long day when it seems to one party or the other that nothing is happening. That is unlikely as it is probable that the mediator will be occupied with one or more of the other parties. A good mediator will make sure that no one feels left out and will, as best he can and with proper regard for confidentiality issues, keep everyone informed as to where things are going.

The time may also come when it looks as though no resolution will occur. In some cases that is simply unavoidable but in many it is at that time that a good mediator will inject new life into the process by one or other means. His skills may well be sorely tested but almost anyone who has regularly attended mediations whether as the mediator or as a representative will know of cases where the seemingly intractable case suddenly falls into place.

It is very much to be hoped that this can be achieved within a reasonable time frame as exhaustion is not a good spur to resolution. Indeed, in a very complex case or one with more than one party on each side, there may be wisdom, despite the costs, of prospectively arranging for a 2 day mediation so that no one feels pressurised or rushed. That, however, should be reserved for rare cases as most should be capable of resolution in a 7 to 8 hour period although 3 to 4 hour mediations have at times proved to be very successful.

16.7.3 The outcome

Assuming that the claim has been resolved, then the representatives must draw up an agreement which reflects what has been agreed and ensure that a person with proper authority signs it. It could include matters peripheral to the main claim such as the provision of a written apology, the naming of a piece of equipment in honour of the deceased, or the confirmation that a criticised procedure has been replaced by an acceptable one.

The possibilities are many and varied and, as the day wears on, and when time allows, it is wise that someone starts to make a full note of the barebones of what might turn into an agreement. Leaving all of the drafting in a complex case until too late in the day is unwise as that is when mistakes and omissions may occur.

Sometimes a further plenary session takes place to explain the agreement reached. Although this is usually the best course time may be short and the parties may not want this. A good mediator will play this by ear.

If the mediation has been unsuccessful then a plenary session may again be convened but may be deemed unwise if emotions are high. The mediator can and should in any event remind both sides of the confidential nature of what has occurred as this has particular relevance when finality has not been achieved.

16.8 EXAMPLES OF ADR IN PRACTICE IN MULTI PARTY ACTION CASES

Mediation has been used successfully in a number of multi party actions in recent years although often the details are not reported.

The Alder Hey organ retention group litigation comprising around 1,100 claims was the first mediation of a group action undertaken by the NHSLA. It was settled after a three-day mediation. The settlement included financial compensation but it was the ability to discuss non financial remedies which ensured a successful conclusion. The families involved produced a 'wish list'. This resulted through the mediation in the provision of a memorial plaque at the hospital, letters of apology, a press conference and contribution to a charity of the claimant's choice. Interestingly the parallel Nationwide Organ litigation failed to settle at mediation.

One of the few reported cases of an ADR scheme is the Leicester Epilepsy litigation. The courts have spoken openly of the advantages to all concerned in resolving a complex case in this way. This was illustrated in this case[24] which, as it involved children, had to have its scheme of resolution approved by the court. In giving judgment approving it Mrs Justice Cox was fulsome in her praise of the pragmatic solution arrived at by the lawyers on both sides. Parents of children were interviewed by a panel of three experts in the presence of solicitors for each side. The experts were able to discuss the parents' concerns with them. The discussions were recorded and the claims valued on the information contained in the records and the transcript of the experts' discussion. There was no need for individual reports which would have made the litigation unmanageable. The experts could make recommendations for additional treatment for the child or for the provision of additional expert advice, such as careers or family planning, which could then be arranged. The parents had a key part to play in this process. As, one of the architects of the Leicester compensation scheme, Paul Balen, said in June 2005:

> 'Right from the outset we were aware that involvement of the parents in the resolution process was critical. Parents have a key part to play in this case. They frequently felt they had let down their children because they had accepted the diagnosis and treatment given by Dr Holton. Many parents described how their children were reduced to drug induced zombies. They had lost years of joy in watching their child's formative years. Whilst no amount of money could replace the years of childhood lost due to misdiagnosis or mistreatment at least the settlement scheme removed the need for a battle in the courts.'

One of the earliest ADR schemes involved the parents of the convicted nurse Beverley Allitt who were claiming compensation for their psychiatric suffering. This was a capital sum scheme. The Health Authority put aside a fixed sum of money to settle all the claims. The claimants hardly surprisingly in the circumstances did not trust the health service and were reluctant to disclose their medical records. The claimants' cases were settled by agreement by the lead solicitors allocating points according to the size of the individual claims so that the pot of money made available was equitably divided. Public accountability for the payment of this money was provided by an opinion from counsel chosen by the claimants' solicitors from a panel of names submitted by the Health Authority.

ADR based compensation schemes have also led to the settlement of individual claims in product liability cases such as those involving the 3M hip prosthesis and Trilucent breast implants.

---

[24] *A N v University Hospitals of Leicester NHS Trust* [2005] EWHC 1416.

16.9   SOME POTENTIAL PITFALLS AND PROBLEMS OF MEDIATION AND ADR

16.9.1   Confidentiality and privilege

The basic premise is that the mediation process is entirely without prejudice and privileged and, in the event that it fails, neither party can refer to what took place. That has been found to be the case on issues of costs – see *Reed Executive plc v Reed Business Information Ltd*.[25] That was a Court of Appeal decision in which it was determined that 'without prejudice' means just that even if with regard to the form of an ADR, what happens during an ADR or on costs. Only in a case of 'unambiguous impropriety'[26] will that position change and it is highly unlikely that an allegedly sham involvement in a mediation could ever fall into such an extreme description.

The seriousness with which this is taken by the courts is by their willingness to enforce the privilege of the process by the granting of an injunction to prevent the parties revealing what happened at a mediation[27] or from relying on documents disclosed for the purposes only of the mediation.[28]

Two areas to have in mind, however, are the issue of a joint experts' report prepared for the mediation process and the use to which the events which occurred may be put in the event of a dispute as to whether there was or was not a concluded agreement.

As to the first, if the joint report is to keep its privileged status, the parties must agree that that should be the case and not seek an order under CPR 35.12(3). This arose in the context of a Technology and Construction Court case – *Aird v Prime Meridian Ltd*.[29] In that case, HHJ Thornton made a r 35.12(3) order pre-exchange of reports (a practice apparently common in the TCC) before a mediation. The Court of Appeal allowed an order against the decision of HHJ Coulson that, as the joint report was prepared for a mediation, privilege should attach to it.

With regard to the latter point, Stuart Isaacs QC sitting as a deputy High Court judge in a Chancery Division case,[30] ruled that the privilege rule could not extend to cover an enquiry into whether a concluded agreement had been reached. That is not really surprising but the ADR Group were seeking to argue that nothing said or done in preparation for, at, or in consequence of the mediation which is liable to disclose the nature of the negotiations can ever be used outside the mediation process in the absence of the unambiguous

---

[25]   [2004] 1 WLR 3026.

[26]   See *Forster v Friedland* (unreported) November 1992 (CA).

[27]   *Venture Investment Placement Ltd v Hall* [2005] EWHC 1227 (Ch).

[28]   *Instance v Denny Bros Printing Ltd* (2000) *The Times*, February 28; *Hunt v Optima* [2013] EWHC 1121.

[29]   [2006] EWCA Civ 1866.

[30]   *Tim Brown v Stephen Rice and ADR Group (Intervener)* [2007] EWHC 625 (Ch).

impropriety of one of the parties – see above. On general principles, that must be taking things too far and would amount to a special and peculiar type of privilege existing for the mediation process that does not apply otherwise.

16.9.2 Getting the agreement right

The importance of ensuring that what is recorded either at the end of a successful round table meeting or mediation truly reflects what the parties have agreed cannot be overstated. Mistakes can be and are made and satellite litigation can ensue.

Having a computer to hand to ensure that a comprehensive and legible document which can be printed off signed and copied to all concerned is the most practical way to deal with the matter. At a mediation one or more of the inevitable lulls as the day unfolds can be productively used to prepare the bare bones of an agreement. What form does it want to be in? Will a court have to approve the settlement? Should there be a Tomlin order to seek to minimise the public part of the agreement? All of these considerations are best thought about in advance and not at 7pm when everyone is keen to get away.

16.9.3 The costs – are they a bar to a mediation at all or can they be kept down?

The costs of mediation are frequently cited as a reason to avoid it and to opt for a simple round table meeting or even not attempt at ADR at all. That is understandable but the potential ADR costs have to be set against the possible need to go to trial. Are the costs really so high? The sliding scale that most mediators, both individual and corporate, adopt so that low value claims cost less is not entirely logical but certainly assists the parties.

Is there a role for mediation or ADR in another form much sooner than hitherto has in practice occurred which can help to limit costs?

It is possible to envisage that a claimant or a proactive defendant in, say, a low value Fatal Accidents Act claim involving a child, might suggest that a mediation at which the understandable grief, anger and, possibly, guilt, however misplaced, of a parent could be aired in a way that no court case would ever allow, should take place after receipt of the letter of claim or the Particulars of Claim. That would keep the costs of the litigation as low as is possible, allowing for the front loading that the CPR mandate.

Of course, both parties must have had the chance to investigate sufficiently to feel comfortable that they can form a sensible view of the merits but that does not need to go as far as a fully pleaded case would go. The costs of the litigation thereby saved, if ADR was successful, would more than offset the costs of a formal mediation.

The earlier the mediation takes place the easier it will generally be to justify the costs incurred and to reduce the influence the issue of costs may have on the eventual outcome. Early mediation is desirable but the cases suitable for resolution early in the process need to be carefully identified.

In the very large quantum cases, especially those involving protected persons and children, claimant's advisers will very frequently say that they cannot form a view about an offer until very many experts have reported and the case been fully worked up. This is a genuine dilemma as such cases are complex and the outcome will affect the client for maybe 50 or 60 years so it has to be got right. However, even these cases can be resolved in the experienced hands of specialist lawyers and an experienced mediator.

Where resolution of breach of duty appears to be reasonably straightforward and even if causation for the whole of the damage may not be established, there is wisdom in trying to obtain at least an outline care report (and quite possibly others dealing with, for example, housing and at least some therapies) as a guide to likely overall value.

16.10   CONCLUSION

Much has occurred in recent years to change the face of litigation in this country. This has been felt in the clinical negligence arena as much if not more than many others. It is likely that there will be more changes to come, especially for the lower value claims where the costs are increasingly becoming out of proportion to the amounts at stake.[31] Court schemes to impose ADR have been trialled, not always with great success, and that is a trend that may well continue and burgeon. In the small claims arena court-based mediation has proved successful.

Anyone litigating in the field of clinical negligence is well advised to become as familiar as possible with ADR in all of its guises. Experience is the best way to educate oneself and allows for an informed decision in later cases as to the most likely method of resolving a case as quickly and as cheaply and painlessly for the client as it can be. For the client – whether claimant or defendant – mediation can have many more advantages than a court hearing. Money invested wisely in mediation perhaps at an earlier stage than previously thought possible or indeed in any other ADR process is likely to pay dividends not least in an arena in which costs recovery by successful parties whether claimant or defendant is becoming increasingly problematic as a result of QOCS so far as defendants are concerned and non-recovery of success fees and insurance premium by claimants.

Obtaining agreement to a mediation, if that is seen to be the preferred course, is much more likely to be forthcoming if the solicitor wishing to pursue that route

---

[31]   Such as the proposed scheme under the NHS Redress Act 2006 which unlike the position in Wales has yet to see the light of day in England.

is able to speak from personal experience of the process. It may be worthwhile attending a mediation of a colleague's case within the firm to get that experience as it is an interesting and not infrequently surprising process that needs to be experienced at first hand. Explaining to a client the rationale for and process of mediation should become second nature to all litigators.

No one should suggest that mediation or ADR generally is a universal panacea and some cases genuinely need to be fully litigated. However, the strong probability is that out of court resolutions will grow in number over the coming years and proper experience and expertise in those areas will be of increasing importance to the clinical negligence practitioner.

APPENDIX

Mediation Agreement

[Name of Mediator]

Mediator

1. Parties

2. Date(s) of mediation

3. Venue

4. The conditions of the mediation

The parties, having agreed to try to settle their dispute by mediation, agree, acknowledge and accept the following:

(i)   that the procedure adopted at the mediation will be determined by the mediator;

(ii)   that the process is voluntary with the result that either party may withdraw from the mediation at any time;

(iii)   that the mediator may withdraw from the mediation if, for any reason, he considers it impossible or impracticable for him to continue;

(iv)   that the process is confidential and 'without prejudice' and that, in consequence, each party will be bound by the provisions of Clause 5 below;

(v)   that the mediator will not give legal advice in connection with the dispute or the terms of any settlement reached and that the parties will be responsible for drawing up a suitable form of written settlement agreement in the event of settlement being achieved;

(vi)   that no agreement reached during the mediation will be binding on the parties until incorporated in a written agreement signed by or on behalf of the parties.

(vii)   that they will make no claim of any kind against the mediator arising from or in connection with (whether directly or indirectly) the mediation and/or any settlement achieved and will indemnify the mediator against any legal action that might be brought by any third party for any act or omission in connection with the mediation;

(viii)   that either before or at the commencement of the mediation they will each nominate one participant at the mediation who will have full authority to agree to a settlement at the mediation.

5. The confidentiality clause

In consequence of the agreement, acknowledgement and acceptance by the parties that the process is confidential and 'without prejudice' it is agreed (without prejudice to the requirements of the general law and save as may be required to secure the implementation or enforcement of any agreement reached during the mediation):

(i)   that no record or other form of continuous transcript or record of the mediation will be made;

(ii)   that all material produced in whatever form for the purposes of the mediation, and any note or other record made during the mediation by any participant, is to be treated as privileged and neither disclosable nor admissible in evidence in any subsequent proceedings of any kind save where it would otherwise have been disclosable or admissible;

(iii)   that all participants in the mediation will maintain confidentiality in respect of all information given and all material produced for the purposes of and during the mediation save as may be (a) required by a court of competent jurisdiction or other competent public authority and (b), so far as the mediator is concerned, reasonably required in his opinion to prevent significant damage to the health or safety of any person or where the failure to disclose information might lead to him becoming the subject of criminal proceedings;

(iv)   that neither party will ask the mediator to provide a witness statement relating to the dispute or the mediation or call him as a witness in any proceedings arising from or in connection with the dispute or the mediation.

6. Costs and expenses

(i)   The parties will, subject to any alternative agreement between them or subject to any order of the court, bear their own costs in relation to the mediation.

(ii) The parties will, subject to any alternative agreement between them or subject to any order of the court, bear equally:

    (a) the costs of providing the mediation venue and any ancillary costs and expenses associated therewith, and

    (b) the mediator's fees and expenses – and the parties' solicitors will remain jointly and severally liable for all such costs, fees and expenses.

(iii) The mediator's fees and expenses will be calculated in accordance with the Schedule to this agreement and will be payable within 14 days of the receipt of any fee note or expenses claim.

SIGNED by . . . . (Name + Firm) on behalf of . . . .
DATE:

SIGNED by . . . . (Name + Firm) on behalf of . . . .
DATE:

TOP TIPS

- All cases may potentially benefit from mediation or ADR *at any stage.*

- A party is brave if not foolhardy to turn his face against mediation or ADR in some form as sanctions could well follow.

- The opportunity for the claimant at a round table meeting or mediation to express his views on what has happened to him to the person being held responsible may not be seen to be a vital part of the process but many claimants find it cathartic.

- No sensible defendant's representative will refuse to allow such an interchange to take place.

- The wise course may be to discuss sensitive matters such as life expectancy in the absence of the client.

- Preparation for round table meetings and mediations is absolutely crucial as much will hang upon the outcome for the parties.

- It is important to ensure that what is recorded at the end of a successful round table meeting or mediation truly reflects what the parties have agreed.

- Early mediation is desirable but the cases suitable for resolution early in the process need to be carefully identified.

CHAPTER 17

ENTITLEMENT TO DAMAGES

In this chapter solicitor David Body reviews the claimant's entitlement to the various heads of damages.

17.1 INTRODUCTION

To achieve best practice in drafting schedules of loss in clinical negligence cases, it is necessary to understand the principles behind this area of the law, and something of the background as to how the whole process has evolved.

17.2 CLAIMING COMPENSATION

In order to seek compensation there must of course be an actionable claim for personal injury, which the Limitation Act 1980 defines as: 'any disease and any impairment of a person's physical or mental condition'.[1]

In the context of clinical negligence cases, assessment of the extent of the 'impairment of condition' is often more complex than many other types of personal injury because of the claimant's pre-existing condition. In many cases, the claimant would have had a level of ongoing injury but for the negligence. This impacts significantly on the value of these claims, and makes the process of valuation generally much more difficult.

It is frequently mentioned that the purpose of compensation is to, '... put the party who has been injured ... in the same position as he would have been in if he had not sustained the wrong for which he is now getting his compensation ...'.[2]

This is generally referred to as the 'full compensation' principle and its ethos underpinned the decision in *Wells v Wells*[3] in which the House of Lords held that the basis of calculation of multipliers should be arithmetic. Ensuring 'full compensation' in a clinical negligence action where an element of ongoing

---

[1] Limitation Act 1980, s 38(1).
[2] Per Lord Blackburn, *Livingstone v Raywards Coal Co* (1880) 5 App Cas 25 at 39.
[3] [1999] 1 AC 345.

injury is not related to the alleged negligence can prove demanding and is all the more reason why the schedule of loss put forward should be accurate, credible, and capable of being relied on at trial.

17.3 GENERAL AND SPECIAL DAMAGES

Assessment of value is split into two heads: general damages (those damages where valuation is imprecise and subjective) and special damages (items that have an exact monetary value, such as loss of earnings and costs of care).

The term 'general damages' incorporates a number of different heads of damage, and is a term for all losses that have to be estimated rather than specified. These will include such things as pain, suffering and loss of amenity, handicap on the open labour market, loss of enjoyment and leisure time, and loss of congenial employment. Loss of marriage prospects and marriage breakdown and loss of use (for example of a vehicle) can also come within the definition.

Technically, all future expenses and losses are general damages because it is not possible to calculate precisely the extent of these losses. However, for the purposes of a schedule of loss, practitioners tend to look at past *and* future economic losses, and in every day discussions, the term 'general damages' is often used only in relation to pain, suffering and loss of amenity. In this way, practitioners are able to separate the non-economic losses (PSLA) and the economic losses, setting out the full extent of all economic losses (both past and future) in the schedule.

For the purposes of this chapter, general damages will mean 'personal loss': the harm and disadvantage that the victim suffers directly and personally because of their injury.

17.4 REDRESS AND WORTH IN CLINICAL NEGLIGENCE ACTIONS

When meeting with a client for the first time, practitioners often explain that the remedy in a clinical negligence action is 'damages', and that the client's wish for a 'guarantee that this will never happen to anyone else' (or other similar forms of redress) is not achievable within a court's judgment.

Because of the very emotive issues within clinical negligence cases, the question of how much the claim is worth is not usually raised by the client at initial interview. The likely amount of compensation is however something that impacts on the whole process of the claim, from initial application for funding of investigations, to settlement negotiations or trial because damages are the only remedy offered by the courts in cases of this sort and because all other associated items of redress tend to be incidental.

For this reason accurate quantification during the investigative process, and in the period leading up to trial, is crucial in order to keep a continuing eye on proportionality, an issue which is particularly important to a third party funder, whether that be the Legal Aid Agency or insurer. In clinical negligence cases particularly, investigations can be very expensive, and can outweigh likely damages. Careful quantification in order to assess the economic viability of claims becomes all important.

The NHS Litigation Authority (a public body answerable to HM Treasury) also places huge reliance on the reserves set for claims faced by the NHS. The same is also true of medical defence organisations and defendant insurers in other PI claims.

One of the recurrent features of clinical negligence practice is the annual announcement of the NHSLA's expenditure on damages and costs and its estimate of future claims; the latter figure may seem to claimant practitioners exaggerated but is directly drawn from full value provision based on schedules of damages served on behalf of claimants – another reason for accurate (rather than overstated) calculation of damages.

17.5 THE EVOLUTION OF SCHEDULES OF LOSS

The Administration of Justice Act 1969 required a change in procedure for the assessment of damages, moving from a global sum assessment to itemisation of individual heads of damage because of the need to account for interest on past losses. Although the trial judge will conventionally award a total lump sum, he must indicate how the lump sum is calculated by itemising the damages under separate heads, as each head is separately appealable.[4] Of course, in order that the trial judge can reach a decision as to the appropriate sum to award, he needs to be aware of what heads of damage are claimed, the level of claim for each, and how each item is calculated.

In *Kirby v Vauxhall Motors Ltd*,[5] Lord Denning said:

> '... it is both proper and helpful for a Judge to itemise the damages; and he should be encouraged to do so for two reasons. First, it shows that the Judge has applied his mind to all the proper considerations and has worked out the damages in the way it should be done. Second, it is a great help to this court on an appeal, so that this court can themselves review the items in computing the overall figure.'

Accordingly, since the 1960s, practitioners have been dividing claims into the various heads of damage.

---

[4] *Jefford v Gee* [1970] 2 QBD 130.
[5] [1969] 113 Sol Jo 736.

17.5.1 The need for a schedule of loss and basic guidance

The schedule of loss is an integral and very important part of any clinical negligence claim for a number of reasons. The schedule states at a glance what the claimant seeks. This, after all, is the basis behind any such claim and the level of detail and care which is put into the preparation of the schedule will be a clear indicator to the defendant as to the level of experience and skill of the claimant's lawyers.

The schedule can set the scene for the defendant's approach to the case. A poorly drafted, incomplete or unconvincing schedule can cause frustration for both sides and delay in resolution of the claim. It may also lead to inappropriate offers of settlement, and create for the client a false expectation of the level of redress that can be difficult to resolve subsequently.

Speculative claims should, on the whole, be avoided.[6] Practitioners should be careful not to claim for items where there is no supporting evidence. If the judge was to find that there was never any chance of a particular head of damage succeeding, costs sanctions could be applied.

However, when drafting the initial schedule, practitioners should be careful to include every relevant element, rather than leave items out. If uncertainty arises from lack of evidence, then it is far better to clarify the position before finalising the schedule, rather than to add in an additional head of loss at a later stage. Adding losses later weakens the credibility of such claims and may prejudice the extent of recovery not only for that one element, but potentially over the whole schedule, as it encourages the defendant to doubt the credibility of the schedule generally. It potentially also causes delays as the defendant needs time to investigate.

It is important that the schedule of loss is realistic. If not, it will provoke the defendant to resist the claim entirely, and could alienate the trial judge. By way of example, in many clinical negligence claims there will be a need for future treatment, but claims for private treatment should be made cautiously. Without cogent evidence that the claimant will pay privately and that the NHS will be unable to provide that treatment, such claims may not succeed and should not be made simply as a matter of course in any claim (see *Woodrup v Nicol*).[7]

17.6 COMPONENTS OF A SCHEDULE

The schedule should provide a template for the trial judge with which to approach the assessment of damages. The judge is obliged to make an award that is just and reasonable to both sides and, for him to be able to do so, the correct and sufficient information must be available.

---

[6]   *Davies v Taylor* [1974] AC 207.
[7]   [1993] PIQR Q104.

The CPR do not state specifically what the schedule of loss should include, but generally speaking one would expect to find:

- the date of preparation/service of the Schedule;
- assumed date of trial;
- date of alleged negligent treatment from which losses commence;
- claimant's date of birth and occupation;
- life expectancy;
- comment on and valuation of general damages;
- heads of past loss;
- heads of future loss;
- interest on both general and special damages;
- details of appropriate multipliers;
- whether periodical payments will be sought.[8]

The schedule should be clear and easy to understand, with a logical progression. This will greatly assist in consideration of the heads of damage at trial, or earlier settlement. A full and detailed schedule will encourage the defendant and the trial judge to adopt it in their consideration of the issues.

The schedule should first set out general damages and interest on them, past economic losses, then interest on past losses, and then future losses set out on a lump sum basis using an annual multiplicand and adopting a multiplier derived from the (Government Actuary's Department) Ogden Tables, currently in their seventh edition.[9] As well as having a logical approach, the schedule should enable future amendment, and so should be well structured and explained with headings for each separate head of loss.

An initial narrative will helpfully set out the background to the claim, and thus to the heads of loss claimed, just as the particulars of claim in a complex clinical negligence case will first discuss the relevant treatment which precedes the alleged negligence. It is also advisable to incorporate a front page of relevant information and statistics that will provide the assumptions on which the schedule is based, and a reference point when working through the heads of loss. This should include:

- date of birth;
- date of alleged negligent treatment leading to the action;
- notional trial date;
- age at notional trial date;
- appropriate multipliers (together with the reasoning behind the multipliers);

---

[8] CPR r 41.5 provides for a statement of whether periodical payments or a lump sum are appropriate in respect of future losses.

[9] https://www.gov.uk/government/uploads/system/uploads/attachment_data/file/245859/ogden_tables_7th_edition.pdf.

- interest on past loss (together with the calculation).

The schedule should finish with a final summary, setting out the totals of each head of loss claimed (including interest) leading to a grand total. This will assist both parties as well as the trial judge when assessing the appropriate award, as it provides a full breakdown of the claim at a glance. In most substantial cases approaching trial there will be a 'round table' (or 'joint settlement') meeting between the parties' lawyers. The schedule will be the key note document for that meeting. It is useful to have this in mind when looking critically at it during preparation.

The key to a successful schedule is presentation, incorporating a logical progression and a good structure. An easy to follow schedule will carry far more weight than one that needs to be pored over to assess properly the extent of loss claimed and will assist in achieving appropriate resolution of the claim. Although the assessment of damages has become more of a science than an art since the Administration of Justice Act 1969 led to the separate itemisation of the various heads of damage, drafting a good schedule is itself something of an art, and requires a certain amount of flexibility to best accommodate the particularities of each individual claim. Practitioners will, over time, find their own preferred style for drafting schedules, which comes with experience (often as a result of having to explain separate heads of damage in negotiations). Adopting a consistent approach to the fundamental aspects of schedules will enable the practitioner to concentrate on the complexities of the claim, rather than having to worry about the basics.

17.6.1   General damages

Traditionally, the schedule of loss only dealt with pecuniary loss but latterly it became more common to see the inclusion of general damages. In this way, both parties have a document which helpfully sets out the full extent of damages sought. It is perhaps the case that schedules in clinical negligence claims less frequently include an assessment of general damages than those for general PI claims. This may be because of the problems of quantification inherent in the assessment of pain, suffering and loss of amenity in a clinical negligence claim.

Initial detailed assessment of general damages is however advisable (where possible) because of the benefit which can be achieved from an early indication of the level of damages that are sought from the defendant. It is critical to ensure that the general damages are properly assessed. If the figure put forward is too low it may be accepted, and the chance to obtain an increase later if necessary will be lost. If it is too high, it may provoke the defendant to prepare detailed argument that a lower sum is appropriate and may adversely colour the judge's view of the claimant's entire damages claim.

17.6.2 Assessment of general damages

The starting point for assessment of damages for PSLA for all PI practitioners (and also the trial judge[10]) is the Judicial College Guidelines for the Assessment of General Damages in Personal Injury Cases, now in its twelfth edition (2013). The current edition reflects decisions of the higher courts on quantum but also helpfully includes an additional column of figures to show the recent 10% uplift in general damages recommended by Sir Rupert Jackson and endorsed by the Court of Appeal in *Simmons v Castle*[11] (see below).

It should be remembered though that the assessment of general damages was traditionally a jury function, representing a conventional figure reflecting social perception of the value of the injury.[12] In attempting to determine the appropriate conventional sum, the judge is effectively seeking to reflect what value society would place on the injury, not an award that the trial judge might consider appropriate.[13] From 1934 the right to trial by jury was a matter of discretion but from the 1960s this discretion was not readily exercised and a judicial tariff of awards (now the JC guidelines) evolved in an attempt to ensure consistency of awards.

For the clinical negligence practitioner, however, the JC guidelines are generally only a starting point in the assessment process because the claim will relate to *additional* injury caused by the treatment, not to the underlying injury itself, nor the ongoing disability caused by the initial injury.

It is therefore necessary to undertake a detailed review of case law relating to similar injuries, in an attempt to find a handful of cases with which to make as accurate an assessment as possible of an appropriate figure that reflects society's view of the value to be attached to the injury. In doing so, one needs to be aware that social perceptions change, and so (generally speaking) the older the case, the less relevant it is likely to be. It is not just a question of uplifting the award to a present day value (which of course is necessary) but a question of using cases that best reflect the current perception of the value of the injury. As a rule of thumb, the most recent awards will be the most relevant. In undertaking an assessment of general damages, clinical negligence practitioners should also refer to:

- Kemp & Kemp
- Lawtel
- Personal and Medical Injuries Law Letter
- Clinical Risk
- Current Law
- Butterworths' Personal Injury Law Service

---

[10] *Heil v Rankin* [2001] QB 272 at [99].
[11] [2012] EWCA Civ 1288.
[12] *Wells v Wells* [1999] 1 AC 345 at 394D-394F.
[13] *Heil v Rankin* at [55].

- The AVMA Medical and Legal Journal.

It is usual for the elements of pain, suffering and loss of amenity to be considered globally, and for the court to award one lump sum. In *Heil v Rankin*,[14] Lord Woolf commented:

> 'In determining what is the correct level of damages for PSLA, it is not usual for the Court to attribute different sums for different aspects of the injury. The Court's approach involves trying to find the global sum which most accurately in monetary terms reflects or can be regarded as reflecting a fair, reasonable and just figure for the injuries which have been inflicted and the consequences which they will have in PSLA. A sophisticated analytical approach distinguishing between pain and suffering and loss of amenity is not usually required.'

In that case the Court of Appeal found that the judicial tariff was too low. It increased the higher awards in the JC guidelines by one third, and then adopted a sliding scale increment to all other awards down to the sum of £10,000. There was considerable pressure on the court by both sides (APIL for claimants, and insurance companies and the NHSLA for defendants) and the decision of the Court of Appeal was seen to be something of a compromise.

More recently there was a further uplift of 10% across the board for general damages awards as a result of the Jackson Reforms, but not as a consequence of a concern that awards remained too low. Rather, this was introduced as a way of helping claimants in meeting the additional risks and costs arising from the introduction of changes to funding through the reforms. The Legal Aid, Sentencing and Punishment of Offenders ('LASPO') Act 2012, which came into force at the beginning of April 2013, encapsulated some of the key reforms recommended by the Jackson Report. Interestingly, though, the 10% increase in general damages did not appear on the face of this Bill as the government took the view that this was an issue for the judiciary.

The issue was confirmed by the Court of Appeal in *Simmons v Castle*.[15] The original judgment was widely criticised for creating uncertainty and was subsequently revised by the court to confirm that the 10% increase applies to general damages in all civil claims where judgment is given after 1 April 2013 and where the claimant has not entered into a CFA/CCFA before that date.

Arguably though, the tariff remains too low. Claimant lawyers often find themselves at a loss when having to explain to their clients why they will only recover what is perceived to be a nominal sum for their injuries. In comparison with other jurisdictions such as Northern Ireland, awards in England and Wales are particularly low. For example, awards for severe brain injury in Northern Ireland are between £300,000 and £550,000.[16] The highest suggested bracket of award in England and Wales is currently £227,975 to £326,700, including

---

[14]   [2001] QB 272.
[15]   [2012] EWCA Civ 1039.
[16]   *Guidelines for the Assessment of General Damages in Personal Injury Cases in Northern Ireland* (4th edn, 2013).

the 10% uplift (according to the JC guidelines). Unfortunately, it seems unlikely that there will be any further significant adjustment for some time. In *Heil v Rankin* the Court of Appeal stated that the exercise,

> '... is not one which should be embarked upon again unless there is real reason to think that once more the level of awards is significantly out of line with the standards which we have identified.'[17]

17.6.3 Interest on general damages

The calculation of interest on general damages involves calculating the period over which interest is payable and applying an interest rate of 2% per annum.

Interest on general damages runs from the date of service of the claim form until the notional trial date. For example, if there is a period of three years between service of the claim form and the trial, the interest rate to apply is 6%. For three and a half years, the interest rate will be 7%. Interest should be calculated to the nearest week.

17.6.4 Past economic losses

No list can ever be exhaustive but will include all of the economic losses caused by and flowing foreseeably from the injury caused by the defendant's negligence. This will include:

* lost earnings;
* the cost of care that has had to be purchased;
* the cost of gratuitous care provided to the claimant by members of his/her family;
* travel expenses;
* equipment purchased.

Each case will have particular losses attaching to it under this heading.

17.6.5 Interest on past loss

A claimant is entitled to claim interest on his damages pursuant to s 35A of the Senior Courts Act 1981 and s 69 of the County Courts Act 1984. Under CPR r 16.4(1)(b), if the claimant is seeking interest, the particulars of claim must include a statement to that effect.

In theory, the claimant is entitled to claim interest on each item of past loss from the date of loss. However, the practice approved by the Court of Appeal in *Jefford v Gee*[18] was to calculate interest on past financial losses from the date of the cause of action to the date of trial at half the normal interest rate. It is

---

[17] At [99].
[18] [1970] 2 QB 130.

usual for losses to accrue incrementally from the date of the negligent treatment and rather than calculate each item of loss separately, the Court of Appeal suggested that an appropriate approach is to award interest on special damages at half the special account rate.

However, this approach may not be appropriate in every case. For example, if all losses were incurred at or close to the time of injury it would be unfair to deprive the claimant of full interest from the date of loss.[19] In such cases practitioners ought to consider claiming the full rate, either from the date of the loss, or where there is a finite period of loss, half way through the period of that loss.[20] The generally adopted (and simplest) approach is to claim half rate on continuing losses, and full rate on losses which have ceased.

The special account rate is set by the Court Funds Office following a direction from the Lord Chancellor and fluctuates from time to time following advice from the Bank of England. Between 1 February 2002 and 1 February 2009 the rate was set at 6% but was reduced to 3% a year on 1 February 2009, to 1.5% on 1 June 2009, and to 0.5% on 1 July 2009 where it has remained ever since. The rate has previously been much higher than this reaching a high of 14.25% in 1989.

Because the rate of interest to apply fluctuates over time, the calculation of interest on any head of loss is complex. Practitioners should refer to tables setting out the rates over the various periods of the loss. Guidance and relevant interest rates are published annually in the *Law Society Gazette*.[21] This is a straightforward and user-friendly guide. Various websites also now provide interest calculators.[22]

17.6.6 Future loss (multipliers and multiplicands)

'Future losses' mean those losses that can be anticipated in the future because of the injury a claimant has sustained. For example a child injured at birth who has both physical and intellectual disability may not be able to achieve any independence in life as an adult without care support; it may be predictable that that child will never be able to earn his or her own living. Claims into the future for lost earnings for pension losses and for the cost of care support are therefore capable of being made.

In 'forecasting' those losses lawyers used the multiplier/multiplicand method of calculation described in *Hodgson v Trapp*,[23] by Lord Oliver:

> 'Essentially what the court has to do is to calculate as best it can the sum of money which will on the one hand be adequate, by its capital and income, to provide

---

[19] See *Prokop v Department of Health and Social Security* [1985] CLY 1037, CA.

[20] *Dexter v Courtaulds Ltd* [1984] 1 All ER 70, [1984] 1 WLR 372.

[21] Prepared by Andrew Morgan, Partner at Field Fisher Waterhouse.

[22] For example Lawtel.co.uk.

[23] [1989] AC 807.

annually for the injured person a sum equal to his estimated annual loss over the whole of the period during which that loss is likely to continue, but which, on the other hand, will not, at the end of that period, leave him in a better financial position than he would have been apart from the accident. Hence the conventional approach is to assess the amount notionally acquired to be laid out in the purchase of an annuity which will provide the annual amount needed for the whole period of loss.'

Earlier, in *Cookson v Knowles*,[24] Lord Diplock said:

'When the first Fatal Accidents Act was passed in 1846, its purpose was to put the dependants of the deceased, who had been the bread-winner of the family, in the same position financially as if he had lived his natural span of life. In times of steady money values, wages levels and interest rates this could be achieved in the case of the ordinary working man by awarding to his dependants the capital sum required to purchase an annuity of an amount equal to the annual value of benefits with which he had provided them while he lived, and for such period as it could reasonably be estimated they would have continued to enjoy them but for his premature death. Although this does not represent the way in which it is calculated such a capital sum may be expressed as the product of multiplying an annual sum which represents the 'dependency' by a number of years' purchase. This latter figure is less than the number of years which represents the period for which it is estimated that the dependants would have continued to enjoy the benefit of the dependency, since the capital sum will not be exhausted until the end of that period and in the meantime so much of it as is not yet exhausted in each year will earn interest from which the dependency for that year could in part be met. The number of years' purchase to be used in order to calculate the capital value of an annuity for a given period of years thus depends upon the rate of interest which it is assumed that money would earn, during the period. The higher the rate of interest, the lower the number of years' purchase ... '

Lord Diplock went on to say:

'The conventional method of calculating [future loss] has been to apply to what is found upon the evidence to be a sum representing 'the dependency', a multiplier representing what the judge considers in the circumstances particular to the deceased to be the appropriate number of years' purchase.'

In his judgment in *Hodgson v Trapp* Lord Oliver referred to this speech of Lord Diplock, pointing out that the 'dependency' referred to is the multiplicand, and the 'number of years' purchase' is the multiplier. Laws LJ, in *Cooke v United Bristol Healthcare*,[25] commented:

'As will be apparent, it is implicit in this reasoning that the two contingencies to which I have earlier referred, that is the effect of accelerated payment and the effect of inflation, are both accommodated by treating the multiplier not simply as a number representing the claimant's life expectancy, but rather as a number which (when applied to the multiplicand) will represent the cost of buying an appropriate annuity to meet the relevant future loss over the predicted period. Thus the

---

[24] [1979] AC 556.
[25] [2003] EWCA Civ 1370, [2004] 1 All ER 797 at paras 11 and 12.

multiplicand remains the figure proved as representing the loss at current prices at the date of trial. Inflation and acceleration are built into the multiplier, and the mechanism for doing that requires that a rate of interest be arrived at as the notional return to be earned on the lump sum over the period in question. This rate of interest is what is known as "the discount rate" .... The fact that the multiplicand remains fixed at current prices is confirmed in Lord Diplock's statement in *Cookson* ... that "[f]or the purpose of calculating the future loss, the 'dependency' used as the multiplicand should be the figure to which it is estimated the annual dependency would have amounted by the date of trial." ...

[A]n appropriate discount rate will depend upon prevailing economic conditions, and so is likely to shift from time to time ... if a *single* discount rate is set for all cases, whether by the courts or by statue ... the full compensation principle will only be achieved in a rough and ready way since actual rates of inflation will differ between different sectors. Thus wages are prone to rise at a faster rate in some sectors than others; and prices likewise.'

The **multiplicand** is simply the future annual loss to the claimant, of each separate head of damage claimed. For example, if at the time of trial the claimant is not working, but prior to the alleged negligence was earning £10,000 net per annum (and it is alleged that his inability to work is solely due to the alleged negligence), the multiplicand for loss of earnings will be £10,000. This figure will remain fixed in most cases, though if for example it can be shown that the claimant would have secured a promotion with significant (predictable) increase in earnings in the future, it may be appropriate to apply different multiplicands to different periods.

The **multiplier** is the figure used to multiply the multiplicand to arrive at an appropriate lump sum for the future years of loss which are claimed. Assessment of future loss must take into account the factors of inflation and the ability to invest a large lump sum. These factors affect the calculation of the multiplier. In *Cooke v United Bristol Health Care*,[26] Laws LJ commented:

'Inflation and acceleration are built into the multiplier, and the mechanism for doing that requires that a rate of interest be arrived at as the notional return to be earned on the lump sum over the period in question. This rate of interest is what is known as the discount rate.'

Traditionally, the courts used a discount rate of 4.5%. Actuarial evidence clearly showed that this was inappropriate but the courts rejected attempts to use such evidence as the basis for calculation of lump sum awards.

In the landmark cases of *Wells v Wells, Thomas v Brighton Health Authority and Page v Sheerness*,[27] it was held that the multiplier should be based on the assumption that the claimant would invest in Index Linked Government Securities (ILGS) with a 3% discount rate. The main policy consideration behind this decision was that investment in ILGS was the most appropriate for

---

[26]   [2003] EWCA Civ 1370, [2004] 1 All ER 797.
[27]   [1999] 1 AC 345.

the claimant in a personal injury case, because it was much more secure than more speculative investment in equities. Although there may be fluctuations in the short term, the long-term return is inflation proof and can be relied upon. However, following *Wells v Wells* the average rate of return has consistently fallen so that the average current rate is nearer 2%.

This prompted claimants to argue that the discount rate should be reduced accordingly. In *Warren v Northern General Hospital NHS Trust (No 2)*[28] the Court of Appeal held that the fall in the rate of return was not such a serious change in economic circumstances that it should disturb the 3% discount rate. It was stated that the applicable rate would stay at 3% until the Lord Chancellor exercised his power under the Damages Act 1996 to change this. That power has since been exercised, and the discount rate is now set at 2.5%.

Sir Michael Ogden chaired a working party which set out actuarial tables for the assessment of future loss. These were first produced in 1984, to 'help in the calculation of future pecuniary losses'. In *Wells v Wells* Lord Lloyd commented: 'The tables should now be regarded as the starting point, rather than a check ... A Judge should be slow to depart from the relevant actuarial multiplier ...'.

The 'Ogden tables'[29] are now in their seventh edition and provide the basis for calculation of future loss for all heads of damage. This most recent edition of the tables was published in October 2011. The changes to the explanatory notes in this edition are minor but the figures have been updated. It was felt that as it was over four years since the last edition a new set of Tables based on the most recent mortality rates produced by the Office for National Statistics (ONS) was required. The result is an increase in life expectancies for males and females and therefore an increase in multipliers. The range of discounts has also been changed to include negative discounts but is unlikely to be useful at present as there has been no change in the discount rate set by the Lord Chancellor (though see below).

The Ogden tables can at times be complex even for the experienced practitioner, and as such care should be taken in using them. It is vital to ensure that the correct multiplier is used in relation to each head of loss, because it may have a huge impact on the final sum claimed. Even a unit difference can relate to tens of thousands of pounds on a large claim.

In 2010 the former Lord Chancellor announced a review of the discount rate after APIL threatened a judicial review on the basis that the 2.5% rate had not changed since 2001. They argued that this meant claimants had been under-compensated since that time as average yields had been lower. In 2012 the Ministry of Justice launched a consultation on setting the personal injury

---

[28] [2000] PIQR Q284.
[29] https://www.gov.uk/government/uploads/system/uploads/attachment_data/file/245859/ogden_tables_7th_edition.pdf.

discount rate looking at two scenarios of whether claimants should be deemed to use minimal risk index-linked government stocks or a mixed investment portfolio.

The consultation paper was published in the summer of 2012 and suggested that using index-linked gilts as the basis for calculating the discount rate applied to personal injury awards could be dropped in favour of a 'mixed portfolio of appropriate investments'. The MoJ stated that they were not consulting on whether to depart from the principles laid down by the House of Lords in *Wells v Wells* in 1998 and moving away from gilts could be 'potentially consistent' with those principles.

In February 2013 the Ministry of Justice launched a second consultation on the discount rate, making it clear that it is considering a change in the law. It said:

> 'This paper is not concerned with the issues addressed in the UK-wide consultation paper on how the discount rate should be set issued by the Ministry of Justice, the Scottish Government and the Department of Justice on 1 August 2012. The August consultation paper and the review of which it forms part is solely concerned with how the discount rate should be set under the present law. The present consultation addresses the question of whether the law should be changed. The two exercises are entirely separate.'

It was also stated that the review would look at whether the legal parameters determining how the discount rate is calculated would produce a rate that is as 'right' as it ought reasonably to be so that the person injured is fully compensated but not over-compensated or under-compensated.

> 'The options are to retain the present law or to change the law so that the rate can be set by reference to higher risk investments, which would produce a higher discount rate and would be expected to produce lower lump sum awards than under the present law.'

The Ministry of Justice also said that any problems with the discount rate could be avoided with the use of periodical payments for future pecuniary loss.

There are wide ranging views on what might come out of this latest review, as to whether the discount rate will change at all, or even that it might actually be reduced from the current 2.5%.

17.6.7 Changes to the 'lump sum' principle, leading to periodical payments

Until 1 April 2005, the principle of full compensation was achieved by empowering the courts to award a lump sum, which once awarded was final. It could not be reopened and the claimant could spend it as he or she chose. This enabled finality and a sense of closure for both parties, but it was seen to be flawed, particularly in terms of the risk of over or under compensating due to the uncertainty of life expectancy.

Parliament has sought to review the lump sum principle in two ways: first by providing for the possibility of provisional damages and latterly by providing for periodical payments in the place of lump sums.

Provisional damages can be awarded where there is a risk of deterioration in the future but which was unpredictable. This allowed the claimant to seek further damages after judgement, if appropriate.

The court may award provisional damages under CPR, r 41.2 where such a claim has been pleaded and the court is satisfied that the conditions of s 32A of the Senior Courts Act 1981 or s 51 of the County Courts Act 1984 have been met:

- There must be proved or admitted a chance (ie a possibility but no more than a possibility) that the claimant will develop some serious disease or suffer some serious deterioration to his physical or mental condition. The chance must be more than fanciful.[30] If the chance is certain or highly probable then the power does not arise.

- It must be proved or admitted that the disease or the deterioration in question that may occur in the future is serious.

- The chance must arise from the act or omission that founds the claim. If it arises from an underlying constitutional condition then there is no claim for provisional damages.

Although provisional damages was the first stage in remedying the shortcomings in the 'lump sum' approach, evolution to the present option of periodical payments has taken time. Taking the concept of the lump sum payment further, Parliament subsequently supported 'structured settlements', the payment of damages over a period of time (usually for the life of the claimant) under the terms of an annuity purchased by the defendant. This enabled the parties together but neither the claimant nor the judge alone to arrange periodical payment of a lump sum without the agreement of the defendant.

This approach led to continuing concern over the appropriateness of final lump sum awards, which led to the judges requiring that in every case involving patients or children, no claim could be settled without the parties demonstrating that they had at least considered whether or not to enter a structured settlement. However, structured settlements could only be achieved by agreement between the parties, and were restricted by the limited availability of commercial annuity products. In practice, structured settlements operated by the purchase of an annuity out of part of the lump sum calculated on conventional principles with a part of that lump sum being retained as a contingency fund.

---

[30] *Wilson v Ministry of Defence* [1991] 1 All ER 638.

In *Wells v Wells*[31] Lord Steyn criticised the lump sum method of compensation in cases of serious injuries where claimants were left with long-term impairment. He felt that in such cases, trial judges simply had to resort to guesswork as to the claimant's future. He proposed that the court should be given power to make an award of periodical payments rather than lump sums where appropriate.

Parliament amended the Damages Act 1996 by enacting provisions in the Courts Act 2003 that enable the court to order payment of future loss by instalments paid regularly over a specified period (usually the lifetime of the claimant). These provisions came into force on 1 April 2005.

There are a number of advantages of periodical payments over a traditional lump sum award:

- They avoid uncertainty over predictions of life expectancy, and ensure compensation for as long as it is needed. Lump sums have a risk of over or under compensating.
- They can help to avoid costly argument over life expectancy.
- They allow greater security for the claimant, and avoid the anxiety of compensation running out if they live longer than expected.
- They avoid the necessity of investment (and thus the need for investment advice), and anxiety over performance of investments.

In calculating the appropriate amount of periodical payment, the heads of loss are used to determine the claimant's annual need, which is then increased in accordance with an appropriate index, on a year by year basis.

Periodical payments may appear similar to the older structured settlements but they are fundamentally different. Structured settlements represent an annuity, purchased by a lump sum payment, because they can be provided only by agreement, and because they depend on there being a market from which annuities for such cases can be readily purchased. Periodical payment orders do not depend on the consent of the parties, and do not require the calculation of a lump sum and its conversion to an annuity. They are designed to cope with annual needs as and when they arise and do not require the purchase of an annuity.

CPR, r 41.5 enables the parties to state in their statements of case whether they regard periodical payments or a lump sum as likely to be more appropriate for all or part of an award for future loss. If it is felt that such indication should be given, brief reasons should be provided before the court requires these. CPR, r 41.6 requires the court to consider and to indicate to the parties as soon as practicable whether periodical payments or a lump sum is likely to be the more appropriate form for all or part of an award of damages. This could well be raised at the first case management conference.

---

[31] [1999] 1 AC 345.

For these reasons, all practitioners must have a working knowledge of the relevant provisions, and be able to form a view on each case as to whether it is appropriate to claim periodical payments, or whether a lump sum award is more appropriate.

17.6.8 Aggravated and exemplary damages

The 'full compensation' principle intends to compensate the claimant rather than necessarily punish the defendant, but there are exceptions where the claimant may be entitled to additional damages in order to punish the defendant.

The court may award aggravated damages where there are aggravating features about a defendant's conduct or motive, which cause the claimant to suffer mental distress such as indignity, disgrace, anger and humiliation. The justification for awarding aggravated damages arises out of exceptional elements in the circumstances at the time the injury was sustained causing the claimant mental distress.

In its report 'Aggravated, Exemplary and Restitutionary Damages'[32] the Law Commission considered that in order to establish a claim for aggravated damages it is necessary to prove (a) exceptional or contumelious conduct or motive on the part of the defendant in committing the wrong, and (b) injury to personality or feelings. These pre-conditions were accepted as correctly stating the law by Dyson J in *Appleton v Garrett*[33] (in which it was held that gross over-treatment by a dental surgeon should lead to an award for aggravated damages).

The purpose of exemplary damages is to punish and deter exceptionally bad conduct, if basic and aggravated damages are inadequate. In *Rookes v Barnard*[34] Lord Devlin identified two categories of case in which an award of exemplary damages might arise:

* Firstly, the restraint of oppressive, arbitrary or unconstitutional action by the servants of the government, as 'servants of the government are also servants of the people and the use of power must always be subordinate to their duty of service'.

* Secondly, where the defendant's conduct is calculated to make a profit, which may extend beyond the compensation payable to the claimant and it is necessary to teach wrongdoers that tort does not pay.

Lord Devlin also ruled that a claimant cannot recover exemplary damages unless he is a victim of the punishable behaviour. He also cautioned against excessive awards and implied that awards should be moderate. He also stated

---

[32] Law Commission: Consultation Paper No 132 (1997).
[33] [1996] PIQR P1.
[34] [1993] QB 507, CA.

that the means of the parties should be material in the assessment of damages and that factors aggravating or mitigating the defendant's conduct are also relevant.

Awards of exemplary damages in clinical negligence claims are vanishingly rare but examples of clinical failures that reflect exceptionally bad conduct are perhaps not quite so rare.

TOP TIPS

- Particularly where an element of ongoing injury is not related to the alleged negligence the schedule of loss put forward should be accurate, credible and capable of being relied on at trial.
- Accurate quantification is crucial in order to be able to readily assess cost–benefit ratios and to keep a continuing eye on proportionality.
- Be careful not to claim for items where there is no supporting evidence.
- Include every relevant element, rather than leave items out. If uncertainty arises from lack of evidence it is far better to clarify the position before finalising the schedule rather than to add in an additional head of loss at a later stage.
- Claims for private treatment should be made cautiously and should not be made simply as a matter of course.
- An easy-to-follow schedule will carry far more weight than one that needs to be pored over to assess properly the extent of loss claimed.
- It is vital to ensure that the correct multiplier is used in relation to each head of loss, because it may have a huge impact on the final sum claimed.
- It is essential to state whether periodical payments are claimed and, if not, that they have been considered.

CHAPTER 18

SCHEDULES OF LOSS

Schedules of loss in clinical negligence cases follow the same principles as other types of personal injury action, and generic rules apply across the spectrum of PI claims. There are, however, differences and complexities with clinical negligence cases that require more of a bespoke approach to drafting schedules, and skills that are honed with experience. In this chapter solicitors Tom Mather, Mandy Luckman and Ian Christian review the compilation of schedules of loss.

18.1 PREPARING A SCHEDULE OF LOSS

The claimant will tell you how the injury he has endured has affected them and how that has changed the way he lives his life and he works/or faces up to his newly recognised inability to work.

The practitioner's job is to translate this narrative into a series of straightforward assertions of calculable loss which 'value' aspects of the claim for damages. Those differences that are literally 'incalculable' will fall under general damages: those to which 'valuation' can be applied will be either past or future economic losses.

The purpose of the schedule is to identify the full extent of the claimant's losses that he would not have incurred but for the negligence of the defendant. All of the losses should be supported by evidence. In the body of this chapter are worked examples which demonstrate how these issues can/should be presented.

18.1.1 Claimants witness evidence

The starting point is the claimant's witness statement. It is useful to ask the claimant to provide 'a day in the life of' account. The statement should include everything the claimant experiences, from the time he gets up in the morning until he goes to bed in the evening. Highlight all of the difficulties that the claimant faces as a result of the injury caused by the alleged negligence. Ensure that every loss claimed in the schedule is detailed in this quantum statement. If necessary then obtain statements from additional witnesses to assist the claimant. Receipts will assist if copies are available.

Quantum statements are witness statements and have to comply with CPR 32.8 and the Practice Direction to Part 32.

Keep the schedule concise and accurate. Avoid heads of loss marked 'to be assessed' wherever possible and do not include losses that are unsustainable. This is a particularly risky approach in view of issue-based costs orders. Always take your client's instructions and ensure that they sign the statement of truth before it is served. This will ensure that the claimant has given appropriate consideration to the document prepared on his behalf to ascertain its accuracy. Should the statement of truth not be signed the document is defective and is open to challenge by the other side under to CPR Pt 22.[1]

18.1.2 Types of schedule

There are two types of schedule:

- A basic or outline schedule may be prepared before or on issue of proceedings. Its purpose will be to outline the anticipated heads of loss giving as much detail as possible although it may not be possible to quantify everything fully if further information is awaited.

- A detailed or final schedule will be drafted following receipt of all medical evidence dealing with condition and prognosis and quantum valuation reports from expert witnesses. This is the schedule to be relied on at trial and in any negotiations that take place.

18.1.3 Content of a detailed schedule of loss

As well as providing an opportunity for setting out the claimant's assessment of his claim for on general damages the schedule will as we have seen deal with both past and future losses.

18.1.3.1 Past loss of income

This will be the loss of salary (net of tax, national insurance and pension contributions) for the period that the claimant has been off work. In order to assess this loss it is usual practice to request 13 weeks pre-injury wage slips to establish an average weekly wage. Alternatively a P60 can be requested. At the same time as requesting the pay slips confirmation should be obtained from the claimant's employer as to whether there have been any salary increases as these will need to be incorporated into the calculation.

If the claimant was self-employed it will be necessary to review his business statement of accounts and/or his tax assessments. If the documents are particularly complicated and the scale of losses justify it, then a forensic accountant may have to be instructed.

Claimants who were in receipt of benefits prior to an injury may have lost some of their benefit entitlement, if they can show that they would have obtained

---

[1] '22.2 (1) If a party fails to verify his statement of case by a statement of truth, the statement of case shall remain effective unless struck out; but the party may not rely on the statement of case as evidence of any of the matters set out in it.'

work but were unable to do so because of their injury. If this is the position then the lost non-recoupable benefits for the period in question should be claimed.

Worked example: lost earnings to trial

At the time of the negligence the claimant was employed by 'X' company. Because of his illness he had to give up work on the 31 May 2005. He has not worked since.

At the time of the accident the claimant's earnings were:

£280 gross per week basic pay for 50 hour working week

£7.74 gross per hour for overtime, he worked on average 12½ hours per week

£14 gross night shift payment which he received twice per week

This resulted in gross weekly earnings of £404.75

This figure is increased in line with average earnings inflation at the start of each new tax year as follows:

3.4.06 = 4.10%

2.4.07 = 4.08%

The net loss of earnings is therefore calculated as follows:

From	To	Net pay	Weeks	Days		Net loss
1.6.05	2.4.06	£307.16	43	3		£13,392.18
3.4.06	1.4.07	£319.12	52	0		£16,594.24
2.4.07	30.3.08	£334.77	52	0		£17,408.04
					Total	£47,094.46

18.1.3.2 Past expenses

The claimant should list all expenses incurred as a result of the injury caused by the defendant's alleged negligence. Any receipts that can be used to support this section will demonstrate the claimant's loss. Should receipts not be available then the details should be included in the claimant's quantum witness statement. Items such as travelling costs, prescription charges or aids and equipment purchased should all be detailed in this section.

18.1.3.3　Gratuitous care

A claim may be put forward for any care or assistance provided to the claimant by family or friends who have not charged for their services in accordance with the principle in *Daly v General Steam Navigation Co.*[2] The value of the services provided may be claimed irrespective of whether the third party has been put to actual expense in rendering those services.

Although the claimant claims the value of the services, any damages awarded to him in respect of this are held in trust for the person who provided the services.

Where no actual fee is incurred by the claimant because the care and assistance was provided on a gratuitous basis, the valuation is more problematic than where professional services were provided. This matter was dealt with in the case of *Housecroft v Burnett*[3] where two possible extreme scenarios were identified: either make an award at the full commercial rate, or assess the cost as nil. It was decided that each case should be looked at on its own merits.

This head of loss is also discounted to reflect the fact that the care provided was on a gratuitous basis and that a professional care rate will include an element of tax and national insurance paid to a professional carer. This discount is conventionally 25%. The pre-discounted rates to be applied may be taken from the British Nursing Associations rates or the Crossroads Charity.

18.1.3.4　Aids and equipment

Any claim for the cost of equipment or aids that the claimant requires as a consequence of his injury needs to be detailed. The cost of the items must be established by reference to a care/occupational therapist expert if necessary. The replacement cost of such equipment also needs to be taken into account. This should be calculated by reference to the replacement period multipliers in the PNBA Facts and Figures at Table A3 assuming a discount rate of 2.5%.

18.1.3.5　Holidays

A Claimant is entitled to recover general damages for the loss of enjoyment of a holiday that he was unable to take as a result of the injury. This should be set out in the narrative. Alternatively he may claim for any additional expenses incurred while on holiday as a result of the injury. This claim should be set out in the schedule.

18.1.3.6　Interest on past losses

The claimant is entitled to recover interest on past economic losses. The mechanism of recovery is explained at para **18.1.3.1** above.

---

[2]　[1980] 3 All ER 696.
[3]　[1986] 1 All ER 332.

18.1.3.7 Future loss of income

It will be necessary to prepare a forecast of the extent of the loss into the future whilst taking into account the claimant's ability to work (if any) in the future. Any future loss is to be claimed net of tax and national insurance contributions.

There are three ways to put forward future loss: total loss, partial loss or defined period loss. A claimant who is wholly unable to work or accept any form of paid employment in the future as a consequence of the injury may claim the loss of his remaining earning capacity to the date of his retirement – this is a claim for a total future loss.

Alternatively there may be arguments that the claimant is in a position to accept other forms of employment albeit with a shortfall in salary. The shortfall should then be claimed and this is known as a partial loss of future earnings. Finally the clamant may be in a position to retrain and thereafter find alternative employment without a reduced salary; this will be a loss for a defined period of time.

18.1.3.8 Smith v Manchester Corporation

The claimant may find himself in a position in which because of his disability it will be more time consuming to find employment in the future and it may not be as well paid. Essentially the claimant now faces a handicap on the open labour market. Should this prove to be the case a remedy may be sought by making a *Smith v Manchester* claim. There are a variety of approaches to this award but all of which are related to the claimant's net annual income.

The sixth edition of the Ogden tables proposes a new system whereby the earnings lost as a consequence of the negligence are calculated using the normal future loss multiplier and the residual earnings are now calculated using a disabled person's multiplier that in fact is significantly lower. Should the courts accept this new approach then *Smith v Manchester* awards will be significantly lower.

18.1.3.9 Future care cost valued commercially

Many claimants will use a care expert in order to value this head of loss which in can be the single most important element of the future loss claim. Such claims will be based on the recommended number of hours of care required and this will be multiplied by the hourly rate using the multiplier derived from the Ogden Tables. Both the number of hours and hourly rate are generally an issue of contention for the parties. It is for this reason that as much information as possible should be set out in the schedule to justify the claim being made.

An example of a claim for future care is demonstrated below:

Future Care Requirements

Reference: Report of 'X' Occupational Therapist dated 'X'

Type of Assistance	Annual Cost	Multiplier	Total
From date of accident to 19/1/08, a period of 141 days			
8 hours per week at a rate of £8.55 per hour	£3,566.05		£1,377.57
From 20/1/08 until claimant leaves home aged 25			
assumed date 20/9/09			
5 hours per week at a rate of £8.55 per hour			
(Table 28 6th edition of Ogden Tables, period of 1.67			
Years = 1.63 × multiplier factor of 0.98)	£2,230.15	1.6	£3,568.24
Care once left family home 21/9/09 until date of			
Revision hip replacement 20/9/2024			
6 hours per week at a rate of £8.55 per hour			
(Table 28 6th edition of Ogden Tables, period of 17.05 × multiplier factor of 0.98)	£2,675.45	12.03	£32,185.66
Total			£37,131.47

18.1.3.10 Pension loss

If a claimant retires early because of ill health he is likely to receive a reduced pension because he and his employer will no longer be contributing towards his pension scheme.

Employees in such a position often take the pension early as a lump sum (rather than receiving it as a periodical payment) and use that lump sum to derive an annual income that mitigates their pension loss. This reduction must be taken into account by claiming payment of a lump sum to compensate for the reduced pension received. In calculating this lump sum, which may well be received far earlier than it would otherwise have been, account will be taken of the comparable pension that can be purchased with the lump sum now being made available compared with the overall pension that would have been achieved had the claimant been able to work longer and contribute more to the scheme.

In order to calculate this reduction a copy of the pension scheme should be requested from the employer to calculate the pension entitlement. The claimant's date of birth and estimated date of trial are needed together with confirmation of the value of ill-health pension at trial. In addition it will be necessary to obtain confirmation of the earnings that the claimant would have received at the date of trial had he continued to work and the age that he had intended to retire. The amount by which the pension was commuted and the amount of the lump sum actually received need to be noted.

No discussion on pension loss would be complete without mentioning the case of *Auty v National Coal Board*.[4] With the recognition of the Ogden tables by the judiciary this case is perhaps more of historical interest than practical value but it does still represent good (if superseded) law.

The case of *Auty* technically applies to defined benefit pension schemes, where the pension is calculated as a percentage of the last year of service, multiplied by the total amount of years in service. In *Auty*, the pension scheme attempted to protect pensions against inflation by index-linking pensions, but there was no guaranteed fund and so payment was dependent on the funds being made available by the government, and also dependent on the effect of inflation. The Court of Appeal assessed damages net of tax, and took no direct account of inflation. It was held that the general rule that inflation should not affect the assessment of compensation for loss in personal injury cases applied to the assessment of compensation for a lost future capital payment such as a pension right. Further, actuarial evidence was not a reliable guide to future inflation or as to whether a future government would provide the coal board with funds to meet index-linked increases. The Court of Appeal adopted a discount rate of 4.5% rather than the present 2.5%, and a discount for contingencies of 27% (which has received much criticism for being too high). Following judicial acceptance of the Ogden tables for calculation of such losses, a detailed knowledge of the principles set out in *Auty* is not required. Adopting the appropriate multiplier from the correct table will enable a calculation that will be accepted by the courts.

Worked example: future pension loss

As a result of the negligence the claimant will be unable to contribute towards his pension fund nor will he have the advantage of his employers contributing to his pension fund. It has been possible to obtain a projection of his actual pension, projected annual pension and lump sum. The damages calculated below will reimburse him so that he can invest these damages in an alternative pension scheme so that the shortfall in income can be made up.

---

[4]   [1985] 1 WLR 784.

Stage 1 to age 40

Claimant's annual pension contributions	
(£40,000 × 3%)	£1,200.00
Employer's annual contributions	
(£40,000 × 3%)	£1,200.00
Employer's additional annual contributions	
(£40,000 × 20%)	£8,000.00
	£10,400.00
Ogden Table 28 multiplier for 6.47 years 5.97	
Total = £10,400.00 × 5.97	£62,088.00

Stage 2 from 40 to age 66

Claimant's annual pension contributions	
(£48,000 × 3%)	£1,440.00
Employer's annual contributions	
(£48,000 × 3%)	£1,440.00
Employer's additional annual contributions	
(£48,000 × 20%)	£9,600.00
Multiplier (21.94 − 5.97) 15.97	
Total = £12,480.00 × 15.97	£199,305.60
Total	**£261,393.60**

18.1.3.11   Accommodation

A seriously injured claimant may require alternative or an adapted property properly to accommodate the extent of his disability. For example, a client in a wheelchair will probably want single storey accommodation with ramps and doors wide enough to allow easy wheelchair access. The claimant's existing property may be suitable if adapted. Alternatively an entirely different property may need to be purchased.

The claimant may claim the increased costs of purchasing the new property net of any existing equity. The most pragmatic formula is that set out in *Roberts v*

Johnstone.[5] The capital costs of buying the property and the mortgage payments on the new property are not recoverable. The claimant will be expected to purchase the property out of his existing capital and consequently will lose the income that the capital would have earned over the period of the award. Damages are therefore assessed by taking a percentage of the net additional capital cost of the accommodation and multiplying it by the appropriate multiplier.

The claimant is also entitled to claim the costs of adapting his existing property. Should the adaptations reduce the value of the property then this is recoverable. Likewise should this increase the value of the property then appropriate credit must be given.

The claimant is also entitled to claim any increased running costs associated with the property.

Worked example: future accommodation costs

Reference: report of 'X' dated 'X'

Head of Claim	Cost	Multiplier	Total
1. *Loss of use of capital from age 21*			
Purchase price of suitable property	289,950.00		
Less:			
Uninjured equity			
Plus:			
Benefit via works	7,000.00		
			296,950.00
Applying *Roberts v Johnstone*			
= £296,950 × 2.5% per annum	7,423.75	23.52	174,606.60
2. *Losses in adaptation – parent's property:*			
Convert garage into bedroom	17,166.97		
Add a dogleg stair lift	9,594.79		

---

[5]   [1989] QB 878.

Head of Claim	Cost	Multiplier	Total
Ground floor WC, shower	32,586.89		59,348.65
Increased heating costs	105.77	33.91	3,586.66

3. Losses in adaptation from age 21

Alteration costs	117,919.53		
Relocation costs	12,200.00		
Less:			
Benefits via works	7,000.00		
	123,119.53 discounted for 12 years early receipt @ 0.7436		91,551.68

4. Increased running costs

Additional running costs	639.03	23.52	15,029.99
Additional Maintenance costs	1,037.85	23.52	24,410.23
Additional building insurance	108.18	23.52	2,544.39
Additional contents insurance	84.50	23.52	1,987.44
Additional council tax	364.42	23.52	8,571.16
Total			**£381,636.80**

18.1.4 Fatal claims

The law relating to fatal claims highlights unresolved issues in relation to calculations of lost dependency. There is consequently uncertainty and the issues are detailed enough to justify a chapter in its own right. This is therefore intended to be only a concise, straightforward approach to dealing with fatal claims.

The Law Reform (Miscellaneous Provisions) Act 1934 (LRMPA) and Fatal Accidents Act 1976 (as amended) (FAA) constitute the material legislation to consider when acting in a fatal case.

The LRMPA allows the claimant to recover a number of heads of damage including: pain and suffering, past loss of earnings, past care/services and miscellaneous costs including funeral expenses if this has been incurred by the deceased. This claim is made on behalf of the deceased's estate.

The FAA provides the mechanism for the claim brought by any dependants of the deceased in respect of their own loss. A dependant will usually claim: bereavement damages, loss of dependency and funeral expenses. Damages for a dependant will be based on the proportion of the deceased's earnings that was expended on the dependant.

The claim must be made in the name of the executor or administrator of the estate within six months of the death. If there is no named personal representative or the period of six months has elapsed, then the claim can only be made by a dependant.

The statutory bereavement award was increased from £10,000 to £11,800[6] for deaths occurring after 1 January 2008 and then increased to £12,980 for deaths occurring after 1 April 2013. This award may only be claimed by a spouse, civil partner or the parents of an unmarried minor.

A dependant can be any of the following to the extent they had an economic dependency upon the deceased:

- a wife or husband or former wife or husband;
- a person living with the deceased as husband or wife for a period of two years prior to the date of death and at the time of death. This includes a same sex partner;
- a parent;
- a person treated by the deceased as a parent;
- a child of the deceased;
- a brother, sister, uncle or aunt of the deceased or their children;
- a person from any marriage to which the deceased was a party at any time and treated by the deceased as a child of the family.

The multiplier should be calculated from the date of death. This is the 'traditional' method set out in *Cookson v Knowles*[7] but has the undesirable effect of reducing the claim for the period between death and the trial which has already been incurred. The 'actuarial' method where the multiplier is calculated from the date of trial and the full dependency calculated up to the date of trial has not yet been adopted by the courts.

---

6 Damages for Bereavement (Variation of Sum) (England and Wales) Order 2007, SI 2007/3489.
7 [1979] AC 556, [1978] 2 WLR 978, [1978] 2 All ER 604, HL.

In a case with no dependant children and a partner who is not working, the multiplicand is conventionally two-thirds (or 66.67%) of the deceased's income.[8] Future loss is calculated by multiplying the balance of the multiplier by the multiplicand at the date of trial.

In a case with dependant children and a working spouse, the multiplicand is generally 75% of the lost income until the end of the period of dependency.

Worked example: loss of dependency

		Calculation using widow's potential earnings
Deceased's annual earnings		£40,000
Dependent widow's annual earnings		£20,000
Combined earnings		£60,000
Dependant's proportion	75%	£45,000
Less dependant's earnings		(20,000)
Annual loss of dependency		£25,000
Multiplier	15	
Total Loss		**£375,000**

In cases where the deceased did not work and thus has no earnings to aggregate in the calculation, the convention is to put a notional value on the loss of the services that the deceased provided to the remaining spouse and to work out a net value.

The claim for past loss of services should cover the actual cost incurred by the claimant up to the date of trial. Services may include the cost of childcare (in which case the cost of employing a nanny will be the applicable yard stick) and/or decorating or gardening or other household activities. In these cases, quotes for the cost of supplanting the deceased's work with professional substitutes used to be provided.

Only one claim is allowed under the FAA and any damages obtained must be apportioned. Any award is subject to the approval of the court if the claim is made by a child or a patient.

---

[8]   *Harris v Empress Motors Ltd* 1983] 3 All ER 561; *Cole v Crown Poultney Packers Ltd* [1984] 1 WLR 212.

18.1.5   Lost years

In 1980 the House of Lords, through the case of *Pickett v British Rail Engineering*,[9] established the principle that where a claimant's life has been shortened, as a consequence of a tortious act, a claim can be brought to recover for the loss of earnings that the claimant would have earned, but for their reduced life expectancy.

The issue of lost years has been explored most recently in the cases of *Lewis v Royal Shrewsbury Hospital NHS Trust*[10] and *Iqbal v Whipps Cross University Hospital*.[11] Both cases considered the position where seriously injured infant claimants (who, following their injuries, were most unlikely to ever have dependants) claimed lost years.

In *Lewis*, HHJ Alistair MacDuff QC came to the view that justice did not demand payment to non-existent dependants during the period when the claimant would not be alive. He took the view that to make an award was too speculative and that the factual circumstances that presented were such that to make an award would compensate for a loss that will not actually be suffered. On the other hand, Sir Rodger Bell, in *Iqbal*, took the opposite view. He found that if the claim for loss of earnings before death is not to be discounted for the lack of dependants then the lack of dependants should not suddenly become determinative against a claim the day after death. Sir Rodger Bell accepted that there are significant uncertainties when evaluating an award for a child, but they are to be accounted for at the stage of assessing the loss rather than by denying the claim altogether.

Lewis remains a first instance decision, but in November 2007 the Court of Appeal gave their judgement in *Iqbal*. The defendant trust had appealed against the decision to award lost years to the claimant on the grounds that such a claim was too remote and that the Court of Appeal had decided in the case of *Croke (a minor) v Wiseman*[12] that lost years claims in these circumstances were impermissible. The Court of Appeal allowed the defendant trust's appeal. However, it was acknowledged that inconsistencies existed in the case law, but these would require correction by the House of Lords. For the time being we seem unable to bring a claim for lost years for seriously injured infant claimants who are most unlikely to ever have dependants.

The different components of a claimant's damages need to be linked together into a coherent statement of overall and complementary losses. The object of the exercise is to present to the defendant a clear unambiguous claim for damages upon which it can decide to settle the case or make a Part 36 offer to test out the claimant's preparedness to compromise.

---

[9]   [1980] AC 136.
[10]   LTL, 14 June 2007 (unreported).
[11]   [2007] EWCA Civ 1190.
[12]   (1982) 1WLR 71.

While overstating a schedule is counter-productive, the careful assembly of a schedule that is internally consistent and thorough will be more likely to maximise the value of the eventual settlement or award.

TOP TIPS

- The claimants witness statement should include all the difficulties he faces as a result of the injury caused by the alleged negligence.

- Keep the schedule concise and accurate. Avoid heads of loss marked 'to be assessed'.

- Always take your client's instructions and ensure that he signs the statement of truth before it is served.

- Should the statement of truth not be signed the document is defective and is open to challenge by the other side under CPR Part 22.

- Any future loss of earnings is to be claimed net of tax and National Insurance contributions.

- The statutory bereavement award was increased from £11,800 to £12,980 for deaths occurring after 1 April 2013.

CHAPTER 19

CURRENT ISSUES IN THE ASSESSMENT OF DAMAGES

Having established entitlement to the damages claimed and set the heads of claim out in the schedule, solicitors David Body and Laura Craig now turn their attention to current issues, the complexity of which require practitioners to be on their toes when calculating quantum.

19.1 INTRODUCTION

This section is intended to provide some assistance in understanding those cases that the courts are currently considering and in so doing prepare practitioners for any further hearings of these cases in the appellate courts.

With so few clinical negligence liability issues being disposed of at trial these days and with Treasury – not to mention media – eyes trained on the levels of compensation being awarded, damages have become the real battleground in clinical negligence litigation. In attempting to assess recent developments, and their implication for the future, the words of Lord Blackburn in *Livingstone v Rawyards Coal Company*[1] remain fundamental:

> 'In settling the sum of money to be given for reparation of damages, you should as nearly as possible get at that sum of money which will put the party who has been injured, or who had suffered, in the same position as he would have been in if he had not sustained the wrong.'

It is this principle which is at the core of the client's claim for damages. Whilst complex actuarial and financial arguments dominate, what in fact is happening is an attempt to achieve Lord Blackburn's century old principle. It is indeed this that drives the scrutiny of where the law currently stands and the likely direction of damages for clinical negligence.

Recent and future developments in damages must be closely observed in an environment where the overriding objective has a new focus on proportionality (of legal costs in relation to damages) and political pressure mounts in the run up to a general election, at the heart of which will be the future of the NHS. The demand for law reform designed to limit the level of damages awarded (and thus limit the NHS' legal bills) to claimant's will undoubtedly make a

---

[1]   (1880) 5 LR App Cas 25.

persuasive manifesto, particularly in the wake of the Jackson reforms[2] and a move to curb the perceived 'compensation culture' that the Government continues to say has emerged in the United Kingdom. In a recent press release[3] the Medical Protection Society again suggested repealing the 1948 Law Reform (Personal Injuries) Act so that future care costs are no longer calculated on the basis of private care, rather than NHS care, an issue that is reviewed later in this chapter.

Four main areas will be dealt with. On 1 April 2006, the Damages Act 1996 introduced periodical payments. As practitioners have begun to utilise periodical payments, analysis has taken place as to whether the annual payment that is awarded allows the claimant to fund the costs that will arise in the future. Such scrutiny of rising costs – particularly labour costs in relation to care – led to consideration of Indexation issues. Away from these two connected issues, The Department for Constitutional Affairs' consultation paper *The Law on Damages* is considered in addition to the 10% increase in general damages post-Jackson.

19.2 PERIODICAL PAYMENTS

Following Lord Steyn's comments in *Wells v Wells*[4] (see **17.2.7** above), there was a review of the efficacy of lump sum awards of compensation which resulted in the implementation statutory power to award periodical payment damages from 1 April 2006. Judges now have power to consider and influence whether damages are paid by a means other than a lump sum.

Judges *may* (a) order that the damages are wholly or partly to take the form of periodical payments; and (b) *shall* consider whether to make that order.[5]

There has been a clear policy decision to provide judges with influence over this decision. It is this shift and the way in which the judges exercise this power that will influence the preparation of clinical negligence claims. To better understand the current position, it is necessary to understand what lay behind this change in policy.

Demographically, life expectancy has increased incrementally (4 months per year) over the last century. This is because of a number of factors including improved public health, as well as medical and rehabilitation techniques. Not only are able bodied people living longer but those injured in accidents are surviving because of new rehabilitation techniques in a way which would have surprised previous generations of clinicians. Consequently, the effect upon quantification of clinical negligence claims has been to introduce uncertainty for the advisers and the claimants when assessing whether a lump sum payment

---

2   See www.judiciary.gov.uk/reports/civil-litigation-costs-review-final-report/.
3   www.independent.co.uk/life-style/health-and-families/health-news/negligence-payouts-bankruptingnhs-8432384.html.
4   [1999] 1 AC 345.
5   Damages Act 1996, s 2(1).

will last a claimant's lifetime. Periodical payments have been presented as a vehicle that will reduce this risk and uncertainty. The benefits of financial certainty and security are fundamental for the able bodied majority, but even more so for those who are disabled.

Periodical payments provide the claimant with a better opportunity of receiving 'full compensation' by ensuring that an annual payment linked to an appropriate inflation index is provided for life.

However, the application of periodical payments started to come unstuck when the cost of providing care (ie a 'labour cost') was being calculated according to the Retail Price Index (RPI – an index based on the cost of goods). As the cost of labour outstripped standard inflation linking the annual payment to RPI would lead to the claimant being unable to afford to recruit and pay carers. It is this concern that has brought about litigation on the appropriate index to be applied.

When considering periodical payments it is still necessary to prepare a schedule as set out in the preceding chapter leading to a calculation of the conventional lump sum. Life expectancy evidence must be obtained and the multiplier/multiplicand approach adopted to calculate (at least to the point of allowing reasonable comparison) what a lump sum would amount to in order to compare this to an annual periodical payment calculation.

Where the parties have settled the case before it comes to trial or judgment the judge will only see the case at the time of endorsing the parties' consent order. Where the claimant lacks capacity, and court approval is necessary, it is incumbent upon the claimant's solicitor to justify at the Approval hearing why a lump sum has been chosen over a periodical payments award.

In such circumstances, it is necessary that the claimant's solicitor obtains financial advice to be able to present to the judge a considered analysis of the effect of periodical payments as against a lump sum. Furthermore, High Court masters or district judges when approving consent orders, will question whether the parties have considered periodical payments and want to see witness evidence to confirm that they have truly done so.

The practical point is that whilst it may appear that periodical payments are only really relevant for maximum severity cases involving children and/or patients, in practice, practitioners must bear in mind periodical payments in **any** case involving future losses.

19.3　INDEXATION

When periodical payments were introduced, analysis began to determine the appropriate index to attach to the annual payment to ensure that the net present value of the award in today's money allowed the claimant to purchase the awarded head of loss as anticipated inflation rises in the future.

Labour economists pointed out that the RPI had a number of problems with its use as an indexation measure. Once this had been appreciated, it became apparent that use of the RPI ran the risk of under-compensating claimants in the future when compared with other more appropriate measures of the likely labour cost increases of providing future care support. The starting point, at least in case-law, is *Flora v Wakom*.[6]

Following a serious injury at work Mr Flora was unable to return to work and required daily care. Liability was admitted but a dispute arose during the course of preparation for the assessment of damages hearing as to the construction of s 2(8) and 2(9) of the Damages Act 1996 which reads as follows:

> '(8) An order for periodical payments shall be treated as providing for the amount of payments to vary by reference to the retail prices index (within the meaning of section 833(2) of the Income and Corporation Taxes Act 1988) at such times, and in such a manner, as may be determined by or in accordance with Civil Procedure Rules.
>
> (9) But an order for periodical payments may include provision –
>
> (a)	Disapplying subsection (8), or
> (b)	Modifying the effect of subsection (8).'

Mr Flora, in his statement of case, pleaded a wage related index as more suitable than the RPI as the mechanism for calculating the sums payable as periodical payments. The defendant objected and sought to strike out these aspects of Mr Flora's statement of case. It was Mr Flora's contention that the RPI, as referred to in s 2(8), identified the default position but that a judge could make an order as identified in s 2(9) for a different index to be applied whenever it appeared just to do so. It was the defendant's position that s 2(8) provided the order that the judge would ordinarily make and that s 2(9) could only be triggered in exceptional circumstances.

Upon the defendant's application, Sir Michael Turner QC, sitting as a deputy high court judge, declined to strike out as unarguable those aspects of the claimant's statement of case to which the defendant objected. He held that the purpose of the Damages Act was to provide full compensation. Periodical Payments would be 'dead in the water' if the court could only use the RPI. The Court of Appeal upheld Sir Michael Turner's judgment, but indicated that they anticipated that a 'basket' of cases would find their way to the appellate courts. Leave to the House of Lords was refused in *Flora* and therefore the case is binding authority for the proposition that it is appropriate for the judge to consider indices other than RPI when deciding the basis upon which periodical payments shall be uprated.

Shortly after *Flora*, the Court of Appeal's anticipated 'basket' was duly constituted, comprising: *Thompstone v Tameside & Glossop Acute Health Services Trust*,[7] *Corbett v South Yorkshire SHA*,[8] *RH v United Bristol*

---

[6]	[2006] EWCA Civ 1103.
[7]	[2006] EWHC 2904.

Healthcare NHS Trust,[9] the majority of which are clinical negligence cases, perhaps because clinical negligence cases often demonstrate the extreme periods over which index linking has effectively to operate.

In these cases the claimants sought to move away from reliance on the RPI, indicating that an earnings based index was more likely to track accurately future care costs than one based on the RPI. The intention of periodical payments is to provide certainty for a lifetime to ensure that, predominantly, the cost of care can continue to be met. To have a system in which the costs of providing care outstrips the annual award that has been made completely undermines the object of introducing of periodical payments.

The claimants, therefore, presented three other indices as more appropriate than the RPI, namely:

- AEI: Average Earnings Index which covers 9 million employees including all occupations.

- ASHE Median: Annual Survey of Hours and Earnings commencing in 1998 based on 1% of employees.

- ASHE 6115 80: Published by the Office of National Statistics with a specific category dealing with the care sector.

These indices were presented as a means of adjusting for inflation in the cost of future care in uprating the periodical payment. At first instance it was held that it was appropriate for the future periodic payments of the claimant's care to be indexed by reference to the ASHE index rather than the RPI.

The defendants appealed this decision and on 16 January 2008 the Court of Appeal handed down its judgment.[10] The defendants' appeal was refused and in summary the following findings were made:

(1) Exceptional circumstances are **not** required before periodical payments can be index linked other than to RPI, in particular to an earnings related measure such as ASHE 6115.

(2) With regards to the index used, the Court's task is to decide which index is appropriate, suitable and best meets the claimant's needs.

(3) If the defendant wishes to re-open the issue of the appropriateness of index linking future care and case management to ASHE 6115 the defendant must produce evidence and arguments significantly different from, and more persuasive than, those deployed in these appeals. Judges should not hesitate to strike out any defences that do not meet that requirement.

(4) The judge's overall aim, when deciding whether to make a periodical payment order rather than a lump sum order, must be to make whatever

---

[8]   (2007) LS Law Medical 430.
[9]   [2007] EWHC 1441.
[10]   [2008] EWCA Civ 5.

order best meets the claimant's needs. This is an objective test, albeit that the judge will have regard to the parties' preferences and all the circumstances of the case.

(5) It would only be in a rare case that it would be appropriate for the defendant to call expert evidence to demonstrate that the form of order preferred by the claimant will not best meet his needs.

The results in the Court of Appeal was a resounding success in favour of the claimant. It has been well established that it is appropriate for earnings to be linked to an index that accurately reflects the cost of wage-related inflation. In making such a finding the Court has rejected emphatically the defendants' arguments and has clearly indicated that these issues are only to be revisited in exceptional circumstances. Not surprisingly the defendants sought leave to the House of Lords on two points:

- whether the Damages Act 1996 can only be modified in exceptional circumstances;
- whether the Court is entitled to take account of the principle of distributive justice (namely that the cost to the NHS would be so great as to reduce money available to patients in the NHS) and whether the principle should be taken into account in these appeals;

but the NHSLA later withdrew this appeal.

Therefore, ASHE 6115 is the appropriate uprating measure for future care and case management. Following this, three judgments were given which clarify the proper form that periodical payments orders should take:

- *RH v United Bristol Healthcare NHS Trust* [2008] EWHC 2423 (QB) (Mackay J, 31 July 2008), [2007] EWHC 1441 (QB), [2007] LS Law Medical 535;
- *RH v United Bristol Healthcare NHS Trust* [2008] EWHC 2424 (QB) (Mackay J, 31 July 2008);
- *Thompstone v Tameside Hospital NHS Foundation Trust* [2009] PIQR P9 (Sir Christopher Holland, 2 December 2008).

Since 2008 periodical payments awards have been linked to ASHE 6115 80th centile, which ensures that many claimants who receive no pay for care is linked to an index that tracks carers earnings.

What is also needed as a result of these changes to the means of paying claims is a new method for the NHSLA to *account* for payment of these claims. Its current practice of accounting in the year in which a PPO award is made for the entirety of the award rather than accounting for it on an amortised basis makes the figures reported every year in the NHSLA's accounts a continual apparently exponentially increasing level of damages paid. While there may be such increases, it needs to be remembered that the gradient of increase is shallower than it appears because of this accounting convention.

It may also be that that the NHSLA does not mind retaining this as a useful stick with which to beat claimant lawyers.

19.4   DCA CONSULTATION PAPER *THE LAW ON DAMAGES*

On 4 May 2007 the Department for Constitutional Affairs (DCA) set out for consultation its paper *The Law on Damages*. Consideration is given here to the chapters of the consultation paper that affect clinical negligence. It remains a comprehensive overview of the heads of loss that practitioners must consider. Key issues and updates, since the paper was first drafted, have been incorporated where appropriate.

The following quotation taken from the introduction to the consultation paper, set out the motivation in sending out the paper for consultation and the thought process behind it:

> 'The Government is committed to tackling the perceptions of a compensation culture and to improving the compensation system for valid claims. It has taken forward a wide-ranging program of work to:
> * stop a compensation culture from developing;
> * tackle perceptions that can lead to a disproportionate fear of litigation and risk adverse behaviour;
> * find ways to resist and discourage bad claims;
> * improve the system for those with a valid claim by providing fair compensation in a more timely, proportionate and cost effective way.'

None of these issues are new. It is clear that the compensation culture myth is at the forefront of minds but, and it is worthy of reinforcement, it is exactly that – 'a myth'. In May 2004 the government's response to the Better Regulation Task Force report *Better Routes to Redress*[11] concluded:

> 'The judicial process is very good at sorting the wheat from the chaff, but all claims must be assessed in the early stages. Redress for a genuine claimant is hampered by the spurious claims arising from the perception of a compensation culture. **The compensation culture is a myth; but the cost of this belief is·very real.**'

It is reassuring that the DCA's introduction leads with the motive of tackling perceptions of a compensation culture, but the first key drive (set out above) is to stop a compensation culture developing. Now, more than ever, claimant representatives must strive to get that message across particularly at a time when, despite the consistent rebuttal by claimant lawyers of the existence of a compensation culture, the reflection of such an idea by the report of the Better Regulation Commission produced by Lord Young in 2010, we find that the Justice Secretary, Chris Grayling is still using that phrase in his introduction of the first reading of the Social Action, Responsibility and Heroism Bill on 22 July 2014.

---

[11]   See http://archive.cabinetoffice.gov.uk/brc/upload/assets/www.brc.gov.uk/betterroutes.pdf.

19.4.1   Wrongful death and bereavement damages (Chapters 1 and 2)

The Law Commission's report *Claims for Wrongful Death*[12] made recommendations for changes to the Fatal Accidents Act 1976. The effects of those proposals and subsequent consultations was to significantly extend the list of those entitled to claim under the Fatal Accidents Act[13] to include deceased children, siblings and long-term partner. The changes came into force on 13 March 2014.

Whether the extended list goes far enough remains to be seen as the natural consequence of any list is that there will remain deserving claimants who are excluded. Despite these repeated recommendations, damages for bereavement can be awarded only to husbands, wives, civil partners, the parents of a child under 18, or mother of an illegitimate child who was under 18 and never married. The parents of a child over 18, children of a deceased parent and parents of a stillborn infant have no such entitlement. APIL advocate an extension of the bereavement damages to mirror the position in Scotland. Furthermore, while it is acknowledged and accepted that there should be a fixed sum of £5,000 to each eligible child, these figures remain worryingly low.

A statutory instrument made on 5 March 2013 effected an increase in the bereavement award under s 1A(3) of the Fatal Accidents Act 1976 in respect of causes of action (ie deaths) on or after 1 April 2013. The sum that may be awarded as damages for bereavement in England and Wales will increase by 10% from £11,800 to £12,980[14] in order to apply a similar element as the 10% increase in general damages which has been introduced in non fatal claims, as a consequence of the Jackson reforms (discussed further below).

19.4.2   Psychiatric illness (Chapter 3)

The Law Commission's report, *Liability for Psychiatric Illness,*[15] recommended introducing statutory provisions in relation to claims for psychiatric illness. The consultation paper rejected that recommendation and concluded that it is preferable to allow the courts to develop the law on liability for psychiatric illness rather than attempt to impose a statutory solution. No changes to the law are proposed.

In *Rabone v Pennine Care NHS Trust*[16] the Supreme Court confirmed that Art 2 of the ECHR[17] imposes an operational obligation on the state to protect mentally ill patients both who are detained and who are not detained under the Mental Health Act 1983 where there was a real and immediate risk of suicide.

---

12   Law Com No 263.
13   Fatal Accidents Act 1976, s 1(3).
14   Damages for Bereavement (Variation of Sum) (England and Wales) Order 2013, SI 2013/510.
15   Law Com No 249.
16   [2012] UKSC 2.
17   European Convention on Human Rights.

The state is now obliged to take positive steps to safeguard a person's life in this situation. This represents a major development in psychiatric illness claims and allows more detailed investigation by a coroner, particularly where a mentally ill patient has died 'in the care of the state'.

19.4.3   Collateral benefits and gratuitous care (Chapter 4)

The Commission's report *Personal Injury Damages*[18] discussed collateral benefits (payments or benefits in kind which a tort victim would not have received but for the tort, eg sick pay, accident insurance, charitable payments, etc).

Recent consideration of this issue arose following *Hussain v New Taplow Paper Mills Ltd*[19] in which Lord Bridge commented upon the principle about collateral benefits which had been established 18 years earlier in *Parry v Cleaver*.[20] This case established the principle that collateral benefits are to be excluded when considering the award of compensation to be paid to the claimant.

Hussain v New Taplow Mills Ltd established the contention that the principal starting point was to be deduction, but, that being said, there are as many exemptions from this contention as examples of it and thus the law is complex and open to significant and costly litigation and appellate rulings. The Law Commission considered whether consistency could be introduced with the preferred approach being that the claimant be compensated once at the full expense of the tortfeasor. This remains a live issue.

So far as gratuitous care is concerned the report recommended that the approach taken by the House of Lords in *Hunt v Severs*,[21] which held that claimants are entitled to recover damages for gratuitous care but must hold the damages on trust for the carer, be replaced by a personal obligation to account for the money to the carer. It also recommends that this should apply for gratuitous care provided by a defendant.

19.4.4   Cost of private care (Chapter 5)

This is a particularly thorny issue in clinical negligence cases. In June 2003 the Chief Medical Officer published his report *Making Amends* in which he recommended that the law should be changed to exempt NHS clinical negligence cases from the provisions of s 2(4) of the Law Reform (Personal Injuries) Act 1948, the effect of which is to entitle a claimant to recover the cost of private health care.

---

[18]   Law Com No 262.
[19]   [1998] AC 514.
[20]   [1970] AC 1.
[21]   [1994] 2 AC 350.

It was proposed that the NHS should provide a 'comprehensive care package, promptly provided and efficiently delivered'. The government currently considers that it would not be appropriate to change the law in relation to clinical negligence claims alone as it would create different provisions for personal injury claims depending on how and where the claimant had suffered the injury.

It is expected that this will remain a head of loss and an issue that defendants will continue to take up with the government.

Aside from a full repeal of s 2(4) there have been suggestions put forward to create an interaction between the public and private provision of care and accommodation services. Generally it is believed by the government that the tortfeasor should pay for the costs of care where possible but that these costs should be based on providing appropriate treatment in a cost effective way.

In recent years, significant court time has been spent hearing arguments on these issues. One of the most prominent judgments came in *Sowden v Lodge* and *Crookdake v Drury*[22] in which Lord Justice Longmore stated in the context of top-up care, that:

> '... while it is for a claimant to assert what are his or her reasonable needs, it is for a defendant to assert that a claimant should be content with local authority residential care to set out in clear terms whether such reasonable needs can be met by such care and whether there is any respect in which they accept that such care does not meet the claimant's reasonable needs.'

This passage, read alongside s 2(4) of the Law Reform (Personal Injury) Act 1948, entitles a claimant, as of right, to decline a care regime provided by the defendant and if the defendant wishes to argue against this then the burden of proving why the claimant should not have a private regime rests with the defendant.

The Court of Appeal in *Crofton v NHSLA*,[23] commenting upon Mr Justice Tomlinson's judgment in *Freeman v Lockett*,[24] stated that in relation to the issue of deductions from an award of compensation and the claimant's right to a privately funded care regime:

> '... provided that no deduction on account of possible receipt of state or local authority funding was made from her award of damages, the claimant could withdraw her application for funding; she wanted to rely exclusively on private funding for her care.'

The position remains that the claimant has a right to a privately funded care package without deduction or credit being given for state provided care. However, there is considerable pressure and judicial wavering in response. It is

---

22   [2005] 1 WLR 2129.
23   [2007] EWCA Civ 71.
24   [2006] EWHC 102 (QB).

anticipated, particularly in clinical negligence cases, that this issue will remain very much at the forefront of the NHSLA's litigation policy as it attempts to shift responsibility for injured claimants from its budget to that of local authority social services departments by arguing that all of this money comes ultimately from the 'same (ie the Government's) pocket'. *Freeman v Lockett* demonstrates how keen the courts can be to see tortfeasor's obligations met by that tortfeasor or his insurers. In the case of the NHSLA, it is to be hoped that the courts maintain the view that when the NHSLA represents tortfeasor health authorities or trusts it meets their obligations in full.

The position was thrown into stark relief in a case heard in February 2008.

The claimant was an adult who will always be a patient. She has 100% judgment on liability. She is receiving superb care, and which all parties agree is excellent, in a private care home funded by her local authority and PCT. The cost of future care is agreed at £3.8m.

The claimant claimed that she should receive full compensation from the defendants and that her deputy should be able to buy care in accordance with advice received from her case manager. The defendants argued that:

(1) there is no financial loss as the claimant cannot be charged for her care either by the PCT (under the NHS Act) or by the local authority (under the National Assistance Act);

(2) if she does not claim what she is entitled to from the council under the National Assistance Act she is not mitigating her loss;

(3) there would be double recovery if the judge ordered the defendants to pay future care costs.

The claimant's case was that:

(1) no victim should be forced to elect to rely on state provision and give up a right to compensation;

(2) a claimant has an absolute right to seek compensation from a tortfeasor;

(3) the judge should accept the word of the deputy that she will not claim for matters in the schedule of future loss from the council and she would offer an undertaking if required;

(4) the mischief of double recovery harming the defendants is less than the mischief of the claimant being forced to rely on council care which is subject to budgetary restraints/political whim, etc;

(5) it is reasonable for the claimant to elect to have privately funded care;

(6) the burden is on the defendant to prove that the claimant is being unreasonable.

The council which had been joined into the action as a Part 20 defendant submitted that the definition of personal injury awards being ring-fenced from councils seeking financial contributions only applies to the PSLA element of damages not where care has been specifically compensated for; that a contrary interpretation runs contrary to government policy requiring state agencies to be recompensed by tortfeasors, and that it is outrageous if it proves to be the case that local community charge payers have to pay for the claimants care over her lifetime whilst the tortfeasor gets away with paying nothing towards it.

The judge held that the amount of damages awarded to the claimant would be disregarded for the purposes of assessing her capital liability to reimburse the local authority and that there was no reason why the claimant should not be able to claim for the cost of future care and accommodation from the defendants. The defendant's appeal to the Court of Appeal was dismissed.

19.4.5 Accommodation expenses (Chapter 6)

In this chapter the Law Commission discusses possible new methods to calculate accommodation expenses arising from the need to buy new accommodation or adapt existing accommodation because of the claimant's injuries.

It seeks views on two possible options: moving to a method whereby the defendant would pay the extra capital cost of the property at the time of trial, and in return receive a charge over the property for the amount paid, repayable on the claimant's death or when the accommodation was otherwise not needed by the claimant; or simply awarding the appropriate extra capital cost to the claimant.

The traditional *Roberts v Johnstone*[25] approach, which provides that the claimant may claim for the cost of the alterations but must give credit for the increasing market value, has significant flaws particularly in a stagnant or falling property market. A major problem is that the claimant may not receive enough capital to purchase the new property at the outset and it is often assumed by judges that the claimant will 'burgle' other heads of loss in order to actually fund a property purchase.

Notwithstanding all the difficulties with the current system, the Law Commission has to date rejected a number of the options that were proposed for reform. Generally it has decided that many of the proposals were unworkable and therefore, having considered and rejected alternatives, it appears as if the *Roberts v Johnstone* principle remains for the immediate future.[26]

Discussion remains ongoing, in particular because the current discount rate is fixed at 2.5% per annum though a review is underway that could result in a change to the discount rate. Claimant advocates have lobbied for a decrease in the rate to reflect the current economic climate though indications from

---

[25] [1989] QB 878.

[26] For a discussion of the policy issues see Robert Weir *Accommodating periodical payments into housing claims* [2008] JIPL 147.

government circles are that the rate may be increased on the basis that everyone is suffering economically and personal injury claimants should not be treated differently.

19.4.6 THE 10 PER CENT INCREASE IN GENERAL DAMAGES

The 10% increase in general damages for pain, suffering and loss of amenity proposed as a means of allowing claimants to meet the newly imposed obligation to pay success fees in the aftermath of the introduction of the Jackson costs shifting qualified one way costs shifting rule was implemented by the decision in *Simmons v Castle*.[27] Following the Court of Appeal's earlier ruling[28] that the 10% increase in general damages would apply to *all cases* decided from 1 April 2013, irrespective of the funding arrangements in place, the ABI applied for a re-hearing to consider whether or not those who benefited from funding agreements entered into before 1 April 2013 and whose entitlement to success fees were still recoverable[29] could also benefit from the 10% increase in general damages.

Having heard argument from the ABI, APIL and PIBA, the court revisited and reformulated its earlier judgment as follows (para 50):

> 'Accordingly, we take this opportunity to declare that, with effect from 1 April 2013, the proper level of damages in all civil claims for (i) pain and suffering, (ii) loss of amenity, (iii) physical inconvenience and discomfort, (iv) social discredit, (v) mental distress, or (vi) loss of society of relatives, will be 10% higher than previously, unless the claimant falls within section 44(6) if LASPO. It therefore follows that, if the action now under appeal had been the subject of a judgement after 1 April 2013, then (unless the claimant had entered into a CFA before that date) the proper award of general damages would be 10% higher than that agreed in this case, namely £22,000 rather than £20,000.'

TOP TIPS

- When considering periodical payments it is still necessary to prepare a schedule leading to a calculation of the conventional lump sum.
- Exceptional circumstances are not required before periodical payments can be index linked other than to RPI.
- It would only be in a rare case that it would be appropriate for the defendant to call expert evidence to demonstrate that the form of order preferred by the claimant will not best meet his needs.
- Collateral benefits are to be excluded when considering the award of compensation to be paid to the claimant.
- A claimant has a right to a privately funded care package without deduction or credit being given for state provided care.

---

[27] [2012] EWCA Civ 1288, [2013] 1 WLR 1239, [2013] 1 All ER 334.
[28] [2012] EWCA Civ 1039.
[29] LASPO 2012, s 44(6).

- The traditional *Roberts v Johnstone* approach has significant flaws particularly in a stagnant or falling property market because the claimant may not receive enough capital to purchase the new property at the outset.

- Remember to factor in the 10% increase to general damages where your funding arrangement has been entered into after 1 April 2013 or where you are dealing with a fatal accident claim, to increase the bereavement damages award in an action where death has occurred on or after 1 April 2013.

APPENDIX 1

MEDICAL GLOSSARY

Introduction

Medical records are usually littered with abbreviations, especially TLAs (three-letter abbreviations). Whilst doctors use these to save time, they serve the additional purposes, often intentional, of making the medical record difficult for the lay person to decipher and enhancing the professional mystique surrounding doctors. They may, usually unintentionally, cause confusion between doctors.

A record might read, '43M, 3/7 CCP, SOBOE, SOA, ^{0}PND PMH: IDDM, H/T Rx: ACE O/E ^{0}A, C, C, J P84/m reg BP 142/80 CVS NAD'

In translation this is: 43-year-old male with a 3-day history of central chest pain, shortness of breath on exertion and swelling of ankles. No paroxysmal nocturnal dyspnoea. Past medical history: insulin-dependent diabetes mellitus and hypertension. Treatment: angiotensin-converting enzyme. On examination: anaemia, cyanosis, clubbing and jaundice absent. Pulse rate 84 per minute, regular. Blood pressure 142/80. No abnormality detected in the cardiovascular system.

Unfortunately there is no universally recognised system of medical abbreviations and ambiguity arises because specialists in different disciplines may use the same abbreviation to denote entirely different conditions. Thus 'PID' may mean pelvic inflammatory disease to a gynaecologist and prolapsed intervertebral disc to an orthopaedic surgeon. Even more confusingly, the same abbreviation may be used to denote similar conditions with crucial differences: 'ALTE' might mean acute life-threatening event to a physician and apparent life-threatening event to a paediatrician.

In previous decades abbreviations were sometimes used by doctors to make, and hide, flippant or even disparaging remarks about patients and their conditions. Examples of some of the least offensive of these are: GOK – God only knows, TALOIA – there's a lot of it about, LGFTD – looks good from the door, GOMER – get out of my emergency room; NFN – normal for Norfolk, and AWTB – away with the birds. Their use is now frowned upon.

Doctors may uses prefixes such as 'O' to denote the absence of a symptom or sign: for example, ^{0}SOB' – no shortness of breath. The symbols '↓' and '↑' are used to denote that something is increasing or decreasing. The '+' sign is sometimes used to indicate that something is present or sometimes that it is severe, but again, and confusingly, there is no universal system. For example 'pain+' may be used by one doctor to mean that a patient has pain but by another to mean that he has a lot of pain. Some doctors use 'pain+++' to denote severe pain.

The denominators 7, 52 and 12 are used to denote days, weeks and months. Thus 3/7 is 3 days, 4/52 is 4 weeks and 5/12 is 5 months.

The following is a list of some of the more commonly used abbreviations but the reader is advised to bear in mind the caveats concerning their use and to exercise caution in their interpretation. A doctor may tell you – as Humpty Dumpty told Alice about words – that an abbreviation means just what he chooses it to mean.

Glossary

Δ	diagnosis
$\Delta\Delta$	differential diagnosis
#	fracture
Ψ	psychiatry
1/7	one day
2/52	two weeks
3/12	three months
Σ	Sigmoidoscopy
A	
AA	Attendance allowance
AAA	abdominal aortic aneurysm
AAL	anterior axillary line
Abdo	abdomen
ABG	arterial blood gases
ABPI	ankle-brachial pressure index
AB_x	antibiotics
ac	before meals (*ante cibum*)
AC	acromio-clavicular
ACL	anterior cruciate ligament
ACTH	adrenocorticotrophic hormone
ACE	angiotension converting enzyme
ACL	anterior cruciate ligament
ADD	attention deficit disorder

ADH	anti-diuretic hormone
ADHD	attention deficit and hyperactivity disorder
ADL	activities of daily living
ADR	adverse drug reaction
A&E	accident and emergency
AE	air entry
AED	automatic external defibrillator
AF	atrial fibrillation OR atrial flutter
AFB	acid-fast bacilli
AFP	alpha fetoprotein
AID	artificial insemination by donor
AIDS	acquired immune deficiency syndrome
AIH	artificial insemination by husband
AJ	ankle jerk (reflex)
AKA	above-knee amputation
AKI	acute kidney injury
Alk phos	alkaline phosphatise
ALL	acute lymphatic leukaemia
ALO	actinomyces-like organism
ALS	advanced life support
ALT	alanine aminotransferase
AMA	against medical advice OR anti-mitochondrial antibodies
AMD	age-related macular degeneration
AML	acute myelocytic leukaemia
ANA	anti-nuclear antibody
ANC	antenatal clinic
ANCA	anti-neutrophil cytoplasmic antibodies
ANF	anti-nuclear factor
APH	antepartum haemorrhage
APMS	Alternative Provider Medical Services
AR	aortic regurgitation
ARB	angiotensin-II receptor blocker
ARDS	acute respiratory distress syndrome
ARF	acute renal failure
ARM	artificial rupture of membranes

AS	aortic stenosis
ASD	atrial septal defect OR autistic spectrum disorder
ASO	anti-streptolysin O
AST	aspartate aminotransferase
A-V	arterio-venous
A/V	anteverted (of the uterus)
AVR	aortic valve replacement
AXR	abdominal x-ray

B

BBV	blood-borne virus
b.d. or b.i.d.	twice daily (*bis [in] die*)
BCC	basal cell carcinoma
BCP	basal cell papilloma
BDD	body dysmorphic disorder
BIBA	brought in by ambulance
BID	brought in dead
BJGP	British Journal of General Practice
BKA	below-knee amputation
BMD	bone mineral density
BMI	body mass index
BMJ	British Medical Journal
BMR	basal metabolic rate
BNF	British National Formulary
BNO	bowels not open
BNP	brain natriuretic peptide
BO	bowels open
BP	blood pressure
BPD	borderline personality disorder OR bi-parietal diameter
BPH	benign prostatic hypertrophy
bpm	beats per minute
BPPV	benign paroxysmal positional vertigo
BS	breath sounds OR bowel sounds OR blood sugar
BSE	bovine spongiform encephalopathy OR breast self-examination
BSO	bilateral salpingo-oophorectomy
BV	bacterial vaginosis

C

C_2H_5OH	alcohol
Ca	cancer OR calcium
Ca^{++}	calcium
CABG	coronary artery bypass graft
CAD	coronary artery disease
CAH	chronic active hepatitis
C&B	choose and book
C&S	culture and sensitivity
CAM	complementary (or alternative) medicine
CAPD	continuous ambulatory peritoneal dialysis
Caps	capsules
CAT	computed axial tomography
CBT	cognitive behaviour therapy
CCF	congestive cardiac failure
CDAT	community drug and alcohol team
CDH	congenital dislocation of the hip (see DDH)
CEA	carcinoembryonic antigen
CF	cystic fibrosis
CFC	chlorofluorocarbon
CFS	chronic fatigue syndrome
CHD	coronary heart disease
CHF	congestive heart failure
CJD	Creutzfeldt-Jakob disease
CK	creatinine kinase
CKD	chronic kidney disease
CLL	chronic lymphocytic leukaemia
CML	chronic myeloid leukaemia
CMV	cytomegalovirus
CO	complains of OR carbon monoxide
C/O	complains of
COAD	chronic obstructive airways disease
COPD	chronic obstructive pulmonary disease
CP	cerebral palsy OR chest pain
CPAP	continuous positive airways pressure
CPD	cephalo-pelvic disproportion

CPK	creatinine phosphokinase
CPN	community psychiatric nurse
CPR	cardiopulmonary resuscitation
Cr	creatinine
CRF	chronic renal failure
CRP	C-reactive protein
CR(T)	capillary refill (time)
CSF	cerebrospinal fluid
CT	computed (axial) tomography
CTG	cardiotocograph
CVA	cerebrovascular accident
CVD	cardiovascular disease
CVP	central venous pressure
CVS	cardiovascular system OR chorionic villous sampling
Cx	cervix
CXR	chest x-ray

D

D&C	dilatation and curettage
D/C	discharge OR discontinue
DDH	developmental dysplasia of the hip
DEXA	dual energy x-ray absorptiometry
DH	drug history
DIB	difficulty in breathing
DIC	disseminated intravascular coagulation
DIP(J)	distal interphalangeal (joint)
DKA	diabetic ketoacidosis
DLA	Disability Living Allowance
DM	diabetes mellitus
DMARD	disease-modifying anti-rheumatic drug
DMD	Duchenne muscular dystrophy
DN	district nurse
DNA	did not attend
DNAR	do not attempt resuscitation
DNR	do not resuscitate
DOA	dead on arrival

DPT	diphtheria, pertussis and tetanus (vaccine)
DRE	digital rectal examination
DSH	deliberate self-harm
DTTO	drug testing and treatment order
DU	duodenal ulcer
DUB	dysfunctional uterine bleeding
D&V	diarrhoea and vomiting
DV	domiciliary visit OR domestic violence
DVT	deep vein thrombosis
D/W	discussed with
Dx	diagnosis
DXT	deep radiotherapy
<u>E</u>	
EBD	emotional and behavioural difficulties
EBM	evidence-based medicine OR expressed breast milk
EBV	Epstein-Barr virus
EC	enteric-coated
ECF	extracellular fluid
ECG	electrocardiogram
Echo	echocardiogram
ECT	electro-convulsive therapy
ECV	external cephalic version
ED	erectile dysfunction
EDC or EDD	estimated date of confinement or delivery
EEG	electroencephalogram
eGFR	estimated glomerular filtration rate
ELSCS	elective lower segment Caesarean section
EM	electron microscope
EMG	electromyogram
EMSI	extra-marital sexual intercourse
EMU	early morning urine
ENT	ears, nose and throat
EOC	epithelial ovarian cancer
EOM	external ocular movements
EPA	enduring power of attorney

EPAU	early pregnancy assessment unit
EPO	erythropoietin
EPU	early pregnancy unit
ERCP	Endoscopic retrograde cholangiopancreatography
ESMI	elderly severely mentally ill
ESR	erythrocyte sedimentation rate
ESRD	end-stage renal disease
ESWL	extra-corporeal shock wave lithotripsy
ETOH	ethanol (alcohol)
ETT	endotracheal tube
EUA	examination under anaesthetic
Ex	examination

F

FB	foreign body or finger's breadth
FBC	full blood count
FBG or FBS	fasting blood glucose or sugar
FBS	fetal blood sampling
FDP	fibrin degradation products
FEV_1	forced expiratory volume in one second
FFP	fresh frozen plasma
FH	family history OR fetal heart
FHH	fetal heart heard
FHHR	fetal heart heard and regular
FH_x	family history
FMF	fetal movements felt
FMH	feto-maternal haemorrhage
FNA	fine needle aspiration
FP10	an NHS prescription form
FROM	full range of movement
FSE	fetal scalp electrode
FSH	follicle stimulating hormone
FVC	forced vital capacity
FWB	full weight bearing
FWG	full warning given
FY1	foundation year 1
FY2	foundation year 2

G

GA	general anaesthetic
GAS	group A streptococcus
GB	gall bladder
GBS	Gullaine-Barré syndrome
GC	gonococcus OR general condition
GCA	giant cell arteritis
GCS	Glasgow coma score
GFR	glomerular filtration rate
GGT	gamma glutamyl transferase
GGPT	gamma glutamyl transpeptidase
GH	growth hormone
GHRF	growth hormone releasing factor
GnRH	gonadotrophin-releasing hormone
GI(T)	gastrointestinal (tract)
GIFT	gamete intra-fallopian transfer
GORD	gastro-oesophageal reflux disease
GPwSI	general practitioner with a special interest
GTN	glyceryl trinitrate
GTT	glucose tolerance test
GU	genitor-urinary
GUM	genitor-urinary medicine
GvH(D)	graft versus host (disease)

H

H/A	headache
HAV	hepatitis A virus
Hb	haemoglobin
HbF	fetal haemoglobin
HBsAg	hepatitis B surface antigen
HBV	hepatitis B virus
HCG	human chorionic gonadotrophin
HCT	haematocrit
HCV	hepatitis C virus
HDL	high density lipoprotein
HDU	high dependency unit
Hg	mercury

HH	hiatus hernia
HIB	haemophilus influenza type B
HIV	human immunodeficiency virus
HOCM	hypertrophic obstructive cardiomyopathy
HPC	history of presenting complaint
HPV	human papilloma virus
HRT	hormone replacement therapy
HS	heart sounds
HS I+II+0	normal first and second heart sounds with no added sounds
HSG	hysterosalpingogram
HSV	herpes simplex virus
HT or H/T	hypertension
HUS	haemolytic uraemic syndrome
HV	health visitor
HVS	high vaginal swab
<u>I</u>	
I&D	incision and drainage
IBD	inflammatory bowel disease
IBS	irritable bowel syndrome
ICP	intracranial pressure
ICS	intercostal space
IDDM	insulin-dependent diabetes mellitus (and NIDDM = non-IDDM)
IE	infective endocarditis
IFG	impaired fasting glycaemia
Ig	immunoglobulin
IGT	impaired glucose tolerance
IHD	ischaemic heart disease
IM	intramuscular
IMB	intermenstrual bleeding
INR	international normalised ratio
IOL	induction of labour OR intraocular lens
IOP	intraocular pressure
IPPV	intermittent positive pressure ventilation
ISQ	the same (*in status quo*)
ITP	idiopathic thrombocytopaenic purpura

ITU	intensive therapy unit
IUCD	intra-uterine contraceptive device
IUD	intra-uterine death
IUS	intra-uterine system
IV	intravenous
IVC	inferior vena cava
IVDU	intravenous drug user
IVF	in vitro fertilisation
IVI	intravenous infusion
IVP	intravenous pyelogram
IVU	intravenous urogram

J

⁰JACCOL	no jaundice, anaemia, clubbing, cyanosis or lymphadenopathy
⁰JADE	no jaundice, anaemia, diabetes or epilepsy
JME	juvenile myoclonic epilepsy
JVP	jugular venous pressure

K

K or K⁺	potassium
KUB	kidneys, ureter and bladder

L

LA	local anaesthetic
LABA	long-acting beta-agonist
LAD	left anterior descending (coronary) artery
LBBB	left bundle branch block
LDH	lactate dehydrogenase
LDL	low density lipoprotein
LE	lupus erythematosus
LFT	liver function test
LH	luteinising hormone
LIF	left iliac fossa
LIH	left inguinal hernia
LKKS	liver, kidney, kidney, spleen
LLL	left lower lobe
LLQ	left lower quadrant
LMN	lower motor neuron

LMP	last menstrual period
LMWH	low molecular weight heparin
LN	lymph node
LOA	left occipito-anterior
LOC	loss of consciousness
LOM	left otitis media
LP	lumbar puncture
LPA	lasting power of attorney
LQTS	long Q-T syndrome
LRTI	lower respiratory tract infection
LSCS	lower segment Caesarean section
LSKK	liver, spleen and kidneys
LTOT	long-term oxygen therapy
LUQ	left upper quadrant
LUL	left upper lobe
LVF	left ventricular failure
LVH	left ventricular hypertrophy

M

mane	in the morning
MAOI	monoamine oxidase inhibitor
^{0}MARCH	no myocardial infarction, angina, rheumatic fever, cerebrovascular accident or hypertension
M,C&S	microscopy, culture and sensitivity
MCH(C)	mean corpuscular haemoglobin (concentration)
mcg or μg	micrograms
MCP	metacarpo-phalangeal
MCUG	micturating cysto-urethrogram
MCV	mean corpuscular volume
MDI	metered dose inhaler
MDR	multiple drug resistant
ME	myalgic encephalomyelitis
MET	maximal exercise test
mg	milligrams
Mg or Mg^{++}	magnesium
MGUS	monoclonal gammopathy of unknown significance
MI	myocardial infarct OR mental illness

MLD	mild learning disability
mm Hg	millimetres of mercury
MMR	measles, mumps and rubella (vaccine)
MND	motor neuron disease
MOI	mechanism of injury
MR	mitral regurgitation OR modified release
MRA	magnetic resonance angiography
MRI	magnetic resonance imaging
MRSA	methicillin-resistant staphylococcus aureus
MS	multiple sclerosis OR mitral stenosis OR morphine sulphate
MSK	musculoskeletal
MSU	mid-stream urine
MT	metatarsal
MTP	metatarsophalangeal
N	
Na	sodium
NAD	no abnormality detected (cynically, 'not actually done')
NAI	non-accidental injury
NBM	nil by mouth
ND	normal delivery
NEC	necrotising enterocolitis
ng	nanograms
NG	nasogastric
NHL	non-Hodgkins lymphoma
NICU	neonatal intensive care unit
NIDDM	non-insulin-dependent diabetes mellitus
NK(D)A	no known (drug) allergies
NMR	nuclear magnetic resonance
NNT	number needed to treat
Nocte	at night
NOF	neck of femur
NOS	not otherwise specified OR no other symptoms
NR	normal range
NRT	nicotine replacement therapy
NSAID	non-steroidal anti-inflammatory drug

NSF	National Service Framework
NSU	non-specific urethritis
NVD	normal vaginal delivery
O	
OA	osteoarthritis
OCD	obsessive-compulsive disorder
OCP	oral contraceptive pill
od	once daily (*omni die*)
OD	overdose
O/E	on examination
OGD	oesophogastroduodenoscopy
OGTT	oral glucose tolerance test
om	every morning (*omni mane*)
OM	otitis media
OME	otitis media with effusion
on	every night (*omni nocte*)
OOH	out of hours
OPD	outpatients department
OSA	obstructive sleep apnoea
OT	occupational therapist
OTC	over the counter
P	
P	pulse
PA	pulmonary artery
PAD	peripheral arterial disease
PAF	paroxysmal atrial fibrillation
PALS	patient advice and liaison service
PAT	paroxysmal atrial tachycardia
PBC	primary biliary cirrhosis
pc	after meals (*post cibum*)
PC	presenting complaint
PCB	post-coital bleeding
PCL	posterior cruciate ligament
PCO	primary care organisation
PCOS	polycystic ovarian syndrome
PCP	pneumocystis pneumonia

PCR	polymerase chain reaction
PCT	primary care trust
PCV	packed cell volume
PD	Parkinson's disease
PDA	patent ductus arteriosus
PE	pulmonary embolus
PEF(R)	peak expiratory flow (rate)
PERLA	pupils equal, react to light and accommodation
PET	pre-eclamptic toxaemia OR positron emission tomography
PETS	paediatric emergency transfer service
PFO	patent foramen ovale
PH	pulmonary hypertension
PHCT	primary health care team
PICU	paediatric intensive care unit
PID	pelvic inflammatory disease OR prolapsed intervertebral disc
PIH	pregnancy-induced hypertension
PIP(J)	proximal interphalangeal (joint)
PKD	polycystic kidney disease
PKU	phenylketonuria
PMB	post-menopausal bleeding
PMH	past medical history
PML	progressive multifocal leucoencephalopathy
PMR	polymyalgia rheumatica
PMS	premenstrual syndrome or Personal Medical Services
PMT	premenstrual tension
PN	percussion note
PND	paroxysmal nocturnal dyspnoea OR post-natal depression
PNS	peripheral nervous system
PO	by mouth (*per os*)
POM	prescription only medicine
POP	progesterone only pill
PPH	post-partum haemorrhage
PPI	proton pump inhibitor

Pr	pulse rate
PR	rectally (*per rectum*)
PRH	pregnancy-related hypertension
PRN	as required (*pro re nata*)
PROM	premature rupture of membranes
PSA	prostate specific antigen
PSM	pan-systolic murmur
Pt	patient
PT	pregnancy test OR prothrobin time
PTCA	percutaneous transluminal angioplasty
PTH	parathyroid hormone
PTSD	post-traumatic stress disorder
PTT	partial thromboplastin time
PUD	peptic ulcer disease
PUO	pyrexia of unknown origin
PUVA	psoralen ultraviolet A
PV	vaginally (*per vaginam*)
PVD	peripheral vascular disease
PVS	persistent vegetative state

Q

qds	four times a day (*quater die semendus*)
qid	four times a day (*quater in die*)
QOF	Quality and Outcomes Framework

R

RA	rheumatoid arthritis
RBBB	right bundle branch block
RBC	red blood cell
RCA	right coronary artery
RCGP	Royal College of General Practitioners
RCT	randomised controlled trial
Rh	rhesus
R(h)F	rheumatoid factor
RICE	rest, ice, compression and elevation
RIF	right iliac fossa
RLS	restless legs syndrome
R/O	rule out

ROA	right occipito-anterior
ROM	right otitis media OR range of motion
RR	respiratory rate
RS	respiratory system or relative risk
RSV	respiratory syncitial virus
RT	radiotherapy
RTA	road traffic accident
RUQ	right upper quadrant
RVH	right ventricular hypertrophy
R_x	treat with (or treatment) (*recipe*)

<u>S</u>

SAH	subarachnoid haemorrhage
SAO_2 or Sats	oxygen saturation
S/B	seen by
SARS	severe acute respiratory syndrome
SBE	sub-acute bacterial endocarditis
SC or S/C	subcutaneous
SCBU	special care baby unit
SCC	squamous cell carcinoma
SE or S-E	side-effect
SH	social history
SHBG	sex hormone binding globulin
SI	suicidal ideation
SIADH	syndrome of inappropriate anti-diuretic hormone
SIDS	sudden infant death syndrome
SL or S/L	sublingual
SLE	systemic lupus erythemtosus
SLR	straight leg raising
SNRI	serotonin and noradrenaline reuptake inhibitor
SNT	soft, non-tender (of the abdomen)
SOAP	subjective, objective, assessment and plan
SOB	short of breath
SOBOE	short of breath on exercise
SOL	space-occupying lesion
SOM	serious otitis media
SOS	if necessary (*si opus sit*)

SR	sinus rhythm OR slow release
SROM	spontaneous rupture of membranes
SSRI	selective serotonin reuptake inhibitor
SSS	sick sinus syndrome
ST or S/T	sore throat
stat	immediately (*statim*)
STD	sexually transmitted disease
SVC	superior vena cava
SVD	spontaneous vaginal delivery
SVT	supra-ventricular tachycardia
SW	social worker
S_x	symptoms
SXR	skull x-ray
T	
T	temperature
T_3	triiodothyronine
T_4	thyroxine
T&A or Ts&As	tonsillectomy and adenoidectomy
^{0}TAB	no tuberculosis, asthma or bronchitis
TAH	total abdominal hysterectomy
TATT	tired all the time
TB	tuberculosis
TCA	tricyclic antidepressant OR to come again
TCC	transitional cell carcinoma
TCI	to come in
tds	three times a day (*ter die sumendus*)
TENS	transcutaneous electrical nerve stimulator
TFT	thyroid function test
TG	triglycerides
THR	total hip replacement
TIA	transient ischaemic attack
TIBC	total iron binding capacity
tid	three times a day (*ter in die*)
TLC	tender loving care
TM	tympanic membrane
TMJ	tempero-mandibular joint

TNF	tumour necrosis factor
TOE	trans-oesophageal echocardigram
TOP	termination of pregnancy
TPHA	*Treponema pallidum* haemagglutination antibody
TPN	total parenteral nutrition
TPR	temperature, pulse and respiration
TR	tricuspid regurgitation
TRH	thyrotropin releasing hormone
TSH	thyroid stimulating hormone
TTO	to take out (medication)
TURBT	transurethral resection of bladder tumour
TURP	transurethral resection of prostate
TWOC	trial without catheter
U	
U&E	urea and electrolytes
UC	ulcerative colitis
UMN	upper motor neurone
URT	upper respiratory tract
URTI	upper respiratory tract infection
USS	ultrasound scan
UTI	urinary tract infection
V	
VA	visual acuity
VDRL	venereal diseases research laboratory
VE	ventricular ectopic/extrasystole OR vaginal examination
VF	ventricular fibrillation
VMB	very much better
V/Q	ventilation:perfusion ratio
VRSA	vancomycin-resistant staphylococcus aureus
VSD	ventricular septal defect
VT	ventricular tachycardia
VUR	vesico-ureteric reflux
VV	varicose veins
VZ	varicella zoster
W	

WBC	white blood cell
WCC	white cell count
WIC	walk-in centre
WPW	Wolff-Parkinson-White syndrome

<u>X</u>

| XR | x-ray |

<u>Y</u>

| Y/O | year-old |

APPENDIX 2

SAMPLE CLINICAL NOTES

(1) SAMPLE CLINICAL NOTES WITH MEDICAL ABBREVIATIONS

09/03/08
SHO on call   46   E/A   Hepatectomy

PC   -   Gallstones had cholecystectomy
                                   5 weeks ago → Ca Gall bladder

PMH

1993   -   Osteomyelitis
2001   -   Pneumonia + Pleurisy
2001   -   ↑ BP

                                   ° Angina/ ° M I/ ° Asthma/ ° CV/ ° RF/ ° TB
                                   ° Anaesthetic Probs

CM   Lisinopril 2.5 mg od

Allergies

          NCDA

FH

          Father   †   (50's)   CVP
          Mother   †   (60's)   MI

          Sister   †   (60's)   Ca

BO   reg
          stool ✓
          petite
          weight   ↓ 1 stone   2 - 3 months
                                           was on low fat diet for gall stones

T   36.5
Sats 97

Trachea central ↔

Chest clear
HS 1 + 11 + 0

Abdo soft
° tender
° masses
BS ✓

PPP
° ankle ° oedema

(2) SAMPLE CLINICAL NOTES IN FULL

09/03/08
SHO on call   46   Emergency Admission   Hepatectomy

<u>Present Complant</u>   -   Gallstones had cholecystectomy
                              5 weeks ago for cancer of the Gall bladder

<u>Past Medical History</u>

1993   -   Osteomyelitis
2001   -   Pneumonia + Pleurisy
2001   -   Increase in Blood pressure

             No Angina/ No Myocardial Infarction/ No Asthma/ No Cardio
             Vascular/ No Renal Failure / Tuberculosis
             No Anaesthetic Problems

<u>Current Medication</u>   Lisinopril 2.5 mg once daily

Allergies

     No current documented allergies

<u>Family History</u>

     Father   died   (50's)   Cardio vascular problem
     Mother   died   (60's)   Myocardial Infarction

     Sister   died   (60's)   Cancer

Bowels   regular
           stools OK
           petite
           weight   decreased by 1 stone in the last 2 - 3 months
                             was on low fat diet for gall stones

Temperature   36.5
Saturations   97

Trachea central   ↔

Chest clear
Heart sounds   1 + 11 + 0

Abdomen soft
Not tender
No masses
Bowel sounds present

Pedal pulses present
No ankle problems, no oedema

APPENDIX 3

MODEL DIRECTIONS FOR CLINICAL NEGLIGENCE CASES (2012) – BEFORE MASTER ROBERTS AND MASTER COOK

Introductory note

These are the Model Directions for use in the first Case Management Conference in clinical negligence cases before the Masters.

A draft order in Word format, adopting the Model Directions as necessary, is to be provided by e-mail to the Master at least 2 days before the hearing.

Parties are required to use the form of order at the end of this document – adapted as necessary. From April 2013 CPR Rule changes will require parties to take as their starting point any relevant Model or Standard Directions

The e-mail addresses of the clinical negligence Masters are:

master.roberts@judiciary.gsi.gov.uk

master.cook@judiciary.gsi.gov.uk

The Model Directions allow the court and the parties to be flexible. For example, sequential exchange of quantum statements (say, with schedule and counter-schedule of loss) may be appropriate. The sequential exchange of expert evidence on breach of duty and causation may sometimes be appropriate.

It would be helpful if dates appeared in **bold** type.

Please note: Solicitors must ensure that the claimant is accurately described in the title to the order: e.g., "JOHN SMITH (a child and protected party by his mother and Litigation Friend, JOAN SMITH). It is never permissible to refer to such a claimant as "JOHN SMITH".

The order should make it clear that it is made pursuant to a Case Management Conference or an application or both.

Please note the role of experts in the preparation of Agendas.

Warning: you must comply with the terms imposed upon you by this order otherwise your case is liable to be struck out or some other sanction imposed. If you cannot comply you are expected to make formal application to the court before any deadline imposed upon you expires.	
on xxxx before Master Xxxx sitting in Room E118 E112 at The Royal Courts of Justice, Strand, London the Master heard the solicitor for the Claimant and the solicitor for the Defendant and made the following Order	*Delete room number as appropriate.*
1) The Claim is allocated to the Multi-Track and is assigned to Master Xxxx for case management.	*All claims issued in the High Court must be allocated to the Multi-track and may well have been allocated earlier. This merely confirms allocation for the avoidance of doubt and confirms the 'docketing' of the claim to the assigned Master.*
2) At all stages the parties must consider settling this litigation by any means of Alternative Dispute Resolution (including round table conferences, early neutral evaluation, mediation and arbitration); any party not engaging in any such means proposed by another is to serve a witness statement giving reasons within **21 days** of receipt of that proposal. That witness statement must not be shown to the trial judge until questions of costs arise.	*The object is to reduce 'door of the court' settlements which are wasteful of costs, resources and judicial time.* *'21 days' can be altered.* *The words* 'and not less than **28 days** before trial' *can always be added after the word 'proposal' by the managing judge if appropriate.* *Not necessary for every Order.* *There can be added:* Such means of Alternative Dispute Resolution adopted shall be concluded not less than **35 days** before trial.
3) Documents are to be retained as follows:	

a) the parties must retain all electronically stored documents relating to the issues in this Claim. b) the Defendant must retain the original clinical notes relating to the issues in this Claim. The Defendant must give facilities for inspection by the Claimant, the Claimant's legal advisers and experts of these original notes on 7 days written notice. c) legible copies of the medical and educational records of the Claimant / Deceased / Claimant's Mother are to be placed in a separate paginated bundle by the Claimant's Solicitors and kept up to date. All references to medical notes are to be made by reference to the pages in that bundle.	
4)	*This and any additional paragraphs to be inserted here may cover various case management directions:* **Amendments** *The following is suggested:* Permission to Claimant / Defendant to amend the Particulars of Claim / Defence in terms of the draft initialled by the Master [or the draft served on xxxx]; the Defendant to serve an amended Defence by xxxx. Costs of and occasioned by the amendments to be borne by (usually, the party seeking permission to amend). [Where no draft is available, but the form of the amendments is not contentious] (Party wishing to amend) to serve draft amended [Statement of Case] by xxxx. If no objection to the draft amendments, response to be served by xxxx, if objection is taken to the draft, permission to restore. **Judgment** *The following is suggested:*

	Judgment for an amount to be decided by the court being xx% of the damages due on a full liability basis.
	Split Trial
	[An order "That there be a split trial" is inappropriate. The following is suggested.]
	A preliminary issue shall be tried between the Claimant and the Defendant as to whether or not the Defendant is liable to the Claimant by reason of the matters alleged in the Particulars of Claim and, if so, whether or not any of the injuries described were so caused; and, if any such injuries were so caused, the extent of the same.
5) Disclosure of documents relevant to the issues of breach of duty and causation and quantification of damages will be dealt with as follows:	*The words 'and category' are optional. Where there is a large number of documents all falling into a particular category, the disclosing party may list those documents as a category rather than individually. See: para 3.2 to Practice Direction 31A.*
a) **By 4pm on xxxx** both parties must give to each other standard disclosure of documents by list and category.	
b) **By 4pm on xxxx** any request must be made to inspect the original of, or to provide a copy of, a disclosable document.	
c) Any such request unless objected to must be complied with within 14 days of the request.	
d) **By 4pm on xxxx** each party must serve and file with the court a list of issues relevant to the search for and disclosure of electronically stored documents, or must confirm there are no such issues, following Practice Direction 31B.	

6) Evidence of fact will be dealt with as follows:

a) **By 4pm on xxxx** both parties must serve on each other copies of the signed statements of themselves and of all witnesses on whom they intend to rely in respect of breach of duty and causation and all notices relating to evidence, including Civil Evidence Act notices.

b) For the avoidance of doubt statements of all concerned with the relevant treatment and care of the Claimant must be included.

c) **By 4pm on xxxx** both parties must serve on each other copies of the signed statements of themselves and of all witnesses on whom they intend to rely in respect of condition, prognosis and loss and all notices relating to evidence, including Civil Evidence Act notices.

d) Oral evidence will not be permitted at trial from a witness whose statement has not been served in accordance with this order or has been served late, except with permission from the Court.

e) Evidence of fact is limited to xx witnesses on behalf of each party.

f) Witness statements must not exceed xx pages of A4 in length.

7) Expert evidence is directed as follows.	*The following text is not designed to be prescriptive, but will cover the essential directions for expert evidence. The directions will identify the disciplines of expertise on which it proposed to rely and, preferably, the names of each expert (or a direction requiring the expert to be named by a date). Where necessary the specific issues which the expert is to address can be identified.*
8) The parties have permission in respect of breach of duty and causation and quantification of damages to rely on the following jointly instructed written evidence of an expert xxxx.	*Delete as necessary* OR experts in the following fields:
a) By xxxx the expert should be agreed and instructed, and if no expert has been instructed by that date the Claimant must apply to court by 4pm the following day for further directions.	*Where it is necessary to confine an expert to specific issues the following subparagraph is appropriate:*
b) By xxxx the expert will report to the instructing parties.	a) The expert's report will be confined to the following issues
c) By xxxx the parties may put written questions to the expert.	i) xxxxx
d) By xxxx the expert will reply to the questions.	ii) xxxxx
e) A copy of this order must be served on the expert by the Claimant with the expert's instructions.	*Whether questions are to be put to the single joint expert is a matter for case management. If they are not required the subparagraphs can be deleted.*
f) A party seeking to call the expert to give oral evidence at trial must apply for permission to do so before pre-trial check lists are filed.	*The following optional subparagraph can be used:*
g) Unless the parties agree in writing or the Court orders otherwise, the fees and expenses of the expert shall be paid by the parties giving instructions for the report equally.	The expert may apply direct to the court for directions where necessary under Rule 35.14 Civil Procedure Rules.

9) In respect of breach of duty and causation the parties each have permission to rely on the following written expert evidence:	*The following can be added for each expert:* confined to the following issues:
a) The Claimant:	
i) an expert in xxxx, namely Mr A, whose report must be served by xxxx.	
ii) an expert in xxxx, namely Dr B, whose report must be served by xxxx.	
iii) an expert in xxxx, namely Ms C, whose report must be served by xxxx.	
b) The Defendant:	
i) an expert xxxx, namely Mr AA, whose report must be served by xxxx	
ii) an expert xxxx, namely Mr BB, whose report must be served by xxxx.	
iii) an expert xxxx, namely Ms CC, whose report must be served by xxxx.	
10) In respect of condition, prognosis and quantification of damages the parties (the Defendants acting jointly) each have permission to rely on the following written expert evidence:	
a) The Claimant:	
i) an expert in xxxx, namely Mr A, whose report must be served by xxxx.	
ii) an expert in xxxx, namely Dr B, whose report must be served by xxxx.	
iii) an expert in xxxx, namely Ms C, whose report must be served by xxxx.	
The Defendant:	

i) an expert in xxxx, namely Mr AA, whose report must be served by xxxx. ii) an expert in xxxx, namely Mr BB, whose report must be served by xxxx. iii) an expert in xxxx, namely Ms CC, whose report must be served by xxxx.	
11) Unless the reports are agreed, there must be a without prejudice discussion between the experts of like discipline by 4pm on xxxx in which the experts will identify the issues between them and reach agreement if possible. The experts will prepare for the court and sign a statement of the issues on which they agree and on which they disagree with a summary of their reasons in accordance with Rule 35.12 Civil Procedure Rules, and each statement must be sent to the parties to be received by 4pm on xxxx and in any event no later than 7 days after the discussion.	*A guide is **8 weeks** after the exchange of reports for the discussion and **7 days** to produce their statement.* *The following direction may be used as appropriate:* Discussions between experts are not mandatory. The parties should consider, with their expert, whether there is likely to be any useful purpose in holding a discussion and should be prepared to agree that no discussion is in fact needed. *Where it is necessary to identify more specifically the areas of discussion, the following may be used (numbering not formatted):* The purpose of the discussions is to identify: The extent of the agreement between the experts; The points of disagreement and short reasons for disagreement; Action, if any, which may be taken to resolve the outstanding points of disagreement; Any further material points not raised in the Agenda and the extent to which these issues are agreed.

| 12) xxxx | **Agendas**
The use of an agenda is not necessary in every case.

Claimants' solicitors and counsel should note the obligation to prepare the draft Agenda jointly with the relevant expert. Experts should note that it is part of their overriding duty to the court to ensure that the Agenda complies with the following direction which may be used (numbering not formatted):

The use of agendas is not mandatory. Solicitors should consult with the experts to ensure that agendas are necessary and, if used, are reasonable in scope. The agenda should assist the experts and should not be in the form of leading questions or hostile in tone. An agenda must include a list of the outstanding issues in the preamble.

The preamble should state: the standard of proof: the Bolam test: remind the experts not to attempt to determine factual issues : remind them not to stray outside their field of expertise and indicate the form of the joint statement. It will also be helpful to provide a comprehensive list of the materials which each expert has seen, perhaps in the form of an agreed supplementary bundle (it is assumed that experts will have been provided with the medical notes bundle).

Otherwise *the following direction may be used (numbering not formatted):* |

	Unless otherwise agreed by all parties' solicitors, after consulting with the experts, a draft Agenda which directs the experts to the remaining issues relevant to the experts' discipline, as identified in the statements of case shall be prepared jointly by the Claimant's solicitors and experts and sent to the Defendant's solicitors for comment at least **35 days** before the agreed date for the experts' discussions.
	The Defendants shall **within 21 days** of receipt agree the Agenda, or propose amendments.
	7 days thereafter all solicitors shall use their best endeavours to agree the Agenda. Points of disagreement should be on matters of real substance and not semantics or on matters the experts could resolve of their own accord at the discussion. In default of agreement, both versions shall be considered at the discussions. Agendas, when used, shall be provided to the experts not less than **7 days** before the date fixed for discussions.
	Where it has been impossible to agree a single agenda, it is of assistance to the experts if the second agenda is consecutively numbered to the first, i.e. if the first agenda has 16 questions in it, the second agenda is numbered from 17 onwards.
13) A copy of this order must be served on each expert by the Claimant with the expert's instructions.	

14) The parties have permission to call oral evidence of the experts in xxxx.	**OR** A party seeking to call oral expert evidence at trial must apply for permission to do so before pre-trial check lists are filed.
15) Any unpublished literature upon which any expert witness proposes to rely must be served at the same time as service of his report together with a list of published literature. Any supplementary literature upon which any expert witness relies must be notified to all parties at least one month before trial. No expert witness may rely upon any publications that have not been disclosed in accordance with this order without the permission of the trial judge subject to costs as appropriate.	
16) Experts will, at the time of producing their reports, incorporate details of any employment or activity which raises a possible conflict of interest.	
17) For the avoidance of doubt, experts do not require the authorisation of solicitor or counsel before signing a joint statement.	
18) If an expert radically alters an opinion previously recorded, the joint statement should include a note or addendum by that expert explaining the change of opinion.	*Note: This does not affect Rule 35.12 which provides that where experts reach agreement on an issue during their discussions, the agreement shall not bind the parties unless the parties expressly agree to be bound by the agreement.*
19) Schedules of Loss must be updated as follows: a) **By 4pm on xxxx** the Claimant must send an up to date schedule of loss to the Defendant.	*Periodical Payments. Parties should, at the first case management conference, be prepared to give their provisional view as to whether the case is one in which the periodical payment of damages might be appropriate.*

b) **By 4pm on xxxx** the Defendant, in the event of challenge, must send an up to date counter-schedule of loss to the Claimant.	*Schedules. Parties are encouraged to exchange Schedules in a form which enables the Counter schedule to be based on the Claimant's Schedule i.e. by delivering a disk with the hard copy, or by sending it as an e-mail attachment.*
c) The schedule and counter-schedule must contain a statement setting out that party's case on the issue of periodical payments pursuant to Rule 41.5 Civil Procedure Rules.	
20) The trial will be listed as follows.	*Usually 6 weeks after the case management conference*
a) **By 4pm on xxxx** Claimant's Solicitors must apply to Queen's Bench Judges' Listing for a listing appointment for a trial within the trial window and give notice of the appointment to the Defendant.	*The Queen's Bench Judges' Listing, in order to maintain the necessary degree of flexibility for listing, will give a 'trial period' rather than a fixed date, but, in order to accommodate the parties' need for certainty as to dates for experts to attend, will, if an approach is made closer to the beginning of the trial period, confirm the date for the trial to begin as the first day of the trial period.*
b) Trial: Judge alone; London	*The trial period will usually be directed to begin at least 2 clear months after the last event besides Alternative Dispute Resolution (this is to allow for Alternative Dispute Resolution).*
c) Category: B	*In relatively modest claims (in term of damages only), the Master may direct:*
d) Trial window: from xxxx to xxxx inclusive.	
e) Time estimate: x days	
f) The parties shall file Pre-Trial Check Lists as directed by the Queen's Bench Judges' Listing.	

	If the parties reach agreement upon breach of duty and causation, the parties are to immediately restore the case before the Master so that alternative directions on the assessment of damages may be considered. *The following subparagraph may be added:* Certified fit for High Court Judge if available.
21) Pre-trial directions are as follows: a) There will be a review case management conference in Room E118 E112 **4 weeks** before the trial window starts with a time estimate of half an hour. b) The case management conference will be conducted by telephone, unless the court orders otherwise. The Claimant must make the relevant arrangements in accordance with Practice Direction 23A Civil Procedure Rules. c) At least **3 clear days** before the case management conference the Claimant must file and send to the Defendant preferably agreed and by email: i) any draft directions; ii) a case summary.	*Delete Room number as appropriate* *This hearing may be vacated by consent provided that all directions have been complied with; no further directions are required; and the Master is given reasonable notice.* *NB the default for a case management conference with a time estimate of "no more than one hour" is by telephone. See Practice Direction 23A paragraph 6.*

22) Not more than **7 nor less than 3 clear days** before the trial, the Claimant must file at court and serve an indexed and paginated bundle of documents which complies with the requirements of Rule 39.5 Civil Procedure Rules and Practice Direction 39A. The parties must endeavour to agree the contents of the bundle before it is filed. The bundle will include a case summary and a chronology.	
23) The parties must file with the court and exchange skeleton arguments at least three days before the trial, by email.	
24) Costs in the case.	*Or other costs order sought* *Note: A party may request the restoration of a CMC or application by letter or e-mail to the assigned Master. If possible the Master should be provided with an agreed list of dates to avoid. Where the application is urgent and the time estimate is no more than 30 minutes, the Master will endeavour to list a hearing at 10.00am as soon as possible. Applications estimated to take more than 30 minutes should be applied for as private room appointments in the usual way.]* *[Both Masters are willing, in appropriate cases, to hear applications by telephone link, provided sufficient notice is given directly to the Master concerned and the relevant papers are provided in advance. E-mails are an acceptable means of communication, provided that they are copied to all parties.]*

	[NOTE: The Court File in cases proceeding before the Masters will not routinely be placed before the Master. Parties wishing for it to be produced should notify the Case Management Section FIVE CLEAR DAYS in advance of the appointment. In all other cases parties should bring with them copies of any filed documents upon which they intend to rely.
25) The parties may, by prior agreement in writing, extend the time for directions, in the Order dated xxxxxx, by up to 28 days and without the need to apply to Court. Beyond that 28 day period, any agreed extension of time must be submitted to the Court by email including a brief explanation of the reasons, confirmation that it will not prejudice any hearing date and with a draft Consent Order in word format. The Court will then consider whether a formal Application and Hearing is necessary.	

Standard Directions for Clinical Negligence Cases outside the RCJ

Warning: you must comply with the terms imposed upon you by this order otherwise your case is liable to be struck out or some other sanction imposed. If you cannot comply you are expected to make formal application to the court before any deadline imposed upon you expires.	
on xxxx before District Judge Xxxx sitting in xxxx	

the Judge heard the solicitor for the Claimant and the solicitor for the Defendant and made the following Order	
9) The Claim is allocated to the Multi-track and is assigned to District Judge Xxxx for case management.	*All claims alleging clinical negligence must be allocated to the Multi-track and may well have been allocated earlier. This merely confirms allocation for the avoidance of doubt and confirms the 'docketing' of the claim to the assigned District Judge.*
10) At all stages the parties must consider settling this litigation by any means of Alternative Dispute Resolution (including round table conferences, early neutral evaluation, mediation and arbitration); any party not engaging in any such means proposed by another is to serve a witness statement giving reasons within 21 days of receipt of that proposal. That witness statement must not be shown to the trial judge until questions of costs arise.	*The object is to reduce 'door of the court' settlements which are wasteful of costs, resources and judicial time.* *'21 days' can be altered.* *The words* 'and not less than 28 days before trial' *can always be added after the word 'proposal' by the managing judge if appropriate. Not necessary for every Order.* *There can be added:* Such means of Alternative Dispute Resolution adopted shall be concluded not less than 35 days before trial.
11) Documents are to be retained as follows: a) the parties must retain all electronically stored documents relating to the issues in this Claim.	

b) the Defendant must retain the original clinical notes relating to the issues in this Claim. The Defendant must give facilities for inspection by the Claimant, the Claimant's legal advisers and experts of these original notes on 7 days written notice. c) legible copies of the medical and educational records of the Claimant / Deceased / Claimant's Mother are to be placed in a separate paginated bundle by the Claimant's Solicitors and kept up to date. All references to medical notes are to be made by reference to the pages in that bundle.	
12)	*This and any additional paragraphs to be inserted here may cover various case management directions:* *Amendments* *The following is suggested:* Permission to amend the Particulars of Claim Defence in terms of the draft initialled by the District Judge. *Judgment (The following is suggested)* Judgment for an amount to be decided by the court being x% of the damages due on a full liability basis. *Split Trial* A preliminary issue shall be tried between the Claimant and the Defendant as to whether or not the Defendant is liable to the Claimant by reason of the matters alleged in the Particulars of Claim and, if so, whether or not any of the injuries described were so caused; and, if any such injuries were so caused, the extent of the same.

13) Disclosure of documents relevant to the issues of breach of duty and causation and quantification of damages will be dealt with as follows:	*The words 'and category' are optional. Where there is a large number of documents all falling into a particular category, the disclosing party may list those documents as a category rather than individually. See: para 3.2 to Practice Direction 31A.*
a) By 4pm on xxxx both parties must give to each other standard disclosure of documents by list and category.	
b) By 4pm on xxxx any request must be made to inspect the original of, or to provide a copy of, a disclosable document.	
c) Any such request unless objected to must be complied with within 14 days of the request.	
d) By 4pm on xxxx each party must serve and file with the court a list of issues relevant to the search for and disclosure of electronically stored documents, or must confirm there are no such issues, following Practice Direction 31B.	
14) Evidence of fact will be dealt with as follows:	
a) By 4pm on xxxx both parties must serve on each other copies of the signed statements of themselves and of all witnesses on whom they intend to rely in respect of breach of duty and causation and all notices relating to evidence, including Civil Evidence Act notices.	
b) For the avoidance of doubt statements of all concerned with the relevant treatment and care of the Claimant must be included.	

c) By 4pm on xxxx both parties must serve on each other copies of the signed statements of themselves and of all witnesses on whom they intend to rely in respect of condition, prognosis and loss and all notices relating to evidence, including Civil Evidence Act notices. d) Oral evidence will not be permitted at trial from a witness whose statement has not been served in accordance with this order or has been served late, except with permission from the Court. e) Evidence of fact is limited to xx witnesses on behalf of each party. f) Witness statements must not exceed xx pages of A4 in length.	
15) Expert evidence is directed as follows.	*The following text is not designed to be prescriptive, but will cover the essential directions for expert evidence. The directions will identify the disciplines of expertise on which it proposed to rely and, preferably, the names of each expert (or a direction requiring the expert to be named by a date). Where necessary the specific issues which the expert is to address can be identified.*
16) The parties have permission in respect of breach of duty and causation and quantification of damages to rely on the jointly instructed written evidence of an expert xxxx. a) By xxxx the expert should be agreed and instructed, and if no expert has been instructed by that date the Claimant must apply to court by 4pm the following day for further directions.	*Delete as necessary* OR experts in the following fields: *Where it is necessary to confine an expert to specific issues the following subparagraph is appropriate:*

b) By xxxx the expert will report to the instructing parties.	The expert's report will be confined to the following issues
c) By xxxx the parties may put written questions to the expert.	xxxxx
d) By xxxx the expert will reply to the questions.	xxxxx
e) A copy of this order must be served on the expert by the Claimant with the expert's instructions.	*Whether questions are to be put to the single joint expert is a matter for case management. If they are not required the subparagraphs can be deleted.*
f) A party seeking to call the expert to give oral evidence at trial must apply for permission to do so before pre-trial check lists are filed.	*The following optional subparagraph can be used:*
g) Unless the parties agree in writing or the Court orders otherwise, the fees and expenses of the expert shall be paid by the parties giving instructions for the report equally.	The expert may apply direct to the court for directions where necessary under Rule 35.14 Civil Procedure Rules.
25) In respect of breach of duty and causation the parties each have permission to rely on the following written expert evidence: a) The Claimant: i) an expert in xxxx, namely Mr A, whose report must be served by xxxx. ii) an expert in xxxx, namely Dr B, whose report must be served by xxxx. iii) an expert in xxxx, namely Ms C, whose report must be served by xxxx. b) The Defendant: i) an expert xxxx, namely Mr AA, whose report must be served by xxxx. ii) an expert xxxx, namely Mr BB, whose report must be served by xxxx.	*The following can be added for each expert:* confined to the following issues:

iii) an expert xxxx, namely Ms CC, whose report must be served by xxxx.	
26) In respect of condition, prognosis and quantification of damages the parties (the Defendants acting jointly) each have permission to rely on the following written expert evidence: a) The Claimant: i) an expert in xxxx, namely Mr A, whose report must be served by xxxx. ii) an expert in xxxx, namely Dr B, whose report must be served by xxxx. iii) an expert in xxxx, namely Ms C, whose report must be served by xxxx. b) The Defendant: i) an expert in xxxx, namely Mr AA, whose report must be served by xxxx. ii) an expert in xxxx, namely Mr BB, whose report must be served by xxxx. iii) an expert in xxxx, namely Ms CC, whose report must be served by xxxx.	

27) Unless the reports are agreed, there must be a without prejudice discussion between the experts of like discipline by 4pm on xxxx in which the experts will identify the issues between them and reach agreement if possible. The experts will prepare for the court and sign a statement of the issues on which they agree and on which they disagree with a summary of their reasons in accordance with Rule 35.12 Civil Procedure Rules, and each statement must be sent to the parties to be received by 4pm on xxxx and in any event no later than 7 days after the discussion.	*The following direction may be used as appropriate:* Discussions between experts are not mandatory. The parties should consider, with their expert, whether there is likely to be any useful purpose in holding a discussion and should be prepared to agree that no discussion is in fact needed. *Where it is necessary to identify more specifically the areas of discussion, the following may be used (numbering not formatted):* The purpose of the discussions is to identify: The extent of the agreement between the experts; The points of disagreement and short reasons for disagreement; Action, if any, which may be taken to resolve the outstanding points of disagreement; Any further material points not raised in the Agenda and the extent to which these issues are agreed.
28) xxxx	*Agendas* *The use of an agenda is not necessary in every case.*

Claimants' solicitors and counsel should note the obligation to prepare the draft Agenda jointly with the relevant expert. Experts should note that it is part of their overriding duty to the court to ensure that the Agenda complies with the following direction which may be used (numbering not formatted):

The use of agendas is not mandatory. Solicitors should consult with the experts to ensure that agendas are necessary and, if used, are reasonable in scope. The agenda should assist the experts and should not be in the form of leading questions or hostile in tone. An agenda must include a list of the outstanding issues in the preamble.

The preamble should state: the standard of proof: the Bolam test: remind the experts not to attempt to determine factual issues: remind them not to stray outside their field of expertise and indicate the form of the joint statement. It will also be helpful to provide a comprehensive list of the materials which each expert has seen, perhaps in the form of an agreed supplementary bundle (it is assumed that experts will have been provided with the medical notes bundle).

Otherwise the following direction may be used (numbering not formatted):

	Unless otherwise agreed by all parties' solicitors, after consulting with the experts, a draft Agenda which directs the experts to the remaining issues relevant to the experts' discipline, as identified in the statements of case shall be prepared jointly by the Claimant's solicitors and experts and sent to the Defendant's solicitors for comment at least 35 days before the agreed date for the experts' discussions.
	The Defendants shall within 21 days of receipt agree the Agenda, or propose amendments.
	7 days thereafter all solicitors shall use their best endeavours to agree the Agenda. Points of disagreement should be on matters of real substance and not semantics or on matters the experts could resolve of their own accord at the discussion. In default of agreement, both versions shall be considered at the discussions. Agendas, when used, shall be provided to the experts not less than 7 days before the date fixed for discussions.
	Where it has been impossible to agree a single agenda, it is of assistance to the experts if the second agenda is consecutively numbered to the first, i.e. if the first agenda has 16 questions in it, the second agenda is numbered from 17 onwards.
29) A copy of this order must be served on each expert by the Claimant with the expert's instructions.	

30) The parties have permission to call oral evidence of the experts in xxxx.	*OR* A party seeking to call oral expert evidence at trial must apply for permission to do so before pre-trial check lists are filed.
31) Any unpublished literature upon which any expert witness proposes to rely must be served at the same time as service of his report together with a list of published literature. Any supplementary literature upon which any expert witness relies must be notified to all parties at least one month before trial. No expert witness may rely upon any publications that have not been disclosed in accordance with this order without the permission of the trial judge subject to costs as appropriate.	
32) Experts will, at the time of producing their reports, incorporate details of any employment or activity which raises a possible conflict of interest.	
33) For the avoidance of doubt, experts do not require the authorisation of solicitor or counsel before signing a joint statement.	
34) If an expert radically alters an opinion previously recorded, the joint statement should include a note or addendum by that expert explaining the change of opinion.	*Note: This does not affect Rule 35.12 which provides that where experts reach agreement on an issue during their discussions, the agreement shall not bind the parties unless the parties expressly agree to be bound by the agreement.*
35) Schedules of Loss must be updated as follows: a) By 4pm on xxxx the Claimant must send an up to date schedule of loss to the Defendant.	*Periodical Payments. Parties should, at the first case management conference, be prepared to give their provisional view as to whether the case is one in which the periodical payment of damages might be appropriate.*

b) By 4pm on xxxx the Defendant, in the event of challenge, must send an up to date counter-schedule of loss to the Claimant.	*Schedules. Parties are encouraged to exchange Schedules in a form which enables the Counter schedule to be based on the Claimant's Schedule i.e. by delivering a disk with the hard copy, or by sending it as an e-mail attachment.*
c) The schedule and counter-schedule must contain a statement setting out that party's case on the issue of periodical payments pursuant to Rule 41.5 Civil Procedure Rules.	
36) The trial will be listed as follows. a) The trial window is between xxxx and xxxx inclusive. b) The estimated length of trial is xx days. c) By 4pm on xxxx the parties must file with the court their availability for trial, preferably agreed and with a nominated single point of contact. They will be notified of the time and place of trial. d) By 4pm on xxxx pre-trial check lists must be sent to the court.	c) 28 or however many days
37) Pre-trial directions are as follows: a) There will be a pre-trial review 4 weeks before the trial window starts with a time estimate of 30 minutes. b) The pre-trial review will be conducted by telephone if the parties so agree, unless the court orders otherwise. The Claimant must make the relevant arrangements in accordance with Practice Direction 23A Civil Procedure Rules.	*NB the default for a case management conference with a time estimate of "no more than one hour" is by telephone. See Practice Direction 23A paragraph 6.*

c) At least 3 clear days before the case management conference the Claimant must file and send to the Defendant preferably agreed and by email: i) any draft directions; ii) a case summary.	
38) Not more than 7 nor less than 3 clear days before the trial, the Claimant must file at court and serve an indexed and paginated bundle of documents which complies with the requirements of Rule 39.5 Civil Procedure Rules and Practice Direction 39A. The parties must endeavour to agree the contents of the bundle before it is filed. The bundle will include a case summary and a chronology.	
39) The parties must file with the court and exchange skeleton arguments at least three days before the trial, by email.	
40) Costs in the case.	*Or other costs order sought*

APPENDIX 4

USEFUL ORGANISATIONS

AVM Support UK

Provide various support services for people affected by Arteriovenous Malformation (AVM).

Tel: 01670 737 231
Email: info@avmsupport.org.uk
Website: www.avmsupport.org.uk

APIL (Association of Personal Injury Lawyers)

3 Alder Court
Rennie Hogg Road
Nottingham NG7 1RX
UK

Tel: 0115 958 0585
Website: www.apil.org.uk

APIL (the Association of Personal Injury Lawyers) was established in 1990 by a group of lawyers working on behalf of personal injury victims and now has approximately 4,500 members. It is an independent, not-for-profit organisation providing accreditation to lawyers specialising in the area of personal injury law.

Aphasia Now

Website: www.aphasianow.org (Website service)

'Aphasia now' is a website started by an aphasia victim who wanted to get in touch with like-minded and other sufferers to learn more about this invisible disability.

Association of Speech and Language Therapists in Independent Practice

Coleheath Bottom
Speen
Princes Risborough
Bucks HP27 0SZ

Tel: 01494 488 306
Fax: 01494 488 590
Website: www.helpwithtalking.com

Can supply details of therapists by region or specific condition.

Brain Tumour Charity

Hartshead House
61–65 Victoria Rd
Farnborough
Hampshire GU14 7BA

Tel: 0808 800 004
Website: www.thebraintumourcharity.org
Email: enquiries@braintumourcharity.org

Brain Tumour UK works to conquer brain tumours through research, education and support.

Brain Injury Association of America

1608 Spring Hill Road
Suite 110
Vienna VA 22182
USA

Tel: + (1) 703 761 0750
Fax: + (1) 703 761 0755
Website: www.biausa.org

Aims to create a better future through brain injury prevention, research, education and advocacy.

Brain and Spine Foundation

3.36 Canterbury Court
Kennington Park
1-3 Brixton Rd
London SW9 6DE

Tel: 020 7793 5900
Fax: 020 7793 5939
help@brainandspine.org.uk

Research, education and information. Booklets on a wide range of neurological conditions and symptoms and an online discussion forum. Helpline is staffed by neuroscience nurses.

Brain and Spinal Injury Charity (BASIC)

554 Eccles New Road
Salford
Manchester M5 5AP

Tel: 0161 707 6441
Helpline: 0870 750 0000
Fax: 0161 206 4558
Website: www.basiccharity.org.uk
Email: enquries@basiccharity.org.uk

BASIC provides a specialist resource at the Neurocare Centre for people and their families in crisis following a traumatic brain injury or neurological diagnosis.

Brain Injury Rehabilitation Trust (BIRT)

(see now The Disability Trust (below))

Brain Tree Training

PO Box 79
Leatherhead KT23 4YT

Tel: 01276 472 369
Website: www.braintreetraining.co.uk
Email: enquiries@braintreetraining.co.uk

Produce home-based cognitive rehabilitation courses for those with acquired neurological injuries.

Brainwave Centre Ltd (*Brainwave Centre for rehabilitation and development*)

Marsh Lane
Huntworth Gate
Bridgewater
Somerset TA6 6LQ

Tel: 01278 429089
Website: www.brainwave.org.uk
Email: enquiries@brainwave.org.uk

Design home-based programmes of rehabilitation for children involving both physical and cognitive techniques.

British Association of Brain Injury Case Managers (BABICM)

PO Box 199
Bury BL8 9EJ

Tel: 07002 222 426
Website: www.babicm.org
E-mail: secretary@babicm.org

BABICM is a professional association that was established in 1996 to promote the development of case management in the field of acquired brain injury.

Child Brain Injury Trust (CBIT)

Child Brain Injury Trust
Unit 1, The Great Barn
Baynards Green Farm
Nr Bicester,
Oxfordshire OX27 7SG

Tel: 01869 341 075
Helpline: 0303 303 2248
Website: www.cbituk.org
Email: info@cbituk.org

The Child Brain Injury Trust (CBIT) supports children, young people and families affected by an acquired brain injury, to enable them to achieve their potential.

Carers UK

Advice line: 0808 808 7777
Website: www.carersuk.org

Carers UK is the voice of carers and the leading campaigning, policy and information organisation for carers.

Chartered Society of Physiotherapy

14 Bedford Row
London WC1 4ED

Tel: 020 7306 6666
Website: www.csp.org.uk

The Chartered Society of Physiotherapy is the professional, educational and trade union body for the country's 45,000 chartered physiotherapists, physiotherapy students and assistants. It aims to support its members and help them to provide the highest standards of patient care.

Cancer BACUP

See now Cancer UK.

Challenging Behaviour Foundation

The Old Courthouse
New Road Avenue
Chatham
Kent ME4 6BE

Tel: 01634 838 739
Website: www.challengingbehaviour.org.uk
Email: info@thecbf.org.uk

Provides an information service, fact sheets, support network to improve the lives and conditions of people with learning disabilities and challenging behaviour, their immediate family and carers.

CRUSE Bereavement care

Tel: 0844 477 9400
Young persons' free phone: 0808 808 1677
Email: help@cruse.org.uk

Care Choices ltd

Valley Court Offices
Lower Road
Croydon
Nr Royston
Herts SG8 0HF

Tel: 0800 389 2077
Website: www.carechoices.co.uk

Care Choices Ltd offers a free residential/care home search service. The
company has a database of care homes, nursing homes, elderly accommodation
and similar establishments throughout the UK.

Carers Trust

32-36 Loman Street
London SE1 0EH

Tel: 0844 800 4361
Fax: 0844 800 4362
Email: info@carers.org

The Carers Trust is the largest provider of comprehensive carers' support
services in the UK.

Contact a Family

Contact a Family
209–211 City Road
London EC1V 1JN

Tel: 020 7608 8700
Fax: 020 7608 8701
Helpline: 0808 808 3555
Textphone: 0808 808 3556
Email Helpline: info@makingcontact.org

Contact a Family is the only UK-wide charity providing advice, information
and support to the parents of all disabled children – no matter what their health
condition. We also enable parents to get in contact with other families, both on
a local and national basis. Each year we reach at least 250,000 families.

Different Strokes

9 Canon Harnett Court
Wolverton Mill
Milton Keynes MK12 5NF

Helpline: 0845 130 7172
Fax: 01908 313 501
Website: www.differentstrokes.co.uk
Email: webcontact@differentstrokes.co.uk

This is a new charity for young stroke survivors aiming to provide access to physio and exercise, information and counselling and advice on further education and job opportunities.

Disabled Living Foundation (DLF)

Ground Floor
Landmark House
Hammersmith Bridge Road
London W6 9EJ

Tel: 0300 999 0004
Helpline: 0300 999 0004
Website: www.dlf.org.uk
Email: info@dlf.org.uk

DLF are the leading source of information on disability equipment. They aim to give advice and information on any aspect of disability presenting problems through providing an information service and answering queries by telephone and letter. Maintains a large equipment display area, which may be visited by appointment.

Disability Rights UK (formerly Alliance Education and Research Association)

Ground Floor
CAN Mezzanine
49-51 East Rd
London N1 6AH

Tel: 020 7250 3222
Fax: 020 7250 8181
Website: www.disabilityalliance.org
Email: enquiries@disabilityrightsuk.org

Aims to promote 'meaningful' independent living for disabled people as well as providing support for carers.

Disability Trust

32 Market Place
Burgess Hill
West Sussex RH15 9NP

Tel: 01444 239 123
Website: www.thedtgroup.org
E-mail: info@thedtgroup.org

The Disabilities Trust is a national charity providing care, rehabilitation and support solutions for people with profound physical impairments, acquired brain injury and learning disabilities as well as children and adults with autism.

Equality and Human Rights Commission (formerly Disability Rights Commission)

Correspondence Unit
Arndale House
The Arndale Centre
Manchester M4 3AQ

Tel: 0161 829 8100
Website: www.equalityhumanrights.com

The Equality and Human Rights Commission is an independent body established under the Equality Act 2006 to challenge discrimination, and protect and promote human rights.

Expert Witness Directory

Website: www.legalhub.co.uk

With over 2,500 experts listed on Legal Hub, it is the most comprehensive database of expert witnesses available. All experts appearing on Legal Hub have agreed to abide by a strict Code of Practice and Terms and Conditions. In addition, The Expert Witness Directory's robust vetting procedure boasts that you can rest assured that all the experts featured on Legal Hub are dependable and reliable.

Headway UK – the brain injury association

Bradbury House
190 Bagnall Road
Old Basford
Nottingham NG6 8SF
United Kingdom

Telephone: 0115 924 0800
Helpline: 0808 800 2244
Fax: 0115 958 4446
Website: www.headway.org.uk
Email: enquiries@headway.org.uk

Headway is a charity set up to give help and support to people affected by brain injury through a network of local Groups and Branches throughout the UK offering a wide range of services, including rehabilitation programmes, carer support, social re-integration, community outreach and respite care. The services available will vary, depending on local needs and resources. Headway UK provides support to the local Groups and Branches and helps to deliver high quality services through guidance on policies, procedures, standards and training.

Headway Ireland

Blackhall Green
Off Blackhall Place
Dublin 7

Tel: +353 (0)1 6040 800
Website: www.headway.ie
Email: services@headway.ie

Independent Living Funds

Independent Living Funds
Equinox House
City Link
Nottingham NG2 4LA

Tel: 0845 601 8815 / 0115 945 0700
Fax: 0115 945 0945
Website: www.gov.uk/government/organisations/independent-living.fund
Email: funds@ilf.gsi.gov.uk

The funds were set up as a national resource dedicated to the financial support of disabled people enabling them to choose to live in the community rather than residential care.

Meningitis Now (formerly Meningitis Trust)

Fern House
Bath Road
Stroud
Gloucestershire GL5 3TJ

Tel: 01453 768000
Helpline: 0808 80 10 388
Fax: 01453 768001
Website: www.meningitisnow.org.uk
Email: info@meningitisnow.org.uk

Funds medical research into the disease. Increases awareness of meningitis and supports sufferers and their families. The trust has produced free information aimed at both health care professionals and the general public. Grants are also available to families affected by meningitis.

Neurological Alliance

Dana Centre
165 Queen's Gate
London SW7 5HD

Tel: 020 7584 6457
Website: www.neural.org.uk
Email: admin@neural.org.uk

The neurological alliance is a forum of a wide range of neurological charities. The alliance pursues the highest standards of service and care for those affected by a neurological condition by consulting its members, influencing policy and working with health and social care organisations.

NHS 111

Tel: 111
Website: www.nhs.uk

Medical advice from trained staff supported by qualified nurses and doctors.

Parkinson's UK (formerly Parkinson's Disease Society (PDS))

215 Vauxhall Bridge Road
London SW1V 1EJ

Tel: 020 7931 8080
Helpline: 0800 800 0303
Email: hello@parkinsons.org.uk

Aims to help patients and their relatives with problems arising from Parkinson's disease, to collect and disseminate information on the disease, to encourage and provide funds for research into the disease.

Relate (national marriage guidance)

Tel: 0300 100 1234
Website: www.relate.org.uk

Aims to support marriage and family life. Relate has a range of literature and can refer to local branches for individual counselling services.

Relatives and Residents Association

1 The Ivories
7–18 Northampton Street
London N1 2HY

Tel: 020 7359 8184
Website: www.relres.org

Provides information and support about care homes.

Royal Association for Disability and Rehabilitation (RADAR)

See now Disability Rights UK.

Royal National Institute for the Blind

Helpline: 0303 123 9999
Email: helpline@rnib.org.uk
Website: www.rnib.org.uk

Supporting people with sight problems.

Stroke Association

240 City Road
London EC1V 2PP

Tel: 020 7566 0300
Helpline: 0303 3033 100
Fax: 020 7490 2686
Website: www.stroke.org.uk
Email: info@stroke.org.uk

Aims to carry out a programme of research, health, education, rehabilitation, welfare, and counselling services, publishing books, posters and leaflets and organising conferences.

SCOPE

6 Market Road
London N7 9PW

Tel: 020 7619 7100
Helpline: 0808 800 3333
Website: www.scope.org.uk
Email: helpline@scope.org.uk

Supporting people with Cerebral Palsy.

Speakability

240 City Road
London EC1V 2PR

Tel: 020 7261 9572
Helpline: 0808 808 9572
Fax: 020 7928 9542
Website: www.speakability.org.uk

Advice line for people with dysphasia (loss of language following stroke or head injury), their families and professionals. Advice on accessing services, benefits, holidays, equipment and computer technology. Also gives advice on self-help groups and speech therapy.

United Kingdom Acquired Brain Injury Forum

UKABIF
PO Box 159
Launceston PL15 0AW

Tel: 0845 608 0788
Website: www.ukabif.org.uk
Email: info@ukabif.org.uk

The United Kingdom Acquired Brain Injury Forum (UKABIF) is a not-for-profit coalition of organisations and individuals that seeks to promote understanding of all aspects of Acquired Brain Injury and to provide information and expert input to policy makers, service providers and the general public to promote the interests of brain injured people and their families.

Vocational Rehabilitation Association

VRA
Armstrong House
First Avenue
Robin Hood Airport
Doncaster DN9 3GA

www.vra-uk.org.uk

The VRA exists to help people working in the field of disability and employment to develop their personal and professional practice and to maintain their awareness of a broad range of disability issues. Members work in the public, private and voluntary sectors, and include both disabled and non-disabled colleagues.

INDEX

References are to paragraph numbers.